D1124566

CHAUCER

CHAUCER

A EUROPEAN LIFE

Marion Turner

PRINCETON UNIVERSITY PRESS

PRINCETON AND OXFORD

Published by Princeton University Press

41 William Street, Princeton, New Jersey 08540

6 Oxford Street, Woodstock, Oxfordshire OX20 1TR

press.princeton.edu

LCCN 2018948733

ISBN 978-069-1-16009-2

British Library Cataloging-in-Publication Data is available

Editorial: Ben Tate and Hannah Paul

Production Editorial: Debbie Tegarden

Text Design: Lorraine Doneker

Jacket Designer: Amanda Weiss

Jacket Art: (top): Hereford *Mappa Mundi*, c. 13th century; (bottom) adapted
from "Steamship Victoria of the Anchor Line," c. 1876

Production: Jacquie Poirier

Publicity: Jodi Price and Katie Lewis

Copyeditor: Cathryn Slovensky

This book has been composed in Garamond Premier Pro

Printed on acid-free paper. ∞

Printed in the United States of America

3 5 7 9 10 8 6 4

For Cecilia, Peter, and Elliot

CONTENTS

⤙–◆•–O–•◆–⤚

PART III: *Approaching Canterbury*

PLATES

>·!·◆◇·○·◇◆·!·◄

(*Illustrations follow page 266*)

ILLUSTRATIONS

Family Trees

Maps

CHAUCER FAMILY TREE

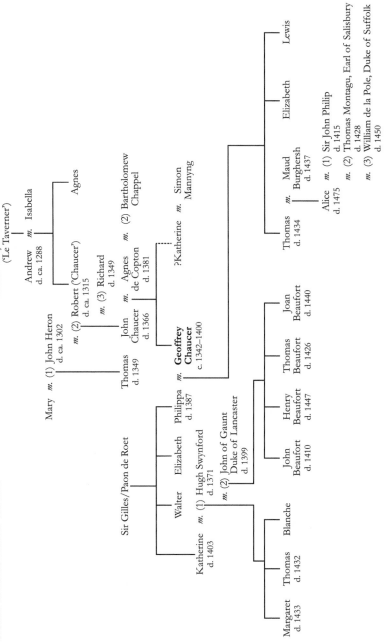

Robert Malyn de Dinehinetune ('Le Taverner')

Andrew *m.* Isabella
d. ca. 1288

Agnes

Mary *m.* (1) John Heron
d. ca. 1302

m. (2) Robert ('Chaucer')
d. ca. 1315

m. (3) Richard
d. 1349

Thomas
d. 1349

John Chaucer
d. 1366

Agnes de Copton
d. 1381 *m.*

m. (2) Bartholomew Chappel

Geoffrey Chaucer
c. 1342–1400 *m.*

?Katherine *m.* Simon Mannyng

Sir Gilles/Paon de Roet

Walter   Elizabeth   Philippa
d. 1387

Katherine
d. 1403

m. (1) Hugh Swynford
d. 1371

m. (2) John of Gaunt
Duke of Lancaster
d. 1399

Thomas
d. 1432

Blanche

John Beaufort
d. 1410

Henry Beaufort
d. 1447

Thomas Beaufort
d. 1426

Joan Beaufort
d. 1440

Margaret
d. 1433

Thomas
d. 1434

Elizabeth

Lewis

Maud Burghersh
d. 1437 *m.*

Alice
d. 1475

m. (1) Sir John Philip
d. 1415

m. (2) Thomas Montagu, Earl of Salisbury
d. 1428

m. (3) William de la Pole, Duke of Suffolk
d. 1450

ROYAL FAMILY TREE

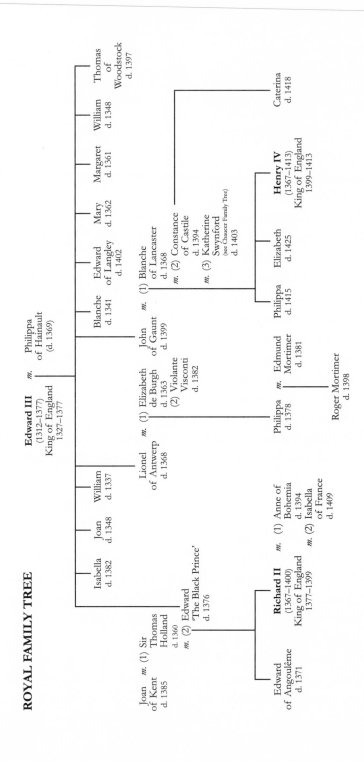

Edward III
(1312–1377)
King of England
1327–1377

m.

Philippa
of Hainault
(d. 1369)

Isabella
d. 1382

Joan
d. 1348

William
d. 1337

Blanche
d. 1341

Mary
d. 1362

Margaret
d. 1361

William
d. 1348

Thomas
of
Woodstock
d. 1397

Joan *m.* (1) Sir
of Kent   Thomas
d. 1385   Holland
               d. 1360

m. (2) Edward
'The Black Prince'
d. 1376

Lionel
of Antwerp
d. 1368

m. (1) Elizabeth
de Burgh
d. 1363

(2) Violante
Visconti
d. 1382

John
of Gaunt
d. 1399

m. (1) Blanche
of Lancaster
d. 1368

m. (2) Constance
of Castile
d. 1394

m. (3) Katherine
Swynford
(see Chaucer Family Tree)
d. 1403

Edward
of Langley
d. 1402

Edward
of Angoulême
d. 1371

Richard II
(1367–1400)
King of England
1377–1399

m. (1) Anne of
Bohemia
d. 1394

m. (2) Isabella
of France
d. 1409

Philippa
d. 1378

m. Edmund
Mortimer
d. 1381

Roger Mortimer
d. 1398

Philippa
d. 1415

Elizabeth
d. 1425

Henry IV
(1367–1413)
King of England
1399–1413

Caterina
d. 1418

ACKNOWLEDGEMENTS

This book has benefited hugely from its early readers: Anthony Bale, Elliot Kendall, and Paul Strohm, acute interpreters, kind interlocutors, willing cocktail drinkers. I also want to extend profound thanks to the careful and thoughtful anonymous readers for Princeton University Press. My editor at the Press, Ben Tate, has been the best of all possible editors, and the rest of the wonderful team at PUP, especially Hannah Paul, Debbie Tegarden, Dimitri Karetnikov, Katie Lewis and Cathy Slovensky, have provided the most supportive and vibrant environment possible. I cannot thank them enough. The British Academy awarded me a mid-career fellowship to work on this book, which allowed me invaluable time to research, write, and think, and I am deeply grateful to them for believing in my project. This book would have taken far longer without their help.

I am also very lucky to work with wonderful colleagues in Oxford, to teach inspiring students here, at Jesus College, Oriel College, and the English Faculty, and to be part of an exceptionally intelligent and kind international community. I can't thank everyone, but here are a few people to whom I am especially grateful for conversations either recent or long ago: Helen Barr, Ardis Butterfield, Chris Cannon, Rita Copeland, Isabel Davis, John Ganim, Alex Gillespie, Vincent Gillespie, Claire Harman, Hermione Lee, Laurie Maguire, Robyn Malo, Katie Murphy, Sophie Ratcliffe, Sebastian Sobecki, Emily Steiner, Helen Swift, Peter Travis, Stephanie Trigg, Dan Wakelin, and David Wallace. In the late stages of the book, Emily Dolmans provided excellent research and editorial assistance, and Tom Broughton-Willett crafted the index. I have learnt a lot from graduate students, especially Hannah Bower and Rebecca Menmuir, and the students who have worked with me on the 'Placing Chaucer' course. Wide-ranging conversations with undergraduates too numerous to mention individually are at the heart of my working life; I feel amazed every day that I get to teach such extraordinary students.

I'm also very grateful to have had the opportunity to give papers about this book at the Universities of Cambridge, Oxford, Sussex, and War-wick; at the Medieval Academy in Atlanta; at the MLA conference in Vancouver; and at the New Chaucer Society Congresses in Reykjavik, London, and Toronto. I often speak at schools, and the opportunity to talk to young people about Chaucer is a huge privilege. It is always inspiring to discuss Chaucer with people who have only recently begun to discover his subtleties, humour, and infinite variety.

Finally, I want to thank my family. My parents, David and Sheelagh, have continued to claim interest in Chaucer, and I'm very lucky to have their unwavering support. My more extended family—especially Katie, Damon, Michael, and Ruby, my aunts Rita and Moira and their families, my Kendall family at the other side of the world, and many friends who are like family, particularly Kirstie Blair, Ned Fletcher, Jessie and Mark Flugge, Camille and Joe Mazarelo, Tim Phillips, Natalie Walker, and Rachel Wevill—are essential to my life and happiness. And everything I do is built on the foundation of the three people with whom I share a home, the lights and loves of my life. Two of them have lived with this book for much of their lives, sustained only by the hope of one day attend-ing a book-launch party featuring a Chaucer cake. Elliot, Cecilia, and Peter, this book is for you.

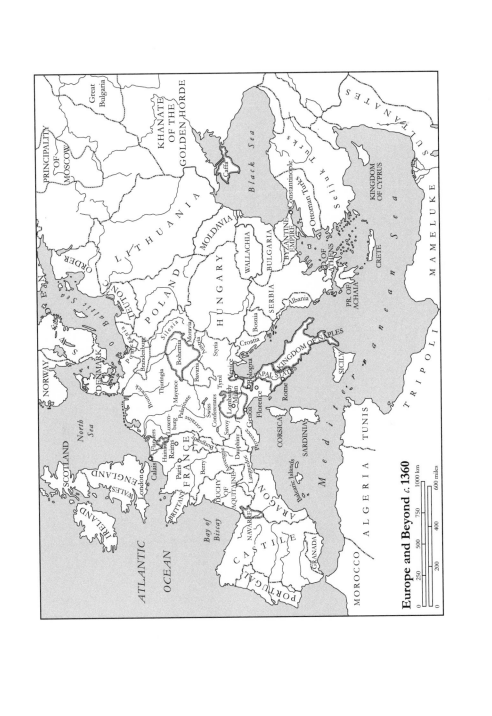

Europe and Beyond *c.* 1360

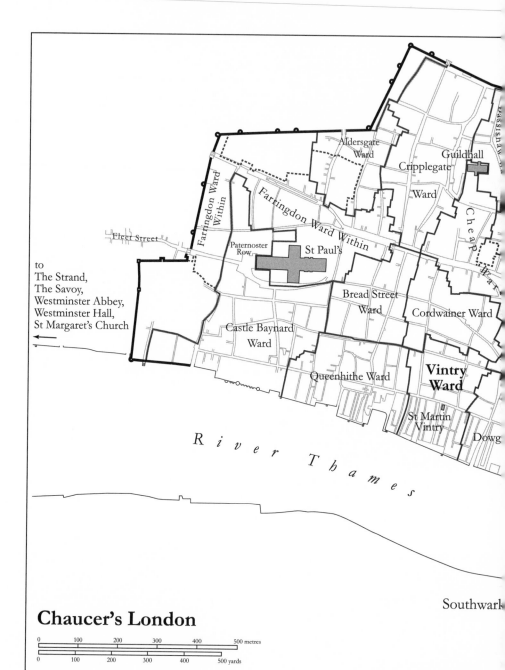

Aldersgate
Ward

Guildhall

Cripplegate

Ward

Farringdon Ward
Within

Farringdon Ward Within

Cheap Wa

Fleet Street

Paternoster
Row

St Paul's

to
The Strand,
The Savoy,
Westminster Abbey,
Westminster Hall,
St Margaret's Church

Bread Street
Ward

Cordwainer Ward

Castle Baynard
Ward

Vintry
Ward

Queenhithe Ward

St Martin
Vintry

Dowg

River Thames

Southwark

Chaucer's London

0   100   200   300   400   500 metres

0   100   200   300   400   500 yards

Broad Street

Ward

Bishopsgate

Bishopsgate Ward

**St Helen's
Bishopsgate**

Cornhill Ward

Lime
Street
Ward

A l d g a t e

Aldgate

Langbourn
Ward

W a r d

Langbourn Ward

Candlewick
Ward

Billingsgate

T o w e r

Bridge
Ward

Ward

W a r d

Thames Street

**Custom
House**

London
Bridge

Liberty of the Tower

**The
Tower
of
London**

R i v e r   T h a m e s

The Tabard Inn

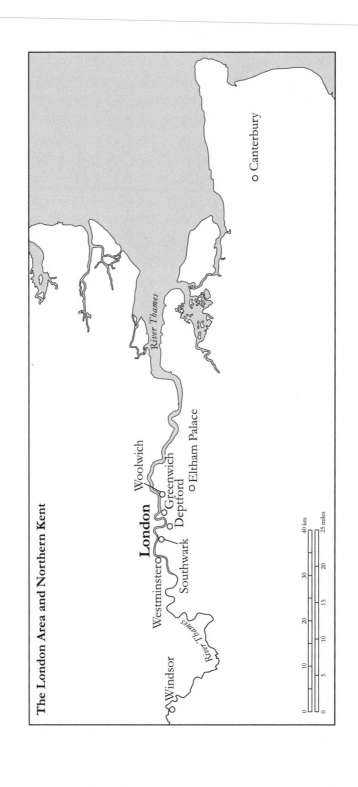

The London Area and Northern Kent

CHAUCER

General Prologue

I am all the writers that I have read, all the people that I have met, all the women that I have loved; all the cities that I have visited, all my ancestors.

—*Jorge Luis Borges*

On 4 July 1378, a bead maker, Simon Wylde de Estland, robbed a haberdasher's shop in London. The victim, Thomas Trewe, made a list of the items that had been stolen: accessories such as caps, laces, threads, and purses; children's clothes of different colours; musical instruments; cushion-frames; and chess sets complete with pieces described in the terms of medieval affinities as a 'familia' (household) or 'mesne' (retinue).[1] The range of items suggests a clientele who cared about their leisure time, who thought about appearance and self-fashioning, and who were interested in their children and their domestic surroundings. Notebooks and hats were jumbled up with pictures of the Crucifixion painted on fabric and items for use in the Mass.

Several details of this case illustrate aspects of the late-medieval use and understanding of space. The shop was located in the area of Paternoster Row, a street directly north of St Paul's churchyard. This area was the centre of both the rosary-selling and the bookmaking trades.[2] Two kinds of products frequently recur in the inventory of stolen items: beads of

---

[1] See Reginald R. Sharpe (ed.), *Calendar of Letter-Books of the City of London: Letter-Book F, 1337–1352* (London: John Edward Francis, 1904), fol. ccxxii, 267–68. Folios ccxvii–ccxxv comprise cases of the delivery of 'infangenthef' (discussed below), 1338–1409. The description and valuation of the contents of the shop are translated and printed in Henry Thomas Riley (ed.), *Memorials of London and London Life in the XIIIth, XIVth, and XVth Centuries* (London: Longmans, Green, 1868), 422.

[2] C. Paul Christianson, 'The Rise of the Book-Trade,' in Lotte Hellinga and J. B. Trapp (eds.), *The Cambridge History of the Book in Britain* (Cambridge: Cambridge University Press, 1999), 3:128–29. 'Paternoster' was another word for 'rosary'; for the making of rosaries in Paternoster Row, see Anne

many different kinds, including wood, jet, and black alabaster, and items relating to book production, such as skins of parchment, inkhorns, pen-cases, quires of paper, and paper covered in leather. People who worked in the same trade tended to cluster together in medieval London,[3] and indeed Thomas Trewe's two formal supporters in his lawsuit were also haber-dashers (John Salle and Richard Spencer), and the accused worked in an associated trade (bead making). The specific location of Trewe's shop is not identified by a street address. Instead, it is described by two different markers: parish (St Ewen's) and ward (Farringdon Within), signifying ec-clesiastical and civic jurisdictions. A fourteenth-century house or shop was located under more than one kind of authority, and the property holder had responsibilities to both ward and parish. As the shop was situated within the city of London itself, the case could be heard under the law of 'infangenthef,' a privilege that allowed the London mayor and aldermen to exercise summary justice (including execution) on thieves within the city. History, law, convention, and social practice all contributed to the particu-lar character of Trewe's shop and to the fate of the man who robbed it.

Geoffrey Chaucer was a Londoner, born and brought up a few streets south and east of Thomas Trewe's place of business. At this time, he resided on the edge of the city, above Aldgate, on the eastern walls of London, but on the day when this case was heard (6 July 1378) he was in Italy, hav-ing been sent on a diplomatic mission to Lombardy.[4] This was his second trip to Italy, and he was particularly suitable for these missions because of his urban background. Although by the 1370s he had become a member of the royal household and a retainer of John of Gaunt, his background was mercantile and urban. His upbringing in the city of London had given him the opportunity to mix with Italians and to learn the language.[5]

Winston-Allen, *Stories of the Rose: The Making of the Rosary in the Middle Ages* (University Park: Pennsylvania State University Press, 1997), 112.

[3] See, for instance, Erik Kwakkel, 'Commercial Organization and Economic Innovation,' in Daniel Wakelin and Alexandra Gillespie (eds.), *The Production of Books in England, 1350–1500* (Cambridge: Cambridge University Press, 2011), 181.

[4] Martin Crow and Claire Olson (eds.), *Chaucer Life-Records* (Oxford: Clarendon Press, 1966), 53–61.

[5] Wendy Childs, 'Anglo-Italian Contacts in the Fourteenth Century,' in Piero Boitani (ed.), *Chau-cer and the Italian Trecento* (Cambridge: Cambridge University Press, 1983), 65–88. Robert R. Ed-wards terms Vintry Ward Chaucer's 'first Italian place,' in 'Italy,' in Susanna Fein and David Raybin, *Chaucer: Contemporary Approaches* (University Park: Pennsylvania State University Press, 2010), 7.

Growing up in a wealthy merchant's house on the banks of the Thames, watching the ships come in bringing products from all over the world, provided a cosmopolitan childhood for the boy who was to become an exceptionally cosmopolitan poet. Items sold in Trewe's shop demonstrate the importance of international trade networks for medieval Londoners. Trewe sold a great deal of paper, for instance, which was almost certainly imported from Italy.[6] He also had *piper quernes* (pepper mills) for sale to feed the affluent class's insatiable appetite for pepper, a luxury product that traversed the world.[7] This appetite had provided the foundation of Chaucer's comfortable upbringing, as his grandmother's first husband had been a pepperer, and she and her subsequent two husbands had continued to live in the heart of the spice traders' quarter. Chaucer's life and his poetry were embedded in and determined by a world of international trade, manuscript exchange, multilingual creativity, and the movement of things and ideas across ever-changing borders.

In writing a biography of Chaucer, I've chosen to tell the story of his life and his poetry through spaces and places, rather than through strict chronology. Each chapter focuses on a particular space that mattered in Chaucer's life, as I attempt to recreate multiple kinds of environment. Some are actual places, such as Vintry Ward or Florence. Some represent contemporary structures that mattered both socially and in the contemporary imagination, such as the Great Household or the Inn. Others are more abstract and draw on key metaphors used by Chaucer, such as the Cage or the Threshold. In every case, my aim in exploring the space is to find out more about Chaucer's imaginative development—as opposed to his emotional life, which I believe is beyond the biographer's reach.[8] The spaces and institutions in which Chaucer lived and worked, and the places that he visited, shaped him as a person and as a poet.[9] I have therefore maintained

---

[6] Edward Heawood, 'Sources of Early English Paper Supply,' *The Library* s4-X (3) (1929): 305–7. See also Orietta da Rold, 'Materials,' in Gillespie and Wakelin, *Book Production*, 12–33.

[7] See Paul Freedman, *Out of the East: Spices and the Medieval Imagination* (New Haven: Yale University Press, 2008), 1–11.

[8] I do not mean to imply that this is inevitably the case for biographers of all subjects, but in the case of a subject who has left no personal correspondence, diaries, or records of conversations, I do not think we can understand that person's emotional life.

[9] Gaston Bachelard argues that the spaces in which we live are the fundamental reflections of our intimate selves. Gaston Bachelard, *The Poetics of Space*, trans. Maria Jolas (Boston: Beacon Press, 1994),

a *roughly* chronological structure, as one of my interests is to track how Chaucer the poet developed to emerge as the confident innovator of the *Canterbury Tales*.

The arrangement of space participates in the very construction of identity: our understanding of the nature of selfhood is contingent upon our understanding of private and public spaces, of the boundaries of the individual. Chaucer lived, for instance, in the public space of itinerant great households, between a set of rooms and an office in London, south of the river in Kent, and in a house in the precincts of Westminster Abbey. His life was also profoundly determined by more abstract institutional spaces, such as Parliament, which was going through a period of rapid change, or the house of Lancaster (headed by John of Gaunt), a shaping influence on Chaucer's entire life and the lives of his children. His travels around Europe gave him access to different modes of living and to multicultural societies. He spent time imprisoned in France, visited international courts in Navarre and Milan, and had opportunities to read and acquire manuscripts of European poetry. Most of his travels involved negotiation and trying to open up and maintain connections, both through marriage and peace talks and through trade agreements. The physical space between different countries was well understood by a man who had ridden from England to Italy at least twice, and who crossed the mountain passes of the Pyrenees in February. The global economy was also vividly present to Chaucer, a boy brought up in the heart of London, where expensive products from as far afield as Indonesia were sold.[10] Later in life, he saw the darkest side of global trade networks when he visited Genoa, where Tartar slaves were for sale, having been trafficked through Caffa and on into Italy.

A recent biographer of Shakespeare, Charles Nicholl, draws on forensics when he cites Locard's Exchange Principle, that 'every contact leaves traces.'[11] To try to understand the imagination of the poet, throughout this book I explore the things that surrounded him, the streets he walked, the

---

3–73. On the 'affective bond between people and place of setting,' see also Yi-Fu Tuan, *Topophilia: A Study of Environmental Perception, Attitudes, and Values* (Englewood Cliffs, NJ: Prentice-Hall, 1974).

[10]On the spice trade, see Freedman, *Out of the East*, 1–11.

[11]Charles Nicholl, *The Lodger: Shakespeare on Silver Street* (London: Penguin Books, 2007), 16.

communities in which he participated, and the structures that he inhabited. As the son of a wine merchant, and as a man who spent many years deeply involved in the wool trade, Chaucer's life was bound up with the movement of *things* between England and the Continent. In his writings, too, Chaucer was interested in materiality, in the literal terms of metaphor and how they signify, in the naturalistic depiction of rooms and objects. To give one example: in Book III of *Troilus and Criseyde*, Pandarus runs to fetch a cushion for Troilus to kneel on as he petitions Criseyde for sexual favour (964).[12] Pandarus's use of a prop underlines his role as author of the episode—a role that Chaucer has dramatically expanded and altered from Boccaccio's version. But the prop itself also merits attention.[13] What did a cushion mean to a fourteenth-century reader? Cushions were highly desirable domestic objects in the later fourteenth century: owning a cushion made a statement. The objects being sold in Thomas Trewe's shop demonstrate the growing importance of interior comfort and an idea of the home at this time. Trewe sold frames for cushions and he also sold quirky items such as a 'flekage,' probably a decorative fly cage to be hung up on the wall, as well as more standard decorative objects such as mirrors.[14] Prosperous merchants as well as members of the higher echelons of society were increasingly interested in spending disposable income on comfortable interiors: soft furnishings such as tapestries and cushions were becoming more and more popular.[15] Pandarus's Trojan house is designed and furnished like a smart fourteenth-century London home, with its large public area, its (semi)private spaces, its lavatory, and its accessories.[16]

---

[12] Quotations from Chaucer's writings are taken from Geoffrey Chaucer, *The Riverside Chaucer*, ed. Larry Dean Benson, 3rd ed. (Oxford: Oxford University Press, 2008).

[13] As James Krasner comments, 'the tangible dynamics of our everyday lives create our identities.' Krasner, *Home Bodies: Tactile Experience in Domestic Space* (Columbus: Ohio State University Press, 2010), 2.

[14] Riley, *Memorials of London*, 422n5. The mirrors are 'specularia,' mistakenly translated by Riley as 'spectacles.' Spectacles were, however, imported and sold in London at this time in large quantities. See Vincent Ilardi, *Renaissance Vision from Spectacles to Telescopes* (Philadelphia: American Philosophical Society, 2007), 71–72.

[15] P.J.P. Goldberg, 'The Fashioning of Bourgeois Domesticity in Later Medieval England: A Material Culture Perspective,' in Maryanne Kowaleski and P.J.P. Goldberg (eds.), *Medieval Domesticity: Home, Housing, and Household in Medieval England* (Cambridge: Cambridge University Press, 2008), 132–33.

[16] For detailed discussions of Pandarus's house, see Saul Brodie, 'Making a Play for Criseyde: The Staging of Pandarus's House in Chaucer's *Troilus and Criseyde*,' *Speculum* 73, no. 1 (1998): 115–40; and

Around the middle of the fourteenth century, well-off Londoners started to build parlours, reception rooms for socializing and conversation separate from the more public great hall. By the later part of the century, we see a multiplication of private chambers on the upper floors of London houses, developing the earlier fashion for having one private room, or 'solar.'[17] Pandarus's house evokes contemporary understandings of the public and private *and* contemporary interest in domesticity and home comforts.

Aristotle explored place in detail in his *Physics*, a widely read text in the late Middle Ages, defining place as the 'innermost motionless boundary' that contains things. He emphasized its *wonder*-ful nature, writing that 'the power of place must be a *marvelous* thing and be prior to all other things.'[18] Medieval commentators supplemented the Greek *topos* idea of place-as-container with the Latin *ubi*, meaning 'where something is.' Scholarly discussions about space and place influenced medieval poetry too; Matthew Boyd Goldie has recently argued that Chaucer evokes debates about Aristotelian ideas in his rhyming of 'place' and 'space' in the 'Knight's Tale,' for instance.[19] More generally, medieval poets were fascinated by the symbolic and imaginative potential of place. Indeed, place functioned as a crucial metaphor in many medieval poems: as Sarah Kay comments, 'Readers are forever being invited to locate themselves on a path somewhere, by some fountain, in some study, or within some garden, castle, or city.'[20] Many poets came to focus not on static places but on the journey through different locations; in dream vision in particular, dreamers often move across multiple places, which represent the complexity of the landscape of the mind. Throughout his work, Chaucer repeatedly uses natural landscapes, buildings, and the movement between various locations to depict psychological journeys; he shows us in detail how our understanding is directed by the kinds of structures we inhabit

H. M. Smyser, 'The Domestic Background of *Troilus and Criseyde,*' *Speculum* 31, no. 2 (1956): 297–315.

[17] John Schofield, *Medieval London Houses* (New Haven: Yale University Press, 2003), 66.

[18] Aristotle, *Physics*, in *The Complete Works of Aristotle*, ed. Jonathan Barnes (Princeton: Princeton University Press, 1984), 1:315–446, 1:212a20 (361), 1:208b32–33 (355); emphasis mine.

[19] Matthew Boyd Goldie, *Scribes of Space: Place in Middle English Literature and Late Medieval Science* (Ithaca: Cornell University Press, 2019), 63–65.

[20] Sarah Kay, *The Place of Thought: The Complexity of One in Late Medieval French Didactic Poetry* (Philadelphia: University of Pennsylvania Press, 2007), 2.

and the objects that we see.[21] Chaucer's specific interest in the contingency and variability of perspective can be compared both with the work of contemporary visual artists such as Giotto and with the work of contemporary scientists.[22] One of the fourteenth century's most original thinkers, the philosopher, mathematician, economist, and astronomer Nicole Oresme developed and refined the arguments of Jean Buridan about the movement of the cosmos and relativity, speculating about the rotation of the earth. In Joel Kaye's words, Oresme formulated 'a fully relativized perspectival system,' arguing, for instance, that if one day the earth revolved and the heavens were still, and the next day the heavens revolved and the earth were still, 'everything would appear exactly the same both today and tomorrow.'[23] At the time of Chaucer's birth, thinkers were newly able 'to imagine the cosmos as a working system with no privileged point of viewing.'[24] Oresme, like Giotto and Chaucer, was fully aware that how you perceive space is determined by where you are standing.[25]

Chaucer repeatedly contrasts the aerial, bird's-eye perspective with the street-level view, and the viewpoint of the idealist with that of the pragmatist. In his earliest poem, the *Book of the Duchess*, Chaucer tells us that you have to look with someone else's eyes in order to understand their perspective (1051). He also, however, makes clear the near-impossibility of escaping one's own standpoint. Even in a dream, his body remains relentlessly present and physical. The *House of Fame* depicts the narrator, Geffrey, caught up by an eagle, who comments upon how heavy the poet-avatar is: 'Thou art noyous [annoying] for to carye!' (574). This whole scene

---

[21] Writing recently about the *House of Fame*, Kathryn McKinley comments that 'Chaucer pursues extremely complex intellectual problems ... by thinking through a set of objects—three buildings and their very material features.' See Kathryn McKinley, *Chaucer's House of Fame and Its Boccaccian Intertexts: Image, Vision, and the Vernacular* (Toronto: Pontifical Institute of Medieval Studies, 2016), 71.

[22] See chapter 6 in this study. For discussion of Giotto and space, see Marvin Trachtenberg, *Dominion of the Eye: Urbanism, Art, and Power in Early Modern Florence* (Cambridge: Cambridge University Press, 1997).

[23] Joel Kaye, *A History of Balance, 1250–1375: The Emergence of a New Model of Equilibrium and Its Impact on Thought* (Cambridge: Cambridge University Press, 2014), 461; Nicole Oresme, *Le Livre du Ciel et du Monde*, ed. and trans. Albert Menut and Alexander Denomy (Madison: University of Wisconsin Press, 1968), 522–23.

[24] Kaye, *History of Balance*, 458.

[25] On medieval optics more generally, see Michael Camille, 'Before the Gaze: The Internal Senses and Late Medieval Practices of Seeing,' in Robert Nelson (ed.), *Visuality Before and Beyond the Renaissance: Seeing as Others Saw* (Chicago: University of Chicago Press, 2000), 197–223.

parodies part of Dante's *Divine Comedy*, but while Dante moves from a partial perspective to revelatory enlightenment, Geffrey remains an embodied presence, limited by his own weight, symbolizing the limitations that prevent any of us from experiencing complete understanding. Chaucer is a deeply secular poet, with no interest in supporting the grandiose claims of the Italian poets laureate who aspired to be poet-theologians.[26] Rather, his brilliance lies precisely in his understanding that all perspective is partial, and that therefore we need to hear as many voices as possible. The *Canterbury Tales* does many different things, but its greatest achievement is to demonstrate the importance of reading each tale, or version of events, in conjunction with other tales, other versions, as Chaucer blends and juxtaposes sources, styles, and genres. In marked contrast to other contemporary tale collections, such as the *Decameron* or the *Confessio Amantis*, Chaucer makes this variation of perspective absolutely central to the text by presenting us with tale-tellers from widely different social backgrounds.

In this biography, I trace the journey of Chaucer's life, from his early experiences of travelling, reading, and beginning his career under the patronage of the royal family, through his centred years at the Custom House in London, where he found time to become a fully fledged and prolific poet, to his mature years in Kent and Westminster, working in various parts of England and writing the *Canterbury Tales*. This is a literary biography, and throughout I am interested in the ways that the texture of Chaucer's poetry illuminates his life, and vice versa. I hope that this book will be of interest not only to scholars and students of literature and history but also to a broader audience: Chaucer's life and writings have much to teach anyone interested in European cultural history and its place in the world.

Chaucer evolved from a poet writing imitative *dits amoureux* (French-inspired love narratives) to a poet of unprecedented innovation and power.[27] His reading was exceptionally varied, and he wrote in an extraor-

---

[26] On Chaucer and Dante, see Karla Taylor, *Chaucer Reads the Divine Comedy* (Stanford, CA: Stanford University Press, 1989). For a recent discussion of what it means to term Chaucer 'secular,' see Megan Murton, 'Secular Consolation in Chaucer's *Complaint of Mars*,' *Studies in the Age of Chaucer* 38 (2016): 75–107.

[27] For more information about the *dit amoureux*, see Sarah Kay, Terence Cave, and Malcolm Bowie, *A Short History of French Literature* (Oxford: Oxford University Press, 2003), 75–80.

dinary range of genres. He did all this while holding down numerous day jobs, travelling frequently, and living through events including the Rising of 1381, several parliamentary rebellions, and finally the usurpation of the throne. His life story is a European story, everywhere dependent on the *translation*—the carrying across—of ideas, texts, and things. It is the story of the development of one of the most surprising imaginations in literary history, an imagination that changed what poetry could do.

PART I

BECOMING

Prologue

Book II of Chaucer's *House of Fame* opens with an address to the audience: 'Now herkeneth every maner man / That Englissh understonde kan' (509–10). The language could hardly be more straightforward; the invitation includes all social classes and emphasizes that the narrator is interested in a local, English audience. However, in the next few lines, he refers to figures from the Bible, Cicero's *Somnium Scipionis*, and the *Aeneid*, appealing to the Muses, and meditating on the nature of thought processes and the workings of the brain. This juxtaposition of tones and textures is entirely typical of Chaucer's poetic style. Indeed, part of Chaucer's talent lies in his ability to be all things to all readers: his texts are funny, accessible, and full of local interest and recognizable details, but they are also highly sophisticated and erudite, rooted in a world of international learning and culture. He can describe a local community, based around a recognizable university town and an abbey, with a blacksmith, carpenter, students, and parish clerks, visualizing even the contemporary shoe fashions worn by the antihero, cut to look like the windows of St Paul's, a building known to all his early listeners and readers.[1] But his

---

[1] This describes the 'Miller's Tale'; the shoe fashions are referred to in 3318.

writings are also steeped in French, Latin, Tuscan, and Hainuyer poetry, he translated late antique philosophy and paid homage to Muslim scientists, he was multilingual, and he was exceptionally well travelled. His ability to bring together the popular and the learned, the global and the local, and the international and the parochial has enabled generations of different kinds of readers to think that their souls are 'congenial' to his.[2] In his own lifetime he wrote texts that (at least aspirationally) addressed the greatest nobles in the land, and that were certainly read by courtiers, but that were read and sold in urban merchants' halls and by brothel owners in inns as well.[3] How did Chaucer gain his international sophistication *and* his interest in writing for a broader audience than a court or great household alone? Were there tensions between Chaucer's fundamental debts to courtly traditions and his emergence as a poet of the marketplace? And why did this cosmopolitan man decide to write in the unpromising vernacular?

Chaucer was born around 1342 in Vintry Ward in London, the area of the city dominated by vintners and hosting more immigrants than any other part of the city.[4] Just over thirty years later, in 1374, he returned to London, to live above Aldgate, and to work on the waterfront, in the Custom House, dealing with wool exports and the flow of international trade on a daily basis. The first section of this book is about what happened to Chaucer between those dates, in the first thirty or so years of his life. These were years of exploration, literal and metaphorical. He was born in London and he circled back to London, but in between he was a prisoner of war in France, a trade envoy in Italy, and a diplomat of some kind in Navarre and also in France. He married a woman whose family came from Hainault, and he travelled extensively around England. Intellectually, by the time he returned to London he had begun making poetry and was ready to embark upon an extraordinary period of writing.

---

[2] The words are Dryden's; for a detailed discussion of this attitude to Chaucer, see Stephanie Trigg, *Congenial Souls: Reading Chaucer from Medieval to Modern* (Minneapolis: University of Minnesota Press, 2001).

[3] Martha Carlin, 'Thomas Spencer, Southwark Scrivener (d. 1428): Owner of a Copy of Chaucer's *Troilus* in 1394?,' *Chaucer Review* 49:4 (2015): 387–401.

[4] Caroline Barron, *London in the Later Middle Ages: Government and People, 1200–1500* (Oxford: Oxford University Press, 2004), 97.

He had read widely in Latin and especially French texts; he had almost certainly written his first long narrative poem (the *Book of the Duchess*) as well as shorter poems and translations; and he was acquainted with many poets and thinkers at the English court. He returned to London ready to begin building his poetic identity: in the next decade, he was to produce almost all of his major works, apart from the *Canterbury Tales*. When he returned to London, Chaucer was a married man and a father of at least two children, and his mother was still alive, although his father had died a few years earlier. He was a retainer both of the king and of John of Gaunt, the duke of Lancaster.

Over the next few chapters, I recreate the environments that mattered most to Chaucer in the early years of his life: his first home in a prosperous, outward-looking, but then plague-stricken city (chapter 1, 'Vintry Ward'), his first job in a structure that influenced his life and poetry in all kinds of ways (chapter 2, 'Great Household'), and his first trip abroad to a country that signified war and poetry to the English (chapter 3, 'Reims and Calais'). I then move on to the French borders in chapter 4, discussing two no-longer-independent countries, Hainault and Navarre, one of which was the home of Chaucer's wife's family, of the queen, and of many contemporary poets, the second of which provided Chaucer with his first experience of a truly multicultural society. The penultimate chapter of this section, chapter 5, focuses on the house of Lancaster, a power base that dominated Chaucer's whole life and supplied the context for his first long poem, and the section ends with chapter 6, about Genoa and Florence, Chaucer's destinations in 1373, cities that brought together art, literature, finance, and trade, and set Chaucer up for his job at the wool customs.

By the time Chaucer returned from Italy in May 1373, he was poised to become a significant poet and, indeed, had embarked on a career of innovative and sophisticated writing. This first section of his life story explores how he entered into adulthood and authorship.

CHAPTER 1

>―!―◆―・O・―◆―!―⋖

Vintry Ward, London

Welcome, O life! I go to encounter for the millionth time the reality of experience.

—*James Joyce,* Portrait of the Artist as a Young Man

In the early 1340s, in Vintry Ward, London—the time and place of Chaucer's birth—a book went missing. It wasn't a very important book. Known as a 'portifory,' or breviary, it was a small volume containing a variety of excerpted religious texts, such as psalms and prayers, designed to be carried about easily (as the name demonstrates, it was portable).[1] It was worth about 20 shillings, the price of two cows, or almost three months' pay for a carpenter, or half of the ransom of an archer captured by the French.[2] The very presence of this book in the home of a merchant opens up a window for us on life in the privileged homes of the richer London wards at this time: their inhabitants valued books, objects of beauty, learning, and devotion, and some recognized that books could be utilized as commodities. The urban mercantile class was flourishing, supported and enabled by the development of bureaucracy and of the clerkly classes in the previous century.[3] While literacy was high in London, books were also appreciated as things in themselves: it was

---

[1] Sharpe, *Calendar of Letter-Books of the City of London: Letter-Book F,* fol. ccxviiib, 255.

[2] Christopher Dyer, *Making a Living in the Middle Ages: The People of Britain, 850–1520* (New Haven: Yale University Press, 2002), x, 240; Crow and Olson, *Chaucer Life-Records,* 24–25.

[3] Michael Clanchy, *From Memory to Written Record: England, 1066–1307,* 3rd ed. (Oxford: Wiley-Blackwell, 2013).

not unheard of for merchants to accept books as payment, as a form of treasure.[4]

The man from whom this book was stolen, Benedict de Fulsham, lived in Vintry Ward, and had worked with wines, as the king's butler, although he was primarily a pepperer, employed in the lucrative spice trade.[5] The thief, Richard de Pembroke, was a tailor, probably a lowly one. Standing as pledges for the prosecution were two local men: one of these men was Richard Chaucer, the step-grandfather of the poet and himself a vintner, although he lived in the neighbouring Cordwainer Ward, a few streets away.[6] The case was heard by the mayor, sheriffs, and aldermen of London on the Wednesday after the Feast of the Translation of St Thomas the Martyr, in the fifteenth year of Edward III's reign. This description of the date (12 July 1341 in our terminology) foregrounds the importance of both the king and the church. Time was measured according to the number of years that the monarch had been on the throne, and according to the moment in the liturgical year, a timescale punctuated by saints' and feast days. On a more microlevel, the very rhythms of the week and the day were determined by the time of the church too: there were meat-eating days and fast days, and the time of day tended to be marked in relation to the canonical hours, such as prime, terce, and nones.[7] But merchant's time moved to a different beat: to the logic of the flow of money, to the rhythms of payment, delivery, debt, and interest, and to the calculation of the cost of delay.[8] For the society into which Chaucer was born, city, church, monarch, and trade guild all exerted their pressures.

London life, then, was carefully regulated and ordered by a number of authorities. Another case, also from around the time of Chaucer's birth, illustrates the street-level policing of life in Vintry Ward. This case—heard

---

[4] William Walworth accepted a romance of Alexander and an Arthurian tapestry as payment for a debt in 1382; see A. H. Thomas (ed.), *Calendar of Plea and Memoranda Rolls of the City of London, 1381–1412* (Cambridge: University Press, 1932), Roll A25, Membrane 5b, 10–11.

[5] *Calendar of Close Rolls Preserved in the Public Record Office: Edward II* (London: HMSO, 1892–98), Membrane 3, 4:624 (29 December 1326).

[6] V. B. Redstone and L. J. Redstone, 'The Heyrons of London,' *Speculum* 12 (1937): 183–95.

[7] City dwellers would hear the prayers being sung. Prime was sung at around 6:00 a.m., terce at about 9:00 a.m., and nones at around 3:00 p.m.

[8] Jacques Le Goff, 'Merchant's Time and Church's Time in the Middle Ages,' in *Time, Work, and Culture in the Middle Ages*, trans. Arthur Goldhammer (Chicago: University of Chicago Press, 1982), 29–42.

on the Wednesday before the Feast of the Circumcision in the seventeenth year of Edward III (31 December 1343)—concerned an 'affray' in Vintry Ward three days earlier.[9] John de Oxford, John de Cleuf, and Henry de Ledham were walking, holding a light before them, when they encountered John Harris, the beadle of the ward, and his men at La Ryole. They passed peacefully, but a little way behind them followed two more of John de Oxford's company, without a light. The beadle asked them what they were doing without a light, and where they were going, and a quarrel broke out. John de Oxford and Henry de Ledham now returned, drew their swords, and assaulted the beadle, wounding him in the right arm. The scenario immediately illustrates the careful policing of the wards. The beadle and his men were actively watching the nighttime streets and were alert to anything being done in darkness. Whether they were engaged in nefarious or innocent pursuits, John de Oxford and his friends were armed and drew their swords at the first hint of trouble. The incident occurred at La Ryole. The name of the street—a version of La Reole, a town in Bordeaux—is testament to the number of Gascon dwellers (many temporary, some more permanent) in Vintry Ward, and to the importance of the wine industry in the fabric of the ward. The name became corrupted to the Tower Royal or La Royal, because the king owned property there, and his mansion became the Queen's Wardrobe. The street reached up to the border of Vintry Ward and Cordwainer Ward, and it is likely that the beadle was policing the boundaries of the ward, the edge of his jurisdiction. Such boundaries were not marked by walls or other physical divisions; streets cut across multiple wards, and parishes could also straddle more than one ward, but everyone knew where the authority of one ward ended and another began.

Violence broke out quickly. John de Oxford, who is depicted as the instigator of this Vintry Ward affray, was a skinner, engaged in the often putrid but very lucrative fur trade. His name tells us his origins, and other contemporary documents identify him as the servant of Henry of Eynsham.[10] Eynsham is a small settlement very close to Oxford, so we see

[9] A. H. Thomas (ed.), *Calendar of Plea and Memoranda Rolls, 1323–1364* (Cambridge: University Press, 1926), Roll A5, Membrane 13, 192–93.

[10] Ibid., Roll A3, Membrane 13b, 122; Roll A3, Membrane 16b, 129.

here immigrant men from the same area working together in London. This was not the only time that John was engaged in fights in the street, and he was even imprisoned in 1340.[11] His standing, however, was not affected: we find him in 1344 designated as one of twelve upstanding skinners with the good of the trade at heart, appointed to inspect the practices of others within the trade.[12]

These cases give us a snapshot of Vintry Ward in the early 1340s, before the demographic and social upheaval brutally wrought by the plague, before the English victories at Poitiers and Crécy, before the dramatic rise of English as a literary language. These were years on the cusp of change. This was the decade in which gunpowder was developed and gold coins were first minted in London; at court Queen Philippa was patronizing Hainuyer poets from her native land; over in France and Italy, Machaut and Boccaccio were writing some of their greatest works—works that were to be hugely influential on Chaucer.[13] While all educated English people knew French (and educated men all knew Latin), Chaucer's Thameside mercantile upbringing gave him the opportunity to mix with Italians and to learn their language—a skill that was to transform not only Chaucer's own poetry but English literature.[14]

Vintry Ward was located on the river, where cargos of Gascon wine were unloaded and stored in the vintners' cellars before the ships were sent back to the Continent, piled high with English wool. To live in the middle of things, at the pulsing centre of a hectic, ever-moving city, is to experience a constant, intoxicating assault on the senses. The sounds of the city came from all sides: sellers shouting their wares, civic proclamations, the snufflings of animals such as pigs who found their way into houses and shops, carts and horses rumbling down the streets, and the bells. There were no public clocks in London yet, though they would arrive soon, and the tolling of the church hours was an important way of structuring the day.[15] The small square mile or so of the walled and gated city supported

[11] Ibid., Roll A3, Membrane 16b, 129.
[12] Ibid., Roll A5, Membrane 22b, 209.
[13] These changes are discussed in detail in later chapters. See especially chapters 3, 4, 6, 10, and 13.
[14] Edwards, 'Italy,' 7.
[15] See W. M. Ormrod, *Edward III* (New Haven: Yale University Press, 2013), 453–54, for clocks in Edward III's reign; see Jacques Le Goff for a groundbreaking discussion of the relationship between

108 parish churches, including Chaucer's parish church, St Martin in the Vintry, so churches could be seen everywhere, punctuating the urban landscape.[16] At street level, the cityscape comprised densely built tenements, many of which were made up of shops fronting the street with living quarters above and behind. Houses extended up about three storeys and down to the cellars, particularly important for the vintners (plate 1). Rooms also overhung the streets, although they had to be at least nine feet up so that a man could ride a horse underneath.[17] In Vintry Ward, there were some magnificent residences, and the impressive houses owned by the wealthy merchants, complete with gardens and courtyards, were juxtaposed with multi-occupancy tenements.

There were, of course, public health problems in the medieval city. Chaucer's family property stretched back to the Walbrook, a river that today is wholly subterranean and that, in Chaucer's day, carried sewage to the Thames. Some people defecated in the open, animals could not easily be controlled, and offal, blood, and dung were transported out of the city in open carts.[18] But civic officials were very much occupied with implementing public health measures. London had an aqueduct for piping water around the city, streets were regularly cleaned, and privies were common. The foremost historian of London cautions that 'there is no reason to suppose that medieval London was unduly squalid,' and that the worst problems developed in the sixteenth century, when the population rapidly increased.[19] Sweet, more exotic smells were also to be found; incense was burnt in every church and a little way to the north of Chaucer's home, near the house of his grandparents, the pepperers congregated around Sopers' Lane. They sold a dazzling array of spices that would bewilder even

merchant's time and church time, and mechanical clocks and the church's hours and offices. He writes that (in Artois) the communal clock was 'an instrument of economic, social, and political domination wielded by the merchants who ran the commune.' See *Time, Work and Culture*, 35.

[16] John Schofield, 'Medieval Parish Churches in the City of London: The Archaeological Evidence,' in Katherine L. French et al. (eds.), *The Parish in English Life, 1400–1600* (Manchester: Manchester University Press, 1997), 37. The description of Chaucer's family home in the deed by which Chaucer quitclaimed the property in 1381 specifies that it was in the parish of St Martin Vintry. Crow and Olson, *Chaucer Life-Records*, 1.

[17] Barbara A. Hanawalt, *Growing Up in Medieval London: The Experience of Childhood in History* (Oxford: Oxford University Press, 1993), 25.

[18] Ibid., 28–29.

[19] Barron, *London*, 255.

the most sophisticated modern cook.[20] The fourteenth-century desire for spices supported an extraordinary trade that brought the products of Southeastern Asia to the shops and tables of London.[21] More commonly, in the streets, cookshops, alehouses, and brewhouses of London, one might eat a hot pie and drink some ale—or, in a tavern, one could drink wine.[22] Wine was the lifeblood of Chaucer's family and their neighbours, and wine created the wealth and royal contacts that established the social identity of the Chaucers, along with other well-off vintners. The English strongly favoured the wines of Gascony; German wines were of much less interest to the medieval English palate.[23] Standing in these streets—in Thames Street, where Chaucer lived, or on one of the myriad lanes, such as Three Cranes Lane or Oxenford Lane, that led off this major thoroughfare—one might touch almost anything: the warm fur worn by prostitutes as well as queens, the smooth stone of a church, a hard silver coin minted nearby in the Tower, the soft dough being taken to the baker's for cooking or the warm loaf of bread being brought back home, the heavy barrels of wine on which the area depended, a sheet of stiff parchment on which crucial accounts were carefully kept.[24] Vintry Ward, ca. 1342, was a place of excitement, business, corruption, entertainment, and opportunity.

For a newborn baby, interiors are more important than streets. Chaucer was lucky. He was born to comfortably off parents who lived in a spacious house, and both his parents, John and Agnes, were alive for his entire childhood and young adulthood. When he was born, his extended family, in similarly affluent circumstances, lived close by. His grandmother, Mary, with her third husband, Richard Chaucer, lived on Watling Street, in Cordwainer Ward, in a house that Mary had originally inherited from her first husband, John Heron, a pepperer. (Her second husband, Robert Chaucer, was Chaucer's grandfather.) Chaucer's uncle, Thomas

---

[20]Freedman, *Out of the East*, 8–12.

[21]Janet Abu-Lughod, *Before European Hegemony: The World System, A.D. 1250–1350* (New York: Oxford University Press, 1991).

[22]See Martha Carlin, 'The Host,' in Stephen H. Rigby (ed.), *Historians on Chaucer: The 'General Prologue' to the 'Canterbury Tales'* (Oxford: Oxford University Press, 2014), 460–81, for a discussion of the different characters and functions of various types of drinking establishments at this time.

[23]Barron, *London*, 84.

[24]In 1351, the city tried to prevent prostitutes from wearing fur; Riley, *Memorials of London*, 267.

Heron, John's constant associate and friend, was based just round the corner from John and Agnes.[25] Chaucer was born at a time when the idea of domesticity and the home was increasingly important.[26] In the middle of the fourteenth century, not only did households seek privacy from outside observers, as lawsuits relating to overlooking and intrusion illustrate, but city dwellers were also concerned with the privacy of the individual within the house, demonstrated by the multiplication of rooms in London houses.[27] The kind of house that Chaucer was born in had private spaces as well as public areas, and contained relatively luxurious furnishings. The Chaucer home—probably 179 Thames Street—certainly had extensive cellars and private rooms.[28] There would have been a large hall, rooms upstairs known as 'solars' or living rooms, bedchambers, and a privy. The family might have all slept in one bedchamber, with apprentices in another bedroom.[29] An inventory of the Vintry Ward home of a prominent vintner, Henry Vanner, taken in 1349, describes a house with a hall, three chambers, a kitchen, a storeroom, a chamber below the hall, a shop, and a cellar.[30] Working from home, or living in the office, were standard practice for medieval merchants, whose houses were also places of business, and the household comprised the nuclear family plus apprentices and servants.[31] Women often took part in running the business, and might keep running it themselves if they were widowed. Households such as Chaucer's were furnished and decorated with tapestries and hangings,

[25] Redstone and Redstone, 'The Heyrons of London'; Lister M. Matheson, 'Chaucer's Ancestry: Historical and Philological Re-Assessments,' *Chaucer Review* 25:3 (1991): 171–89.

[26] Goldberg, 'Fashioning of Bourgeois Domesticity.'

[27] The Assize of Nuisance heard cases relating to the invasion of privacy, for instance, complaints about windows overlooking the property of others. For discussion, see Barbara Hanawalt, *The Wealth of Wives: Women, Law, and Economy in Late Medieval London* (Oxford: Oxford University Press, 2007), 142–43. For the multiplication of rooms in London houses, see Schofield, *Medieval London Houses*, 93. In chapter 7, I discuss public and private spaces and the problems of privacy in detail.

[28] Thomas Bestul, 'Did Chaucer Live at 177 Upper Thames Street?,' *Chaucer Review* 43:1 (2008): 1–15; Crow and Olson, *Chaucer Life-Records*, 8–11. Matheson shows that John Chaucer probably moved into this house between 1337 and 1339 ('Chaucer's Ancestry,' 184).

[29] Schofield, *Medieval London Houses*, 71.

[30] Guildhall Record Office, Husting Roll 77, item 66. See also A. R. Myers, 'The Wealth of Richard Lyons,' in T. A. Sanquist and M. R. Powicke (ed.), *Essays in Medieval History Presented to Bertie Wilkinson* (Toronto: University of Toronto Press, 1969), 306.

[31] Goldberg, 'Bourgeois Domesticity,' 135–36.

comfortable beds and cushions, and display objects, such as silver plates and cups.[32] He would have had a cot to sleep in and soft coverings to keep him warm.

Simple things matter to babies: being warm, having good-quality milk—his mother would have been well nourished, and generally mothers breast-fed their children themselves, until their child was between one and three—and being comfortable.[33] Most of all, of course, babies need to be loved. We can't hope to find out anything about John and Agnes's emotional connection with their son, but most medieval parents loved their children, as do most modern ones,[34] and contemporary accounts and advice manuals demonstrate that parents cared about the same eternal issues of childcare as new parents do today—most pressingly, often, how do you help the baby get to sleep? How do you soothe them? Bartholomeus Anglicus, writing in the thirteenth century, recommended rocking a baby to sleep, and singing to them, methods that are still the preeminent ways of getting babies to sleep.[35] Very wealthy households even employed someone as a 'rocker' in nurseries.[36] Parents or nurses and babies sometimes co-slept, not simply because of lack of space but for comfort.[37] Indeed, a scurrilous story was spread that the real John of Gaunt had been accidentally smothered by a nurse in this way and replaced in the royal nursery by a butcher's son.[38] Some advice manuals reveal neglect and abuse: William of Pagula's manual, written about fifteen years before Chaucer's birth, warns that parents must not tie a baby into a cot or leave

---

[32] Ibid., 126–28, 132–35; Felicity Riddy, '"Burgeis" Domesticity in Late-Medieval England,' in Kowaleski and Goldberg, *Medieval Domesticity*, 29–30.

[33] Nicholas Orme, *Medieval Children* (New Haven: Yale University Press, 2001), 58, 66.

[34] Many historians have written about medieval parents' attitudes to their children, and about the medieval conception of childhood. For an excellent discussion of the issues and the relevant historiography, see Barbara A. Hanawalt, 'Medievalists and the Study of Childhood,' *Speculum* 77:2 (2002): 440–60.

[35] Bartholomaeus Anglicus, *On the Properties of Things: John Trevisa's Translation of Bartholomaeus Anglicus, 'De Proprietatibus Rerum,'* ed. M. C. Seymour (Oxford: Clarendon Press, 1975), book 6, chapter 4, 299.

[36] Paul B. Newman, *Growing Up in the Middle Ages* (Jefferson, NC: McFarland, 2007), 67.

[37] Orme, *Medieval Children*, 78.

[38] Marion Turner, 'Conflict,' in Paul Strohm (ed.), *Middle English: Oxford Twenty-First Century Approaches to Literature* (Oxford: Oxford University Press, 2007), 266–67.

them unattended for too long.[39] Contemporary London records tell of tragedies and atrocities—a baby eaten by a pig, others killed by fire along with their parents in cramped living quarters, and, rarely, infanticide.[40] Chaucer's young life, though, was privileged, and he is likely to have been cossetted and protected, insulated from some of the most egregious dangers of city life.

We do not know Chaucer's exact date of birth, but it was probably in 1342 or 1343. In 1386, he declared that he was more than forty years old, and that he had borne arms for twenty-seven years. If he first bore arms in 1359 (on the French campaign in which he was taken prisoner), he is likely to have been sixteen or seventeen at that point, possibly a little older.[41] He was born, then, when Edward III had been on the throne for about fifteen years, after his father, Edward II, had been deposed in 1327. Edward and Phillippa of Hainault already had several children, including Edward the Black Prince, Lionel of Antwerp (one of Chaucer's first employers), and John of Gaunt, who was to be very important in Chaucer's life, and who was almost exactly the same age as him. Babies were born at home and baptized within a day or so at the parish church. Baptism was a fairly traumatic experience for the brand-new baby, as it involved immersion in water three times. The baby, with father and godparents, but not the mother—who was not allowed to enter the church until she underwent the churching ceremony a few weeks after birth, and who anyway would have been recovering from the difficulties of giving birth without much medical help—gathered in the porch or doorway of the church. The baby, as a non-Christian, could not enter the church before she or he had been instructed, exorcised, blessed, and named. The party then went to the font, near the door, for the anointing and baptism ceremony. The ritual had several different parts; its central purpose was to bring the child into the Christian community so that she or he had the chance of ultimate salvation. This entry into the Christian community also, of course, made the

[39] Colin Platt, *The Parish Churches of Medieval England* (London: Chancellor, 1995), 49.

[40] Hanawalt, *Growing Up*, 64, 26–27; Richard H. Helmholtz, 'Infanticide in England in the Later Middle Ages,' *History of Childhood Quarterly* 1 (1974–75): 282–390; Barbara Hanawalt, *Crime and Conflict in English Communities, 1300–1348* (Cambridge, MA: Harvard University Press, 1979), 154–57.

[41] Crow and Olson, *Chaucer Life-Records*, 24.

baby a member of an earthly group, the large community of Christians and the small, local community of the parish. The godparents, who usually lived nearby and hence were on hand, gave gifts and often the name; they became the child's spiritual family. The child's name—in this case, Geoffrey—was repeated twenty-four times during the service, in a symbolic establishment of his identity as a valued individual, set now on his path in life, with the support of his parents, their friends (the godparents), and the structures of the parish.[42]

St Martin Vintry offered a secure parish home. One of four churches in Vintry Ward—the others were St Michael Paternoster, St James Garlickhythe, and St Thomas Apostle—it was the church most specifically associated with the wine merchants; it provided an identity with a long history and a prestigious pedigree. Three hundred years earlier, not long after the Norman Conquest, it had been termed the *baermannecyrce*, the church (*cyrce*) of the carriers or porters (the *baermanne*—the men who bore things). It was, in other words, the church of merchants, of traders. There are several references to it as *baermanecherche* throughout the twelfth and thirteenth centuries.[43] In 1299, it was rebuilt, largely at the expense of Matthew Columbars, who had left money for this purpose in his will. He was a Bordeaux wine merchant who had been the king's chamberlain, or taker of wines, throughout England, responsible for choosing and buying the king's wines. His arms were placed in the east window of the church.[44] The church, dedicated to St Martin, patron saint of the vintners' company, was dominated by the wine trade. A few years after Chaucer's baptism, for instance, the wealthy John Gisors, alderman, mayor, MP, and politician, scion of a patrician family that had long been dominant in London trade and politics, was buried in the church, before the rood.[45] Chaucer, the son of a prominent vintner, became part of a community that offered protection and stability.

Unlike the Gisors family, Chaucer's own family did not have a long London provenance. His great-great-grandfather, Robert le Taverner, or

---

[42] Orme, *Medieval Children*, 24–37.

[43] Henry A. Harben, *A Dictionary of London* (London: Herbert Jenkins, 1918), 387.

[44] Ibid., 387; Schofield, 'Medieval Parish Churches,' 50.

[45] Reginald R. Sharpe (ed.), *Calendar of Wills Proved and Enrolled in the Court of Husting, London, A.D. 1258–A.D. 1688* (London: John C. Francis, 1890), Roll 78 (248), 1:643.

Robert de Dinehinetune, was from Ipswich, in Suffolk. He was also known as Malen or Malyn of London, which suggests he traded in the capital as well as in East Anglia. Malyn seems to have been the family name, with Dinehinetune referring to their village, and taverner to their trade. His son, Andrew de Dynyngton, was married to Isabella, and was based in Ipswich.[46] Their son, Robert, went to London, where he became the apprentice to a mercer, John de Dowgate, also known as John le Chaucer. This John de Dowgate/Chaucer, had business dealings with John Heron, a wealthy pepperer. In 1302, John de Dowgate/Chaucer was involved in a street fight and eventually died of his wounds. He left a quarter of his business to his apprentice, Robert, who took his name as a token of respect.[47] And when John de Dowgate's friend, John Heron, died, Robert married his widow, Mary. This couple were Chaucer's grandparents, the parents of his father, John Chaucer. Robert held royal appointments, as deputy to the king's butler, Henry de Say, in London, in 1308,[48] and as collector in London for customs on wine levied on merchants from Aquitaine in 1310.[49] Robert and Mary's son, John, was born around 1312, and Robert died two or three years later.[50] Meanwhile, he still had family connections back in Ipswich, notably his sister, Agnes, who had married Walter de Westhale. Mary Chaucer, widowed for the second time, married again, this time to Richard Chaucer—we do not know if he had a relationship to Robert or to Robert's erstwhile master. In 1324, anxious to secure John Chaucer's inheritance from his own father (her brother), Agnes de Westhale abducted her nephew, hoping to marry him to her daughter. This dramatic episode is attested to in the subsequent lawsuits: Agnes and Geoffrey Stace (whom she would later marry) kidnapped John, a child of about twelve, from Cordwainer Street and carried him off. His stepfather, Richard, and halfbrother, Thomas Heron, pursued the abductors to Ipswich, where they robbed Agnes of £40 worth of property. John was returned to his parents

[46] Matheson, 'Chaucer's Ancestry,' 172.

[47] Ibid., 179–81.

[48] *Calendar of the Patent Rolls Preserved in the Public Record Office: Edward II* (London: Eyre and Spottiswoode, 1894–1904), Membrane 20, 1:143 (15 November 1308), http://sdrc.lib.uiowa.edu/patentrolls/e2v1/body/Edward2vol1page0143.pdf.

[49] Walter Rye, 'Chaucer's Grandfather, Robert le Chaucer,' in Edward A. Bond and Walford D. Selby (eds.), *Life-Records of Chaucer* (London: N. Trübner, 1886), 3:128.

[50] Matheson, 'Chaucer's Ancestry,' 175.

unharmed, and unmarried. After protracted lawsuits, the Chaucer family was awarded enormous damages of £250 by a London court in 1327.[51]

Family squabbles, jealousies, and infighting dominated high politics in England at this time too. In 1326, Queen Isabella, her lover, Roger Mortimer, and her teenage son, Edward of Windsor, had invaded England and taken up arms against Edward II, Isabella's husband and Edward of Windsor's father. Towards the end of the year, the king was captured. London strongly supported Isabella and Prince Edward and pushed for the deposition of Edward II and his replacement by his son. In January 1327, Edward II was indeed deposed, although he was not killed, and his son was crowned on 1 February. That night, a Scottish army attacked England, and plans were formed for a counterattack.[52] In the summer, John Chaucer and his half-brother Thomas Heron, along with a troop of Londoners, took part in a shambolic campaign against the Scots. The following year, as tensions mounted in the country and Henry, earl of Lancaster, mobilized against Mortimer, John Chaucer was amongst a group who rode to fight with Lancaster against Isabella and Mortimer. This venture too collapsed, and a number of Londoners were summoned to appear at the Court of Hustings in 1329; those who failed to appear, including John Chaucer, were outlawed.[53] However, this is unlikely to have had much force or meaning, especially as Edward III was shortly to topple Mortimer and have him executed, with the support and help of the earl of Lancaster.

In the 1330s, John Chaucer entered into sober adulthood and became established as a wine merchant. His name often crops up in city records in association with other well-respected merchants. He travelled to Europe; for instance, in 1338 his name appears in a list of men to whom the king issued letters of protection just before an English army went to fight in France, basing itself at Antwerp. Vintner Henry Picard and John Heron also figure in this list.[54] He shipped wool between Ipswich and Flanders

[51] Crow and Olson, *Chaucer Life-Records*, 3. Redstone and Redstone, 'Heyrons of London,' 185–86.

[52] Ormrod, *Edward III*, 64–65.

[53] Redstone and Redstone, 'Heyrons of London,' 186–88.

[54] Thomas Rymer, *Foedera* (London, 1704–35), 5:51–52. John Heron may have been another family connection, and he also seems to have taken part in the 1327 foray with John Chaucer and Thomas

around the time of Chaucer's birth.[55] Chaucer's mother was Agnes de Copton, daughter of John de Copton, and niece of Hamo de Copton, who owned quite a lot of property in and around the city.[56] In material terms, both of Chaucer's parents brought wealth to the marriage and both were Londoners and owners of London property. By 1342, around when Chaucer was born, John's name appears, consenting to city legislation about wine, alongside other well-known vintners, such as Thomas Gisors and John de Stodeye.[57] In the 1360s, John Chaucer appears in the records as a supporter of Richard Lyons, a merchant who rose to extraordinary wealth and influence, was impeached by the Good Parliament, emerged relatively unscathed, but was then executed by the rebels during the Rising of 1381.[58] The inventory for Lyons's house in Kerion Lane, at the heart of Vintry Ward and very close to the Chaucer residence, survives and bears witness to the lifestyle of the richest residents of the ward.[59] As well as detailing the contents of his ship, several taverns, and a shop, the inventory divides the house into the following rooms: 'sale,' 'parlour,' 'principale chamber,' 'seconde chambre,' 'tierce chambre,' 'chapel,' 'garderobe,' 'naparie,' 'petit garderobe,' 'chapman chaumbre,' 'autre chambre pur autres,' 'panetrie et botellie,' 'cusyne,' 'larder,' 'stable,' and 'comptour.' Featherbeds, occasional tables, chandeliers, chaise longues, and cushions abound.[60] Chaucer grew up surrounded by solid wealth, amongst people who cared about comfort and about lovely things.

The structures and communities of late-medieval London were idiosyncratic. A family's identity was strongly tied both to ward and to parish. The ward was the bigger structure. London was divided into

Heron, and in the 1328 venture alongside John Chaucer; see Redstone and Redstone, 'Heyrons of London,' 186–88. Crow and Olson suggest that the John Chaucer in this record could have been a different John Chaucer (*Chaucer Life-Records*, 4), but the presence of Heron and Picard makes it very probable that this is indeed the poet's father.

[55] Crow and Olson, *Chaucer Life-Records*, 4.

[56] Ibid., 7–8.

[57] Sharpe, *Calendar of Letter-Books: Letter-Book F*, fol. lxiii, 78; Thomas Milbourn (ed.), *The Vintners' Company, Their Muniments, Plate, and Eminent Members* (London: Vintners' Company, 1888), 5. See also Anne Crawford, *A History of the Vintners' Company* (London: Constable, 1977), 35.

[58] See 9 December 1364, in Thomas, *Calendar, 1364–1381*, Roll A10, Membrane 4b, 11. Lyons's career is discussed in more detail in subsequent chapters in this study, especially chapters 7 and 12.

[59] National Archives, E 199/25/72.

[60] Myers, 'Wealth of Richard Lyons,' 307–29.

twenty-four wards at this point (in 1394 Farringdon was split in two, making twenty-five). The ward was an instrument of city government: the wardmote, a gathering of all the men in the ward, both householders and servants, under the direction of the ward's elected alderman, met to elect jurors or advisors to the alderman, hear new civic legislation, discuss necessary public health and safety measures, and complain about antisocial and illegal behaviour. Being part of a ward meant taking some of the collective responsibility for making sure that the streets were clean, that precautions were taken against fire, and that brothel owners were made notorious. Ordinary householders knew that they could be the focus of criticism and accusation if they built illegal extensions, threw dung onto the street, or ignored price controls.[61] The wards had markedly different characters. In 1304, a list of aliens (foreigners) who protested about paying a tax demonstrates that they were living in only eight of the twenty-four wards. Vintry Ward had the most immigrants, mainly from Gascony, the hub of the wine trade. Adjoining Dowgate was the home of Germans and people from the Low Countries; those from Spain, Italy, and Provence lived in the wards of Cordwainer, Cheap, and Langbourn.[62] While there are certainly cases in which we see Londoners closing ranks against foreigners, we can also find cases in which European immigrants were treated with notable equity. One case, centering around the nonpayment of money owed for wine, which should have been paid on a quay in the Vintry, involved a Gascon merchant and a London apprentice. It went before a jury deliberately comprised half of Gascons, before going to the arbitration of four members of the vintners' guild, and the decision was in favour of the Gascon merchant.[63] The existence of nearby Olde Iuwerie, however, so named after the expulsion of the Jews in 1290, reminds us that not all immigrants, or descendants of immigrants, were treated equally.[64]

As a riverside ward, the Vintry must have been strongly influenced by *all* the immigrants and products arriving at the docks and being transported further into the city; it was a borderland, a transition point between

[61] Barron, *London*, 122–23.

[62] Ibid., 97.

[63] Thomas, *Calendar, 1381–1412*, Roll A29, Membrane 11, 162.

[64] Kathy Lavezzo, *The Accommodated Jew: English Antisemitism from Bede to Milton* (Ithaca: Cornell University Press, 2016), 109–11.

the English market and the rest of the world. Ships arrived every day. They brought wine from Gascony, England's most important import, but they also brought skins, furs, and leather from Spain; fish, timbers, beeswax, grain, iron, zinc, and copper from German and Baltic lands; squirrel skins from Lithuania, Poland, and Hungary; other skins from Russia, Finland, and Estonia; spices and silks from the Far East via numerous middlemen; glass, paper, and fustian from Italy; and sugar, fruits, and alum from the Mediterranean.[65] To see these ships unload, to experience the shops of London, to live in a wealthy household complete with luxury fabrics and sophisticated spices and wines, was to be aware of a global economy on a vast scale. References to products in Chaucer's poetry often include their place of origin—'cloth of Reynes' (*Book of the Duchess*, 255); 'a steede of Lumbardye' ('Squire's Tale,' 193); 'outlandish [foreign] ware' (*The Former Age*, 22)—suggesting that their provenance added to their value; people cared about the origin of their goods. The wharfs of Vintry Ward and the Thames itself were the doors and road that led to this greater world, a world everywhere evident within the ward itself.

Being part of a parish provided a different kind of identity. But just as the ward made its wealthiest members feel part of a global network, part of the superstructure of London, and part of a local community, so the parish rooted its members in international Christendom, in the English church, and in the diocese, while primarily being a local organization. Crucially, laypeople in the parish were not the passive recipients of the church's services. They had responsibility for the upkeep of parts of the church, gave money to the church, and assisted with regular duties, such as locking up holy oil, chrism, and the host, and covering and locking the font. Some parishioners gave generous bequests.[66] The church was more than a place of worship for parishioners; it was a community centre where people might go for meetings, or to trade, or even for a cockfight.[67]

---

[65] Barron, *London*, 86.

[66] In 1350, John Gisors left detailed instructions for the provision of a chantry at St Martin Vintry in his will: the chaplain was to have his own chamber, a chalice, a two-volume missal, a portifory, a psalter, vestments, and a cope of fine linen; he also provided garments for the deacon and subdeacon and various vessels and cloths of silk and gold. Sharpe, *Calendar of Wills*, Roll 78 (248), 1:643.

[67] Katherine French, *The People of the Parish: Community Life in a Late Medieval English Diocese* (Philadelphia: University of Pennsylvania Press, 2001), 1, 30.

Every church was supposed to contain a diverse range of objects, according to surviving lists of diocesan instructions. Above all, each church was supposed to have a range of books, including a manual, ordinal, missal, collect book, a *legenda* (of saints' lives and scriptural lessons for readings), a number of music books, and a copy of the statutes of the synod. Not all churches had all these things, but they do all seem to have a reasonably wide range of items.[68] Chaucer's parish church also contained an altar to St Thomas Martyr: Thomas à Becket, the great London saint whose shrine at Canterbury was to provide the never-reached goal of the *Canterbury Tales*. As well as attending weekly Mass, Chaucer, along with the other parishioners, heard instruction four times a year on six points: the fourteen articles of faith, the ten commandments of the law and two of the Gospel, the seven works of mercy, the seven deadly sins, the seven virtues, and the seven sacraments. Since the Fourth Lateran Council of 1215, confession to one's parish priest was mandatory every Lent; at this time the priest, if he were conscientious, also inquired into the confessant's religious knowledge.[69] Each church was staffed by a few men—perhaps a deacon and subdeacon, as well as the priest; at the least a parish clerk and perhaps a holy water clerk or boy.[70] In the poll tax of 1381, St Martin Vintry returned three chaplains as well as the rector.[71] St Martin Vintry would have been a constant part of Chaucer's life, perhaps from the very day of his birth, certainly from the first few days, a place for worship and instruction, but also a place of gathering and belonging.

We do not know if Chaucer had siblings. There is a much later reference to Katherine, wife of Simon Mannyng, as Chaucer's sister, and Chaucer did have connections with Simon, mainprising him (standing surety for him in law) in 1386.[72] Most wealthy families in this period ended up with only two or three surviving children, so it would not be unusual if Geoffrey were the only child to survive.[73] It is very likely that he did have siblings who died either at birth or in infancy; certainly all children saw

[68] Platt, *Parish Churches*, 27–29.

[69] Ibid., 48.

[70] Ibid., 61–62.

[71] A. K. McHardy, 'Taxation of the Clergy, 1379–81: Poll Tax of 1381 in the City of London,' in *The Church in London, 1375–1392* (London: London Record Society, 1977), 25–27, *British History Online*, http://www.british-history.ac.uk/london-record-soc/vol13/pp25-27.

[72] Crow and Olson, *Chaucer Life-Records*, 285–89.

[73] Orme, *Medieval Children*, 53.

infant mortality at close hand in this era. Whether or not he had siblings as playmates, Chaucer was brought up in a district where everyone knew everyone else and where his father was a well-known personage; his childhood was embedded in his parents' social networks, and it was probably highly social. Toys tend to be ephemeral and few have survived, but those that have bear witness to the essential similarity of many aspects of play across the centuries. Medieval children, it turns out, liked playing with toy cooking sets, dolls, and knights on horseback; in other words, they engaged in imitative and imaginative play, acting out what they saw adults doing and pretending to be grown-ups themselves.[74] Very wealthy children had more technical, mechanical toys.[75] Children played outside, particularly with balls, and also went swimming and fishing; inside they learnt games of skill, memory, and chance, such as dice, backgammon, draughts, chess, and cards.[76] Young children spent a lot of time with their parents and often followed the parent of the same gender: records of accidents show us that boys seem to have been outside more with their fathers, while girls led a more domestic existence.[77] We can't know what kind of child Chaucer was—confident or introverted, the centre of attention or an observer, imaginative or orderly, careful or physically bold—but we can be sure that his early life was inflected by his father's business. The life of a merchant's son was infused with trade, with the products and practitioners of international importing and exporting, and with London retail too; business was everywhere in the houses and streets in which Chaucer spent his early years.

In 1347, John Chaucer got a new job: in February, he was appointed as deputy to the king's butler, John de Wesenham, in Southampton; a couple of months later he was also made the deputy for collecting customs on cloth and beds exported by foreign merchants from Southampton, Portsmouth, Chichester, Seaford, and Shorham.[78] The position of deputy

---

[74] On medieval toys, see Patricia Clare Ingham, *The Medieval New: Ambivalence in an Age of Innovation* (Philadelphia: University of Pennsylvania Press, 2015), 75–76; and J. Allen Mitchell, *Becoming Human: The Matter of the Medieval Child* (Minneapolis: University of Minnesota Press, 2014), 59–116.

[75] Orme, *Medieval Children*, 168–72.

[76] Ibid., 178–79.

[77] Barbara Hanawalt, 'Childrearing among the Lower Classes of Late Medieval England,' *Journal of Interdisciplinary History* 8:1 (1977): 8; Orme, *Medieval Children*, 67.

[78] *Calendar of the Patent Rolls Preserved in the Public Records Office: Edward III* (London: Eyre and Spottiswoode, 1891–1916), Membrane 30, 7:253; Membrane 15, 7:276.

butler was essentially that of a tax collector, but one with specialist knowledge of wines.[79] The king's butler appointed several deputies to oversee the purchase of wines in different ports, and both John's father and his stepfather had held similar appointments.[80] John's second role, exacting customs on the export of woolen cloths and beds, reflected the complexities of the wine trade as merchants tried to fill up their ships in both directions.[81] The king's butler and his deputies were frequently accused of corruption: in 1333 the butler's deputies were removed from office and in 1339 and 1345 they were warned against extortion under pretence of purveyance. In 1351 a statute was passed forbidding the evil practices of the king's butler and his deputies.[82] Certainly, anyone doing this job would have to be streetwise at the least; it was normal to use such positions for personal profit. Although the war with France was causing some difficulties for the wine trade, and coastal ports were at risk of attack—Southampton had been raided by the French in 1338 and further attacks were feared—the wine trade remained very lucrative.[83]

Merchants in Southampton lived well: a will from 1349 mentions silver vessels, silk, lengths of fine cloth, carpets, bed-hangings, feather-beds, chests, doublets, tunics, and robes, evidence of a healthy disposable income and of the same kind of taste as London merchants and indeed aristocrats.[84] While not nearly as important as London, Southampton was a major port and, like London, its dependence on international trade gave it a cosmopolitan atmosphere: in the thirteenth century a local merchant owned products from all over Europe, ate imported fruits, and kept an African monkey as his pet.[85] The Chaucers may not, however, have spent much of their time there: it is likely that they travelled back to London regularly; perhaps indeed Agnes and Geoffrey stayed there most of the

[79] George Unwin (ed.), *Finance and Trade under Edward III* (Manchester: Longmans, Green, 1918), 282.

[80] For Richard Chaucer's appointment in London on 6 October 1341, under Reymund Seguyn, see *Calendar of the Patent Rolls: Edward III*, Membrane 9, 5:289.

[81] Unwin, *Finance and Trade*, 251, 296–97; Margery Kirkbride James, *Studies in the Medieval Wine Trade*, ed. Elspeth M. Veale (Oxford: Clarendon Press, 1971), 168.

[82] Unwin, *Finance and Trade*, 289–90.

[83] James, *Medieval Wine Trade*, 9, 16; Colin Platt, *Medieval Southampton: The Port and Trading Community, A.D. 1000–1600* (London: Routledge and Kegan Paul, 1973), 107–9.

[84] Platt, *Medieval Southampton*, 102.

[85] Ibid., 103.

time. John certainly would have continued his own business dealings in the city, and they still owned their property there. But John was also now closely involved in the king's business, particularly in purchasing wine and sending it to the king's residences at Winchester, Salisbury, Oxford, and Odiham, and provisioning other castles such as Porchester, Carisbroke, and Marlborough.[86] He was perhaps making or consolidating the contacts that were to enable him to place his son in a royal household in the middle of the 1350s.

After John had been in this job for a year, unimaginable catastrophe struck: for the Chaucer family, for the country, for the whole of Europe and Asia, probably the most devastating catastrophe that the world has ever known. The ships that brought wine, spices, metals, timber, skins, fabrics, and fruits also brought a terrifying disease. The story of the Black Death is well known: it spread from the East, inexorably travelling across Europe, hitching a ride on the trade networks so fundamental to the Asian, North African, and European economies. It was a monstrous, agonizing, and brutal disease. It is possible that half of England's people died. It reached every corner of the country; it was indiscriminate in the toll it exacted.[87]

Many writers have speculated about the effect of the Black Death on the mentality of the survivors. Some suggest that it caused a carpe diem attitude, others that it led to increased emphasis on piety and religion. Literary critics point to a 'reciprocity between the depth of the pandemic's impact and the vigor of creative expression, particularly within the evolving category of literature,' in the years that followed.[88] Contemporary commentators desperately searched for a reason behind it, blaming the Jews, general immorality, or bad air.[89] Boccaccio—whose works would later change the trajectory of Chaucer's poetic career—wrote his magnum opus, the *Decameron*, just after the plague. He writes passionately about the behaviour of the people in plague-stricken Florence, painting a fictional picture of inverted moral codes and desperation. The ten wealthy protag-

[86] James, *Medieval Wine Trade*, 182.

[87] Dyer, *Making a Living*, 271–72.

[88] Jamie C. Fumo, *Making Chaucer's 'Book of the Duchess': Textuality and Reception* (Cardiff: University of Wales Press, 2015), 66.

[89] See documents in Rosemary Horrox (trans. and ed.), *The Black Death* (Manchester: Manchester University Press, 1994), 56–57.

onists retreat from the city to the countryside, to tell stories and while away the time until the plague passes. Indeed, the rich did suffer less than the poor, as they did not live in such close proximity to each other, and they had more freedom of movement, but no class of people was immune—one of the king's daughters, Joan, died in Bordeaux in 1348.[90] The plague came to the Bordeaux region in the early months of 1348 and, from John Chaucer's point of view, was disastrous for the wine trade. While in 1308–9 (a bumper year) 102,724 tuns were exported from Gascon ports, in 1348–49, only 5,923 were exported.[91] There were human tragedies about to hit the Chaucer family when the plague came to England. In April 1349, all of John and Agnes's London relatives were wiped out. Possibly, it was their absence in Southampton that saved John and his family from perishing as well, through contact with their close relatives Richard Chaucer and Thomas Heron. The plague struck Southampton too, of course, as it struck everywhere, and the terror of the epidemic affected everyone. Yet, as historians have pointed out, recent archaeological evidence reveals that bodies were neatly laid out in cemeteries, not tipped into mass pits, and institutional records show that government went on much as usual. The records suggest a surprising continuity, demonstrating that the structures and institutions of the country were remarkably robust.[92]

The horrors of the Black Death must be seen in the context of a society in which death routinely struck people down at a much younger age than is the case today, where death appeared even more random and unpredictable than it does to us. Tragedy was the condition of life, as it always is, but in a far more extreme way: parents regularly saw their babies stillborn and experienced child after child dying; many more women died in childbirth, as minor infections could easily be fatal in an age before antibiotics. We have not experienced anything on the scale of the Black Death; no event, either natural or man-made, in the twentieth or twenty-first century has destroyed that kind of proportion of the general population. The differences in our attitudes to and expectations about death

[90] Dyer estimates that among the rich, mortality was about 27 per cent, among the clergy 42–45 per cent, and among peasants between 40 and 70 per cent. *Making a Living*, 272.

[91] James, *Medieval Wine Trade*, 26.

[92] Dyer, *Making a Living*, 273.

make it clear that our society would react very differently to a plague on the scale of what happened in 1348–49. Many people have written about the fact that Western culture today is a culture that excludes death, where dead bodies are not usually viewed, where death is taken out of the home and into a medical context and funeral industry, where death is, in many ways, taboo.[93] This was not the case in the Middle Ages. That doesn't mean that people did not mourn the loss of their family and friends just as much as we do today, but it does mean that people had different horizons of expectation and thought differently about the place of death in their lives.

The cycle of life and death is one of the great leitmotifs of medieval poetry, memorably expressed by Chaucer in many of his poems. The *Canterbury Tales* opens with the image of April succeeding March, spring succeeding winter, life succeeding death, masterfully linking this imagery with human sickness both physical and spiritual:

> Whan that Aprill with his shoures soote
> The droghte of March hath perced to the roote,
> And bathed every veyne in swich licour
> Of which vertu engendred is the flour;
> Whan Zephirus eek with his sweete breeth
> Inspired hath in every holt and heeth
> The tendre croppes, and the yonge sonne
> Hath in the Ram his half cours yronne,
> And smale foweles maken melodye,
> That slepen al the nyght with open ye
> (So priketh hem nature in hir corages),
> Thanne longen folk to goon on pilgrimages,
> And palmeres for to seken straunge strondes,
> To ferne halwes, kowthe in sondry londes;
> And specially from every shires ende
> Of Engelond to Caunterbury they wende,

---

[93]Jean Baudrillard, *Symbolic Exchange and Death*, trans. Iain Hamilton Grant (London: Sage, 1993).

The hooly blisful martir for to seke,

That hem hath holpen whan that they were seeke. (1–18; plate 2)

The church's cycle of Lent and Easter mirrors the natural cycle of the seasons as spring and regeneration succeed winter. The extraordinary opening sentence culminates in a celebration of the thaumaturgic power of saintly relics ('The hooly blisful martir,' 17), as the pilgrimage brings spiritual healing to the pilgrim. The very cadences of these lines, with two parallel clauses, both beginning 'Whan . . .' (1, 5) building up to a decisive 'Thanne' (12) powerfully suggest that the cycles—of the seasons, the crops, the church year, human sin and recovery, and human life and death—have a balance and an order. That order is not a fair one—suffering and death strike unannounced and horrifically—but the cycle of life is inevitable. A passionate concern with these cycles of life and death suffuses the poetry of Chaucer, and of many of his contemporaries.[94] However, Chaucer is ultimately not interested in *dwelling* on that which we cannot change; rather, he depicts the choices and circumstances of particular individuals, at particular places and particular times. Indeed, in the opening of the *Canterbury Tales*, Chaucer quickly moves away from his distancing depiction of the eternal cycles of life to focus, instead, on what happened 'in that seson on a day, / In Southwerk at the Tabard as I lay' (19–20). He shifts our perspective from the eternal to the temporal, from the sacred to the secular, from the cosmic to the street-level. Both this juxtaposition of perspectives and the ultimate focus on a viewpoint in medias res, rather than an omniscient view from above, are hallmarks of Chaucer's poetics.

Chaucer's own family starkly experienced the tragedy of life in April 1349. In London, Thomas Heron made his will on 7 April, bequeathing all his tenements to John and making him his executor.[95] Five days later, when Richard Chaucer made his will, Thomas was already dead. Richard provided for two chantries, one in St Mary de Aldermarie and one in St Michael de Paternoster, for himself and for the souls of Thomas and of Richard's late wife, Mary, Chaucer's grandmother, whose tomb was in

[94] See, for instance, my discussion of the *Book of the Duchess* in chapter 5.
[95] Sharpe, *Calendar of Wills*, Roll 76 (169), 1:544.

St Mary Aldermarie.[96] We do not know exactly when she died; Richard's will was proved in July.[97] John Chaucer had now lost his parents, stepfather, and brother, and these losses made him a much richer man. Agnes also lost relations: her uncle, Hamo de Copton and her cousin Nicholas de Copton (Hamo's son) both died, and Agnes inherited their substantial property.[98] Nicholas's will is dated on the same day as Richard Chaucer's, 12 April. John now resigned his customs job and went back to London—but a changed London. It is impossible to know how he and his wife felt about profiting from this terrible tragedy. It had altered their—and everyone's—lives materially and emotionally; those who survived had new challenges to face.

When the 1350s started, Chaucer, aged seven or eight, was back in London with his parents. They were in very affluent circumstances but, like so many others, must have been reeling from the psychological fallout of the worst disaster in recorded history.[99] The Chaucer family was not alone in benefitting financially from the horrors of the plague: those who survived found they could command higher wages and a better standard of living, and there was a little more social mobility in the decades following the first arrival of the disease.[100] There were also, however, attempts to intervene in the market for the benefit of those at the top.[101] The Statute of Labourers tried, unsuccessfully, to fix wages at pre-plague levels but it could not hold back the changed economic conditions that the shortage of labour caused. In 1350, the mayor and aldermen of London issued new regulations to try to control wages and prices: this document has the aim of amending and redressing 'the damages and grievances' of the people of the city, who have been suffering from 'masons, carpenters, plasterers, tilers, and all manner of labourers' taking 'unreasonably more than they

---

[96] Ibid., Roll 77 (59), 1:590.

[97] Lister Matheson suggests that she may have died shortly before April 1339, when Thomas Heron granted a property to Richard Chaucer, perhaps because he had inherited the family home (originally his own father's house) on Mary's death. 'Chaucer's Ancestry,' 183.

[98] Sharpe, *Calendar of Wills*, Roll 77 (107), 1:600; 'The soke of Aldgate,' in G.A.J. Hodgett (ed.), *The Cartulary of Holy Trinity, Aldgate* (Leicester: London Record Society, 1971), fol. 175v, 197–99. *British History Online*, http://www.british-history.ac.uk/london-record-soc/vol7/pp197-199.

[99] Dyer points out that on a global scale, the Black Death exceeded in mortality any other known disaster. *Making a Living*, 233.

[100] Ibid., 279.

[101] Kaye, *History of Balance*, 391–97.

have been wont to take.' Amidst the detailed regulations about exactly how much different kinds of labourers could be paid, and exactly how gloves, shoes, and different kinds of wine should be priced, over and over again we see the phrase 'not take more than they were wont to take.'[102] Civic authorities and the government tried hard to fix the economy at pre-1349 levels, to override the dramatically changed conditions. Labourers and the poor, however, had died in such numbers that the balance of society had changed, and the lower classes had a little more power. This kind of legislation reveals attempts to maintain a status quo that had gone forever. Instead, this was an era of economic and social change and development, of 'newfangleness'—a word that Chaucer himself would later coin.[103] Sumptuary laws sought to prevent social mobility and to maintain class stratification by prescribing what fabrics people of different social statuses could wear, but such legislation had very little effect and indeed was almost immediately repealed.[104] People now were a little less bound to remain metaphorically or physically in the place where they were born. Of course, mercantile families were more used to experiencing the quick rise of new men than were laboring peasants or the aristocracy. The fact that all aspects of life are dependent on economics, on wages and prices, supply and demand, had always been evident to men such as John Chaucer and his associates. So the new zeitgeist was an intensification of the usual condition of mercantile society, less of a shock than it might have been to long-established landed gentry, for example. Nonetheless, from the 1350s onward, there was a clear perception that things had changed, that the world was a more uncertain and unpredictable place.

Chaucer was now at the age when infancy was thought to end and childhood to begin. This was the time when children might attend school and generally start to live a more structured kind of existence. Many boys

---

[102] Riley, *Memorials of London*, 253–57 (translated from *Letter-Book F*, fol. clxxxi).

[103] The *Middle English Dictionary* assigns the first recorded usages of the word to Chaucer, although this does not, of course, demonstrate definitively that he was the first to use the word. See Hans Kurath, Sherman M. Kuhn, and Robert E. Lewis (eds.), *Middle English Dictionary* (Ann Arbor: University of Michigan Press, 1952–2001), available online at https://quod.lib.umich.edu/m/med/. On Chaucer and the new, see Ingham, *The Medieval New*, 112–40.

[104] October 1363, in Given-Wilson (ed.), *Parliament Rolls of Medieval England* (Woodbridge: Boydell and Brewer, 2005), Membrane 3, no. 25, 5:165–66 (hereafter, PROME). The law was repealed at the subsequent parliament (January 1365). PROME, Membrane 2, no. 11, part 2, 5:182.

and girls who learnt to read did so initially in the home.[105] Learning the alphabet and entering literacy was then, as it is now, associated with a domestic, maternal kind of learning that also, paradoxically, begins to separate the child from the mother, as does the earlier entry into language itself.[106] As Chaucer moved beyond the home, primary scene of the entry into literacy, he entered into a new reading scene, the male-dominated space of the schoolroom. There were several local schools, including one at St Paul's Cathedral, which Chaucer might have attended. The schoolboy lived a structured life, attending school from early in the day, wearing a long gown, carrying his writing materials with him.[107] Schools were also places of discipline and corporal punishment: in a neat example of poetic justice, in 1301 an Oxford teacher fell out of a tree and drowned while cutting rods to beat his pupils.[108]

At school, the focus was on learning Latin. The school alphabet was comprised of twenty-four letters (there was no 'j' or 'w') and the symbols for 'et,' 'con,' and 'est.' The alphabet was recited like a prayer, beginning with the sign of the cross and ending with 'Amen.'[109] Later in the century, Trevisa wrote that since 1349—that is, after the plague—English had supplanted French as the language of teaching in schools.[110] However, Christopher Cannon has recently argued persuasively that this account is misleading and that Trevisa's views were skewed by his experiences of Oxford grammar schools, which were not representative of the rest of the country. Cannon argues that Trevisa's account misrepresents the role of French as well as the role of English and that surviving textbooks strongly suggest that students were immersed in Latin from a young age—in other

[105] Nicholas Orme, *Medieval Schools: From Roman Britain to Renaissance England* (New Haven: Yale University Press, 2006), 60–61.

[106] Miri Rubin writes that the ABC 'epitomizes the acquisition of the formal properties of language, that learning which removes the child from the breast where it first learns to speak into the world of grammar. ABC is innocence and its loss.' Rubin, *Mother of God: A History of the Virgin Mary* (London: Allen Lane, 2009), 278. See also Georgiana Donavin, *Scribit Mater: Mary and the Language Arts in the Literature of Medieval England* (Washington, DC: Catholic University of America Press, 2012), 163–84.

[107] Orme, *Medieval Schools*, 133.

[108] Ibid., 145.

[109] Ibid., 56.

[110] Ibid., 75, 87. There is evidence that, from the 1340s, some textbooks included English translations of verb paradigms, for instance, John Cornwall's *Speculum Grammatice*, discussed in Orme, *Medieval Schools*, 106.

words, that a vernacular was not routinely used in teaching Latin.[111] Cannon also argues that what Chaucer learnt at school 'shaped his writing ever afterwards,' and indeed that the extraordinary outpouring of poetry in the last decades of the fourteenth century can be connected with the training received in schoolrooms during these years, as the teaching of grammar 'licensed experimentation and exploration,' through the encouragement of independent composition and improvisation.[112]

Boys such as Chaucer, who went to school, experienced books en masse in the schoolroom. St Paul's, for instance, had a very large library: in 1328, William Tolleshunt left a sizeable collection of books for the school, including Hugutio, Isidore, Priscian, and books on logic, law, and medicine.[113] Boys owned their own books and passed them on. Books were not always worth a fortune and were not always luxury objects. In 1337, for instance, John Cobbledick left twenty-nine books to Oriel College, worth a total of £9, 2s (around 6s each, less than Chaucer's first employer was to spend on his paltok [tunic] and leggings, as we shall see in chapter 2).[114] A manuscript of *Troilus* was valued at 20 shillings in 1394 (the same price as the portifory discussed at the beginning of this chapter).[115]

The space of the schoolroom itself was different from schoolrooms today. The master sat in a chair of authority, raised up, surveying the room, while the boys sat in benches around the edges.[116] Perhaps the most obvious association is the panopticon, a conceptual space in which the teacher is all-important and the boys under his surveillance. Another way of thinking of this bookish space, though, is the theatre. This was a space for performance, and performativity reflected the spirit of education at this time more generally.[117] At school, boys engaged with set texts not by mindlessly

---

[111] Christopher Cannon, *From Literacy to Literature: England, 1300–1400* (Oxford: Oxford University Press, 2016), 17–34.

[112] Cannon, *Literacy to Literature*, 8, 13, 85.

[113] Orme, *Medieval Schools*, 154. See also Edith Rickert, 'Chaucer at School,' *Modern Philology* 29:3 (1932): 257–74.

[114] Charles F. Briggs, 'The Clerk,' in Rigby, *Historians on Chaucer*, 187–205, 197. See chapter 2 in this study for Chaucer's paltok.

[115] Carlin, 'Host,' 477.

[116] Orme, *Medieval Schools*, 153, 162.

[117] Seth Lerer, *Children's Literature: A Reader's History from Aesop to Harry Potter* (Chicago: University of Chicago Press, 2008), 5.

learning but by parsing, translating, paraphrasing, writing commentaries, and debating morals. Dialectic and argument were the essence of the experience of the medieval schoolboy: 'disputations . . . were the heart and soul of the educational curriculum.'[118]

It is instructive to look at some of the foundational books that medieval schoolboys grappled with in the schoolroom. Aesop's *Fables* are perhaps the most iconic of 'childhood' texts. At the heart of the medieval school curriculum, they are still read by children and adults alike today, and they are deliberately provocative texts. Medieval children were encouraged to be scholarly but also to interpret for themselves. Indeed, in the Aesop they had before them, they saw active reading exemplified: they read not a text that even pretended to be by Aesop but a version by Avianus, who had translated Babrius's Greek verse translation of Aesop's text into Latin verse; or by Romulus, who had translated Phaedrus's Latin verse translation of Aesop into Latin prose; or by Walter of England, who had compiled a set of Latin verse based on Romulus.[119] Texts appeared with glosses and commentaries, and sometimes summaries were added. In Avianus's version, a later writer added *promythia* and *epimythia* at the beginning and end of the fables, to point to a moral.[120] Some fables contain morals in the voice of a character, some in the voice of a narrator. Some fables have no obvious moral at all. Thus, the collection includes, for instance, the fable of the crow and the jar, in which the crow is able to raise the water level on the jar and quench his thirst by dropping pebbles into the container, demonstrating the superiority of foresight over effort, or the fable of the ant and the grasshopper, in which the ant profits from hard work and the grasshopper is not allowed the fruits of the ant's labour. In contrast, the collection also includes the story of the traveller and the satyr, in which the traveller is punished for being able to warm his fingers and cool his food with his breath, or the story of the monkey's

---

[118] David C. Fowler, *Life and Times of John Trevisa, Medieval Scholar* (Seattle: University of Washington Press, 1995), 68; Thomas L. Reed, *Middle English Debate Poetry and the Aesthetics of Irresolution* (Columbia: University of Missouri Press, 1990), 43–55; Peter Travis, *Disseminal Chaucer: Rereading the Nun's Priest's Tale* (Notre Dame: University of Notre Dame Press, 2010), 57.

[119] Lerer, *Children's Literature*, 41–43.

[120] 'Introduction to the Fables of Avianus,' in J. Wight Duff and Arnold M. Duff (trans.), *Minor Latin Poets*, Loeb Classical Library 434 (Cambridge, MA: Harvard University Press, 2014), 2:675. Promythia introduce a fable; epimythia provide a moral at the end.

twins, in which the favourite twin ends up abandoned, and the spurned baby ends up as the lucky one. An explicit moral is included for this story, but it is hardly satisfying, especially for the monkey who has been abandoned to predators ('many come to like what once they slighted; and hope, changing the order of things, carries the lowly back into happier fortune').[121] Such stories encourage debate and dissent over their meanings. In the schoolroom, Chaucer learnt to argue for argument's sake, to play with rhetoric, to defend a position, however indefensible. These early experiences infused Chaucer's later poetry. Most notably, as Peter Travis has magisterially demonstrated, the multigeneric, debate-dominated 'Nun's Priest's Tale' returns the reader to 'foundational curricular experiences,' to a time when Chaucer was 'most intimately engaged in the craft of literary analysis, imitation, and production.'[122]

For an increasingly independent child, the streets of London offered many kinds of excitement. Londoners were accustomed to civic entertainment and performances, from mayoral ceremonies, plays, and fairs to pillorying, rough music, and hangings.[123] Much later in Chaucer's life, he was living in Aldgate when Vintry Ward became the centre of the worst atrocity of the Rising of 1381: the mass murder of immigrant workers, pulled out from the sanctuary of St Martin Vintry and slaughtered in the street.[124] In Chaucer's childhood, the blood that flowed in Vintry Ward usually came from animals. In 1368, the jurors of several wards, including Vintry, held inquests about who was throwing offal and other remnants from the slaughtering of animals into the Thames, and who was carrying the animal parts through the streets, spilling blood and animal organs into the lanes.[125] At the other end of the spectrum, the streets of Vintry Ward also played host to the most important men in the country, who attended feasts in the ward and used it as a thoroughfare. A feast hosted by Henry Picard in the late 1350s or early 1360s became known as the Feast of the

[121] Avianus, 'The Monkey's Twins,' in Duff and Duff, *Minor Latin Poets*, 2:736–37.

[122] Travis, *Disseminal Chaucer*, 54–57, 83.

[123] Anne Lancashire, *London Civic Theatre: City and Pageantry from Roman Times to 1558* (Cambridge: Cambridge University Press, 2002), 52–55; Hanawalt, *Growing Up*, 33.

[124] V. H. Galbraith (ed.), *The Anonimalle Chronicle: 1333 to 1381* (Manchester: Manchester University Press, 1970), 145–56; translated in R. B. Dobson, *The Peasants' Revolt of 1381* (London: Macmillan, 1970), 162.

[125] Thomas, *Calendar, 1364–1381*, Roll A13, Membrane 6, 93.

Five Kings; a generation later, in the early fifteenth century, Lewis John hosted the sons of Henry IV at a feast in Vintry Ward at which Chaucerian poems were performed.[126] One of my favourite Vintry Ward streets—'Knight riders streete'—was so named because knights were armed at the Tower Royal and then rode through this street on their way to Smithfield for jousting.[127] And sometimes dramas that began inside the houses of Vintry Ward played out in the streets. Joan and William Sharpyng, whose marriage was breaking apart because of William's impotence, came into conflict on the streets of Vintry Ward in the early 1370s, as William repeatedly assaulted her there while attempting to prevent her consulting her lawyer.[128] The streets of Vintry Ward were spectacular, cosmopolitan, filthy, smelly, banal, beautiful, violent, and changeable.

Chaucer entered his teens while living in this dynamic urban environment, learning languages and business skills, enjoying the comfortable lifestyle of his wealthy parents, mixing with people he had known all his life, secure in his Thames Street home in the Vintry. But he was about to move out of his comfort zone and into a quite different mode of life. By the time the Black Prince, fresh from his incredible victory at Poitiers, triumphantly entered London in 1357 with his prisoner, the French king, to be greeted by elaborate pageants and displays, Chaucer was no longer living with his parents in Vintry Ward. He had begun his career and was now living and serving in an aristocratic great household.

[126] The five kings are usually said to be the kings of England, France, Scotland, Cyprus, and Denmark, but they were not all in England at the same time. There probably was a lavish feast including some kings, but the story has been embroidered over time. See C. L. Kingsford, 'The Feast of the Five Kings,' *Archaeologica* 67 (1916): 119–26. A note in Ashmole 59 accompanying Scogan's Moral Balade reads: 'Here folowethe nexst a moral balade to my lord the Prince, to my lord of Clarence, to my lord of Bedford, and to my lorde of Gloucestre, by Henry Scogan, at a souper of feorthe merchande in the Vyntre in London, at the hous of Lowys Johan.' Katherine Forni (ed.), 'Scogan's Moral Balade,' in *The Chaucerian Apocrypha: A Selection* (Kalamazoo, MI: TEAMS Middle English Texts, 2005), 148–52.

[127] John Stow, 'Vintrie warde,' in C. L. Kingsford (ed.), *A Survey of London; Reprinted from the Text of 1603* (Oxford: Clarendon Press, 1908), 245, *British History Online*, http://www.british-history. ac.uk/no-series/survey-of-london-stow/1603/pp238-250.

[128] Thomas, *Calendar, 1364–1381*, Roll A15, Membrane 3, 117–18; Roll A19, Membrane 7, 173–74.

CHAPTER 2

Great Household

[P]ut not youre handes in youre hosen youre codware for to clawe.
—*John Russell,* Boke of Nurture

In the middle of the 1350s, when Chaucer was about fourteen or fifteen years old, he stopped living in one place and started living in a conceptual structure. This moving place is hard for us to imagine but was absolutely central to the lives and imaginations of Chaucer and the people he knew. This chapter focuses on the amorphous space of the great household, a dynamic structure that brought with it a complicated set of expectations about how to live. The household was 'the central institution of society'; indeed, the post-1350 Middle Ages has been termed 'the age of the household.'[1] Until this point, Chaucer had spent almost his whole life, apart from the family's brief sojourn in Southampton, living in the same place, surrounded by familiar faces. He had been a privileged child, with rich parents who employed servants and apprentices. Now, he moved out of this cossetted existence, this comfort zone, and started to make his way in the world. He entered a great household, almost certainly as a page. His employer was Elizabeth de Burgh, countess of Ulster, a great heiress in her own right. She was the wife of Lionel of Antwerp, son of Edward III, and she was also first cousin to Blanche of Lancaster, who was to marry

[1]David Starkey, 'The Age of the Household,' in Stephen Medcalf (ed.), *The Later Middle Ages* (London: Methuen, 1981), 225.

John of Gaunt.[2] Elizabeth and Lionel had one child, Philippa, born in 1355, through whom the later Yorkist claim to the throne was traced. Although Chaucer first appears in Elizabeth's accounts, shortly afterwards he was fighting in Lionel's troops, and it is clear that he worked for both of them.[3] This household, then, was headed by a young, very wealthy couple; it was a household with the closest possible connections not only to the king and queen but to many of the greatest families in the land. In many ways, it must have been a dazzling environment; Elizabeth and Lionel's lives were punctuated by royal visits, Garter festivities, tournaments, and feasts; they lived surrounded by beautiful, sumptuous things. Throughout Chaucer's poetic career, the structure and material environment of the great household were of vital importance to his imagination. Dream visions, such as the *Book of the Duchess* and the *House of Fame*, are built upon the relationship between great lord or lady and subjected clients; *Troilus and Criseyde* depicts the problems of the public modes of living that the great household demanded; tales, including the 'Manciple's' and the 'Knight's,' meditate in different ways on what it means to be part of the affinity of a great lord. And many of Chaucer's poems luxuriate over the lifestyle and objects of the great household—the clothes, the food, the soft furnishings, the opportunities for dalliance and games.[4]

Great households headed by wealthy aristocrats were itinerant institutions that moved between different houses. A household was a structure: a lord or lady; their dependents; their extensive retinue of household officers, servants, and hangers-on; their horses and other animals; and a

[2] Elizabeth de Burgh's father was William de Burgh, 3rd earl of Ulster. He was the greatest landowner in Ireland and was also the heir to huge properties in England through his mother, Elizabeth de Clare, sister and coheir of Gilbert de Clare, 8th earl of Gloucester. William was murdered in 1333 in a particularly messy episode of Irish politics. His wife was Maud (also known as Matilda) of Lancaster, daughter of Henry, 3rd earl of Lancaster, a giant of the English political scene in the reign of Edward II, and sister of Henry of Grosmont, who became the first duke of Lancaster. Elizabeth's mother became a nun at Campsey Ash in Suffolk, which appears frequently in Elizabeth's accounts. See also Frances Underhill, *For Her Good Estate: The Life of Elizabeth de Burgh* (Basingstoke: Palgrave Macmillan, 2000), 109; this is a biography of the grandmother of the Elizabeth de Burgh for whom Chaucer worked; I refer to her throughout by her most usual title, the Lady of Clare.

[3] Very wealthy aristocratic married couples often had separate households—that is, separate officers, servants, budgets, and furnishings—even though the two households might usually live together. It is possible that Lionel and Elizabeth only sometimes separated their accounts, perhaps when they were apart; it also seems likely that they merged their households when Lionel came of age in 1359.

[4] The household is discussed in many chapters of this book, particularly in chapters 5 and 14.

vast quantity of furnishings and furniture, all of which piled into carriages and carts and then unloaded into manor houses littered around the country. These households travelled frequently, usually sending purveyors in advance to acquire foodstuffs, spending money but also putting pressure on rural markets, covering around fifteen miles a day as they went between bases.[5] Everything centred around a person rather than around a particular building or place: the ultimate example of this was, of course, the king, who was the moving centre of government and law, so much so that a specific legal system operated within twelve miles of wherever he was ('the verge').[6] Each household was a complicated administrative machine, focused around serving the desires of its lord and/or lady, and each household formed a microsociety by itself. The household provided everything: a position in such an institution was not just a job, it was a whole way of life. Employees ate and slept in the household, wore the clothes of the household, were entertained in the household, received medical care from the in-house physician and, if they were lucky, annuities, the medieval equivalent of pensions. The household protected and controlled its members; it was its own self-contained world.[7] Although Chaucer now moved in exalted circles, in other ways he must have seen a sharp downturn in his own standard of living, as he had to bed down where he could and perhaps, as a page, undertake some relatively menial jobs. He now lived in a world in which his own desires were of negligible importance.

Adolescence is a time of intense physical and psychological transition, a time when identity is reshaped. The theory of the seven ages of man suggested that infancy ended at around seven, childhood at around fourteen, when one entered into adolescence. Chaucer's early life maps rather neatly onto this pattern, with the end of infancy coinciding with a kind of end of innocence wrought by the plague, and the end of childhood

[5] C. M. Woolgar, *The Great Household in Late Medieval England* (New Haven: Yale University Press, 1999), 187.

[6] Chris Given-Wilson, *The Royal Household and the King's Affinity* (New Haven: Yale University Press, 1986), 48–52.

[7] Richard Firth Green comments that the household was a 'complete environment,' and that 'every medieval man of substance gathered a "familia"'; *Poets and Princepleasers: Literature and the English Court in the Late Middle Ages* (Toronto: University of Toronto Press, 1980), 19, 13.

marked by his taking up his first job. In 1357, he appears in Elizabeth's household accounts,[8] though he may have entered the household slightly earlier (the accounts are fragmentary). Now, instead of having servants, he *was* a servant; his own desires and wants had to be subjugated to the will of his employers. A servant must learn what they are supposed to say, how they are supposed to respond, how to please the person at the centre of the household. They must learn to put their own wishes aside and to obey complicated regulations about where they are allowed to go, where they can eat, how they should behave. A servant in a great household would learn, in short, how to be a performer, how to craft an identity that would please the employer but that might be quite different to the face that he or she showed to his or her peers. Indeed, one of the reasons that boys from wealthy households were willing to become pages in such institutions was that such a position taught them etiquette and social skills; how to live in the highest echelons of society.[9] Such a position also, of course, provided opportunities for advancement and patronage of many kinds. In Chaucer's case, he was to move on to the greatest household of all—that of the king—which position in turn led to myriad jobs later in his life. As a part of a great household, a page worked as a general helper, errand runner, and attendant, but he also had the opportunity to take part in games—ball games, chess, and backgammon were all popular—practice riding, hunting, and swordsmanship; participate in music, dancing, and story-reading or telling; and perhaps gain further education from a household clerk.[10] Chaucer became a highly educated man, and one who was trusted on diplomatic missions and with sensitive documents; his household training, whether from an early age or later on in his household career, when he worked for the king, gave him the preparation for these jobs. Members of great households, indeed, often had time on their hands: Edward II's household ordinances indicate that his retainers had only the vaguest sense of what they were supposed to be doing and seem to have spent much of their time hanging around,

[8] See Edward Bond, 'New Facts in the Life of Geoffrey Chaucer,' in *Life-Records of Chaucer*, 3:97–113, and Crow and Olson, *Chaucer Life-Records*, 13–18.
[9] Crow and Olson, *Chaucer Life-Records*, 18; Green, *Poets and Princepleasers*, 21.
[10] Crow and Olson, *Chaucer Life-Records*, 18.

providing prestige simply through their existence as part of a large retinue.[11]

What kind of things did Chaucer see in this new environment? Perhaps most importantly, he saw constant movement as the household packed up and travelled the country; his environment frequently changed, and the household adapted all the time to new circumstances. At the same time, he also saw the power of the wealthy to remake environments according to their own desires as they commandeered the resources of the neighbourhood and re-formed their comfortable world in Yorkshire, Woodstock, or Windsor. Places were pulled into shape rather than being accepted for what they were. The records, fragmentary as they are, nonetheless go into detail about the kind of objects that were important to Elizabeth: cushions, embroidered for the joust at Smithfield ('tapetis quichssens maculatis ad hastiludia in Smetheueld'), curtains, canopies, and cords for beds ('lecto de rubeo weorstede cum iii ridellis et dimidio celare de rubeo canabo'), clothes for herself and her servants.[12] The details of the accounts—payments for ribbons of gold and silver cloth ('de argento de cipre' 'aureo de cipre'), for lengths of red velvet ('ulnis rubei veluetti'), or for two minstrels of the queen of Scotland ('ii munestrallis Regine Scocie') paint a picture of the environment of Elizabeth's household.[13] That environment was characterized by luxurious fabrics and beautiful objects of display: the world in which Chaucer now lived was intensely glamorous.

Most children are accustomed to being observers. This is particularly the case for children who spend time watching their parents work, as medieval children did. While most servants were expected to be silent, unobtrusive observers, this was not true of the kind of servant that Chaucer became in his teens. On the contrary, Chaucer now became an object to be observed, and he had to learn how to show himself to his most fashionable advantage. He was now a beautiful object of display. The first time that Geoffrey Chaucer appears before us in documentary records, he does

[11] See 'The Household Ordinances of Edward II,' in T. F. Tout, *The Place of the Reign of Edward II in English History* (Manchester: Manchester University Press, 1914), 267–318.

[12] Bond and Selby, *Life-Records of Chaucer*, 3:109, 111.

[13] Ibid., 109–113. The queen of Scotland was Joan, daughter of Edward II and Isabella, and therefore sister of Edward III.

not appear as a poet, customs officer, diplomat, or soldier. Instead, he steps off the page as a fashion plate, dressed to the nines in clothes so breathtakingly fashionable and daring that contemporary commentators condemned them as causing the wrath of God to descend on England in the shape of the plague. At Easter 1357, Elizabeth de Burgh paid 4 shillings for a paltok for Chaucer, and a further 3 shillings for black and red hose and a pair of shoes.[14] In the early 1360s, the critique of fashion focused on these specific garments: 'particoloured and striped hose which they tie with laces to their paltoks . . . they go about with their loins uncovered,' 'paltoks, extremely short garments . . . which failed to conceal their arses or their private parts,' 'shoes with long toes.'[15] According to these chroniclers, young men were going about in short tunics and long, two-coloured leggings or tights, laced up together provocatively in such as way as to emphasise the genitals indecently. John of Reading explicitly blamed this kind of clothing for causing the plague (which had returned in the early 1360s); the *Eulogium* author too had feared a judgement from God for such outrageous sartorial choices. The two chroniclers cited here were writing in 1362 and 1365; the *Eulogium* author emphasizes that this fashion craze swept England in 1362. John Newbury's account of the expenditure of the king's great wardrobe in 1361 demonstrates that Edward had a paltok made that year to be worn at Christmas; these accounts go on to demonstrate that in 1361–62, members of the court circle, but not their valets or servants, were enthusiastically wearing paltoks; by 1363–64, the paltok had had, in the words of a fashion historian, 'amazing success,'[16] and was now being worn more widely, by squires as well as the nobility. In 1357, then, Elizabeth's household was ahead of the game, at the cutting edge of fashion, leading the way where, a few years later, the king and his entourage were to follow. The paltok, always written about in fashion history as a new item of clothing in the 1360s, was in fact being sported several years earlier, by no less a person than the teenage Chaucer. This detail

[14] Ibid., 14–15.

[15] Frank Scott Haydon (ed.), *Eulogium historiarum sive temporis*, Rolls Series 9 (London: Longman, Brown, Green, Longmans, and Roberts, 1858–63), 3:230–31; John of Reading, *Chronica Johannis de Reading et Anonymi Cantuariensis, 1346–1367*, ed. James Tait (Manchester: University Press, 1914), cited in Horrox, *The Black Death*, 132–34.

[16] Stella Mary Newton, *Fashion in the Age of the Black Prince* (Woodbridge: Boydell Press, 2002), 55.

in the household accounts gives us a surprising insight into the kind of world into which this adolescent boy had been catapulted; the household in which he was living and working was interested in the new, in style, in trendsetting, in ostentatiously creating and displaying its image. And even the bodies of the most menial members of the household were vehicles for staging that image, and could be used for making statements about how modern, confident, and risqué this community was. Wastoure, the free-spending aristocrat in the contemporary poem *Wynnere and Wastoure*, defends all the money that he spends on fashion against the criticism of the hoarding merchant-figure, Wynnere, saying, 'And if my peple ben prode, me payes alle the better' ('And if my retinue are proudly dressed, that pleases me more' [433]).[17] The convention of clothing servants marked their bodies as owned by their employers: when Walter, in the 'Clerk's Tale,' has his peasant fiancée stripped and reclothed 'in swich richesse,' this symbolizes his takeover of her identity; when he repudiates her and sends her away, her clothing is taken away too, as she is now free of his total control.[18] Phoebus, in the 'Manciple's Tale,' is even crueller: when he turns out his devoted and truthful servant (the crow), he mutilates him and his appearance, tearing out his white feathers, and then turns him black, marking him and his descendants forever as the victims of the unjust anger of a great lord with power over the bodies of those who served him.[19]

The fact that Chaucer was paid in clothing is entirely symptomatic of the way the great household worked. It was an institution that focused obsessively on the body, on sensory experience, on the arts of living. Food, clothes, and beds and bed decorations were all important: proportionately, food preparation and eating took much more time, and textiles cost much more money than they do today.[20] Ensuring the comfort of those at the apex of the household was the primary job of all the other members of this

[17] Stephanie Trigg (ed.), *Wynnere and Wastoure*, EETS 297 (London: Oxford University Press, 1990).

[18] See Carolyn Dinshaw, *Chaucer's Sexual Poetics* (Madison: University of Wisconsin Press, 1989), 133–34.

[19] Louise Fradenburg, 'The Manciple's Servant Tongue: Politics and Poetry in *The Canterbury Tales*,' *ELH* 52:1 (1985): 103–4.

[20] Woolgar, *The Great Household*, 111; Goldberg, 'The Fashioning of Bourgeois Domesticity,' 127–28.

community, from the steward to the page of the saucery. The body of the lord or lady, cleaned, dressed, and generally ministered to by household servants, adorned in silks, jewels, and furs, seated on or near an elaborately decorated bed, was the symbolic heart of the household. Beds, indeed, were often not for sleeping in but for signifying a level of intimacy and trust; the presence of a bed conveyed the idea of intimate space—and it was intimacy with the body of the lord or lady that conferred status on the other members of the household.[21] Getting close to that body, serving in the chamber rather than the hall, was the goal for retainers.[22] And household life ensured that the body of the lord or lady did little in private: the household accounts of Elizabeth, Lady of Clare (Elizabeth de Burgh's grandmother) tell us that before she went through menopause, she paid laundresses high wages and gave them gifts of squirrel fur, presumably to recompense them for the laborious and unpleasant work of thoroughly washing out large quantities of bloodied cloths.[23] The household must generally have been aware of menstrual cycles, conjugal visits, early signs of pregnancy, stomach upsets—of all the things that today most of us like to keep secret. And the body of the *servant* was also symbolically central to the status of the household. The relationship between employee and employer was not exclusively concerned with offering a service in return for a wage; the employer was responsible for the body of the servant, for keeping that body well fed, rested, appropriately clothed, and generally presentable. As a member of the household, then, one's body was not really one's own; and, indeed, it was difficult to marry, and impossible to live in a private, domestic setting. It may have been that Chaucer met his future wife within Elizabeth's household, at this early stage of his life. A 'Philippa Pan,' who appears along with Chaucer in Elizabeth's records,

---

[21] Wilson 'Royal Lodgings,' 44. See also W. M. Ormrod, 'In Bed with Joan of Kent: The King's Mother and the Peasants' Revolt,' in Jocelyn Wogan-Browne et al., *Medieval Women: Texts and Contexts in Late Medieval Britain; Essays for Felicity Riddy* (Turnhout: Brepols, 2000), 277–92. For a recent discussion of medieval beds, see Hollie L. S. Morgan, *Beds and Chambers in Late Medieval England: Readings, Representations and Realities* (York: York Medieval Press, 2017).

[22] The thirteenth and fourteenth centuries saw great lords retreating more and more from hall to chamber and taking meals in more private spaces. Given-Wilson, *The Royal Household*, 29; Green, *Poets and Princepleasers*, 35–37. Contemporary poets criticized this separation; see William Langland, *Piers Plowman: The B Version; Will's Visions of Piers Plowman, Do-Well, Do-Better and Do-Best*, ed. George Kane and E. Talbot Donaldson (London: Athlone Press, 1975), 412, Passus X, lines 98–103.

[23] Underhill, *For Her Good Estate*, 76.

may be the Philippa, daughter of Sir Paon de Roet, whom Chaucer later married. For adolescents and young people, removed from their families, living and sleeping in close proximity to their peers, surrounded by luxury and excitement, seeing their fellow servants all the time, day and night, the atmosphere must have been laden with sexual frisson and opportunity.

Privacy was not valued in the fourteenth century in the way that it is today. Chaucer's 'Reeve's Tale,' in which husband, wife, daughter, and two overnight guests all sleep in the same room, resulting in mistaken identities and rapes, illustrates the forced intimacy that could result from the domestic arrangements of the poor. But for the rich as well, great household living made privacy for sexual intercourse extremely difficult, both because of the press of people and their expectation of access, and because of domestic architecture. In the 'Manciple's Tale,' the servant is represented as a caged bird, whose privileged access to the intimate spaces of the house has allowed him to see his master's wife committing adultery. From his cage, he 'Biheeld hire werk, and seyde never a word' (241); an image of the servant who sees all kinds of things that he might rather not see—and he ends up being punished brutally for telling the truth to his master. The difficulty for even the most privileged in society of finding a private space, even for the most intimate acts, is particularly clearly demonstrated in *Troilus and Criseyde*. When Criseyde is persuaded to stay the night at Pandarus's house, where Troilus is waiting for her, she has in attendance some of her own male servants, her niece, and 'other of hire wommen nyne or ten' (Book III, 598). Criseyde's uncle and her most trusted women all accompany her to her bed, in a small closet, and her women all sleep 'at this closet dore withoute, / Right overthwart [directly opposite]' specifically within earshot (684–86). Indeed, the door is left open, and when Pandarus has managed to smuggle Troilus into the closet via a trapdoor, he quietly shuts the door, confident that the ladies are all asleep, and that the storm outside is luckily loud enough to mask the noise (743–49). The long, involved conversation, and then the night of sex that follows, have to take place in this claustrophobic context, in an atmosphere fraught with anxiety about who might hear what.[24] In a house with corridors,

---

[24] Paul Strohm discusses the retinue as a major obstacle to privacy in the poem in 'The Space of Desire in Chaucer's and Shakespeare's Troy,' in Andrew James Johnston, Russell West-Pavlov, and

there would be no need for the complicated trapdoor arrangement; in a house with multiple private rooms, the other women would be sleeping in separate rooms; indeed, in a non-household-based social system, Criseyde would not move around the city accompanied by a dozen or more attendants. All the details of this scene are dependent upon certain social and architectural assumptions. In his use of the closet, Chaucer depicts extremely fashionable and new ways of arranging space. There are no references to 'closets' in London documents such as inventories until the sixteenth century, and Chaucer's uses of the term in *Troilus* are the first recorded uses of the term in any kind of text.[25] Other writers, including Gower and Trevisa, use the word shortly afterwards, so the idea of the closet—a small, private space off the bedchamber—was clearly coming into fashion at this time. Pandarus and Criseyde are shown making use of arrangements of space that were new in Chaucer's London.

One's opportunities to do secret things are much greater if one has hallways and corridors, if rooms are not accessed through other rooms. In Edward III's massive building and remodeling projects at Windsor and Westminster in the 1350s and 1360s, space was used in new ways. The major chambers still interconnected, but galleries were provided, giving the king alternative routes around his residences that allowed him to bypass all the people hanging around in the elaborate series of chambers. In order to reach Edward's bedroom at Windsor, one passed through the great chamber (Chaucer probably never got further in than this in his long career of household service),[26] then a formal audience chamber, then the king's private dining chamber, then the second chamber where the king's immediate attendants might wait and sleep. It is easy to see why galleries (or indeed trapdoors, as we see in *Troilus*) would be very appealing to those

---

Elisabeth Kempf (eds.), *Love, History and Emotion in Chaucer and Shakespeare: 'Troilus and Criseyde' and 'Troilus and Cressida'* (Oxford: Oxford University Press, 2016), 46–60.

[25] Schofield, *Medieval London Houses*, 81; Kurath, Kuhn, and Lewis, *Middle English Dictionary*.

[26] In later records, from the 1360s through to the 1380s, when Chaucer worked in the court, he is usually identified with the household, not the chamber, but three records do link him with the 'camera regis': he is termed a 'vallectorum camera regis' (1368), a 'scutiferi' of the chamber (1373), and a valet of both household and chamber (1385). But whenever lists distinguish between chamber and household, Chaucer is always in the household group. Green suggests that the blurring of lines might suggest that Chaucer, while working primarily at a greater distance from the king, might have had some chamber duties. Crow and Olson, *Chaucer Life-Records*, 100, 104–5, 126; Green, *Poets and Princepleasers*, 68.

who lived in this very public, communal way—all the more so if they had affairs of sexual intrigue to conduct.[27]

For less important members of the household, the problems were different: they did not have private rooms at all, and although others might have been less interested in whom the groom was sleeping with than in the lord or lady's behaviour, there was the practical problem of where to do it, if one usually slept in a room with many others. Household servants were not supposed to bring spouses with them, but at court there were regular prostitutes, and presumably it was accepted that sex need not be a private activity.[28] And perhaps those engaging in nonmarital sex were innovative in the locations they chose—in the *Canterbury Tales*, adultery takes place in a tree and is planned for a garden—these scenes are symbolic, and both relate, in slightly different ways, to ideas of Eden and the fall, but nonetheless, perhaps people did have sex outdoors more when they lacked their own bedrooms. People who were having illicit sex tried to avoid unwanted pregnancies in a number of ways. Chaucer's Parson warns against contraception ('drynkynge venenouse herbes thurgh which she may nat conceyve'), abortion ('putteth certeine material thynges in hire secree places to slee the child'), and anal sex (intercourse 'in place ther as a child may nat be conceived' [576–77]).

Household servants did sometimes marry each other, as Chaucer and Philippa did, but their existence within the household precluded domesticity; they would not have had their own quarters at court, and it must have been difficult to find opportunities for real intimacy.[29] But couples were sometimes given extra money on their marriage, and members of the king's household seem to have served in rotation, spending some of their time on other jobs in the gift of the king, and, we presume, maintaining their own establishment for their families.[30] Edmund Rose, for instance, a valet in the countess of Ulster's service and a yeoman to Edward III, married Agnes Archer, damsel of queen Philippa, and was given a grant of 40 marks a year in consideration of his service and marriage. His other

[27] Wilson, 'The Royal Lodgings of Edward III at Windsor,' 47–50.

[28] Given-Wilson, *The Royal Household*, 60.

[29] The marriage of servants was discouraged; see Kate Mertes, *The English Noble Household, 1250–1600: Good Governance and Politic Rule* (Oxford: Basil Blackwell, 1988), 180.

[30] Given-Wilson, *The Royal Household*, 22.

appointments included working as a bailiff errant in Norfolk, being the keeper of Puyl Castle, and acting as a commissioner to decide whether or not a certain man was an 'idiot.' Some of his jobs were sinecures—when he was granted custody of the small seal for recognisances of debts in Norwich, he was mandated to appoint a deputy so he could remain attendant on the king.[31] This was all typical of the experience of royal service: one picked up grants and salaries here and there, moved about, and might not always be physically with the king.

Much of the business of the household was concerned with the most basic bodily needs: making sure that all of its members were fed and housed. The right to all one's meals, bedding, clothing at certain times of year (and special clothes such as mourning liveries, when appropriate) was part of each member of the household's employment package—and comprised the entirety of the remuneration for pages.[32] A huge proportion of time and money was spent on sourcing, preparing, serving, and eating food.[33] In large households, there would be more than one sitting for meals, and each meal could take two or three hours: typically, dinner would be served at 10:00 or 11:00, and supper at 4:00 or 5:00.[34] Many of the departments of the household would be based around food and drink: a large household might divide the business of food preparation into the buttery, pantry, kitchen, cellar, larder, spicery, saucery, scullery, poultery, and confectionary: positions in the king's household included subclerk of the spicery, esquire fruiterer, and naperer (a household official in charge of the table linen).[35] The physical organization of the household offices created a layout deeply familiar to many of us: the modern structure of a pub derives from the bar of the pantry or buttery at which rations

[31] Crow and Olson, *Chaucer Life-Records*, 17, 69, 95; National Archives, E 101/93/12; *Calendar of the Patent Rolls: Edward III*, Membrane 4, 10:324 (16 December 1355), Membrane 21d, 10:445 (10 June 1356), Membrane 32, 6:111 (24 July 1343), Membrane 22, 6:450 (6 March 1345), Membrane 25d, 13:202 (10 October 1365); *Calendar of the Patent Rolls Preserved in the Public Record Office: Richard II* (London: Eyre and Spottiswoode, 1895–1909), Membrane 16, 1:187 (23 March 1378), Membrane 40, 3:94 (16 January 1386).

[32] Green, *Poets and Princepleasers*, 21.

[33] See Christopher Dyer, *Standards of Living in the Later Middle Ages: Social Change in England, c. 1200–1520*, rev. ed. (Cambridge: Cambridge University Press, 1998), 55–70, for a detailed discussion of aristocratic spending on food.

[34] Woolgar, *The Great Household*, 88.

[35] Ibid., 17; Given-Wilson, *The Royal Household*, 13.

were doled out.[36] The household travelled around with live animals to use for meat, such as poultry, partridges, piglets, and doves, while also acquiring meat locally; preserved meat was also used, and sides of meat would be hung for curing in the kitchen and the hall. The range of departments attests to the range of foodstuffs used in the great household; fish and preserved fish were especially important, as most households would have three days on which meat was not eaten or was reduced; spices were a vital part of the upper-class diet and, in testament to the household's in loco parentis role to its younger servants, children through to teenagers were given extra allowances of milk to drink.[37] To give some indication of the scale of great household living: Elizabeth's grandmother's pantry milled flour and baked bread about twice a week, producing as many as 2,360 loaves on a baking day; the brewhouse brewed ale every four or five days, producing around 900 gallons each time.[38]

The business of eating was intertwined with mannered behaviour; treating the body in a ritualized way was central to household etiquette. It was usual to wash before meals, after sleep, and after going to the privy; items such as soap, toothpicks, and combs are itemized in accounts; those who wished to emphasise their particularity might adopt an eccentricity, for instance, using a silver fork for eating peas, as Piers Gaveston did.[39] The distribution of liveries and clothes tended to rank people according to how much cloth they were given; all were marked as belonging to the lord, but each had their own value, written on their bodies with lengths of material.[40] Living in a great household meant living in an environment in which people were intensely interested in constructing an image of sophistication, elaboration, and taste, an image that depended on regimenting bodies, and shaping them into stylized constructions. When you ate, with whom you ate, what you wore, which rooms you were allowed to enter in the household, what kind of bedding you received, and where you were allowed to

---

[36] Woolgar, The Great Household, 1.

[37] Ibid., 114–28.

[38] Underhill, For Her Good Estate, 69–70.

[39] Woolgar, The Great Household, 157, 167–68. Incidentally, Piers Gaveston was married to Elizabeth's great-aunt (Margaret, sister of Elizabeth of Clare).

[40] When Chaucer and his wife, Philippa, received mourning liveries in 1369 for the death of Queen Philippa, Chaucer received significantly less material than his wife did. Crow and Olson, Chaucer Life-Records, 98–99.

put your bed: all these aspects of life, which might strike us as profoundly personal, were out of the control of the household servant, and all these conditions expressed exactly where he or she stood in the pecking order.

As a teenage page, Chaucer was a relatively unimportant member of the household, but his time with Elizabeth and Lionel offered him extraordinary opportunities and experiences. At Easter 1357, they were in London, where Chaucer's daring outfit was purchased, and they went on to Windsor for the St George's Day celebrations. In May, Elizabeth bought more clothes for Chaucer, and also for herself, in preparation for spending Pentecost at Woodstock, with the court. The household travelled north after this, passing through Doncaster and ending up at Hatfield Manor House, in south Yorkshire, in July. They may have stayed there for several months; certainly, they spent Christmas 1357 there. In 1358, the earl and countess were at Windsor again for the St George's Day festivities, were at Smithfield for a tournament in the early summer, and were celebrating the betrothal of their daughter, Philippa, to Edmund Mortimer, along with the betrothal of John of Gaunt to Blanche of Lancaster, and princess Margaret (Lionel's sister) to John Hastings, earl of Pembroke. This triple betrothal—of two of Edward III's children and his only grandchild—took place in the Queen's Chapel in the summer.[41] They continued to travel widely, for instance, to Liverpool, Reading, and London, where they visited the lions in the Tower and also attended the funeral of Queen Isabella, widow of Edward II, at the church of the Friars Minor in Newgate Street. In 1359, they attended the wedding of Blanche of Lancaster and John of Gaunt in Reading in May.[42]

The partial accounts that have survived undoubtedly have many gaps but nonetheless give us all kinds of information about what Chaucer's life was like at this time. This was probably the period in his life in which he travelled most widely around England, billeting wherever he could while travelling, but then gaining access to luxurious palaces, castles, hunting lodges, and manors. The year was marked by festivals in the Christian calendar: Christmas, Easter, Pentecost, and the newly fashionable St George's

---

[41] Ormrod, *Edward III*, 391.

[42] See Bond and Selby, *Life-Records of Chaucer*, 3:97–13. The accounts are excerpted and discussed in Crow and Olson, *Chaucer Life-Records*, 13–18.

Day, and these festivals were occasions for hospitality and consumption. At Christmas and New Year 1357–58, for instance, Elizabeth and Lionel entertained John of Gaunt and his entourage at Hatfield; they gave payments to a wide range of people at this time, including Chaucer himself, Gaunt's attendants, and messengers, who brought letters from Blanche of Lancaster, and from Ireland.[43]

Chaucer entered aristocratic service at a moment of exceptionally conspicuous display and magnificence, and witnessed some of the most sumptuous demonstrations of royal self-fashioning in medieval England. Edward III was at the height of his success in these years; he was in the prime of his life and, with the help of his spectacularly able—and lucky—eldest son, was achieving extraordinary military victories in these early years of the Hundred Years' War. Crécy in 1346 allowed the English to feel confident in their king, and the king took every advantage of his position to reinforce and burnish his image. His return from France was marked with tournaments, spectacle, and, interestingly, dressing up. At one point, Edward appeared as a pheasant (a decade earlier he had ordered a hat decorated with tigers, trees, a castle, and a man riding a horse, picked out in pearls and in gold and silver plate).[44] He also, around June 1348, founded the Order of the Garter, mapping this new idea onto an earlier, unrealized plan to found a Round Table. Over the next few years, he and his image makers worked to present an image of Windsor as Camelot, Edward as a new Arthur—garbed in cloth of gold imported via Venice from the Far East. The first formal Garter meeting was held on St George's Day 1349, and over the next few years, Edward commissioned extensive building and painting work at Windsor, patronizing some of the finest craftsmen and artists in Europe. In 1356, the Black Prince, heir to the throne, had his great military victory at Poitiers, a victory crowned with the capture of the French king himself. At the St George's Day celebration in the subsequent year—probably the first one at which Chaucer was in attendance on Elizabeth and Lionel—this victory gave an extra reason for euphoria. The importance of the celebrations

[43] Ibid., 14–15.

[44] See Ormrod, *Edward III*, 299–321; the reference to the pheasant costume is on 299–300; the tiger hat appears on 315.

was such that, as Parliament was sitting in April 1357, a recess was called for 21–23 April. Less than a fortnight later, on 5 May, the Black Prince and Jean II of France docked at Plymouth. Now began a frenetic display of the glory of the English court, beginning with an elaborate entry into London and reaching its zenith in the Garter celebrations of 1358. Heralds were sent to France, Germany, and the Low Countries to announce these jousts.[45] Chaucer was at most an observer at these spectacles, a watcher, not a participant, someone who existed to facilitate the enjoyment of others, a cog in a complicated machine. And the role of observer was, of course, to be central to his poetic identity: the watcher and recorder, a standard narratorial persona in dream vision especially, poems often penned by courtiers, gained new particularity in Chaucer's poetry as he perfected the persona of hapless bystander in poem after poem.

Chaucer's life was now punctuated by peripheral attendance on these most dazzlingly glamorous events, and by other gatherings of the royal family, for instance, at the now-vanished hunting lodge at Woodstock, near Oxford, at Pentecost 1357. Nothing can have been ordinary in a lifestyle defined by travel and change, but his existence when the household was living on its own must have been less extravagant and more predictable than when it was a satellite to the Garter celebrations, or to Gaunt's wedding, for instance. When households were not travelling or attending spectacular celebrations, they ran according to regular rhythms. On a daily basis, these rhythms were based around meals, of course, and religious services; on a weekly basis, on dietary changes on certain days (usually Wednesday, Friday, and Saturday); and on an annual basis, on the festivals of the church year. Food was intertwined with religion; there were days of abstinence, fasting, and changes in diet that marked the religious calendar on both a weekly and a yearly scheme.[46]

Hatfield Manor House in Yorkshire seems to have been the nearest to a regular home that Elizabeth and Lionel had. This house still exists, and is still lived in. Although little is visible of the medieval structure, it is still possible to discern the dimensions of the original great hall (around

---

[45] Ormrod, *Edward III*, 299–321, 387–91. See also Stephanie Trigg, *Shame and Honour: A Vulgar History of the Order of the Garter* (Philadelphia: University of Pennsylvania Press, 2012).

[46] Woolgar, *The Great Household*, 90–91.

140 square metres, or 15.8 by 9, not a vast structure) beneath the smaller rooms mapped on top of it by subsequent centuries; and one can still look through one of the twelfth-century narrow windows, set deep in the one-metre-thick stone walls, that Chaucer knew. There may have been a complex of buildings here, with a separate kitchen block. Although legend tells of a vast medieval residence here, on the site of Edwin of Northumbria's palace, it seems to have been a manor house of relatively modest proportions.[47] Chaucer certainly met John of Gaunt here at Christmas 1357 (although they might, of course, have met before as well).[48]

Owned by the de Warrenne family, Hatfield was seized by Thomas of Lancaster early in the fourteenth century during his private war with John, earl of Warenne (who had abducted Thomas's wife),[49] and was then held by the Crown, passed back to John, and returned to the Crown again in 1347. It was a convenient location for stopping off between London and major centres in the north, such as York, and was particularly prized for its hunting—many records refer to people hunting, trespassing, or poaching around Hatfield. When Edward Balliol, erstwhile king of Scotland and a de Warrenne on his mother's side, resided there in 1356, he was said to have 'hunted extremely.' Edward III and Philippa also spent time there; one of their children who died in infancy, William, was born there in 1336, and later, the house was held by the queen in right of her son, Edmund of Langley.[50] Elizabeth and Lionel treated it as a temporary home. The arrival of members of the royal family with their extensive entourage, and the demands they made on local markets, must always have caused considerable upheaval in the area. Situated a few miles from Doncaster, at this time a market town, Hatfield was only a small settlement. In the Vintry, entertainment, culture, friends, and social life could be found in many places; now everything was concentrated on the world of the household. Hatfield was a particularly appealing location for Elizabeth and Lionel, as it was only about ten miles from the Isle of Axholme,

[47] Julian Birch and Peter Ryder, 'Hatfield Manor House, South Yorkshire,' *Yorkshire Archaeological Journal* 60 (1988): 65–104.

[48] Crow and Olson, *Chaucer Life-Records*, 18.

[49] John's wife, Joan de Bar, was a close friend and cousin of Elizabeth, Lady of Clare, Elizabeth de Burgh's grandmother. See Underhill, *For Her Good Estate*, 107.

[50] Birch and Ryder, 'Hatfield Manor House,' 84–91.

where the Mowbray family had their main residence. John Mowbray (II) had been married to Elizabeth's aunt, Joan of Lancaster; their children, John, Eleanor, and Blanche, were thus Elizabeth's first cousins. And John (III) was also closely connected to Lionel and his family—John was knighted in 1355 by the king and the duke of Lancaster (his uncle) along with twenty-six others, including Lionel and John of Gaunt.[51]

Elizabeth's accounts mention a gift to a servant who came from Axholme to Hatfield in December 1357: he had been unable to come the usual way (about ten miles) because of the ice ('congellacionem aquarum') and so had come via Blyth—making it a forty-mile journey (one way) in the middle of winter.[52] The life of those in the retinue of great lords and ladies was not all about attending Garter celebrations and reading romances: they had to minister to their employers' wants, however inconvenient, uncomfortable, and perilous this might be. Indeed, at times, their duties could be deeply unpleasant and even illegal. Great lords maintained their incomes through exacting feudal dues from as many subjects as they could, often intimidating people with far less power than themselves. In *Wynnere and Wastoure*, Wynnere, who represents the landed aristocracy, rebuts accusations that he, 'prikkede with powere [the chief justice's] pese to distourbe!' (rode out with force to disturb [the chief justice's] peace) (317); this kind of personal intimidation by a great lord, and, usually, his private army of retainers, was an everyday part of late-medieval life. Men such as Chaucer, serving within the retinue of a great lord, would certainly have been aware of the tactics that men (and women) of power employed, and may themselves have taken part in intimidation and coercion.

The great household was not just important to Chaucer for the couple of years in which he served Elizabeth and Lionel. It remained vital to his

[51] Rowena E. Archer, 'Mowbray, John (I),' 'Mowbray, John (II),' and 'Mowbray, John (III),' in *The Oxford Dictionary of National Biography*, online ed. (Oxford: Oxford University Press, 2008; hereafter, *ODNB*), https://doi.org/10.1093/ref:odnb/19450; https://doi.org/10.1093/ref:odnb/19451; and https://doi.org/10.1093/ref:odnb/19452. The Lady Mowbray mentioned in Elizabeth's accounts is not her aunt, as has usually been assumed, as Joan had died by 1344, but John's third wife, Elizabeth de Vere.

[52] Bond and Selby, *Life-Records of Chaucer*, 3:111.

material circumstances throughout his life, and was also of central imaginative importance in the literature that he read and wrote, both in obvious and in more ambiguous ways. Although we don't know what Chaucer was doing in the first half of the 1360s, he was almost certainly attached to a princely household, perhaps still Lionel and Elizabeth's, John of Gaunt's, or the Black Prince's—this would make particular sense given his trip to Navarre in 1366, as Aquitaine (the Black Prince's base from 1363–70) would be a natural starting point for the journey. From 1367, Chaucer received an Exchequer annuity from Edward III, which was confirmed by Richard II when he inherited the throne. Chaucer relinquished this annuity in 1388 but received a new allowance in 1394 from Richard, which was confirmed by Henry IV when he usurped the throne in 1399.[53] So, for most of his adult life, Chaucer was attached in various ways to the king's household. This did not mean that he was living in the household as he did when he was a page. Rather, it meant that the king called on him for various duties: diplomatic missions abroad, usually to negotiate peace or marriages, or journeys within England, for instance, to free a Genoese ship that had been impounded in Dartmouth in 1373.[54] He received perks such as 'Christmas robes' and other livery robes, and his attendance was expected at state events, such as the funerals of Philippa of Hainault and Joan of Kent, for which he was given mourning livery in 1369 and 1385.[55] Chaucer's wife was also a devoted household servant, and her roles often involved her physically attending and living with the ladies that she served. Indeed, this may have provided an escape route for Philippa from a less-than-perfect marriage. Philippa was a 'domicella' of the queen's chamber in 1366, and she continued to receive an allowance from the royal Exchequer until her death.[56] However, she did not remain in active service at court; rather, she moved to the household of John of Gaunt, where she served his second wife, Constance, from 1372.[57] Chaucer also received an annuity from Gaunt

[53] Crow and Olson, *Chaucer Life-Records*, 94–143.
[54] For his diplomatic trips, see ibid., 29–62; for the Dartmouth journey, see ibid., 40–42.
[55] Ibid., 94–107.
[56] Ibid., 67–85.
[57] Ibid., 85–93.

himself from 1374, although they had certainly been connected for many years by this point.[58] Indeed, this relationship was the most important relationship of Chaucer's life.[59]

All of Chaucer's jobs from the middle of the 1350s to the middle of the 1370s were household-based and connected to the king or to his sons. This household environment provided him with the literary experience that made him into a fledgling poet. A manuscript likely assembled by Oton de Graunson, poet and friend of Chaucer (University of Pennsylvania, MS Codex 902, formerly MS French 15) exemplifies the kind of poetry being read around the court in the middle and, to some extent, the later part of the century, poetry by Machaut, de la Mote, Graunson, Margival, and Deschamps.[60] Poets such as Jean de la Mote and Froissart, both Hainuyers who wrote in French, worked at Edward and Philippa's court, and Chaucer may have known them personally.[61] The poetry of Machaut was particularly fashionable and may have been popularized after the French king Jean's imprisonment in England. MS Codex 902 contains short French poems signed 'Ch,' which some critics have speculated may be Chaucer's own early writings. We can't prove this authorship attribution, but this is certainly the kind of poetry that Chaucer was reading as a young adult.[62] And in the list of his works in the Prologue to the *Legend of Good Women*, Alceste mentions 'many an ympne [hymn] for [Love's] halydayes, / That highten balades, roundels, virelayes' (F-Prologue, 422–23).[63] Chaucer styles himself as someone who is interested in different kinds of verse form, and in writing lyrics about love—which could have been in French or English. Some of the extant short poems could fall within this group, but much has probably been lost. The courtly French poetry in MS Codex 902 exemplifies the poetic culture of the great household in

---

[58] Ibid., 271–74; this annuity rewards service already given. In 1369 Chaucer seems to have fought in Gaunt's company in France; see ibid., 106–7 and 31–32.

[59] See chapter 5 in the current study.

[60] The manuscript is discussed in James I. Wimsatt (ed.), *Chaucer and the Poems of 'Ch,'* rev. ed. (Kalamazoo, MI: TEAMS Middle English Texts, 2009). For Graunson as compiler, see 88–90.

[61] See chapter 4 for further discussion of Hainuyers at the English court.

[62] Wimsatt, *Chaucer and the Poems of 'Ch,'* especially 1–15 and 53–90.

[63] There are two versions of the Prologue, conventionally termed the F-Prologue and the G-Prologue. The earlier F-Prologue is discussed in detail in chapter 14, and the changes between the F- and G-Prologues are explored in chapter 18.

the years when Chaucer was maturing. This culture is characterized by an interest in experimenting with verse form and rhyme, and it is overwhelmingly French. It is also dominated by one subject matter—love—although love was often a metaphor for other kinds of relationships.

Indeed, the poetry that Chaucer read and wrote was also poetry of the great household in that much of it was overtly concerned with the relationship between client and patron. Poems such as Machaut's *Jugement du Roi de Behaigne* and *Jugement du Roi de Navarre*, and Chaucer's own *Book of the Duchess*, dramatized this relationship, depicting the poet as a sympathetic servant, peripheral to and utterly focused on the far more important emotions and love affairs of the great lord.[64] Other contemporary poems, *Sir Gawain and the Green Knight* and *Wynnere and Wastoure*, refer to the daily calculation of rations for each member of the great household in their poems, and in myriad other ways too depict an inside view of life in such a household.[65] Chaucer, along with his friend Sir John Clanvowe, used the language of retaining in dream vision poetry to conceptualise the subject's submission to Love, imagining the narrator as 'withheld' (retained) in a household structure.[66] Chaucer's contemporary and friend, John Gower, used the great household as a major structural

[64] The literature of courtly love more generally, with its focus on the disdainful, powerful Lady and the abject, servile male lover, is often read as a displaced depiction of the relationship between feudal lord and vassal. The lover/servant figure is utterly subjected to the power of the dominant lady, who must be obeyed at all costs.

[65] D. Vance Smith, *Arts of Possession: The Middle English Household Imaginary* (Minneapolis: University of Minnesota Press, 2003), 11. In contemporary literature, the household in general was central to many poets' imaginations and using architectural structures allegorically was a standard trope. The idea of the soul as a house, an allegory that structures texts such as Hugh of St Victor's *De anima*, the early Middle English *Sawles Warde*, and parts of *Ancrene Wisse*, informs Chaucer's 'Tale of Melibee' too, in which Melibee himself is represented as a fortified house, his wisdom as his wounded daughter, and his careful pragmatism as his wife Prudence. Henry of Grosmont (father of Blanche of Lancaster and uncle of Elizabeth de Burgh) compared his body to a sophisticated great house, with his heart as a cesspit; in contrast, the Virgin's heart was like a cistern receiving water from gutters and clarifying it. See Henry of Lancaster, *The Book of Holy Medicines (Le Livre de Seyntz Medicines)*, ed. Catherine Batt (Tempe, AZ: Arizona Centre for Medieval and Renaissance Studies, 2014). The *Gawain* poet refers to God as a king, 'honeste in his housholde and hagherlych served.' Robert J. Menner (ed.), *Purity: A Middle English Poem* (New Haven: Yale University Press, 1920), 18.

[66] G-Prologue in the *Legend of Good Women*, 76; *Book of Cupid*, 289 in V. J. Scattergood (ed.), *Works of Sir John Clanvowe* (Cambridge: D. S. Brewer, 1975). Elliot Kendall, *Lordship and Literature: John Gower and the Politics of the Great Household* (Oxford: Oxford University Press, 2008), 66; Lee Patterson, 'Court Politics and the Invention of Literature: The Case of Sir John Clanvowe,' in David Aers (ed.), *Culture and History, 1350–1600: Essays on English Communities, Identities, and Writing* (Detroit: Prentice-Hall, 1993), 10.

device in his work, using metaphors of service to represent the self as a complicated structure with chamberlains, secretaries, and other household officials playing their parts.[67] Thomas Usk, early reader of Chaucer, imagines his relationship with Lady Love as a relationship between retainer and great lord, in which he wears her livery and is explicitly one of her 'retinue.' Usk, like Chaucer, was someone with connections in the city and the court: he worked for a livery company in London and was enmeshed with mayoral politics, but also aspired to and briefly gained an appointment based in the king's household, when he became one of the king's serjeants-at-arms.[68]

In moving from a merchant's household to a noble household, Chaucer crossed social boundaries, moving from a trading, monetary environment dominated by families who had often only recently gained wealth to an environment where luxurious lifestyles were supported by landed wealth and where long-standing semifeudal relationships were supposed to be mutually beneficial. But imagining these two worlds as starkly opposed is to misrepresent history. Written around the mid-1350s, *Wynnere and Wastoure* emphasises Edward III's dependence on merchants for finance, and satirizes two contrasting ways of life. Wynnere sees himself as a careful saver, but Wastoure condemns him as a miser with no social conscience or desire to spread his wealth in the community. Wastoure argues that he himself spends lavishly and that that expenditure extends to the poor; Wynnere claims that Wastoure spends what he does not have, neglecting his lands and responsibilities in order to fight and squander money. The two are, in fact, dependent on each other—one to supply, the other to consume. The poem reflects contemporary unease at the rise of mercantile values while also criticizing irresponsible landowners whose lifestyle of feasting and fighting was not underwritten by good lordship. It also, however, sets up a false dichotomy when it implies that mercantile and aristocratic values oppose each other. Throughout this period, merchants had court positions, became landowners, married into the gentry and nobility, and were sometimes themselves knighted; nobles and royalty were

---

[67] Kendall, *Lordship*, 65–98.
[68] Marion Turner, 'Usk and the Goldsmiths,' *New Medieval Literatures* 9 (2007): 139–77.

heavily involved with banking and trade.[69] And any individual great household needed both to accumulate and to spend; these contradictory impulses existed in constant tension.[70] Nonetheless, when Chaucer took up his job with Elizabeth, he not only experienced the novelty of becoming a servant, an inferior, he also came into contact with different ways of life: the itineracy, the overwhelming focus on spectacle, the absence of the kind of work that produced things, made this a markedly different lifestyle from that to which he was accustomed. John and Agnes Chaucer were undoubtedly consumers of luxuries, but they were also *providers* of commodities. Lionel and Elizabeth consumed and encouraged consumption on a large scale: the consumption of food, drink, textiles, clothes—the 'ostelementz' (household goods) that Boethius condemned—was the primary business of their lives.[71] In *Wynnere and Wastoure*, consumption is as conspicuous as possible: the king wears an astonishing belt that itself tells a story, depicting birds so lifelike that they seem to tremble at the hawks' approach (96–100); a feast is described (332–65) that begins with a boar's head, bucks' hindquarters, venison, pheasants, and pies, and continues through an array of birds, including geese, snipe, bitterns, larks, linnets, and woodpeckers—the table and its dishes described, scathingly, as appearing like a jeweled cross (343). The diners are thus depicted (by the disapproving miser-figure, Wynnere) as blasphemous in their consumption; the lord as utterly unconcerned with real need, providing one night of lavish excess when regular meals are required (365).

In a short poem, *To Rosemund*, Chaucer's persona imagines himself as an object of consumption, as something to be eaten. This poem plays with

---

[69] Given-Wilson, *The Royal Household*, 149–53. In chapters 6 and 7, I discuss in detail the king and royal government's relationship with the wool trade in particular. A good example of a merchant family that crossed over into the highest aristocracy is the de la Poles. William de la Pole (d. 1366) was a Hull merchant whose son Michael became the 1st earl of Suffolk; Michael's grandson (another William) married Alice Chaucer, the poet's granddaughter, and their son John married Elizabeth, the sister of Edward IV and Richard III. For the career of the first William de la Pole, see E. B. Fryde, *William de la Pole: Merchant and King's Banker* (London: Hambledon Press, 1988).

[70] See Vance Smith's comment on *Wynnere and Wastoure* as being 'about the ethical and logistical difficulties of possessing the household,' and the household's 'profoundly antithetical, agonistic tendencies.' *Arts of Possession*, 76, 81.

[71] See Chaucer's translation in the *Riverside Chaucer*; *Boece*, book 2, prosa 5, 119, p. 415.

the conventions of love poetry, building up to the last stanza, which opens with:

> Nas never pyk walwed in galauntyne
> As I in love am walwed and ywounde,
> For which ful ofte I of myself devyne
> That I am trewe Tristam the secounde. (17–20)

The speaker asserts that he believes he is a second Tristan, fabled lover of Isolde, because of the extent of his love; he is steeped and wrapped in love even more than a piece of pike is steeped in 'galantine.' The sauce makes something quite ordinary into something desirable; just as love was supposed to be a transforming passion. A galantine sauce was made of bread, vinegar, and varying spices; a fifteenth-century cookbook gives a recipe for pike in galantine, advising 'cast the sauce under him and above him that he be al yhidde in the sauce.'[72] The image, then, is of the lover utterly encased by this sticky mess, his identity hidden and subsumed. The speaker is totally powerless, hidden by the sauce and ready to be consumed, to be eaten by the object of desire. The lines parody the courtly love relationship, which itself represents a feudal, service relationship. The comic aspect of the image, the ludicrousness of imagining oneself as a sauce-covered dead fish, is entirely typical of Chaucer's irreverence towards *fin amor*. And his construction of himself not as consumer but as consumed makes his persona a servant-figure, whose body is subject to the will of the master or mistress. The choice of this image reminds us of Chaucer's familiarity with luxuries, not as a consumer but as someone who, in the Vintry, saw the spices arriving on ships and sold in shops and, in the great household, saw cooks preparing elaborate meals and servants serving them—and Chaucer may have helped with these jobs himself when he was a page. As Hiatt writes, this image 'disorients,' it brings the 'market, the pantry, the economy' into the poem.[73] In another short poem, *The Former Age*, 'galantine' is a shorthand for elaborate fine dining.

---

[72] London British Library MS Harley 4016, printed in Thomas Austin (ed.), *Two Fifteenth Century Cookery Books*, EETS 91 (London: Oxford University Press, 1888, repr. 1964), 101.

[73] Alfred Hiatt, 'Genre without System,' in Strohm, *Middle English*, 277–94.

Chaucer declares that in a seemingly idyllic pastoral golden age, man ate and drank simply:

No man yit in the morter spyces grond
To clarre ne to sause of galantyne. (15–16)

The twist—and there is always a twist—is that this 'former age' is not simply held up as a model of simple pleasures; in contrast, at this time it turns out that people ate 'mast, hawes, and swich pounage' (nuts, berries, and such pig food [7]); they slept on grass and leaves, peacefully admittedly, but with no 'doun of fetheres' (45); their lifestyle was a series of negatives: no dyes for their clothes, no ships, no money, no cities, no 'outlandish ware' (22)—overseas merchandise—sold by merchants. Indeed, no one knew better than Chaucer how much aristocratic, luxurious living depended on mercantile activity, and while he understood the drive to criticize modernity, he also made clear that few would really want to give up their beautifully dyed clothes, their wine, or their 'paleis-chaumbres' (41).[74] This is the first use of 'paleis-chaumbre' in English, its very novelty emphasizing how fashionable Chaucer was, how aware of new kinds of domestic space, of trendy kinds of clothes (the paltok) and food—such as the 'sause of galantyne.'

Galantine in French cooking developed into a meat dish cooked in aspic, and often elaborately decorated. Although the word probably derives ultimately from the Latin 'gelata' (jelly), which itself derived from 'gelare' (to freeze or coagulate), the dish came to be related to the Old French word 'galant' (sophisticated), deriving from 'galer' (to make merry), as the dish evolved into something playfully decorated. We can perceive a similar pun in the Middle English 'galuntyne': 'galaunt' as a noun meant a 'man of fashion,' particularly one who dressed extravagantly, and as an adjective meant merry or gaily dressed. Chaucer uses variants of this word in the 'Miller's' and 'Cook's' Tales, and a macaronic (multilingual) poem from about 1380 (known by modern editors as 'On the Times') includes a long

---

[74] The poem is one of Chaucer's 'Boethian' lyrics. In part 2 of this book, I discuss Chaucer's response to Boethius's *Consolation* in detail, especially Chaucer's discomfort with contemptus mundi and Neoplatonic thought. See especially chapters 8 and 9. For further discussion of *The Former Age*, see A. S. Galloway, 'Chaucer's *Former Age* and the Fourteenth-Century Anthropology of Craft: The Social Logic of a Premodernist Lyric,' *ELH* 63:3 (1996): 535–54.

attack on the figure of the 'galaunt' as a symbol of what is wrong with the contemporary world.[75] The critique of the 'galauntes' (117) focuses on their attempt to change their bodies through fashion.[76] 'On the Times' attacks galauntes for padding their clothes ('Brodder then ever God made,' 129), and making themselves swell at the shoulders ('humeris sunt arte tumentes' [They puff out (their) shoulders artificially], 130), building up to the statement that 'Goddes plasmacoun / non illis complacet ergo' (God's shaping of them / therefore is not pleasing to them [135–36]).[77] In *To Rosemund*, the 'galaunt' pun relates the dead fish covered in sauce to the bland man covered in fashionable clothes, which serve to mask his essential ordinariness. The word 'yhidde,' used in recipes, emphasizes this sense of disguise, of a stylized self-fashioning appropriate both to lover and to servant; one who is transforming his identity to please his master or mistress.

The idea of relating food to fashion is entirely commensurate with a holistic sense of culture that pertained in the fourteenth century, in which food, clothes, and indeed manuscripts were all objects of sumptuous display. Food (through vivid colours, or through sculpting food into shapes, such as castles) or clothes (such as Edward III's tiger-scene hat, the king's belt-tableau in *Wynnere and Wastoure*, or even Chaucer's shocking paltok and hose) could be entertaining, could provide spectacle, in the same way that performing a poem or acting a scene could amuse and delight. In great households in the thirteenth century, meals were punctuated by 'entremets,' edible delicacies, which evolved into 'subtleties,' interesting, nonedible pieces of art, and pageants, incorporating live performers, who

---

[75] This poem is discussed by Richard Firth Green, 'A Poem of 1380,' *Speculum* 66:2 (April 1991): 330–41; and Andrea Denny-Brown, *Fashioning Change: The Trope of Clothing in High and Late-Medieval England* (Columbus: Ohio State University Press, 2012), 148–78.

[76] However, in many ways, the so-called invention of fashion in the middle of the century involved making clothes fit *more* precisely to the shape of the body, replacing less structured forms. As Denny-Brown writes, the 'vast majority of recent scholarship on medieval costume locates the birth of Western fashion in the virtual revolution of European dress that emerged in and around the 1340s.' Denny-Brown, *Fashioning Change*, 8. See also Newton, *Fashion in the Age of the Black Prince*; for a discussion of different views about fashion's emergence, see Sarah-Grace Heller, *Fashion in Medieval France* (Cambridge: D. S. Brewer, 2007), 46–60.

[77] The poem is printed in James M. Dean (ed.), *Medieval English Political Writings* (Kalamazoo, MI: TEAMS Middle English Texts, 1996), 140–46. The translations are taken from Dean's gloss.

could entertain the diners.[78] An education in fine food and clothes was not irrelevant to the education of a future writer; Chaucer was learning the arts of entertainment in myriad ways as he experienced life in a great household.

But being part of a great household also conferred serious responsibilities—if the lord went to war, his household went with him. This is what happened to Chaucer in autumn 1359, when he was only sixteen or seventeen years old.

[78] Woolgar, *The Great Household*, 160.

CHAPTER 3

Reims and Calais

Galfrido Chaucer capto per inimicos in partibus Francie in subsidium
redempcionis sue . . . xvi li. (As a contribution to the ransom of
Geoffrey Chaucer, captured by enemies in France, £16)
—*Edward III Wardrobe Accounts, 1359–60*

Reims was a city of great symbolic importance in France, the place where
kings were crowned. Legend has it that Clovis was simultaneously baptized and crowned there by Bishop Remigius in 496, when a dove
descended from heaven bearing an ampula of holy oil.[1] Clovis became
king and priest at once, and future kings were crowned in the same place:
every French king except one between 1131 and 1825 was crowned in
Reims. The oil, supposedly received directly from God, marked French
kings as superior to all other kings, comparable with the Old Testament
prophets, and invested with thaumaturgic powers—the miraculous ability to cure scrofula.[2] The archbishop of Reims crowned and advised the
king, and he became known as 'First Peer of the Realm.'[3] Through a false
etymology that connected Reims with Remus, the city was also associated
with Rome and imperial power.[4] It was a militant city: another legend

---

[1] Anne Walters Robertson, *Guillaume de Machaut and Reims: Context and Meaning in His Musical Works* (Cambridge: Cambridge University Press, 2002), 18.

[2] Jacques Le Goff, 'Reims: City of Coronation,' in Pierre Nora (ed.), *Realms of Memory: The Construction of the French Past III: Symbols*, trans. Arthur Goldhammer, English edition ed. Lawrence D.
Kritzman (New York: Columbia University Press, 1998), 193, 194, 205, 233.

[3] Robertson, *Guillaume de Machaut and Reims*, 19.

[4] Le Goff, 'Reims,' 219. The name came from the Remi, a people from Germania who settled in this
area. Le Goff, 'Reims,' 193.

claimed that, earlier in the fifth century, Bishop Nicasius protected and defended his people against the invading Vandals, and was ultimately slaughtered in the church itself. The place of his murder was marked with a stone known as the Rouelle; today a slab in the pavement marks the spot. The story of Nicasius defined the role of the archbishop as active and military; he was expected to be a warrior-prelate and to defend this sacred city of kings.[5]

Reims was a place that focused on endless repetition, on replaying the same ceremony as a triumph of ahistoricity, of sacred time.[6] But there was nothing sacred about Calais, a town defined by change. A borderland, an occupied territory, and a trading hub, famous for its brave bourgeoisie, this town on the edge of France became part of England in 1347 and remained in English hands until 1558. While Reims was conceptually a place rooted in history, connected to Rome, Remus, and early Christianity, in the 1350s Calais was primarily a place of the now: its most famous story related to its capitulation in 1347. After a siege of almost a year, and having been abandoned by the French army, the burghers of Calais agreed to surrender in order to avoid starvation. According to Froissart, they agreed to Edward's conditions, and the six most prominent citizens delivered themselves up to the English king, barefooted and bareheaded, with halters around their necks. He intended to kill them, in punishment for all the English lives lost in the siege, but his heavily pregnant wife interceded for them, and he granted her their lives.[7] It was an archetypal scene of queenly intercession of the type that monarchs often staged, and that would be played out again and again in Chaucer's works (the 'Knight's Tale' and the 'Wife of Bath's Tale' stage exactly this scene of male kingly violence being neutralized by queenly abjection and pleas for peace). The heroes of this story are not kings or archbishops but the bourgeoisie, testament to Calais's urban, mercantile identity. In the 1350s, Edward ruled Calais in right of the French Crown, but its nature was changing as more Londoners settled there—and as the garrison became more and more securely established.[8] In 1360, as we shall see, Calais was assigned to

[5] Robertson, *Guillaume de Machaut and Reims*, 22.
[6] Le Goff, 'Reims,' 194.
[7] Jean Froissart, *Chronicles*, trans. Geoffrey Brereton (London: Penguin, 1968), 103–10.
[8] Jonathan Sumption, *The Hundred Years War II: Trial by Fire* (London: Faber and Faber, 1999), 20.

England in perpetuity,[9] and in 1363 the wool staple was moved there, making it a crucial centre for trade. But when Chaucer arrived there in 1359, these changes were yet to come.[10] It was a place in process, being changed dramatically and roughly by the immediate forces of history as it was pushed into the role of England's military stronghold on the Continent.[11]

In sharp contrast, in Reims, a city whose wealth was in fact founded on the cloth and fabric trade, the burghers were systematically excluded from the coronation ceremonies, allowed to attend only a few minor events. They were also marginalized through their representation in the riot of sculpture on the cathedral, where the few depictions of more ordinary citizens are hidden away amongst flora and fauna. Reims' identity, projected through its architecture and its coronation ceremony, focused on the symbiosis between Church and Crown, between bishops, canons, and monks on the one hand and king, counsellors, and knights on the other.[12] Indeed, the bourgeoisie were often depicted as usurers and heretics by the archbishop and canons of the cathedral: in the thirteenth century, cloth traders in particular were at great risk in Reims (there were mass burnings of alleged heretics nearby), and the windows that were glazed at this time (the 1230s) reflected the antipathy between church and merchants. The stained glass took the triumph over usury and heresy as a major theme, and depictions of Cain harnessed the common local association of Cain with heresy, Jews, usury, and, specifically, the textile trade.[13] The ecclesiastical authorities took care to attack the bourgeoisie in the very fabric of the iconic cathedral itself.

Chaucer did not get into Reims. It was a destination-not-reached, as Canterbury was to be for his pilgrims. But Reims was the goal for the army of which Chaucer was a member: in 1359 Edward III, supported by a huge army, laid determined siege to the city for several weeks, intending to seize it and, perhaps, to have himself crowned there as king of France.[14]

---

[9] Ibid., 447.

[10] Ormrod, *Edward III*, 482–83; David Wallace, *Premodern Places: Calais to Surinam, Chaucer to Aphra Behn* (Malden, MA: Blackwell, 2004), 41.

[11] Sumption, *Trial by Fire*, 18–24.

[12] Le Goff, 'Reims,' 215–16.

[13] Meredith Parsons Lillich, *The Gothic Stained Glass of Reims Cathedral* (University Park: Pennsylvania State University Press, 2011), 8–9, 89, 122.

[14] Ormrod, *Edward III*, 400–402.

And, while Chaucer—still a teenager—was taking part in this uncomfortable and unsuccessful siege, in which he was captured and held prisoner by the enemy, one of his greatest poetic influences, Machaut, was himself within the walls of Reims, seeing events from exactly the opposite perspective.

A few months later Chaucer was in Calais, where the treaty that ended this campaign was ratified. It was a place to which Chaucer was to return over and over again on his trips abroad, and a place that was of ongoing importance to him as a traveller, messenger, diplomat, and, later, customs officer. Reims, city of kings, archbishops, ceremony, and sacred history, and Calais, town of merchants, exchanges, treaties, and mixed identities, represent two very different aspects of 'France' (although Calais, indeed, was technically not France at all). Chaucer's first known trip abroad focused on impregnable Reims, but began and ended in Calais. And this seems deeply appropriate: later in life, Chaucer was to be a poet not of order and enshrined hierarchies but of heterogeneous voices and the marketplace. Indeed, David Wallace has written about Calais as 'epiphenomenal of the Chaucerian poetic' in its hybridity, adding that Calais in the later fourteenth century also represents England itself in its complicated cultural mix.[15]

This was probably Chaucer's first visit to France; indeed, it was probably his first trip abroad. But poetry in French, by French and Hainuyer poets, was well known to educated members of the king's household. Chaucer might well have already encountered French lyric and romance, and over the next few years, French poetry became part of the fabric of his mind. The most important secular poetic text in Chaucer's heritage was the *Roman de la Rose*, termed by critics 'the great foundation text of the European Middle Ages,' and 'the central medieval love story.'[16] In the *Book of the Duchess*, the *Rose* was the poem painted on the walls, alongside the story of Troy, portrayed in the glass windows, symbolizing together the two most influential stories in the poetic tradition (321–34). The *Rose* focuses on an almost-universal, transformational experience: the

[15] Wallace, *Premodern Places*, 60.
[16] David Wallace, 'Chaucer and the European *Rose*,' *Studies in the Age of Chaucer* 1 (1984): 67; James I. Wimsatt, *Allegory and Mirror: Tradition and Structure in Middle English Literature* (New York: Pegasus, 1970), 64.

youthful experience of sexual desire or, put another way, the experience of falling in love for the first time. Set in the garden of pleasure, this dream vision builds up to the plucking of the rose, despite numerous obstacles. In poetic terms, it is one of the great medieval allegories, and it is a text that strongly influenced both the French poets that Chaucer read earlier in his career and the Italians that he encountered in the 1370s. Written by two authors (Guillaume de Lorris and Jean de Meun), the first part is generally seen as a key 'courtly love' text; the second, longer section is darker and more satirical. While the idea of the art of love dominates the poem, it is encyclopaedic in its interests, ranging across a wide array of subjects. Chaucer tells us in the Prologue to the *Legend of Good Women* that he translated the *Roman de la Rose* (F-Prologue, 328–29), and this translation is also obliquely mentioned by his contemporary, Deschamps, and by Lydgate a generation later.[17] While we lack a critical consensus on whether or not the whole or parts of the extant Middle English *Romaunt of the Rose* are indeed Chaucer's translation, the evidence is that he certainly did embark on a translation at some point, probably early in his career.[18] We also see evidence of the *Rose*'s influence everywhere in Chaucer's work. Figures such as La Vielle, Faux Semblant, and the Ami were models for the Wife of Bath, the Pardoner, and Pandarus. The allegorical aspects of the *Rose* were influential on Chaucer's dream visions; the more satirical and naturalistic elements of de Meun's continuation conditioned Chaucer's later writings.[19] Even more fundamentally, the most important aspect of the *Rose* for Chaucer's poetic development was de Lorris's development of the narrator figure. Barbara Nolan terms Lorris the 'master' of the technique of separating the perspectives of narrator and audience, suggesting multiple points of view, and making the audience part of a 'conspiracy' with the author.[20]

---

[17] Deschamps praises Chaucer as a translator who has sown the rose in England; see chapter 14 in this study for discussion. For Lydgate, see Charles Dahlberg, 'Introduction,' in Geoffrey Chaucer, *The Romaunt of the Rose*, ed. Charles Dahlberg (Norman: University of Oklahoma Press, 1999), 17.

[18] For the critical debate, see Dahlberg, 'Introduction,' 3–70.

[19] See Charles Muscatine's characterization of the two *Rose* authors' different modes. *Chaucer and the French Tradition: A Study in Style and Meaning* (Berkeley: University of California Press, 1957).

[20] Barbara Nolan, *The Gothic Visionary Perspective* (Princeton: Princeton University Press, 1977), 141. See also David Lawton, *Chaucer's Narrators* (Cambridge: D. S. Brewer, 1985), 62–75.

The *Rose* was one of the key inspirations behind the development of the *dit amoureux*, or tale of love, in fourteenth-century French literature, and this genre underpins Chaucer's earliest forays into narrative poetry. And the French writer that had the most immediate effect on Chaucer (most directly in the *Book of the Duchess*) was Guillaume de Machaut, the prolific composer and poet who produced an extraordinary number and range of texts: poems, songs, motets, dits, and the first complete Mass cycle. Machaut was an expert in the art of the *dit amoureux*, the 'lyrical narrative' love poem, told in the first person, and usually involving narratorial frames, debate, and some kind of judgement or resolution.[21] While the *dits* are overtly about love and the experience of desire, they are also poems about poetry. They meditate on authority, how to reframe source material, and the practice of poetic making. Machaut was particularly adept at both utilising and challenging the authoritative texts that preceded him (such as the *Rose*, but also older classical and late antique texts by authors such as Ovid and Boethius). He also developed a hesitant, unreliable, narratorial persona, often depicted as somewhat comic and as ineffectual.[22] This dual focus on irreverence towards the past and on the unreliability of any narrative filter was to be crucial to Chaucer's entire poetic development. In all of his long poems, Chaucer created distancing narratorial personae, often representing biased readers and hapless interpreters as, throughout his career, he emphasized the need for readers to be active participants in texts. He developed his own poetics in response to a wide range of intellectual currents, most notably, Italian ideas that he encountered in the 1370s, but all such ideas were themselves dependent on French literature of the thirteenth and fourteenth centuries.[23] French culture was

[21] For the *dit amoureux*, see Kay, Cave, and Bowie, *A Short History of French Literature*, 75–80.

[22] See Deborah McGrady, 'Guillaume de Machaut,' in Simon Gaunt and Sarah Kay (eds.), *The Cambridge Companion to Medieval French Literature* (Cambridge: Cambridge University Press, 2009), 109–22; Kevin Brownlee, *Poetic Identity in Guillaume de Machaut* (Madison: University of Wisconsin Press, 1984); Helen Swift, 'The Poetic I,' and Anne-Helene Miller, 'Guillaume de Machaut and the Forms of Pre-Humanism in Fourteenth-Century France,' both in Deborah McGrady and Jennifer Bain (eds.), *A Companion to Guillaume de Machaut* (Leiden: Brill, 2012), 15–32 and 33–48.

[23] For further discussion on the *Roman*'s influence on Middle English poetry, see Stephanie A. Viereck Gibbs Kamath, 'The *Roman de la Rose* and Middle English Poetry,' *Literature Compass* 6:6 (2009): 1109–26.

at the heart of Chaucer's education as a poet, both before and after his experiences in the Hundred Years' War.

For those associated with the English court in the second half of the fourteenth century, then, France meant two things: war and the poetry of love. While English political life was underpinned by the ongoing conflict, English high cultural life was infused by French poetry. These two elements collide in Chaucer's encounter with Machaut's Reims in December 1359. By the time Chaucer embarked on this campaign, the war with France had been rumbling on for twenty years. The English were certainly having the best of it; by this point, they had had custody of the French king for more than three years. The Battle of Poitiers in 1356 had ended in the English capturing huge numbers of prisoners: receipts from those prisoners, not including the king and his son, came to at least £300,000—three times what Edward III had spent on this expensive war over the previous year—and the gains also included horses, armour, clothes, and other objects taken from the defeated.[24] This pitched battle, then, proved extraordinarily lucrative even before one begins to consider the unique political capital that the English gained by imprisoning the French king. One result of his capture was, as one would expect, chaos and infighting in France, a situation that could only benefit France's enemies. But although so much capital could be gained from an individual battle, such battles were rather unusual in this conflict, which in general proceeded more by crop-burning, harassment, and the destruction of food trains and supplies than by actual battles. Both sides were highly conscious of the economics of war. The English destroyed crops, villages, and towns, making sure that they both depleted sources of revenue and created the need for what revenue that there was to be spent on rebuilding and defences.[25] The French retreated within walled cities, taking all their food supplies with them and burning what they left in the fields, leaving the invading armies without access to food and ensuring that they had to arrange and bring huge baggage trains and stores with them.[26] It was a war, then, that had appalling effects on the countryside and on civilians, a state of affairs made

[24] Sumption, *Trial by Fire*, 248.
[25] Ibid., 185–86.
[26] Ibid., 425–27.

worse by the effects of the plague and by the emergence of numerous independent companies of thugs who roamed the countryside and pillaged for their own profit.

The situation in France in 1358 and early 1359 had been increasingly chaotic. In the absence of John II, Charles, count of Evreux and king of Navarre, John's most troublesome relative and subject, had been even more troublesome than usual. The succession disputes of the fourteenth century went back to Philip III, who had three sons who survived to adulthood. One became Philip IV, the father of Louis X, Philip V, and Charles IV. When all three in turn reigned and died without sons, the throne passed not to the son of their sister Isabella, England's Edward III, nor to Louis X's daughter's son, Charles of Navarre, but to Philip VI, whose father, Charles of Valois, was brother to Philip IV. Philip VI was thus first cousin to his predecessor, Charles IV, and to Isabella. Charles of Navarre's French royal blood was the strongest of all, as his father was the son of Louis d'Evreux, the third surviving son of Philip III and brother of Philip IV and Charles of Valois. Charles was therefore descended from Philip III through both his mother and his father. Charles and Edward III were both debarred from the throne by the Salic law, which discounted the female line, although this was much disputed.

The conflicts of the middle of the fourteenth century were played out between a triangle of competing interests: first, the French Crown, held in turn by Philip VI, John II, and Charles V; second, the English Crown, held by Edward III; and third, Charles of Navarre. It was a family quarrel. The triangular aspect is important, as Charles of Navarre frequently switched sides throughout these years, negotiating with the English as a way of putting pressure on the French king to give him concessions. Although Charles was king of Navarre, he was not very interested in his kingdom, preferring to jockey for land, power, and influence in France, a far more important political player. In the 1350s, Charles assassinated Charles de la Cerda (also known as Charles of Spain), constable of France and the king's favourite; repeatedly treated with the English; plotted with the dauphin; and was himself imprisoned by John and eventually escaped. His own conflict with the dauphin (during John's imprisonment in England) was swept up in the Jacquerie revolt of the French peasantry in 1358. At times, Charles was hugely popular in France and had enormous bargaining power; at other times he dramatically overplayed his hand.[27]

For many Chaucer scholars, Charles is best known not for his political and military machinations but as patron of Machaut, for whom Machaut wrote his *Jugement du Roi de Navare* (*Judgement of the King of Navarre*), a sequel to the *Jugement du Roi de Behaigne* (*Judgement of the King of Bohemia*) (Machaut's earlier patron had died at Crécy in 1346). These poems, love debates about the sorrows of betrayal and bereavement, about gender, patronage, and service, poems that experiment with the construction of narratorial and authorial voices, exerted strong influences on Chaucer's poetry. And the *Jugement du Roi de Navare*, in particular, set on 9 November 1349, engages explicitly with the contemporary horrors of the plague and of the Hundred Years' War, as powerful men with 'Towers, troops, catapults, or arbalests' (l. 75) destroy the land.[28]

In 1359, John's advisors saw Charles as a bigger threat than Edward, and they signed a treaty with England that was greatly to Edward's advantage, and detrimental both to France and to Charles (as it transferred many of Charles's French lands to England).[29] They were willing to sacrifice almost anything to gain John's freedom. But the dauphin and the Estates-General rejected the treaty, John remained in prison, and Edward prepared to invade France, and to conquer Reims.[30] As the year wore on, Charles made peace with the dauphin, but his brother, and many of his troops, allied with the English. Indeed, some of the soldiers and leaders under Navarrese command were themselves English, notably Rabigot Dury, whose identity has not been fully unraveled, and Robert Scot.[31] Mercenaries of many nationalities were eager to fight for the English, in the hope of plunder, and Edward actually dismissed many hundreds of willing soldiers, because he had too many mouths to feed.[32] This was the

---

[27] Ibid., 124, 141, 155, 163–68, 199, 206–14, 294–98, 327–50.
[28] These poems are translated in Barbara K. Altmann and R. Barton Palmer (eds. and trans.), *An Anthology of Medieval Love Debate Poetry* (Gainesville: University Press of Florida, 2010).
[29] Sumption, *Trial by Fire*, 400–401.
[30] Ibid., 402–4.
[31] Ibid., 420–22, 205.
[32] Ibid., 427.

constant and insurmountable problem for Edward and his generals: the difficulty of feeding the army, when the French had made it impossible for them to live off the land. And Edward made extraordinary efforts to keep the army marching on its stomach: for this particular campaign, he commissioned leather boats, milling machines, and portable ovens to provide fresh fish and bread to the troops.[33] This army was no ramshackle force but a very well-equipped and supplied set of men.

Edward landed at Calais on 28 October 1359. The massive English army separated into three columns: one led by the king, another by the Black Prince, and the last by Henry, duke of Lancaster. It is usually thought that Lionel's company (seventy men plus valetti) served under the Black Prince.[34] Chaucer marched through France in late autumn 1359, through a ravaged and abandoned landscape of burnt crops and evacuated houses. The French watched from within their walled towns, and guerilla groups attacked English foraging parties. The weather was against the English; they proceeded through cold rain, waded through mud, and were unable to find adequate drinking water or fodder for the horses. In these dispiriting circumstances, the whole army converged near Reims between 28 and 30 November 1359.[35] It was during this march that Chaucer was at Rethel, a town about twenty-five miles from Reims. In a contemporary account, the *Scalacronica*, Thomas Gray tells of the Black Prince's march via St Quentin and Rethel, describing the French burning Rethel to prevent the English army from getting through. According to Gray, the prince forced a passage nonetheless, moving on to Château-Porcien.[36] Twenty-seven years later, Chaucer himself told a story about this campaign, in a sworn testimony to the High Court of Chivalry, on 15 October 1386. Describing himself as more than forty years old, and having borne arms for twenty-seven years, Chaucer gave evidence in the Scrope-Grosvenor controversy,

---

[33] Ormrod, *Edward III*, 399.

[34] Crow and Olson, *Chaucer Life-Records*, 27; Derek Pearsall, *The Life of Geoffrey Chaucer: A Critical Biography* (Oxford: Blackwell, 1992), 41.

[35] Sumption, *Trial by Fire*, 427.

[36] Thomas Gray, *Scalacronica: The Reigns of Edward I, Edward II, and Edward III, as Recorded by Sir Thomas Gray and Now Translated by Sir Herbert Maxwell* (Glasgow: Glasgow University Press, 1907), 147.

which centred on the question of which family had the right to bear arms *azure a bend or*. Chaucer's evidence supported the Scropes, who went on to win the case. He asserted that when he was 'devaunt la ville de Retters,' he saw Richard le Scrope bearing these arms, and Henry le Scrope bearing them with a white label (indicating that he was not head of the family or heir), and that he saw these arms throughout 'le dit viage tanqe le dit Geffrey estoit pris' (the same campaign during which the said Geoffrey was captured).[37] The anecdote draws us a little picture of the campaign: of the English nobility and soldiers assembled in rural France, with their coats of arms as marks of identity. It also provides us with rough evidence about Chaucer's age: the 'xl ans et plus' is a general statement, in line with how others describe their age in these depositions, and suggests a birth date in the early 1340s, as discussed earlier. He was probably around seventeen on this campaign: the average age for first bearing arms, using the evidence given in this particular case, was nineteen; almost all witnesses first bore arms between the ages of fifteen and twenty-three.[38]

The teenage Chaucer, then, on his first military campaign, in a company with all the most glamorous military commanders and princes of the day—Henry, duke of Lancaster, the Black Prince, and the king himself—but enduring miserable conditions, advanced to Reims, city of culture, coronation, and kings. By 4 December, they were at the walls of the city and on the 18th, the army came down for a close blockade. At one point they tried to storm the city but were beaten back. For weeks, the army surrounded the city, assailed by freezing rain, and with an ever-decreasing food supply.[39] From within the city, though, things looked ominous. The English, after all, had had victory after victory over the previous thirteen years; they had held the French king for three years now, and Edward had famously besieged Calais for almost a year, starving the inhabitants into submission. Within the walls, Machaut composed a motet.[40] In heartfelt language he compares the besieged Remois to Daniel in

---

[37] Crow and Olson, *Chaucer Life-Records*, 370–74.

[38] Pearsall, *Life of Geoffrey Chaucer*, 11.

[39] Sumption, *Trial by Fire*, 427–32.

[40] See Robertson, *Guillaume de Machaut and Reims*, 202–6, for the argument that Motet 21 was composed in December 1359/January 1360.

the lions' den; he implores God to strike down the plunderers; he declares:

Iam nostra virtus deficit
Nec os humanum sufficit
Ad narrandum obprobria
Que nobis dant vecordia,
Divisio, cupiditas
Fideliumque raritas,
Unde flentes ignoramus,
Quid agere debeamus.
Circumdant nos inimici,
Sed et nostri domestici
Conversi sunt in predones:
Leopardi et leones,
Lupi, milvi et aquile
Rapiunt omne reptile.
Consumunt nos carbunculi.

[Our strength is now failing,
Nor does the human voice suffice
To tell of the shameful things
Given us by this madness,
Division, avarice,
And scarcity of the faithful,
For which reason we, weeping, know not
What we should do.
Our enemies surround us,
Even our countrymen
Have been changed into brigands:
Leopards and lions,
Wolves, birds of prey, and eagles
Snatch away every creeping thing.
Carbuncles consume us.]

The lyrics suggest not only terror and hatred for the attackers but anxiety about treachery and internal divisions. The whole is set in an apocalyptic context, as the contemporary conflict is imagined in biblical terms.[41]

While Chaucer camped outside the walls, Machaut, forty years his senior, poured out his emotions within the city. Deschamps, another great poet and Chaucer's contemporary, may also have been in Reims during the siege: he says he was, but as his account is lifted from another source, his eyewitness claims may be poetic licence.[42] Along with the other citizens, Machaut was rostered for guard duty under Gaucher de Châtillon, who organized the defence of Reims.[43] There were four major gates in the walls of the city: the Porte de Mars, the Porte de Venus, the Porte de Ceres, and the Porte de Bacchus (or Bazee).[44] The Porte de Mars had been the weak spot in the city's defences: it housed one of the archbishop's residences and opened out onto the countryside. This third-century gate was a beautifully preserved Roman arch with elaborate carvings; the tableaux carved on its inner passages included an image of the Roman she-wolf suckling Romulus and Remus, legendary founders of Rome and Reims.[45] The current archbishop, Jean de Craon, had repeatedly refused to fortify this gate, and had only done so at all under great pressure; he was suspected of treachery by the Remois and was disliked for his alliances with predatory nobles. Indeed, the archbishops of Reims had often clashed with the townspeople: they protected their houses and power and were unwilling to pay for defences and building works.[46] The Porte de Mars specifically had been a flashpoint for civic unrest in the thirteenth century when the bourgeoisie attacked the law court that the archbishop had established there, and where he held heresy trials.[47] The simmering tensions between town and archbishop could have led to disaster now for Reims, had it not been for the dominant will of the captain of the city, who managed to force the cathedral chapter to accede to his will. This exceptionally able and

---

[41] Quoted in ibid., 327; discussed 192–206, 219–23.

[42] Eustache Deschamps, *Eustache Deschamps: Selected Poems*, ed. Ian S. Laurie and Deborah M. Sinnreich-Levi, trans. David Curzon and Jeffrey Fiskin (New York: Routledge, 2003), 5.

[43] Sumption, *Trial by Fire*, 429.

[44] Robertson, *Guillaume de Machaut and Reims*, 11–14.

[45] Ibid., 17.

[46] Sumption, *Trial by Fire*, 427–29.

[47] Lillich, *Gothic Stained Glass*, 9.

energetic man, de Châtillon, built walls, taxed the inhabitants and the rural refugees, walled-up gates, dismantled drawbridges, dug extra ditches, had a whole forest (owned by the cathedral chapter) cut down for building materials, requisitioned horses and carts, and called all citizens to arms.[48]

Faced with this formidable defence, and suffering in the bad weather and from lack of supplies, the English sent out bands to plunder what they could in the surrounding area—a group from the Black Prince's division, for instance, took Cormicy by digging a mine to destroy the castle keep.[49] But they soon realized that there was nothing more to squeeze out of the district, and that they were not going to take the city. They abandoned the siege on 11 January 1360 and planned to march around Paris, causing trouble and finding supplies as they went, while a new supply train was organized from Lower Normandy. As the army proceeded, they wreaked destruction everywhere they went and were themselves constantly harried by small groups that picked off anyone foraging for food or sleeping without guards.[50]

It was about this time that Chaucer was taken prisoner, probably during some skirmish in the countryside around Reims or towards Burgundy—although he could have been captured earlier in the campaign.[51] He was ransomed on 1 March, when the king paid £16 for his release.[52] At around the same time, Richard Sturry, king's esquire, was ransomed for £50 and Sir William de Graunson, knight of Burgundy, for £20. At the other end of the scale, Richard Dulle, archer, was worth 40 shillings and John de York, king's carter, and his seven fellows, £12 as a job lot. Two of the queen's valets went for £16 together; one of the countess of Ulster's valets for £10.[53] So Chaucer was valued at considerably more than a valet, but much less than a king's esquire. It is also worth noting that he may have already been friends with men such as Richard Sturry, a man who pops up many times in Chaucer's life and who was a member of the so-called Chaucer circle of chamber knights with literary interests and ascetic religious leanings.

[48] Sumption, *Trial by Fire*, 429.
[49] Gray, *Scalacronica*, 148.
[50] Sumption, *Trial by Fire*, 431–33; Ormrod, *Edward III*, 402–3.
[51] Ormrod, *Edward III*, 404; Sumption, *Trial by Fire*, 433; Pearsall, *Life of Geoffrey Chaucer*, 41.
[52] Crow and Olson, *Chaucer Life-Records*, 24.
[53] Ibid., 24–25.

Chaucer was to travel abroad with Sturry again in 1377 when they both served as English representatives in the peace negotiations at Montreuil.[54] As a teenager, Chaucer was already in the right places to make connections that lasted throughout his life.[55]

Ransom culture had developed into big business in the High Middle Ages. One argument is that it was borrowed from the war practices of Muslim cultures; another that the rise of the tournament, with its emphasis on capture rather than killing, may have influenced how real wars were conducted.[56] It was ransom culture that made war so potentially profitable and that encouraged men to flock to join Edward's army; chroniclers from these decades repeatedly comment on the easy fortunes to be made from ransoms and looting.[57] The rules of war decreed that a prisoner must agree to surrender—through a sign (a hand up) or a word ('Je me rends' or 'Rançom')—and must then give his oath to his captor, ideally accompanied by a material pledge, such as his right gauntlet.[58] The captor was then the master of the prisoner, who was not free until the ransom was paid but instead owed obedience to his captor.[59] The phrase 'prisoner of war' was not yet used—the most common phrasing for what happened was 'pris . . . par/pour fait de guerre' (taken by act of war).[60] There was a convention, however, that such prisoners had a particular status. If gentlemen, they were not supposed to be manacled, and they were not usually kept in a dungeon, or in the pit of a prison, but in a chamber higher up in the building.[61] Their prisons might be castles, palaces, hotels, houses, or city gates—and we have no idea where Chaucer was kept, or in what degree of comfort or discomfort. What we do know is that he experienced, for a relatively short time but perhaps for as long as a couple of months, what it was like not to be a free man, to be under the physical control of someone else, with one's movements curtailed and limited, at the mercy of one's enemies.

[54] Ibid., 50.

[55] For Sturry, see especially chapter 15.

[56] Rémy Ambühl, *Prisoners of War in the Hundred Years War* (Cambridge: Cambridge University Press, 2013), 2–3.

[57] Ibid., 99.

[58] Ibid., 106–7.

[59] Ibid., 19.

[60] Ibid., 5.

[61] Ibid., 121, 118.

Years later Chaucer wrote in some detail about war, captivity, tournaments, and violent death in the longest, grandest, and densest of the *Canterbury Tales*: the 'Knight's Tale.' The tale draws on many sources, particularly Boccaccio's *Teseida*, and also Statius's *Thebaid* and Boethius's *Consolation of Philosophy* (a foundational text of prison literature). At many points, Chaucer makes clear and deliberate changes to his sources. Those changes demonstrate the particular slant that Chaucer put on this story, and the changes work together to make the conflict between Athens and Thebes more like the war in which Chaucer fought, and to emphasise the inglorious and horrific aspects of that war. In one of the most powerful descriptive passages in his poetry, Chaucer depicts the temple of Mars, god of war, drawing heavily on Boccaccio. In the source passage, Boccaccio describes land devastated by war, the taking of spoils, people in chains, shattered citadels.[62] Chaucer develops this into:

> The careyne in the busk, with throte ycorve;
> A thousand slayn, and nat of qualm ystorve;
> The tiraunt, with the pray by force yraft;
> The toun destroyed, ther was no thyng laft. (2013–16)

He chooses to concentrate on details such as a corpse, killed in the woods, not in the heat of battle; on the sheer numbers of the dead; on the work of tyrants; and on total devastation: 'ther was no thing laft.' Other details, such as, 'The shepne brennynge with the blake smoke' (2000) illustrate the effect of the war on the countryside and on ordinary life. Indeed, Chaucer goes on to insert images of death and injury that one would not usually associate with Mars:

> The hunte strangled with the wilde beres;
> The sowe freten the child right in the cradel;
> The cook yscalded, for all his longe ladel. (2018–20)

The images are of a world turned upside down: the hunter is hunted by his prey; a baby is consumed where she should be safest, in her cot; a cook is burnt by his own implements—over which he should be able to exercise

---

[62] William E. Coleman, 'The Knight's Tale,' in Robert M. Correale and Mary Hamel (eds.), *Sources and Analogues of 'The Canterbury Tales'* (Cambridge: D. S. Brewer, 2005), 2:168–69.

control. The implication is that war turns all society, all order, on its head, and affects everybody, even the totally innocent. This monstrous image, of the pig eating the baby, is given even more emphasis by another addition of Chaucer: a few lines later, he describes a statue of Mars accompanied by a figure of a wolf eating a man ('A wolf ther stood biforn hym at his feet / With eyen rede, and of a man he eet' [2047–48]). While the Porte de Mars of Reims portrayed a wolf nourishing Romulus and Remus, the animal world working in conjunction with the forces of human history that were protecting those with an imperial, conquering, warlike destiny, Chaucer's Mars is a force of destruction that sets animals to attack and consume abject human beings. And the folly of thinking that forces of Mars can be harnessed and made to work with mankind is strongly indicated in Chaucer's addition of Conquest to Mars's temple: Conquest sits: 'With the sharpe swerd over his heed / Hangynge by a soutil twynes threed' (2028–29). Rather than being a glorious destiny, military victory is simply a brief and precarious moment in the turn of Fortune's wheel.

Earlier in the tale, Chaucer describes how the two heroes, Palamon and Arcite, are taken prisoner by Theseus. In Boccaccio's version, after the two wounded men are found amongst the bodies on the battlefield, Teseo questions them, treats them mercifully, summons a doctor, and has their wounds treated as he would if they were his own relatives. He considers executing them, but decides that would be excessive, and instead keeps them imprisoned, but comfortably.[63] Chaucer's depiction differs sharply, and each change serves to criticize Theseus and to bring attention to the tyrannical aspects of the military hero and conqueror. There is no questioning, no mercy, no doctor, and no treatment. And while in Boccaccio, Teseo's decision to imprison them seems merciful in comparison to the alternative—execution—Chaucer presents different alternatives, and has Theseus choosing the crueller course. He writes that Theseus:

> . . . ful soone hem sente
> To Atthenes to dwellen in prisoun
> Perpetuelly—he nolde no raunsoun. (1022–24)

[63] Coleman, 'Knight's Tale,' 2:143.

By raising the question of ransom, foregrounding it as a cultural possibility, Chaucer makes Theseus's actions seem ruthless. The very structure of the lines—whereby 'Perpetuelly' is delayed and placed in an emphatic position at the beginning of the line—stresses the endlessness and hopelessness of their fate. And, to make this hopelessness and refusal to ransom even more pointed, Chaucer tells us about it again eight lines later: 'For everemoore; ther may no gold hem quite' (1032), and yet again a little later in the tale ('Perpetuelly; us gayneth no raunsoun' [1176]). He does not change the facts of the source—that they are imprisoned—but he utterly changes what those events suggest about Theseus, the military conqueror, by repeatedly raising ransom as a refused possibility.[64]

Chaucer, in common with many other fourteenth-century poets, was intensely interested in psychological freedom and constraint, in the relationship of the subject to those who had power over him or her, in subjection and subjectivity, in identity and self-definition. In the *Romaunt de la Rose*, love is explicitly compared to a prison:

> . . . as man in prisoun sett
And may not geten for to et
But barly breed, and watir pure,
And lyeth in vermyn and in ordure;
With all this yitt can he lyve,
Good hope such comfort hath hym yive,
Which maketh wene that he shall be
Delyvered, and come to liberte.
In fortune is [his] fulle trust;
Though he lye in strawe or dust,
In hoope is all his susteynyng.
And so for lovers, in her wenyng,
Whiche Love hath shit in his prisoun. (2755–67)

The passage does two important things. First, it compares being in love to being in prison, making clear that the important factor here is not literal constraint but psychological subjection to forces out of one's control

---

[64] See David Aers's excellent discussion of Chaucer's changes to Boccaccio's *Teseida* in *Chaucer, Langland, and the Creative Imagination* (London: Routledge and Kegan Paul, 1980), 176–77.

(the captor, the lady, one's own emotions). Second, the lines suggest that the mind can battle these constraints, whether they are literal or not: hope, belief, and faith can overcome external factors. These ideas are philosophically thoroughly Boethian, but the poetry of the late Middle Ages frequently transferred the issue to the context of courtly love. Machaut was influenced by Baudouin de Condé's *Li Prison d'Amours*, as was Froissart, who wrote the *Prison amoureuse*—for someone who was, indeed, in prison (Wenceslas of Brabant).[65] In Chaucer's 'Knight's Tale,' the protagonists are both literally in prison and psychologically imprisoned by love. Indeed, Chaucer takes the idea of imprisonment further when he suggests that captor, as well as captive, is constrained and limited. Just as Palamon and Arcite are imprisoned 'in a tour' (1030), in a 'grete tour' (1056), so Conquest itself, sitting under the dangling sword, is 'in a tour' (2027). The walls might be defensive, but the effect is the same: what is outside is threatening, and the conqueror is a prisoner of his actions, and subject to external forces, symbolized by the sword hanging by the thinnest of threads.

Chaucer did not need to be imprisoned to have the tools to think about the effects of subjection and loss of freedom on the psyche. Machaut's *dits amoureux* examined with great complexity the relationship between a poet and his patron, and the way that service and expectation determined what could be said. Machaut's work explored both the nature of selfhood and the nature of the authorial self. In the *Jugement du Roi de Navare*, Machaut describes the fate of a betrayed man, someone who loses the anchor of his personality when his mistress abandons him: his descent into madness is physical and violent, as he loses his sensory abilities and his social understanding. Physically tied up by his friends in response, his madness continues, and he is eventually allowed to roam free, physically and psychologically adrift from all coordinates (2286–2314).[66] His subjectivity fragments when he can no longer shape his identity through subjection to a mistress-lord. Machaut's most interesting explorations of

---

[65] See V. A. Kolve, *Chaucer and the Imagery of Narrative: The First Five Canterbury Tales* (Stanford, CA: Stanford University Press, 1984), 93–96. See also Jean Froissart, *La Prison Amoureuse*, ed. Laurence de Looze (New York: Garland, 1994).

[66] Guillaume de Machaut, *The Judgement of the King of Navarre*, Garland Library of Medieval Literature 45, Series A, ed. and trans. R. Barton Palmer (New York: Garland, 1988).

identity focused on self-presentation and the role of the author: he was one of the earliest poets to experiment with authorial personae, making explicit the instability of the 'I' by consciously fracturing it. In the *Jugement du Roi de Navare*, he overtly separates his voice into 'Guillaume' and 'The Author,' but the two become blurred, with the persona sometimes stepping outside of his role and sounding like the author (3141, 4027). These techniques of self-projection and self-protection were developed and finessed by Chaucer in all of his major poetic works: the figure of the narrator, the constraints of the author, and the obscurity of the self were subjects to which he returned time and again. In more than one way, then, Chaucer's early encounters with France helped him to think about subjectivity and the constraints placed on identity and expression.

The campaign dragged on through the spring of 1360, as Edward's army besieged Paris, but we do not know what Chaucer was doing at this point. In April a terrible storm destroyed many horses and equipment, and disease was spreading through the army.[67] It was time to make terms. On 7 May, France and England agreed on the Peace of Brétigny, sealing it the next day, and on 18 May, Edward and his sons went back to England.[68] Lionel's troops were paid until the end of May, but presumably Chaucer remained in household employment with Lionel and Elizabeth.[69] In October, when the campaign was rounded off by the completion of the treaty in Calais, Chaucer was there too, in Lionel's company. This frontier town was a place where multiple nationalities and identities converged, a place dominated by the military garrison at this point, but soon to become a crucial European trade centre. It had become an uncanny place for the French: known and not-known, once theirs but now culturally and demographically changed almost beyond recognition. They viewed it with suspicion and dislike, characterizing the town as hell's mouth.[70]

Eustache Deschamps, whose poems are dense with patriotic and xenophobic comments (Hungary is hellish, Bohemia is characterized by lice,

[67] Ormrod, *Edward III*, 404; Sumption, *Trial by Fire*, 443.
[68] Ormrod, *Edward III*, 405–7.
[69] Crow and Olson, *Chaucer Life-Records*, 28.
[70] Wallace, *Premodern Places*, 63.

fleas, pigs, and mould, people from Hainault and Brabant are obsessed with mustard),[71] writes one poem about nearly being captured by the English in Calais, when his friend (Oton de Graunson, also Chaucer's friend and fellow poet) plays a joke on him, disavowing him and only claiming him at the last moment. Deschamps focuses on the language mix in muddy Calais, inserting English words into his French poem and giving an aural impression of the hybridity of the town.[72] He also riffs on the idea that the English are tailed and devilish, physically and morally a strange set of creatures. In another poem, Deschamps gives a visceral description of his uncomfortable, insomniac experience of spending the night in Calais:

> Est cilz aise qui ne se puet dormir
> Et qui ne fair toute nuit que viller,
> Puces sentir, oyr enfans crier,
> Sur un matra as sur cordes gesir,
> Avoir ors draps et sur dur orillier;
> Est cilz aise qui ne se puet dormir
> Et qui ne fait toute nuit que viller?
> Et, d'autre part, oir a grant mer bruir,
> Et les chevaulx combatre et deslier?
> C'est a Calys; Granson, veillés jugier:
> Est cilz aise qui ne se puet dormir
> Et qui ne fait toute nuit que viller,
> Puces sentir, oyr enfans crier?

> [Can a man be comfortable all night
> Who cannot get to sleep, who lies awake
> Hearing kids cry, feeling fleas bite,
> On a mattress of cords, for heaven's sake!
> And the pillow's hard, the sheets are a filthy sight.
> Can a man be comfortable all night
> Who cannot get to sleep, who lies awake

---

[71] 'That country really is a hell on earth,' 'Lies, fleas, pigs, mould,' 'Always, never asking, mustard'; Deschamps, *Selected Poems*, 189, 195, 115.

[72] Wallace, *Premodern Places*, 54; Ardis Butterfield, *The Familiar Enemy: Chaucer, Language, and Nation in the Hundred Years War* (Oxford: Oxford University Press, 2009), 140–41.

And also hears the waves of ocean break
And horses slipping ties, the sounds of a fight?
This is Calais, Oton de Granson! am I right?
Can a man be comfortable all night
Who cannot get to sleep, who lies awake
Hearing kids cry, feeling fleas bite?][73]

Deschamps powerfully evokes how discomfort feels: the noises are not dramatic but they are persistent—waves, horses, fights, babies. And his body is assailed by minor irritations impossible to ignore: dirt, insects biting, a hard, lumpy bed. The intimate details of his nighttime misery evoke an image of Calais more generally—after all, he characterizes the experiences thus: 'This is Calais.' The town is imagined as a place of wretched annoyances, a restless place where there is no repose, and where the senses are under attack. The lines are dense with verbs, imitating this sense of restlessness, crystallised in the last line: 'puces sentir, oyr enfans crier?' There are no adjectives, adverbs, articles, or prepositions here, just two stark nouns and three verbs. Two of the verbs, 'sentir' and 'oyr,' are locked together by internal rhyme, mirroring the assault on the senses that the words evoke, as the poet simultaneously feels the bites and hears the cries. Calais is not depicted as a horrific, monstrous place; it is just really unpleasant, irritating, and uncomfortable.

This facility for writing about the pedestrian is one of the most interesting aspects of Deschamps's poetry. A poet whose life and career paralleled Chaucer's closely in a number of ways (both were born in the 1340s and worked as royal administrators), he too brought the quotidian, the visceral details of life, into poetry.[74] Moving away from topics related to courtly love or patronage, he expanded the subject matter of the French lyric, writing poems about, for instance, his own ugliness ('Among all other uglies, I should be the king'), or the benefits of sleeping alone (he discusses how annoying it is when your co-sleeper takes all the blankets).[75] Chaucer scholars know him best for his address to Chaucer as 'grant translateur': they were aware of each other's work, and certainly had mutual

---

[73] Deschamps, *Selected Poems*, 98–99.
[74] Ibid., 1–2.
[75] Ibid., 110–11, 164–65.

friends.[76] Back in 1360, like Machaut, Deschamps watched the assault on his country with horror, and his later comments on Calais continue his general dislike for foreign places—another poem emphasizes that 'Paris is beyond compare.'[77]

Deschamps's comments about Calais were written more than twenty years later, when the town had expanded hugely after the transfer of the wool staple,[78] but Machaut wrote about his impressions of Calais in 1360 itself, when he accompanied another one of his patrons there for the treaty signing. Jean, duke of Berry, was to be handed over to the English as guarantor of his father's ransom.[79] Machaut's comments demonstrate that the image of Calais as uncomfortable and foreign was clearly established by this point. He disparagingly termed it 'une ville petiote' (a small village), 'De barat pleinne et de riote' (a place full of uproar and license), and also full of 'avolez' (strangers).[80]

The Treaty of Brétigny gave Edward III a much-enlarged and sovereign Aquitaine in return for his renunciation of his claim to the French throne. Edward also gave up his rights to Normandy, Touraine, Anjou, and Maine, and a ransom for John II was agreed upon. When the treaty came to be ratified, however, the provisions relating to John's formal renunciation of his rights in the territories being assigned to Edward were put into a separate agreement, so Edward did not renounce his claim to the throne, nor John his rights over the lands granted to the English. These renunciations were never actually made, leaving the door wide open for either party to renege on the treaty (which they did).[81]

Lionel seems to have arrived in Calais on 13 October, joining his father and brothers, and the peace was concluded on 24 October.[82] The two kings, their families, and their principal advisors swore to uphold the treaty, and John was released from his long imprisonment. We know

[76]Wallace, *Premodern Places*, 52–53; Butterfield, *Familiar Enemy*, 143–44; Wimsatt, *Chaucer and the Poems of 'Ch,'* 79–82. See also chapter 14 in this book.

[77]Deschamps, *Selected Poems*, 63.

[78]I discuss the wool staple in detail in chapters 6 and 7.

[79]Ormrod, *Edward III*, 422.

[80]Machaut, *Fontaine amoureuse*, 2809–12, cited in Wallace, *Premodern Places*, 41.

[81]John le Patourel, 'The Treaty of Brétigny, 1360,' *Transactions of the Royal Historical Society* 10 (1960): 19–39.

[82]Crow and Olson, *Chaucer Life-Records*, 19–20.

that Chaucer was with Lionel in Calais because during the two and a half
weeks that Lionel was there (13–31 October), he made a payment of 9
shillings to Chaucer, for Chaucer to travel back to England 'cum lit-
teris' (with letters).[83] These were probably personal letters to friends or relatives, as payments for carrying messages relating to affairs of state came
from the king's privy wardrobe.[84] Soon after arriving in Calais, then,
Chaucer was on the move again, continuing his lifestyle of frequent travelling in the service of his noble employers, an itinerant and tiring way of
life. Other payments in the same account sheet tell us something about
the men surrounding Lionel: the payment immediately after Chaucer's is
to John Tregettour.[85] A 'tregettour' was an entertainer, a kind of min-
strel, who might play music, sing, recite poems, and do tricks. Chaucer
lived in a world where oral performance was still valued, even as the written word was ever more important. Indeed, Chaucer himself was already
involved in his work life with the written word: this basic task of conveying letters was something that he continued to do in later life, as he engaged in diplomacy and message delivery of varying kinds. In an era before
telephones or telegrams, trusted messengers were hugely important politically, and Chaucer repeatedly fulfilled this task.

And it seems appropriate that Chaucer was a go-between from Calais,
city of in-betweenness, a national no-place, with an identity coming into
being and founded on what it was not—neither culturally France nor
geographically England. Chaucer would have travelled back, as Lionel
did a few days later, on a well-worn route, via Deal, Sandwich, Wingham,
Canterbury, Boughton, Ospringe, Sittingbourne, Rochester, and Dartford.[86] This route would become deeply familiar to Chaucer on his travels
over the next few decades, as he went to Europe many times on political
business. His travels of 1359–60 introduced him to war, imprisonment,
peace treaties, and high-level diplomacy. It also introduced him to the
city with which Machaut, a formative influence for Chaucer when he
started to construct his own poetic identity, was closely connected, and

[83] Ibid., 19.
[84] Ibid., 20.
[85] Ibid., 19.
[86] Ibid., 19.

to the town that was to become the central point in the English wool trade, which gave Chaucer his living for much of his adult life. Over the next couple of decades, Chaucer's encounters with the Continent continued to shape his political, cultural, and personal life.

Between 1366 and 1378, Chaucer travelled abroad at least eight times, and very likely more.[87] In 1366, he went to Navarre; in 1368, to an unspecified place in Europe; in 1369, he fought in northern France with Gaunt; in 1370, he went to France or Flanders; and in 1373 he visited Genoa and Florence.[88] At the end of Edward's reign, he made more journeys: in 1376 and 1377 he was involved in more than one trip to places including Flanders, Paris, and Montreuil, before travelling to Italy again in 1378, this time to Lombardy.[89] A 1381 record refers to multiple journeys made in the previous few years.[90] In the 1370s, Chaucer had decisively moved on from military campaigns to the more congenial world of negotiation. In Lombardy, that negotiation involved trying to bring mercenaries over to fight for England, but Chaucer's own role involved talking, not fighting.[91] In 1381, Richard gave Chaucer a gift of £22 to compensate for some of his journeys taken over the previous several years: it specifies that his trips had been 'causa tractatus pacis' (to treat of peace) in the time of Edward III and 'causa locucionis habite de maritagio' (to talk about making a marriage) between Richard and a daughter of the king of France, during Richard's reign.[92] These two aims—making peace and forming marriage alliances—dominated Chaucer's trips to France and elsewhere: in Lombardy too he was discussing Richard's possible marriage with a Visconti bride. Even when his journeys involved trade discussions, as his 1373 trip to Italy did, the motivation was bringing differing interests into alignment—not subjugation and destruction, as had been the aim in 1359.[93] Compromise, not conquest, was Chaucer's forte.

---

[87] We have no records of Chaucer's whereabouts between 1360 and 1366; he was probably involved in diplomacy and household service either for the king or his sons. See chapter 4 for discussion.

[88] See Crow and Olson, *Chaucer Life-Records*, 29–40 and 64–66 for discussion of these journeys, several of which are discussed in subsequent chapters.

[89] Ibid., 42–61.

[90] Ibid., 49.

[91] He was negotiating with John Hawkwood, the famous English mercenary; see chapter 13 for discussion.

[92] Crow and Olson, *Chaucer Life-Records*, 49.

[93] For the trade negotiations in Italy in 1373, see chapter 6.

CHAPTER 4

Hainault and Navarre

> [I]n the older imagining, where states were defined by centres, borders
> were porous and indistinct, and sovereignties faded imperceptibly into
> one another.
>
> —*Benedict Anderson,* Imagined Communities

Neither Hainault nor Navarre exists as an independent political entity
today: Hainault has been split between France and Belgium, Navarre
between France and Spain. The changing map of Europe reminds us that
not only do borders change but so do political structures. In the fourteenth century, the county of Hainault was an imperial fief under the
authority of the Holy Roman Empire but on the borders of France and
French in language and culture. Navarre was an independent monarchy,
but its ruler, Charles d'Evreux, also had extensive French lands, for which
he did homage to the king of France. Indeed, Charles was born and
brought up in France and patronized French poetry extensively, as discussed in chapter 3. The ruling houses of Hainault and Navarre were
both largely defined by their relationship with France, and their courts
were French in style. Both countries influenced the Hundred Years' War,
and both were important to Chaucer in the mid-1360s.

The sovereign state was a far less dominant political construct in the
fourteenth century than it is today. Many rulers did not enjoy sovereign
status but did homage for their lands to an overlord, such as the French
king or the Holy Roman Emperor. Some (such as the count of Flanders)

did homage to different lords for different bits of their territory.[1] Rulers such as the English king were sovereign over some of their lands but owed homage for others.[2] And the church extended power that was not limited by territory;[3] all secular rulers in Western Europe coexisted in varying degrees of discomfort with church courts, church taxes, and church authorities—the Schism and the Golden Bull highlighted some of the tensions between ecclesiastical and secular authorities in the fourteenth century.[4] Meanwhile, organisations such as the Hanseatic League, based on trade, wielded political and military power and illustrated a mode of political living quite different from the sovereign state.[5] Borders fluctuated greatly in all the countries of Europe—neither France, nor Italy, nor Germany, nor Spain existed in anything like their present form—and the wars over territory were largely sustained by mercenaries, whose loyalties were for sale.[6] These individuals and their companies did not fight for their country; they were willing to fight for anyone who could pay, although they sometimes specified that they would not fight against their own overlord. The frequent demise of male lines and the importance of dynastic marriages often brought territories under new spheres of influence and altered the balance of power in a region. And a great deal of high culture crossed borders with ease: painters and minstrels travelled from court to court, beautiful objects were sold and given within trade networks and between allies and spouses, and educated men and women across Europe read much of the same literature and valued the same leisure

[1] Walter Prevenner, 'The Low Countries, 1290–1415,' in Michael Jones (ed.), *The New Cambridge Medieval History: Volume VI, 1300–1415* (Cambridge: Cambridge University Press, 2000), 570.

[2] Tensions between England and France often flared up over the question of whether and in what form the English king would do homage for his Continental territories.

[3] Hendrik Spruyt comments that 'the modern state defines the human collectivity in a completely novel way. It defines individuals by spatial markers, regardless of kin, tribal affiliation, or religious belief,' arguing that medieval systems of rule were often nonterritorial and overlapping. *The Sovereign State and Its Competitors* (Princeton: Princeton University Press, 1994), 34–35.

[4] The papacy was based at Avignon from 1309 to 1377, during which years the papacy was strongly influenced by the French Crown. During the Great Schism (1377–1417), there were two popes, one at Rome and one at Avignon. The Golden Bull (1356) formalized the procedure for electing an emperor, enshrining the power of the electors and sidelining the papacy.

[5] See Spruyt, *Sovereign State*, 126.

[6] Kenneth Fowler, *Medieval Mercenaries* (Oxford: Blackwell, 2001).

occupations.[7] At the same time, this was the century of the vernacular, when local languages flourished as the languages of literature, gaining a dominance that they were never to lose. The year 1366, upon which this chapter focuses, was the year of the Statutes of Kilkenny, which banned the Anglo-Irish from using the Irish language, playing Irish sports, or intermarrying with Irish women.[8] These statutes were not effective or enforced, but they reveal English political anxiety about the relationship between language and colonial politics and a specific desire to promote the English language. In many other ways too the 1360s was a transitional decade for Englishness: this was the decade in which Parliament was first opened in English and English was used in the law courts. Around the end of the 1360s and the beginning of the 1370s, Langland and Chaucer began to write great English poems.[9]

But the milieu of courts and great households that sustained Chaucer when he was in his teens and twenties was profoundly international. These households were populated by people from many different countries; they were multilingual, itinerant, and involved in far-flung trade networks; their heads patronized poets and artists from across Europe; and their marriages frequently involved cultural exchange. For instance, Lionel, Chaucer's employer in 1360, was born in Antwerp; Lionel's grandfathers were the count of Hainault and the king of England; his grandmothers were both French princesses. He himself married an Anglo-Irish heiress first and then a Lombard. Lionel spent the early 1360s in Ireland (and oversaw the Statutes of Kilkenny); his older brother spent many years ruling Aquitaine; his younger brother was later to claim to be king of Castile. The sons of Edward III, with whom Chaucer was closely connected, looked to Europe to provide them with power bases and adventures. And their retainers often travelled widely too and spent long periods of time in different countries.

[7] Malcolm Vale, *The Princely Court: Medieval Courts and Culture in North-West Europe, 1270–1380* (Oxford: Oxford University Press, 2001).

[8] H. F. Berry (ed.), *Statutes and Ordinances and Acts of the Parliament of Ireland, King John to Henry V* (Dublin: HMSO, 1907), 432–35.

[9] John H. Fisher, *The Emergence of Standard English* (Lexington: University Press of Kentucky, 1996); Christopher Cannon, *The Making of Chaucer's English: A Study of Words* (Cambridge: Cambridge University Press, 1998).

Chaucer himself vanishes from the record between October 1360 (when we saw him in Calais) and February 1366, by far the longest gap in his adult life-records. In 1366, he reemerges in Navarre, and either during this year or earlier, he married a woman from a Hainault family. These border countries punched above their weight when it came to political influence— the one (Hainault) largely because of clever and fortuitous marriage alliances, the other (Navarre) because of the strategic importance of its mountainous passes and because of the French landholdings of its duplicitous ruler. The role that these now-vanished countries played in Chaucer's life, and in shaping English politics and culture more generally, demonstrates the artificial and changing nature of political boundaries, the difficulty in identifying exactly what a nation might be.

Hainault was a county in what is now northern France and Belgium, incorporating the cities of Valenciennes, Mons, Cambrai, and Charleroi, an independent feudal state within the Holy Roman Empire. In the thirteenth century, it was ruled by the Avesnes family, who also gained control of Holland and Zeeland in 1299, greatly increasing their power. At the same time, heightened tension between England and France from the late thirteenth century led English kings to seek marriage alliances with the Netherlands in order to bolster their influence on the northern borders of France.[10] One of Edward I's daughters, Margaret, became duchess of Brabant in 1290; another, Elizabeth, countess of Holland in 1297.[11] England had a close relationship with Hainault,[12] and when Queen Isabella sought allies against her husband, Edward II, she found them in this county—where the countess, like Isabella, was a French princess (Isabella and Jeanne were first cousins). William I, who ruled from 1305 to 1337, was keen to extend his influence through marriages and had achieved a marriage for one of his daughters, Margaret, with Louis of Bavaria, the future Holy Roman Emperor, in 1324. In 1326, another of his daughters, Philippa, was betrothed to Edward, the future king of England, as William gambled on Isabella, Mortimer, and Edward's ability to

---

[10] Vale, *Princely Court*, 5–7.
[11] Ibid., 95.
[12] Ormrod, *Edward III*, 127.

defeat the incumbent king. His understanding of the situation was undoubtedly profoundly shaped by his brother's ability and willingness to supply large numbers of troops and money to aid Isabella and Mortimer's invasion of England. The deposition of Edward II was achieved with the crucial help of John of Hainault (also known as John of Beaumont) and his seven hundred or so troops. John and his soldiers continued to be a vital part of Edward III's fighting force; in 1327 Edward's army included about five hundred Netherlandish men fighting under John. In the same year, Philippa arrived in England and was married to Edward on 26 January 1328, in York Minster. In 1330, she was crowned queen and gave birth to her first child, Edward of Woodstock (the Black Prince).[13] Several Hainuyers now made successful and influential careers in England, and the culture of the Hainault court infused the court of Edward and Philippa. Chaucer numbered many Hainuyers, including, of course, his wife's family, amongst his close associates, and he certainly read the work of Hainault poets, some of whom he knew personally. Without Hainault, English political and cultural life in the mid-fourteenth century would have looked very different.

The court of Hainault under William I was a centre of culture and magnificent display. Indeed, since the twelfth century, the counts of Hainault had been renowned for their literary patronage and cultural interests. William I owned many books of different kinds; some valuable, deluxe books included a Lancelot, a romance of Merlin, and parts of a French Bible.[14] One of his minstrels, Jean de Conde, has left twenty thousand lines of poetry, including moral tales, fabliaux, narratives, and lais. Many other epic poems and romances can be associated with the Hainault court, including the *Roman de Perceforest*.[15] William's brother, John, also patronized poets and chroniclers, and the *Voeux de Heron*, a poem about the beginning of the Hundred Years' War, may have been written by a member of his household.[16] Hainault also hosted many *puys*—poetry competitions

[13] Ibid., 38–41, 65–71, 84, 88.

[14] Vale, *Princely Court*, 272.

[15] Jean Devaux, 'From the Court of Hainault to the Court of England: The Example of Jean Froissart,' in C. T. Allmand (ed.), *War, Government and Power in Late Medieval France* (Liverpool: Liverpool University Press, 2000), 2–4.

[16] Devaux, 'From the Court of Hainault,' 5.

that took place in towns and encouraged performance and social rivalry between musicians and poets.[17] *Puys* also encouraged the cultural interaction of the urban elite and members of the court, a dynamic mix that models Chaucer's own social and cultural milieu. William also knew the value of visual culture: he spent lavishly on goldsmiths' work and was an indefatigable organizer of jousts.[18] While the Hainault court had its own tradition of cultural patronage, the cultural mix was infused by the influence of William's wife, Jeanne of Valois, who came from the French court and whose mother was the sister of Robert of Naples, greatest of fourteenth-century literary patrons and sponsor of Petrarch and Boccaccio at his dazzling Neapolitan court.[19]

Queen Philippa's influence on English court culture was wide-ranging. The poets Jean de la Mote and Jean Froissart came to England in her wake. She gave her husband gifts such as a silver cup and ewer decorated with the Worthies, including Charlemagne, Arthur, Roland, Oliver, Gawain, and Lancelot, and a manuscript that shows evidence of the labour of both English and Hainault text workers.[20] She entered wholeheartedly into a culture of display and extravagance, and she and her countrymen and women were perceived as leaders and innovators of fashion.[21] Chandos Herald, who wrote the *Life of the Black Prince*, was from Hainault;[22] Philippa herself helped to found an Oxford college, and she also commissioned a startlingly unusual tomb sculpture from a Brabançon artist, Jean de Liège, who depicted her in individual and realistic form.[23] Jean de la Mote worked for Philippa and Edward in the 1330s and again in the 1340s and 1350s; in between he wrote for Simon of Lille, the French king's goldsmith.[24] De la Mote wrote an elegiac dream vision for Philippa—*Li Regret*

---

[17] Ibid., 6.

[18] Vale, *Princely Court*, 273; Devaux, 'From the Court of Hainault,' 9.

[19] Gervase Mathew, *The Court of Richard II* (New York: W. W. Norton, 1968), 2–4.

[20] Ormrod, *Edward III*, 13–15; Devaux, 'From the Court of Hainault,' 10.

[21] Ibid., 128; Newton, *Fashion in the Age of the Black Prince*, 9. John of Reading attacks Hainuyers as the origin of outrageous fashions; cited in Horrox, *The Black Death*, 131.

[22] Devaux, 'From the Court of Hainault,' 18.

[23] Juliet Vale, 'Philippa [Philippa of Hainault] (1310x15?–1369),' in the *ODNB*, https://doi.org/10.1093/ref:odnb/22110.

[24] Nigel Wilkins, 'En Regardant Vers Le Pais de France: The Ballade and the Rondeau, a Cross-Channel History,' in Mark Ormrod (ed.), *England in the Fourteenth Century* (Woodbridge: Boydell Press, 1986), 299; Ormrod, *Edward III*, 457.

Guillaume—to commemorate the death of her father; it provided Chaucer with a model for his own elegiac dream vision on the death of Blanche of Lancaster, the *Book of the Duchess*.[25] This poem also draws heavily on Froissart's *Paradys d'amour*.[26] Froissart, perhaps the most famous Hainuyer, described himself as made by Philippa, shaped by her patronage and desires: 'Car elle me fist et crea' ('For it was she who created me' [237]).[27] He too wrote at the English court, working for Philippa throughout the 1360s.[28] These writers wrote in French, but they were strongly connected with English interests—which were intertwined with Hainault's during these decades. Thus, de la Mote was fiercely attacked by the French poet Philippe de Vitry for his English associations, and responded (in French) by emphasizing his lack of connection to France: 'Ne je ne sui point de la nacion / De terre en Grec Gaulle' ('And I in no way belong to the nation / Of the Land in Greek called Gaul'; *La Response*, 9–10).[29] Hainault identity was sui generis—fundamentally shaped by international and especially French literature, but with its own character, both in terms of dialect and interest. On the basic level of subject matter, Froissart's chronicles pay especial attention to Hainault heroes, and de la Mote's elegy was for the Hainault count.

Philippa of Hainault, then, was the centre around which much of this Hainault culture revolved. Chaucer's first employer, Elizabeth de Burgh, had been brought up in Philippa's household as a child, and Lionel was Philippa's second surviving son. At some point in the 1360s, Chaucer became attached to the royal household itself, bringing him closer to the queen. And his wife, Philippa de Roet, not only worked for the queen but was herself from a Hainault family. Chaucer's father-in-law, Sir Gilles de Roet, known as Paon, was a knight from Hainault. He owned some land there—which one of his English grandsons later tried to claim—and was connected with the comital family. His career is impossible to piece together properly from the fragmentary evidence that we have. According

---

[25] Wimsatt, *Chaucer and the Poems of 'Ch,'* 5–7, 65.

[26] See, for example, Butterfield, *Familiar Enemy*, 269–84.

[27] The quotation is from Jean Froissart, *Le Joli Buisson de Jonece*, ed. Anthime Fourrier (Genève: Droz, 1975).

[28] Ormrod, *Edward III*, 457.

[29] Wimsatt, *Chaucer and the Poems of 'Ch,'* 67–68.

to Froissart, he was one of Philippa's knights—perhaps he went to England in the train of Philippa when she first married Edward, or perhaps he came later.[30] Froissart also tells us that he was present at the siege of Calais and, along with another Hainuyer, Eustace d'Aubrichecourt, was sent to escort the burghers of Calais out of the town.[31] Froissart suggests, then, that Paon was working for the English Crown in the 1340s in some capacity. He then worked for Philippa's sister, Margaret, the countess of Hainault—there are several references to him between 1349 and 1352 in her accounts. In 1349, she sponsored his daughter, Elizabeth, presenting her to a prebend in a nunnery.[32] Paon is referred to as Margaret's 'master of the house' (*maistre valet de sen osteil*),[33] and there are references to his going on pilgrimage to the shrine of St Druon at Sebourch in Hainault, to his journeys into Holland and Zeeland, and to his expenses.[34] The exact timing of these payments locates him as a retainer of Margaret's at the height of a civil and familial war in Hainault-Holland-Zeeland.

After William I's death in 1337, his son, William II, had ruled and died childless. Hainault then passed to his sister, Margaret, in 1345 (Philippa was another sister), who was married to the emperor, Louis of Bavaria. Her son, William, acted as her representative, but tensions soon built up and a civil war ensued between Margaret and her son. This was partly a war between the aristocracy and the towns, with their respective factions, known as the Hooks and the Cods. Edward III initially supported Margaret and won a victory in May 1351, but in July William fought back decisively. Shortly after this, Edward made peace with William, who later became William III, and he married Maud of Lancaster (daughter of Henry, duke of Lancaster and sister of Blanche). Margaret continued to rule Hainault until her death, while William had control of Holland and Zeeland. After Margaret's death he gained Hainault too, but

---

[30] Jean Froissart, *Oeuvres de Froissart: Chroniques*, ed. Joseph Kervyn de Lettenhove (Brussels: V. Devaux, 1867–77), 15:238. Froissart is not always reliable, however.

[31] Ibid., 5:215.

[32] Léopold Devillers (ed.), *Cartulaire des Comtes de Hainaut, de l'avènement de Guillaume II à la mort de Jacqueline de Bavière* (Brussels: F. Hayez, 1881), 1:321.

[33] Ibid., 766.

[34] Ibid., 753, 764, 766.

he suffered from a mental illness and was confined from 1358, while his brother, Albert, assumed the regency and then the title.

The payment made to Paon on 9 July 1351 specifies *frais et despens* (expenses and costs) in his journeys to Holland and Zeeland, which suggests that he accompanied Margaret there during the war. He may well have also been with the countess in England for William's wedding in 1352. In the *Register of the Black Prince* there are also references to Walter de Roet, who was probably Paon's son: he is mentioned as a yeoman of the chamber and was sent by the Black Prince, with the ubiquitous Eustace d'Aubrichecourt (one of the most interesting Hainuyers) to Margaret's court, to claim money from Stephen Maulyons, clerk to Margaret, in 1355.[35] Paon seems also to have had a connection to the Black Prince: according to Paon's (no longer extant) tombstone, he was Guienne King of Arms, the chief herald of Aquitaine, but we do not know at what point in his life he held this position.[36]

Crucially, Paon's connections with the ruling house of Hainault allowed him to place two of his daughters, Katherine and Philippa, in the households of the queen of England and her daughters-in-law. Katherine de Roet worked for Blanche of Lancaster in the 1360s and was governess to her children by John of Gaunt; in the 1370s she was to become John's mistress, mother of the Beaufort line, and, eventually, duchess of Lancaster. We do not know how Philippa's career started. She may or may not be the 'Philippa Pan' who appears in Elizabeth de Burgh's household accounts alongside the teenage Chaucer, as discussed earlier in chapter 2. But by 12 September 1366, Philippa de Roet had become Philippa Chaucer and is mentioned in the royal accounts as a lady of the queen's chamber.[37] The likelihood is that she had already served the queen for some time in order to merit the receipt of a life annuity. It is possible that this grant was prompted by her marriage or by her promotion within the chamber. What

---

[35] *Register of Edward the Black Prince, Preserved in the Public Record Office: Part IV, 1351–1365* (London: HMSO, 1933), fol. 68d, 114–15; fol. 96d, 162.

[36] The tomb was destroyed, but its inscription had been noted in the seventeenth century and was later printed. See John Weever, *Antient Funeral Monuments of Great Britain, Ireland, and the Islands Adjacent* (London: William Tooke, 1767), 413.

[37] Crow and Olson, *Chaucer Life-Records*, 67–68.

we do know is that by early autumn 1366, Chaucer was married to a lady from Hainault who was in attendance on the queen, and who had connections with the Hainault court and with the households of both the Black Prince and John of Gaunt (through her siblings). Indeed, the de Roet family seems to have had a strong tradition of working in the service of ruling families: Paon, Walter, Katherine, and Philippa all had careers in the service of the most important figures in Hainault and England; the one exception, Elizabeth, gained her position through the patronage of the countess of Hainault. Working in great households was the automatic way of life for this family. And the de Roets' ability to move easily between Hainault and England is testament to the international character of the greatest households; Hainuyers were very much at home in England in the second and third quarters of this century.

Chaucer's marriage fixed him more securely within the orbit of the court and also connected him with Hainault, bringing him closer to Hainault culture and politics. Hainuyers continued disproportionately to influence European conflicts and power struggles, mainly due to their military and diplomatic skills. Indeed, when Chaucer was in Navarre, Eustace d'Aubrichecourt (erstwhile companion of Chaucer's father-in-law in Calais and brother-in-law in Hainault) was there too, being paid huge sums by Charles of Navarre to keep him onside.[38] What, then, was going on in Navarre at this moment, and what were all these people doing there?

Like Hainault, Navarre mattered because it was a border country. It is easy to think of the Hundred Years' War as essentially a war between France and England and to forget how different 'France' and 'England' were at this time (in terms of their borders, dependent territories, and cultural and linguistic diversity), and that many other countries were also part of this conflict. Both Hainault and Navarre bordered France, and the ruling families had many ties with both the French and English Crowns. Edward III's grandmother had been the queen of Navarre in her own right—Joan I of Navarre. Joan was also the great-aunt of Maud and Blanche

---

[38] Jean-Auguste Brutails (ed.), *Documents des Archives de la Chambre des Comptes de Navarre* (Paris: É. Bouillon, 1890), 142.

of Lancaster, and of Elizabeth de Burgh.[39] Charles of Navarre (great-grandson of Joan I) was a central figure in French politics throughout the middle of the fourteenth century, as has already been seen. Navarre, sandwiched between Aquitaine, Castile, and Aragon, was embedded in Spanish as well as Anglo-French conflicts, and during the 1360s, these Spanish conflicts became an arena on which France and England could play out their own rivalries. Navarre became a magnet for all kinds of people in 1366 as mercenaries circled amidst frantic and treacherous diplomacy. As Castile exploded into civil war, usurpation, and fratricide, and the Black Prince prepared to embark on another military exploit, Navarre found itself at the centre of the storm.

What happened in Castile resulted directly from the Treaty of Brétigny, discussed in chapter 3. Once France and England were at peace, the bands of mercenaries roaming around France became a serious problem for the French Crown.[40] The conflicts in Spain offered France an opportunity for getting rid of these destructive plunderers while installing a French ally in strategically important Castile. The French king had reason to dislike Pedro I of Castile. Pedro had married a French princess, Blanche of Bourbon (sister of Philip VI of France), whom he had immediately repudiated in favour of his Spanish mistress. He then imprisoned his young wife and she died in unclear circumstances. Although the rumour that Pedro murdered her is unproven, his behaviour towards her was certainly abhorrent. This was not an isolated atrocity. Pedro's father had had many illegitimate children by his mistress, and after his death, Pedro's mother had her rival killed. Pedro and his half-brother, Enrique de Trastámara, became embroiled in an ongoing conflict, and Pedro

---

[39] Blanche of Artois married Henry I of Navarre, by whom she had Joan of Navarre. Blanche's second husband was Edmund Crouchback (son of Henry III of England); their children included Henry, earl of Lancaster. His son, Henry of Grosmont, duke of Lancaster, was thus half-nephew to Joan, and his children (Maud and Blanche) were her great-nieces. Elizabeth de Burgh's mother, another Maud of Lancaster, was Henry of Grosmont's sister, so Elizabeth had the same relationship to Joan as did Maud and Blanche. Joan of Navarre married Phillip IV of France and was mother of Isabella, who was to marry Edward II. Joan's three sons all became kings of France; the eldest, Louis, left a daughter, Joan II of Navarre, who was the mother of Charles of Navarre.

[40] Fowler notes that the peace of Brétigny was the catalyst for the formation of the mercenary Great Companies. *Medieval Mercenaries*, 1.

murdered Enrique's twin, Fadrique.[41] These internecine problems within Castile took place against the backdrop of ongoing tensions between Castile and Aragon, so it made sense for Enrique to seek the support of Pedro's enemies: Aragon and France. From the French point of view, this provided a chance to evict the mercenary companies that were causing so much damage in France, and they were willing to do this at almost any cost.[42] Pedro, meanwhile, allied with England (and Aquitaine), as the English emphatically did not want a pro-French Castile controlling shipping routes from Spain. Charles of Navarre was, literally and metaphorically, in the middle. His friendship was widely sought because he controlled the mountain passes through the Pyrenees as well as a number of other crucial borders.

In 1362, England signed an Anglo-Castilian treaty with Pedro, and Charles of Navarre also allied with Pedro.[43] In 1365, large numbers of mercenaries started to move from France to Spain, with the blessing of the French pope and the ostensible aim of crusading against the Moors in Granada. The massive funding for these companies came from three sources. Two of them—the pope (based at Avignon) and the French Crown—wanted to get the mercenaries out of their territories.[44] The third—Aragon—wanted to vanquish Pedro and conquer Castile for Enrique. The companies on whom all this depended were a motley crew of fighters of different nationalities, most notably Bertrand du Guesclin (who was French) and Hugh Calveley (who was English). Companies that had formerly fought against each other now happily came into alliance; for them, war was a business. In a panic, Pedro sent messengers to England in the autumn to beg for assistance, and Edward ordered that English and Gascons must not take part in the French-funded expedition, although the Black Prince had been accommodating about letting

---

[41] Peter Linehan, 'Castile, Navarre, and Portugal,' 638–39; Fowler, *Medieval Mercenaries*, 160–63.

[42] Margaret Wade Labarge, *Gascony: England's First Colony, 1204–1453* (London: Hamish Hamilton, 1980); Sumption, *Trial by Fire*, 480–81, 530. Fowler writes that although 'the Spanish expedition certainly removed a large number of the companies across the Pyrenees . . . the problems posed by the mercenaries were far from over in France.' *Medieval Mercenaries*, 154.

[43] Sumption, *Trial by Fire*, 543, 481.

[44] Fowler, *Medieval Mercenaries*, 119–21.

English and Gascons join the alleged 'crusade.'[45] Edward's orders arrived too late to stop his subjects taking part in the campaign and indeed Calveley played a major part. Meanwhile, Charles of Navarre was secretly negotiating with Pere IV of Aragon and concluded a treaty late in 1365.[46] Charles agreed to provide soldiers and in return Navarre was not to be damaged; Charles also received other benefits, including a pension for his oldest son. This treaty remained secret, as Charles was still officially allied with Castile. On New Year's Day 1366, the troops were in position. That day, Pere IV of Aragon gave a great feast for the leaders of his army, Bertrand and Hugh, the French and English mercenaries.[47] Now they prepared for their campaign, which began in February 1366. Charles of Navarre remained undecided, having made treaties with both Pedro and Pere, and he focused on strengthening his own defences.[48] He also recruited some important mercenaries to his own cause (of self-protection), using vast rewards to entice Eustace d'Aubrichecourt, that Hainauyer who crops up repeatedly in this story, to his service.

This was the scene when Chaucer arrived in Navarre in that very month. The companies, in nearby Aragon, were poised to invade Castile, and convenient routes lay through Navarre. Charles was frantically trying to secure his kingdom as best he could. Edward III was attempting to rein in English soldiers now working for Aragon-France-Enrique. As one historian comments, during this particular month, 'the activity was frenzied,' as Charles fortified his towns and cities and prepared to resist invasion.[49] The document concerning Chaucer is dated 22 February 1366, and was issued at Charles's palace in Olite, his fortress town (plate 3). It is a safe-conduct for Chaucer and three companions, plus their servants, horses, and goods, allowing them to come and go all over the country of Navarre, by day and by night. Chaucer would have found many men of his acquaintance in Olite at this particular moment. On 13 February, Charles had issued a safe-conduct to Jean Manart, squire of the Black Prince, who had

---

[45] Sumption, *Trial by Fire*, 544.
[46] Fowler, *Medieval Mercenaries*, 171; Sumption, *Trial by Fire*, 534.
[47] Sumption, *Trial by Fire*, 533.
[48] Fowler, *Medieval Mercenaries*, 173–74.
[49] Ibid., 174.

arrived with gifts;[50] on 6 March, Charles gave a safe-conduct to Thomas de Alberton, squire of Edward III, on his way to Castile (like Chaucer, Thomas married a Hainault lady-in-waiting to Philippa).[51] Charles also bought the homage of numerous English squires and knights during these weeks: on 4 March John Carsewall, Michael Londelo, William Bouteiller, Norman de Suinford, Robin de Ares, and Robert Briquet all entered into this kind of transaction, and several other Englishmen also appear in nearby records.[52] Others, such as John Devereux or Sir Stephen Cosington, received larger payments.[53] Some of these men are well known from other records: Cosington, for example, was a highly valued retainer of the Black Prince, and his annuity was greatly increased after his service to the prince at Poitiers.[54] Englishmen serving in Aquitaine flocked to Charles's court to take advantage of his urgent desire for experienced soldiers at this time.

Most notably, Charles spent enormous amounts on recruiting Eustace d'Aubrichecourt. D'Aubrichecourt was a career soldier who had served in Ireland, in Gascony, and in the Hundred Years' War, and who was a founder member of the Order of the Garter.[55] In 1359 he had been commanding opportunist bands of soldiers in France when he was captured and ransomed by the French Crown; he then went to join Edward's army and was instrumental in plundering supplies for the besieging army at Reims in early 1360. Later that year, he married Philippa of Hainault's niece, the daughter of her sister, Joanna of Hainault and Wilhelm, duke of Juliers. D'Aubrichecourt's wife, Isabella/Elizabeth von Julich, had first been married to the earl of Kent (whose sister, Joan, was married to the

[50] Brutails, *Documents des Archives*, 139.

[51] Ibid., 147. For his wife, Mary, see *Calendar of the Patent Rolls: Edward III*, Membrane 8, 13:126 (18 April 1365), Membrane 37, 15:115 (17 June 1371); *Calendar of the Patent Rolls: Richard II*, Membrane 16, 4:246 (11 March 1390); *Calendar of the Patent Rolls: Henry IV* (London: Eyre and Spottiswoode, 1903–9), Membrane 19, 4:350 (24 November 1411); *Calendar of Close Rolls: Richard II* (London: HMSO, 1914–27), Membrane 32d, 3:444 (4 November 1387).

[52] José Ramón Castro (ed.), *Catálogo del Archivo General de Navarra: Seccion de Comptos; Documentos: Vol. VI, Años 1366–1367* (Pamplona: Editorial Aramburu, 1954), 66–69, 72–77, 114.

[53] Ibid., 56, 114.

[54] *Register of the Black Prince*, fol. 52, 88; fol. 93d, 152; fol. 154, 269; fol. 103d, 178–79; fol. 171, 301; fol. 180d, 319; fol. 207, 373; fol. 285, 555.

[55] Ormrod, *Edward III*, 304. He is termed 'Sanchet' in this context, and some historians have thought that this is a different d'Aubrichecourt, perhaps Eustace's brother, but Ormrod argues that this is indeed Eustace d'Aubrichecourt, also citing unpublished work by Richard Barber in support of this point of view (note 23).

Black Prince). A few years later, he was fighting for Charles of Navarre in Normandy.[56] He planned to fight with du Guesclin and others in Spain but was deflected to Navarre instead, as Charles offered him huge rewards. It is likely that d'Aubrichecourt brought over troops and equipment to protect Navarre—and the change of plan presumably suited him well given his long-term connections to Edward III.[57] Indeed, on 24 January 1366, he swore to serve Charles and his successors against all enemies except for Edward III and the Black Prince, in return for '1,000 libras' a year.[58] His name recurs over and over again in the Navarrese records at this time.[59] On the day that Charles issued Chaucer's safe-conduct (22 February), he was also writing an order to the chatelaine of St-Jean-Pied-de-Port to allow the war machinery of d'Aubrichecourt through to defend the northern frontier.[60]

The route from England to Navarre lay through Aquitaine, and Chaucer must have come through the Black Prince's territory. He may have come from England, on the orders of the king, or have come directly from the Black Prince, if he had been working in Aquitaine. Chaucer certainly had many connections there; later on in Chaucer's life he was often closely connected with men who had spent time working for the Black Prince and his wife in the 1360s. Some of those men—such as Lewis Clifford, later a poetic intermediary between Chaucer and Deschamps and probably godfather to Chaucer's younger son[61]—were also caught up in Navarrese politics.[62] Whether he spent much time in Aquitaine or not, Chaucer certainly passed through the region, a place that had been a part of his mental landscape since early childhood when his father traded continually with Gascony. Following the Treaty of Brétigny, England held a much-enlarged Aquitaine in complete sovereignty, and from 1362 to 1368, the Black Prince ruled the new Principality of Aquitaine.[63] He went there

---

[56] Sumption, *Trial by Fire*, 391, 406–10, 432, 514, 521.

[57] Fowler, *Medieval Mercenaries*, 175–76.

[58] Castro, *Catálogo del Archivo General*, 28–29.

[59] For instance, see ibid., 54, 56, 78, 116, 226, 342.

[60] Brutails, *Documents des Archives*, 142.

[61] For Clifford's role as poetic intermediary in 1385–86, see chapter 14; for further discussion of Clifford and his likely role as godfather to Lewis Chaucer, see chapter 15; for Lewis Chaucer, see chapter 9.

[62] For Clifford in Navarre, see Thomas A. Reisner and Mary E. Reisner, 'Lewis Clifford and the Kingdom of Navarre,' *Modern Philology* 75:4 (1978): 385–90. See also Peter Fleming, 'Clifford, Sir Lewis (c. 1330–1404),' in *ODNB*, https://doi.org/10.1093/ref:odnb/50259.

[63] Labarge, *Gascony*, 146–49.

with his wife, Joan, whom he had married in 1361. The marriage was initially scandalous—the Black Prince was the most eligible man in Europe, and he chose to marry his thirty-three-year-old cousin, who had several children, and who had already been married twice. And she had had these two husbands not in succession but *at the same time*: after a secret marriage to Thomas Holland, she then married the earl of Salisbury; when Holland protested, the pope annulled the second marriage. She therefore brought a scandalous past and no diplomatic value; this really was a love match.[64] The couple held magnificent court, and their reign in Aquitaine was known for its extravagant display and conspicuous consumption.[65] Their sons—Edward of Angoulême, who died young, and Richard of Bordeaux, who became Richard II—were both born during these years in Aquitaine.

After travelling through Bordeaux, Chaucer crossed the Pyrenees. The most important of the mountain passes was the hamlet of Roncesvalles, famous as the site of the defeat of Charlemagne and the death of Roland, memorialized and fictionalized in the *Song of Roland*. Roncesvalles was also particularly known in England for the Chapel and Hospital of St Mary Rounceval at Charing Cross, under the authority of the mother-house at Roncesvalles, an Augustinian monastery. The Charing Cross satellite was to be the imagined home of the Pardoner when Chaucer came to write the 'General Prologue.' Roncesvalles was—and still is—on the pilgrimage route to Santiago de Compostela, so its monks were accustomed to the presence of visiting foreigners, but it was an isolated and otherworldly place. Chaucer was only about twenty-three or twenty-four when he made this trip, and although he had already travelled around England and been taken prisoner in France, the experience of travelling across mountain paths in wintertime, through an area populated by bears and wolves, was unlike anything else he had experienced. When I visited Roncesvalles one February, the month that Chaucer arrived in Navarre, there was snow on the ground and fog in the air, and the tiny settlement felt cut off, exposed, and very much open to nature (plate 4). But despite the cold quiet of the mountains, Chaucer did, of course, have

[64] Ibid., 150.

[65] Richard Barber, *The Black Prince* (Stroud: Sutton, 2003), 184.

his entourage of colleagues, servants, and horses; he was not alone or unsupported. On the contrary, he was travelling in some style—and entering a small country teeming with his acquaintances.

Olite offered a marked contrast to the mountain passes of the Pyrenees. The capital of Navarre at this time, it was a sophisticated town, home to Charles's beautiful palace, surrounded by olive groves, and boasting elaborate churches and protective walls. The landscape contrasts with the mountains and rushing river of Roncesvalles; Olite is surrounded with greenery and gentle hills, although a desert lies to the south. In February, Olite is not warm, but it is still sunny and far more pleasant than Chaucer's homeland at that time of year. Many aspects of the town would have been familiar to Chaucer: it has Roman remains and medieval walls, and the churches have the same kind of iconography as the churches in London. The king, who issued Chaucer's safe-conduct, was the patron of Machaut, who was a vital influence on Chaucer, especially on his early poetry. In many ways, to visit a town such as Olite was to be reminded of international, French-centred high culture, and of the homogenizing power of the church.

In other ways, however, Olite was an alien place to Chaucer. An English traveller here experienced that strange tension between the familiar and the unknown that often characterizes an immersion in a different culture. Chaucer's perspective must have shifted constantly, as on one hand he moved in a familiar cultural milieu and even met up with many men known to him from the English court, but on the other he saw those aspects of life specific to the Iberian peninsula. In particular, he now saw at firsthand the operation of a multicultural society. The street that immediately leads up to Charles's palace is the Rúa de la Judería (Street of the Jews), testament to the close relationship between the Jewish community and the court (plate 5). Indeed, the day before he issued Chaucer's safe-conduct, Charles ordered the Jews of Pamplona to allow the Jews from the suburbs and countryside to take refuge in the city, as the soldiers coming from Aragon might target them.[66] Relations between the Christian rulers and the Jewish communities were a constant political issue in the Iberian peninsula. In Castile, Pedro protected the Jews and was attacked for

[66] Brutails, *Documents des Archives*, 141.

this by Enrique, who himself persecuted and massacred Jews.[67] In Navarre, Jews were a prominent part of the cultural mix. They lived alongside Muslims and Christians, in a border country in which groups including Gascons, Basques, Navarro-Aragonese, and Castilians, all mingled. Many Jews worked as moneylenders, but they also did a huge range of other jobs: they were silversmiths, embroiderers, vets, doctors, irrigation specialists, grape growers, and mill owners. Charles II had a trusted Jewish physician, and his favourite juggler was a Jew. Jews could own property and land, and could therefore farm. Their oaths had full value, and if a Jew went to court, he or she took a Jewish witness and observer. Although they also suffered many injustices, such as heavy taxation and sometimes violence, their position was better than it was or had been in most other parts of medieval Europe. Their frequent appearances in the account books indicate that they were an obvious presence around the royal court.[68] England, in contrast, had expelled its Jewish population in 1290.

When proclamations were made in Tudela, they were made in markets and city squares on Thursdays, in mosques on Fridays, in synagogues on Saturdays, and in churches on Sundays.[69] Navarre had a religious mix unlike any community in England or France at this time. Muslim communities tended to be rural, although Tudela, in particular, had an important Muslim quarter. Muslims could, but did not have to, live in this area, and non-Muslims could live there too. Again, Muslims were engaged in diverse activities. Many worked as muleteers and providers of packhorses; others were horse doctors and blacksmiths. They were also involved in manufacturing harnesses and saddles, and in manufacturing weaponry. In the 1360s, a Muslim, Amet Alhudaly, was master crossbowman to Charles II, and master of the ordnance of his castles. A few years earlier, in a striking example of cultural tolerance, Charles had asked Pere IV of Aragon to give safe-passage to some Navarrese Muslims on their way to Mecca.[70]

It is not my intention to idealise the situation of non-Christians in Navarre. Their lives were precarious; their situation often difficult, some-

[67] Clara Estow, *Pedro the Cruel of Castile: 1350–1369* (Leiden: Brill, 1995), 155.
[68] Béatrice Leroy, *The Jews of Navarre* (Jerusalem: Magnes Press, Hebrew University, 1985), 10, 22, 34–35, 50–54, 90, 104, 140–42.
[69] Leroy, *Jews of Navarre*, 9.
[70] L. P. Harvey, *Islamic Spain, 1250–1500* (Chicago: University of Chicago Press, 1990), 140–45.

times intolerable. But their lives and communities were embedded in and constitutive of Navarrese society. For the first time, Chaucer visited a country in which people of three major religions cooperated to make society work. He may have hired horses from Muslims or had contact with Jewish doctors or bankers at court. Whether or not he did, he experienced life in a country where different religions coexisted, often amicably, where accommodations were made to take into account different sets of cultural norms.

Chaucer's safe-conduct covered 22 February to 24 May. In the middle of February, Pere IV was at Saragossa; Pedro I at Burgos—each only about fifty miles from Pamplona.[71] The Aragonese army planned to launch their attack through Navarre, and at the end of February, Hugh Calveley struck north and invaded Navarre, followed by Bertrand du Guesclin. Charles of Navarre frantically tried to pay them off to keep looting to a minimum. On 10 March, Hugh went into Castile, and by 28 March, Pedro had fled. The next day, Enrique was crowned.[72] Meanwhile, the Black Prince and Edward III were considering intervening. In May, Sir Thomas Holland and Sir Neil Loring (the Black Prince's stepson and chamberlain) were sent to Aquitaine from England, with some troops and sappers. The prince was recruiting troops in Gascony, and in June Edward III was requisitioning shipping for a larger force.[73] By this point, Pedro had sought refuge in Portugal.

This period, then, in which Chaucer was in Navarre, was a time of extreme political tension. Navarre was invaded during this time, and by English troops who (from the English Crown's perspective) ought not to have been fighting against Pedro. Charles himself had double-crossed his allies, and it was unclear which, if any, side he was on. Many English individuals were being retained by Charles, as he desperately tried to improve his position.

What was Chaucer doing in the middle of these intrigues? Given that his previous and subsequent career involved working for the household of the king and his sons, and that in later years he was sent on

---

[71] Sumption, *Trial by Fire*, 534.
[72] Ibid., 536–37.
[73] Ibid., 544; David Green, *The Black Prince* (Stroud: Tempus, 2001), 157.

many diplomatic missions to Europe, it is reasonable to assume that he was a messenger of either the king or the Black Prince. Although he is not identified as an employee of the Crown, the fact of the safe-conduct makes it likely that he was there on some kind of official business. Unlike so many of his compatriots, he did not swear fealty to Charles or take advantage of Charles's policy of retaining English squires and knights at this point. Again, this suggests that he was in the service of the English Crown, not travelling independently. Perhaps he was gathering information or bringing messages to Charles; perhaps he was also negotiating with English soldiers. Certainly, travelling on a diplomatic mission for the king is exactly what we would expect Chaucer to be doing, given his employment over the following couple of decades. He may well have gone on to Castile, to take messages to Pedro—although in the case of Thomas de Alberton, travelling to Castile a couple of weeks later, the Navarrese document does record the fact that he was en route to Castile, and Chaucer's safe-conduct does not state this.[74] Perhaps Chaucer's mission was more varied and Alberton's purpose was solely to get through Navarre and onto Castile. Given the political situation, it is likely that Chaucer went to see Pedro himself in Burgos, to take him messages from Edward or the Black Prince, to find out his plans, and perhaps to discuss the support that the English were willing to offer. He could even have gone in the company of Arnaud Amanieu, the Gascon lord of Albret, one of the Black Prince's most important subjects, who went to Burgos from Navarre at exactly this time (the last few days of February), accompanied by *otros caballeros* (other knights) and urged Pedro to shore up his own position by buying the services of some of the mercenary companies.[75] If Pedro had taken such action this would, of course, have suited England very well and saved them a great deal of trouble. Pedro, however, refused to spend his money, and the lord of Albret returned to Charles's court in Navarre.

What Chaucer saw in Navarre was realpolitik par excellence. Charles of Navarre—who had allied with both sides, just as in earlier years he had

[74] Brutails, *Documents des Archives*, 147.

[75] Pedro López de Ayala, *Cronicas de los Reyes de Castilla: Don Pedro, Don Enrique II, Don Juan I, Don Enrique III* (Madrid: Antonio de Sancha, 1779), 1:397. Fowler, *Medieval Mercenaries*, 179.

frequently flirted with the English before returning to the French—was one of the most pragmatic and self-interested politicians of the day. The mercenaries provided a different kind of example of the pragmatics of war; Hugh Calveley, one of the leaders of the Aragonese army, was fighting alongside du Guesclin, whom he had fought against in France. Edward III, not knowing the details of what was going on in Southern Europe, had even appointed Calveley as one of his commissioners to stop English and Gascon men from joining du Guesclin.[76] Calveley was now fighting against Pedro I; the following year he returned with the Black Prince to reinstate Pedro. Indeed, many of the mercenaries did the same, thinking nothing of selling their services to opposing sides in succession. D'Aubrichecourt was an interesting example of someone who acted essentially independently of borders, although he always kept a loyalty to England—which was not, of course, the country of his birth.

But while national loyalty and national borders must have seemed fluid and porous concepts to anyone watching events in the French and Spanish domains at this time, in other ways boundaries were of the greatest importance. Indeed, Navarre gained its strategic significance precisely because of its natural walls, the Pyrenees. When Chaucer was in Navarre, Charles was preoccupied with building walls. Chaucer was surrounded by the preparations for defence. During February, Charles's activity reached fever pitch. He reinforced fortifications, commanded trees to be felled to shore up defences, ordered people to get within the walled towns, appointed captains, strengthened the borders, and engaged the services of seasoned campaigners.[77] A few years earlier, Chaucer had been outside the walls of a city under siege (Reims), and a few years later, he would find himself living on the walls of London when they were breached by a rebel army. Now he was inside the walls of cities that were preparing to be attacked by rampaging military companies of great power and little control. From the watchtowers of Olite, one could see across to the next hilltop village, which could send signals reporting on what could be seen in Aragon. The Navarrese knew that hostile armies were coming, and were frantically trying to protect themselves.

[76] Sumption, *Trial by Fire*, 544.
[77] Fowler, *Medieval Mercenaries*, 173–75.

The symbolic force of walls must be different if one lives in a culture of walled cities, where the success or failure of military adventures depends on whether or not the walls hold. Much of Chaucer's poetry circles around images of enclosure, crystallised in the proverbial image of the mouth, walled with teeth and lips as a way of containing the tongue and speech: 'God of his endelees goodnesse / Walled a tonge with teeth and lippes eke, / For man sholde hym avyse what he speeke' ('Manciple's Tale,' 322–24). It is a wonderful image for a diplomat to use as it brings together verbal negotiation and physical defences, discussion and siege, treaties and self-protection. *Troilus and Criseyde*, a poem set within and then outside a besieged walled city, is suffused with images of enclosure as both protecting and suffocating. And one of Chaucer's short poems, *The Former Age*, meditates explicitly on the function of walls in society. The poem sets the violence, extravagance, and conspicuous consumption of contemporary life against an imagined past of plain living, peace, and moral simplicity (as discussed in chapter 2). One of the key differences between the two societies is walls. He tells us that in the former age people had 'Ne toures heye and walles rounde or square' (24), that the people slept 'withoute walles' (43), and that Nimrod (legendary founder of cities) had not yet made 'his toures hye' (59). But Chaucer makes it resoundingly clear that if you don't have walls and cities, you lose all the luxuries and comforts of life too. Armies, he says, besiege cities 'the cite for to asayle' (40) when there is something worth taking there: 'bagges' and 'fat vitaile' (38). If you are starving and only have 'mast' (nuts) to eat, then no one will bother attacking you.[78] Walls and towers, both words that recur in this poem, are inevitable parts of comfortable life—if you want the clothes, the food, the bed, and the products, you also have to put up with the envy, the acquisitiveness, the betrayal, and the murder.[79]

[78] Later in this book, in chapter 8, I discuss at length how Chaucer differentiates himself from Boethius, partly through his redeployment of the terms of Boethius's metaphors. Chaucer's interest in materiality and the senses is a central aspect of his attitude to philosophy and poetics. See also chapter 9.

[79] While the poem suggests that contemporary societies defend themselves behind impenetrable walls, it also depicts those societies as open to foreign products and merchants. Modernity subjects and colonizes nature and animals—instead of sharing food with animals, they are pressed into service and turned into luxury objects, just as the outdoor life is replaced with the ostentatiously made environment. For further discussion of the poem, see Galloway, 'Chaucer's *Former Age*.'

Chaucer's description of 'Doublenesse, and tresoun, and envye, / Poyson, manslawhtre, and mordre in sondry wyse' (62–63) could certainly have been applied to what happened next in the Iberian imbroglio. Pedro travelled to Aquitaine and made a plan with the Black Prince and Charles of Navarre. In essence, they were to invade Castile and depose Enrique. The Black Prince was to pay the troops; Pedro left his daughters as hostages and promised to pay him back and also to give him land concessions. Charles too was to receive territory to expand Navarre.[80] Predictably, Charles then changed his mind and made a treaty with Enrique, agreeing to close the passes to the Black Prince's troops. The Black Prince ordered Hugh Calveley—who was now fighting for England and Pedro—to invade Navarre from the south, and Charles quickly capitulated, agreeing to open the passes and disclaiming his treachery.[81] When the Black Prince marched through Navarre with his army, on his way to confront Enrique, Charles paid a mercenary, Oliver de Mauny, to pretend to kidnap him, so he could be out of the way until it was all over.[82] The Black Prince won a decisive victory at Najera and reinstated Pedro on the throne of Castile. At this point, however, it all went wrong. Pedro was incensed at the Black Prince's desire to ransom, rather than execute, the prisoners. The Black Prince became ill, and many of his soldiers died. And Pedro refused to pay the Black Prince back, although the costs had been massive and disastrous for Aquitaine.[83] So the Black Prince left, and a couple of years later Pedro was dead, killed by his brother, Enrique, with the help of du Guesclin and Oliver de Mauny. Chaucer later wrote about his death in the 'Monk's Tale,' depicting du Guesclin through his coat of arms ('The feeld of snow, with th'egle of blak therinne / Caught with the lymrod coloured as the gleede' [2383–84]), as Deschamps also did in a ballade, and de Mauny through a pun 'wikked nest' (mau-ni [2386]). Pedro is 'this worthy kyng' (2390), a comprehensible description if one remembers that John of Gaunt married Pedro's daughter, Constance, as his second wife, and through her claimed to be king of Castile, and that Philippa

---

[80] Barber, *Black Prince*, 189–91.
[81] Sumption, *Trial by Fire*, 548.
[82] Ibid., 549; Linehan, 'Castile,' 642.
[83] Sumption, *Trial by Fire*, 555–59; Ormrod, *Edward III*, 440–42.

Chaucer worked for Constance for several years. Chaucer probably removed his reference to Enrique's illegitimacy ('Thy bastard brother') when Gaunt and Constance's daughter married Enrique's grandson in 1386.[84]

In the late 1360s, both Chaucer and Philippa were attached to the court itself, Chaucer as an esquire of the king's household and Philippa as one of the queen's ladies.[85] Shortly after Chaucer's visit to Navarre, Philippa is named as Chaucer's wife, and a year or two later, she gave birth to Thomas Chaucer.[86] In the first few months of 1366, almost certainly while Chaucer was abroad, there were also other dramatic changes in his family: his father died and his mother remarried almost immediately. His father was still living on 16 January, when he appears on a legal record; on 13 July, Chaucer's mother, Agnes, appears in a property record as the wife of Bartholomew Chappel, another London vintner.[87] Within less than six months, then, Chaucer lost his father and gained a stepfather. We do not know anything about how these events affected Chaucer. But for anyone, the death of a parent and the decision to marry and have children are events that encourage one to take responsibility. Involvement in the cycles of life and death—bereavement and parenthood—also brings home with particular emphasis the profound mutability of life. Chaucer's mother's immediate remarriage enacts the kind of pragmatic response to change that Chaucer depicted (with sympathy) in the figure of Criseyde or the figure of Venus (in the *Complaint of Mars*). Chaucer often suggests that we have a choice about whether to submit to the 'tragic' path of Fortune's wheel, to accept what happens, or to adapt and seize what one can out of a situation. One can choose to 'maken vertu of necessitee,' as Chaucer repeatedly tells us—this is a statement that is at the heart of his poetry ('Knight's Tale,' 3042; *Troilus and Criseyde*, Book IV, 1586; 'Squire's Tale,' 593). This important phrase, with its balancing of agency ('maken') against those things that are out of one's control ('necessitee'), with each aspect

---

[84] *Riverside Chaucer*, 933, note to line 2378.

[85] Chaucer was named as a king's squire and granted a life annuity in June 1367. See Crow and Olson, *Chaucer Life-Records*, 123–35. The records relating to Philippa are on 67–93.

[86] We do not know the exact date of Thomas Chaucer's birth. He was a mainpernor in a case on 8 July 1389, so he was presumably twenty-one by this point, which would give a birth date of before 8 July 1368. See Albert Croll Baugh, 'Kirk's Life-Records of Thomas Chaucer,' *PMLA* 47:2 (1932): 463.

[87] Crow and Olson, *Chaucer Life-Records*, 8.

equidistant from 'vertu' (strength), sums up the opportunities and limitations of existence.

The mid-1360s were crucial years for Chaucer, years in which he expanded his horizons and lived a very international life while simultaneously becoming more rooted to an English base, as a messenger of the king and as a father. On the one hand, he travelled to Aquitaine, to Navarre, perhaps to Castile, and shortly afterwards (in 1368) undertook further journeys on the Continent.[88] He was also reading widely in poetry by French and Hainuyer authors, amongst other things, and was perhaps himself writing poems in French, and translating the *Roman de la Rose*.[89] Many of his associates were not English born, and he became further rooted in a Hainault environment through his marriage. On the other hand, unlike the mercenaries who sold their services in short-term contracts to different overlords, Chaucer worked for the English Crown—in effect for the English government. He always came back to this base, and he increasingly had responsibilities to his family. He was not an adventurer. But to be an educated Englishperson at this time demanded an international outlook; the court (like the city of London) was full of people of varying nationalities, the fashionable literary texts were mainly written in French, the queen and her ladies brought Hainault culture to the forefront. Aquitaine, like Calais, was English territory, and the borders of England were in a constant state of change. England, like other nations, was and is a process, always becoming something that it was not before.

---

[88] Ibid., 29–30.

[89] Wimsatt, *Chaucer and the Poems of 'Ch,'* 1–2. For the dates of composition of the *Roman de la Rose*, see Charles Dahlberg's introduction in Chaucer, *Romaunt of the Rose*, 24–27.

CHAPTER 5

Lancaster

Many a servant unto his lord seith
That al the world spekith of him honour.
                    —*Thomas Hoccleve,* La Male Regle

At the end of his earliest extant narrative poem, Chaucer famously names the greatest nobleman of the day, the duke of Lancaster, in a series of multilingual puns. The Black Knight retreats to his stronghold:

A long castel with walles white,
Be Seynt Johan, on a ryche hil. (1318–19)

The 'long castel' represents John of Gaunt's principal title, duke of Lancaster; the 'walles white,' his dead wife, Blanche, in commemoration of whom the poem has been written; 'Johan' is his own given name; the 'ryche hil' denotes his role as earl of Richmond. Lancaster, for Chaucer, did not connote the town in the northwest: it meant this enormously powerful man, the duke of Lancaster, and his vast network of lands, properties, and influence. Indeed, the fact that Chaucer gets the etymology of Lancaster wrong—'Lan' comes from the river Lune, not 'long'—symbolizes his lack of interest in Lancaster itself. For Chaucer, 'Lancaster' was a person and a huge range of places—including the castles of Hertford, Tutbury, Pontefract, Kenilworth, Dunstanburgh, Knaresborough, and Leicester, and the Savoy Palace. John of Gaunt held land all over England as the richest and most powerful nobleman in the country. After his second marriage, to Constance of Castile, Gaunt combined the royal arms of England with the arms of Castile: his coat of arms then prominently featured two golden castles.[1] Lancaster meant not just one place but seigneurial power at its most imposing, symbolized by gleaming, protective castles, designed to dominate and to enclose. But Lancaster was not, for Chaucer, associated only with male militarism and power: Gaunt gained his title and his lands through his wife, the 1st duke of Lancaster's coheiress and the woman about whom Chaucer wrote the *Book of the Duchess*. And by the end of his life, Chaucer's own sister-in-law was Gaunt's third duchess of Lancaster—and her connection with Gaunt had already been invaluable to Chaucer's family for decades.

John of Gaunt was Chaucer's contemporary. Born in 1340, in Ghent, he was Edward III and Philippa of Hainault's third surviving son. Ten years younger than the Black Prince, he seems to have spent part of his adolescence in the household of his glamorous oldest brother, and they remained close.[2] On 2 May 1359, Gaunt married Blanche of Lancaster, one of the greatest heiresses of the day, daughter of Henry of Grosmont, 1st duke of Lancaster, a towering presence both at Edward's court and in military and diplomatic affairs on the Continent. Gaunt and Chaucer certainly met at Hatfield in 1357–58, as discussed in chapter 2, and they might have met before. Although there was a wide social gulf between the prince and the page, it is a mistake to think that this gulf precluded any but the most glancing or transactional of interactions. The two boys were the same age and clearly shared at least some of the same interests. Gaunt was an intelligent and cultured man, and members of the royal family were accustomed to mixing with men from the London mercantile classes. Indeed, Edward III was not an inaccessible king; his court was known for its openness, and Chaucer's family had long had connections with the court.[3] In Elizabeth and Lionel's household, Chaucer was not the kind of servant who was relegated to the kitchens; he was a smartly dressed, ornamental young man, able to play games, recite poetry, and generally take part in household culture. His early encounters with

[1] P. E. Russell, *The English Intervention in Spain and Portugal in the Time of Edward III and Richard II* (Oxford: Clarendon Press, 1955), 167–69.

[2] Anthony Goodman, *John of Gaunt: The Exercise of Princely Power in Fourteenth-Century Europe* (Harlow: Longman, 1992), 30–31.

[3] On the accessibility of Edward and his court, see Ormrod, *Edward III*, 533.

Gaunt were the beginning of a profoundly productive relationship for Chaucer with the man who was to become the greatest landowner in the kingdom.[4]

The Lancaster inheritance had been formed a century earlier, when Edmund Crouchback, younger son of Henry III and Eleanor of Provence, was given a parcel of lands, principally deriving from the forfeiture of Simon de Montfort after the Barons' War, and was created earl of Lancaster and of Leicester. He and his wife, Blanche of Artois (queen of Navarre), had two very influential sons: Thomas of Lancaster, the 2nd earl, who was executed for his role in condemning Piers Gaveston, and Henry of Lancaster, the 3rd earl. Henry was one of the architects of the overthrow of Edward II, and subsequently led opposition to Mortimer's tyranny—as we saw earlier, Chaucer's father rode to his support in 1328–29. Henry and his wife, Maud Chaworth, were the parents of seven children, including Maud, mother of Elizabeth de Burgh, Chaucer's first employer, and Henry of Grosmont, the leading nobleman at the court of Edward III. Henry of Grosmont was singled out amongst Edward's subjects for favours: he was the second person ever to be created duke in England (the Black Prince, the heir to the throne, was the first); his county of Lancaster was raised to the status of a palatinate, giving him sovereign rights in the county; he was also given the rights to mint his own coins in Bergerac; he was a founding member of the Order of the Garter; and he led English diplomacy in France. In the campaign of 1359–60, in which Chaucer was captured, the army was divided into three, led by the king, the Black Prince, and Henry; Henry subsequently led the peace negotiations at Brétigny, at which Chaucer was present. He was also an author, penning the Anglo-Norman penitential tract, *Le livre de seyntz medicines*, which draws together the languages of medicine and religion in its meditation on the sickness of the soul.[5]

---

[4] Biographers have adopted radically different viewpoints about Chaucer's relationship with Gaunt, ranging from William Godwin's inclusion of Gaunt in the title of his biography of Chaucer to James R. Hulbert's insistence that Gaunt did not patronize Chaucer at all—Hulbert's book does not even mention Katherine Swynford. I discuss biographers' attitudes to Chaucer and Gaunt in more detail in 'Chaucer,' in *A Companion to Literary Biography*, ed. Richard Bradford (Oxford: Wiley-Blackwell, 2018), 378.

[5] See Kenneth Fowler, *The King's Lieutenant: Henry of Grosmont, First Duke of Lancaster, 1310–1361* (London: Elek, 1969), and Henry of Lancaster, *Le livre de seyntz medicines*, ed. E. J. Arnould (Oxford:

Given the very prominent position that Henry held at Edward's court, and the fact that his estate was to devolve to his two daughters, the marriage between John of Gaunt and Henry's daughter Blanche was entirely predictable. Less predictable was the death of Henry's older daughter Maud, without children, which meant that her half of the vast Lancastrian inheritance also came to Blanche and her husband. Henry died in 1361, Maud in 1362. In the same year, John of Gaunt was made duke of Lancaster; in 1377 he was given palatine rights for his life, and in 1390 these rights were extended to his heirs. His landholdings as duke of Lancaster gave him a power base unrivalled by other great magnates, especially when coupled with his position as the son of Edward III. By the time his father died, John was his eldest surviving son and perfectly placed to dominate domestic politics for the first part of the minority of Richard II. He suffered reverses: he was effectively public enemy number 1 in 1376–77, when broadsides were pinned up impugning his birth, and again in 1381, when the rebels particularly targeted his Savoy palace. Richard II turned against him in the middle of the 1380s, and he focused his attention on Iberia for a while, escaping domestic politics. Although Gaunt had good years again between 1389 and about 1395, the later 1390s were a deeply uncertain time for the house of Lancaster, culminating in the exile of Gaunt's son Henry (and, after Gaunt's death, Henry's disinheritance). The 1360s and early 1370s, however, were the years of Gaunt's youth and glamour, when he enjoyed the wealth and power that his unique position as son of the king and owner of the Lancastrian inheritance brought to him, a time when he felt he had everything to play for on the European stage.[6]

In the 1360s, Chaucer's and John of Gaunt's paths crossed in a number of different ways. They had both been involved in the 1359–60 campaign and in the subsequent peace negotiations. As I discussed in chapter 4, the effects of Brétigny led to the problems in Spain; Chaucer was in

---

Anglo-Norman Text Society, Blackwell, 1940).

[6] For Gaunt's life, see Goodman, *John of Gaunt* and Sydney Armitage-Smith, *John of Gaunt: King of Castile and Leon, Duke of Aquitaine and Lancaster, Earl of Derby, Lincoln and Leicester, Seneschal of England* (London: Constable, 1964). See also Simon Walker, *The Lancastrian Affinity, 1361–1399* (Oxford: Oxford University Press, 1990). His life and impact on Chaucer are discussed throughout the current study; see especially chapters 7, 8, 10, 12, 18, 19, and 20. On the broadsides accusing him of being the son of a butcher of Ghent, see Turner, 'Conflict,' 267.

Navarre in 1366, and in 1367 Gaunt was there, fighting alongside his brother in the campaign to reinstate Pedro the Cruel. Gaunt's wife, Blanche, died in 1368; during the 1360s she had given birth to five children, three of whom survived—Philippa, Elizabeth, and Henry of Bolingbroke, the future Henry IV.[7] Henry was born around the same time as Thomas Chaucer, and they were to be connected in many ways throughout their lives.[8] In 1369, Chaucer seems to have fought in Gaunt's company in northern France. The evidence for this is that his name appears in a list of wages of war paid to knights, esquires, and others in 1369. Chaucer's name is listed alongside others in the king's household, with a payment of £10.[9] It was a damp squib of a campaign: there was no pitched battle, the army plundered in Artois, Picardy, and Normandy, and then returned to Calais at the end of October.

In 1370 and 1371, Gaunt was in Aquitaine, where the Black Prince, now very ill, made him his lieutenant. Gaunt was effectively in charge of Aquitaine until the summer of 1371, when he gave up the command due to lack of funds. In September of that year, he married Constance of Castile, the daughter of Pedro the Cruel, through whom John claimed the throne of Castile and Leon. And it was in the late 1360s and early 1370s that the de Roet sisters rose to prominence in Gaunt's entourage. Philippa Chaucer worked as an attendant on Constance and was granted an annuity of £10 by Gaunt in 1372. From this point until her death in 1387 Philippa received a salary and gifts from Gaunt.[10] Her position was undoubtedly enhanced by her sister's relationship with Gaunt. We do not know exactly when Katherine's affair with Gaunt began. She worked in Blanche's household from around 1365 and married one of Gaunt's tenants, Sir Hugh Swynford; she was widowed in 1371, having given birth to at least three children (Thomas, Blanche, and Margaret Swynford).[11] Katherine later received payments for the wardrobe and chamber expenses of Gaunt's le-

[7] For Henry's life, see Chris Given-Wilson, *Henry IV* (New Haven: Yale University Press, 2016).

[8] 'Thomas Chaucer of Ewelme,' in J. S. Roskell, *Parliament and Politics in Late Medieval England, Volume III* (London: Hambledon Press, 1983), 151–92. In this study see, especially, chapters 18 and 20.

[9] Crow and Olson, *Chaucer Life-Records*, 31, 106–7.

[10] Ibid., 85–93.

[11] Thomas Swynford was probably Henry Bolingbroke's 'closest boyhood companion'; see Given-Wilson, *Henry IV*, 24. For Margaret's connection with Chaucer's daughter, see chapter 8 in this study.

gitimate daughters as she acted as their 'maistresse' in the 1370s, the person who oversaw their education and behaviour.[12] This gave her an official position in the Lancastrian household. Katherine bore four children to Gaunt in the 1370s: John, Henry, Thomas, and Joan Beaufort. These children—all of whom went on to hold important titles and positions—were first cousins to Chaucer's children. Although John of Gaunt formally renounced Katherine in the wake of the Rising of 1381, their relationship continued, and she eventually became his third wife in 1396. This allowed John to petition for and to receive both papal bulls and an Act of Parliament legitimating the Beaufort children.[13] Gift patterns and appointments made demonstrate not only that Katherine had an excellent relationship with Gaunt's three legitimate children by Blanche, but that those children also had close relationships with the Swynford, Beaufort, and Chaucer children, all of whom seem to have spent a lot of time together as children in various Lancastrian great houses.[14] Throughout the 1370s, when all of the offspring of Gaunt, Katherine, and the Chaucers were children, Philippa Chaucer was working at least intermittently for Constance, and Katherine also had an official role in the Lancastrian nursery. The life of Chaucer's family was thus intimately bound up with the life of Gaunt's family.[15] Indeed, in 1386, Philippa Chaucer was admitted to the fraternity of Lincoln Cathedral along with Henry Bolingbroke, John Beaufort, Thomas Swynford, and Robert Ferrers (who was to marry Joan Beaufort). In the same year, Thomas Chaucer was in Spain with John of Gaunt, at the beginning of his long and extremely

[12] Eleanor Lodge and Robert Somerville (eds.), *John of Gaunt's Register, 1379–1383*, Camden Third Series (London: Offices of the Society, 1937), folio 94b, 2:302–3, no. 963 (25 July 1376) and folio 96b, 2:307, no. 984 (7 September 1381); National Archives, DL 28/3/1 M5.

[13] Goodman, *John of Gaunt*, 363–64; Given-Wilson, *Henry IV*, 101; PROME, Membrane 2, no. 28, 7:322–23 (January 1397).

[14] Gaunt's legitimate children were brought up with the Swynfords and Beauforts; see Given-Wilson, *Henry IV*, 24. Philippa's role attending Constance, and the fact that payments were sometimes made to her in Lincolnshire (Crow and Olson, *Chaucer Life-Records*, 80–93), where Katherine had her property, makes it likely that Philippa and Geoffrey's children spent time with their cousins and the children of Gaunt and of Katherine. Thomas and Elizabeth Chaucer received extremely generous patronage from Gaunt, and the much-later-born Lewis Chaucer also appears in Lancastrian contexts. See chapters 8, 9, and 18.

[15] I am in agreement here with Strohm, who argues in *The Poet's Tale* that Katherine's relationship with Gaunt was of fundamental importance in determining Chaucer's relationship with Gaunt. See Paul Strohm, *The Poet's Tale: Chaucer and the Year that Made 'The Canterbury Tales'* (London: Profile Books, 2016), 27–45.

lucrative career of Lancastrian service, which followed seamlessly from a childhood probably spent in Lancastrian nurseries. From 1374, Chaucer received an annuity of £10 from Gaunt. As far as we know, this income continued for Chaucer's whole life. It was given to Chaucer in recognition both of the services that Chaucer had rendered to Gaunt and of those that Philippa had rendered to Queen Philippa and to Constance.[16]

On the only occasions in his poetry in which Chaucer explicitly asks for favour, he addresses the house of Lancaster. When he directly addresses Richard II, in *Lak of Stedfastness*, it is to advise, not to request. But in *The Complaint of Chaucer to his Purse*, Chaucer asks Henry to think about his 'supplicacion' (26), a request detailed in the refrain addressed to his purse: 'Beth hevy ageyn' (7). It is ostentatiously a begging poem. In the earlier *Fortune*, too, Fortune asks three or two princes to intervene with the 'pleintif's' 'beste frend' (32, 40, 48) to procure 'som beter estat' for him (79). The princes here are generally taken to be the dukes of Lancaster, York, and Gloucester, and the friend is the king.[17] These brief references are interesting because they are so unusual—Chaucer doesn't usually ask for anything through his poems and probably never got anything through his poems. But if he were going to ask someone for help, it would be the house of Lancaster. And the only poem that he did certainly write in response to a real incident in someone's life was written about the death of the duchess of Lancaster, Gaunt's wife.[18]

The moment in Gaunt's life that has been imaginatively rendered for us by Chaucer had taken place in 1368. After nine years of marriage, having given birth to five children, Blanche was still only in her midtwenties when she died, probably either in childbirth or of the plague. This was a woman whom Chaucer knew, at least distantly, and who possibly patronized his early work, a woman for whom his sister-in-law worked. He tells us in the 'Introduction to the Man of Law's Tale' that he wrote the story

[16] Crow and Olson, *Chaucer Life-Records*, 271–74.

[17] I discuss this in more detail in chapter 18. There is one other short poem in which Chaucer, more obliquely, asks for favour, when he asks Scogan to remember him at court ('Mynne thy frend, there it may fructyfye!'). *Lenvoy de Chaucer a Scogan*, in *Riverside Chaucer*, 655, line 48.

[18] It has sometimes been suggested that Blanche herself patronized Chaucer's poetry, but the evidence is problematic. I discuss this in chapter 20.

'In youthe' (57). That, of course, is an imprecise category, but it flags the poem as early in his writing life. The poem could have been written very soon after Blanche's death, in 1369 or 1370, or perhaps to coincide with the elaborate annual memorial service for Blanche, inaugurated in 1374. The argument that it would be inappropriate for Chaucer to depict Gaunt in the figure of the inconsolable Black Knight after his second marriage (in 1371) does not hold water: his marriage was a matter of international relations, and Gaunt saw no inconsistency between being married (and indeed also keeping a beloved mistress and second family) and at the same time lavishly and publicly mourning Blanche in St Paul's and paying for a tomb for himself and Blanche to be constructed in 1374. But it certainly makes sense for the poem to have been written when the memory of Blanche's death had not faded too much, probably not later than 1374 and perhaps as early as 1369. Gaunt officially lost the title of earl of Richmond in 1372, and given the importance of that title in the poem, the poem was probably written before that date, although it is perfectly possible that Chaucer did not keep immediately abreast of Gaunt's every change of title.[19]

The previous few years had been personally grim for John of Gaunt. Two sons had died in infancy in the mid-1360s. In 1368, his wife died and, a month later, his brother Lionel also died. In 1369, his mother, Philippa of Hainault, died. His oldest brother had become ill and his father was in decline. Not only were his closest relations of all generations dying, but the plague had also returned to England, with all its attendant horrors and memories. Chaucer himself had not suffered this kind of cluster of tragedy but, as discussed in chapter 4, he had recently undergone the death of his father and the birth of his first child; the cycles of life were vividly present to him. And in this context, Chaucer penned an elegiac poem that he names twice in his other works, once as 'the book of the Duchesse (*Retractions*, 1086) and once as 'the Deeth of Blaunche the Duchesse' (F-Prologue to the *Legend of Good Women*, 418).

---

[19] For the arguments about date, see Alastair Minnis, *The Shorter Poems* (Oxford: Oxford University Press, 1995), 80; Michael Foster, 'On Dating the Duchess: The Personal and Social Context of *Book of the Duchess*,' *Review of English Studies*, n.s., 59:239 (2008): 185–96; Fumo, *Making Chaucer's 'Book of the Duchess*,' 18–27.

Why did Chaucer decide to write a long narrative poem *in English*?[20] His emergence as poet must have been a long time coming. This exceptionally literary man was steeped in French and Hainuyer poetry and had already been writing short poems, perhaps his translation of the *Roman de la Rose*, perhaps his lost *Book of the Lion*.[21] The *Book of the Duchess* responds to a number of recent texts, most notably, Machaut's *dits*—including the *Fontaine Amoureuse*, written in 1360—and Froissart's *Paradys*, penned in England in 1362. It also responds to other poems by Hainuyers, such as Jean de la Mote's elegy for the queen's father—another courtly memorial poem.[22] It is in the genre of the *dits amoureux*: a poet-narrator overhears a wretched, agonized courtly lover-patron, who talks through some of his emotions. This was a French genre, and the *Book of the Duchess* is French in its form, written in an English version of the octosyllabic couplets used by poets such as Machaut but adapted to the four-stress pattern of English verse. The idea of writing in English was gaining in momentum at this time. Chaucer may already have read manuscripts, such as the 'Auchinleck' manuscript, a vernacular manuscript dating from the second quarter of the fourteenth century and containing a wide range of secular and religious material (some of which was even in octosyllabic couplets).[23] He was writing at the beginning of an explosion of English poetry (by poets including Gower, Langland, and the *Gawain* poet, as well as Chaucer himself). But no one had written this *style* of poem in English before, and it is extraordinarily interesting that Chaucer now made his intervention into the world of stylized courtly letters in a language that had not previously been a language of literature at the English court. An audience accustomed to hearing syllabic French verse, metrically determined by syllable count rather than stress patterns, was now confronted with

---

[20] Pearsall terms Chaucer's choice an 'extraordinary decision.' *Life of Geoffrey Chaucer*, 73. See also D. Vance Smith, 'Chaucer as an English Writer,' in Seth Lerer (ed.), *The Yale Companion to Chaucer* (New Haven: Yale University Press, 2006), 87–121.

[21] He mentions his *Book of the Lion* in the *Retractions*; it was likely a translation of Machaut's *Dit du Lyon*.

[22] James I. Wimsatt, *Chaucer and the French Love Poets: The Literary Background of the 'Book of the Duchess'* (Chapel Hill: University of North Carolina Press, 1968).

[23] National Library of Scotland Advocates, MS 19.2.1. See https://auchinleck.nls.uk.

English accentual-syllabic verse.[24] English, like other Germanic languages, is a stress-based language, and the metrical force of the iamb is determined by the balance between the stressed and unstressed syllables. This also allows poets to construct particular effects through playing with that metre, for instance, by omitting the first unstressed syllable to start a line with an emphatic beat (for example, line 5: 'Purely for defaute of slep'). While Chaucer's verse is metrically unusually regular and carefully constructed, both his use of informal diction and filler phrases and his adherence to the rhythms of aural English (precisely through his attention to iambs) give his poems a conversational tone.[25]

In choosing to write in English, he may have been inspired by Hainuyer poets' penning poems for their Hainault patroness, and have elected to complement this trend at the English court by writing an English poem for an English prince, about his dead English wife.[26] It might have been a way of marking himself as part of a group of contemporary poets and yet claiming his own ground. Chaucer was tapping into a pan-European trend: in the fourteenth century, writing in the vernacular was itself an international fashion.[27] His choice to write a poem that is in many ways a homage to writers such as Machaut and Froissart, a poem dependent on the forms developed by those poets, positions Chaucer as a participant in a sophisticated and cosmopolitan poetic milieu, not as a combative little Englander showing the French the superiority of English letters.[28] Such an idea could only have seemed ludicrous to a multilingual man such as Chaucer, whose deep and engaged reading of his French and Hainuyer contemporaries is evident in almost every line of the *Book of the Duchess*. He himself was to foreground the problems and novelty of writing in

---

[24] Insular French verse did use stress patterns; see Martin J. Duffell, *New History of English Metre* (London: Legenda, 2008), 75–77.

[25] See 'Versification,' in the *Riverside Chaucer*, xxxviii–xli for an overview of Chaucer's metre. See also Christopher Cannon, 'Chaucer's Style,' in Pietro Boitani and Jill Mann (eds.), *The Cambridge Companion to Chaucer* (Cambridge: Cambridge University Press, 2004), 236–37; and Duffell, *English Metre*, 73–85.

[26] Butterfield speculates that Froissart's picard *Paradys* 'impel[led]' Chaucer to write the *Book of the Duchess*; *Familiar Enemy*, 293.

[27] Elizabeth Salter, 'Chaucer and Internationalism,' *Studies in the Age of Chaucer* 2 (1980): 71–79.

[28] See Butterfield, *Familiar Enemy*, 269–91. See also Fumo, *Making Chaucer's 'Book of the Duchess,'* 74–78.

English in his *Complaint of Venus*. He points out here that it is hard to find sufficient English rhymes (80), thus drawing attention to his own virtuosity in nonetheless managing to do so, characteristically presenting himself as hapless while expertly negotiating poetic form, coining words, and alluding to contemporary (in this case French) poetry. He addresses Oton de Graunson in this poem, 'flour of hem that make in Fraunce' (82), a Savoyard poet associated with the English court in the last quarter of the fourteenth century. He too, like Chaucer, was patronized by John of Gaunt: indeed, Graunson's and Chaucer's names appear together twice in Gaunt's *Register*, receiving payments from Gaunt.[29]

Chaucer's own poetic voice is indeed idiosyncratic, but his difference from his contemporaries is not primarily determined by language choice but by the kind of poetry he chose to write and, in particular, the nature of his interest in the development of the 'I' figure. His predecessors shared with him an interest in the depiction of subjectivity, and in the crafting of narratorial personae. Chaucer was participating in a poetic conversation with men such as Machaut, Froissart, and Graunson. But Chaucer, as many critics have noted, departs from the courtly personae of the *dits amoureux* tradition to create narrators characterized by a startlingly comic pragmatism.[30] This is not unprecedented—there are comic elements in Machaut's narrator-personae, and Jean de Meun certainly juxtaposes the domestic and the courtly—but Chaucer dramatically develops the figure of the hapless, misdirected, often literal-minded, narrator.[31] Chaucer thus gently satirizes aspects of conventional courtly poetry by refusing to maintain the illusions of the poetic world. He does this largely through self-mockery. We *never* see Chaucer present his narratorial persona as a figure of divine inspiration or poetic genius. Quite the contrary. For

[29] Haldeen Braddy, 'Messire Oton De Graunson, Chaucer's Savoyard Friend,' *Studies in Philology* 35:4 (1938): 522–23; Sydney Armitage-Smith (ed.), *John of Gaunt's Register, 1372–1376*, Camden 3rd series (London: Offices of the Society, 1911), fol. 223b, 1:299–300, no. 1662 (20 January 1375); Lodge and Somerville, *John of Gaunt's Register, 1379–1383*, fol. 33a, 2:99, no. 296 (11 May 1380).

[30] David Lawton, for instance, discusses Chaucer's 'radical change of persona,' in *Chaucer's Narrators* (Cambridge: D. S. Brewer, 1985), 52; Muscatine discusses the narrator's 'realism' and 'intense comic practicality,' in *Chaucer and the French Tradition: A Study in Style and Meaning* (Berkeley: University of California Press, 1957), 103, 105.

[31] See my earlier discussion in chapter 3. On Machaut's poetic personae, see also Brownlee, *Poetic Identity*; Swift, 'The Poetic I'; and Miller, 'Guillaume de Machaut and the Forms of Pre-Humanism in Fourteenth-Century France.' On Jean de Meun, see Cannon's discussion in 'Chaucer's Style,' 237.

instance, the narrator offers to give Morpheus, god of sleep, a feather bed (251). This detail comes directly from Machaut, but Chaucer's narrator takes the offer much further, emphasizing all the accessories that will come with the bed, where the fabrics come from, and how very comfortable it will be. The dream vision is thus brought into the docks and shops of London, where such goods arrived and were sold; the classical god is made into a customer, and the everyday, mercantile world pierces the courtly fantasy of the dream-vision genre.[32] Crucially, this is done through the construction of a narrator who diverges dramatically from the poet and who, at times, functions as a comic and yet truth-telling figure. And the tensions between the aristocratic and the mercantile, the classical and the contemporary, and the ideal and the actual were tensions that animated and produced much of Chaucer's poetry throughout his career. Chaucer's first narrative poem is already 'Chaucerian' in its concerns and in its narrative positioning, but it is operating very much within a tradition and is making fairly conventional moves. In this, it differs utterly from subsequent poems—most notably the *House of Fame*, a poem in which we see the influence of Dante prompting Chaucer to full-blown parody and to an extraordinary meditation on what poetry is, where it comes from, and where it might go next. With the *Book of the Duchess*, Chaucer is taking interesting, but early, steps.

The *Book of the Duchess* meditates on how we can move on from trauma and emotional collapse. The poem depicts a lovelorn, insomniac man who falls asleep reading Ovid's story of Ceyx and Alcyone, a tragic depiction of bereavement. Failing to read the ending—which moves on to transformation and reunification after death—the narrator instead fantasises about the God of Sleep and falls into his dream vision. Moving from a chamber of stained glass, which is painted with the story of Troy and the

---

[32] J. Stephen Russell discusses the 'gross mercantile description,' as a 'parody,' in *The English Dream Vision: Anatomy of a Form* (Columbus: Ohio State University Press, 1988), 162. Muscatine comments that the 'array of bedroom finery . . . would do credit to a mercer's apprentice'; he does not note that the feather bed detail itself is not Chaucer's own, however. He also particularly discusses the awakening of Morpheus, commenting that its 'realism' is 'startling' and adding that '[t]he mind behind the narrative tears so bluntly through the finery of the traditional rendering that we need hardly know the tradition to feel the shock of the passage in its context.' *Chaucer and the French Tradition*, 104–5. For a detailed recent discussion of the bedchamber in the *Book of the Duchess*, see Sarah Stanbury, 'The Place of the Bedchamber in Chaucer's *Book of the Duchess*,' *Studies in the Age of Chaucer* 37 (2015): 133–61.

Roman de la Rose, through a field and forest, he is then led by a whelp into a lush clearing, where a Man in Black laments for his lost love. The rest of the poem comprises a debate between the two men, in which the narrator seems not to understand the Man in Black's extended chess metaphor, nor the reason for his misery. He encourages the Man in Black to talk and talk, remonstrates against his idealizing rhetoric, and advises hope, until he is cut short by the stark 'She ys ded' (1309). The mourner returns to his castle, where the bells are tolling; the dreamer awakes with a book still in his hands.

In the *Book of the Duchess*, the Man in Black is a man destroyed by grief, a man who has become a personification of sorrow—'y am sorwe, and sorwe ys y' (597)—and who is unable to believe in the possibility of consolation. White is dead, and he can find no way of accepting that tragic fact. The landscape, though, reveals that nature thinks differently, as spring inexorably returns and the earth—we are explicitly told—does indeed forget the death that it has suffered. Chaucer's avatar moves into a garden-like space, clearly differentiated from the hunting ground: now he is in a 'floury grene,' full of 'gras, ful softe and swete' and 'floures fele [many],' where the trees are no longer close together but instead stand 'by hymselve' (398, 399, 400, 419). Chaucer describes this idyllic space in detail:

> For both Flora and Zephirus,
> They two that make floures growe,
> Had mad her dwellynge ther, I trowe;
> For hit was, on to beholde,
> As thogh the erthe envye wolde
> To be gayer than the heven,
> To have moo floures, swiche seven,
> As in the welken sterres bee.
> Hyt had *forgete* the povertee
> That wynter, thorgh hys colde morwes,
> Had mad hyt suffre, and his sorwes;
> All was *forgeten*, and that was sene,
> For al the woode was *waxen* grene;
> Swetnesse of dew had mad hyt *waxe*. (402–15; emphasis mine)

The earth does not dwell on the harshness of winter; it ostentatiously forgets (twice repeated within four lines) and puts on a riotous display of fertility. It displays seven times more flowers than there are stars in the sky and everything is growing: 'waxe,' like 'forgete,' is insistently repeated. Such performative, excessive forgetting might not be a desirable human response to death but nor is performative, excessive remembering, the kind of remembering that idealises the lost love-object to such an extent that the griever can never be reconciled with the loss. Time passes, the earth forgets, and people have to forget too—for what is the alternative? It is presented in the figure of the Black Knight, that embodiment of sorrow, darkness, and stasis, a solipsistic, isolated individual, trapped in the language of desire and regret.

The Man in Black takes the aristocratic language of courtly love seriously, just as so many of his Chaucerian successors do—Troilus, Palamon, the eagles in the *Parliament of Fowls*—and his language itself becomes an issue for debate. This is in the tradition of the *pastourelle*, the European poetry that placed the noble lover's courtly voice in dialogue with the demotic voice of a plebian rural lover, who often pretended not to understand his love language.[33] This was a technique that Chaucer was to finesse, expand, and adapt in multiple ways, such that the juxtaposition of contrasting discourses and genres became a signature part of Chaucer's poetics. In the *Book of the Duchess*, the clash is much gentler than is the clash between, for instance, Troilus and Pandarus, or the Knight and the Miller, but it is certainly there. We see it in the narrator's seeming puzzlement over the chess metaphor, for instance, part of his relentless literalism. But we also see it in the two speakers' *attitudes* to love. In lines 1037–53 Chaucer dramatizes the clash between an absolute and a relative perspective:

---

[33] The *pastourelle* flourished in the thirteenth century and was revived in the fourteenth century by, amongst others, Froissart. See James I. Wimsatt, *Chaucer and His French Contemporaries: Natural Music in the Fourteenth Century* (Toronto: University of Toronto Press, 1991), 205. See also John Scattergood, 'The Love Lyric before Chaucer,' in Thomas G. Duncan (ed.), *A Companion to the Middle English Lyric* (Cambridge: D. S. Brewer, 2005), 39–67; Butterfield, *Familiar Enemy*, 93, 387; Rosanna Brusegan, 'Le Jeu de Robin et Marion et l'ambiguïte du symbolism champêtre,' in H. Braet, J. Nowé, and G. Tournoy (eds.), *The Theatre in the Middle Ages* (Leuven: Leuven University Press, 1985), 119–29. For pastourelles in MS Penn 15, see William W. Kibler and James I. Wimsatt (eds.), 'The Development of the Pastourelle in the Fourteenth Century: An Edition of Fifteen Poems with an Analysis,' *Mediaeval Studies* 45 (1983): 22–78.

For certes she was, that swete wif,
My suffisaunce, my lust, my lyf,
Myn hap, myn hele, and al my blesse,
My worldes welfare, and my goddesse,
And I hooly, and everydel.'
'By our lord,' quod I, 'ye trowe yow wel!
Hardely, your love was wel beset;
I not how ye myghte have do bet.'
'Bet? Ne no wyght so wel,' quod he.
'Y trowe hyt wel, sir,' quod I, 'parde!'
'Nay, leve hyt wel!' 'Sir, so do I;
I leve yow wel, that trewely
Yow thoghte, that she was the beste
And to beholde the alderfayreste,
Whoso had loked hir *with your eyen*.'
'With myn? Nay, alle that hir seyen
Seyde and sworen hyt was soo.' (Emphasis mine)

This interaction is sandwiched in the middle of long, hyperbolic mono-
logues by the Man in Black. Three times, the narrator praises White in
language that the Man in Black thinks is lukewarm: the narrator says that
the Black Knight couldn't have done better, that he thinks she was a good
choice, that he understands that the Black Knight thought that she was
the most beautiful woman in the world, and that anyone who had looked
with his eyes would have thought the same. This is the crucial difference
between their perspectives: the Black Knight denies that his opinion is subjective: 'With myn? Nay, alle that hir seyen / Seyde and sworen hyt was soo.'
The debate here keeps circling the same point: what the narrator says is
never enough for the Black Knight, because he insists that White was
indeed the best woman in the world by an objective standard, while the
narrator insists that people see things differently. To the Black Knight—
who is, of course, someone of social and political authority as well as a
lover—his perspective is sovereign, there is no room for debate. By emphasizing the subjectivity of perspective, the narrator challenges not only the
authoritative voice but the very concept of an authoritative voice.

Indeed, the *Book of the Duchess*, and the poems from which it draws its inspiration, are all intensely interested in what it means to be a subject—in all senses of the word. Following in the tradition of the *dits amoureux*, Chaucer's poem explores what it means to write from the first-person perspective, and in the process Chaucer plays with the possibilities, traps, and limitations of that viewpoint. It is well known to Chaucer scholars that this is the first narrative poem in English to begin with 'I'—and that the 'I' is a translation.[34] The opening line ('I have gret wonder, be this lyght' [1]) closely imitates the first line of Froissart's *Paradys d'amour* ('Je sui de moi en grant merveille').[35] And this is only the beginning of a densely interwoven web of intertextuality; the *Book of the Duchess* pays overt homage to many of Chaucer's French and Hainault contemporaries, and the depiction of the Black Knight (the Gaunt figure) should be seen primarily within its poetic, rather than biographical, context. Like all of Chaucer's long poems, this is a poem that is (in part) about poetry and poetic identity.[36] The relationship between poet-narrator and patron in this poem is highly conventional, most obviously imitating Machaut's poetic depictions of his persona interacting with several of his actual patrons— such as John of Luxembourg, king of Bohemia, Charles of Navarre, and Jean, duke of Berry. The *Book of the Duchess* draws extensively on Machaut's poems, especially the *Jugement du Roi de Behaigne* (*Judgement of the King of Bohemia*) and the *Fontaine Amoureuse*. In both of these poems, the narrator is an observer of someone else's grief. The emotional centres of the poems are the poet's social superiors—noblemen (and, to a lesser degree, noble ladies); the poets are supporting characters in their own lives. As the titles suggest, the *Jugement du Roi de Behaigne* and its sequel, the *Jugement du Roi de Navare* (*The Judgement of the King of Navarre*), explicitly place Machaut's real-life patrons in a position of authority and power. And Machaut's poems constantly explore the selfhood of the poet-narrator and its subjection to patronage: in the *Fontaine Amoureuse*, the poet and

---

[34] See Butterfield, *Familiar Enemy*, 272.

[35] Wimsatt, *Chaucer and His French Contemporaries*, 178; Butterfield, *Familiar Enemy*, 293; Arthur W. Bahr, 'The Rhetorical Construction of Narrator and Narrative in Chaucer's the *Book of the Duchess*,' *Chaucer Review* 35:1 (2000): 43–59.

[36] In this, Chaucer imitates his predecessors too; Wimsatt comments that in Machaut's *Fonteine*, 'the characters are obsessed with poetry.' *Chaucer and His French Contemporaries*, 83.

the nobleman dream the same dream; in the *Jugement du Roi de Navare*, the lady and the king ultimately condemn the poet for writing the *Jugement du Roi de Behaigne*; in *Le voir dit*, Machaut presents himself as old, ill, impotent, and ridiculous, in contrast to the stereotypical courtly lovers of the *Jugement* poems or the *Fontaine*.[37]

When Chaucer, then, chooses to write a poem about a social superior (a kind of patron) lamenting the loss of his love, and to present his own persona as an observer, he is doing precisely what one might expect a reader of Machaut to do (although his decision to make his persona so bewildered and funny is not so expected). These choices tell us very little about his own relationship with Gaunt, and a great deal about his bedtime reading. But of course, the *Book of the Duchess* is not simply an imitation of Machaut and Froissart. John of Gaunt and Blanche were real people with real connections to Chaucer, and Chaucer, like Machaut, wanted the favour of influential royal personages. Just because it was conventional to write about oneself as subject to a patron does not mean that poets were not indeed subject to patrons.

Fourteenth-century poets wanted to write about selfhood and relationships. Butterfield terms Machaut's interest in the post-Poitiers collapse of the French princely subject 'almost obsessive,' and adds that Froissart 'pushes the first person mode itself further into the spotlight' through his insistent use of the 'je.'[38] And these poets choose to write about selfhood in specific, socially inflected ways. In Chaucer's *Book of the Duchess*, and Machaut's *Judgement* poems and the *Fontaine*, the poets are not writing about the private emotional life of the narrator, nor about the experiences of their patrons from an assumed detached perspective, but instead are exploring interactions between servant-figure and patron. These poets were much more interested in how identity is constructed through networks of political power, through relationships that were primarily (though not exclusively) male-male, than rather in how identity might be formed through relationships based on sexual intimacy and companionship. The relationships that matter most in these poems are not, in the end, the

---

[37] Butterfield comments on the 'careful, clever double subjectivity' of the *Fontaine*, discussing its focus on the 'fracture and dissolution' of the subject. *Familiar Enemy*, 277.

[38] Ibid., 279–80.

relationship between the nobleman and his lost love but the relationship between the narrator and his social superior. In the *Book of the Duchess* or the *Fontaine Amoureuse*, the absence of the woman makes this focus particularly striking—all the more so in the *Book of the Duchess*, because Blanche is not just absent but dead. The female perspective is missing in this poem: we can only access her through contrasting male perspectives.

The relationship between a client and a patron is a relationship that demands a meditation on subjection and subjectivity. Being an individual in society (unless you are, say, Henry VIII or, to a lesser extent, Richard II) requires impulse control, compromise, thinking before you speak, considering the perspectives and concerns of others as well as yourself, empathy, and strategy. In a relationship with your prince, all of these requirements are hugely heightened. The court poet forever struggles, not only with the classic question of how to speak truth to power but with the issue of how selfhood is split and compromised by politics and power. Selfhood becomes a performed practice in which one is always acting a part, always dissembling, always conscious of the difficulty of trying to influence someone much more powerful than oneself. While it was formerly claimed by some influential early-modern scholars that an awareness of the self as divided and performative came about only in the sixteenth century, scholars such as James Simpson have convincingly argued that 'the theatrical and divided self is not specific to the Renaissance; it is specific to certain kinds of community.' The kind of community to which Simpson points is the court, characterized as 'enclosed,' 'attractive,' and 'threatening.'[39] It encourages an anxiety about the self, a hyperawareness of the need to self-fashion and to perform.

In the *Book of the Duchess*, Chaucer constructs a persona that is ostentatiously inadequate: he can't read very intelligently, is fascinated by material comforts, and seems not to understand what he hears. At the same time, he manages to expose the inadequacy of the rhetoric of courtly love, and to coax his interlocutor into what any post-Freudian reader can see is a textbook analyst's talking cure. The issue is not whether he is

[39] James Simpson, *Oxford English Literary History: Volume 2, 1350–1547; Reform and Cultural Revolution* (Oxford: Oxford University Press, 2004), 246. See also Stephen Greenblatt, *Renaissance Self-Fashioning: From More to Shakespeare* (Chicago: University of Chicago Press, 2005).

'really' very stupid or very clever. Rather, this is a fragmented persona performing different roles, not a consistent character.[40] In Froissart's first
line, he opposes 'je' and 'moi' as *Je* sui de *moi* en grant merveille' (emphasis
mine).[41] In the *Book of the Duchess*, the 'I's' observation of himself is taken
a step further when he steps outside of himself to observe what he is like,
describing himself as a 'mased thyng' (12), just as Skelton, 130 years later,
would step outside himself to describe his own paranoid courtier persona
as a 'mased man' (*Bouge of Court*, 83).[42] This 'mased thyng' in the *Book of
the Duchess* is obsessively described as empty in a series of lines that focus
explicitly on 'nothing' (no-thing), 'defaute' (lack), and falling.[43] And this
is a poem that goes on to portray the idea of 'remade interiors' both
through an externalised fantasy of domestic soft furnishings and through
the macabre depiction of a reanimated corpse.[44] The inside of the self and
its capacity for change is a central theme of the poem, and this depiction of
selfhood is embedded in an awareness that the self can look at itself, perform, split, and dissemble. The *Book of the Duchess* clearly does not represent Chaucer and Gaunt in any simple way. But the tensions surrounding
the very idea of selfhood and subjectivity in the poem illuminate for us the
pressures surrounding subjectivity in a fourteenth-century courtly context, as poets tried to negotiate an awareness of performative selfhood and
the compromising of the self by networks of power.

Chaucer also, like many of his contemporaries, demonstrates the superiority of communication over isolation, open doors over walled enclosures.[45] In the *Book of the Duchess*, the interior of the self is insistently
troped through different kinds of spaces and landscapes, spaces that are

---

[40] A. C. Spearing discusses this as the difference between the narrating and the experiencing 'I,'
emphasizing that there is no 'unitary textual I' in the poem. *Textual Subjectivity: The Encoding of Subjectivity in Medieval Narratives and Lyrics* (Oxford: Oxford University Press, 2005), 155.

[41] While French chroniclers started using 'Je' instead of the third person to begin their chronicles
from around 1300, Froissart seems to be the first person to use 'Je' to start a narrative *dit*. Butterfield,
Familiar Enemy, 275. For further discussion of Froissart's personae, see Philip E. Bennett, 'The Mirage
of Fiction: Narration, Narrator, and Narratee in Froissart's Lyrico-Narrative Dits,' *Modern Language
Review* 86:2 (1991): 285–97.

[42] John Skelton, *The Complete English Works of John Skelton*, ed. John Scattergood, rev. ed. (Liverpool: Liverpool University Press, 2015).

[43] Butterfield, *Familiar Enemy*, 291.

[44] L. O. Aranye Fradenburg, *Sacrifice Your Love: Psychoanalysis, Historicism, Chaucer* (Minneapolis: University of Minnesota Press, 2002), 79–112.

[45] I discuss this at length in chapters 7, 8, and 9.

connected to class and social position as well as to sources of imaginative inspiration.[46] The settings of the poem include a 'real' chamber, a painted dream chamber, a field, a forest, a clearing, and a castle, many more *kinds* of location than we typically see in such poems.[47] In Chaucer's first long narrative poem, he already demonstrates his facility for using places and journeys to represent psychological states and changes. In particular, in the *Book of the Duchess* and the later *House of Fame*, Chaucer sets the stony castle against other, more open, and less iconic structures, depicting enclosure as psychologically oppressive; open spaces, movement, and collaboration as essential for mental and poetic development.[48] But in the *Book of the Duchess*, the journey is stunted and ultimately closed-down, in contrast to the far more expansive and open-ended *House of Fame*.

The *Book of the Duchess* is a poem about enclosing frameworks, be they dreams, narratives, or walls.[49] Both the Black Knight and fair White are insistently connected to impenetrable stony castles. The Black Knight begins as a 'whit wal or a table,' ready to be written on, to be formed through his subjection to the Lady (780). But her death leaves him utterly bereft, unable to function. When he leaves his castle, he is able, briefly, to communicate with a sympathetic servant-figure, but the interaction ultimately breaks down, and the experiences of the poem return him to his walled castle, to mourn alone. This is a return to an enclosed and isolated self, marked with his names and titles, some of which are the legacy of his relationship with White. His identity is represented by the classic

[46] For a more substantial discussion of the spaces of the *Book of the Duchess* and the *House of Fame*, see Marion Turner, 'Chaucer,' in *Oxford Handbooks Online*, ed. James Simpson, http://www.oxford handbooks.com/view/10.1093/oxfordhb/9780199935338.001.0001/oxfordhb-9780199935338-e-58.

[47] In *Pearl*, for instance, the dreamer moves from a garden to a dream garden, from which he can see across a river to a city.

[48] Theorists of metaphor suggest that the metaphor of the self as a container is an intrinsic part of the language that we speak; see George Lakoff and Mark Johnson, *Metaphors We Live By* (Chicago: University of Chicago Press, 1980), 25–32. However, in cultures that place less importance on private, enclosed spaces, different kinds of spaces more appropriately represent selfhood. Lynn Staley, for instance, has recently suggested that the semi-enclosed croft might be a more useful image of medieval life than the aristocratic castle. Lynn Staley, 'Enclosed Spaces,' in B. Cummings and J. Simpson (eds.), *Cultural Reformations: Medieval and Renaissance in Literary History* (Oxford: Oxford University Press, 2010), 113–32. James Simpson has argued that Chaucer's geographical and topographical imagination tends to privilege 'relatively insignificant places' over 'places of powerful cultural resonance.' James Simpson, 'Chaucer as a European Writer,' in Lerer, *The Yale Companion to Chaucer*, 55.

[49] Maud Ellmann, 'Blanche,' in Jeremy Hawthorn (ed.), *Criticism and Critical Theory* (London: Edward Arnold, 1984), 103–4.

fortress or castle, its stones separating him from others. He has not found resolution or community.[50] His description of Blanche also obsessively emphasizes how closed in she is: this stresses her chastity, of course, but also more generally suggests a completed, walled-in self (939–47).[51] The Black Knight makes the explicit comparison to an ivory tower ('a tour of yvoyre', 946)—she is so untouchable that she looks like a smooth ivory surface, a building that cannot be entered, made of hard, impenetrable material. The description links her to the perfectly enclosed Mary, by echoing the Song of Songs ('sicut turris David collum tuum' [Thy neck is as the tower of David], 4:4), and also figures her, again, as a chess piece, carved out of ivory, a beautiful and inhuman object. And, of course, the ending description of the Black Knight again implicates her: the 'long castel' (1318) with white walls reminds us of her first name and her family name, as well as memorializing the land, buildings, and possessions that she represented in life and that she brought to her marriage. In a very real way she, like any late-medieval heiress, represented actual castles and places to her husband. The ending of the poem, with its emphasis on her death, also reminds us that she is herself walled in a tomb: indeed, to be so complete and walled in can only really be accomplished in death. The castle identity is sterile, deadly, unfriendly to collaboration, progress, or inspiration.

The narrator chooses radically different structures to represent himself and his own search for imaginative space. At the beginning of the poem, he is sitting upright in bed in his chamber, unable to sleep, when he asks someone to fetch him a romance. When it is brought, he reads it rather than playing a game of chess or backgammon. The notable aspect of his place of sleep is that it is not wholly private; there is a servant there whom he can ask to bring him a book, and there are people available with whom

[50] As Fradenburg argues, the white wall of his interiority, a 'wall of wonder,' is transformed into an exterior 'defensive wall, a material sign of seigneurial power.' Fradenburg, *Sacrifice Your Love*, 106.

[51] The female body is frequently depicted as an enclosure, as I discuss in chapters 8 and 14. For discussion, see, for instance, Peter Stallybrass, 'Patriarchal Territories: The Body Enclosed,' in Margaret W. Ferguson, Maureen Quilligan, and Nancy Vickers (eds.), *Rewriting the Renaissance: the Discourses of Sexual Difference in Early Modern Europe* (Chicago: University of Chicago Press, 1986), 123–42; Roberta Gilchrist, 'Medieval Bodies in the Material World: Gender, Stigma and the Body,' in Sarah Kay and Miri Rubin (eds.), *Framing Medieval Bodies* (Manchester: Manchester University Press, 1994), 43–61.

he could play a game—there is some potential for connecting with others in this space. When he dreams himself into a dream chamber, he finds himself in the middle of a riot of the senses: the sound of the birds singing is described in great detail, and the narrator tells us that the birds are sitting on the roof of his chamber, on the tiles, singing so that his chamber rings with their song. The windows and walls are painted with the story of Troy and with the *Roman de la Rose*, the most important stories in contemporary poets' heritage. The sun shines through the windows and through these stories to reach the narrator. For all the sound and light, there is also a sense of distance: the windows are all shut and, we are explicitly told, there are no holes at all (324). The sound and the light are being filtered through to the narrator—the room is connected with its surroundings—but the song and sunlight are separated from him by the roof, walls, and windows that are described so materially.[52] He needs to leave the chamber to communicate properly with others. In a passage dense with active verbs, he tells us:

> I was ryght glad, and up anoon
> Took my hors, and forth I wente
> Out of my chambre; I never stente. (356–58)

The first person appears in every line; the emphatic initial 'took' and 'out' along with the rhyming verbs 'wente' and (never) 'stente' stress his movement beyond the chamber. The book-lined chamber has proved insufficient: he needs to go beyond the room, to talk to people as well as to read books, in order to find material for a poem and to develop his imagination. Imaginative and empathetic development takes place outside, in a place of wonder—and the very fact of change, of movement, is productive.

The scene, though, is clearly circumscribed by convention and artifice, ostentatiously denying its imaginative independence and proclaiming its dependence on the books back in the chamber. The outside encounter between poet-client and mourning lover-aristocrat figure was deeply familiar to Chaucer's immediate audience from their knowledge of the

---

[52] See Helen Barr, *Transporting Chaucer* (Manchester: Manchester University Press, 2015), 10–12, for a discussion of this scene as a refraction of the annunciation into a scene of literary transformation; I discuss this in chapter 19.

Jugement du Roi de Behainge and the *Fontaine Amoureuse*. Later, in the *House of Fame*, Chaucer more confidently demonstrated how his poetry was born from a union of books and firsthand knowledge, but we can already see his interest in the authority/experience, reading/living nexus. Here, the narrator offers no interpretation of his experience; rather, he proclaims how unsatisfactory it was—back in his room he declares, 'This was my sweven; now hit ys doon' (1334). The poet-dreamer has not yet found the spaces of inspiration—and we have to wait for the *House of Fame* for a portrayal of the spaces where poetry can be formed with more freedom. The spaces of the mind have allowed only very limited mental change, only a little bit of interaction with other minds. But it is clear that the space where some psychological progress can be made is an open space; medieval poets knew well that collaboration was at the heart of the human as well as the poetic project.[53] Chaucer did not aspire to write alone, and he makes this explicit in the *House of Fame*.[54] And feudal structures tended to bring people together in an unproductive, noncollaborative (because overtly hierarchical) way: the poem constructs the ultimate symbol of feudal power—the castle—as a space hostile to effective communication and interaction. Poets needed to find other spaces for experimentation and inspiration. In Chaucer's subsequent dream poems, he would depict a chaotic garden-based cacophony of birds (in the *Parliament of Fowls*) and the extraordinary wickerwork house (in the *House of Fame*) as poetic spaces that challenged conventional axes of power and allowed multiple poetic voices to flourish. But in the *Book of the Duchess*, he had yet to find an answer to the question of where poetic voices might find a place to experiment.

The poem is filled with anxiety about the oppressive demands placed on a poet operating under patronage, in the shadow of the enclosing gold castles of John of Gaunt's coat of arms. And Chaucer himself moved away from this kind of poetry, and from this kind of client-patron poetic relationship. Only in the Prologue to the *Legend of Good Women* does

[53] Butterfield writes about love poetry as 'a public, international, collective, and openly generative activity.' *Familiar Enemy*, 274.

[54] See chapters 7 and 9. In contrast, Petrarch promoted *otium*—peaceful leisure—as the ideal condition for writing, not in complete isolation but communing only with a select, like-minded group. He wrote two tracts relevant to this idea: *De vita solitaria* and *De otio religiosa*. See chapter 16 for discussion.

Chaucer return to presenting himself as the insecure vassal of a royal patron. The rest of his poems veered dramatically away from the Machaut-inspired scene of a court servant interacting with a noble patron. Instead, poems such as the *Parliament of Fowls*, the *House of Fame*, and the *Canterbury Tales* explode the idea of an authoritative voice by depicting, respectively, a parliament, a chaotic house of tidings, and a dizzying array of pilgrim voices. Many of the concerns of his later poems are already present in the *Book of the Duchess*—mistrust of authority, skepticism about a sovereign voice, cynicism about courtly love, the clash of discourses, the unreliable narrator—but he chose radically different modes and incorporated a new range of sources in order to explore these ideas further and to foreground diverse genres, registers, and voices. There is no evidence that Chaucer wrote his subsequent long poems for Gaunt,[55] or in the hope of Gaunt's reading them, although Gaunt may have appreciated Chaucer as an intellectual and have seen him as part of a cultured group that he maintained.[56]

If we take 'Lancaster' as signifying a kind of poetry, it was a route that Chaucer tried and from which he veered away. If we take 'Lancaster' as signifying sociopolitical influence, however, it overshadowed Chaucer's life until the end, and it decisively shaped the future of his descendants too. His interests became firmly aligned with Gaunt's: in his negotiations in Genoa, and in his subsequent long-held job at the Custom House, Chaucer was representing royal—that is to say, Gaunt's—interests, not the interests of his own birth community, the merchants of the city of London.[57] Just as Gaunt flirted with Wycliffite thought without leaving the orthodox fold, so Chaucer consistently associated with the so-called Lollard knights, men who were attracted by aspects of Wycliffe's beliefs but who maintained devotional lives within the church.[58] Many of Chaucer's friends—men

---

[55] In this I agree with Pearsall's critique of those who have tried 'to prove how every one of Chaucer's writings turns upon some event in [Gaunt's] exciting life.' *Life*, 83. However, Pearsall also downplays the connection between Chaucer and Gaunt more generally. In my view, the evidence does clearly point to Gaunt as Chaucer's most consistent sponsor in other areas of his life. That does not mean that Gaunt and Chaucer were friends, but it is beyond doubt that throughout his life Chaucer gained significant benefits from his connections with the house of Lancaster.

[56] See Lynn Staley, *Languages of Power in the Age of Richard II* (University Park: Pennsylvania State University Press, 2005), 187–88.

[57] See chapters 6 and 7.

[58] For the Lollard knights, see Kenneth Bruce McFarlane, *Lancastrian Kings and Lollard Knights* (Oxford: Clarendon Press, 1972); and Nigel Saul, *Richard II* (New Haven: Yale University Press,

closely associated with him both in administrative documents and in poetic circles, such as Clanvowe and Graunson, for instance—were also connected with Gaunt.[59] Chaucer's life was profoundly bound up with 'Lancaster': his finding favour under Richard II and associating closely with Ricardians did not break the link; Philippa Chaucer's death did not break it; John of Gaunt's death did not break it; Henry Bolingbroke's usurpation of the throne did not break it. This connection was an absolute constant, in some ways *the* absolute constant—for a man who did not have an influential birth-family network of his own, and whose marriage seems to have been a failure or at least to have involved extensive separation.[60] The relationship with these people far above him on the social scale formed and controlled many aspects of Chaucer's life and identity from his teenage years to his grave. For part of the late 1380s and early 1390s, his annuity from Gaunt may well have been his only income; he also received money from Henry, and Henry increased Chaucer's Exchequer allowance when he became king.[61] Chaucer's wife's rooms were decorated with expensive hanaps (elaborate goblets) given to her by John of Gaunt, and Chaucer himself wore clothes given to him by Lancastrian men—such as the fur for a scarlet gown bestowed on him by Henry in 1395.[62] Gaunt also helped Chaucer's children throughout the 1370s, 1380s, and 1390s. He paid very large sums for Chaucer's daughter to reside in two extremely prestigious nunneries (in 1377 and 1381), and retained his son (Thomas): he took him to Spain in 1386, gave him a life annuity in 1389, doubled his annuity in 1394, and arranged a spectacular marriage for him around 1395.[63] Lancaster—Chaucer's 'long castel' (1318)—extended its shadow over Chaucer's whole life and gave him (and especially his son) huge advantages—but Chaucer's poetry slipped away from the constraints of its claustrophobic control.

1997), 293–303. I discuss the Chaucer circle below, especially in chapter 15. For Gaunt's piety, orthodoxy, and relationship with Wycliffe, see Goodman, *John of Gaunt*, 241–71.

[59] For further discussion, see Staley, *Languages of Power*, 188.

[60] See chapter 8.

[61] See chapters 18 and 20.

[62] For the hanaps, see Crow and Olson, *Chaucer Life-Records*, 88–91; for the annuities, see ibid., 271–74 and 525–34; for the fur, see ibid., 275.

[63] See chapters 8 and 18; see also chapter 9 for Lewis Chaucer's Lancastrian connections.

CHAPTER 6

>─┤─◆>─•─O─•─<◆>─┤─≺

Genoa and Florence

It's the economy, stupid.

—Campaign slogan for Bill Clinton

In the famously sensual description of Alison, the adulterous Oxfordshire heroine of the 'Miller's Tale,' Chaucer describes her as 'softer than the wolle is of a wether [sheep]' (3249). At first sight, this is a deeply mundane, domestic image: her flesh is soft and receptive, like the coat of an animal known for its softness—and its stupidity. She is also compared to other animals—a kid, a calf, a weasel—and in the course of the magisterial 'effictio' (a traditional head-to-toes description, although this version suggestively circles around Alison's middle), we hear not only about how it feels to touch her but about how she tastes, sounds, smells, and looks. The description though, as well as objectifying and animalizing Alison, also likens her to the most important trading product of fourteenth-century England: wool. And, incidentally, Cotswold wool (from Oxfordshire and Gloucestershire) was the softest wool, and had taken over from wool from the north and east as the most desired wool—necessitating an increased focus on southern ports (such as Southampton) rather than eastern ones. This soft wool was the foundation of England's wealth, and it was woven through the centre of Chaucer's life. Genoese interest in England was based on the wool trade. To understand Chaucer's visit to Genoa, we have to try to grasp something of world economics in the fourteenth century: how the Crusades, the slave trade, ship design, European politics, and the desirable products of the Middle East and beyond all affected the trading systems that crisscrossed the world. But we also have to understand how the world system affected and was affected by English sheep.[1] The English wool trade was a cog in a series of interlocking wheels, and Chaucer was increasingly involved in this complicated system in the 1370s. His trip to Genoa, like his subsequent job in the London Custom House, was all about wool.

Chaucer went to Genoa in late 1372 and early 1373. The Exchequer accounts run from 1 December 1372 to 23 May 1373, covering travel to Genoa, on to Florence, and back to England again.[2] The commission to Chaucer, termed a king's esquire, authorized him to negotiate with the Genoese about the appointment of a seaport for the use of Genoese merchants, that they: 'habere possint (inhabitacionem) [in] aliquo loco seu villa aliquia super costeram maris in regno Anglie pro applicacione taritarum et navium dicte civitatis cum bonis et mercandisis'[3] (could have a place in some location or some town on the coast of the sea in England for putting in the tarits and ships of the said people with goods and merchandise). He travelled with Genoese companions: John de Mari, Sir James (Jacobi) Provan, and two Genoese crossbowmen. Chaucer's position in the royal household, his family connection with Gaunt, and his long knowledge of trading matters all made him a suitable diplomat for this mission, but it is probable that his knowledge of Italian made him particularly useful. His mission may sound straightforward enough—to discuss Genoese trading possibilities in England, a relationship that one would imagine could easily be mutually beneficial. But behind the neutral-sounding life-record swirled chaotic and competing currents; Chaucer's mission was a highly controversial one and pitted him against the interests of his parents' associates and his own future associates in London. It involved him in political conflicts that escalated to the confrontations of the Good Parliament and led to notorious murders in London later in the decade. To understand what happened, we need to approach the journey from multiple directions—Genoa, London stapler interests, and the English court.

---

[1] Alwyn Ruddock writes that from the thirteenth century, 'the demand for English wool in Italy was almost insatiable.' *Italian Merchants and Shipping in Southampton* (Southampton: University College, 1951), 15.

[2] Crow and Olson, *Chaucer Life-Records*, 34–37.

[3] Ibid., 33; translation mine.

In earlier centuries, Genoa had partly been sustained through conflict and then cooperation with emerging Islamic states. Muslim raiders had pillaged Genoa in 935, but in the eleventh century, the Genoese and the Pisans launched a successful raid on Mahdia in Tunisia, using the profits to build the cathedral in Pisa and the church of San Sisto in Genoa.[4] The Crusades then gave rise to a 'frenzy of shipbuilding,'[5] which left Genoa and Venice as great naval powers, middlemen between Western Europe and Eastern Europe, Asia, the Middle East, and Africa. In the 1260s, Genoa made a treaty with the Greeks, gaining trading advantages in both Constantinople and, crucially, Caffa on the Black Sea.[6] This was the decade in which Genoa constructed its magnificent harbor mole, as the city began to approach the height of its power.[7] Ever evenhanded in its willingness to sell to whomever could buy, Genoa now took to supplying Tartar slaves from the slave markets of the Crimea to the Egyptian mamluks, to fight on the Muslim side against Christian Crusader strongholds.[8]

It had been difficult for Genoa to establish regular trading relationships with the important centres of Bruges and Flanders while Muslims had control of the straits of Gibraltar, but by the end of the thirteenth century, a Castilian-Genoese fleet had defeated the Muslim forces, allowing Genoa to develop its trade with Northern Europe.[9] This was important for Genoa because English wool and Flemish cloth made from that wool were extremely desirable products. In 1287 in England, twenty-two sacks of wool were put into a Genoese galley. In these last decades of the thirteenth century, Italian companies displaced Flemish traders as the major exporters of English wool; these Italian companies were principally Florentine and Luccan. They mainly traded from the north and east of England, from ports such as Boston and Hull.[10] English merchants,

[4] Trevor Dean (trans.), *The Towns of Italy in the Later Middle Ages* (Manchester: Manchester University Press, 2000), 4.

[5] Abu-Lughod, *Before European Hegemony*, 111.

[6] Steven A. Epstein, *Genoa and the Genoese, 958–1528* (Chapel Hill: University of North Carolina Press, 1996), 150.

[7] Ibid., 148.

[8] Abu-Lughod, *Before European Hegemony*, 244, 274.

[9] Ibid., 122.

[10] T. H. Lloyd, *The English Wool-Trade in the Middle Ages* (Cambridge: Cambridge University Press, 1977), 71–72; Wallace, *Premodern Places*, 95.

however, were starting to organize themselves more effectively and to see how much they were giving up to foreign middlemen. In 1313, the idea of a staple was established: staple towns were towns through which wool for export had to pass. Initially, these towns were abroad, in Flanders, Artois, and Brabant, and the rule applied only to wool going to these countries (to supply the flourishing cloth trade).[11] Later, in 1326, English staple towns were established, and only English merchants could buy wool outside these towns; alien merchants then bought wool in the staple towns and paid customs dues there.[12] The staple was a complicated and changing idea, but its origins certainly lay in giving English merchants more power over the wool trade. As the fourteenth century progressed, the story of the wool trade became very much about English stapler interests pitted against the interests of aliens, who were often allied with the king. A vignette that we see repeated in slightly different ways across the century goes like this: on 9 May 1317, Edward II wrote to the mayor and bailiffs of Great Yarmouth about a Genoese complaint. Antonio di Negro complained that someone stole his ship, *La Mariotte of Amela*, and its cargo. After an investigation, the jurors responded that they had discovered that the ship was captured by some evildoers from Scotland, and they did not know their names or where it was taken.[13] This is, in essence, the story of Janus Imperial, which played out in 1379 and the years immediately following: a Genoese diplomat-merchant was openly murdered in London, and while the royal interest pressed for results, London juries obstinately refused to make headway, stonewalling repeatedly with bland statements about accident and self-defence.[14]

The Genoese, then, were extending their interest in Northern Europe in the fourteenth century, although the heart of their power still lay in the East, in Pera (their trading base at Constantinople), and in Caffa, in the Crimea. Caffa was a truly international place, packed with people of

[11] On the important role of Flanders across the period, see especially Wallace, *Premodern Places*, 91–138.

[12] Robert L. Baker, 'The Establishment of the English Wool Staple in 1313,' *Speculum* 31:3 (1956): 444–53.

[13] Robert S. Lopez and Irving W. Raymond (eds.), *Medieval Trade in the Mediterranean World: Illustrative Documents* (New York: W. W. Norton, 1967), 322.

[14] Paul Strohm, *Theory and the Premodern Text* (Minneapolis: University of Minnesota Press, 2000), 112–31.

diverse nationalities and religions and trading products, including Grecian wine, Ligurian figs, linen from Champagne, silk from China, carpets from Samark, fur from the Urals, and Indian spices.[15] The bases around the Black Sea formed the western end of the Silk Road and Caffa was also an entrepôt for grain from Bulgaria and the Danube plain. Most notoriously, it was also a centre for the slave trade.[16] In the fourteenth century, Genoa underwent a number of crises—the emergence of Catalonia as a major naval power, political problems within the city, a commercial recession[17]—but the most notorious one allegedly came from Caffa: the Black Death. The Genoese Gabriele de'Mussi gave an account of what happened. In 1346, a Tartar army was besieging Caffa when it was struck by a terrible disease. The sick survivors lost interest in fighting, but they:

> ordered corpses to be placed in catapults and lobbed into the city in the hope that the intolerable stench would kill everyone inside . . . And soon the rotting corpses tainted the air and poisoned the water supply, and the stench was so overwhelming that hardly one in several thousand was in a position to flee the remains of the Tartar army. Moreover one infected man could carry the poison to others, and infect people and places with the disease by look alone . . . As it happened, among those who escaped from Caffa by boat were a few sailors who had been infected with the poisonous disease. Some boats were bound for Genoa, others went to Venice and to other Christian areas. When the sailors reached these places and mixed with the people there, it was as if they had brought evil spirits with them: every city, every settlement, every place was poisoned by the contagious pestilence.[18]

It may well not be true that the plague reached Europe because of the Tartars' deployment of biological warfare,[19] although Genoese ships were

[15] Iris Origo, 'The Domestic Enemy: The Eastern Slaves in Tuscany in the Fourteenth and Fifteenth Centuries,' *Speculum* 30 (1955): 321–66.

[16] Dennis Deletant, 'Genoese, Tatars, and Rumanians at the Mouth of the Danube in the Fourteenth Century,' *Slavonic and East European Review* 62:4 (1984): 511–30.

[17] David Abulafia, 'Genoa and the Security of the Seas: The Mission of Babilano Lomellino in 1350,' *Papers of the British School at Rome* 45 (1977): 272.

[18] Horrox, *The Black Death*, 17–19.

[19] Mark Wheelis, 'Biological Warfare at the 1346 Siege of Caffa,' *Emerging Infectious Diseases* 8:9 (2002): 971–75.

probably partly culpable for bringing the plague-infested rats to European ports. But the story bears witness to fears about cultural exchange and trade. The dead, infectious Tartar bodies took a symbolic place in markets within Caffa, which usually displayed live, healthy Tartar bodies, ripe for forced military or sexual service.

The Genoese and their restless, acquisitive trading ways were blamed for the plague, as they were blamed for all kinds of things, characterized as scattered, avaricious, and Jew-like by numerous medieval writers.[20] The plague also had disastrous effects on their population and their manpower—and therefore, it hugely increased the market for slaves. While England dealt with the fallout from the Statute of Labourers as its response to the labour shortage after the plague, Italy made use of slaves, relatively easily available via Caffa, from where the plague itself had come. In 1363, a decree in Florence, for instance, permitted the unlimited import of slaves, as long as they were not Christian.[21] When Petrarch describes the Tartar slaves at Venice in 1367, he writes: 'a strange, enormous crowd of slaves of both sexes, like a muddy torrent tainting a limpid stream, taints this beautiful city with Scythian faces and hideous filth.'[22] The language of the plague haunts the description: the foreign slaves are viewed with suspicion, not pity, with visceral disgust, not self-examination. Indeed, in a neat demonstration of the fact that contemporaries saw no problem with being both Christian humanists and slave owners, a slave bought in Genoa was partially paid for with Seneca's *Moral Letters to Lucilius* and an Office of Our Lady.[23]

Genoa was going through various problems in the third quarter of the fourteenth century as it struggled with the aftermath of the plague. It was warring with Venice in the 1350s; it briefly accepted overlords from elsewhere in Italy (the Lombard Visconti family) and then threw them out in

---

[20] Wallace, *Premodern Places*, 182, 184.

[21] Origo, 'Domestic Enemy,' 324.

[22] 'insolita et inextimabilis turba servorum utriusque sexus hanc pulcerrimam urbem scithicis vultibus et informi colluvie, velut amnem nitidissimum torrens turbidus inficit.' Francesco Petrarch, *Prose*, ed. Guido Martellotti (Milan: Ricciardi, 1955), 1118, quoted and discussed in Wallace, *Premodern Places*, 191.

[23] Wallace, *Premodern Places*, 190.

favour of returning to a doge as the ruler (1367); there were ongoing rivalries between different groups within the city. A law was passed prohibiting anyone from shouting for or against the Guelfs or the Ghibellines (broadly speaking these were the pro-papal and pro-imperial groups). The plague returned in 1361, and a plague of locusts hit in 1365. In 1370, a Ghibelline doge, Domenico Campofregoso, was elected, in alliance with a Guelf.[24] In retrospect, we know that Genoa was beginning to decline in power, but at the time it was not evident that the downturn would be permanent. Instead, Genoa was seeking to expand in particular areas—and in the 1370s, the Genoese had their eyes firmly fixed on England and its fabulous sacks of wool. In these years, the Genoese became the most prominent group of Italians in England,[25] and they were able to make major inroads into the wool market because of the dubious antics of the people surrounding the increasingly incapable Edward III.

In the second half of the fourteenth century, the Calais staple was the most important economic issue in London and in the court. The Calais staple was set up in 1363: this meant that all wool exported from England had to go via Calais.[26] The government of the town was placed in the hands of a company of twenty-six English merchants—the merchants of the staple—who had control over the wool trade, and were able to fix prices and impose duties.[27] Almost immediately, this system ran into problems, and in 1365 separate provision was made for the government of the town and the staple.[28] Edward III also started to sell some licences that allowed Italians to ship wool directly to Italy. In 1369, the staple was abolished and English merchants were banned from exporting wool, but these decisions were reversed in 1370.[29] Around the same time, against a backdrop of renewed war with France, the return of the plague, and rising prices, Nicholas Sardouche, an Italian merchant accused of corruption, was pardoned by

[24] Epstein, *Genoa*, 220–27.

[25] Ruddock, *Italian Merchants*, 40.

[26] Lloyd, *English Wool Trade*, 211.

[27] Christian Drummond Liddy, *War, Politics and Finance in Late Medieval English Towns: Bristol, York and the Crown, 1350–1400* (Woodbridge: Boydell Press, 2005), 130. Liddy helpfully summarises the debate between Unwin and Lloyd about whether or not the company had a monopoly.

[28] Liddy, *War, Politics, and Finance*, 131.

[29] Lloyd, *English Wool Trade*, 215–17.

the Crown (1369) and then murdered in London (1370).[30] In mid-December 1371, the Crown started selling licences to merchants to evade the staple and, despite loud protests from the English stapler merchants, this practice continued and became a major source of complaint in the Good Parliament of 1376.[31] Overall, while the staple was being enforced, aliens accounted for about a quarter of wool exports; from 1372 to 1375, the figure is around 40 per cent.[32] In Southampton (a better port for Genoans than London, because their boats, tarits, fared better in deep water ports), in 1362–68, aliens exported about 211 sacks each year. In almost twenty-two months between 1369 and 1371, they exported 1056.5 sacks. From March 1371 to March 1372, they exported 1857 sacks of wool.[33] So, as the 1370s commenced, aliens were strengthening their position in the English wool trade, to the detriment of English merchants.

Why was this happening—and what were its effects? By selling licences direct to Italian merchants, the Crown directly received the higher duties. The Crown also developed relationships with these merchants that could be useful for negotiating loans and in diplomacy.[34] For English stapler merchants, this was disastrous, as the staple lost its duties and its control. Furthermore, if Italian merchants were coming to Southampton, for instance, rather than Calais, they were selling the products that they brought with them directly within England rather than using London middlemen. Many of the products that they brought with them pertained to the cloth trade, a rapidly growing industry in England. If they sold to provincial clothiers themselves, rather than via London merchants, then the merchants lost out on their cut. While the Genoese had been sailing to Continental hubs to buy their wool, English traders bought commodities such as spices, woad, soap, alum, olive oil, iron, and almonds in Flanders or France—and then sold these things at a profit back in England. Furthermore, if the Genoese were bringing these products not to London, but to Southampton, then many provincial buyers would go to Southampton

---

[30] Pamela Nightingale, *A Medieval Mercantile Community: The Grocers' Company and the Politics and Trade of London, 1000–1485* (New Haven: Yale University Press, 1995), 233.

[31] Lloyd, *English Wool Trade*, 218–20.

[32] Ibid., 222.

[33] Ruddock, *Italian Merchants*, 43.

[34] Nightingale, *Medieval Mercantile Community*, 226.

to buy them, bypassing London altogether.[35] All Londoners were potentially the losers in this situation.

An added complication at this time was that there was a great deal of suspicion and resentment about who exactly was profiting from these licences, and about who was acting in the name of the Crown. Edward, now in his late fifties, suffered some kind of health crisis in August 1371, and for the last years of his life (he died in 1377), his health was in decline.[36] His eldest son, the Black Prince, who died the year before his father, had been ill since the Spanish campaign of 1367. In his biography of Edward III, Mark Ormrod writes that in these years: 'the court and council of Edward III, once famed for their openness and accessibility, came to be seen as closed shops, dominated by the influence and ambition of the few.'[37] Alice Perrers, the king's mistress, was one of the most notorious of the inner circle. Richard Lyons, London financier, was another target of mistrust. Many of the officials at the heart of the court came from a Lancastrian background: John, Lord Neville, a retainer of Gaunt's, was steward of the household from 1371 to 1376; Lord Latimer, Neville's father-in-law, was chamberlain; Richard le Scrope, another Lancastrian retainer, was treasurer from 1371 to 1375; and Sir John Ypres, controller of the royal household from 1368 to 1376, was also a Lancastrian retainer.[38] Those in powerful positions were certainly not acting as one unified group—on the contrary, they were often at odds with one another, and many were motivated by personal profit.[39] But several did share a connection with Gaunt. Indeed, Gaunt returned to England with his second wife, Constance, on 4 November 1371, and was mainly in England for the next couple of years—and during this time, he was the effective leader of domestic government.[40]

A few years later, the behaviour of Crown officials during the early and mid-1370s came under sharp (and of course biased) scrutiny in the Good Parliament of 1376 (a parliament alluded to by Langland in beast-fable

---

[35] Ibid., 235.
[36] Ormrod, *Edward III*, 529–30.
[37] Ibid., 533.
[38] Goodman, *John of Gaunt*, 55.
[39] Ormrod, *Edward III*, 536.
[40] Goodman, *John of Gaunt*, 48; Ormrod, *Edward III*, 529.

form in *Piers Plowman*). The first specific point that the Commons made was that:

> Whereas the staple of wool and of other merchandises of the staple and bullion were formerly ordained in parliament to be at Calais and nowhere else overseas, for the great profit of the king and the realm and for the strengthening and improving of the said town of Calais through the coming and continual residence of merchants there; the same staple and bullion since have been, and still are, in great part withdrawn and almost completely ruined, at the procurement and counsel of the king's said intimates and of others of their faction for their singular profit, to the great prejudice and damage of the king and his realm and in destruction of the aforesaid town of Calais.[41]

The detailed accusations against the king's intimates again prioritise the undermining of the staple. The first accusation against Richard Lyons is as follows:

> And especially because the said Richard, by agreement made between him and some of our lord the king's privy council, in order to have their singular profit and advantage thereon, has procured many letters patent and writs of licence to be made, to carry a great quantity of wool, woolfells, and other merchandises elsewhere overseas than to the staple of Calais.[42]

From the perspective of the Commons, those close to the king were selling licences and pocketing the vast proceeds, while the Calais staple, the Crown coffers, and the interests of London generally were all neglected.

In the early 1370s, then, those around the king were profiteering by negotiating with Italian merchants to allow them to ship wool direct, evading Calais and its duties, to the fury of many Londoners. Stapler merchants such as William Walworth and Nicholas Brembre (who would later become staunch supporters of Richard II) were firmly set against this cabal. Indeed, another accusation made by the Good Parliament was that Lyons and Latimer had refused to allow the Crown to accept an interest-free loan from Walworth and the other staplers, with the only condition being the

---

[41] PROME, Membrane 2, no. 16, 5:300 (April 1376).
[42] PROME, Membrane 3, no. 17, 5:300 (April 1376).

enforcement of the staple, instead themselves making a loan to the Crown at 50 per cent interest.[43] The stapler merchants, and indeed many other London traders, were profoundly anxious about and resentful towards Crown policy, Gaunt, Italian moneymen, and those London merchants such as Lyons who were working against stapler interests. Despite the unrest and dissatisfaction with Crown policy towards the Italians in the early 1370s, the Crown pressed ahead with a treaty with Genoa. This peace treaty, made in February 1371, renewed a treaty of 1347. A few days later, a writ directed to the sheriffs of London forbad the molestation of Genoese merchants.[44] On 17 September 1372, treaties for freedom of commerce between England and Genoa were confirmed.[45] The year 1372 had been significant in Gaunt's life: this was almost certainly the year that he began his affair with Katherine Swynford, a relationship that would last until his death. It is impossible to know exactly when their relationship became sexual, but 1372 saw a marked increase in Katherine's status and rewards, and their eldest son was probably born in 1373 or perhaps even 1372.[46] In that year, Chaucer's wife, Philippa (Katherine's sister), was serving Constance, Gaunt's wife, and was given a payment by Gaunt in August.[47] In all likelihood Constance, Gaunt's children, Katherine, Philippa, and the de Roet sisters' own children were all living together as one fluid household in Hertford and Tutbury castles.[48] Geoffrey and Philippa had at least two children by this point—Thomas and Elizabeth—who were probably being brought up around the Lancastrian nurseries, as discussed in chapter 5. At the end of this year, Chaucer was sent on his mission to Genoa, in the service of the Crown. His interests were now very specifically

---

[43] 'At the time when the said loan of the said 20,000 marks was made to the king, the said William Walworth, in the name of himself and of his companion merchants of the said staple of Calais, offered the said Lord Latimer to make a loan of £10,000 to our said lord the king, without taking any interest by usury or otherwise; by such agreement that they could be repaid the said £10,000 into their own hands from the subsidies due to the king from their wool etc. then next to cross to Calais; and also by agreement that the king would grant them that no such licences would be granted thereafter to carry wool etc. elsewhere than to the staple of Calais.' PROME, Membrane 4, no. 27, 5:305 (April 1376).

[44] Crow and Olson, *Chaucer Life-Records*, 39n3.

[45] Ibid., 39. National Archives, E 30/273.

[46] Armitage-Smith, *John of Gaunt's Register, 1372–1376*, 1:169–70, nos. 409–10 (15–16 May 1372); 1:182–83, no. 446 (20 June 1372); 2:56, no. 988 (1 May 1372).

[47] Crow and Olson, *Chaucer Life-Records*, 85–87.

[48] Ibid.

tied up in the Crown and Gaunt, rather than in the mercantile city of London, where his origins lay.

It should now be clear that the idea of providing the Genoese with a fixed property on the coast of England that they could use as a trading centre was not a straightforward mission. The context of the violent disputes in England at this time about the evasion of the staple make it clear that this was a highly controversial scheme, one that would be anathema to the staplers of London. At this point in his life—shortly after he had been serving with Gaunt overseas, when his sister-in-law was bearing Gaunt's children and his wife working for Gaunt's wife, and when he himself had recently written an elegy for Gaunt's first duchess—Chaucer was certainly acting for Gaunt. The mission—Chaucer's first visit to Italy as far as we know—took him to a sophisticated, cosmopolitan city. Chaucer was no provincial; he had always lived in luxurious environments and was used to seeing sumptuous display; he had also travelled to other fairly exotic locales, such as Navarre. Genoa, nonetheless, was something different: a city packed with produce from the Middle East and beyond, whose citizens tended to spend heavily on clothing, jewellery, food, and drink, enjoying a high standard of living. Even fairly ordinary people were used to products such as spices, cotton shirts, and raisins, and many people were extremely widely travelled.[49] A description from earlier in the fourteenth century describes Genoa's commerce lavishly:

> There is always a great abundance of merchandise from the Levant, overseas, and all other places. Who could list all the types of precious brocades, sendals, velvets, cloth of gold, feathers, ermine, squirrel, and other furs? Who could list all the goods that are brought there, the pepper, ginger and musk, the spices large and small . . . the pearls and precious stones and marvelous jewels.[50]

Just as its products came from all over the world, the physical description of the city emphasizes its maritime character—it is on the sea, dominated by the port, and by the mole built into the harbor.[51] The art in the city

[49] Epstein, *Genoa*, 161.
[50] Dean, *Towns of Italy*, 22.
[51] Ibid., 21–22.

also bore witness to Genoa's liminal position: the frescos at the Duomo in Genoa are attributed to a Byzantine painter of the early fourteenth century, and although the style is largely Byzantine, the content is Tuscan.[52] The slave markets demonstrated in a very different way Genoa's role as a pivot—transporting human flesh from east to west and south. While Chaucer was used to markets and exotic commerce, he was not used to slaves, nor to the ubiquity that luxury products had here. Genoa was a sensual and brutal place where everything—even humans—could be openly bought and sold. It was also a city-state, now ruled by an elected doge.

Chaucer was in Genoa during an international political crisis. Peter I of Cyprus had been murdered in 1369, a death that was to become one of the 'modern examples' in Chaucer's 'Monk's Tale,' alongside the death of Peter of Castile (Pedro the Cruel), killed in the same year. And Peter of Cyprus had visited London back in 1363 and subsequently became renowned/notorious for the capture of Alexandria, one of the campaigns highlighted in Chaucer's description of his Knight.[53] Peter's son, Peter II, was a child when his father was killed, and was not crowned until 1372. In January that year he was crowned as king of Cyprus, and in October as king of Jerusalem. It was at this coronation that Genoese representatives fought with their maritime rivals, the Venetians, over precedence, ultimately sparking off a conflict between Genoa and Cyprus. By March 1373, Genoa sent seven galleys to raid Cyprus, following this with a larger force later that year. The Genoese ended up winning huge concessions from Cyprus and dramatically improving their position in this lynchpin location. While Chaucer was there in early 1373, then, Genoa was embroiled in this conflict as it established itself as the colonial overlord of Cyprus.

Chaucer travelled on to Florence. His expense documents refer to the trip as a journey 'vers les parties de Jeene et de Florence' (to parts of Genoa and Florence) 'in servicio regis' (in the service of the king) and 'in negociis regis' (on the business of the king).[54] His companion, Jacob Provan, had been in Florence just over a year earlier (18 December 1371), to negotiate an

[52] Robert S. Nelson, 'A Byzantine Painter in Trecento Genoa: The *Last Judgment* at S. Lorenzo,' *Art Bulletin* 67 (1985): 548–66.
[53] Ormrod, *Edward III*, 452–53. 'General Prologue,' 51.
[54] Crow and Olson, *Chaucer Life-Records*, 34–35.

agreement with two Florentines to provide shipping vessels for Edward III.[55] The Florentine Bardi family, who had long been the most important providers of loans to Edward, had lent the king the vast sum of ten thousand nobles just a few months before Chaucer's visit (16 August 1372).[56] So, although we do not know exactly what Chaucer was doing in Florence, Edward had his fingers in more than one Florentine pie at this particular historical moment. Chaucer's mission was almost certainly financial and involved negotiating with the wealthy merchant companies of the city— companies that were also fundamentally connected with the extraordinary artistic revolution that had taken place in the city earlier in the century. Chaucer arrived in Florence at a time of Dante fever, when members of 'literary, civic, and mercantile circles' were likely talking about their new plan to honour their great vernacular poet.[57] Shortly after he left the city, in June 1373, the citizens of Florence presented a petition, which was approved by the Council of the Commune on 13 August, asking Boccaccio to give lectures on Dante. The ageing poet gave the first lecture on 23 October.[58] While there is no evidence that Boccaccio and Chaucer met, Chaucer may at this point have encountered some of his poetry, as well as that of Dante. Florence in the mid-late fourteenth century claimed Boccaccio as their cultural spokesman, and he, in turn, eulogized twin artistic masters from earlier in the century, one a painter, the other a poet: Giotto and Dante. In the *Amorosa Visione*, a poem very close to the *House of Fame* in a number of ways, Boccaccio 'extolled the work of Giotto, the absolute master of realism . . . and raised the figure of Dante to a height above any other artist, ancient or modern.'[59]

Throughout his poetic career Chaucer demonstrated an intense interest in the individual perception of reality. He prioritized not an 'objective' or divine viewpoint but a viewpoint conditioned by the physical position and preconceptions of the viewing subject. For instance, in the *House of Fame*, the narrator obsessively repeats 'I saugh,' reminding us that what

---

[55] National Archives, E 30/264.

[56] *Calendar of the Patent Rolls: Edward III*, Membrane 24, 15:196–97 (16 August 1372).

[57] David Wallace, *Chaucer and the Early Writings of Boccaccio* (Woodbridge: D. S. Brewer, 1985), 5.

[58] Vittore Branca, *Boccaccio: The Man and His Works*, trans. Richard Monges (New York: Harvester Press, 1976), 182.

[59] Ibid., 63.

we, the readers, 'see' is filtered through his interpretative lens.[60] The very pictures that he sees are also presented as biased interpretations, telling the story of Aeneas and Dido first from the perspective of Aeneas/Virgil, then of Dido/Ovid. The subjectivity of actual and metaphorical vision had been of interest to earlier French poets such as Jean de Meun, who wrote about optics and the distorting effects of mirrors in the *Roman de la Rose*; French poets such as Machaut and Froissart were also concerned with the idea of the partiality of perspective.[61] Trecento artists had found new and stunning ways of engaging with the subjectivity of perspective: they 'enabled, for the first time, the individual viewer's empirical experience of reality to be acknowledged and made part of the description of religious truths in pictures.'[62] In the first half of the fourteenth century, Giotto had focused on producing a more realistic imitation of nature through creating an illusion of three-dimensional space and modeling more plastic and rounded figures.[63] His works of art do not aim to show a scene in its entirety, but assume a particular viewpoint, from which particular objects can be glimpsed; bodies and structures are shown in part and, by implication, spill over the edges of the frame.[64] Giotto even used the space of the setting so that the viewer needed to stand in a certain position to achieve the ideal viewpoint of the work of art.[65] His interest in depicting perspective as partial, and space as realistic, contrasted dramatically with traditional 'flat' art, with its focus on the symbolic. Dante stands at the boundary between these two ways of perceiving reality: the *Divine Comedy* depicts the different spheres of the afterlife in clearly separated, hierarchical and fixed positions, above and below each other, and in his persona's

---

[60] The use of 'I saugh' is particularly discussed by Marilynn Desmond, *Reading Dido: Gender, Textuality, and the Medieval 'Aeneid'* (Minneapolis: University of Minnesota Press, 1994), 131–35.

[61] Guillaume de Lorris and Jean de Meun, *Le Roman de la Rose*, ed. Armand Strubel (Paris: Librarie General Francaise, 1992), 18173–286. For a discussion of Machaut and Froissart's 'debate about subjectivity,' see Butterfield, *Familiar Enemy*, 276–282, quote at 282.

[62] Michael Hagiioannu, 'Giotto's Bardi Chapel Frescoes and Chaucer's *House of Fame*: Influence, Evidence, and Interpretations,' *Chaucer Review* 36:1 (2001): 30.

[63] See, for instance, Lauro Martines, *Power and Imagination: City-States in Renaissance Italy* (Baltimore: Johns Hopkins University Press, 1988), 249.

[64] See, for instance, Trachtenberg, *Dominion of the Eye*. Trachtenberg discusses Giotto's *Apparition at Arles*, in the Bardi Chapel of Santa Croce, on pp. 179–80, describing its 'precision of visual location' and its 'virtual viewpoint slightly to the left of centre.'

[65] Ibid., 180.

moment of transcendent understanding in the *Paradiso (33)*, we see that there is an objective truth. But the poem is filtered through a personal and incomplete viewpoint by someone who is himself learning and confused.[66]

The innovations of Giotto were fundamentally rooted in politics and economics. The rise of the *popolo*—the middle and lower classes as opposed to the aristocratic feudal elite—had changed the social and political structures of late-medieval Italian city-states. Art historians have argued that as the *popolo* gained representation and triumphed over the idea of feudal social fixity, so they transformed the way people perceived the world. Lauro Martines writes that Giotto's art would not have been possible without the rise of these classes, and that his style 'served the outlook and psychic needs of a triumphant popolo,' as in his work, their way of seeing the world 'finds its expression in style.'[67] Indeed, in the context of intellectual history more generally, Joel Kaye has shown how the development of 'the monetized urban marketplace of the thirteenth and fourteenth centuries,' enabled 'perceptual shifts,' including 'relativistic determinations, probabilistic reasoning, the focus on motion and change rather than essences and perfections.' Exploring the connection between the flourishing of self-regulating economic systems and the expression of a more relativistic view of the world by scientists and artists alike is fundamental to Kaye's work. His analysis of a 1317 manuscript of *La vie de Saint Denys*, for instance, reveals two different layers of visual narrative: the one timeless, eternal, and hierarchical, the other contemporary, self-organising, and freighted with 'relativized meaning.' The link between urban, mercantile activity and an intellectualized understanding and artistic depiction of relativity lies at the heart of Kaye's analysis: 'relativity replaces hierarchy as the basis of order and identity.'[68]

Economic change *directly* affected artistic production too: Giotto and his followers were patronized extensively by the merchants and banking families of Florence and elsewhere. In the great Florentine church of Santa

[66]Charles Muscatine, 'Locus of Action in Medieval Narrative,' *Romance Philology* 17:1 (1963): 118–19.

[67]Martines, *Power and Imagination*, 46–58; quotes at 333 and 249.

[68]Quotes in this paragraph are from Kaye, *History of Balance*, and appear on 14, 277, and 7, respectively. For his discussion of *La vie de Saint Denys*, see 267–82.

Croce, Giotto frescoed both the Bardi Chapel and the adjacent Peruzzi Chapel (plate 6). These were two of the most important Italian merchant-banking families; both appear frequently as creditors of Edward III. Nearby, Giotto's pupil Taddeo frescoed the chapel of the banking Baroncelli family. The Bardi—with whom Chaucer was likely negotiating in 1373—also had particular connections with Boccaccio. His family had been their agents and fattori (bailiff-farmers) and Boccaccio had worked in the Bardi bank.[69]

Given Chaucer's interest in culture, the compact nature of Florence, the centrality of worship to everyday life, and the close relationship between the Bardi family and Santa Croce, the overwhelming likelihood is that Chaucer saw the art of Giotto and consciously experienced the artistic revolution that had taken place. Santa Croce was the Bardi family's favourite church.[70] There, Chaucer could see extraordinary experiments with the depiction of space, light, and movement. Most dramatically, the dynamic frescos emphasise that any representation is partial, in both senses: the scene continues beyond the frame, and the eye is directed to certain foci. Giotto's paintings are also intensely invested in spatial dynamics. As well as portraying depth and the individual's situation within an environment, Giotto and his school were particularly interested in city scenes. The frescos are packed with loggias, arcades, buildings, and carefully delineated interiors, and characters reach across and move through boundaries.[71] In this context, it is particularly interesting to remember that both Boccaccio and Chaucer write poems in which their avatars are stimulated by seeing frescos to embark on their own journeys.[72] Both the *Amorosa Visione* and the *House of Fame* depict the poet-narrator viewing paintings and then himself moving through a variety of different spaces, unable to gain a complete understanding of what his guide wants to show him. Boccaccio's poem ends with a resolution while Chaucer's remains errant.[73] The point

[69] Branca, *Boccaccio*, 277–78.

[70] Hagiioannu, 'Giotto's Bardi Chapel Frescoes,' 30.

[71] Martines, *Power and Imagination*, 250–51.

[72] The use of visual art to stimulate the production of a literary text has a classical history, most famously in *Aeneid* II. For a discussion of the *Amorosa Visione* and the *House of Fame*, see McKinley, *Chaucer's 'House of Fame.'*

[73] See Giovanni Boccaccio, *Amorosa Visione: Bilingual Edition*, trans. Robert Hollander, Timothy Hampton, and Margherita Frankel, with an introduction by Vittore Branca (Hanover: University Press of New England, 1986).

is not that Chaucer was (necessarily) consciously inspired by Giotto's experimentation, nor even that Chaucer's mental landscape was conditioned by the extraordinary artistic environment of 1370s Florence, although it would be very odd if this were not the case. Rather, I would emphasise that the same broad social and economic factors enabled the production both of visual art and of poetry that was especially interested in partiality, in incompletion, in imperfect perspectives. Chaucer, like Boccaccio and Giotto, could not have made the kind of art that he produced if the rise of the mercantile class had not taken place.

The Italian poets that inspired Chaucer wrote about Giotto explicitly in their works. In the *Purgatorio*, when Dante directly addresses the issue of Fame, he uses Giotto and Cimabue (whose crucifix hung at Santa Croce) as his examples. He writes: 'O empty glory of human powers, how briefly lasts the green on its top, unless it is followed by an age of dulness! In painting Cimabue thought to hold the field and now Giotto has the cry, so that the other's fame is dim' (11.91–96).[74] Petrarch praised artists including Simone Martini and Giotto and indeed owned a Giotto panel himself.[75] In the *Decameron*, Boccaccio describes the naturalism of Giotto's art, writing that his painting: 'looked not like a copy but like the very thing.'[76] And in the *Amorosa Visione*, an ostentatiously 'Florentine' poem, written about fifteen years after Giotto painted the Bardi Chapel at Santa Croce, and just after Boccaccio had returned to Florence, he writes:

> I do not believe human hand was ever
> extended with so much genius
> as every single figure there made manifest
> unless by Giotto, from whom beautiful Nature
> hid no resemblant part of herself
> in the art on which he sets his seal. (4.13–18)[77]

---

[74] Dante, *The Divine Comedy, Book 2: Purgatorio*, trans. John D. Sinclair (New York: Oxford University Press, 1961), 146–47. Subsequent references are to this translation.

[75] See Michael Baxandall, *Giotto and the Orators: Humanist Observers of Painting in Italy and the Discovery of Pictorial Composition, 1350–1450* (Oxford: Clarendon Press, 1971), 51–53.

[76] Giovanni Boccaccio, *The Decameron*, trans. Guido Waldman (Oxford: Oxford University Press, 1993), 6.5, 394.

[77] On the *Amorosa Visione* as a Florentine production, see the introduction to the text, ix–x, and Branca, *Boccaccio*, 60.

In earlier works too, Boccaccio had demonstrated his interest in ekphrasis (the powerful verbal description of visual art), which Chaucer was to imitate closely: the *Teseida* and the 'Knight's Tale' temples are good examples.[78] While we already see, in the early *Book of the Duchess*, Chaucer's interest in the idea of using art to represent literature and in showing art as inspirational for a poet, he developed these concepts dramatically in the *House of Fame*, after his encounters with Italy, its art, and its literature. Most notably, the nine-line description of the artistic rendering of Troy and the *Romance of the Rose* (*Book of the Duchess*, 326–34) contrasts dramatically with the nearly 250-line description of the representation of the *Aeneid-Heroides* in the *House of Fame* (143–380).

In fourteenth-century art and literature, we see a fascination with spatial relationships and the movement through space. Indeed, as Michael Baxandall comments, medieval audiences had a strong 'sense of close relation between the movement of the body and movement of the soul and mind.'[79] Giotto's experiments with perspective, his interest in gestures, and his careful representations of urban architecture find a literary equivalent in Boccaccio's innovative depiction of multiple locations and the narrator's movement through a series of triumphs in the *Amorosa Visione*.[80] In the *House of Fame*, Chaucer carefully delineates different kinds of spaces, describing landscapes, the interiors of rooms, and buildings in unusual detail. He also pays close attention to his avatar's movement across thresholds and in and out of spaces. His psychological development is mapped through his movement across different kinds of location.[81] Many late-medieval dream poems show the protagonist moving through symbolic realms. But the sheer variety of locations, and the specific emphasis on the body of the narrator in that space—the eagle comments on his weight (574)—distinguishes Chaucer's work as more intensively focused

---

[78] For a discussion of Chaucer's use of ekphrasis, see Andrew James Johnston, 'Ekphrasis in the *Knight's Tale*,' in R. Howard Bloch et al. (eds.), *Rethinking the New Medievalism* (Baltimore: Johns Hopkins University Press, 2014), 181–97.

[79] Michael Baxandall, *Painting and Experience in Fifteenth-Century Italy* (Oxford: Clarendon Press, 1972), 60.

[80] See 'Introduction' in Boccaccio, *Amorosa Visione*, xv.

[81] See Turner, 'Chaucer,' in *Oxford Handbooks Online*.

on the psychology of space and on the movement of the individual through the world.[82]

Chaucer's journey in 1373 reminds us that trade and economics were at the heart of royal policy and the courtly world, just as they were at the centre of the mercantile milieu. They were also a global business—just as the kind of literature in which Chaucer was interested was a fundamentally international phenomenon. Chaucer was travelling for the Crown, to further international wool trading and banking; he was talking about warehouse locations, tariffs, and the relationship between native and foreign merchants. The softness of a sheep mattered not only to farmers and merchants: it mattered to Gaunt, who personally owned swathes of sheep-farming land and also had an interest in royal taxes; it mattered to the Genoans, who knew that the softness of English wool was a crucial European money-spinner; it mattered to Edward III's advisors, who were getting rich on wool-export licences; and it certainly mattered to Chaucer, who was about to spend a decade at the centre of the wool trade. Economics were the driving force behind artistic development too: Giotto's innovations were enabled by the changing social structures of Italian cities; the idea of the tale-telling Canterbury *compaignye*, imitating a mercantile *puy* (a European guild-like society that sponsored poetry competitions), would not be possible in a feudal society; the *Decameron* set out to appeal to lower-class and female readers (and was disparaged by Petrarch for this appeal 'ad vulgus' [to the multitude]).[83] Indeed, the *Decameron*, with its array of stories of far-flung journeying set within an intricate and stable frame, and the *Canterbury Tales*, with its less complete structure but its greater interest in diverse and varying perspectives, are both texts that depend upon a mercantile genesis and audience.[84] Both texts were written by clerkly accountants, sons of men involved in mercantile life, poets who

---

[82] See chapter 9 for a discussion of the astral journey in the context of Neoplatonic journeys.

[83] See Wallace's discussion of Petrarch's *Seniles* 17:3 in *Chaucerian Polity: Absolutist Lineages and Associational Forms in England and Italy* (Stanford, CA: Stanford University Press, 1997), 283.

[84] The *Decameron*, with its completed project of ten days of ten stories has a far more architecturally complete frame than the *Tales*. The *Tales*, with its socially mixed pilgrim company, offers far more variation in perspective than the *Decameron*, whose tellers all come from the same social circle. For the genesis of the *Tales*, see part II in the current study, especially chapters 12, 13, and 14.

depended upon trade for their livelihood.[85] In contrast, Petrarch spent many years living as a client of the despotic Visconti—and had a very different idea of whom literature was for, and how it should be written.[86] Boccaccio's biographer calls the *Decameron* a '*chanson de geste* of the paladins of commerce,' pointing out that the landscapes and environments of the *novelli* mirror the places where Italian merchants directed their business.[87] The trading routes that crisscrossed the world found their poets in men such as Boccaccio and Chaucer—and Chaucer was actually on an international trade mission when he had his first opportunity to encounter the art and literature of Tuscany. It is entirely appropriate that when Chaucer came to Florence, perhaps Europe's greatest centre of art, architecture, and literature at this particular moment in history, he came not on a poetic but on an economic mission. Without the economic changes of thirteenth- and fourteenth-century Europe, the kind of visual art that Giotto made and the kind of poetry that Boccaccio and Chaucer wrought could not have been produced. Chaucer, experiencing the Bardi-sponsored art of Giotto, was perfectly poised to become the poet of the counting house.

[85] Most critics would now accept that Chaucer knew the *Decameron* in some form. For the relationship between the *Canterbury Tales* and the *Decameron*, see Helen Cooper, 'The Frame,' in Correale and Hamel (eds.), *Sources and Analogues*, 1:7–13; and Leonard Michael Koff and Brenda Dean Schildgen, *The 'Decameron' and the 'Canterbury Tales': New Essays on an Old Question* (Madison, NJ: Fairleigh Dickinson University Press, 2000).

[86] See chapter 13 for a discussion of the Visconti and chapter 16 for a short discussion of Petrarch's idealization of *otium* (leisure). See also Wallace, *Chaucerian Polity*, for a thorough discussion of the kind of poetic and political models that Petrarch and Boccaccio offered Chaucer.

[87] Branca, *Boccaccio*, 276–97, especially 283; quote is on 297.

PART II

BEING

><+>+O+<+><

Prologue

Chaucer's life up to 1374 was a time of exploration, journeying, *becoming*. He travelled, made contacts and acquired semi-patrons and friends, married and had children, read widely, and began to write poetry. He established his identity as a cultured European man, with aspirations of becoming a cosmopolitan man of letters. The subsequent decade or so was a time of consolidating and continuing, a time of *being*. Although he still travelled (particularly around the end of the 1370s) and continued, crucially, to read all kinds of new things, he led a far more settled existence than he had heretofore. For most of 1374 to around 1385, Chaucer lived in London, doing the same job, traversing the same streets, and living close to both his daughter and his mother until 1381.[1] His route from his rooms over Aldgate to his office at Wool Quay must have become boringly, or comfortingly, familiar. These were years of extraordinary upheavals for the city: the Good Parliament, the Rising of 1381, and the battles over the mayoralty were all crises for London.

These were years of dazzling creative experimentation for Chaucer. He wrote an enormous quantity of poetry during these years: the *House of*

---

[1] I discuss the precise date at which he left London in chapter 11; his mother and sister's residence in London until 1381 is explored in chapter 8.

Fame, the *Parliament of Fowls*, the 'Knight's Tale,' *Troilus and Criseyde*, and the first version of the *Legend of Good Women* belong to these years, as well as his translation of Boethius. Fresh from one trip to Italy (1373), and embarking on another a few years into his job (1378), trips that were instrumental in introducing him to the writings of Dante, Petrarch, and Boccaccio, he was now in a situation where he found time to give full rein to his creative talents and to write poems that were boldly experimental and profoundly unusual—and heavily influenced by Italian poetry. Chaucer now tried out a number of different modes and voices as he worked out what kind of poet he wanted to be. We see him in these years writing dream vision, romance-tragedy, philosophy, and debate. The *House of Fame*, like the *Book of the Duchess*, utilizes the eight-syllable line. *Boece* translates prose and verse—'prosimetrum'—into prose. The majority of Chaucer's work, however, was written in the ten-syllable line. It was only after Chaucer's devouring of the *Teseida* that he began to write in the decasyllabic line, an innovation in English poetry, but a line similar to the hendecasyllable or *endecasillabo* used by Dante, Petrarch, and Boccaccio.[2] The earliest poems in which Chaucer used this line were probably the *Parliament of Fowls*, *Anelida and Arcite*, and the 'Knight's Tale,' all poems heavily influenced by the *Teseida*. These three poems all use the same length line but are formally distinct in other ways: the *Parliament of Fowls* is in rhyme royal; the 'Knight's Tale' in an early version of the heroic couplet; *Anelida and Arcite* experiments with a number of forms and inserts some octosyllabic sections as well as stanzas of varying lengths. (Indeed, this poem showcases Chaucer's fascination with formal poetic innovation.)[3] Through his regularizing of the iambic rhythm, Chaucer now invented the iambic pentameter.

In these most 'centred' years of Chaucer's life, it is noticeable that he wrote poems about where he was: London. The *House of Fame* and *Troilus and Criseyde* both manifestly depict London in refracted form: the

[2] See chapter 13. See also Martin J. Duffell, *A New History of English Metre* (London: Legenda, 2008), 85–87 and Wallace, 'Chaucer's Italian Inheritance,' in Boitani and Mann, *Cambridge Companion to Chaucer*, 36–57.

[3] For a discussion of the textual complexities of *Anelida and Arcite*, see A.S.G. Edwards, 'The Unity and Authenticity of *Anelida and Arcite*: The Evidence of the Manuscripts,' *Studies in Bibliography* 41 (1988): 177–88.

House of Fame sketches the move from court to city as the transition from Fame to Rumour, from old authority to the contemporary new. Indeed, movement between spaces, perspectives, and varying traditions is fundamental to Chaucer's life *and* poems in these years. *Troilus and Criseyde* depicts London as Troy, drawing on the popularity of the idea of New Troy in the 1380s. The *Parliament of Fowls* evokes Westminster rather than the city itself when it sketches a recognizable English Parliament in avian form, complete with a lively Commons. Of course, these poems are not only about London, nor are they about London in a journalistic way: they are, above all, embedded in numerous literary traditions and in a world of poetic allusion and play. But they are obviously 'London' texts.

Two strands of argument dominate the chapters in this section. The first relates to identity. Chaucer, I suggest, was deeply concerned with subjectivity as a connected and collaborative process. His engagement with Neoplatonic thought, and particularly with Boethius, Cicero, and Dante, involved a rejection of intellectual isolation and an embracing of the material aspects of existence.[4] He frequently contrasts the astral and the street-level perspective—to the advantage, perhaps surprisingly, of the latter. The constraint of human life became, for Chaucer, an opportunity and a fundamental part of his creative identity. His lived engagement with new, more private modes of living, and his profound belief in the need to live with others enacted a tension between older modes of life and modernity. Every one of the poems written during this period overtly meditates on the interaction of the public and the private life. Crucially, Chaucer's interest in individual subjectivity does not equate to unproblematic admiration for a private life. *Troilus and Criseyde*, for instance, is a poem of extraordinary psychological depth that reveals an equivocal attitude towards privacy/secrecy. In chapters 7, 8, and 9 ('Counting House,' 'Cage,' and 'Milky Way,' respectively), I explore Chaucer's understanding of how we live, and his deployment of metaphor, puns, and imagined spaces, to explore the porous nature of identity, as something constructed through our relations with others. Chaucer, I argue, saw selfhood as inevitably and productively embedded in communities, however antagonistic those

---

[4] This is particularly the subject of chapters 8 and 9.

communities might be. In chapter 10 ('Tower'), I focus particularly on Chaucer's awareness of the self as an economic subject, and the relationship of selfhood to craft, making, and forging. Chapter 11 ('Troy') explores Chaucer's awareness of the self's containment by political, social, and discursive structures, looking at the London of the 1380s and Criseyde's Troy in parallel.

The final three chapters of this section deal particularly with my second major concern: how the poet of the counting house became the poet of the *Canterbury Tales*. Throughout Chaucer's most famous work, he was to speak in the assured voice of a narrator able to ventriloquize multiple voices, genres, and perspectives, and to do so while disclaiming responsibility. In chapter 12 ('Parliament'), I suggest that the emergence of the Speaker as the common voice of Parliament helped Chaucer to develop the distinctive voice of the *Tales*. In chapters 13 and 14 ('Empire' and 'Garden'), I discuss the literary roads deliberately not taken by Chaucer. He formed his characteristic voice partly in constructive opposition to the Italian poet-theologians, and the theories of empire and sovereignty that they represented. We see him experimenting one last time with the role of court poet, and rejecting that role, and the limitation and subjection that it entailed in his courtly *Legend of Good Women*. However, in both the *Legend of Good Women* and in the *House of Fame*, Chaucer took formal and thematic steps that led him towards the project of the *Canterbury Tales*.

Many of the chapters in this section range across the entire decade or so that I'm considering, and sometimes beyond. For instance, the counting house was Chaucer's place of work for the whole of this period. Similarly, three crucial parliaments were held in 1376, 1386, and 1388.[5] Empire was particularly important to Chaucer in his trip to Lombardy in 1378 and in his subsequent profound engagement with Dante, but it was of continuing relevance across the entirety of Richard's reign. Many London spaces were important in Chaucer's life when he took up his job as clerk of the king's works between 1389 to 1391, so chapters 8, 9, and 10 in particular consider his engagement with London during those years as well

---

[5] The Good, Wonderful, and Merciless.

as earlier. And while we know roughly when many of Chaucer's texts were written, we do not have exact dates: texts such as *Boece* and *Troilus and Criseyde* belong to Chaucer's years at the Custom House, but we can't pin them down precisely. Most of Chaucer's texts were probably written, revised, and circulated in different forms, so they do not belong to one particular year. I analyse many of his poems through a variety of different lenses: the *House of Fame*, for instance, is discussed in some detail in chapters 7, 8, 9, and 13.

As a set, this group of chapters builds up a picture of some of the spaces, institutions, and imagined locations that were most important to Chaucer during his London years. At the end of this period, he was still only in his early or mid forties, ready to embark on his most surprising and enduring poetic enterprise, as the poet of the *Canterbury Tales*. How did he get there?

CHAPTER 7

Counting House

> [G]rown-up games are known as 'business.'
>
> —*Augustine,* Confessions

For approximately a decade of Chaucer's life, he had a regular place of work. Between the mid-1370s and mid-1380s, Chaucer spent a great deal of time doing the same kind of thing in the same kind of place. The counting house and its surrounding rooms, including the weighing room, at Wool Quay in the port of London, became Chaucer's habitual environment, a place in which he dwelled by day, and which inevitably affected his modes of thought and imagination. When Chaucer worked in great households, including the royal household, there was little or no division between work and leisure. Part of the job involved eating, or listening to stories, or playing games—providing a certain kind of courtly or aristocratic ambience. Similarly, on diplomatic trips, he was always on duty. This kind of life did not abruptly end for Chaucer: he went on several trips abroad in the 1370s and 1380s, and remained a member of the king's household. However, his principal job, as controller of the wool custom, was a different kind of job, a job that took place in a particular place at particular times. And that place of work was physically separated from the place where Chaucer slept. Although many of us do sometimes work at home, most of us are used to a geographical separation between home and workplace—and until the advent of the Internet, the majority of people doing paid jobs in the twentieth century had a clear sense of separation between work and home environment. But in the fourteenth century, space was not divided in this way, and merchants, as we saw in chapter 1, usually did a good deal of their work at home. Shops might occupy the ground floor of a house with living quarters above; goods might be kept in cellars under the house.[1] In the 'Cook's Tale,' the corrupt apprentice lives and works with his master; when he is sacked, he loses his livelihood and his home, and his response is to send his bed and his clothes to his friend's house—to live in a dual place of business, where a shop and a whorehouse coexist in a home. This mixing up of work and home was much more common than the mode of life into which Chaucer had entered at Wool Quay.

But even when work and home-life occupied the same building, there were increasing attempts to demarcate different areas for different purposes in Chaucer's lifetime. Chaucer is the first person to use 'countour' in English to designate a specific room, a counting house.[2] In the late fourteenth century, we start to hear of merchants having counting houses in their own dwellings.[3] The very idea of a place of work, a specific location where accounts were made and written up, was growing in importance, whether that place was located in or out of the home. In this chapter, I recreate something of Chaucer's own lived experience of sitting in a counting house at the commercial heart of London, keeping and rendering accounts, weighing wool and competing interests, measuring his days with formulaic yet highly politicized numbers.

Chaucer's move to London in 1374 changed the way that he lived and worked. Instead of being embedded in one capacious space, a great household, he went between separate spaces—from apartment to office and back again. But his appointment to the position of controller of customs was a continuity of his previous life in terms of allegiances, interests, and the kind of political and economic work in which he had recently been involved. It is easy to imagine a dramatic contrast between a glamorous trip to Italy and working as an accounts keeper in a warehouse, but these jobs were economically very closely aligned in their focus on wool and, specifically, on competing Crown/London/foreigner interests relating

---

[1] Schofield, *Medieval London Houses*, 59.

[2] Kurath, Kuhn, and Lewis, *Middle English Dictionary*, s.v. 'countour' (definition 1).

[3] Sarah Rees Jones, 'Women's Influence on the Design of Urban Homes,' in Mary C. Erler and Maryanne Kowaleski, *Gendering the Master Narrative: Women and Power in the Middle Ages* (Ithaca: Cornell University Press, 2003), 195.

to the wool trade.[4] Chaucer returned from Genoa in the middle of 1373. As discussed in chapter 6, his job there had been to try to arrange for the Genoans to have a base in England so that they could trade directly with English wholesalers, a move counter to the staplers' interest (and to London's interests more generally) and one calculated to infuriate the wool merchants of London—such as Nicholas Brembre, William Walworth, and John Philipot. Chaucer had been working for the Crown, which in these days of Edward's decline meant John of Gaunt and some of Edward's cabal of advisors. Later that year, Chaucer was again involved in the affairs of the Italians—who were viewed with profound suspicion by the London monopolists—when he was sent to Dartmouth in August to deliver to its master a Genoese ship (a tarit) that had been taken into custody.[5] There is no doubt that Chaucer was given the job of controller at the desire of John of Gaunt. The duke of Lancaster returned to England from Bordeaux in April 1374, and spent most of his time at the Savoy from May until early July.[6] During this time Chaucer received a wine grant (23 April), the lease on the Aldgate apartment (10 May), the appointment as controller (8 June), and, alongside Philippa, an annuity directly from Gaunt (13 June).[7]

The controllership was a major administrative job, as wool was by far England's most important export and the Crown's major source of revenue. The tax money went, of course, to the Crown, but the nature of royal finances at this time meant that those owed money by the Crown were often given the right to take it from the wool revenue. The finances surrounding the wool export trade were in the charge of two principal officers: the collector and the controller. Their jobs involved levying taxes on wool exports and making sure that wool exporters were not evading duties. The job of the controller of customs was to serve the *royal* interest. Paul Strohm has argued that Chaucer was appointed essentially as an ally of the collector, Nicholas Brembre, in a kind of 'conspiracy,' but I read the

---

[4] London here signifies the monopolist stapler interest.

[5] Crow and Olson, *Chaucer Life-Records*, 40–41.

[6] Anthony Goodman, *John of Gaunt: The Exercise of Princely Power in Fourteenth-Century Europe* (Harlow: Longman, 1992), 53.

[7] Crow and Olson, *Chaucer Life-Records*, 112, 144–45, 148–50, 271.

politics of 1374 somewhat differently.[8] The collectors were merchant princes of London, men who were themselves major wool exporters and were keen to promote the interests of the merchant oligarchy and the wool staple at Calais.[9] They were monopolists, virulently against the Crown selling of licences to evade the staple; their agenda was to prevent foreigners (mainly Italians) from muscling in on the wool trade in England. The controllers, in contrast, were supposed to promote royal interests.[10] At this historical moment, the Crown was happily making money from selling licences to Italians, and allowing foreigners a very substantial share in the market, to the fury of the London monopolists. Strohm suggests that the London wool men were, at this point, 'flush with success,' as the monopoly was operating, and that they had 'veto power' over Chaucer's appointment.[11] The staple had indeed been renewed in 1370, but the Crown had been selling licences to evade it since 1371, and these licences were granted right up until 1376.[12] During the staple, aliens had handled 25 per cent of the wool trade, but between 1372 and 1375, they handled nearly 40 per cent.[13] In these years, most of the wool trade was diverted from Calais, and much of it was in the hands of aliens.[14] The numbers of woolsacks going to Calais and elsewhere in these years according to the Exchequer accounts were: 1372–73: 11,483 (Calais), 15,731 (elsewhere); 1373–74: 5,973 (Calais), 17,662 (elsewhere); 1374–75: 11,221 (Calais), 16,416 (elsewhere); 1375–76: 14,054 (Calais), 6,941 (elsewhere).[15] Only in 1375–76, as the

[8] Strohm, *The Poet's Tale*, 90.

[9] On the kind of 'well-established burgess collectors' who held office until the early 1390s, see Anthony Steel, 'The Collectors of the Customs in the Reign of Richard II,' in H. Hearder and H. R. Logan (eds.), *British Government and Administration: Studies Presented to S. B. Chrimes* (Cardiff: University of Wales Press, 1974), 28; and Olive Coleman, 'The Collectors of Customs in London under Richard II,' in A.E.J. Hollaender and William Kellaway (eds.), *Studies in London History Presented to Philip Edmund Jones* (London: Hodder and Stoughton, 1969), 184.

[10] See, for instance, Lee Patterson, *Chaucer and the Subject of History* (Madison: University of Wisconsin Press, 1991), 37.

[11] Strohm, *Poet's Tale*, 97.

[12] Lloyd, *English Wool Trade*, 217–21.

[13] Ibid., 220.

[14] George Holmes, *The Good Parliament* (Oxford: Clarendon Press, 1975), 80. The Exchequer rolls show that between 1371 and 1375, much more wool went to locations other than Calais than went to the staple port (81).

[15] Ibid.

political situation became increasingly fraught, do we see a partial swing back to the staple. These then were difficult years for the wool monopolists— all the more so as there was a general decline in wool exports in the 1370s. Indeed, Brembre himself was to be ousted from his collectorship in 1375. He was only reinstated in late 1377, after the Good Parliament's hard-hitting attack on Gaunt, Edward's advisors, and the Crown practice of selling licenses to evade the staple.[16] The addition to Chaucer's appointment that was controlled not by the Crown but by the city was his rent-free Aldgate apartment: he received this under the auspices of the mayor, Adam de Bury, one of the cabal surrounding Edward III and associated with the monopolists' archenemy, Richard Lyons.[17] Adam de Bury was impeached in the Good Parliament of 1376 along with the rest of Edward's most notorious profiteers. Some of the other men associated with court corruption at this point were associates and friends of Chaucer: Richard Sturry and Philip de la Vache.[18] Chaucer's own recent negotiations with the Genoese made him fully cognizant of the relationships between the Crown and the Italians. Gaunt, antagonistic to Brembre and to the London oligarchs in general, supportive of many of the profiteers surrounding Edward who were benefitting from the selling of licences to Italians, at the height of his relationship with Chaucer's sister-in-law (who bore him four children during the 1370s), put Chaucer in this role to represent the Crown, and the Crown's interests were diametrically opposed to Brembre's.[19] Things were going so badly for the wool merchants at this time that they tentatively began a new strategy: late in 1374, after all these appointments had been made, Brembre participated in a joint loan to the king.[20] But policy did not change and we hear in the Good Parliament of further loan offers from Walworth and the other staplers, made with the condition that the king reinstate the staple, being refused while high-interest

[16] *Calendar of Close Rolls Preserved in the Public Record Office: Edward III* (London: HMSO, 1896–1913), Membrane 15, 14:166–67; *Calendar of Fine Rolls Preserved in the Public Record Office* (London: HMSO, 1911–39), Membrane 21, 8:293; Membrane 27, 9:7; Membrane 16, 9:132. For the Good Parliament, see '1376 April,' in PROME, 5:289–94, and Holmes, *Good Parliament*.

[17] Crow and Olson, *Chaucer Life-Records*, 144–45.

[18] Ormrod, *Edward III*, 535.

[19] See Nightingale, *Medieval Mercantile Community*, 240–42, for Brembre's role as defender of the staple and antagonist to men collaborating with the Crown to sell licences.

[20] See 10 December 1374, *Calendar of the Patent Rolls: Edward III*, Membrane 7, 16:36.

loans from Latimer and Lyons were accepted.[21] Although a few years later, in Richard II's reign, Brembre (along with other monopolists) became a staunch Crown supporter—and lost his life for it—in these later years of Edward's reign, he was emphatically not a supporter of Crown policy.[22] Chaucer was put into this job as a Crown client, on the side of the Italians and in support of maximizing profit for the Crown and for the major wool growers (such as Gaunt personally).[23] Of course, this is not to say that there was any personal antagonism between Chaucer and Brembre, or that they did not work well together. There is no evidence that they were either friends or enemies; they had much shared history in London mercantile families, and as the years went on, politics changed for both of them. But in the mid-1370s, Chaucer was in a tricky situation in the Custom House. Brembre too was in difficulties, as his demotion in 1375, the rejection of the monopolists' loan, and the continuing success of the aliens demonstrate. In 1376 and 1377, the political climate changed completely: the Good Parliament, the Bad Parliament, the impeaching of Edward's corrupt advisors, the death of the Black Prince and then of Edward himself, John of Gaunt's dramatic quarrel with London, and the beginning of the reign of the child-king Richard II altered many of the contours of the political landscape.

As the years passed in the counting house, the merchant-capitalist wool men of London became more powerful in the city. Chaucer's years as controller were punctuated by two major political events in and around London: the Good Parliament and the Great Rising (Peasants' Revolt) of 1381. Although these were events of very different tenor, both the 1376 parliament and the 1381 revolt expressed widespread dissatisfaction with how government was operating, with Crown advisors, with foreigners, and with John of Gaunt.[24] The Good Parliament attacked and impeached Edward's most notorious advisors, including Lyons, and also singled out Edward's mistress, Alice Perrers. While there obviously had been a culture of extreme profiteering at Edward's court in the 1370s, the Commons

[21] PROME, Membrane 3–4, nos. 17–29, 5:300–307 (April 1376).

[22] It was in the 1380s that Brembre 'rapidly developed into an ardent royalist.' Steel, 'Collectors,' 35.

[23] Wool growers were best served by a multiplication of markets (Strohm, *Theory and the Premodern Text*, 126), the Crown by selling high-price licences to aliens.

[24] See especially chapters 11 and 12.

was not simply a scourge of corruption. Rather, it was promoting a protectionist agenda that allowed a crude and savage xenophobia full rein. They claimed that 'many of those who are held as Lombards are Jews and Saracens and secret spies; and that recently they have brought into the land a most horrible vice which should not be named.'[25] The Italian merchants and bankers faced the full fury of the Commons, and it soon became clear that the session had established an atmosphere of such prejudice that Italians could now be murdered with impunity in London's streets.[26] Chaucer, whose working and personal life had always been profoundly cosmopolitan, and who had travelled on long journeys across Europe with Italians and negotiated with them in some depth, was connected with the targets of Parliament in many ways. This is not to say that he himself was in trouble but that 'good' would not have been his own adjective of choice to describe this assembly.

Gaunt was, at this point, the de facto leader of government and chair of the parliament, because his father and older brother were both dying;[27] he was ostentatiously left out of the new list of advisors demanded by the parliament. Nonetheless, during the parliament he took a generally conciliatory tone and indeed had no problem with his father's mistress being attacked, for instance. The Commons were led by Sir Peter de la Mare, steward of Edmund Mortimer, earl of March (husband of Philippa, daughter of Chaucer's first employers, Elizabeth and Lionel). The staplers of London backed the Commons, who were protesting against Lyons and others' evasion of the staple and the Crown's refusal to enforce the staple: on 24 July 1376, the *Letter-Books* record that no more licences were to be issued to bypass the staple. Most of Parliament's decisions were quickly reversed, and after the death of the Black Prince and as the king's health continued to deteriorate, Gaunt became more powerful. He also started to forge an alliance with John Northampton, draper, who was to become

---

[25] PROME, Membrane 8, no. 58, 5:318 (April 1376).

[26] Strohm, *Theory and the Premodern Text*, 112–31. See also F.R.P. Akehurst and Stephanie Cain Van D'Elden (eds.), *The Stranger in Medieval Society* (Minneapolis: University of Minnesota Press, 1997).

[27] The *Anonimalle Chronicle* reporter describes him as 'lieutenant of the king to hold parliament' (lieu tenant le roy detener le parlement). *Anonimalle Chronicle*, fol. 314v, 83. The Black Prince died on 8 June; Edward III lasted another year, dying on 21 June 1377.

the champion of small tradesmen and artisans in London, and who was also to be Brembre's archenemy in the early 1380s. But in general, Gaunt was perceived as hostile to the interests of Londoners. In early 1377, Gaunt's feud with London came to a head. He was actively supporting John Wycliffe, who was preaching the disendowment of the church and who, at this point, found quite a bit of aristocratic support—particularly amongst a group of knights with whom the Black Prince, Princess Joan, and Chaucer himself were connected.[28] When the bishop of London examined Wycliffe at St Paul's, Wycliffe came escorted by Gaunt and Henry Percy. Accounts differ as to exactly what Gaunt threatened London with: he allegedly proposed that the mayor of London be replaced by a captain, or that Percy's jurisdiction over the Marshalsea be extended to London, or threatened William Courtenay, the bishop. Whatever the details, it seems clear that Gaunt acted in such a way as to threaten London's liberties. A mob rose against him, while he and Percy were at the house of Sir John Ypres (a London merchant of Flemish origin, with close connections to Gaunt and to the court faction), eating oysters. When they heard of the danger, they leapt up and rowed quickly across the river to Kennington, seeking sanctuary with Princess Joan. In response, the Londoners reversed Gaunt's arms (a sign of illegitimacy) and pinned up scurrilous stories about him, accusing him of being the son of a butcher of Ghent, a changeling child.[29] Incandescent with rage, Gaunt demanded very heavy penalties; finally, the Londoners agreed to a change of officials in the city. However, the staplers remained in the ascendancy. Although the mayor had to step down, the staplers elected none other than Brembre as replacement mayor.[30] Later in the year, Edward III died and his young grandson, the ten-year-old Richard, became king. Some of Edward's advisors were subsequently pushed out by the people surrounding Richard. Brembre and his associates gradually gained more favour from the court, making loans to the Crown and obtaining a new charter for the city protecting the city's liberties and attacking aliens.[31] Gaunt and his brothers continued to work for

[28] See chapter 15 for discussion of the so-called Lollard knights. For Wycliffe, see Anne Hudson and Anthony Kenny, 'Wyclif [Wycliffe], John,' in the *ODNB*, https://doi.org/10.1093/ref:odnb/30122.

[29] Turner, 'Conflict,' 267.

[30] Nightingale, *Medieval Mercantile Community*, 252.

[31] Ibid., 254–55.

different interests and to clash with London: when Gaunt's brother, Thomas of Woodstock, found his servants attacked and his house broken into in London, he specifically blamed Brembre.[32] Parliament was held away from London (in Gloucester), and it overturned the charter, gave privileges to aliens, and allowed aliens to avoid the staple.[33] The city, however, remained firmly in stapler hands: Brembre's first year as mayor was followed by three of his allies taking office—the next mayors were John Philipot, John Hadle, and William Walworth. Chaucer continued to work closely with these men while also maintaining a good relationship with Gaunt, and with the Crown more generally. In 1378, he embarked on his trip to Lombardy—again singled out to be the Crown's man in Italy. He undoubtedly had an excellent knowledge of the Italian language, as well as of Italian economics and trade; this time, though, he went to talk marriage, not wool, the exchange of women, not sheep.

As tends to happen in minority rules, things did not go well in the early years of Richard's reign. In London, the murder of the Genoese ambassador, there to negotiate wool-trading rights, demonstrates how high feelings ran about Italian trade. Janus Imperial was pursuing the exact plan that had taken Chaucer to Genoa in 1373: the establishment of a Genoese commercial base in Southampton.[34] More generally in the country, the notorious poll tax was viewed with loathing by a people who did not understand where their tax money was going but suspected it went into the pockets of Richard's courtiers and relatives. The 1381 revolt will be dealt with more fully in other chapters; suffice it to say that Gaunt was a major target, and his great palace, the Savoy, was burnt to the ground. The wool men came out of the revolt well: Walworth, Philipot, and Brembre accompanied Richard to his meeting with the rebels at Mile End, and were knighted for their services. But later that year, John Northampton, Gaunt's protégé at this point and the supporter of the small men of London, gained the mayoralty for two years and made changes to city government.[35] Northampton's group was associated with guilds including the mercers,

---

[32] Ibid., 256–57.

[33] Ibid., 257. PROME, Membrane 1, nos. 74–76, 6:101–3 (October 1378).

[34] Strohm, *Theory and the Premodern Text*, 112–31.

[35] Ruth Bird, *The Turbulent London of Richard II* (London: Longmans, Green, 1949), 26–29.

drapers, and goldsmiths; Adam Bamme, who worked extensively for Gaunt, was a prominent member of the group; Thomas Usk and Adam Pynkhurst, who were both connected with Chaucer's poetry (as discussed below), were also associated with them. So there is no reason to think that Chaucer would have had a problem with this group—quite the contrary. Equally, when Brembre returned to power in 1383–85 and Northampton was banished, many members of the stapler faction had been Chaucer's colleagues for years. And, crucially, while in the 1370s Brembre and his friends had been largely an anti-Crown group, now they were firmly supporting the new king and the new group around him. The court had changed; Gaunt's relationship with Richard was periodically and increasingly uneasy, and the politics of London changed too.[36] Chaucer—neither a crony of Lyons, Perrers, and Bury in the 1370s, nor a passionate Ricardian in the 1380s, but a man who did his job and above all retained his friendship with Gaunt—maintained a decent relationship with the Crown when the regime changed, and his longevity in the Custom House suggests he did his job to the Crown's satisfaction. But it is a mistake to see him as consistently the ally of Brembre and the staplers, just as it is a mistake to see Brembre as consistently the ally of the Crown during these years.

Looking at Chaucer's years in London, it is evident that the different areas of his life often overlapped: personal and professional, home and work. As Caroline Barron has shown, Chaucer was a member of a number of different communities—ward, parish, Custom House, court, literary-intellectual, familial—and these communities intersected like a complicated Venn diagram.[37] For instance, one of Chaucer's colleagues at the counting house, John Warde (collector, 1375–77), was also his alderman in Aldgate Ward (from 1369 to 1377 and from 1379 to 1380), as well as being mayor of London in 1375–76. Chaucer interacted with him about local business regarding nuisance, defence, and the problems of everyday living, as well as dealing with the politics of the Custom House. All men in the ward were obliged to attend the wardmote four times a year,

---

[36] For the notorious case of the Carmelite friar who accused Gaunt of treason in 1384, see Thomas Walsingam, *The Chronica maiora of Thomas Walsingham, 1376–1422*, trans. David Preest (Woodbridge: Boydell Press, 2005), 725–27.

[37] Caroline Barron, 'Chaucer the Poet and Chaucer the Pilgrim,' in Rigby, *Historians on Chaucer*, 24, 28–29; Patterson, *Chaucer and the Subject of History*, 32–41.

so there is no doubt that Chaucer did indeed play at least some part in local business, which included, for instance, checking local weights and measures, just as Chaucer inspected the weights at the Custom House. All men older than fifteen, except knights and clerks, were obliged to take communal responsibility for the ward, to make sure justice was being done and business honestly conducted.

The London to which Chaucer returned was a building site. As London recovered after the second wave of the plague in the late 1360s, it entered into a period of redevelopment and building.[38] In particular, people were building *up*, adding storeys to their houses to increase and vary their living space, and thus adding to the crowded feeling of London's narrow streets.[39] The interiors of these houses meanwhile offered more opportunities for demarcating space and for private or semiprivate chambers, part of the general trend towards living in less communal or public ways, a trend that continued to develop in the fifteenth century.[40] These were interesting times: Chaucer's years in London were to witness dramatic confrontations between reformer and bishop, between smaller-scale merchants and artisans and the monopolist-oligarchs and, most famously, between the rebels of 1381 and their victims, who ranged from government officials to poor immigrants. Despite all of this chaos and conflict, Chaucer was also returning to a city he knew intimately, the city of his youth, packed with acquaintances, the city in which his mother lived.

The counting house itself changed during Chaucer's tenure. The Custom House occupied a large riverfront site of around 0.375 hectares near the Tower of London, situated between Lower Thames Street and the river. Outside the building was a wooden jetty projecting out into the Thames; beyond this, ships were moored, the vehicles of London's constant traffic with the Continent.

There was probably some kind of house near here for weighing the wool from the late thirteenth or early fourteenth century—that is, shortly after the wool custom was introduced in 1275. The site itself was privately

---

[38] Schofield suggests there was a 'resurgence of construction' in 1369–83; *Medieval London Houses*, 3.

[39] Schofield discusses the increasing trend for multistorey buildings in the late fourteenth century (ibid., 3).

[40] Ibid., 93, 70.

owned; from 1378 it was leased and then owned by John and Emma Churchman. They rebuilt the Custom House, and then added a further extension before summer 1383. Archaeologists estimate that the medieval Custom House was about 24 metres by 10 metres, with an addition of 17 by 9.[41] The tronage or weighing hall, where the parcels of wool were processed and assessed, was the heart of the building; the counting house, where the accounts were kept and the money sorted out, was its brain. Churchman's extension comprised 'a small chamber for a latrine and a sollar over the counting-house 38 feet by 21½ broad, containing two chambers and a garret, as a further easement for the customers, controllers, and clerks.'[42] Greater attention to comfort, privacy, and the division of tasks and spaces lies behind the construction of extra chambers and a latrine. This was an increasingly elaborate complex. The provision of the latrine demonstrates a care and attention for the people working in and visiting the building. Its 'fine timber drain' was recently unearthed by archaeologists, suggesting that this structure was carefully designed and built.[43] The chambers might have had a number of purposes, as there were many different people working in and visiting this site. Apart from the collectors and controller, there was also the troner and peser, who weighed the merchandise in the tronage (weighing) hall. This position was held by Richard Fillongley, esquire of the king. There were two searchers, one in London and one at Gravesend, who seized goods and prevented illegal exports and imports, and at least four packers and porters. Frequent visitors to the building included the wool merchants themselves and their agents, and an array of the king's creditors and grantees who were claiming money from the wool subsidy.[44]

For Chaucer's first year in office (1374–75), and for the last few years that he held the job (1382–86), he also held the position of controller of the petty custom, working with another set of staff and another collector. The petty or new custom was levied on merchandise not covered by the wool (or ancient) custom or by butlerage (levied on wine imported by

[41] Tim Tatton-Brown, 'Excavations at the Custom House Site, City of London, 1973,' *Transactions of the London and Middlesex Archaeological Society* 25 (1974): 117, 128, 141, 143–45.

[42] *Calendar of the Patent Rolls: Richard II*, Membrane 37, 2:299 (18 July 1383).

[43] Tatton-Brown, 'Excavations,' 140.

[44] Crow and Olson, *Chaucer Life-Records*, 151–75.

aliens), including wine, cloth, and worsted. While Brembre, as we have seen, was a stapler and merchant-oligarch, a stalwart of the city and defender of the collective interests of the great wool merchants, the collector in the petty custom when Chaucer started the job was quite a different kind of politician: Richard Lyons. This notorious businessman was infamous for his corrupt practices and was to be one of the major targets of the Good Parliament, and one of the most notable victims of the Rising of 1381. Probably an illegitimate Fleming, Lyons was a generation older than Chaucer and had been an associate of Chaucer's father. Both wine merchants—although Lyons had his finger in many other pies as well—they were connected in 1364 when John Chaucer stood surety for Lyons, and after his death Lyons was buried in St Martin Vintry.[45] In 1365, Lyons had acquired the monopoly on the sweet wine trade in London when the mayor, Adam de Bury (the man who gave Chaucer his London rooms, as we saw earlier), licenced only three London taverns to sell sweet wine (from Italy). All three taverns belonged to Lyons. In the 1370s, he profiteered by selling licences to evade the staple, buying up loans at a discount and reclaiming their full value from the Treasury, and lending money at exorbitant rates of interest. He farmed the petty custom from 1372–75. His rapacious individualism and antistapler activity earned him the hostility of the powerful merchants of London, as well as of the Commons more generally, and he was impeached in 1376. At this point, an inventory was taken of his wealth, and much of his property was sold off. However, this was a temporary setback. The Good Parliament's decisions were swiftly reversed, Lyons was pardoned, and he continued to accumulate more property and wealth, although not to hold office in London. When he died, he owned thirty messuages (houses), a toft (land), sixty shops, twelve cellars, six gardens in London and the northern suburbs, two shops and seven gardens in Southwark, a manor in Kent, two in Essex, and more land in Kent and Essex.[46] It was not high but popular politics that finally brought him down: five years after his impeachment, he was murdered by the rebels

[45] Thomas, *Calendar, 1364–1381*, Roll A10, Membrane 4b, 11 (9 December 1364); Roger L. Axworthy, 'Lyons, Richard,' in the *ODNB*, https://doi.org/10.1093/ref:odnb/52191.

[46] Myers, 'Wealth of Richard Lyons,' 301–5.

in 1381. As a corrupt profiteer, self-motivated Crown advisor, and foreigner, he embodied all of the insurgents' greatest resentments.

Richard Lyons, then, was someone with whom Chaucer had been familiar since his own childhood in Vintry Ward, and they were now colleagues a few metres down the road from the Vintry. As an extremely wealthy merchant, Lyons's own lifestyle reveals to us something of contemporary trends in using space, particularly how business spaces were now being constructed in houses and separated from other areas of the house. As well as associating with Chaucer in the counting house at Wool Quay, Lyons had his own counting house at home. He was in the forefront of a growing trend to designate a room in the house as a business room, a trend that demonstrates an interest in separating work and leisure—as Chaucer was now doing with his 'office job' in contrast to his fluid work in the king's household. The very idea of a counting house at home immediately suggests a desire to place business into its own space, rather than letting it seep into all areas of life. But when we look more closely at these home counting houses, we see that this division was not convincingly enacted. When Lyons was impeached, a detailed inventory was made of his house, room by room. His 'comptour' or counting house contained standard business items, such as many different weights. It also contained an astonishingly diverse array of other items, including ribbons, coral, a nutmeg shell made into a cup, a decorated copper bowl, a pair of silver scissors, a mirror, forty-three pearls, some broken pieces of gold, and four books in French and English. Some of these items may have been precious goods to be traded, some may have been personal valuables that Lyons liked to keep in a secure room, some may have been beautiful *objets* that he simply liked to have around him while he worked. The nature of the kind of work that Lyons did—trading in elaborate materials, jewels, and wines— meant that items that might seem like luxurious leisure goods to most of us were tradeable commodities to him. But that is not the whole story. Many of the items are not valued highly—he was not keeping them here merely for security: the coral is valued at 1s 6d, for instance; one of his books at only 1s. The room is a place of beauty and thought, a place of glittering jewels, soft fabrics, novelty items, and various books (diverse treatises, a book about chancery, a book that may have been a Brut [a romance/chronicle about the legendary history of Britain], and a saints' lives collection).[47] None of the books were valuable, and while some were clearly related to work (the 'livre de la chauncellerie appellee regestre'), others were not ('livre appellee legend sanctorum en engleis'). It is fascinating that this court-connected Flemish immigrant was evidently reading in English as well as in French, and that he kept these books lying around his own workroom. Fifteen years later, an inventory was made of another merchant's counting house in London. Richard Toky's counting house also contained objects clearly related to accounting and other business practices: weights, paper, pen, an ink-horn, a cheap book of statutes.[48] The other items in his counting house lacked the eclectic exoticism of Lyons's collection: Toky favoured a wide array of armour and weaponry (which may have been kept there for security), and some conventional alabaster religious images, reminiscent of the Italian merchant Datini's motto 'For God and for Profit.'[49] Lyons's fascinating collection of items suggests that the boundaries between work and leisure remained extremely porous, even as interior design created a greater illusion of separation than had previously been the case.

The existence of books and paper in counting houses reminds us of the primary importance of record-keeping in Chaucer's job, and in mercantile life generally. The counting house at Wool Quay was the place where Chaucer kept accounts in his own hand, as his job demanded that he do. While the wool custom was a fixed amount on each sack of wool, levied at two rates for native and foreigner, the petty custom was more complicated because it varied according to the quality of the goods, although it also included fixed tunnage and poundage duties. The basic taxes for native merchants were, for the wool custom, 50 shillings for each sack of wool or lot of 240 woolfells and 100 shillings for each last of leather. Foreign merchants paid 53s 4d for each sack of wool and 106s 8d for each last of leather. Tunnage was 2s per tun of wine; poundage 3d per pound

[47] Ibid., 326–27. Vance Smith compares this counting house with 'the space of romance,' as the other place 'in which such objects and interests converge.' *Arts of Possession*, 53.

[48] The inventory dates from 26 October 1391; Thomas, *Calendar, 1381–1412*, Roll A33, Membrane 2b, 212 (4 December 1393).

[49] Iris Origo, *The Merchant of Prato: Francesco di Marco Datini, 1335–1410* (Boston: Nonpareil Books, 1986), 114.

weight of goods.[50] The regular taxes were supplemented by extra subsidies, both on wool and on the petty custom: while the wool subsidy was in Chaucer's hands, along with the wool custom, the petty subsidy was consistently farmed out to others. Even from this very brief description, it should be clear that Chaucer was dealing with a varied system of taxes. While customs' accounts were not new, in other areas of London mercantile life, there was a new interest in keeping written records in the later fourteenth century. The great livery companies started to keep detailed records and accounts, and to establish places to keep these records. The provision of halls was bound up with the maintenance of records as the companies simultaneously rooted themselves in time and place, in history and geography.[51] Men such as Thomas Usk and Adam Pynkhurst wrote records for (important, antiwool monopolist, anti-Brembre) livery companies (the Goldsmiths and the Mercers) while also selling their scrivener skills elsewhere. Both were connected to Chaucer: Usk as an early reader and imitator, Pynkhurst as the scribe of early Chaucer manuscripts (probably including the Ellesmere Chaucer; plates 2, 7, and 8) and almost certainly the addressee of *Chaucers Wordes Unto Adam, His Owne Scriveyn*.[52] Pynkhurst was also the writer of other documents connected to Chaucer, such as his request for a deputy at the Custom House in 1385.[53] This was a culture in which record-keeping was increasingly important, and in which identity was fashioned partly through the production and preservation of relatively formulaic writing. The accounts of, for instance, the Goldsmiths, with their lavish descriptions of processions, demonstrate the close relationship between different kinds of accounts—narrative and numerical. And men such as Pynkhurst and Usk were accustomed to writing in multiple languages, just as Chaucer kept his Latin accounts and wrote fiction in English.

What, then, was Chaucer recording in the ambiguous space of the counting house at Wool Quay? None of his own account books have survived, but a wealth of similar documentary material—the collectors'

[50] Crow and Olson, *Chaucer Life-Records*, 150.

[51] Turner, 'Usk and the Goldsmiths,' 145–57.

[52] See chapter 11 for a more detailed discussion of Pynkhurst.

[53] Simon Horobin, 'Adam Pinkhurst, Geoffrey Chaucer, and the Hengwrt Manuscript of the *Canterbury Tales*,' *Chaucer Review* 44:4 (2010): 355.

accounts, accounts of the petty subsidy, similar accounts from other ports or from a slightly earlier or slightly later date—gives us a clear picture of the kind of records he was keeping.[54] He was recording the names of the ships containing the products, the names of the merchants who had goods on the ships, the amount of goods, and the dues.[55] When merchants paid their dues, a receipt, known as a cocket letter, was drawn up in two copies and sealed with the cocket seal, one half of which was held by the collector and one half by the controller. One copy was given to the merchant, the other passed on to the Exchequer. On average, Chaucer sealed more than one thousand cockets each year, but these would tend to be issued not on separate occasions but in groups, as several merchants would have shipments of wool on the same ship.[56] He dealt with imports and exports. He worked closely with the troner and peser, who weighed the merchandise in the tronage hall; he also had to work closely with the collectors, as their independent accounts were supposed to match each other's, and each had to seal each other's half of the cocket into a bag.[57] Chaucer was also supposed to inspect the packers' books, and, indeed, in 1380 when the packers were accused of employing untrustworthy deputies, Chaucer and the collectors were mandated to employ responsible packers who would do the job themselves.[58]

Frequently, Chaucer would have to give up custody of his part of the cocket seal to creditors of the king, who were authorized to collect their repayments at a certain rate from the wool custom. When this was the case—as it was, for instance, from April 1376 when Richard Lyons and several others had Chaucer's cocket—he still needed to seal cockets but had to get the seal back from the creditor or his agents.[59] This must have been so cumbersome that it is hard to believe it happened each time the controller needed to use his seal. But it is likely that he had to communicate very frequently with these moneylenders or their employees: this was

---

[54] Collectors' accounts, mentioning Chaucer by name as surveying the documents, do survive. See National Archives, E 122/71/4 and E 122/71/9.

[55] Crow and Olson, *Chaucer Life-Records*, 190–96.

[56] Ibid., 179.

[57] Ibid., 178.

[58] Ibid., 175–76.

[59] Ibid., 179–80.

a job that demanded cooperation; it simply couldn't work unless collector, controller, and creditor—as well as the more menial employees—worked closely together. Chaucer was certainly not spending his days sitting alone in the counting house, totting up lines of figures. And although the accounts were largely made up of names, lists of goods, and columns of numbers, the cockets themselves were narrative in style. They took the form of letters, or certificates, written in the name of the king, and specifying who had paid duties, whether he was native or alien, what the goods were, and when the cocket was issued. The merchant could use his own copy to demonstrate that he had paid taxes and that his goods were being legally transported, so that he could avoid being charged again.[60] The sheer number of cockets sealed, and the plethora of similar documents that surrounded Chaucer in the counting house, remind us that, like Hoccleve or Usk, Chaucer's 'professional responsibilities had less to do with self-expression than with the endless reduplication of a language of grave bureaucratic anonymity.'[61] His day job involved writing in the voice of the bureaucratic machine, but those formulaic documents told all kinds of stories: about the treatment of foreigners (the place of origin of merchants was always specified, as the charges were different), about the international networks of trade, and about the working relationships between merchants and shipowners. The surviving documents tell us fragments of fascinating tales: the collectors' (Brembre's and Philipot's) accounts for 1380–81, for instance, compiled under the survey of Chaucer, include payments made by 'Affrikano Petro' (African Peter), who was transporting wool on John Double's ship.[62]

Chaucer also had to work with the king's creditors, who sometimes were actually in possession of his half of the cocket seal, and who frequently were being paid back their loans from the wool revenue in particular. The most notable lender to the king at this time was Matthew Janyn or Chenyn. He was a Lombard merchant who lent so much money to the king that he was given the Crown jewels as security. His large loan of 6,000

[60] For examples, see ibid., 176–77.

[61] Ethan Knapp, *The Bureaucratic Muse: Thomas Hoccleve and the Literature of Late Medieval England* (University Park: Pennsylvania State University Press, 2001), 19.

[62] National Archives, E 122/71/4. This has been discussed in a blog by Euan Roger: http://blog.nationalarchives.gov.uk/blog/civil-servants-tale-geoffrey-chaucer-archives-part-two/.

marks was repaid on the wool custom; he then continued to take 1 mark from each sack of wool, and to retain the cocket seal, taking payment of a large amount owed to Catalonian and Aragonese merchants, for whom he was acting. We see Janyn being paid consistently from 1380–84.[63] Chaucer was thus in frequent contact with well-off Italians—or their agents—at exactly the period when he was reading Italian literature in great depth. Rather than there being a clear contrast between writing accounts by day and reading Dante by night, Chaucer's work on Wool Quay kept him in touch with all things Italian, and, indeed, he may have bought Italian books from the merchants with whom he was in contact in the counting house.[64]

Chaucer's London life was not the life of an anonymous commuter, writing anonymous bureaucratic documents and retreating, unseen and uncared about to his apartment. It was a life of intersecting communities and politics, jostling interests, and competing colleagues. Even the mechanics of Chaucer's writing life involved collaboration. Critics have usually assumed that he wrote rough versions of his texts either on wax tablets or on parchment or paper, and then took them to a scribe who made a fair copy.[65] He must have been well acquainted with the shops of Paternoster Row, the centre of the bookmaking trades, as discussed at the beginning of this book. We know that Chaucer worked with scribes such as Adam Pynkhurst, who seems to have worked part-time out of the Mercers' base at the Hospital of St Thomas Acon.[66] We might imagine Chaucer carrying his papers through the city to his scribes, who took Chaucer's 'makyng' and wrote it 'newe,' after which Chaucer himself might have to 'correcte'

[63] *Calendar of the Patent Rolls: Richard II*, Membrane 17, 2:4; Membrane 14, 2:7; Membrane 19, 2:46; Membrane 25, 2:102; Membrane 31, 2:154.

[64] Nick Havely, 'The Italian Background,' in Steve Ellis (ed.), *Chaucer: An Oxford Guide* (Oxford: Oxford University Press, 2005), 315–16.

[65] A. I. Doyle and M. B. Parkes, 'The Production of Copies of the *Canterbury Tales* and the *Confessio Amantis* in the Early Fifteenth Century,' in M. B. Parkes and Andrew G. Watson (eds.), *Medieval Scribes, Manuscripts and Libraries: Essays Presented to N. R. Ker* (London: Scolar Press, 1978), 167. See also Daniel Wakelin, *Scribal Correction and Literary Craft: English Manuscripts, 1375–1510* (Cambridge: Cambridge University Press, 2014), 87–94; Linne R. Mooney, 'Chaucer's Scribe,' *Speculum* 81:1 (2006): 121.

[66] Mooney, 'Chaucer's Scribe,' 111. On Pynkhurst's 'shop,' see also Alexandra Gillespie, 'Books,' in Strohm, *Middle English*, 98–99.

the version (*Chaucers Wordes Unto Adam, His Owne Scriveyn*; 4, 2, 6). Some of the work might have taken place in Pynkhurst's or Chaucer's homes.[67] Certainly, the physical production of Chaucer's texts did not take place in large public scriptoria *or* in isolation; it usually involved two people (Chaucer and scribe) who either passed the text back and forth for correction or even partly worked together. Christopher Cannon has recently suggested an interestingly interactive model of composition, arguing that Chaucer may have dictated his poems to scribes acting as secretaries, perhaps using a partial copy as a prompt.[68] In this model, there is no authorial original or stem text; rather, Chaucer kept the text partly in his head and added bits, changed stanzas around, or missed bits out as he reworked the text through multiple dictations. There is no doubt that the production of each text was a social and collaborative enterprise; it may even be the case that the text was partly built through the interactive process of dictation. This does not mean that scribes were *creatively* involved in the texts (although they might have been at times).[69]

The intersections between the different areas of Chaucer's life are further demonstrated by his use of the language of accounting in his poetry—and by the change in how he used such language. In the *Book of the Duchess*, which was probably written *before* Chaucer started work at Wool Quay, he imagines a mathematician in his counting house.[70] After describing the bewildering array of animals in the dream garden that he has entered, the narrator states:

---

[67] Linne R. Mooney, 'Locating Scribal Activity in Late Medieval London,' in Margaret Connolly and Linne R. Mooney (eds.), *Design and Distribution of Late Medieval Manuscripts in England* (York: University of York Press, 2008), 183–204. For a recent argument that Chaucer is not the author of the poem, see Eric Weiskott, 'Adam Scriveyn and Chaucer's Metrical Practice,' *Medium Aevum* 86:1 (2017), 147–51.

[68] Christopher Cannon, ' "Wyth her owen handys": What Women's Literacy Can Teach Us about Langland and Chaucer,' *Essays in Criticism* 66:3 (2016): 277–300.

[69] Indeed, one of the key aspects of Cannon's argument is that the scribes tended to use final 'e's' nonmetrically precisely because they were not thinking about Chaucer's poetic metre but simply using their own spelling practices. Ibid., 293–94.

[70] As discussed in chapter 5, it is possible that the poem was written in 1374 to coincide with the construction of Blanche's tomb and the inauguration of the annual commemoration of her, although an earlier date is more likely. In June 1374 Gaunt sent six cartloads of alabaster to London for an 'ymage' for Blanche's tomb; there was a solemn commemoration that September and annually thereafter. Goodman, *John of Gaunt*, 257.

Shortly, hyt was so ful of bestes
That thogh Argus, the noble *countour*,
Sete to *rekene* in his *countour*,
And *rekene* with his *figures* ten—
For by the *figures* mowe al ken,
Yf they be crafty, *rekene* and *noumbre*,
And telle of every thing the *noumbre*—
Yet shoulde he fayle to *rekene* even
The wondres me mette in my sweven. (434–42; emphasis mine)

The ostensible point of these lines is that even a great mathematician would fail when faced with this dream: numerical skill can't compass the wonder that the narrator faces. So there is a suggestion that plodding accountancy has no business with dreamscapes and fantasy. The language of the passage is dense with the language of accounting: in seven lines there are four uses of 'rekene,' and two each of 'countour,' 'figure,' and 'noumbre.' 'Countour' is rhymed with itself, and 'noumbre' is also rhymed with itself. In each case, the word changes its meaning slightly: 'countour' means first 'mathematician' and then 'counting house'; 'noumbre' is first a verb and then a noun. But there is little semantic variation or punning across the mathematical language; ambiguity is always there, but it is not exploited as it is in, say, the 'Shipman's Tale,' where the differing meanings of 'tail-lynge' as accounting, having sex, and telling tales jostle with each other for supremacy.[71] This passage from the *Book of the Duchess* is dominated by an aesthetics of repetition: the same words are not only insistently repeated, they are even rhymed with each other. Argus sits in his counting house cut off from wonder, the limitation and sameness of his occupation reflected by the limited lexicon used to describe it. The dreamer, in contrast, is living the experience of 'the wondres me mette in my sweven.' This is one way in which Chaucer depicted accounting, before he was enmeshed in the counting house at Wool Quay. Over the next decade, he became an experienced accountant and financial record-keeper, and he wrote about 'rekenynge' in quite different ways.

---

[71] See, for example, Jonathan Hsy, *Trading Tongues: Merchants, Multilingualism, and Medieval Literature* (Columbus: Ohio State University, 2013), 45.

The difficulty of separating working life from other domains is a key issue in Chaucer's writings about accounting. Chaucer's use of puns and metaphor demonstrates the interplay between different aspects of life. In modern English too, we *spend* time; we face a final *reckoning*; we *account* for our movements. While accounting was punningly connected to sex and to narrative, it was metaphorically linked to the meaning of life on an eschatological scale. The puns have been much discussed: in Anglo-Norman, 'countour,' as in a metal counter or a table or board, is almost identical to 'contur,' a narrator, which itself puns on 'con,' or vulva, as money, stories, and sex mingle.[72] Similarly, in the 'Shipman's Tale,' 'taillinge' is accounting, telling tales, and having sex. When the narrator wishes us all a plethora of 'taillinge' (434), he is playing on all these meanings—economic success, sexual pleasure, and storytelling. In a world where the only sanctioned sexual activity—marital sex—was termed a debt to be paid, economics and sex were inevitably intertwined.[73] The connection between accounting and telling tales is perhaps less predictable. The word 'wrecan,' in Old English means 'utter' or 'tell.' Ezra Pound's translation of it in his *Seafarer* as 'reckon,' with its twentieth-century meaning of 'count,' reveals how the word changed over time: for Chaucer it has both meanings, although he more often uses it with 'count' as the primary meaning. Thus, the user of the astrolabe should 'Rekene than the nombre of degres' (*Astrolabe*, II.27.9); the Shipman should 'rekene wel his tydes' ('General Prologue,' 401); the narrator of the *Romaunt of the Rose* can't 'reken[e] every tree' (1390). But the Squire speaks of 'al that myghte yrekened [told] be' (427) about the falcon; and the Knight tells us that he 'rekned and rekne shal' (1933) all the circumstance of love.

Rekenynge—the word that Chaucer uses to describe his day job in the *House of Fame* (653)—also functions as a metaphor for Judgement Day.[74] The best examples of this come in the 'Parson's Tale':

[72] *Anglo-Norman Dictionary*, s.v. 'countour [1]' and 'contur [1].' See also Hsy, *Trading Tongues*, 45.

[73] The Wife of Bath, for instance, draws a connection between sex and economic debt in 'The Wife of Bath's Prologue,' 129–30 and 152–59.

[74] For discussion of Judgement Day in Chaucer, see Helen Cooper, 'Four Last Things in Dante and Chaucer: Ugolino in the House of Rumour,' *New Medieval Literatures* 3 (2000): 39–66.

'He shal yeven acountes,' as seith Seint Bernard, 'of alle the goodes that han be yeven hym in this present lyf, and how he hath hem despended, / [in] so muche that ther shal nat perisse an heer of his heed, ne a moment of an houre ne shal nat perisse of his tyme, that he ne shal yeve of it a rekenyng.' ('Parson's Tale,' 253–54)

Here, the extended metaphor is particularly effective because it simultaneously works on the literal and figurative level. The individual should indeed engage in charity and material generosity, but more importantly, he needs to have used his talents and time appropriately. Time is key here: he needs to give a reckoning of—account for—every moment of his life. Time is spent, and we will be judged—by the ultimate accountant—on how we spent it. The accountancy metaphor is set up before the tale begins, when we see the scales of justice hanging in the sky, cosmic versions of the scales that Chaucer saw every day in the tronage hall ('Parson's Prologue,' 11). Elsewhere in the 'Parson's Tale,' it is not time but words themselves for which we must account: 'we shullen yeven rekeynynge of everich ydel word' (166). Language becomes a currency in the eschatological account. And in the 'Man of Law's Prologue,' the metaphor sharply veers back to the literal, when the Man of Law imagines the poor man commenting on the rich man, that 'somtyme he rekene shal, / Whan that his tayl shal brennen in the gleede' (110–11). The reference is obviously to hell, but the rich man's burning nether body (tayl) is also his account book. The poor man is using accounting metaphorically to talk about the rich man *rekening*—totting up his evil deeds—but the language is especially effective because the poor man is also making reference to the rich man's own rapacious *rekening* in this life. In other words, when a merchant faces his reckoning, the language of rendering accounts becomes particularly loaded.

People run into problems in Chaucer's texts when they try to separate different areas of their life, spatially and figuratively. In the *House of Fame*, Chaucer comically portrays himself as doing his 'rekenynges' (653) by day in one place, and then trudging home to Aldgate, to sit alone at his literary books:

But of thy verray neyghebores,
That duellen almost at thy dores,
Thou herist neyther that ne this;
For when thy labour doon al ys,
And hast mad alle thy rekenynges,
In stede of reste and newe thynges
Thou goost hom to thy hous anoon,
And, also domb as any stoon,
Thou sittest at another book
Tyl fully daswed ys thy look;
And lyvest thus as a heremyte,
Although thyn abstynence ys lyte. (649–60)

Here the separation between the domain of the counting house and the domain of poetry is signalled spatially: Geffrey physically leaves the wool quay—'thou goost hom to thy hous anoon' (655)—and pursues his literary interests while closed off from the world. When he reads alone, he 'herist neyther that ne this': he is deaf to his neighbours. He cannot speak, he is 'domb as any stoon.' His eyesight is affected ('fully daswed ys thy look'), and he is like one who is fasting ('a heremyte'), although in fact his 'abstynence ys lyte' (649–60). These lines continually emphasise the senses, making it clear that by coming home and reading silently and alone, ignoring his neighbours, Geffrey is cutting off his sensual connection with the world.[75] His senses are numbed, and his reading is profitless—he has no tidings, no inspiration, and needs divine help. His lack of success with his reading is profoundly connected with his attempting to read in an isolated and disembodied way, separated from communities and the messiness of everyday life.

The merchant of the 'Shipman's Tale' attempts to do his job in isolation from his household. He closes the door of his counting house—a marked moment, particularly as this is the first recorded instance in English of the 'countour-dore' (85). His wife even has to bang on that closed door

[75] See Marion Turner, 'The Senses,' in Peter Brown (ed.), *A New Companion to Chaucer* (Oxford: Wiley-Blackwell, forthcoming); R. M. Smith, ' "Mynstralcie and Noyse" in the *House of Fame*,' *Modern Language Notes* 65:8 (1950): 521–30; David Bevington, 'The Obtuse Narrator in Chaucer's *House of Fame*,' *Speculum* 36:2 (1961): 288–98.

to get his attention (213) as she tells him to stop his 'rekenynges' (218). Chaucer describes a very up-to-the-minute domestic set-up, with a special counting house in which one can be segregated from the household. But his separation enables the monk and the wife to plan their adultery—and their sensual engagement is sharply contrasted with the merchant's sensual deprivation. He is fasting and indeed no one in the household can dine until he emerges from his place of business so that they can all go to Mass and dinner (215–23). Chaucer suggests that this kind of separation is problematic, that everything is connected, overlapping, interlinked. The idea of the countour's mathematics as cut off from wonder is a warning, not a reflection of inevitable practice. On the contrary, Chaucer luxuriates in the puns and metaphors that reveal the fundamental links between accounts, judgement, time, narrative, and sex. Interestingly, although for many people, as Sarah Stanbury comments, 'privacy was becoming a desirable good,' Chaucer seems to have had decidedly mixed feelings about the trend towards more private modes of living.[76]

Both the *House of Fame* and the 'Shipman's Tale' end with the suggestion of a different way of life from the life of bookish isolation: the merchant takes accounting into the bedroom in an exuberant, albeit profoundly commercial, bout of sex, while Geffrey starts listening to his neighbours and entering fully into the chaotic and tale-filled life of the mercantile city, when he encounters the House of Rumour. These engaged modes of life are more accurate depictions of contemporary London life than the image of the closed room. In late fourteenth-century London, the idea of spatially separating work and leisure was in its infancy, and coral, fiction, mirrors, and novelty cups lived in rooms of accounts, weights, and measures. Chaucer knew that we need vigorous interaction in order to be emotionally connected and creatively productive; we need to live, work, and write with others. While each person's perspective is singular and separable from any other perspective, as Chaucer repeatedly shows us in his writings, those perspectives are not formed in isolation. On the contrary, each point of view is embedded, contingent, and weighted down in space and time.

[76] Sarah Stanbury, '"Quy la?": The Counting House, the *Shipman's Tale*, and Architectural Interiors,' in Susanna Fein and David Raybin (eds.), *Chaucer: Visual Approaches* (University Park: Pennsylvania State University Press, 2016), 42.

CHAPTER 8

Cage

It's part of being a watcher, forgetting who you are and putting
yourself in the thing you are watching. That is why the girl who was
me when I was small loved watching birds. She made herself disappear,
and then in the birds she watched, took flight. It was happening now. I
had put myself in the hawk's wild mind to tame her, and as the days
passed in the darkened room my humanity was burning away.

—*Helen Macdonald,* H is for Hawk

As Chaucer settled down to his new patterns of life in the counting house,
he entered into a period of intense reading, translating, and writing. One
of his core endeavours during these years was his translation of Boethius's
Consolation of Philosophy, the single text that did more to change and shape
Chaucer's patterns of thought than any other. Boethius's focus on what
Bachelard calls intimate immensity[1]—the dual perspective of caged
imprisonment and expansive, astral perspectives—shaped Chaucer's own
understanding of space and time. At the same time as he was immersed
in Boethius, his own daughter Elizabeth inhabited the 'cage' of the nunnery, just around the corner from Chaucer's apartment, a cage that proved
to be far less constraining than we might imagine. When Chaucer writes
about enclosed spaces, he repeatedly suggests that constraint, subjection,
and enmeshed perspectives are a fundamental and energizing part of
the human condition. In Chaucer's Boethian-inspired writings, the lived

[1] Bachelard, *Poetics of Space*, 183–231.

experience of late-medieval urban life meets late-antique philosophy to create fascinating, idiosyncratic ideas about the productive limits of individual identity. Over the next two chapters, I explore Chaucer's philosophical understanding of space and time through the images of the cage and the Milky Way, linking his attitudes to these spaces with his relationships with his children, and with the jobs that he did both during and after his London years. While these chapters focus on Chaucer's intellectual and imaginative development, my argument is that his patterns of thought were shaped by the material conditions of his life. In the present chapter, a close examination of the image of the cage-prison reveals Chaucer's fascination with material culture, and with the constrained nature of identity. We need first to plunge into the *Consolation* itself in order to understand how and why Chaucer transformed Boethius's attitudes to identity and materiality—and precisely why for Chaucer, in direct contrast to his predecessors, the cage is a *positive* place to inhabit.

When he embarked on his translation, Chaucer was fully engaged with the *Consolation*, using the Latin original, Jean de Meun's prose French translation, and the commentary tradition to help him construct his own English *Boece*. In choosing to translate this text, he was very much in tune with the European intellectual world. Indeed, there were multiple translations of Boethius in the fourteenth century, as medieval thinkers engaged with the text and its commentary tradition with enthusiasm: in this century there were at least eight Italian translations alone. Influential texts, including Bernardus Silvestris's *Cosmographia* or Alain de Lille's *De Planctu Naturae*, were deeply indebted to the *Consolation*.[2] The poetic texts that most influenced Chaucer—such as the *Divine Comedy*, the *Romance of the Rose*, and the *Teseida*—were themselves imbued with Boethian thought: it was from Boethius that medieval poets took the structure of the debate form as a way of exploring spiritual psychology, the concept of the Boethian perspective, and the struggle between poetry and philosophy. From Boethius they learnt the power of allegory and of the dream-vision structure that made a female authority figure the instructress of the narrator. In Boethius, Chaucer found not only the depiction of an unreliable

[2] Winthrop Wetherbee, 'The Consolation and Medieval Literature,' in John Marenbon (ed.), *The Cambridge Companion to Boethius* (Cambridge: Cambridge University Press, 2009), 282–83.

and flawed narrator who goes through a process in parallel with the reader but also the dramatization of a writer trying to find his own language and mode beyond the shadows of his ancestors. In the *Consolation*, Lady Philosophy drives the Muses away, not because poetry has no place in the text—it obviously does—but because the author needs to find his own voice,[3] just as Geffrey in the *House of Fame* has to leave behind the classical authorities to find new tidings of his own.

Boethius was fundamentally concerned with time and space and, indeed, with their interconnection, 'the space of lif infinit' (book 5, prosa 6, 466). The form of the *Consolation*, alternating prose and metre, itself aestheticises a philosophy of time: the temporal sequence of prose is ruptured by the poetry, which comes from out of time and out of the story of the narrative. Thus time, as experienced in day-to-day life, is contrasted with an extratemporal divine perspective, and the very harmony of God's time is made visible and audible in the harmony of metre.[4] A similar contrast is evident in Boethius's treatment of space, where the cage of embodied imprisonment is contrasted with the flight of philosophy, with the important caveat that it is not literal imprisonment that matters, but the internal limitation of the self. The prisoner is 'enclosed in so greet angwyssche of nede' (book 2, prosa 4, 412); Philosophy attaches 'fetheris' to his 'thought' so that it 'mai arisen in heighte,' so that the prisoner can return 'unto thyn house' and 'unto thi contree' (book 4, prosa 1, 441). Indeed, the metaphor of the journey is fundamental in this text: Boethius takes the idea of the 'methodos' of a mode of enquiry and makes it into a 'via'—a way, a journey, to a true home, Augustinian style.[5] The prison, or cage, is the body enclosing the soul: God 'encloseth with membres the soules' (book 3, metrum 6, 427), and the soul desires to return to its spiritual home, outside the body, with the divine.

Boethius describes this natural longing through the image of the caged bird. The bird longs to be 'on the heghe braunches,' 'in the wode'; she sees the 'agreables schadwes of the wodes' and seeks 'oonly the wode,' 'desyrynge the wode with hir swete voys.' She rebels against the cage: she is 'enclosed

---

[3] Seth Lerer, *Boethius and Dialogue* (Princeton: Princeton University Press, 1985; repr. 2014), 101.

[4] See Eleanor Johnson, 'Chaucer and the Consolation of Prosimetrum,' *Chaucer Review* 43:4 (2009): 461–65. She develops her argument further in *Practicing Literary Theory in the Middle Ages: Ethics and the Mixed Form in Chaucer, Gower, Usk, and Hoccleve* (Chicago: University of Chicago Press, 2013).

[5] Lerer, *Boethius and Dialogue*, 8.

in a streyte cage,' and skips 'out of hir streyte cage,' refusing to be tempted by the 'honyed drynkes and large metes' that men offer her (423). This example is part of a series of examples in book 3, metrum 2, all focused on the idea that 'Alle thynges seken ayen to hir proper cours, and alle thynges rejoysen hem of hir retornynge ayen to hir nature.' The exempla are specifically linked to men looking towards the 'verray fyn of blisfulnesse' as 'naturel entencioun' leads them 'to thilke verray good' (book 3, prosa 3, 423).

This Boethian image of the cage was one to which Chaucer often returned. He translated the passage as part of his translation of the whole text, and he drew very closely on book 3, metrum 2 in the 'Manciple's Tale,' and also in the 'Squire's Tale.' Both tales include birds as characters more generally, but in both tales the idea of the bird in a cage is also used as an image of human behaviour, in a direct reworking of the *Consolation*. When Chaucer reworks Boethius in the 'Manciple's Tale,' the image is turned on its head: the Manciple uses the caged bird who flees to the forest as an image for the adulterous woman who seeks extramarital sex. For the Manciple, when the bird eschews the comforts offered it by its owner and desires the 'forest that is rude and coold,' it reveals its baseness: it wants 'wormes and swich wrechednesse' rather than refined food (170–71). Its desire to *leave* the cage is driven by disreputable and dirty needs of the body, in stark contrast to Boethius's focus on the cage itself as the place of the body, and the woods as the place of beauty, freedom, song, and flight.

When Chaucer reworks Boethius, he characteristically inserts a different take on material culture, modernity, and *things* in general. A good example of this approach comes in *The Former Age*, a poem that draws extensively on book 2, metrum 5, but inserts ambiguity about the relative value of the simple life versus modernity as the narrator lingers over the joys of materially and technologically advanced life.[6] A particularly interesting moment comes in the first verse. Boethius's words: 'They weren wont lyghtly to slaken hir hungir at even with accornes of ookes' (book 2, metrum 5, 415) become, in *The Former Age*, '[t]hey eten mast [acorns and beechnuts], hawes [hawthorn berries], and swich pounage [pig food].' In

---

[6] Of course, none of Chaucer's narrators are reliable or replicate an authentic authorial voice. But the frequency with which Chaucer articulates this perspective certainly demonstrates a refusal to endorse Boethius's philosophical perspective.

Chaucer's poem, eating plain food is no longer solely a sign of purity and natural living; rather, it also demonstrates a debasement as the people of this former age are eating food fit for pigs. The implication is that in lacking the developments of civilization they also lack a measure of what makes us human. A thorough reading of the *Consolation* reveals that there is another passage of relevance here: in book 4, metrum 3, Lady Philosophy tells the story of Ulysses. When Circe turns his men into pigs (swyn), they exchange their human food 'for to eten akkornes of ookes' (446). The repetition of the same phrase draws an obvious parallel within the *Consolatio* between the simple people of the first age and the animalized victims of Circe. Chaucer's specific reference to pig food encourages us to think about both parts of Boethius's text and reinforces the idea that avoiding the luxuries of life need not be a moral imperative. Indeed, across the three mythological metra in the *Consolatio*, the relationship between human and animals represents the struggle between the divine aspects of man and the lower part of his nature. In the third, triumphant mythological metrum, Hercules subdues the animals and thus 'disservide eftsones the hevene,' and reaches 'the sterres' (book 4, metrum 7, 457).[7] Being like an animal in this part of the *Consolatio* does not suggest following one's nature in a positive way (as the caged bird longing for the woods represents the soul longing for heaven); rather, animals stand for 'erthly lust' (457). The simplicity of living like an animal is not only a rejection of human possibility in terms of civilisation but also a rejection of the potential of the human mind and soul. Somewhat counterintuitively, the luxurious food of *The Former Age* represents not (or not only) a prioritization of base bodily needs but rather makes humans' bodies different from those of animals, more refined, like Ulysses's men, not Circe's pigs.

Again, in the 'Squire's Tale,' leaving the luxuries of the cage for the natural wood is wholly negative (610–20).[8] The bird flies to the 'wode' because he wants to eat 'wormes,' driven by a love of 'novelries' for their own sake. He rejects 'gentillesse,' and this rejection is revealed in his

---

[7] Lerer discusses the three mythological metra as staging the prisoner's movement upwards. *Boethius and Dialogue*, 168.

[8] As Susan Crane writes, 'Chaucer resists the philosophical clarity of Boethius's position on "kynde."' Susan Crane, *Animal Encounters: Contacts and Concepts in Medieval Britain* (Philadelphia: University of Pennsylvania Press, 2013), 131.

eschewing not only the comforts of the cage—its owners 'strawe hir cage faire and softe as silk, / And yeve hem sugre, hony, breed and milk'—but also the care that they lavish on him: 'nyght and day take of hem hede.' So it is a rejection of refined feelings and care as well as a rejection of refined material aspects of life. In both the 'Manciple's' and the 'Squire's' Tales, the bird's desire for the woods reveals the blunted vulgarity of its nature. It does not appreciate civilization or refinement. And in both tales, seeking worms is a metaphor for lust-based, adulterous sex (by the wife in the 'Manciple's Tale' and by the male lover in the 'Squire's Tale'), while the beautiful, comfortable cage and edible delicacies represent a monogamous, loving relationship. Both tales also feature an actual bird in a cage, a bird that in one tale represents a betrayed lady and in the other a brutalized court servant—in both cases these birds are truthful and broadly sympathetic characters; in neither case do they want to leave their cages. The bird who leaves the cage is the male who betrays the falcon in the 'Squire's Tale' and the woman who betrays Phoebus in the 'Manciple's Tale.'

What was a cage to Chaucer? Or indeed to Boethius? This is Boethius's image of the bird in its cage (book 3, metrum 2):

Quae canit altis garrula ramis
Ales *caveae* clauditur *antro*;
Huic licet inlita pocula melle
Largasque dapes dulci studio
Ludens hominum cura ministret,
Si tamen *arto* saliens *texto*
Nemorum gratas viderit umbras,
Sparsas pedibus proterit escas,
Silvas tantum maesta requirit,
Silvas dulci voce susurrat.

[The babbling bird which sings on the high branches is enclosed in *the hollow of a cage*; in this it is allowed a cup smeared with honey and ample meals; playing, the attention of man takes care of it with sweet devotion. If, however, leaping from the *tight web*, it sees the beloved shadows of the woods, it crushes with its feet its scattered dishes, it misses the woods with so much sorrow, it murmurs for the woods with its sweet voice.] (Translation and emphasis mine)

The phrases used to describe the cage are ambiguous. First, the location is described as 'caveae . . . antro.' 'Antro' has a range of meanings, including cave, tomb, and hollow, while 'cavea' can mean basket, crate, cage, coop, stall, beehive, fence, enclosure. Common sense tells us, of course, that the primary meaning is not beehive here, but the fact that the word can refer to more open structures, such as a basket or a coop, alerts us to the idea that a cage itself might not be the kind of prison-like structure that we tend to imagine. There is no reference here to a door being closed or opened; the structure is not necessarily something that can be sealed. This is further emphasized by the next description of the location, as 'arto . . . texto.' While 'arto' means tight, narrow, scarce, or strict, 'textus' has meanings such as framework, web, plait, woven fabric. None of its meanings suggest the enclosure of a modern cage. A 'textus' tends to be made out of something soft—such as spider's silk or cloth of some kind. These two phrases are translated by Jean de Meun as 'l'estraite cage' and 'sa maison estroite,' and by Chaucer, in both instances, by 'streit cage.'[9] Some of the complexities of Boethius's description are thus flattened out by his translators. But in choosing 'cage' to translate 'cavea,' Chaucer was not removing the connotations of coop or basket latent in the Latin word; similarly, in translating 'textus' as 'cage,' he was not replacing an open structure with a necessarily lockable one. The range of meanings of the word 'cage' in the fourteenth century was extensive. It was used to describe prisons but also to describe more open structures such as coops. Chaucer uses the word 'cage' twice in his description of the House of Rumour, a structure that is open, full of windows and holes, and unguarded. He describes the house as being 'mad of twigges, falwe, rede, / And grene eke, and somme weren white, / Swiche as men to these cages thwite' (1936–38). He then goes on to say that such twigs are also used to make different kinds of baskets. The emphasis on twigs, and the visual image of them as woven into baskets, is far more reminiscent of a nest than it is of a modern cage. Forty lines later, we are told that the House of Rumour is 'shapen lyk a cage' (1985). In between, the insistence on the fact that 'this hous hath of entrees / As fele as of leves ben in trees / In somer, whan they grene been' (1945–47) again associates the House with the natural world and indeed with the nest. While the Manciple and Squire use the Boethian image of the cage to contrast the cage with nature, in the *House of Fame* the two are brought together, as the cage is nest-like and organic. And it is a place from which things constantly emerge; tidings are not imprisoned here. By aligning the cage with the House of Rumour, Chaucer also compares it with the 'Domus Dedaly' or 'Laboryntus' (1920–21), a structure that is not closed off, even if it is difficult to find a way out. When Boethius writes about the 'hous of Didalus,' he creates an image of psychological enmeshing and interlacing: the prisoner tells Lady Philosophy that she 'hast so woven me with thi resouns the hous of Didalus, so entrelaced that it is unable to ben unlaced, thow that otherwhile entrist ther thow issist, and other while issist ther thow entrest' (book 3, prosa 12, 438–39).[10] Like the 'textus' of book 3, metrum 2, the image is not of an impenetrable enclosure but of a woven space, hard to escape but soft, not permanently entrapping. For Chaucer, this enclosing structure is also a space that offers protection, opportunity, and even movement.

The image of the 'cage' was also used as a metaphor for the womb, particularly the Virgin's womb. For instance, in Maidstone's *Penitential Psalms* (ca. 1390), he writes, 'A blissful brid was brought in Cage,' and Capgrave, around 1450, wrote 'Lych to the glas I lykne that maydenes kage.' The idea of the female body as an enclosure has a long history, and there is extensive critical literature about the use of this motif.[11] Chaucer refers to men treating their wives as caged animals (in the 'Miller's Tale,' John keeps

---

[10] For a reading of the House of Rumour as an intuitive representation of the neuroplasticity of the brain, see Ashby Kinch, ' "Mind Like Wickerwork": The Neuroplastic Aesthetics of Chaucer's House of Tidings,' *postmedieval* 3 (2012): 302–14. Classical memory techniques provide another important model for thinking about the mind as an architectural structure: see Mary Carruthers, *The Book of Memory: A Study of Memory in Medieval Culture*, 2nd ed. (Cambridge: Cambridge University Press, 2008).

[11] See, for instance, Stallybrass, 'Patriarchal Territories, 123–42; and Gilchrist, 'Medieval Bodies in the Material World,' 43–61. The Song of Songs 4–5 is a good example of the depiction of the female body as a locked enclosure.

Alison 'narwe in cage' [3224]), but we might also think about literally enclosed women if we think about women and cages—nuns and anchorites. But what was the cage of the cloister like? It was precisely in his early years in London, in the 1370s, that Chaucer had reason to be closely interested in the life of a nunnery, through his intimate family connection with a life of enclosure. Three years after he started work at the Custom House, his daughter became a nun at St Helen's Bishopsgate (plate 9), a stone's throw from Chaucer's Aldgate apartment, and Elizabeth remained there for four years, less than a third of a mile—a five-minute walk—from Chaucer's rooms. We know very little about this girl, but an exploration of the spaces in which she lived makes it clear that she did not vanish into a kind of voluntary prison when she took the veil—far from it. Her cage resembled a twiggy nest far more than it did a barred prison. And thinking about Chaucer's daughter reminds us of the diverse social networks, many of them facilitated by women, in which he was embedded in his London years.

In 1377, when Richard II took the throne, he exercised a traditional royal prerogative to nominate two girls to become nuns at prestigious nunneries: one at Barking Abbey, an exceptionally wealthy and aristocratic house, the other at St Helen's Bishopsgate in London, also a rich foundation, albeit a notch under Barking, and unusual in having strong mercantile, city connections.[12] In terms of St Helen's, this was the only time that a monarch ever exercised this alleged prerogative, so it may have been invented for the occasion. Richard was at this point ten years old, and his uncle, John of Gaunt, was directing affairs, so it is clear that Gaunt was very keen to place these girls in comfortable and indeed fashionable surroundings. The identity of the two girls makes Gaunt's involvement very obvious. The girl nominated to Barking on 27 July 1377 was Margaret Swynford, daughter (by her first marriage) of Katherine, now Gaunt's beloved mistress and mother of his own children. The girl nominated to St Helen's Bishopsgate was Elizabeth Chaucer, first cousin to Margaret, niece

[12] For the nominations, see *Calendar of the Patent Rolls: Richard II*, Membrane 15, 1:20 (27 July 1377). For the wealth of Barking and St Helen's, usefully set in the context of the wealth of sixty-one nunneries, see Roberta Gilchrist, *Gender and Material Culture: The Archaeology of Religious Women* (New York: Routledge, 1994), 129–30.

of Katherine, and daughter of Philippa, lady-in-waiting to Gaunt's wife, Constance. We know nothing of Elizabeth prior to this point; it is most likely that she was born around the mid- to late 1360s and was between eight and twelve.[13] Margaret was a similar age. This was very young to become a nun, but not unheard-of, and there were other children in nunneries as lodgers and pupils, so a child-nun would not be isolated.[14] The records do make it clear that Elizabeth is entering St Helen's as a nun, not as a student herself.[15] In some ways, though, entering into the priory at this time would have been fairly similar to entering into a great household, in terms of the standard of living, educational opportunities, and social interactions available.

Nunneries were an essential part of the social fabric, not places of removal and separation. They were businesses: they owned land and other property, collected rents, and went to court.[16] Far from being separated from others, the nuns in these religious houses were outnumbered two to one by lodgers, servants, and other lay members of the household.[17] Within such houses, important nuns occupied private sets of chambers and ate luxurious food.[18] This does not mean that the nuns were irreligious, or that prayer was unimportant, but it demonstrates that nuns who came from wealthy backgrounds maintained their standard of living once they entered the cloister. Indeed, within nunneries, there was a developing trend for more private modes of living, a trend that mirrors lifestyle changes in secular life too and that was a source of anxiety. In 1387, for instance, William of Wykeham sent injunctions to the nunneries under his diocesan

---

[13] We first hear of Geoffrey and Philippa being married in 1366, although the marriage could have taken place earlier. Katherine married Sir Hugh Swynford at a similar time, and he died in 1371.

[14] Paul Lee, *Nunneries, Learning, and Spirituality in Late Medieval English Society: The Dominican Priory of Dartford* (York: York University Press, 2001), 160–62. Eileen Power, *Medieval English Nunneries, c. 1275 to 1535* (Cambridge: Cambridge University Press, 1922), 261–64.

[15] *Calendar of the Patent Rolls: Richard II*, Membrane 15, 1:20 (27 July 1377).

[16] Nancy Bradley Warren, *Spiritual Economies: Female Monasticism in Later Medieval England* (Philadelphia: University of Pennsylvania Press, 2001), 67; Lee, *Nunneries*, 50–51.

[17] Ibid., 66.

[18] On private quarters and eating, see Marilyn Oliva, *The Convent and the Community in Late Medieval England: Female Monasteries in the Diocese of Norwich, 1350–1540* (Cambridge: Boydell Press, 1998), 102–3n171; on the diet at Barking, see 'Charthe longynge to the Office of the Celeresse of the Monasterye of Barkynge,' in William Dugdale, *Monasticon Anglicanum* (London: Longman, 1817–30), 1:442–45.

control, exhorting the nuns to eat communally and warning them against holding private property.[19]

Chaucer surely visited his daughter; her placement in St Helen's makes particular sense if we remember that her father was living very close by, and her grandmother, Chaucer's mother, also lived in the city. Indeed, it is likely that Chaucer stayed with his mother at times if his utilitarian Aldgate rooms became too dreary for him.[20] St Helen's was a welcoming place for visitors. Sixty years later, Dean Reynold Kentwode visited St Helen's and wrote detailed recommendations for reform; the practices that he describes and prohibits were clearly entrenched, so his injunctions give us an insight into what this house was like when Chaucer's daughter was there. Kentwode makes it clear that 'there is moche coming in and owte unlefulle tymys,' and urges the nuns not to allow a secular visitor to 'be lokkyd withinne the boundes of the cloystere,' nor to come in after compline, except for women servants and girl pupils. He goes on to recommend that a trustworthy woman be in charge of the keys, to keep people out of the cloisters after compline and at other inappropriate times. He adds that no secular woman should sleep there without special permission. The prioress is urged to sleep in her 'dortour' by night, and the nuns should refrain from 'daunsyng and revelyng' except at Christmas and other 'honest tymys of recreacyone.' It is noticeable that even the reforms allow for regular, if regulated, dancing and parties in the priory. Other injunctions are elliptical: the prioress is urged not to 'use nor haunte any place with inne the priory, thoroghe the wiche evel suspeccyone or sclaundere mythe aryse; weche places for certeyne causes that move us, we wryte not here inne owre present iniunccyone.'[21] We can only speculate about what might lie behind this cryptic warning. But we consistently hear that the priory is a social space, a space penetrated by outsiders as a matter of course, a space embedded in its London surroundings.

---

[19] Richard Luce (ed. and trans.), 'Injunctions Made and Issued to the Abbess and Convent of the Monastery of Romsey after His Visitation by William of Wykeham, 1387,' *Hampshire Field Club and Archaeology Society Proceedings* 17, part 1 (1949): 34, 38.

[20] Strohm reconstructs Chaucer's dingy rooms in *The Poet's Tale*, 52–61.

[21] Reynold Kentwode's injunctions date from 21 June 1439. Dugdale, *Monasticon Anglicanum*, 4:553–54.

The spaces of the priory are a constant concern for Kentwode. He frequently worries about who is inside 'the boundes,' making detailed recommendations about what kind of person (a 'sadde woman and discrete') can be in charge of the keys, and ordering that the nuns should not be able to unlock the postern door and get into the churchyard. He also makes specific recommendations about changing the way the church and its outbuildings are divided, which lets us know their prior layout. For instance, Kentwode wants a door to be built on the 'nonnes quere'—the nuns' part of the double church, which was half the nuns' place of worship (the north side), and half a parish church (the south side), the two halves placed side by side. Kentwode's injunction suggests that the two halves were not firmly separated, and indeed he specifies that the door should be provided so that strangers don't look at nuns, nor nuns at strangers. Even more intriguingly, he wants the prioress to make 'a hache of conabyll heyth, crestyd with pykys of herne to fore the entre of yowre kechyne' to keep strangers out. He here specifies that the kitchen should be closed off with a door—perhaps a split stable-type door—with horned spikes on the top. The symbolism of the 'pykys of herne' is fascinating: presumably, these would be aesthetically impressive and also intimidating. Is the idea partly that the spikes would discourage people from climbing in? In which case, were there people who did indeed want to climb into—or out of—the priory? There are cases of nuns running away and marrying.[22] The detail that Kentwode supplies reveals how much patterns of behaviour are perceived as being tied to the arrangement of space. The fortified door is to be a guarantee of the nuns' morality; a more complete enclosure will protect them from the moral infections and physical incursions of the secular world. St Helen's social and spatial practices were typical: Wykeham's injunctions to Romsey Abbey issued in 1387 similarly complain about, 'the great traffic and concourse of secular people of either sex through your cloister,' and go on to lay down rules about when doors can and cannot be opened, and about who should have guardianship of the doors.[23]

---

[22] Minnie Reddan and Alfred W. Clapham, *Survey of London, Vol. IX: The Parish of St Helen Bishopsgate* (London: Batsford, London County Council, 1924), 8.

[23] Luce, 'Injunctions,' 41.

The environment into which Chaucer's daughter was placed was an environment familiar to her, and to her father. The great patron of St Helen's Bishopsgate was Adam Fraunceys. Mercer, wine merchant, property developer, wool exporter, collector of customs in London for several years in the 1360s, stalwart city official, alderman, MP, and twice mayor of London, Fraunceys would have been well known to Chaucer, and indeed to Chaucer's father.[24] Fraunceys had long had business dealings with St Helen's, dating back to 1348 when he leased land from them, and he may well have ended up residing in his house in the close of St Helen's.[25] He endowed two chantries at St Helen's, and when he died, he left property and rents to the nuns in general and also to a named sister, Katherine Wolf, probably a relative.[26] He died in 1375, so by the time Elizabeth was professed, a Mass was said daily for his soul, and his anniversary was elaborately commemorated. Fraunceys's daughter, Maud, married John Montagu, 3rd earl of Salisbury, as her third husband: he was one of the so-called Lollard knights, with whom Chaucer was socially and culturally connected. Indeed, the poet Christine de Pisan was to praise Salisbury's own poetry and his affection for poetry.[27] St Helen's itself had a fascinating literary connection: the Puy, London's own mercantile poetry competition, had chosen the priory for the annual celebration of a Mass for dead members.[28]

Elizabeth only stayed at St Helen's for four years. In 1381, she transferred to Barking Abbey, where her cousin already lived. John of Gaunt paid lavishly for this transfer: he expended £51 8s 2d.[29] She was still there in 1397 and presumably stayed there until her death. Gaunt's generosity is of a piece with his constant sponsorship of Thomas Chaucer, and indeed

---

[24] Stephen O'Connor, 'Fraunceys, Adam,' in the *ODNB*, https://doi.org/10.1093/ref:odnb/52176; Stephen O'Connor, 'Finance, Diplomacy, and Politics: Royal Service by Two London Merchants in the Reign of Edward III,' *Historical Research* 67 (1994): 18–39; Stephen O'Connor (ed.), *Calendar of the Cartularies of John Pyel and Adam Fraunceys: Mayors and Merchants of London, 14th Century* (Cambridge: Cambridge University Press, 1995).

[25] O'Connor, *Cartularies*, 63.

[26] Ibid., 22.

[27] McFarlane, *Lancastrian Kings and Lollard Knights*, 175; Christine de Pisan, *The Vision of Christine de Pizan*, trans. Glenda McLeod and Charity Cannon Willard (Cambridge: D. S. Brewer, 2005), 106. Chaucer was with Salisbury in Montreuil in 1377. Crow and Olson, *Chaucer Life-Records*, 50.

[28] Reddan and Clapham, *Survey of London*, 4.

[29] Crow and Olson, *Chaucer Life-Records*, 546.

Chaucer's other son, Lewis Chaucer, also appears in Lancastrian records. The Chaucer children were clearly viewed by Gaunt as part of his household, which makes sense given his relationship to Katherine alone, quite apart from Philippa and Geoffrey's services to him. But why did Elizabeth move in 1381? Gaunt issued the warrant for the payment on 12 May—that is, before the Rising of 1381, so the horror of the rebels' behaviour in London was not a factor. Instead, I would tentatively point to another document: Chaucer's quitclaim of the property in Vintry Ward on 19 June 1381.[30] What this quitclaim reveals to us is that Chaucer's mother had died. She had previously owned this property, after the death of John Chaucer, and Chaucer inherited it from her, not from his father. As this is the first reference to the property being in Chaucer's ownership, it is reasonable to assume that she died not long before this date and that Chaucer immediately, or fairly quickly, handed it over to the long-term tenant, Henry Herbury. Until 1381, Chaucer had a mother and a daughter living very close to him. Elizabeth, a child in London, very likely saw her grandmother regularly, and her death might have made London a much lonelier place for her—notwithstanding the presence of her father. Her move to Barking might then have been strongly motivated by the desirability of being near another female relative (her cousin Margaret) now that she no longer had her grandmother to support her.

Chaucer was losing women in droves. His wife does not seem to have lived regularly with him: Gaunt paid her allowance to her in Lincolnshire between 1378 and 1383, where she could either have been attending Constance at one of Gaunt's manors or staying with her sister Katherine at her Lincolnshire manor, Kettlethorpe.[31] Now, in one year, his daughter moved away and his mother died. In the previous year, he had had some kind of encounter, almost certainly sexual, perhaps nonconsensual, with Cecily Champaigne, a relationship that, however it started, ended disastrously with lawsuits and damages.[32] Critics have written a great deal

[30] Ibid., 1–2. See page 10 and note 1 for Agnes Chaucer and Bartholomew Chappell's possession of the property after John Chaucer's death.

[31] Ibid., 80, 87–88.

[32] Ibid., 344–45; Christopher Cannon, '*Raptus* in the Chaumpaigne Release and a Newly Discovered Document Concerning the Life of Geoffrey Chaucer,' *Speculum* 68 (1993): 74–94; Christopher Cannon, 'Chaucer and Rape: Uncertainty's Certainties,' *Studies in the Age of Chaucer* 22 (2000): 67–92;

about this case; some have been keen to make it clear that Chaucer could not have been a rapist, often using his sympathy for female characters as 'evidence' in his favour; others have tried to explore what it means for us as critics if we believe that he was a rapist. It is the most controversial of all the life-records.[33] What we know is that Chaucer was accused of 'raptus'— almost certainly an accusation of sexual rape. He paid the accuser off, and the case was dropped. Another document about the case makes no mention of 'raptus': this might be because Chaucer and his powerful male supporters fought to have that damaging accusation struck off the record, or it might be because the extreme accusation was only included in the first place as a bargaining chip.[34] We don't know. Indeed, Chaucer did father a child around this time; that boy could have been Cecily's child, although this is highly unlikely; almost certainly he was a late child of Chaucer's marriage. That child is little Lewis, described as ten years old around 1391.[35] And all this took place just before the Rising of 1381, with its traumatic violation of boundaries and destruction of certainties.

We have no evidence that Chaucer had any successful relationships of any kind with women in the last couple of decades of his life. Indeed, the sexual relationships that we know about in Chaucer's life both ended badly—one may have been violent, the other was at best a marriage that petered out. Of course, he may have had all kinds of relationships that we don't know anything about. But the ones that we do know about were problematic. At the beginning of the 1380s, one woman was taking him to court while another was mainly living apart from him. We could endlessly speculate about Chaucer's attitude towards women, in his life and in his writings; indeed, critics have long debated whether he was a misogynist or women's friend.[36] What happened between Chaucer and Cecily

H. A. Kelly, 'Meanings and Uses of Raptus in Chaucer's Time,' in *Inquisitions and Other Trial Procedures in the Medieval West* (Aldershot: Ashgate, 2001), 101–65. Pearsall suggests Chaucer sold his parents' house to fund payments to Cecily (*Life of Geoffrey Chaucer*, 136–37).

[33] For a discussion of critics' attitude to the case, see Susan S. Morrison, 'The Use of Biography in Medieval Literary Criticism: The Case of Geoffrey Chaucer and Cecily Chaumpaigne,' *Chaucer Review* 34:1 (1999): 69–86. I discuss biographers' attitudes to Cecily in 'Chaucer' (2018), 378–79.

[34] On the two different documents, see Cannon, 'Raptus,' 93.

[35] *A Treatise on the Astrolabe*, Prologue, 24, p. 662. See chapter 9 in this study.

[36] Dinshaw, *Chaucer's Sexual Poetics*; Elaine Tuttle Hansen, *Chaucer and the Fictions of Gender* (Berkeley: University of California Press, 1992); Catherine Cox, *Gender and Language in Chaucer* (Gainesville: University Press of Florida, 1997); Jill Mann, *Feminizing Chaucer* (Woodbridge: D. S.

Champaigne cannot be recovered by us; it remains uncertain, unknowable perhaps to anyone but the two of them.

The women with whom Chaucer was connected tended to be independent. He was himself no John, or January, or Walter, keeping women in cages under his own control. His wife Philippa had her own job and her own money, and this did not change after she had children. She lived in great households, and in her sister's household far more than she lived with her husband. She moved in higher social circles than he did, entered into a grand fraternity in company with some of the most important people in the land, and moved herself and her children largely into her sister's orbit. Agnes Chaucer, Geoffrey's mother, had been a property owner in her own right. Cecily Champaigne sued him, in her own name, and it paid off. She didn't retreat and keep silent out of shame. Chaucer centred two of his dream poems around real women: Blanche of Lancaster and Anne of Bohemia. And Chaucer's own daughter, by entering prestigious nunneries, was in fact put in a position to be in many ways more independent than a married woman, to live a comfortable and intellectually free life, a life of figs and books.[37] Her cousin became the abbess at Barking, which meant becoming a major businesswoman and manager. In London more generally, Chaucer would have known female artisans, *femmes sole* who traded in their own right, guildswomen, and property owners.[38] His life gave him multiple experiences of women as thinking and independent beings, strong women, even though they underwent all kinds of legal and social constraints. There is no evidence that Chaucer ever acted as a controlling patriarch within his family, or that he had *any*

Brewer, 2002); Sheila Delany, *The Naked Text: Chaucer's 'Legend of Good Women'* (Berkeley: University of California Press, 1994).

[37] 'Charthe longynge to the Office of the Celeresse of the Monasterye of Barkynge,' in Dugdale, *Monasticon Anglicanum*, 1:444.

[38] For instance, there were female blacksmiths; see Jane Geddes, 'Iron,' in John Blair and Nigel Ramsay (eds.), *English Medieval Industries: Craftsmen, Techniques, Products* (London: Hambledon Press, 1991), 186. See also Helen M. Jewell, *Women in Medieval England* (Manchester: Manchester University Press, 1991); Caroline M. Barron, 'The "Golden Age" of Women in Medieval London,' in A. K. Bate and Malcolm Barber (eds.), *Medieval Women in Southern England*, Reading Medieval Studies 15 (Reading: Graduate Centre for Medieval Studies, University of Reading, 1989), 35–58; Caroline Barron and Anne Sutton (eds.), *Medieval London Widows, 1300–1500* (London: Hambledon Press, 1994); Barbara Hanawalt (ed.), *Women and Work in Pre-Industrial Europe* (Bloomington: Indiana University Press, 1986).

family or intimate experience of women who lived under the direct and exclusive financial and spatial control of men.

The cages that Chaucer controlled were not metaphorical cages for women. They were actual bird enclosures. When he was appointed as clerk of the king's works—the job that gave him jurisdiction over the works on the Tower, amongst many other royal properties—he was given responsibility for the royal mews at Charing Cross, home of the king's falcons ('mutas nostras pro falconibus nostris juxta Charryngcrouch').[39] Birds of prey were of central importance to royal and aristocratic modes of living in late-medieval Europe. The mews had been built more than a century earlier, in 1274–77, on the site that now houses the National Gallery in Trafalgar Square. The mews were built around a preexisting chapel to St Eustace. They consisted of the homes for the birds, set in a turfed garden, containing a lead bath with a metal image of a falcon. The London aqueduct piped water here, which emerged through four brass spouts ending in leopards' heads. There were dovecotes, providing food for the falcons, kennels, a house for cranes (that the falcons could fly at), and a falconers' hall. This hall was rebuilt a few years later, with a kitchen, a storage room, and a garderobe. Solars were built for the falconers and the chaplains, and a wall made of earth and thatched with reeds divided the mews from the road.[40] The birds' own residential areas would also have been open: usually mews were not locked enclosures but airy rooms, sometimes allowing room to fly, although the birds were tethered by their jesses. The birds were brought out for baths and carefully tended, given their high value. And the mews were not, of course, their permanent home: they came here only for the nonhunting, moulting season, so that they could grow their new feathers in safety and avoid injuring them when they were nascent and vulnerable. Although aspects of the care of birds of prey were cruel—some falconers sewed up the eyes of birds to train them—it was impossible to train a bird effectively without taking care of them, developing relationships of trust, and, in particular, paying careful attention to their senses. Adelard of Bath, a philosopher and mathematician, who wrote a falconry

---

[39] Crow and Olson, *Chaucer Life-Records*, 403; 'our mews for our falcons next to Charing Cross' (translation mine).

[40] H. M. Colvin et al. (eds.), *History of the King's Works* (London: HMSO, 1963–82), 1:550–51.

treatise in the twelfth century, advised the falconer to sing to his bird when feeding her, so that the bird would associate gentle music with food. Bathing was another ritual designed to calm the birds.[41] Rather than sewing up the eyes, birds could be calmed by being hooded, and curtains were also provided in the Charing Cross mews. The birds, then, lived in a place with running water piped in and fabric curtains at their windows—a luxurious mode of living available to few medieval humans. At Lionel of Antwerp's wedding to Violante Visconti in 1368 (at which Chaucer might even have been present),[42] the guests were plied with gifts of hunting birds at the second, fourth, and fifth course: at the fifth course, they were given six peregrine falcons with hoods of velvet, decorated with pearls, buttons, and rings of silver.[43] The birds were thus associated with luxury, with the highest pleasures of a refined, civilized, exclusive existence. The formel's preference for the beautiful cage of the 'Squire's Tale' that Canace crafts for her makes absolute sense in this context. And indeed, her bedchamber-like mew, with its hangings and paintings, may not function as amusing anthropomorphizing fantasy but as realistic depiction of the mews in which royal birds spent the spring and summer months. Birds did sometimes sleep in bedchambers, where perches could be part of the furniture.[44] In *Troilus and Criseyde*, Chaucer repeatedly uses the mew as an image of a room or hiding place, a space that offers protection and safety and allows the metaphorical bird to look out.[45] When Troilus returns from literal hawking, he sees Criseyde appearing at 'hire wyndow' looking '[a]s fressh as faukon comen out of muwe' (Book III, 1783–85). Troilus's hiding place, from which he can look out via a 'litel wyndow,' is also described as a 'mewe' (Book III, 601–2); its secrecy conveys power to Troilus. The mew is a place of security, but it

---

[41] Robin Oggins, *The Kings and Their Hawks: Falconry in Medieval England* (New Haven: Yale University Press, 2004), 24–25.

[42] Chaucer went on a trip abroad in 1368. We don't know where he went, and although it is possible he attended Lionel's wedding, we do not have any evidence for this. For his trip overseas at this time, see Crow and Olson, *Chaucer Life-Records*, 29–30.

[43] Oggins, *Kings and Their Hawks*, 111.

[44] Ibid., 6.

[45] See also Book I, 381; Book IV, 496; and Book IV, 1310.

is not closed off from the world: its windows are crucial in both of these scenes.[46]

Of course, the luxuriousness of the Charing Cross birds' privileged and cossetted existence, tended with medicines, lovingly bathed, jealously nurtured, should not make us forget their lack of liberty. The idea of training the birds was that they would internalize their subjection so that they would come willingly back to hand. In essence, this is the relationship that humans have with pets.[47] If we imagine this as a metaphor for a human relationship—for instance, the relationship between Walter and Griselda, January and May, Phoebus and his servant—the relationship is clearly monstrous, and is presented as such by Chaucer. But there are other ways of thinking about cages, birds, and constraint. Medieval Christian culture sometimes imagined the relationship between master and bird as a positive image for God's relationship with the soul. In a fifteenth-century poem (which may reflect an older tradition), in BL MS Add. 37049, Christ is the falconer, winning back sinners to grace by showing them his wounds, representing the meat used to lure back a hawk.[48] This idea may be reflected in a carving in the Angel Choir of Lincoln Cathedral, of an angel wearing a falconer's glove and offering meat to the hawk on his wrist.[49] This image of the benefits of voluntary captivity turns Boethius's metaphor of the caged bird inside out: for Boethius, departing from the cage and flying to the woods represented reaching for the divine, for one's true home; in the iconography described above, it is the return to captivity that represents the return to God. But the crucial difference is that the captivity is chosen.

Chaucer too is interested in voluntary constraint, and in thinking about the caged creature in nongendered terms, as a way of exploring identity more generally. In his reworkings of Boethius, Chaucer suggests that total freedom is the freedom literally to eat worms, or pig food, to exist apart

---

[46]Machaut also presents his narrator as hiding in a mew (en mue) like a hawk (esprevier) and then going to the window (fenestre); see The Judgement of the King of Navarre, 459–60 and 465.

[47]Kathleen Walker-Meikle, Medieval Pets (Woodbridge: Boydell Press, 2012), 1–4, 42–43, 51.

[48]Discussed in Jessica Brantley, Reading in the Wilderness: Private Devotion and Public Performance in Late Medieval England (Chicago: University of Chicago Press, 2008), 132.

[49]Oggins, Kings and Their Hawks, 134, fig. 15.

from the conventions of society. As many philosophers have suggested, subjection is a precondition of self-awareness.[50] Chaucer's interest in the subject configures identity as productive constraint, formed through relationships—some of them subjected—with others. The cage that is really a nest, the nest that is really a cage is a porous enclosure, a place of security and openness, constraint and comfort, limitation and opportunity.

Boethius wrote at a time in which the area of literary studies was moving from the public to the private, from forum to classroom or study, from the polis to the individual.[51] In cultural terms, Chaucer wrote at a historical moment that saw the rapid development of a public sphere fuelled by the growth of all kinds of textual production.[52] Boethian allegory is reconfigured by Chaucer into a more social and material commentary on how to live and how to be. Boethius was writing as an isolated man on the equivalent of death row, Chaucer as a person enmeshed in communities. For Chaucer, we are all in cages, the question is how to make a virtue out of that necessity.

[50] Christopher Cannon, 'Enclosure,' in David Wallace and Carolyn Dinshaw (eds.), *The Cambridge Companion to Medieval Women's Writing* (Cambridge: Cambridge University Press, 2003), 109–23.

[51] Lerer, *Boethius and Dialogue*, 3–4.

[52] See David Lawton, *Voice in Later Medieval English Literature: Public Interiorities* (Oxford: Oxford University Press, 2017); Anne Middleton, 'The Idea of Public Poetry in the Reign of Richard II,' *Speculum* 53:1 (1978): 94–114; Karma Lochrie, *Covert Operations: The Medieval Uses of Secrecy* (Philadelphia: University of Pennsylvania Press, 1999); Sheila Lindenbaum, 'London Texts and Literate Practice,' in David Wallace (ed.), *The Cambridge History of Medieval English Literature* (Cambridge: Cambridge University Press, 1999), 284–310; Clanchy, *From Memory to Written Record*; Marion Turner, 'Imagining Polities: Social Possibilities and Conflict,' in D. Vance Smith and Holly Crocker (eds.), *Medieval Literature: Criticism and Debates* (Abingdon: Routledge, 2014), 403–6; and Turner, 'Conflict.'

CHAPTER 9

Milky Way

Humanity is not forever chained to this planet and our visions go
rather further than that.

—*Neil Armstrong*

From this cage, Chaucer looked at the stars, as many prisoners do. He
wrote about the stars and planets in many of his texts and wrote a prose
treatise about the astrolabe. He had read astronomical texts ranging from
Macrobius's *Commentary on the Dream of Scipio* with its discussions of the
exact mass of the sun and the circumference of the earth to Masha'Allah
ibn Atharī's *Compositio et operatio astrolabii*, a key source text for *A Treatise on the Astrolabe*, to Nicholas of Lynn's *Kalendarium*, a contemporary
practical text to which Chaucer refers by name.[1] He was particularly fascinated by the idea of flight. In both the *Parliament of Fowls* and the *House
of Fame*, he writes about a human ascent to the stars, and many of his other
writings—such as *Troilus and Criseyde*, the 'Squire's Tale,' and *Boece*—also
imagine supernatural flight. Chaucer was the first person to write in English about the 'Milky Wey' and the 'Galaxie' (*House of Fame*, 936–37).[2]
And he was writing at a time in which university scholars debated the

[1] Macrobius is mentioned several times by Chaucer and, in particular, his *Commentary* is a key
source for the *Parliament of Fowls*. Macrobius, *Commentary on the Dream of Scipio*, trans. with intro.
and notes by William Harris Stahl (New York: Columbia University Press, 1952). For the sources of *A
Treatise on the Astrolabe*, see *Riverside Chaucer*, 1092–93. Nicholas of Lynn is mentioned in the Prologue to the *Treatise* in *Riverside Chaucer*, 663, line 86.

[2] The terms are then used in the late 1390s by John Trevisa in his translation of Bartholomaeus's *De
Proprietatibus Rerum*.

possibility of other worlds and infinite space; medical manuscripts were illustrated with 'zodiac men,' showing the relationship between health and the stars; and astronomy was one of the core subjects of the quadrivium. Perhaps the most arresting element of Chaucer's depiction of 'Geffrey's' unwilling astral flight is his persistent physicality: 'noyous' to carry (*House of Fame*, 574), his bodily mass resists his elevation, and his escape to the spheres leads him inexorably back to a very London-like space.

In his interests in flying and in the stars and planets, Chaucer was very much of his moment. Philosophers and scientists fantasized about flying machines throughout the late-medieval period.[3] In the literary-mythological sphere, stories about Icarus, flying horses, and Phaethon were repeated and analysed in detailed commentaries.[4] Speculative thought about the cosmos and what lay beyond the universe increased dramatically after 1277, a date sometimes said to mark the beginning of modern science.[5] Ironically, it was theological anti-Aristotelianism that partly enabled these thought experiments: the 1277 Paris condemnations censured Aristotelian doctrines—such as the assertion that there were no other universes—for limiting the power of God. These condemnations stimulated thinkers to write about infinite space and the possibility of other worlds.[6] Thomas Bradwardine, for instance, the fourteenth-century Oxford scholar and archbishop of Canterbury, some of whose work Chaucer certainly knew, wrote about the infinite void space of the cosmos.[7] Later in the century, in a particularly striking assertion of God's ability to transcend the laws of space, Albert of Saxony wrote that God:

[3] For discussion, see Ingham, *The Medieval New*, 112.

[4] Craig A. Berry, 'Flying Sources: Classical Authority in Chaucer's *Squire's Tale*,' *English Literary History* 68:2 (2001): 287–313.

[5] This was the view of Pierre Duhem; see *Études sur Léonard de Vinci, ceux qu'il a lus et ceux qui l'ont lu* (Paris: A. Hermann, 1906), 2:412. For discussion and critique of Duhem's claim, see Richard Newhauser, 'Inter scientiam et populum,' in Jan A. Aertsen, Kent Emery, and Andreas Speer (eds.), *Nach der Veruteilung von 1277/After the Condemnation of 1277*, Miscellanea Mediaevalia 28 (Berlin: Walter de Gruyter, 2001). See also Philip Knox, Jonathan Morton, and Daniel Reeve (eds.), *Medieval Thought Experiments: Poetry, Hypothesis, and Experience in the European Middle Ages* (Turnhout: Brepols, 2018).

[6] See especially the discussion in William F. Woods, *Chaucerian Spaces: Spatial Poetics in Chaucer's Opening Tales* (Albany: State University of New York Press, 2008), 61–69. See also Linda Tarte Holley, *Reason and Imagination in Chaucer, the 'Perle'-Poet, and the 'Cloud'-Author: Seeing from the Centre* (New York: Palgrave Macmillan, 2011), 26.

[7] Chaucer mentions Bradwardine in the 'Nun's Priest's Tale,' 3242. See also Woods, *Chaucerian Spaces*, 65.

could place a body as large as the world inside a millet seed. . . . Within that millet seed, God could create a space of 100 leagues, or 1000, or however many are imaginable. A man inside that millet seed could traverse all those many leagues simply by walking from one extremity of the millet seed to the other.[8]

This kind of thought experiment lies behind Symkyn's mockery of the Cambridge students in the 'Reeve's Tale,' when he says, 'Ye konne by argumentes make a place / A myle brood of twenty foot of space' (4123–24)—although the students, of course, have the last (violent) laugh when they do indeed turn the mundane small room into a place of sexual opportunity and rape.[9] They also alter their hosts' perceptions of space when John moves the cot. Specific interest in the skies was increasing exponentially in the West: astrolabes became much more widespread in the thirteenth and fourteenth centuries, especially as small, portable, flat astrolabes were developed (plate 11).[10] Richard II himself had a strong interest in astronomy—and astrology and geomancy—and John of Gaunt also commissioned astronomical books.[11] In Paris, thinkers such as Oresme speculated about the rotation of the earth and imagined what an eye would see from the heavens as he demonstrated the relativity of perspective.[12] And a great scientific and practical leap forward was made when mechanical clocks were invented, many of which were based on astrolabes.[13] The development of the public clock radically changed how time (and labour) were measured and imagined.

[8] Albert of Saxony, *De caelo et mundo*, in *Quaestiones et decisiones physicales insignium virorum* (Paris: Iodoci Badii & Conradi Resch, 1518), book 1, question 9, 93v, col. 2. Discussed in Woods, *Chaucerian Spaces*, 61–71.

[9] See discussions by Sheila Delany, *Medieval Literary Politics: Shapes of Ideology* (Manchester: Manchester University Press, 1990), 108; Peter Brown, *Chaucer and the Making of Optical Space* (Oxford: Peter Lang, 2007), 136–42; and Peter Brown, 'The Containment of Symkyn: The Function of Space in the "Reeve's Tale,"' *Chaucer Review* 14:3 (1980): 225–36.

[10] See Alexander Murray, 'Purgatory and the Spatial Imagination,' in Paolo Acquaviva and Jennifer Petrie (eds.), *Dante and the Church: Literary and Historical Essays* (Dublin: Four Courts Press, 2007), 77.

[11] Linne R. Mooney, 'Chaucer and Interest in Astronomy at the Court of Richard II,' in Geoffrey Lester (ed.), *Chaucer in Perspective: Middle English Essays in Honour of Norman Blake* (Sheffield: Sheffield Academic Press, 1999), 139–60.

[12] Kaye, *History of Balance*, 461–62.

[13] Murray, 'Purgatory,' 78–84. On the development of clocks, see also Le Goff, 'Merchant's Time and Church's Time,' 34–37.

In some of his writings about the stars and planets, Chaucer describes the experience of looking up to the skies (particularly in the later *Treatise on the Astrolabe*, discussed below); in others he imagines what it might be like to look down from an astral perspective. In both the *House of Fame* and the *Parliament of Fowls*, Chaucer describes the experience of being transported to the stars and looking down at the earth. It is appropriate that these astral flights happen in dream poems: journeys into the immensity and vastness of space mirror the journey into the depths of the self represented by the dream. For many late-medieval writers, the idea of flight and the idea of ascending to the stars were both figures for the separation of soul from body. Avicenna, for instance, used the flying man as a central image in his argument about the nature of the soul and the role of the senses. He referred to the idea in three different places in his work as a central statement of his Neoplatonism (understood here to mean a loose philosophical position that took as a central tenet the idea that mind or thought preceded and could escape from the material). The flying man is suspended, unable to see, and positioned in such a way that his limbs do not touch each other, and the air or void around him is such that he cannot feel it. Cut off from his senses and his physicality, he is nonetheless aware that he has a soul. Avicenna uses the image to affirm a body/soul duality: flying represents spiritual escape.[14] In Neoplatonic thought, one could go beyond the senses to commune with the divine: in the twelfth-century *Anticlaudianus*, for instance, Alain de Lille depicts a chariot whose wheels symbolize Arithmetic, Music, Geometry, and Astronomy, pulled by the flying horses of the five senses, driven by Reason, which takes Intelligence up to heaven. There, Intelligence leaves behind Nature, the senses, the arts, and Reason, to enter into the world of Theology and seek a soul.[15] In the celestial realm, the senses are abandoned along with education and reason.

---

[14] See Juhana Toivanen, 'The Fate of the Flying Man: Medieval Reception of Avicenna's Thought Experiment,' in Robert Pasnau (ed.), *Oxford Studies in Medieval Philosophy* (Oxford: Oxford University Press, 2015), 3:64–97.

[15] See books 4 and 5 of Alan of Lille, *Anticlaudianus, or, The Good and Perfect Man*, trans. and comm. J. J. Sheridan (Toronto: Toronto University Press, 1973), 117–55.

The image of flight as a separation from bodiliness also animates Boethius's image of the flight from the cage, discussed in chapter 8. Boethius also famously wrote about looking down from the spheres and seeing the tiny earth below as an unimportant point, an image used by Boccaccio in the *Teseida* and Chaucer in *Troilus*. Boethius imagines the soul 'unbownden fro the prysone of the erthe' and travelling 'frely to the hevene,' stating that it then 'despiseth' all earthly things and rejoices that it is 'exempt fro alle erthly thynges.'[16] In book 4, Lady Philosophy tells the prisoner that she can fix feathers into his thought to help him to 'despiseth the hateful erthes' so that he can travel through air, clouds, fire, and the firmament until he reaches the stars and sun and is 'imaked a knyght of the clere sterre,' glossed in Chaucer's text by an explanation that the thought is made God's knight 'by the sekynge of trouthe to comen to the verray knowleche of God.' The soul then dwells in the stars 'in alle the places there as the schynynge nyght is ypainted' and travels further on to the 'dredefulle clerenesse of God.' This is the soul's true home and it remembers: 'here was I born, her wol I fasten my degree, here wol I duelle.'[17] Macrobius describes a very similar understanding of the soul's relationship both to the body and to the stars when he writes that the soul 'withdraws from the body, so to speak, under the guidance of philosophy,' and should have 'no dread of the dizzy heights of the complete ascension to the celestial realms' (121). Indeed, Cicero's *Somnium Scipionis*, another key text about astral flight well known to Chaucer, is animated by the idea that the soul's origin, true home, and eventual destination is in the outer reaches of the universe. As Macrobius writes in his commentary: 'the purpose of the dream is to teach us that the souls of those who serve the state well are returned to the heavens after death' (92). Cicero thus also uses the image of flight to the stars to discuss the idea of the body as a prison and to affirm a belief in the self-moved soul (76) although, crucially, his text advocates a commitment to safeguarding the commonwealth and to the life of the polis while on earth. Dante, whose *Divine Comedy* was profoundly

---

[16] Book 2, prosa 7, 419.
[17] Book 4, metrum 1, 441.

influential on Chaucer in the 1380s, also writes in *Paradiso* 22 about the experience of looking down through the seven spheres to the earth:

> And all seven showed me that is their magnitude and what their speed and at what distance their stations. The little threshing-floor that makes us so fierce all appeared to me from hills to river-mouths, while I was wheeling with the eternal Twins. Then to the fair eyes I turned my eyes again. (148–54)[18]

As it was for Boethius, for Dante the experience of looking down allows him to see how tiny and unimportant the things of the world are; he looks instead at the things of heaven, freeing himself from the ferocity of the world. Drawing on a number of sources, including Dante, Macrobius, and Boethius, Boccaccio describes Arcite ascending to the spheres after death and laughing as he looks down on the earth, and this is the most immediate source for Troilus's ascent to the spheres and contemptuous laughter.[19] The tone of this moment, however, is made deeply problematic by its placement in what has famously been called 'a nervous breakdown in poetry,' an anxious buildup of conventional tropes, none of which give satisfactory closure to this extraordinarily complex poem.[20]

Gaston Bachelard writes at length about immensity, describing a feeling that can arise from looking into the forest, the sea, or the constellations, or from aesthetic, particularly musical, experiences. He suggests that one feels 'freed from the powers of gravity,' as if in 'high places,' adding that the dreamer 'sees himself liberated from his cares and thoughts,' as 'he is no longer shut up in his weight, the prisoner of his own being.'[21] The authors discussed above—Boethius, Dante, Cicero, Macrobius—all suggest that flying to the stars offers an escape from the body, a chance for the soul to be itself. Liberation and escape are fundamental here.

---

[18] Dante, *The Divine Comedy, Book 3: Paradiso*, trans. John D. Sinclair (New York: Oxford University Press, 1961).

[19] *Teseida*, book 11, 1–3; *Troilus*, Book V, 1807–27.

[20] E. Talbot Donaldson, *Speaking of Chaucer* (New York: Norton, 1970), 91; Rosemarie P. McGerr, *Chaucer's Open Books: Resistance to Closure in Medieval Discourse* (Gainesville: University Press of Florida, 1998), 96–118.

[21] Bachelard, *Poetics of Space*, 187–95.

In the *House of Fame* and the *Parliament of Fowls*, poems steeped in Chaucer's reading of exactly these authors, Chaucer does not suggest this. On the contrary, Chaucer's texts characteristically move from an astral perspective, a bird's-eye view, to a vision of chaotic human life. The body remains insistently present throughout dreams, astral flights, and supernatural journeys. These dream visions—especially the *House of Fame*—ostentatiously refuse to engage with the theological and philosophical transcendence of their Neoplatonic sources;[22] poetry remains, for Chaucer, an endeavour embedded in his world, and the Milky Way leads him back to his own lived experience.

Book II of the *House of Fame* opens with Geffrey being seized by his prosaic, down-to-earth eagle guide, who shouts at him and comments on his weight. The particular force of this detail is that it reminds us of Geffrey's body: this body has not been left behind, the soul has not been 'withdrawn from the body,' as Macrobius puts it, nor 'freed from gravity,' 'no longer shut up in his weight' in Bachelard's terms. This is not that kind of astral journey. The eagle goes on to attack the idea of isolation, criticizing Geffrey's antisocial bookish tendencies and encouraging participation in the life of his neighbourhood (648–60). While writers such as Alain de Lille suggested that freedom from the senses enabled a higher mode of being, a greater communion with the divine, here, the eagle describes a lack of connection with the senses as a problematic disability when he mocks Geffrey as deaf ('thou herist neyther that ne this' [651]), dumb (656), and part-sighted (658).[23] In other words, he is encouraging an engagement with the senses (and therefore the body), not a transcendence of them. After his detailed discussion of sound itself—a force that acts on everything around it, sending ripples out from itself like a stone hitting the water (789–806)—we come to a section of the text that makes explicit reference to most of the texts about flight discussed above. Geffrey is compared to Alexander the Great, Scipio, Daedalus, and Icarus (915–20). He then himself starts thinking about what he has read:

[22] Taylor, *Chaucer Reads the Divine Comedy*; Vincent Gillespie, 'Authorship,' in Marion Turner (ed.), *A Handbook of Middle English Studies* (Oxford: Wiley-Blackwell, 2013), 135–54.

[23] See also Turner, 'The Senses,' and chapters 7 and 16 in the present study.

And thoo thought y upon Boece,
That writ, 'A thought may flee so hye
Wyth fetheres of Philosophye,
To passen everych element,
And whan he hath so fer ywent,
Than may be seen behynde hys bak
Cloude'—and al that y of spak.
Thoo gan y wexen in a were,
And seyde, 'Y wot wel y am here,
But wher in body or in gost
I not, ywys, but God, thou wost,'
For more clere entendement
Nas me never yit ysent.
And than thoughte y on Marcian,
And eke on Anteclaudian,
That sooth was her descripsion
Of alle the hevenes region,
As fer as that y sey the preve;
Therfore y kan hem now beleve. (972–90)

His paraphrase of Boethius's description of soaring beyond the clouds, a description that sets the world, the body, and exile against the stars, the soul, and home, is immediately followed by Geffrey's assertion that he 'wexen in a were' and could not work out if he was there 'in body or in gost.' 'Were' is glossed in the *Riverside Chaucer* as 'state of doubt, perplexity,' and indeed this is an accepted meaning of the word, and it makes sense here. But 'were' also means fish-trap, as Linda Tarte Holley points out, and Chaucer uses it with this meaning in both the *Parliament of Fowls* (138) and *Troilus and Criseyde* (Book III, 35), texts that belong to the same creative period as the *House of Fame*.[24] The idea that Chaucer here juxtaposes Philosophy's feathered flight with a prison-like trap in a stream fits very well with the *House of Fame*'s constant movement between different kinds of spaces: chamber and desert, icy monument and open wickerwork cage. It also chimes with Rebecca Davis's recent reading of the poem that

---

[24] Holley, *Reason and Imagination*, 64.

focuses on the eel trap at the end of the poem as an alternative to monu-mental structures.[25] Geffrey, then, tells us that when he thinks about thought, rather than soaring free, he feels trapped and, specifically, he doubts whether he is really free from his body—as Boethius would expect him to be. The pattern of his thought then moves on, not to philosophy but to empirical astronomy. He mentions two Neoplatonic thinkers, but focuses on their descriptions of heaven as if it were a 'real' place, saying that he will now believe their authority because he has himself experienced it. But his muddled thinking is then blatantly displayed as he refuses to listen to the eagle's discourse on the stars and the zodiac, comfortably assuring him that he believes 'hem that write of this matere' as completely as if he had seen the places himself, but he would rather not look on the bright stars for the sake of his sight. Geffrey thus disclaims intellectual cu-riosity or the kind of scientific thirst to see proofs for oneself that, a few lines earlier, he had been asserting. He manages to close down philosophy and astronomy here, to construct himself as pragmatic and dull, and com-prehensively to reject a transcendent reading of the heavenly journey.

We even see this relentless demystifying in the description of the Milky Way. The eagle urges Geffrey:

Se yonder, loo, the Galaxie,
Which men clepeth the Milky Wey
For hit ys whit (and somme, parfey,
Kallen hyt Watlynge Strete). (936–39)

These novel translations of Greek and Latin terms are set alongside the deeply familiar 'Watlynge Strete,' a phrase that compares the galaxy to a street in London, and to the road cutting across England from Kent up to the northwest. This demystification also occurs at a linguistic level in the longer passage quoted above, where multisyllable rhymes, Latin names, and striking new words pile up at the ends of four subsequent lines—'Marcian, Anteclaudian, description, region' (985–88)—to be followed by a couplet

---

[25] Rebecca Davis, Fugitive Poetics in Chaucer's House of Fame, *Studies in the Age of Chaucer* 37 (2015): 101–32. Jessica Lockhart has recently argued that the House of Rumour represents a fish weir; see *Everyday Wonders and Enigmatic Structures: Riddles from Symphosius to Chaucer* (University of Toronto, unpublished PhD dissertation, 2017), 179–223.

of striking simplicity, monosyllables, and comfortingly familiar words: 'As fer as that y sey the preve; / Therfore y kan hem now beleve' (989–90). Juxtaposition is one of the cornerstones of Chaucer's art; he uses it in these descriptions of the heavens to separate himself from a philosophical and reverent understanding of the galaxy, bringing his discussion of the stars back to what we can know empirically, and to his interest in using space travel as a way of talking about contemporary social, political, and poetic life, rather than about God and the origin of souls.

Indeed, from the very start of the poem, his journey has been focused on a search for poetic inspiration and subject matter. The *House of Fame* shows us, over and over again, that poetic inspiration is not to be found in splendid isolation or in the immense spaces of the universe or of the self. Sitting alone in a tower room; standing, a tiny figure, in a vast desert; soaring beyond the spheres, all prove to be unproductive, dispiriting experiences. The eagle explains to Geffrey that he would be better listening to the gossip of his neighbours, and the urban cacophony of the chaotic House of Rumour ends up depicting a scene that manifestly represents the origins of Chaucer's greatest poetic masterpiece. This is all the more striking if we return, briefly, to Chaucer's source texts. In the *Somnium Scipionis*, Scipio is exhorted to ignore the 'gossip of the common herd,' as 'gossip is confined to the narrow bounds of the small area at which you are gazing' (chap. 7, 76). The music of the spheres and the grandeur of the Milky Way provide a perspective from which earthly gossip can be ignored. In the *House of Fame*, however, earthly gossip becomes something that can be harnessed and used to produce poetry, and this is Geffrey's concern: he is interested only in what he can do in *this* life. This is not to say, of course, that this is all that Chaucer himself was interested in. But his poetry firmly eschews the theological ambitions of Dante and remains defiantly rooted in the life of the city around him. Rather than looking down, or looking up, Geffrey ends up next to and within the House of Rumour, taking a ground-level view.

Several of Chaucer's texts move structurally from the bird's-eye perspective to a street view. In the first half of the *House of Fame*, Geffrey flies to the Milky Way and describes the experience of looking down:

And y adoun gan loken thoo,
And beheld feldes and playnes,
And now hilles, and now mountaynes,
Now valeyes, now forestes,
And now unnethes grete bestes,
Now ryveres, now citees,
Now tounes, and now grete trees,
Now shippes seyllynge in the see. (896–903)

Most readers of this book will have had the experience of looking down from an aeroplane, and all will have seen aerial and satellite pictures and other representations of the earth from the sky. For medieval writers to imagine the bird's-eye perspective involved an imaginative leap unknown to us. Chaucer is not seduced by its marvellous possibilities: his text moves on and ends with the viewer in the middle of a scene of chaos, not watching from above. He rushes about within the house—'as I alther-fastest wente' (2131)—hardly able to perceive what is going on, caught up in a crowded environment where everyone is scrambling for the best position and treading on each other's toes.

Similarly, the *Parliament of Fowls* is structured by a trajectory that moves from a flight to the spheres and an aerial perspective, to an embedded perspective in a confusing experience of shouting and disorder. The description of Scipio's flight emphasises the distant perspective that he gains: he looks down on Carthage (44) and up to the Galaxy (53); he sees 'the lytel erthe' and that 'erthe was so lyte' (57, 64). But the dreamer, who goes to sleep full of 'busy hevynesse' (89) does not lose his sense of his body once he is dreaming. Just as the 'noyous' Geffrey was 'hente' (seized, 574, 543) by the eagle, so the dreamer here is repeatedly 'hente' (120, 154) by Africanus, and is 'shof' (shoved) (154) through the gate. Africanus also physically takes his hand (169) and looks into his face (155). Immediately after Africanus first seizes him, the dreamer finds himself at a gate. Unable to see beyond, he pauses on the threshold, not knowing whether to go on, to see what is inside. The decision is taken away from him when Africanus forces him bodily in. After his guide forces him out of his frozen, 'astoned' fear (141–54), we then move through the landscape with the dreamer for around two hundred lines (ca. 141–315). As he walks through the garden, the dreamer does not see everything at once. Lacking the bird's-eye perspective, he carefully and pointedly describes the experience of moving through space, of seeing the landscape unfold before one. The dreamer perceives a thick wood 'where that I myne eyen caste / Were trees' (172–73). As he moves through the environment, he sees different things: the garden, the river, the fish, the birds, the rabbits. He looks at things close up and far away: 'And ferther al aboute I gan aspye' (194). This is a textured vista: some things are close, some things are glimpsed at a distance, or only just catch his eye—'in a prive corner in disport / Fond I' (260); 'But thus I let hire lye, / And ferther in the temple I gan espie' (279–80). As he moves closer to a distant structure—the temple—the dreamer uses emphatic initial prepositions in a series of stanzas to position himself in relationship to what he is viewing. One stanza begins, 'Aboute the temple' (232), the next 'Byfore the temple' (239), the next 'Withinne the temple' (246), as he moves closer to and finally enters Venus's abode. He reminds us that perception can be hazy: 'Derk was that place, but afterward lightnesse / I saw a lyte' (263–64). He also emphasizes the fact that what he sees is changing because he is himself moving: 'saw I, as I wente' (253), 'Forth welk I tho' (297). He does not stop and establish himself in a viewing position until he reaches a location remarkably similar to the overcrowded corner of the House of Rumour where Geffrey ends up. In the *Parliament of Fowls*, the dreamer's place to observe, 'So ful was that unethe was there space / For me to stonde, so ful was al the place' (314–15). The clumsy repetition of 'so ful was' reflects a stunned response to the packed parliament scene. The dreamer then seems to stay put in his location, watching events unfold from his own little hemmed-in niche.

In the previous two hundred lines, then, Chaucer has meticulously described the experience of one's perspective changing as one moves through a landscape; of seeing a scene open up as different things reveal themselves; of seeing things at a distance and then close up. This is a very particular way of thinking about space, and it is a different experience of space to the bird's-eye view, though both approaches recognize that *what* one sees is dependent on *how* one sees—in other words, on where one is located.

When he lived in London, Chaucer constantly moved between liminal, upstairs rooms, both in Aldgate and in the counting house, and the streets that he traversed between home and work. That kind of transition of perspectives is played out time and again in his writings, and while his texts are often framed by the perspective from on high, it is the descent to the street, to be where other people are, that forms the creative heart of his poetry.

The juxtaposition of these two ways of positioning oneself is peculiarly characteristic of Chaucer's writing. We can see the same kind of pattern in the 'Nun's Priest's Tale,' for example. The tale begins with a depiction of the whole: 'A yeerd she hadde, enclosed al aboute / With stikkes, and a drye dych withoute' (2847–48) and ends with chaotic noise ('they skriked and they howped. / It semed as that hevene sholde falle' [3400–3401]), as the narrator scrambles for position and becomes part of the crowd himself, inserting the plural personal pronoun into the text: 'oure dogge' (3383).[26] And now, the shrieking crowd is comprised of people with multiple interests and perspectives (just like the rebels of 1381, to whom they are compared): the widow's concern for Chauntecleer is quite different from Pertelote's; the animals have no understanding of their function in the economy or their relationship to the wider world. Chaucer's most famous lines—the opening of the 'General Prologue'—use the same structure. Here, we move from the big picture of the seasons, weather, nature, the zodiac, through people in general, England, Canterbury, and Thomas à Becket's body, to end up in medias res again: with the narrator '*in*' Southwark (20; emphasis mine), surrounded by 'wel nyne and twenty in a compaignye' (24)—once more, the perspective is fractured into many different points of view. We might also note that in all these experiments with perspective, birds are prominent. From the eagle of the *House of Fame*, to the competing birds in the *Parliament of Fowls*, to Chauntecleer and his wives in the 'Nun's Priest's Tale,' to the 'smale foweles' of the 'General Prologue' (9), the example of those that can see in a way that humans cannot see (especially in a pre-flying-machine era) serve to remind us of different ways of perceiving—all the more so in the 'Nun's Priest's Tale,' where the plot hinges on Chauntecleer's ability to fly.

---

[26] See Helen Barr's discussion of the importance of this pronoun in *Socioliterary Practice in Late Medieval England* (Oxford: Oxford University Press, 2001), 126.

Chaucer's poems, then, often move from an overview to a confused perspective, a position from which the narrator cannot see everything and struggles to discern things through the jostling crowd. He focuses on a lived experience of space rather than the conceptual, totalizing perspectives offered by the bird's-eye view. Late-medieval thinkers were increasingly interested in mapping and organizing space through diagrams, charts, and plans. One scholar has described the late thirteenth century as 'a golden age for the spatial imagination,' adding that through the late thirteenth and early fourteenth century there was a 'sharp growth in spatial consciousness.' He points to the development of portolan charts and then maps, to the invention and spread of the portable plane astrolabe, to changes in painting techniques prefiguring the rise of perspective, and to work on optics as factors that illustrate a heightened interest in the representation of space.[27] Chaucer had available to him pictorial depictions of 'whole' cities in manuscript illuminations and on city seals, and in the fourteenth century, Brunetto Latini's totalizing idea of the city as an organic body became part of London's official image of itself, when it found its way into the city's *Liber Custumarum*.[28] Kathleen Biddick links the urge to totalize history, in the form of universal histories, to graphic and spatial taxonomies and miniaturizing, pointing out that such histories were illustrated with diagrams, schemata, genealogies, and *mappae mundi*.[29] The desire to understand, control, and clearly represent space as an entity lies behind the cartographic impulse, and that desire necessitates a denial of spatial complexity and unwieldiness, of the subjective lived experience of space.[30] This is, in essence, the distinction between *voyeur* and *flaneur* (watcher and walker) in recent writing about space.[31] It is striking

[27] Murray, 'Purgatory,' quotes at 89, 73.

[28] Keith Lilley, *City and Cosmos: The Medieval World in Urban Form* (London: Reaktion, 2009), 135–37. The 'book of customs' is a late-medieval compilation of documents such as laws and letters pertaining to London governance.

[29] Kathleen Biddick, 'Becoming Collection: The Spatial Afterlife of Medieval Universal Histories,' in Barbara Hanawalt and Michal Kobialka (eds.), *Medieval Practices of Space* (Minneapolis: University of Minnesota Press, 2000), 234.

[30] Jerry Brotton writes: 'one of the most basic objectives of human understanding is to impose some kind of order and structure onto the vast, apparently limitless space of the known world' through an 'abstraction of terrestrial reality.' *A History of the World in Twelve Maps* (London: Allen Lane, 2012), 2.

[31] See Michel de Certeau, 'Walking in the City,' in *The Practice of Everyday Life*, trans. Steven Rendall (Berkeley: University of California Press, 1984), 91–110. See also Jonathan Hsy, 'City,' in Turner,

to me that *A Treatise on the Astrolabe*, a text that aims at making sense of the most mysterious parts of our universe, and comprehending them in the palm of our hands, is a very carefully organized and structured text. The manuscripts are divided up into books, sections, and subheadings, as the careful ordering of the material reflects the attempt to order space.[32] Verbal and graphic attempts to totalize urban space were increasingly common in the late-medieval era, and these attempts were, by and large, 'dehumanizing' in their removal of inhabitants' own perceptions of space. An excellent example comes from fourteenth-century Marseilles. Analysis has demonstrated that while the majority of those living in the city described their addresses in terms of their vicinity or neighbourhood, professional notaries usually used street names to identify property. These street names were often made up by the notaries, who thus constructed an impersonal and transparently connected city in contrast to the city of intimate neighbourhoods known best by those who lived there. Daniel Lord Smail suggests that as notaries depended for their living on communication between people who did not know each other well, it suited them to imagine the city as an impersonal, connected network, rather than to use the model of the city as a cluster of intimate artisanal groups who would be less likely to use notaries between themselves. His point is essentially that 'the relationship between power and geography is indeed longstanding.'[33]

This understanding of city space as intimately connected neighbourhoods rather than a crisscrossing grid of streets is certainly germane to the London Chaucer knew. A key Chaucer life-record details his relinquishing of his family home to its long-term tenant in 1381. The home is identified in this way:

> quodam tenemento situato in parochia Sancti Martini in Vinetria Londonie inter tenementum Willelmi le Gauger versus orientem et tenementum quod quondam fuit Johannis le Mazelyner versus occidentem et

---

Handbook of Middle English Studies, 315–29.

[32] For a recent discussion of the forms of the text, see Lisa Cooper, 'Figures for "Gretter Knowing": Forms in the *Treatise on the Astrolabe*,' in Thomas A. Prendergast and Jessica Rosenfeld, *Chaucer and the Subversion of Form* (Cambridge: Cambridge University Press, 2018), 99–124.

[33] Daniel Lord Smail, 'The Linguistic Cartography of Property and Power in Late Medieval Marseilles,' in Hanawalt and Kobialka, *Medieval Practices of Space*, 59.

extendit se in longitudine a vico regio de Thamystrete versus austrum usque ad aquam de Wallebroke versus aquilonem.[34]

This is rather a 'belt and braces' approach, describing the tenement in meticulous detail. We begin with the parish, which is thus marked as the crucial descriptive factor, and the fact that the parish is St Martin in the Vintry means that both the local church and the trade with which the area is connected are flagged. Next, we move from east to west to south to north. We are told who owns the tenements to the east and west of Chaucer's— but these names are historic, dating from earlier documents about the house. The former, indeed, had died almost forty years earlier. So here, local knowledge is implied: people would know that that house had been William le Gauger's even though he had died in 1343.[35] Next, we are given the street as the southern boundary to the address, and the Walbrook as the northern boundary. In contrast to modern descriptions of this address— which tend to be number plus street (177 or 179 Thames Street)—the fourteenth-century description is three-dimensional rather than two-dimensional, giving a sense of the whole property, not merely its frontage.[36]

Chaucer's deposition in the Scrope-Grosvenor trial at the Court of Chivalry in 1386, however, does indeed focus on the frontage of a property. He describes how he was walking down Friday Street when he saw a sign: a coat of arms hanging out in the street.[37] This trial was all about a surface—who had the right to use this sign as a symbol of their family— and the point of Chaucer's testimony is that he saw this symbol and deduced wrongly from it, because it was not being used to signify what it 'should' have signified: the Scrope family. So there is something particularly appropriate about the surface, street-level focus. But at the same time, the symbolism of the scene constructs a deeper spatial awareness quite different from that conjured up in Marseilles when notaries were making up street names themselves. This street name signifies, as Strohm has discussed, a long history of trade, its name reminding contemporaries of the (contentious) fish trade. And the coat of arms inserts a long, aristocratic

[34] Crow and Olson, *Chaucer Life-Records*, 1.
[35] Ibid., 9.
[36] Bestul, 'Did Chaucer Live at 177 Upper Thames Street?'
[37] Crow and Olson, *Chaucer Life-Records*, 370–71.

family history into the mercantile street.[38] I would add to this that the coat of arms, like the astrolabe, is an attempt to spatialize or to diagramatize time itself. Just as the astrolabe seeks to tell the time by ordering space in terms of the positions of stars, so the coat of arms spatially represents and miniaturizes a long family history, distilling it into something small and portable. Time itself can be carried around both in the shape of an astrolabe and in the shape of a flag advertising one's family identity. This is what is at stake in the Scrope-Grosvenor controversy: the usurpation of that identity and the theft of history and time.[39]

Space and time were therefore family matters at their essence. It is not a coincidence that Scipio is shown the spheres and exhorted to behave ethically on earth by his father and grandfather. Chaucer's relationship to the spaces of London was marked by his own family: he gave up his father and mother's house, embedded in the Vintry Ward, just a few years before he gave testimony in the Scrope-Grosvenor trial about which family was allowed to mark time (their own family history) and space (by hanging up their sign outside their place of residence) by the coat of arms *azure a bend or*. And when Chaucer comes to write about the astrolabe—in other words, about space and time's intimate connections—he does so with his son, constructing his treatise as a family text in a manner unique in his corpus.

A Treatise on the Astrolabe is precisely about what we can learn from looking up. It teaches its readers how they can use an informed understanding of the space above them to tell the time, and how, if they know the time, they can find celestial objects in space. The astrolabe spatializes time by utilizing lines of longitude and the movement of astral bodies to pin down time in a particular location—thus also making clear the contingency of time, its dependence on longitude. In itself, the portable astrolabe also miniaturizes space, bringing the vast immensity of the heavens into the tiny space of a handheld object. This early scientific instrument purports to make sense of the awe-inspiring vastness of the Milky Way and to deploy it for the benefit of the user. The audaciousness of capturing the

---

[38] Strohm, *Theory and the Premodern Text*, 5–7.

[39] For a discussion of heraldry, see D. Vance Smith, 'Institutions,' in Strohm, *Middle English*, 160–76.

stars—astrolabe means 'star-catcher'—is even more acute in the context of Chaucer's treatise, as he sets out to teach a young boy how he too can make sense of the mysteries of the universe.

The primary purpose of this text about the distant regions of the galaxy is not to inspire awe, nor to lift the soul from the mundanities of ordinary life. On the contrary, this text sets out to make the stars useful in everyday life. It is also Chaucer's most transparently social text: the only substantial text that he wrote that is manifestly a didactic text, his only substantial text in which he openly declares that he is writing for a real person, in response to a request, the only time in his entire corpus in which he addresses himself to a family member. Here, more than anywhere else in Chaucer's writings, the gap between Chaucer the person and his narratorial persona collapses almost completely; here we get the closest we ever do to an 'authentic' voice. He begins the *Treatise* in this way:

> Lyte Lowys my sone, I aperceyve wel by certeyne evydences thyn abilite to lerne sciences touching nombres and proporciouns; and as wel considre I thy besy praier in special to lerne the tretys of the Astrelabie. (Prologue, 1–5, p. 662)

He tells us that he writing for his son, because his son is gifted at maths and sciences, and because his son has asked specially to learn how astrolabes work. Chaucer then goes on to tell us that he has given Lewis an astrolabe (8), and that Lewis is ten years old (24). He explains that because Lewis knows little Latin as yet, he will write in English (25–28). Stating the purpose of the treatise, Chaucer claims that he wants Lewis to have 'the gretter knowing of thyn oune instrument' (67–68), and that he wants to 'techen the worken the verrey practik' (70, p. 663). There may well have been two intended audiences for this treatise—the individual Lewis and a broader group, perhaps Chaucer's habitual readers, perhaps a more specific group.[40] But there is no reason to doubt that it really was written for Lewis.

---

[40] This is the view of most critics. See, for example, Sigmund Eisner and Marijane Osborn, 'Chaucer as Teacher: Chaucer's *Treatise on the Astrolabe*,' in Daniel T. Kline (ed.), *Medieval Literature for Children* (New York: Routledge, 2003), 155–87; Edgar Laird, 'Chaucer and Friends: The Audience for the *Treatise on the Astrolabe*,' *Chaucer Review* 41:4 (2007): 439–44.

We know very little about Lewis Chaucer. Apart from this treatise, there is one additional document in which he appears. In 1403, he turns up alongside his older brother, Thomas Chaucer, as part of the garrison at Carmarthen Castle in Wales, in company with their cousins, Katherine Swynford's children, Henry Beaufort, Sir Thomas Beaufort, and Sir Thomas Swynford, all under the command of John Beaufort (Gaunt and Katherine's oldest child), now earl of Somerset.[41] That is all we know about him. The *Treatise* provides us with some knowledge of his age. This text is usually dated to around 1391, as it makes calculations based on this year. If Lewis were ten in 1391, he was born around 1381. But, as scholars have pointed out, the date for the *Treatise* is not fixed—it makes calculations for a number of years in the 1390s, and one critic has argued for a date as late as 1397; a date in the late 1380s is also possible, although unlikely, given the specific references to dates in the 1390s (and in any case, the date of composition must be after 1386, when Nicholas of Lynn wrote his *Kalendarium*).[42] The much later dates seem less likely too, as Lewis was fighting by 1403. So Lewis was almost certainly born in Chaucer's London years, and probably in the early 1380s. Whether he was born in 1378 or 1387, this was a child born in difficult circumstances.[43] He was a late child of a somewhat-estranged couple who lived largely apart, a child whose mother died when he was very small. Philippa Chaucer died in 1387; Lewis was either a few years old or an infant (it is even just possible that she died in childbirth or shortly afterwards). His appearance in 1403 demonstrates that he was part of the Chaucer-Beaufort-Swynford group—the cousins caught up under the protection of Gaunt, who remained supporters of their relative, or relative once removed, Henry

[41] Crow and Olson, *Chaucer Life-Records*, 544–45. See also National Archives, E 101/43/22, printed by E. A. Lewis, 'Carmarthen Castle: A Collection of Historical Documents Relating to Carmarthen Castle from the Earliest Times to the Close of the Reign of Henry VIII,' *West Wales Historical Records* 4 (1914): 4–5.

[42] Andrew Cole, 'Chaucer's English Lesson,' *Speculum* 77:4 (2002): 1154–55. Cole suggests that the *Treatise* postdates the 'General Prologue' to the Wycliffite Bible (ca. 1395–97).

[43] It is possible, though not probable, that he was the son of Cecily Champaigne, given that Chaucer's connection with her—possibly rape—occurred in 1380–81. However, this is very unlikely, given Lewis's surname and connection with Thomas Chaucer and the Lancastrian group generally, as discussed above.

Bolingbroke, when he took the throne. The likelihood is that Lewis spent large chunks of his childhood in a household with Gaunt-Swynford associations: perhaps Katherine Swynford's household (he was closer in age to her children than he was to his own siblings), perhaps Thomas Chaucer's (he was much older than Lewis, and indeed was married in the mid-1390s). When Chaucer wrote the treatise, his other children were grown-up, in their twenties, and well established, thanks to Gaunt's patronage; Lewis was much younger, and was suffering a much more difficult childhood in emotional terms.

And this text is an emotional text, a text that focuses on Lewis's vulnerability and Chaucer's love for him. Chaucer repeatedly calls him 'litel' (1, 28) and 'of tendir age' (24). He also repeatedly addresses him as 'my' son (1, 28), marking his protectiveness and responsibility over him. This vocabulary also transfers to other things across the 'Prologue.' Not only is Lewis little, but the astrolabe is little, and the *Treatise* is little: Chaucer is writing a 'litel tretys' (11, 42) about 'so small an instrument portatif aboute' (73). This is a world in miniature, fit for a child. And not only does Lewis belong to Chaucer but so does English: Chaucer writes about 'my lighte Englissh' (51) and 'myn Englissh' (63) just as he writes about 'my sone' and 'my litel sone.' Both English and Lewis are homely, domesticated things 'owned' by Chaucer, part of his basic being, not imported from elsewhere or grafted onto him. In the early part of the *Treatise* in particular, Chaucer writes in a simple style: he tells us that he will repeat himself for pedagogical reasons (47–49); he uses vivid and domestic visual imagery ('like to the clawes of a loppe [spider], or elles like the werk of a wommans calle [hairnet]');[44] he adapts from sources that use conditionals and subjunctives, replacing these more complex sentence structures with straightforward indicative anecdotes.[45]

Chaucer had plenty of literary, conventional precedent for writing a text addressed to his son or to another young boy, but what Chaucer does is different in emphasis. In his astrolabe treatise, Adelard of Bath claims that he is writing at the request of Henry Plantagenet, but describes him as fourteen years old, and as a competent Latinist, now interested in Arab

---

[44] *Treatise*, Part I, section 19, lines 2–4, p. 667.
[45] Eisner and Osborn, 'Chaucer as Teacher,' 160–61.

learning. Martianus Capella, mentioned by Chaucer in the *House of Fame* as a source for his knowledge of astronomy, stages his *De nuptiis* in the context of a conversation with his son: Martianus junior speaks forthrightly to his father and urges him to get on with the story.[46] In the *Commentary on the Dream of Scipio*—a text that was profoundly important to Chaucer—Macrobius more emotionally addresses his own son: 'my son Eustachius, my joy and boast in life,' 'Eustachius, my son dearer to me than life itself.'[47] Chaucer's text stands out for its explicit emphasis on Lewis's extreme youth and his vulnerability: reading the 'Prologue' drives home to us the fact that Lewis is little and dependent; that the text has to be tailored to his abilities; that he needs looking after. As critics we often avoid and look down on attempts to sentimentalise authors, but Chaucer's affective relationship with his son is a crucial part of this text. And the evidence of the *Treatise* reveals to us both that Chaucer related to those that he loved through writing—that was his gift to his son, rather than a financial legacy—and that his writing practices were (probably) interestingly contingent. Spurred by a request, he embarked on research and writing. The extraordinary variety of his output may owe something to this willingness to respond to suggestions and ideas.

The clear pedagogy of this text works to categorise and explain the mysteries of the galaxy. Indeed, the text is highly regulated: it is divided into books, and each book is further divided into short sections with subtitles and numbered sections. But there are moments when this practical, even prosaic, text is punctuated by glimpses of aesthetic wonder. Chaucer's words reflect the experience of gazing at the night sky when he describes looking up: 'In som wynters nyght whan the firmament is cler and thikke sterred' or when he refers to 'this merveylous arisyng.'[48] Even in the city, the night skies in the fourteenth century would have been startlingly different from those that most of us see today through the haze of industrial

[46] William Harris Stahl, Richard Johnson, and Evan Laurie Burge (eds.), *Martianus Capella and the Seven Liberal Arts* (New York: Columbia University Press, 1971–77), 2:4 (book 1, part 2).

[47] It is also worth noting that Macrobius's commentary is about a text—Cicero's *Somnium Scipionis*—that is itself structured around a dreamer meeting his father and grandfather and listening to their advice. The idea of patriarchs passing on wisdom to male descendants is key to Cicero's text. Seth Lerer also points to Macrobius's more elaborate address to his son in his preface to the *Saturnalia*; see Seth Lerer, 'Chaucer's Sons,' *University of Toronto Quarterly* 73 (Summer 2004): 909.

[48] *Treatise*, Part II, section 23, lines 1–2, p. 675; and Part II, section 19, line 6, p. 674.

pollution and electric light. When he deviates from the pragmatic, however, Chaucer simply pauses for a moment on beauty: never, in the *Treatise*, do the spheres become an excuse to ponder theology. In many late-medieval texts, contemplating the galaxy—and particularly flight to the galaxy— was a way of thinking about the immortality of the soul, Neoplatonism, and the possibility of experience beyond the world of the senses. We might not expect such explorations in a scientific treatise written for a young child. But in Chaucer's dream visions too, he ostentatiously refuses to follow in the path of Alain de Lille, or Dante, for instance, both of whom suggested that astral flight led to transcendent experiences of truth.

For many people, their relationships with their children are the part of their life in which they think most acutely about time: about what will remain after their death, about things that will not come again, about the stages of life that both their child and they themselves are going through, and about the importance of not dying too soon. Lewis will not always be little; he will grow up precisely because of the existence of the time that he is learning to measure. The Scropes are trying to fix their own past and future as a family with a history; the Vintry Ward document memorializes the history of the spaces of London as the history of families. Thinking about the immensity of space does not encourage Chaucer to isolate himself from the things of the world and laugh at their inconsequentiality. On the contrary, he structures his texts in such a way as to suggest a *progress* between the galaxy and the cage/parliament/riot/pub.[49] And few aspects of life are as likely to discourage contemptus mundi as parenthood. Chaucer chooses to link his scientific exploration of the stars to his own fatherhood, in an emotional rather than a conventional way. In other words, he emphasizes his own affective ties to the world, his interest in claiming a piece of time and space for himself and his child. Even if that space is crammed and hedged in, it still provides a perspective of infinitely more interest and diversity, Chaucer suggests, than the view from above.

---

[49] See *House of Fame*, *Parliament of Fowls*, 'Nun's Priest's Tale,' and the 'General Prologue,' respectively.

CHAPTER 10

> ╾┼◆╾○╾◆┼╼

Tower

By Juliu Caesar the Tour founded of old
May be the hous of Mars victoriall,
Whos artillery with tonge may not be told.
London, thou art the flower of Cities all.

—Anonymous; attributed to Dunbar, 1501

The best place to gain a view from above in 1380s London was not, of course, from the spheres or from a flying machine but from London's most imposing building. Next door to the counting house stood London's most iconic and awe-inspiring edifice: the Tower of London (plate 10). With the White Tower at its heart, this castle complex was at once defensive, residential, and symbolic, built by William the Conqueror as a physical reminder of his power, 'looming over the humble buildings of the conquered city.'[1] To access the massive Tower, a visitor had to pass multiple drawbridges, gates, portcullises, and causeways, passing through Lion Tower, where the roars of the animals made for an alarming welcome.[2] Such was its image as a centre of conspicuous consumption and ostentatious otherness that in the thirteenth century, one could watch a tethered polar bear fishing in the Thames from its Tower home.[3] In Chaucer's lifetime the kings of France and Scotland were kept in luxurious

---

[1] Edward Impey and Geoffrey Parnell, *The Tower of London: The Official Illustrated History*, rev. ed. (New York: Merrell, 2006), 18.

[2] Ibid., 34–36.

[3] Ibid., 29. Henry III was sent a polar bear from Norway in 1251; the sheriffs of London were ordered to provide a cord long enough to enable him to fish in the Thames.

imprisonment here,[4] and it was also the scene for the performance of power, as extravagantly theatrical processions—for coronations, tournaments, and royal entries—began at the Tower before sweeping through London.[5]

For Chaucer, however, this was not a place of intimidating power and mystique: on the contrary, he was involved in the behind-the-curtain (wall) workings of this extraordinary set of buildings. When he worked at the Custom House, virtually next door to the Tower, he walked past the Tower every day, and during these years the Tower was often the scene of spectacle—most notoriously during the Rising of 1381, the only time in the Tower's history that it has been forcibly invaded. Once, Chaucer collected his allowance direct from the warden of the mint within the Tower.[6] Chaucer's own involvement with the Tower actually intensified after he left London. Chaucer was appointed to the role of clerk of the works on 12 July 1389, for a wage of 2s a day. He was responsible for a number of buildings in the southeast of England, but during his tenure, the Tower occupied far more of his energies than any of the others. The expenditure on works by the Tower accounted for more than half of his total expenditure, as he was in charge of extending and repairing the wharf, and also repairing other buildings and houses near the wharf.[7] He dealt with the nitty-gritty of building upkeep and maintenance, employing workers and supervising the moving of materials to extend the wharf.[8] The Tower's meaning in his life is aptly demonstrated by the list of stock at the Tower that he had to take responsibility for in 1389: for Chaucer, this shining fortress housed a pile of bits and bobs of dubious value, including a frying pan, a bucket, a bell named Wyron, four broken wheels, and a ram with a broken cord.[9] The

[4]David of Scotland was there between 1346 and 1357; John of France arrived in 1360, having spent the previous few years of his imprisonment at other English castles and palaces—the Savoy, Hertford Castle, and Somerton Castle. Ormrod, *Edward III*, 389–408.

[5]Richard II began his coronation procession from the Tower; London tournaments often involved processing from the Tower to Smithfield for the jousts, as in 1376: Ormrod, *Edward III*, 547. See also Lancashire, *London Civic Theatre*, 46–47.

[6]Crow and Olson, *Chaucer Life-Records*, 438.

[7]Ibid., 402, 412, 470–71.

[8]Ibid., 402–76.

[9]'i fryingpanne,' 'i bekettum,' 'i campana vocatur Wyron,' 'iiii rote omnino devastantur,' 'I ramme cum toto apparatus excepta i drawing corda que frangitur et devastator.' Ibid., 407.

story of the Tower in Chaucer's lifetime is a chaotic story of industry, dirt, conflict, and the collapsing of the façade of power. This space mattered to Chaucer across and beyond his London years. Most fundamentally, as the home of the mint, as well as of numerous artisans and workshops, it was an emblem of how economics determines selfhood. And the last quarter of the fourteenth century was a period of dramatic economic upheaval.

Chaucer was born at the same time as two major changes entered into English life: the development of guns and the production of gold coins. The manufacturing of guns and advanced weaponry, and the growth of gold coinage, bills of exchange, and promissory notes into recognizably modern banking systems, are two developments that have shaped our world in ways difficult to quantify. Chaucer lived through extraordinary transitions. These developments came at the same time as the plague, with its consequences for the movement of labour and class, and the growth of anxiety about the performance and clothing of the self.[10] In this chapter I think about the Tower—the place where money and weapons were made—as a symbol both of royal power and of economic transition. It was a place of industry, technology, and making, a place that represented the new economic realities of late fourteenth-century England.

Theorists of space emphasise that towers are places that convey dominance. Henri Lefebvre writes about the phallic 'verticality and political arrogance of towers,' while Gaston Bachelard writes that:

> From the top of his tower, a philosopher of domination sees the universe in miniature. Everything is small because he is so high. And, since he is high, he is great, the height of his station is proof of his own greatness.[11]

The White Tower, 36 by 32.6 metres across and 27.5 metres tall, might today be dwarfed by the skyscrapers of the financial district, but in the

---

[10] For sumptuary laws, see F. E. Baldwin, *Sumptuary Legislation and Personal Regulation in England* (Baltimore: Johns Hopkins University Press, 1926); N. B. Harte, 'State Control of Dress and Social Change in Pre-Industrial England,' in D. C. Coleman and A. H. John (eds.), *Trade, Government and Economy in Pre-Industrial England* (London: Weidenfeld & Nicolson, 1976), 132–65. See also chapter 2 in this study.

[11] Henri Lefebvre, *The Production of Space*, trans. Donald Nicholson-Smith (Oxford: Blackwell, 1991), 261, 262; Bachelard, *Poetics of Space*, 173.

fourteenth century, it was a building that dominated its environment and that was supposed to be impregnable.[12] However, during Richard's reign, it was repeatedly penetrated by aggressive forces: in 1381 by a crowd of rebels, and six years later by a group of magnates (known as the Lords Appellant), who had moved against the king in Parliament in 1386 and who almost certainly deposed the king in the Tower in 1387. What happened at the Tower in 1381 has never been satisfactorily explained. The rebels, coming mainly from Kent and Essex, were angered by the poll tax, by the erosion of traditional rights and the aggressive assertion of seigneurial authority, by the malign influence of the king's advisors and officials, by the power of John of Gaunt, and by the presence of foreign immigrant workers.[13] Londoners opened the gates to them—and suspicion later fell (probably unfairly) on the merchant-capitalist monopolists who would in general have loathed the rebels' desire for greater rights for the disenfranchised, but who would have heartily approved of their attacks on Gaunt and on foreigners. They entered through Aldgate, directly underneath Chaucer's apartment, sweeping through the streets that he walked every day—and attacking targets metaphorically as well as literally close to home for Chaucer: Gaunt and people who wrote documents for a living in particular. The rebels repeatedly attacked the offices of writing, burning books, rolls, and remembrances at the Temple, for instance.[14] Another target was the Hospital of St John and its priory. Just outside the city, they burnt Gaunt's Savoy palace to the ground and also destroyed the records at Lambeth. They released prisoners and slaughtered foreigners indiscriminately, massacring a large group of Flemings who had taken refuge in St Martin Vintry, and also killing Richard Lyons—doubly damned as a former court intimate and as a foreigner. Richard II, who was only fourteen, was in the Tower, together with his mother, Princess Joan, his half-brothers, his cousin Henry of Derby (Gaunt's son), various magnates, Simon Sudbury (archbishop of Canterbury and chancellor), Thomas Hales (treasurer), William Appleton (physician), and John Legge (serjeant-at-arms and juror).

---

[12] Impey and Parnell, *Tower of London*, 16.

[13] Dobson's *The Peasants' Revolt of 1381* is an extremely useful collection of accounts of the revolt.

[14] Steven Justice, *Writing and Rebellion: England in 1381* (Berkeley: University of California Press, 1994); Susan Crane, 'The Writing Lesson of 1381,' in Barbara Hanawalt (ed.), *Chaucer's England* (Minneapolis: University of Minnesota Press, 1992), 201–21.

Sources agree that the rebels entered the Tower and ran fairly wild there—we later find payments for mending the door that they broke.[15] They also found and executed Sudbury, Hales, Appleton, and Legge. How did this happen? How did this ragtag force gain entry to the supposedly invulnerable Tower without a protracted siege?

The accounts vary. The carefully terse account in the *City of London Letter-Book* tells us clearly that they entered the Tower by force. Froissart, often an unreliable chronicler, tells us that when Richard and his entourage came out to meet the rebels at Mile End, a group of them gained entry. Even more unlikely is Knighton's statement that the victims came out voluntarily from the Tower. Walsingham tells us that the king allowed the rebels to enter the Tower, the *Eulogium* writer that the king and his knights were too frightened to defend the Tower; the *Anonimalle Chronicle* does not explain how they got in; nor does the *Westminster Chronicle*. It is impossible that they could actually have entered by brute force: they must have got in either while the gates were open and badly defended or because the frightened inhabitants let them in. The *Anonimalle Chronicle* describes their entry as happening after protracted negotiation and discussion, which makes it plausible to imagine a kind of appeasement going on; Walsingham tells us that Richard: 'allowed the rebels to enter the Tower and to search the most secret places there at their wicked will, like someone who could deny them nothing with safety.'[16] The picture we get is of a king and court paralysed with fear, not knowing what to do, incompetent and vacillating—and this is certainly the impression given by Gower's fictionalized account in the *Vox Clamantis*.[17] Across the accounts, the Tower is

---

[15] Frederick Devon (ed.), *Issues of the Exchequer: Being a Collection of Payments Made out of His Majesty's Revenue, from King Henry III to King Henry IV Inclusive* (London: John Murray, 1837), 216–17 (20 September 1381). Cited in T. F. Tout, 'Firearms in England in the Fourteenth Century,' in *The Collected Papers of Thomas Frederick Tout* (Manchester: Manchester University Press, 1934), 2:268.

[16] 'The Peasants' Revolt according to the *City of London Letter Book H*,' in Dobson, *Peasants' Revolt*, 210 (the entries that follow are all from this source); 'The Rebels in London according to Froissart,' 190–91; 'The Rebels in London according to Henry Knighton,' 182–83; 'The Rebels in London according to Thomas Walsingham,' 171; 'The Peasants' Revolt according to the Continuator of the "Eulogium Historiarum,"' 207–8; 'The Rebels in London according to the *Anonimalle Chronicle*,' 160–61; and 'The Peasants' Revolt according to the "monk of Westminster,"' 201.

[17] See book 1 of the *Vox Clamantis*, in John Gower, *The Complete Works of John Gower: Vol. 4, The Latin Works*, ed. G. C. Macaulay (Oxford: Clarendon Press, 1902), 20–81, translated in John Gower, *The Major Latin Works of John Gower: The Voice of One Crying, and the Tripartite Chronicle*, trans. Eric W. Stockton (Seattle: University of Washington Press, 1962), 49–112; for discussion, see Sylvia

not a place of power, refuge, and authority: it is an open, vulnerable structure. Its permeability is such that the rebels not only penetrate its outer walls, they get into the queen mother's bedroom and threaten to enter the queen mother herself—an old lady, and the most important lady in the kingdom. In the ultimate violation of authority, order, and boundaries, they suggestively play in her bedroom, in one account breaking her bed, in another demanding kisses from her.[18]

This image of the Tower as helpless in the face of attack was seen again six years later, in Richard's crisis of government in 1387. The Lords Appellant (Thomas of Woodstock, duke of Gloucester; Richard FitzAlan, earl of Arundel; Thomas Beauchamp, earl of Warwick; Henry Bolingbroke, earl of Derby; and Thomas Mowbray, earl of Nottingham) had asserted their displeasure with the king and his favourites in the Wonderful Parliament of 1386, and were now dominant. Indeed, in a few weeks time they were to execute some of Richard's most trusted friends. They had just won a military victory at Radcot Bridge, and Richard's bid to oppose them was in tatters. This was the situation when they came to meet him in the Tower on 27 December. Before they came, he sent them the keys to the gates and the armouries, so that they could send an advance party to search for ambushes. After they arrived, they almost certainly deposed him, as the Whalley Abbey account tells us and as Gloucester's later confession suggests, but quickly reinstated him when it became clear that Gloucester wanted the throne for himself, leapfrogging Gaunt and Henry's claims. The Tower, then, was the scene of Richard's greatest humiliation.[19]

In accounts of both 1381 and 1387, the Tower's function as panoptic viewing platform, a high place from which the watcher can survey lower beings from a position of superior authority and perspective, is subverted. The *Anonimalle Chronicle* tells us of Richard watching the fires from high up in a garret in 1381; he sees the city in flames and tries to make

---

Federico, *New Troy: Fantasies of Empire in the Late Middle Ages* (Minneapolis: University of Minnesota Press, 2003), 1–28; Marion Turner, *Chaucerian Conflict: Languages of Antagonism in Late Fourteenth-Century London* (Oxford: Oxford University Press, 2007), 56–92; Ormrod, 'In Bed with Joan of Kent.'

[18] 'Rebels in London according to Froissart,' 191, and 'The Rebels in London according to Thomas Walsingham,' 172, in Dobson, *Peasants' Revolt*. See also Ormrod, 'In Bed with Joan of Kent.'

[19] See McFarlane, *Lancastrian Kings and Lollard Knights*, 33–34; Anthony Tuck, *Richard II and the English Nobility* (London: Edward Arnold, 1973).

proclamations and promises, but to no avail.[20] In 1387, according to Knighton, Henry took Richard high on the walls of the Tower to see the crowd calling for the deaths of Richard's friends. The chronicler writes that 'comes Derbeye alexit regem murum Turris petere' (the earl of Derby had induced the king to go up onto the walls of the Tower).[21] The verb 'alexit,' with its meanings of 'allure/entice/induce,' draws a sketch of Henry cunningly persuading the king to go to the threshold with him in order to see the reality of what lies outside. When Richard sees the clamouring crowds, Gloucester tells him that they represent less than a tenth of the people who wanted to accompany the Lords Appellant 'ad destruendum et exterminandum falsos proditores regis et regni eius' (to destroy and exterminate the false betrayers of the king and the kingdom). This sinister scene depicts the king being held hostage in his own stronghold: while the Lords pursue the accustomed rhetoric of claiming that their army is mobilized not against the king but against his evil advisors, their massive show of force aims at coercing Richard into giving up his friends and his entire royal strategy. The Lords make it clear to Richard that if he wants to retain his throne—and indeed his life—he must submit. The seemingly superior perspective that the Tower gives in fact underlines the isolation and vulnerability of the watcher, who has no control over the menacing crowds outside. The king's gaze does not prove his greatness or domination, as Bachelard suggests it should; rather, it proves his utter vulnerability—all the more so in 1387, as his enemies are already within.

Indeed, the king and court's power was so fragile throughout this last quarter of the fourteenth century that the Tower could only function as a symbol of authority, domination, and glory through a massive suspension of disbelief. We see this particularly strikingly in 1376, when a procession started from the Tower, featuring a sumptuously arrayed woman dressed as the Lady of the Sun, starring in the ceremonial progress from the Tower to Smithfield for a tournament.[22] This took place in February, and the Lady of the Sun was Alice Perrers, loathed mistress of the king

[20] 'The Rebels in London according to the *Anonimalle Chronicle*,' 158–59.

[21] Henry Knighton, *Knighton's Chronicle*, ed. and trans. G. H. Martin (Oxford: Clarendon Press, 1995), 426–27.

[22] Most historians have thought that this took place in 1375; Ormrod demonstrates that it was in 1376 in *Edward III*, 547.

(Edward III), who just a few weeks later in April was to be attacked by the Good Parliament, accused of all kinds of corruption, especially bribery and maintenance, and expelled from court, and who, the following year, was openly tried in the first parliament of Richard II's reign, and subsequently exiled, her property forfeit.[23]

Far from exemplifying the quasi-divine glory of monarchy, aristocracy, and chivalry, as the Tower and royal processions were supposed to do, Alice actually demonstrated the multiple meanings of the Tower far more accurately. It was the place of the mint, and it was associated with commerce, trade, loans, and economic progress. Alice too was strongly linked with acquisition, financial corruption, and the circulation of conspicuous wealth. Indeed, the sideways reflection of her in *Piers Plowman* imagines Alice as Lady Mede, a personification of the problems of untrammelled capital.[24] Chaucer also imagines golden, sun-like, sexually available women as coins, linking the circulation of women with the circulation of money. In his late poem, the *Complaint to His Purse*, the purs is 'my lady dere,' whom he wants to shine 'lyk the sonne bryght,' with unequalled 'yelownesse' (2, 10, 11). He addresses this golden lady of the sun with a series of puns: his purse/lady is light/wanton; he wants her to be heavy /pregnant; he wants to hear her lovely jangling/voice (1, 3, 7, 9).[25] In the 'Miller's Tale,' this identical set of associations—money/woman/gold/sun /purse—is specifically associated with a noble made *in the Tower*. This is the only time that Chaucer explicitly writes about the Tower of London, and he does so to foreground its function as home of the mint. Describing Alison, he writes: 'Ful brighter was the shynyng of hir hewe / Than in the Tour the noble yforged newe' (3255–56). The mint had a family connection for Chaucer: his mother's uncle, Hamo de Copton, from whom she inherited tenements outside Aldgate, had been a 'moneyer' in the

---

[23] See PROME, Membrane 6, no. 45, 5:313 (April 1376); Holmes, *Good Parliament*, 88–106, 135–39; W. M. Ormrod, 'The Trials of Alice Perrers,' *Speculum* 83:2 (2008): 366–96; W. M. Ormrod, 'Who Was Alice Perrers?' *Chaucer Review* 40: 3 (2006): 219–29.

[24] David Aers, 'Class, Gender, Medieval Criticism and *Piers Plowman*,' in Britton Harwood and Gillian Overing (eds.), *Class and Gender in Early English Literature: Intersections* (Bloomington: Indiana University Press, 1994), 59–75; Clare Lees, 'Gender and Exchange in *Piers Plowman*,' in ibid., 112–30; and Stephanie Trigg, 'The Traffic in Medieval Women: Alice Perrers, Feminist Criticism, and *Piers Plowman*,' *Yearbook of Langland Studies* 12 (1998): 5–29.

[25] See chapter 20 for further discussion.

Tower, with the job of fashioning the blanks and striking the coins.[26] Richard Lyons, his father's associate and his own colleague at the petty custom, was warden of the mint from 1375 to 1376. This was a political appointment; the person in more immediate charge was the master, and this role was held from 1363 to 1394 by Walter de Bardi, a member of the famous Italian banking family.[27] In 1390, when he was clerk of the king's works, Chaucer certainly had dealings with Bardi: on 27 October 1390, he was assigned £25 to be collected from Bardi.[28] When Chaucer writes, briefly, about the Tower, he is writing about it as a place where money was made: a place of industry and workshops, where skilled workers melted, poured, formed, shaped, and stamped metal, a place at the heart of the economy of England. And the status and fate of the actual money coined in the Tower was a vexed issue indeed in Chaucer's lifetime.

Alison is associated here not just with general money but with a very specific coin, the noble, a coin that had been born around the same time as Chaucer. Although there had been some gold coinage in Italy in the thirteenth century, it was not until the discovery of the gold mines of Hungary in the 1320s that Northern Europe began to mint gold coins.[29] The next thirty years saw the transformation of Europe from an area that mainly used silver for currency to an area that mainly used gold.[30] Edward III's first gold coin, the 1344 florin, was overvalued and therefore short-lived, but later that year the noble was produced. This changed English money permanently: although most everyday money remained silver, by the end of the century most of the currency was gold, if measured in terms of total value rather than number of coins.[31] The noble was symbolically rich too: it depicted Edward III on his ship, bearing his

[26] Hodgett, *Cartulary of Holy Trinity*, fol. 161, 180, no. 926, refers to Hamo and his relationship to Agnes and John Chaucer. On moneyers, see Jessica Freeman, 'The Mistery of Coiners and the King's Moneyers of the Tower of London, c. 1340–c. 1530,' *British Numismatic Journal* 70 (2000): 67–82.

[27] Martin Allen, *Mints and Money in Medieval England* (Cambridge: Cambridge University Press, 2012), 85–86.

[28] Crow and Olson, *Chaucer Life-Records*, 438.

[29] Pál Engel, *Realm of St Stephen: A History of Medieval Hungary, 895–1526*, trans. Tamás Pálosfalvi and ed. Andrew Ayton (London: I. B. Tauris, 2001), 155–56.

[30] Peter Spufford, *Money and Its Use in Medieval Europe* (Cambridge: Cambridge University Press, 1988), 267.

[31] Allen, *Mints and Money*, 359.

weapons, almost certainly commemorating his victory at Sluys, and his recapturing of his ship, the *Christopher* (Christ-bearer)—thus neatly making Edward himself a Christ figure, complemented by the biblical motto: 'But Jesus passing through their midst went His way.'[32] It also, until the Treaty of Brétigny, proclaimed that Edward was king of France.

The arrival of gold coinage onto the scene in England both enhanced the position of the Italians and deepened the resentment between Italian and English entrepreneurs. The noble was launched by Percival Porche of Lucca, and for the next twenty years, control of the mint veered from being mainly under Italians in the 1340s to being under a series of Englishmen in the 1350s, before Walter de Bardi took it over for the long term.[33] At the same time, money-changing suddenly became big and controversial business. In the same year as the introduction of the noble, an exchange was set up to change gold for silver, and was assigned to Italian merchants, who were also given authority to run exchanges in York and Canterbury.[34] In 1352 a statute forbad anyone except the king's exchanger to change money for profit, but corruption was rampant: one of the charges against Adam de Bury in the Good Parliament was that he had been holding an exchange in his own house.[35]

The errancy of gold was a constant concern. From 1344 to 1364, gold nobles could be exported, but silver could not. The rationale was that if gold coins could be exported, this would help to keep silver bullion in England, but the outflow of gold was such that from 20 January 1364, the export of both gold and silver was expressly forbidden, except by royal licence.[36] And so began the attempt to retain gold that became increasingly desperate as the century wore on, and reached crisis point in the late fourteenth and early fifteenth centuries. Gold vanished. It wore away, it was hoarded, it was transformed into plate and other objects, and it was shipped

[32] See D. Vance Smith's discussion in '*Piers Plowman* and the National Noetic of Edward III,' in Kathy Lavezzo (ed.), *Imagining a Medieval English Nation* (Minneapolis: University of Minnesota Press, 2004), 240–42.

[33] Allen, *Mints and Money*, 81–86.

[34] Ibid., 215–16.

[35] John H. Munro, 'Bullionism and the Bill of Exchange in England,' in *The Dawn of Modern Banking* (New Haven: Yale University Press, 1979), 191; and Allen, *Mints and Money*, 220.

[36] Munro, 'Bullionism,' 191.

abroad.[37] For the economy to function smoothly, new coins had to be minted, but the supply of bullion into the mint rapidly diminished in the last quarter of the fourteenth century.[38] Between around 1380 and around 1410, England (and indeed Europe more generally) experienced 'bullion famines,' as mining of both silver and gold declined. The adoption of gold had led to a great deal of silver being sent out of Europe to the Islamic world and Asia, and the seams of silver at the great silver mines at Freiberg and Kutná Horn in Bohemia and in the lesser mine of Iglesias in Sardinia, were running thin.[39] Around 1380, there was a fall in the yield of the Hungarian gold mines too.[40]

As the productivity of the mines was wholly out of England's control, anxiety coalesced around what was happening to existing coins: where were they going, and how could they be kept in circulation in England? The 'Canon's Yeoman's Tale,' which is not really a tale about alchemy—making gold—but is instead a story about how easily gold can vanish, taps into serious anxieties about gold in the last twenty years of the fourteenth century. In this tale, £40 worth of gold nobles vanishes as the duped priest hands it over to the canon, who disappears. The promise of 'multi-plying' (transmuting base metals into gold [1391]) instead causes men to 'empten . . . grete and hevye purses' (1404), turning out to be 'the cause grettest of swich scarsetee' (1393). Those who allege they can make gold instead make it disappear—there is no magic solution that will increase the gold supply. The disappearance of gold occupied Parliament and the Crown obsessively in these years. Unlike other European countries, England did not resort to frequent debasement of the currency: Parliament was violently against debasing and, as one economic historian has commented, 'no other country even approached such conservatism in its

[37] Edwin S. Hunt and James M. Murray, *A History of Business in Medieval Europe, 1200–1550* (Cambridge: Cambridge University Press, 1999), 63.

[38] See Munro, 'Bullionism,' 178. In the 1350s, the amount of silver and gold minted in kilograms was, respectively, 1091.9 and 1759.3; in the 1360s the figures were 1071.1 and 2121.9. In the 1370s, there was a dramatic downturn: 354.7 and 606.0, and in the 1380s, things got even worse: 257.0 and 313.9. The 1390s were not as bad as the 1380s, but still bad: 233.9 and 539.8, and in the 1400s, the nadir was reached: 48.6 and 149.1. Munro, 'Bullionism,' 180.

[39] Ibid., 186; Hunt and Murray, *History of Business*, 172.

[40] Engel, *Realm of St Stephen*, 187.

mint policies.'[41] The Crown was able to do this because, in contrast to other European countries, it had a strong Parliament: this meant that Parliament could get its wishes heard, and also that it could implement taxation so that the Crown did not have to rely on debasement to finance its wants.[42] This lack of debasement meant that English currency stayed strong. Not debasing was good for landowners, because the value of their rents remained the same, and for consumers, for whom prices did not go up. In other countries that relied on debasing, landlords suffered, and the peasantry, who paid fixed dues, benefitted, as did producers of export goods.[43] The refusal to debase intensified the Crown's obsession with keeping precious metals in England. In the late fourteenth century, there was a ban on importing foreign coins (because they might be clipped or counterfeited) and exporting bullion and coin; laws also required exporters to deposit bullion at the mint and importers to export goods of the same value as their imports (so that they were not sending money out of the country). There were also repeated attempts to control foreign exchange transactions and to limit the use of credit.[44]

Merchants were thus hampered in many ways by the strong 'bullionist' mentality. Time and again, Parliament anxiously debated issues relating to retaining bullion in these years and, unsurprisingly, anxieties about vanishing gold and silver became intertwined with other acute anxieties: about foreigners, the church, and documentary culture. As John Munro writes, it is the 'bullionist mentality that helps to explain both royal and public hostility to the bill of exchange.'[45] All aspects of English finance were fundamentally connected with the Italians at this time. As we have seen, an Italian even controlled the mint, as well as the exchange, appropriately located in Lombard Street. The bill of exchange—which was first developed in Genoa in the late twelfth century—was the 'most important financial innovation of the High Middle Ages.'[46] It made it possible for

---

[41] Munro, 'Bullionism,' 191.

[42] Spufford, *Money and Its Use*, 316–18; Munro, 'Bullionism,' 187.

[43] Spufford, *Money and Its Use*, 318.

[44] Munro, 'Bullionism,' 187.

[45] Ibid., 198.

[46] Hunt and Murray, *History of Business*, 65.

someone to receive money in one currency and to pay it back in a different currency, at a later date and in a different place. The exchange rate was determined in such a way as to give the issuer of the bill a profit (in other words, this was really usury or lending at interest). Italian banking families, with their reliable and extensive networks in different cities, dominated the use of the bills. The bill allowed, for instance, an English cleric to pay a sum of money to an Italian exchanger in London whose partner would then, on his behalf, remit payment to the pope in Avignon or Rome. But as English gold was flowing to the exchanger's coffers, it was widely seen as a way of exporting bullion. Anxiety about the loss of bullion was exacerbated by frustration that so much money flowed to the pope and to parent houses of alien religious foundations, especially as this was all done through the means of Italians—yet more foreigners taking money from England. Indeed, it is likely that the principal use of bills of exchange was for ecclesiastical payments.[47] In the Good Parliament—which, as we have seen, moved harshly against those selling licences to Italians, and accused Lombards of being Jews, Saracens, and homosexuals—the Commons petitioned for a ban on the bill of exchange, which they called 'lettre de Lumbard.' They asked that '[n]o man should be so presumptuous as to make payment or send overseas any of the good money of this land, secretly or openly, by the letter of a Lombard or in any other manner[.] And no Lombard or other should make such letters.'[48] The article that followed was an attack on the pope and his collector, accusing Lombards of being spies, sending letters to Rome that spilt English secrets. With this context in mind, we can see that the protest against bills of exchange is part of a general paranoia about foreign influence in England, and in particular about foreigners operating secret networks—the kind of accusation that is repeated against groups of different countries, religions, or ethnicities in myriad times and places. In 1380, when Parliament ordered that gold, silver, or anything else 'par letter d'eschange' could not be sent out of the kingdom for the profit of aliens, they were making it impossible for

---

[47] Munro, 'Bullionism,' 200; Michael Prestwich, 'Italian Merchants in Late Thirteenth and Early Fourteenth Century England,' in *Dawn of Banking*, 77–104.

[48] PROME, Membrane 13, no. 103, 5:334 (April 1376).

aliens to hold ecclesiastical benefices in England, or for alien parent houses to receive money from English foundations.[49] Many of these same anxieties motivated the rebels of 1381, who also suspected foreigners, the church establishment, particularly alien foundations, and writing itself.

It did not make sense, however, for the Crown to lump Italian merchants in with the papacy and the church more generally. Instead, while Londoners focused on the iniquities of merchants, who were perceived as threatening their own profits and business opportunities, the Crown focused on the papacy itself, whose wealth was always a source of distress to English monarchs. A good example of how these rival antiforeigner tensions played out is the case of the Florentines in the late 1370s. The pope had placed Florence under interdict in 1375, which meant that people all over Europe had licence to exclude them from business and abuse them with impunity. The interdict was sent to England in spring 1376 (while the Good Parliament was under way), but the Crown refused to publish it. In January 1377, William Courtenay, the bishop of London, published it in London in direct opposition to the wishes of the Crown. We have to see this in the context of Gaunt's support of Wycliffe's attack on church property and Courtenay's censuring of Wycliffe, which took place in February 1377 (three months later, Wycliffe was condemned by the pope). The Florentines were now in an extremely precarious position in London, and they appealed to the king, asking him to take them (and their goods) into the Tower itself for their own safety. He agreed, and they took refuge there. The king then took them under his personal protection, making them his legal chattels, which allowed them to stay and trade in a cunning bit of legal manipulation.[50]

As the bullion crisis got under way in the 1380s, political and economic worries centred around counterfeiting. The noble made in the Tower, the coin that Alison resembles, was threatened by a new pretend noble, a coin made in Burgundy by Philip the Bold, a coin that was supposed to be equivalent to the English noble but that had a lower gold content. Richard II made attempts to ban the use of Flemish nobles in England in 1389,

[49] PROME, Membrane 3, no. 37, 6:83 (January 1380).
[50] Richard C. Trexler, *The Spiritual Power: Republican Florence under Interdict* (Leiden: Brill, 1974), 64–66.

1392, and 1394—and in 1397 Philip banned English nobles from his own lands. This new concern was no longer about Italians fraudulently taking English money but about Flemings bringing in their own pretend money and tricking the English that way. It is a different angle, but the focus on money as something absolutely bound up with national identity and threatened by foreigners is a constant across this period. There is also a consistent preoccupation with being deceived: for instance, the *City of London Letter-Books* recount stories such as that of John Tilney, paltok maker, who was tricked by John Grey's substituting counters for gold 'ferlings' in a chest, in a story with strong similarities to the 'Canon's Yeoman's Tale.'[51]

Chaucer's famous reference to English currency—'in the Tour the noble yforged newe'—repays the closest of reading. The reference is to a newly made coin—hence, it is shining, as it has not yet been passed from hand to hand; it is unused. The specific mention of the English Mint—the Tower—underlines the fact that this is an authentic coin, and it is an English coin. It is what it looks like. And yet Chaucer also emphasizes its inauthenticity: like all money, it is a representation; it is also a made object, something that has been crafted in a forge. And here, we come to a crucial ambiguity: the verb 'yforged.' Most obviously in this context, the past participle draws our attention to the fact that the coin has been made in a workshop, fired and beaten in a furnace by skilled artisans. This meaning, however, was not the word's only or even most obvious meaning in the late fourteenth century. This is itself the first recorded usage of the verb 'to forge' being used to mean 'to coin.' In the 1380s, it was also used—by Chaucer and also by the writer of the Wycliffite Bible—with the more general artisanal meaning of 'to form or fashion something at a forge.' Chaucer uses the word in the 'Knight's Tale,' describing smiths forging 'sharpe swerdes on his styth' (2026), and in the *Complaint of Mars*, comparing true lovers to metal 'that is forged newe' (201). But the word is also used with a variety of meanings relating to deception, just as today we talk of forging documents, of forgers and forgery. In the first half of the fourteenth century, the word was used with the meaning of counterfeiting a document; around the middle of the century, there are examples of

---

[51] Reginald Sharpe (ed.), *Calendar of Letter-Books: Letter-Book H* (London: John Edward Francis, 1907), fol. lxvb, 67–68 (29 May 1378).

its being used with a general meaning of 'plotting.'[52] Again, Chaucer is the first person that we know of to have used the word to mean 'to compose a story, to imagine, to tell a lie.' In the 'Parson's Tale,' he writes: 'Another lesynge comth of delit for to lye, in which delit they wol forge a long tale and peynten it with alle circumstances' (610). Here, the liar forges, as in *makes up*, a story, but, crucially, the liar also forges, as in *makes* or crafts a tale. The idea of the lie as a physical made object is emphasized as the metaphor continues: after having been forged, this object is painted ('peynten . . . with alle circumstances'). This draws on the Ciceronian trope of the colours of rhetoric that Chaucer explicitly references elsewhere ('Colours of rethoryk been to me queynte'; 'Franklin's Prologue,' 726), which itself suggests an artisanal approach to rhetoric, but the connection is much clearer in the 'Parson's Tale' quotation, where both 'forge' *and* 'paint' have clear, pragmatic, artisanal meanings. Weaponry, coins, and fictions are all things that are forged in Chaucer's writings. It was common at this time for a poet to be termed a maker or a craftsman, and the artisan was often seen in parallel with the poet.[53] Chaucer is tapping into this convention, but the emphasis on deceit and counterfeiting adds another angle: the seeming solidity of the made object can, like a story, be deceptive, untrue, a copy rather than an embodiment of honest truth. But medieval culture did not have a simple binary attitude towards truth /nature versus deception/human culture: in the *Romance of the Rose*, it is Nature who operates the forge.[54]

In the second reference to the noble in the 'Miller's Tale,' the coin is not there at all; it is imagined as a substitute for a tool—a tool that becomes an

[52] See 'forgen' in Kurath, Kuhn, and Lewis, *Middle English Dictionary*.

[53] Mary Carruthers, 'The Poet as Master Builder: Composition and Locational Memory in the Middle Ages,' *New Literary History* 24:4 (1993): 887. See also Lisa Cooper, *Artisans and Narrative Craft in Late Medieval England* (Cambridge: Cambridge University Press, 2011); Kellie Robertson, *The Labourer's Two Bodies: Labour and the 'Work' of the Text in Medieval Britain, 1350–1500* (New York: Palgrave Macmillan, 2006). Robertson writes about 'a continuum of work on which manual and intellectual labours occupied adjoining positions'; Cooper suggests that poets were thinking about 'making' in material terms with particular intensity in the late fourteenth and early fifteenth centuries (59).

[54] Nature 'toute s'entente metoit / A forgier singulières espieces' (put all her attention on forging individual creatures); *Roman de la Rose*, 15900–904, in Guillaume de Lorris and Jean de Meun, *The, Romance of the Rose*, trans. Charles Dahlberg, 3rd ed. (Princeton: Princeton University Press, 1995), 270. Discussed by Cooper, *Artisans*, 100. For an important recent book on nature, see Kellie Robertson, *Nature Speaks: Medieval Literature and Aristotelian Philosophy* (Philadelphia: University of Pennsylvania Press, 2017).

instrument of violence and sexual warfare.[55] The smith, whose job is, of course, forging, lends Absolon his plough blade or 'kultour,' hot from the fire, saying, 'were it gold, / Or in a poke nobles alle untold, / Thou sholdest have' (3779–81). Forgery here retains its deceptive suggestiveness: the thing that has been forged as a farming implement is used as a substitute for a weapon (for, in fact, the swords of the 'Knight's Tale'), and is explicitly compared to another object that could be forged—the noble. And this object—not-money—is then used in an act of mock-sex or mock-sodomy, although it is not a penis, and it is deployed on a body that is not the body it is supposed to be (Alison's) but is instead Nicholas's, just as Alison, in the previous episode, substituted a nether hole of some kind for her face. This becomes a tale of dizzying substitutions—of things forged, or forgeries.[56]

The equivalence suggested here between an instrument of violence and a gold coin is peculiarly appropriate. Not only were both metal objects forged in furnaces, but the noble itself commemorated a military victory, with its depiction of Edward III in triumph after the battle of Sluys. Moreover, that battle was almost certainly the first battle at which the new technology of guns and gunpowder was used by the English.[57] At around the same time as the noble was first made, the Tower also became host to workshops for manufacturing, and armouries for storing, gunpowder and guns. Chaucer was not only born in the same half decade as the noble, but also in the same half decade as gunpowder (in England)—and both nobles and gunpowder were birthed in the Tower. When Chaucer visited the Tower as clerk of the works, he was visiting a place of industry and technology, the crucible of advanced weapons manufacture. And his job there in 1389–91 was also dependent on warfare: he was extending the wharf primarily to facilitate the shipping of arms and supplies for the Hundred Years' War. The role of the Tower of London in the arms business had

[55] As Cooper notes, there is a 'long literary tradition of associating the forge and metallurgical work with sexual desire, procreation, and male potency.' *Artisans*, 100.

[56] Maura Nolan discusses the play between artifice and nature in the description of Alison, arguing against the idea that the two are set against each other. She convincingly argues that this is a poem that celebrates substitution and materiality. 'Beauty,' in Strohm, *Middle English*, 208–14, 218–20.

[57] J. R. Partington, *A History of Greek Fire and Gunpowder* (Baltimore: Johns Hopkins University Press, 1960), 103; Thomas of Walsingham, *Historia Anglicana* (London: Longman, 1863–64), 1:227.

changed substantially during Chaucer's lifetime: the privy wardrobe had been established and fixed at the Tower, with responsibility for arms amongst other goods, and the Tower simultaneously developed from a place where arms were kept to the principal working armoury of the realm, manufacturing, repairing, storing, and transporting arms.[58] Just as the mint comprised noisy, smelly, dangerous workshops, so the making of weapons was a messy industry. Nuisance cases were brought against London armourers during this period, complaining both of the smoke and of the effect on neighbouring properties of the violent blows struck to make the weapons.[59] When Chaucer became clerk of the works, England was temporarily at peace with France, but nonetheless was concerned with the preparations for war. During the 1380s new castles had been built, at least partially to defend the country against French attacks. For the first time, castles were designed with guns in mind: Cooling Castle, near the Kent estuary and a project of Henry Yevele's, had holes for 'arkets,' muzzle-loaded firearms that were forerunners of the rifle.[60]

When Chaucer mentions a gun in the *House of Fame*, he uses it as a simile: just as Alison shines *like* a noble, the sound of Aeolus's trumpet reverberates: 'As swifte as pelet out of gonne / Whan fyr is in the poudre ronne' (1643–44). These similes need to be comprehensible to the audience in order to work, but by choosing inventions of his own lifetime, Chaucer also ensures the 'newfangleness' of his poetry. Not many of his audience would have much or any experience of guns and gunpowder, although they would be aware of its existence. (Similarly, the noble was not a coin used every day as it was of too high value for ordinary transactions.)[61] T. F. Tout characterized the years up to 1360 as the 'experimental' stage of cannon, arguing that it was not until after 1369 that guns and gunpowder became really significant to English armies. In the 1370s, there was 'unprecedented activity' in the Tower workshops, and after around 1380,

---

[58] Roland Thomas Richardson, The Medieval Inventories of the Tower Armouries, 1320–1410 (DPhil thesis, University of York, 2012), 269; Malcolm Mercer, 'King's Armourers and the Growth of the Armourers' Craft in Early Fourteenth-Century London,' in J. S. Hamilton (ed.), *Fourteenth-Century England VIII* (Woodbridge: Boydell, 2014), 1–20.

[59] See Geddes, 'Iron,' 175, for a case brought against Stephen ate Fryth in 1377.

[60] Norman Pounds, *The Medieval Castle in England and Wales: A Social and Political History* (Cambridge: Cambridge University Press, 1990), 255. For Yevele, see below.

[61] Allen, *Mints and Money*, 360.

firearms are constantly mentioned in accounts of battles and sieges.[62] In the 1380s, we find references to early handguns, 'pelotgunnes'; in 1387, three small bronze cannon 'vocatos handgonnes' were sent to Berwick.[63] This was an age of innovation and development in the armaments industry and this innovation was centred around the Tower.

As a result, Chaucer experienced the Tower as a place of industry and technological advancement, a place of smoky workshops and forges, teeming with artisans of all kinds—not as a place of awe-inspiring feudal power. Castles, of course, had multiple purposes. Lefebvre writes that medieval urban space 'was fated to become the theatre of a compromise between the declining feudal system, the commercial bourgeoisie, oligarchies, and communities of craftsmen.'[64] In thinking about a castle's mixed spaces, the work of architectural historian Matthew Johnson is useful: he has shown that the ostensible defensive purposes of Cooling Castle (mentioned above, and built in the 1380s) are deceptive. The imposing front walls of the towers are merely a façade, as they are open at the back, for instance, amongst a host of other features that question its defensive purposes.[65] A copper plate on the gatehouse proclaims in English:

> Knowyth that beth and schul be
> That I am mad in help of the cuntre
> In knowynge of whyche thing
> Thus is charter and wytnessyng.

More important, perhaps, than whether or not the castle really was made 'in help of the cuntre' is the assertion in the first part of that line 'I am mad [made].'[66] Like a coin, gun, or tool, a castle itself is a made object, a demonstration of many kinds of artisanal skills. And it is with that aspect of the Tower—its very fabric—that Chaucer was primarily concerned in his role as clerk of the king's works.

---

[62] Tout, 'Firearms,' 242–45.

[63] Richardson, 'Inventories,' 266, 172.

[64] Lefebvre, *Production of Space*, 269.

[65] Matthew Johnson, *Behind the Castle Gate: From Medieval to Renaissance* (London: Routledge, 2002), xv–xvi.

[66] For discussion of this poem, see Cristina Maria Cervone, 'John de Cobham and Cooling Castle's Charter Poem,' *Speculum* 83:4 (2008): 884–916.

Chaucer supervised multiple employees in his job; perhaps the most interesting of them is Henry Yevele, pioneer of the perpendicular style, and the greatest architect of his age. Usually described as a master mason, Yevele illustrates the fluid boundaries between artist and artisan in this era. Starting off as a mason, he became one of the greatest architectural designers in English history, responsible for the masonry at Westminster Hall, where he worked with the equally impressive carpenter Hugh Herland, who made the hammer-beam roof. Yevele became a rich and successful man, with a hand in innumerable building projects, including castles, colleges, tombs, and churches, and served in London as warden of London Bridge, where he owned property. Indeed, he had acquired a great deal of property by the time of his death. For the first time in English architectural history, there are references in the records to one man (Yevele) designing building works, and others executing it according to Yevele's 'devyse.' Yevele was thus explicitly acknowledged to be a designer, an artist, and a skilled craftsman and labourer.[67] As clerk of the king's works, Chaucer worked with a range of different craftsmen: carpenters, glaziers, smiths, joiners, plumbers, and masons all lived at the Tower and were paid by Chaucer.[68] In this job, more than at any other time in his life, he was in very frequent contact with various kinds of makers—in contrast to his experience in the counting house, where he mainly associated with merchants and bankers.

Both Yevele and Herland appear alongside Chaucer in 1369, receiving exactly the same mourning livery after Queen Philippa's death.[69] As indentured members of the king's household, they were entitled to a certain amount of payment in kind; as employees contracted to do specific jobs, they received fixed amounts of money. These two aspects of Chaucer's employment conditions illustrate the economic and cultural transition taking place in the late Middle Ages. Broadly speaking, in the early Middle Ages, up until around the twelfth century, rulers and lords lived

[67] John H. Harvey, *Henry Yevele, c. 1320–1400: The Life of an English Architect*, 2nd ed. (London: Batsford, 1946), 39.

[68] Harvey discusses the range of craftsmen living at the Tower in Harvey, *Henry Yevele*, 23–24.

[69] Crow and Olson, *Chaucer Life-Records*, 99. Yevele and Chaucer are both listed as esquires of lesser degree, while Herland has the less important position of valet, although he received the same livery: 'troys aunes de drap de colour noir court.'

mainly on the products of their demesnes and by the services of vassals; those vassals who were rewarded—such as bureaucrats and warriors—tended to be paid in benefits such as land, food, and clothes. Money did, of course, exist, but it had a lesser role than it was to have in later centuries. From the thirteenth century, rulers increasingly depended on taxes, and lords on rents and farms: demesne lands were leased out for money, services were often commuted for cash payments, and paid servers were largely recompensed in money.[70] Money was increasingly collected and brought to the centre before being recirculated and moved out again. There is a major conceptual difference between being paid with products that have an intrinsic value and being paid with money, the value of which is representational, and which can be exchanged according to your own desires. Chaucer represents this very contemporary economy in the 'Knight's Tale,' where the artisans are paid in 'mete and wages' (1900)—food and money—for making Theseus's theatre, and, figuratively, the God of Love pays his servants: 'Hir wages and hir fees for hir servyse' (1803). Here, 'wages' refers to fixed amounts of money, and 'fees' specifically refers to 'renumeration other than wages for service'; other examples given by the *Middle English Dictionary* include occasions in which 'fee' refers to ale, an arrow, and armour. Even in the realm of metaphor, the God of Love's retaining system reflects the mixed rewards that were common in Chaucer's world. Absolon, in the 'Miller's Tale,' similarly offers Alison a range of food and drink, and money (3378–80). For men in Chaucer's position, there were obvious benefits to receiving a set salary (rather than household benefits), particularly in terms of the freedom one had to spend it: this had all kinds of knock-on effects, such as being able to choose where to eat and with whom; it allowed one to create part of one's life away from the control of one's employer. Moneyed salaries were also, however, subject to problems relating to inflation, for instance, that would not affect payment in kind. More seriously, the actual payment of salaries was anything but straightforward in the late fourteenth century, and Chaucer had to go through all kinds of contortions to receive the money that he was owed. For many of us today, the vast majority of our

---

[70] Spufford, *Money and Its Use*, 379; Dyer, *Making a Living*, 137–45, 178–83.

money is virtual—we never see it as it moves from one bank account to another with the press of a button. But Chaucer had to find out where the money physically was and go and get it, and if he couldn't wrest it out of the hands of his superior, he might decide to employ someone better placed to do so, at a cost to himself. When Chaucer was owed an allowance or expenses, he went to the Exchequer and was given a physical object: a tally stick with notches in it indicating how much he was owed. He then had to take this to the appointed Crown debtor, who was supposed to give him the money in return for the tally stick, which the debtor could then take to the Exchequer when his accounts were audited.[71] It is easy to see how problematic such a system could be, and how fraught with potential delays and excuses.

The *Chaucer Life-Records* are full of accounts of Chaucer's difficulties with money. He was often in debt, but those debts may well represent not an overall imbalance in his income and spending but problems of cash flow. His creditors are sometimes linked to his jobs, which may relate to his promising work-related payments from the Exchequer but then being unable to extract the money, leaving the supplier unrecompensed. One of his creditors was John Churchman, owner of the Custom House site and later himself a collector of customs; another was Isabella Buckholt, widow of a deputy of a previous clerk of the king's works, who probably also worked for Chaucer.[72] It was often difficult to secure funds in advance of expenditure, and Chaucer found himself seriously out of pocket in the course of his role as clerk of the king's works in particular, a job that at times required major expenditure. On 6 April 1391, he was given tallies for the enormous total of £213 6s 8d. However, £66 13s 4d of this was supposed to come from the farm of the forest of Rockingham, and Sir William de Thorpe, who had control of the revenue there, died that same month and Chaucer did not receive the money. In order to balance the books, Chaucer was credited with having lent the sum to the Crown, and he did not get it back for more than two years, on 22 May 1393.[73] He must have paid out this money himself and had a long wait for its repayment.

[71] Crow and Olson, *Chaucer Life-Records*, 136.
[72] Ibid., 384–87, 397–401.
[73] Ibid., 441, 469.

He was also out of pocket by a further £20 19s 2d for general extra expenditure; this was noted in the audit of June 1391, but not paid in full until July 1392. If we remember that Chaucer's annual salary as clerk of the works was £36 10s, it is clear that he was bearing enormous debts for the Crown. Indeed, frustratingly for Chaucer, the Exchequer paid off his smaller debt in measly installments (while delaying for longer the payment of the larger debt): in December 1391, the Crown owed him in total almost £90 from the two debts, and made him a payment of just £3 13s 4d.[74] For Chaucer, the transition to a money economy did not simplify life in a straightforward way; in many ways it made life more complicated. Even those complications, though, participated in the transition to greater autonomy for the employee, who was him/herself less subjected and more active both in the pursuit and the expenditure of wages.

The transitional nature of the economy is also signalled in the physical properties of money itself. Not all money is the same. Gold cannot have the same intrinsic, life-preserving qualities as food or clothing, but coins that partly or wholly maintain their value even if melted down, because their metal has a value that transcends the mint's authority, function differently to money that is representational, such as paper money, which substitutes for an authority that is not itself present. There is a *thingly* quality to medieval money lacking from our banknotes today. Indeed, thinkers have commented on premodern culture's different valuation of *things* in general. Most notably, Bruno Latour argues that the scientific revolution of the seventeenth century involved an intense focus on dividing subject from object, people from things and nature, as man asserted his (and it was usually his) separation from the matter that he tested and upon which he worked. More recently, there has been a reaction against this separation, an acknowledgement that there is a continuum between humans and things, and between culture and nature. Latour argues that there are aspects of the premodern mentality that are more in tune with the enmeshing of people and things than the Enlightenment mentality tends to be. He writes about premodern people's 'obsessive interest in thinking about the production of hybrids of Nature and Society, of things

---

[74] Ibid., 457, 467–69.

and signs, their certainty that transcendences abound, their capacity for conceiving of past and future in many ways other than progress and decadence, the multiplication of types of nonhumans.'[75] Again, we see Chaucer poised at a time of transition; the extraordinary figure of the Canon's Yeoman, one of the most fully realized individuals in the *Canterbury Tales*, is, in Lee Patterson's words, 'eager to dominate the natural world' while also bespeaking a 'yearning . . . for the value-laden, animated universe of traditional religion.'[76] The fact that he describes his own identity as blurring with the identity of the objects with which he works—as he gradually changes colour (727–28)—illustrates the ambiguities of his subject position. He self-consciously imagines himself into an objectified position: he becomes a thing, a spectacle, but his is the active hand that makes himself into an object.

The animate universe existed not only in relics and sacramental thought;[77] we can also see its traces in, for instance, the bell named Wyron that Chaucer inherited at the Tower or in the wearing of charms or amulets to ward off illness or to protect in battle that were specifically legislated against by the Court of Chivalry in the 1380s.[78] The animated power that 'things' had is reflected in the word itself: as Robertson points out, both Chaucer and Shakespeare use 'thing' to refer to people, as well as to 'objects.'[79] But while some people increasingly made their own choices and, through the money economy, were able to move from a prescribed place of work and life to form their own associations and even to write their own narratives, these same changes also led to the development

---

[75] Bruno Latour, *We Have Never Been Modern*, trans. Catherine Porter (Cambridge, MA: Harvard University Press, 1993), 133. See also Kellie Robertson, 'Medieval Things: Materiality, Historicism, and the Premodern Object,' *Literature Compass* 5:6 (2008): 1060–80.

[76] Lee Patterson, *Temporal Circumstances: Form and History in the Canterbury Tales* (New York: Palgrave Macmillan, 2006), 175.

[77] For discussion of the belief in objects as living, see Caroline Walker Bynum, *Christian Materiality: An Essay in Religion in Late Medieval Europe* (New York: Zone Books, 2011), 20–24; and Seeta Chaganti, *Medieval Poetics of the Reliquary: Enshrinement, Inscription, Performance* (Basingstoke: Palgrave Macmillan, 2008).

[78] For discussion of these, see Turner, 'Imagining Polities,' 398–406. On amulets, see also Don C. Skemer, *Binding Words: Textual Amulets in the Middle Ages* (University Park: Pennsylvania State University Press, 2006).

[79] Robertson, 'Medieval Things.'

of a heavy bureaucracy that textualised and objectified other people in a relentless homogenization of identity.[80]

In this world in which humans were objects as well as subjects, and things could have an agency and a value in themselves, the issue of subjectivity and selfhood was vexed indeed. The contrast between the 'Knight's Tale' and the 'Miller's Tale' is not a contrast between the ideal and the debased, or love and lust, nor is it primarily about knightly chivalry versus mercantile vulgarity, or even about romance versus fabliau, although this is a key part of the tale.[81] But the bigger contrast is between a life of complete subjection and a life in which the individual has a bit of choice. The image of the Tower is a key image for delineating this contrast. Palamon and Arcite, who subscribe to the beliefs that 'Al is this reuled by the sighte above' (1672) and that 'A man mot nedes love' (1169) are trapped 'in a tour, in angwissh and in wo' (1030). Syntactically and metaphorically, their physical entrapment parallels their agony: they are mentally as well as physically trapped. I have discussed the idea of the prison of love in chapter 3: Palamon and Arcite develop identities (to some extent) through subjection to higher powers—Theseus, Emily, Love, Venus, and Mars. This enclosing Tower contrasts sharply with the economic 'Tour' of the 'Miller's Tale.' Alison is by no means a liberated woman, but she does have some degree of choice; she makes some decisions for herself, unlike Emily, denied the opportunity to walk in the woods wild (2309), outside her own entrapment by Theseus. The sensual delight of the 'Miller's Tale' partly illustrates the emergent classes' ability to seize the day; to take action for happiness and amusement.

The 'Knight's Tale' betrays the constructedness of the allegedly natural hierarchy that puts everyone in a predetermined place and discourages the kind of errancy celebrated in the 'Miller's Tale'—and showcased even more dramatically in the figure of the Canon's Yeoman. It does this partly through an exposure of the workings of the theatre of power. Roger

---

[80] Kellie Robertson, 'Authorial Work,' in Strohm, *Middle English*, 441–58. She writes explicitly about the problems of trying to 'textualise personhood' at this time.

[81] On the Knight/Miller, see especially David Aers, *Chaucer, Langland and the Creative Imagination*, (London: Routledge and Kegan Paul, 1980), 175–95.

Dymmok, writing against the Lollards in the 1390s, emphasized the importance of goldsmiths, treasure, and luxury in general in creating an awe-inspiring image of political power.[82] Critics have written insightfully about Theseus's self-conception as architect and constructor, shaping his world by clearing land and constructing buildings, although his attempts to assert control do not succeed.[83] I would add that in the 'Knight's Tale,' we see how the illusion of power and stability is created not by a divinely ordained Theseus but by skilful artisans—people who are themselves itinerant, socially dynamic, and able to change their own position and environment. Theseus summons every 'crafty man' in the country 'to maken and devyse' (1897, 1901) the theatre (just as Chaucer himself was in charge of building the lists for the jousts at Smithfield in 1390).[84] Chaucer reminds us of the material aspects of art: when the Knight describes the emotive pictorial depiction of a woman in labour, he adds that the artist: 'With many a floryn he the hewes boghte' (2088).[85] Art is made, and power enforced, not through skills or talents that float separately from the mechanics of society but by buying materials and then crafting them. Theseus similarly presents himself in a carefully constructed way, making sure he is framed 'at a wyndow set' so that he seems 'as he were a god in trone'; he is there 'to [be] seen' (2528, 2529, 2531). Indeed, the world of the 'Knight's Tale' is noticeably concerned with the made aspects of Theseus's life: both the 'Knight's Tale' and the 'Miller's Tale' are interested in smithies, metalwork, and the use of made objects in the world. The scene in the Oxford smithy in the 'Miller's Tale' discussed above, in which the ploughshare is taken from the fire and used as a weapon, parodies the focus on making weaponry in the 'Knight's Tale': the smyth forges 'sharpe swerdes on his styth' (2026), and the armourers 'with fyle and hamer' (2508) ride around.[86] The Knight's gaze lingers over the actual making of the trappings of chivalry when he describes how one could see:

---

[82] See discussion in chapter 18.

[83] See, for instance, Kathryn L. Lynch, 'The Meaning and Importance of Walls in Chaucer's Poetry,' in Robert Edwards (ed.), *Art and Context in Late-Medieval English Narrative* (Cambridge: D. S. Brewer, 1994), 109–12.

[84] Crow and Olson, *Chaucer Life-Records*, 449.

[85] See Robert Epstein, ' "With many a floryn he the hewes boghte": Ekphrasis and Symbolic Violence in the *Knight's Tale*,' *Philological Quarterly* 85 (2006): 49–68.

[86] See Cooper's discussion of the forge, *Artisans*, 94–102.

> devisynge of harneys
> So unkouth and so riche and wrought so weel
> Of goldsmythrye, of browdynge, and of steel;
> The sheeldes brighte, testeres, and trappures,
> Gold-hewen helmes, hauberkes, cote-armures. (2496–2500)

Indeed, all kinds of things are *wrought* in the 'Knight's Tale,' as we are continually reminded of the crucial role of artisans in constructing the illusion of a feudal, divinely ordered society. Theseus sets himself up as the master builder, following the natural order of things, but not only does the repeated collapse of his plans and structures work against him, we also see how other people's artistry and independence are necessary to Theseus's plans. And their very art questions his worldview: they depict the horrors of war, love, and chastity in the temples that he commissions; they challenge the principles that he holds dear both in portraying the forces of chaos in the world and by themselves exceeding their remit and revealing Theseus's own limited control.[87]

Chaucer's own experiences of the Tower were only about feudal power insofar as they exposed the constructedness of that power. More importantly, Chaucer's interactions with the Tower illustrate for us his close connections with all kinds of artisans, and the complicated role that money played in his life. It is well known that in the *Canterbury Tales* Chaucer describes the traditional three estates of those who fight, those who work, and those who pray (Knight, Plowman, and Parson). This feudal social model, however, contrasts strongly with the chaotic variety of the world that Chaucer knew and that dominates the Canterbury group (populated by, for instance, the Miller, the Canon's Yeoman, the Pardoner, the Friar, the Guildsmen, the Merchant, the Shipman, the artisanal Wife of Bath, and the Cook). The Parson, an ethical and devout figure, stays in one place, preferring not to leave the boundaries of his parish. His tale makes it clear that he understands personhood according to a clearly laid-out set of external values (the seven deadly sins); people are

---

[87] Peggy Knapp argues that we see here art overflowing 'its conceptual mission' and that Theseus 'got more than he bargained for.' 'Aesthetic Attention and the Chaucerian Text,' *Chaucer Review* 39:3 (2005): 248.

objectified, categorized, and ultimately homogeneous.[88] His opposite is the Canon's Yeoman, a figure of modernity, restive, errant, relentlessly subjective, a quasi-scientist consumed by desires, crafting his own language, examining and constructing his own sense of self. The former avoids London, while the latter is fundamentally of the city. Although Chaucer's own life experience placed him firmly in the realm of modernity as a socially mobile man, moving in the money economy, interested in science, vernacular experimentation, and the formation of identity, he is not unaware or uncritical of the problems of leaving the security of less autonomous ways of life. Chaucer's concerns about the problems and insecurities inherent in crafting identity are neatly summed up in the wonderfully ambivalent idea of the *forged* self, made and counterfeited in the artisanal spaces of the Tower of London.[89]

---

[88] See discussion in chapter 19. See also Larry Scanlon, *Narrative, Authority, and Power: The Medieval Exemplum and the Chaucerian Tradition* (Cambridge: Cambridge University Press, 2007), 3–26.

[89] For Thomas Usk's imaginative construction of himself as forged and tested silver, see Turner, 'Usk and the Goldsmiths,' 167–69.

Plate 1. Medieval merchant's house, Southampton

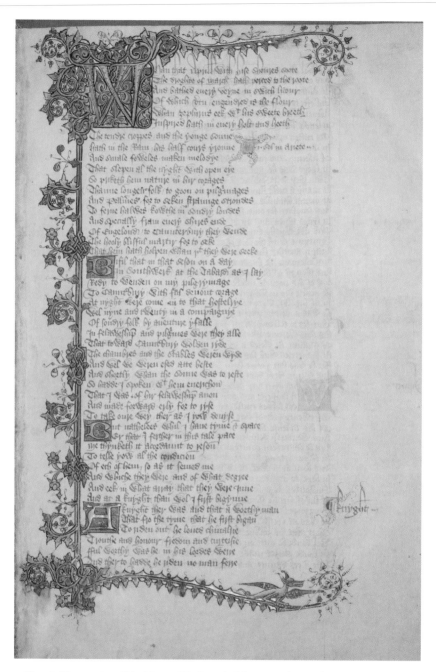

Plate 2. The opening of the 'General Prologue' of the *Canterbury Tales*, The Ellesmere Chaucer, c. 1400–1410

Plate 3. Old palace, Olite, Navarre

Plate 4. Iglesia de Santiago, Roncesvalles, Navarre

Plate 5. Rúa de la Judería, Olite, Navarre

Plate 6. Giotto, Death of St Francis, Florence, Santa Croce (Cappella Bardi), c. 1325

Plate 7. Scribal comments on the 'Wife of Bath's Prologue,' The Ellesmere Chaucer, c. 1400–1410

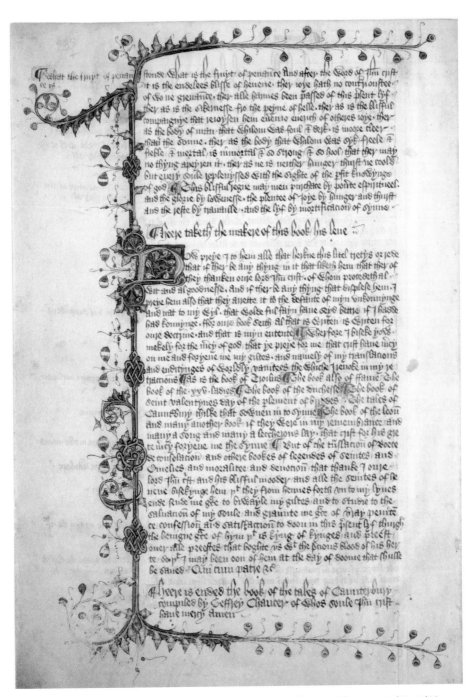

Plate 8. Chaucer's Retractions, in the *Canterbury Tales*, The Ellesmere Chaucer, c. 1400–1410

Plate 9. St Helen's Bishopsgate

Plate 10. The Tower of London

Plate 11. Astrolabe, c. 1370.

Plate 12. Sculpture of a poet laureate, fourteenth century, Castello Sforzesco, Milan

Plate 13. Visconti coat of arms (the 'biscione'), Castello Visconteo, Pavia

Plate 14. Tomb of Bernabò Visconti sculpted by Bonino da Campione, 1357–63, Castello Sforzesco

Plate 15. Medieval walled garden, Royal Palace of Olite, Navarre

Plate 16. Richard II, the Westminster portrait, c. 1395

Plate 17. Chaucer's tomb, Poets' Corner, Westminster Abbey, 1556

Plate 18. Portrait of Chaucer, in Thomas Hoccleve, *The Regiment of Princes*, c. 1411–20

Plate 19. Alice Chaucer's tomb, Ewelme, Oxfordshire, c. 1470s

CHAPTER 11

✥━┥◀▸━◉━◂▸┥━✦

Troy

On my right I then thought I saw New Troy, which was powerless as
a widow.

—*John Gower*

Troy, like Rome, was a place of central importance for Chaucer and his
contemporaries. In later fourteenth-century political discourse and literature, the city was used both to explore contemporary political and social
problems and to consider the place of the self in history. In poem after
poem of the 1380s and early 1390s, we see a Trojan idyll undercut by brutal political reality, as poets explored the fate of the individual in the context of the march of time. Troy, for a late fourteenth-century writer or
reader in the London area, was very much two places. It was the legendary city, home of Priam, Hector, Paris, and Aeneas, origin point of Rome
and the *translatio imperii* (translation of empire). And it was also the current incarnation of that *translatio*: London itself. There was an extraordinary concentration on London-as-Troy in the last quarter of the fourteenth
century. John Gower, Richard Maidstone, and the *St Erkenwald* poet all
call London either Troy or New Troy, and the *Gawain* poet too writes
about Britain's Trojan origins. Both Richard II and the mayor, Nicholas
Brembre, call London New Troy or Little Troy.[1] Troy, the city that
destroyed itself through internal betrayal and corruption, is a conflicted
place in poems of the 1380s. Readers of manuscripts of the *Aeneid* begin to

---

[1] For discussion of New Troy in this period, see Federico, *New Troy*; and Turner, *Chaucerian
Conflict*, especially chapter 3.

make marginal notes on their texts, drawing comparisons between events in ancient Troy and events in contemporary London—in particular the Rising of 1381.[2] Chaucer himself writes about Troy in many of his poems, most notably the *House of Fame*, the *Book of the Duchess*, and the 'Nun's Priest's Tale,' as well as *Troilus and Criseyde*. Indeed, Helen Cooper has suggested that in the *House of Fame* (1470), he places himself—'Englyssh Gaufride'—in a group of poets who write about Troy, defining his poetic work by its Trojanness.[3] In both the *Book of the Duchess* and the *House of Fame*, stories of Troy symbolize the literary habitus that shaped Chaucer's creative background.

Both the Troy of *Troilus and Criseyde* and the London of the early 1380s were places split between a shining surface of processions, set pieces, feasts, and parties, and an underbelly of violence, betrayal, and fatal conflicts. City records and Chaucer's poem both oscillate between these different facets of urban life. The politics of spectacle, and the politics of language use, are key issues both in the poem and in 1380s London, a place newly staging itself through glorious processions—and a place where books were burned by rebels and mayors alike and where the politics of representation were under pressure in the guildhall. In *Troilus and Criseyde*, Chaucer meditates on the self's relationship with political, social, and discursive structures that constrain and determine individual choice, actions, and modes of speech. The pressured spaces of Troy closely mirror the spaces of contemporary London.[4]

Troilus and Criseyde, Chaucer's most sustained Trojan poem, is very much a product of Ricardian London, as opposed to Edwardian London. The capital after 1377 was a city reinventing itself in the wake of the Good Parliament, a city now embarking on representing itself through public spectacle and pageantry, a city in which the ruling oligarchs were facing (and ultimately seeing off) unprecedented challenges.[5] *Troilus* is ostentatiously connected with contemporary London: Chaucer states that he is placing it under the correction of Gower and Strode (V, 1856–57), his

---

[2] Christopher Baswell, 'Aeneas in 1381,' *New Medieval Literatures* 5 (2002): 7–58.

[3] Cooper, 'Four Last Things in Dante and Chaucer,' 58–60.

[4] See Strohm, 'The Space of Desire in Chaucer's and Shakespeare's Troy.'

[5] For example, Gordon Kipling, *Enter the King: Theater, Liturgy, and Ritual in the Medieval Civic Triumph* (Oxford: Oxford University Press, 1998).

friends and associates in Southwark and London. He also mentions *Troilus* in his poem to 'Adam scriveyn'—Adam Pynkhurst, scribe of the Mercers' Company and therefore deeply implicated in London politics. Our first known reader of Chaucer's poem is Thomas Usk, scribe of the Goldsmiths' Company, and a factionalist who worked first for Northampton and then in the Ricardian-Brembre interest.[6] And by the early 1390s, *Troilus and Criseyde* was being used as a payment for a debt in Southwark.[7] Its specific connections with contemporary Londoners—Strode, Gower, Pynkhurst, and Usk—distinguish it from Chaucer's previous poems as a text conceptually and materially embedded in the contemporary city.

Produced after his second trip to Italy,[8] in the wake of a deep engagement with Dante, Boethius, and, in particular, Boccaccio, *Troilus and Criseyde* is a polished and self-consciously 'literary' poem.[9] It plays with styles from the Petrarchan sonnet, to letters, to complaint, mixing together genres such as epic, romance, lyric, tragedy, and history. Through his blending of sources and his changing of emphases, Chaucer particularly calls our attention to the dark side of Trojan history.[10] Chaucer also interweaves a developing naturalism into this literary poem: through his interest in circumstantial detail, conversational patterns, demotic language, concrete and realistic incidents, and most of all psychology, he writes a poem that is far more varied and subtle than Boccaccio's version,

---

[6] On Pynkhurst, see Mooney, 'Chaucer's Scribe,' and Lawrence Warner, 'Scribes, Misattributed: Hoccleve and Pinkhurst,' *Studies in the Age of Chaucer* 37 (2015): 55–100, discussed below. On Usk, see Turner, 'Usk and the Goldsmiths.'

[7] See chapter 16 in this study and Carlin, 'Thomas Spencer.'

[8] The 1378 trip is discussed in detail in chapter 13.

[9] I agree with the *Riverside Chaucer* that 'a date of composition 1382–1385 seems likely,' though work on the poem at an earlier date seems probable too. It is important to remember that the poem, like all long works, was written over a period of time, and that quite different versions are extant. Although there are various reasons for dating the poem to the early 1380s, the only firm piece of information we have is that Usk had read it and used it in his own long prose work, which he had written before his death in March 1388. For a summary of some of the arguments, see *Riverside Chaucer*, 1020. See also articles by John Livingston Lowes, 'The Date of Chaucer's *Troilus and Criseyde*,' *PMLA* 23 (1908): 285–306; Robert Kilburn Root (ed.), *The Book of Troilus and Criseyde* (Princeton: Princeton University Press, 1959); and George Lyman Kittredge, *The Date of Chaucer's Troilus and Other Chaucer Matters* (London: K. Paul, Trench, Trübner, 1905). See also Barry Windeatt, *Oxford Guides to Chaucer: Troilus and Criseyde* (Oxford: Clarendon Press, 2002), 3–11.

[10] Lee Patterson, *Negotiating the Past: The Historical Understanding of Medieval Literature* (Madison: University of Wisconsin Press, 1987); Eugene Vance, *Mervelous Signals: Poetics and Sign Theory in the Middle Ages* (Lincoln: University of Nebraska Press, 1986).

Il Filostrato.[11] *Troilus and Criseyde* explores the minds of individuals in a way quite different from Chaucer's other poems and from his sources. While Criseyde is a character of great complexity and depth, whose words and thoughts are distinct from each other, Troilus is a man trapped by surfaces, unable to escape the conventional language of romance and to find a language of emotion that he can call his own. In contrast to Boccaccio, Chaucer focuses on Criseyde's interiority and the complexity of human relationships.[12] He is fascinated by how the self functions in political society, by the question of who has a voice, and who is silenced—questions that were to occupy him in poetic terms across his whole career.

In 1380s London, as a new mayor attempted to change electoral practice, to widen representation, and to undermine oligarch monopolies; as rebels burned books and focused their anger on clerks and writing; and as English increasingly appeared in local government documents, broadsides, mayoral proclamations, and poetry, the issue of whose voice could be heard was foregrounded everywhere. The turbulent early 1380s were quiet years for Chaucer personally, however. The evidence of the *Life-Records* suggests that he was keeping his head down in these years, doing his job, collecting his allowances, and generally staying out of the limelight. There were no major trips during these years. Philippa was in attendance on Constance of Castile, now Gaunt's duchess, receiving gifts from Gaunt alongside other ladies-in-waiting.[13] Given the amount of writing that Chaucer produced during these years, it is clear that he was able to devote substantial chunks of his time to poetic making. The first few years of Chaucer's time at the Custom House (the mid- and late 1370s) were years marked by the political chaos of Edward's death, Gaunt's mauling at the

[11] Wimsatt argues that Chaucer and Jean de Meun draw on Ovid and the art of love tradition and on the tradition of cosmic fables (Cicero, Boethius, etc.) to develop their realism. See James I. Wimsatt, 'Realism in *Troilus and Criseyde* and the *Roman de la Rose*,' in Mary Salu (ed.), *Essays on Troilus and Criseyde* (Cambridge: D. S. Brewer, 1979), 43–56.

[12] James Simpson argues that Chaucer's version forms a powerful critique of 'Boccaccio's framing of his story as a narrative designed to serve the interests of masculine suffering.' 'Chaucer as a European Writer,' 75–76.

[13] Crow and Olson, *Chaucer Life-Records*, 90–91. For instance, in 1380, when she receives a silver-gilt hanap made by Adam Bamme, a London goldsmith and associate of Usk and Northampton at this point, she is named alongside Blanche of Trumpington and Lady Sanche Blount, also ladies-in-waiting to Constance. Lodge and Somerville, *John of Gaunt's Register, 1379–1383*, fol. 35b, 2:111–12, no. 327 (2 January 1380).

Good Parliament, and the conflict between the staplers and the court, in which Chaucer, as Gaunt's man and as the diplomat who had negotiated with Genoa, was implicated. In these years he went on journeys abroad to France, Flanders, Lombardy, and, closer to home, embarked on his disastrous relations with Cecily Champaigne. But during the following years—from around the middle of 1380 to late 1384—he had a much more settled and even pace of life. The evidence is that he did his office job and wrote his poems. While these were relatively quiet years for Chaucer, around him the city was erupting in utter chaos. These were the years not only of the Rising of 1381 but also of vicious and sometimes brutal conflicts over city government, conflicts dominated by the rivalry between Brembre and his followers and the Northampton faction, who mounted a radical challenge to the urban oligarchy.[14] These were also the years in which Richard began to assert himself, and John of Gaunt suddenly found himself in newly murky political waters. As a royal servant, retained by Gaunt, working with Brembre, recently involved in marriage negotiations for the king, and living over the gate through which the rebels entered in 1381, Chaucer's life was touched in all kinds of ways by the political maelstrom, yet he simply got on with his life and managed to find time and space to write extraordinary and innovative poetry. His most substantial poem from these years—indeed his *only* really substantial, *complete* poem—is concerned with the ebb and flow of personal and political fortune, and with the discrepancy between surface and depth.

Throughout *Troilus and Criseyde*, Chaucer goes out of his way to emphasise the negative aspects of Troy, focusing much more attention than Boccaccio does on Troy as a city that is internally divided and responsible for its own destruction, and insistently reminding us of the Trojans' wilful ignoring of the ominous example of Thebes and its fall.[15] The attractive surface of Troy, with its dinner parties, book groups, and festivals, is everywhere offset by political and personal betrayals, secret stratagems, intimations of rape, and aggressive and bloody imagery. By opening with

---

[14] The classic account remains Bird, *Turbulent London*. See also Pamela Nightingale, 'Capitalists, Crafts and Constitutional Change in Fourteenth-Century London,' *Past and Present* 124:1 (1989): 3–35; Lindenbaum, 'London Texts,' 284–310.

[15] Patterson, *Chaucer and the Subject of History*, 132–36.

Calchas's betrayal, by emphasizing that Antenor, adored by the Trojans, will later betray and destroy Troy, and by demonstrating the Trojans' ignoring of Cassandra, Chaucer portrays Troy as a city of treachery, a city that self-destructs.[16]

The very structure of *Troilus* ('fro wo to wele, and after out of joie,' Book I, 4) makes it clear that happiness is preceded and succeeded by misery, in well-known Boethian style. But the poem also shows us that even the glittering surface of Trojan life at its peak is only made possible by a sustained and determined denial of what is happening beneath and indeed by an insistence on dwelling on the surface itself, on representation and performance. In other words, this is not a poem that simply contrasts the lows and highs of Fortune's wheel. Towards the end of Book III (1716–43), Troilus, having consummated his relationship with Criseyde, is at the peak of that wheel, and the narrator describes for us his ecstatic happiness, building up to his Boethian song:

> In suffisaunce, in blisse, and in singynges,
> This Troilus gan al his lif to lede.
> He spendeth, jousteth, maketh festeynges;
> He yeveth frely ofte, and chaungeth wede,
> And held aboute him alwey, out of drede,
> A world of folk, as com hym wel of kynde,
> The fresshest and the beste he koude fynde;
>
> That swich a vois was of hym and a stevene,
> Thorughout the world, of honour and largesse,
> That it up rong unto the yate of hevene;
> And, as in love, he was in swich gladnesse,
> That in his herte he demed, as I gesse,
> That there nys lovere in this world at ese
> So wel as he; and thus gan love hym plese.
>
> The goodlihede or beaute which that kynde
> In any other lady hadde yset

---

[16] Turner, *Chaucerian Conflict*, 41–44.

Kan nought the montance of a knotte unbynde,
Aboute his herte of al Criseydes net.
He was so narwe ymasked and yknet,
That it undon on any manere syde,
That nyl naught ben, for aught that may bitide.

And by the hond ful ofte he wolde take
This Pandarus, and into gardyn lede,
And swich a feste and swich a proces make
Hym of Criseyde, and of hir wommanhede,
And of hir beaute, that withouten drede
It was an hevene his wordes for to here;
And thanne he wolde synge in this manere:

These four stanzas depict Troilus at his most joyful, in love with the whole
world, embracing his community, distributing largesse in a world of affection, music, and luxurious celebration. The stanzas are dominated by
rhetoric and hyperbole: the tricolons ('suffisaunce'/'blisse'/'singinges';
'spendeth'/'jousteth'/'maketh festynges'), the superlatives ('fresshest and
the best'), and the emphasis on the expansive and absolute nature of Troilus's experience ('al his lyf,' 'alway,' 'a world of folk,' 'thoroughout the world,'
'yate of heven,' 'in this world,' 'an hevene') create an atmosphere of dizzying excess. The narrator has taken on Troilus's characteristic rhetorical
habits—Troilus tends to speak in absolutes and superlatives—to create an
idea of Trojan life that is breathtakingly solipsistic. The world is not really
ringing with delight at Troilus's chivalric successes; rather, to him his own
little community is all that matters in the world. And the inward-looking
nature of Troilus and his comrades is a real problem when we remember
that all of this excessive partying is happening in a war zone, in a city under
siege, where people are dying in battle while this prince and his friends
change their outfits and sing songs. Even the verse form mirrors the sense
of excess: the first and last of the four stanzas quoted above are not end-
stopped. This is unusual in the poem and tends to reflect an overspilling
of emotion, a lack of control, as the content is not contained within the
formal patterning of rhyme royal with its concluding couplet. The image
of the knot also reminds us of the imagery of trapping and knots that

dominates the poem, as we are told the story of Criseyde's entrapment by Troilus and Pandarus, and that Troilus will slide knotless through her own heart by the end (Book V, 769).

The whole passage is about the surface, the performance of a courtly lover. Troilus changes his clothes often, and as others make 'swich a vois . . . of hym and a stevene,' so he makes 'swich a proces' of Criseyde. That is the point of the scene: the focus is on talking about something, not on the actual person or the relationship. Physically absent, Criseyde is not even mentioned until many stanzas into the description of Troilus's happiness, and in the final stanza quoted above, her absence is made troublingly obvious when 'by the hond ful ofte he wolde take' leads us breathlessly into the next line, where we find not 'This Criseyde' but 'This Pandarus.' Troilus is not with his lover but with his friend and helper, the person he can talk to about his lover or, more importantly, about his own feelings of love. Troilus's connection with Criseyde provides him with subject matter for the role of courtly lover, which he can play perfectly well in her absence. And indeed, throughout *Troilus and Criseyde*, Troilus creates a perfect, divinized image of Criseyde through language and convention that ultimately does not bear comparison with the actual woman herself, a person who is flawed, vulnerable, and changeable, as humans tend to be. She has been *made*, or *forged*—like the art and buildings constructed by artisans in the 'Knight's Tale' (discussed in chapter 10). To Troilus, from his first song in Book I to his final song in Book V, she is a star and a goddess, not allowed to be anything less than an eternally beautiful and unchangeable statue. In Troilus's focus on the surface—of Criseyde, and in terms of his own performed behaviour—he rejects the complex interiority of the heroine that Chaucer is at such pains to delineate in microscopic detail.

If we read the records carefully, we can draw two contrasting pictures of London in the early 1380s akin to the glittering surface and treacherous depths of Chaucer's Troy. One of the most glorious city spectacles of these years was the elaborate ceremonial entry of Queen Anne into London.[17] The idea of a marriage between Richard and Anne had de-

---

[17] These spectacles continued later in the reign too; notably in 1392, after the quarrel between Richard and London, the reconciliation pageantry was described in Trojan terms by Richard Maid-

railed the negotiations that Chaucer had been undertaking with Bernabò Visconti four years earlier.[18] This marriage was the cornerstone of an Anglo-imperial-papal alliance constructed in opposition to France and Avignon. The two participants in the marriage were both fifteen years old—Richard had his birthday mere days before the wedding. The *Westminster Chronicle* tells us that Anne arrived in London on 18 January and was 'received with signal honour by the citizens of London and, seated upon a charger, was escorted with great pomp to Westminster.' Two days later, she was married, and two days after that, crowned queen.[19] The Goldsmiths' Accounts, penned by Thomas Usk, give us a wealth of detail about the ceremonial welcoming of Anne to London. These kind of ceremonial royal entries were a new thing in London: 1377, when Richard became king, was probably the first occasion in which guilds sponsored pageants for a royal entry. Increasingly, London put on spectacles, pageants, mummings, and elaborate gift-giving ceremonies, often for courtly guests. While there had in the past been formal entries into London, these had not been accompanied by the kind of performative spectacle that now became the norm. Indeed, the last quarter of the fourteenth century marked the beginning of a steady increase in urban spectacle, as city oligarchies gained in power and status, and cities expressed and formed their identities through cultural display.[20] In 1382, a summer castle was erected in Cheap (probably reused from 1377), and three virgins leaned out of it to scatter leaves; there were also minstrels, elaborate painted ornaments, and accessories such as 'silverskins.' The payments make it clear that this event provided work for many skilled craftsmen, including painters and carpenters, and payments are also recorded for fabrics and for clothing. The companies all marched in red and white, but each guild had

---

stone. See Richard Maidstone, *Concordia (The Reconciliation of Richard II with London)*, ed. David Carlson and trans. A. G. Rigg (Kalamazoo, MI: TEAMS Middle English Texts, 2003), lines 18, 39, 212; Federico, *New Troy*, 1–7, 19–28; Turner, *Chaucerian Conflict*, 63.

[18] I discuss this in chapter 13.

[19] L. C. Hector and Barbara F. Harvey (ed. and trans.), *The Westminster Chronicle, 1381–1394* (Oxford: Clarendon Press, 1982), 23.

[20] Kipling, *Enter the King*, 6, 28; Sheila Lindenbaum, 'Ceremony and Oligarchy: The London Midsummer Watch,' in Barbara Hanawalt and Kathryn L. Reyerson (eds.), *City and Spectacle in Medieval Europe* (Minneapolis: University of Minnesota Press, 1994), 171–88; Lancashire, *London Civic Theatre*, 55–56; Turner, 'Usk and the Goldsmiths.'

its own accessories to distinguish it. The goldsmiths were able to use this opportunity to advertise their own products and skills; they 'had the red part of their clothing barred with silver wire and powdered with silver pearl trefoils, and each of the seven score men of the said mistery wore on their left side a large gold clasp with gemstones, and on their heads they wore chaplets covered in red material powdered with the said trefoils.'[21]

Chaucer was not a member of a city company, nor was he a citizen of London. But he was an inhabitant of London, an important official on the quayside, a member of the king's household, a diplomat who had been involved in many different negotiations for possible brides for Richard, and a client of John of Gaunt. This kind of spectacle—and probably this very one—were part of his imaginative world. He was also aware of and perhaps involved in the annual commemorations of Blanche's death at St Paul's, which centred around her beautiful and elaborate tomb. This had been celebrated just two months before Anne's entry, and involved Gaunt entering the city with a large retinue and proceeding to the tomb.[22] Plays took place in London, the most likely place for Chaucer to have watched drama and picked up his knowledge of those that 'pleyeth Herodes upon a scaffold hye' ('Miller's Tale,' 3384).[23] Jousts were staged at Smithfield—some were held to celebrate Anne and Richard's wedding, and a decade later Chaucer was himself responsible for erecting the scaffolds.[24] However much or little Chaucer took part in or personally observed feasts, drama, processions, and other spectacles, he was certainly aware of the social surface of London life, and of the increased emphasis on spectacle in the reign of Richard II.

At the same time, in these years, London was in political and institutional turmoil. The smooth surface covered a deeply divided city where everyone's allegiances were complicated and multiple. As we have seen in chapter 7, Chaucer returned to London while Gaunt was riding high, and

[21] Lisa Jefferson (ed.), *Wardens' Accounts and Court Minute Books of the Goldsmiths' Mistery of London, 1334–1446* (Woodbridge: Boydell, 2003), 196–99.

[22] Goodman, *John of Gaunt*, 91.

[23] For instance, the clerks of London put on plays lasting five days at Skinners' Well around 29 August 1384, at about the same time as John Northampton's trial. Hector and Harvey, *Westminster Chronicle*, 95; E. K. Chambers, *The Medieval Stage* (Mineola, NY: Dover Publications, 1996), 2:118–19; W. O. Hassell, 'Plays at Clerkenwell,' *MLR* 33 (1938): 564–67.

[24] Goodman, *John of Gaunt*, 92; Crow and Olson, *Chaucer Life-Records*, 449.

while the profiteering court cabal was locked in conflict with the monopolist staplers. The Good Parliament saw London's varied interests almost
entirely united against Gaunt, the Italians, and Edward's advisors.[25] Men
who would become implacable enemies in the 1380s were temporarily
allies against the threats to the city's liberties posed by Gaunt and the
court. In 1376, the staplers, prominent amongst whom was Brembre, and
the group led by Northampton, made an 'unmistakeable alliance.'[26] The
staplers were demanding an end to the sale of licences to evade the staple;
Northampton's group wanted the franchise (essentially a retail monopoly
for Londoners) restored so that they could control the London cloth trade
and restrict alien trade. But the alliance between different groups in London did not last, and indeed Northampton and his allies felt that they had
been betrayed by the staplers, when the court agreed to the staplers' demands
but not those of Northampton: on 24 July the king confirmed the Good
Parliament's ordinance and forbad the evasion of the staple. However, the
franchise was not mentioned.[27] In the wake of the impeachment of his
former allies in the city, Gaunt now sought a new way to intervene in
London and joined forces with Northampton, a fellow enemy of the staplers.[28] While Northampton wanted to open city government to a wider
range of people, to lower prices, and to break the power of the great merchants, Gaunt's interest was in weakening the city as a power bloc to enable
the court influence to gain power at the expense of the powerful men of
London. In the late 1370s, Gaunt moved against Brembre's associates
Walworth and Philipot, getting them removed as treasurers; Parliament
also moved against the murderers of the Genoese ambassador—men
certainly motivated by the interest of the wool monopolists.[29] And Gaunt's
brother (the future Appellant) made a personal accusation against Brembre and was paid off by him.[30] By 1381, John Northampton was mayor,
supported by Gaunt, and the traditionally powerful men of the city were
suffering an (as it turned out temporary) eclipse.

[25] Bird, *Turbulent London*, 44; Nightingale, *Medieval Mercantile Community*, 243–53.

[26] Nightingale, *Medieval Mercantile Community*, 243.

[27] Ibid., 244; Sharpe, *Calendar of Letter Books: Letter-Book H*, fol. xl, 31.

[28] Nightingale, *Medieval Mercantile Community*, 245–51.

[29] See Strohm on the murder of Janus Imperial in *Theory and the Premodern Text*, 112–31.

[30] Bird, *Turbulent London*, 45–48.

The years 1381–83 were exceptional in London's history. Sandwiched between mayoralties of some of the richest and most powerful men in the city, for these two years John Northampton tried to institute reforms that radically changed who had power in the city and how the poor could live. In the wake of the Good Parliament, Northampton and his supporters had brought in reforms to elections that allowed more people in the city to have a say in who elected the members of the common council and the mayor, and in who could become an alderman.[31] The thrust of these changes was to make it difficult for the same men to have a stranglehold on power. These reforms were quickly repealed in 1384 after Brembre had taken over.[32] During his mayoralty, Northampton also brought in a series of regulations designed to ease the plight of the poor and attack corruption. These included banning people from offering more than a farthing at baptisms, marriages, and requiems, to prevent the poor from being pressured or coerced into offering more than they could afford. Bakers and brewers were required to make bread and ale in farthing measures, extra farthings were to be produced at the Tower, and sellers were obliged to give change.[33] Overall, Northampton had a programme of promoting the interests of the less powerful in London against the interests of the oligarchs and monopolists.

He was supported by Gaunt, for Gaunt's own reasons. It is unlikely that Gaunt had any particular interest in the price of bread in London, although he *was* interested in church corruption—again for his own reasons. And he was very interested in attacking the vested power interests of London, men who were complicit in the repeated attacks on Gaunt in the late 1370s, and who were attempting to counter royal power in London. Northampton gave him a way of meddling in London and keeping down the merchant capitalists—against whom he had been pitted in the 1370s in the conflicts surrounding the wool trade, as we have seen. When we see the Crown promoting Northampton's election in 1382, this tells us that Gaunt was still in control of this part of royal policy at least, as Gaunt consistently

[31] Nightingale, *Medieval Mercantile Community*, 245–51.
[32] Bird, *Turbulent London*, 30–43.
[33] Sharpe, *Calendar of Letter-Books: Letter-Book H*, fol. cxliv, 183.

supported Northampton.[34] But it was exactly in the next few years that Richard began to separate himself from Gaunt, and to form his own political group. As Richard grew into precarious adulthood—or thought he did—Gaunt lost the dominant position that he had managed to hold on to for about a decade.

Looking at the shifting power groupings in late fourteenth-century London politics more generally, it is difficult and often confusing to talk about 'sides,' 'parties,' or 'factions.' One reason for this is that people changed their position frequently: Brembre moved from anticourt Londoner in the 1370s, when Gaunt and Edward's advisors were hand in glove with the Italians who threatened Brembre's and his friends' designs upon the wool trade, to close intimate of the court in the 1380s, when he became Richard's banker and supporter. His different policies and alliances in these decades supported an unchanging underlying agenda—his own enrichment and the power of (oligarch-controlled) London. Another reason is that people often made temporary alliances that at first glance may have seemed surprising, as individuals or groups whose general aims and positions were quite different could come together for a common cause. People supported the same policy but for very different reasons, making alliances perhaps on the principle that 'my enemy's enemy is my friend.'

The Rising of 1381 was a cataclysmic event that exposed not only the divisions but also the confused alliances within contemporary London and its environs. It was also a moment that perfectly demonstrated the surface/depth split: Richard II rode to the rescue, declaring to the underprivileged that he would be their champion and then promptly went back on his word and destroyed them and their movement. If one looks at the varied demands of the rebels, and the grievances aired during the revolt, an inconsistent picture of allegiances and common causes emerges. For example, some great merchants of London shared the rebels' loathing for Gaunt, foreigners, and scribal culture. Books were burned both by the rebels in 1381 and by the oligarch mayor, Nicholas Exton, in 1387. In the revolt, clerks were consistently associated with Gaunt, foreigners, and other

[34] Bird, *Turbulent London*, 76.

agents of doom as foci of the rebels' fury.[35] The rebels targeted clerks and their documents, and demonstrated a profound suspicion of those who worked in the writing offices. As we have seen, 'literary' scribes are consistently connected with Northampton-supporting, not Brembre-supporting, guilds. The insurgents revealed an acute distrust of the way that writing was employed and a belief that representation (e.g. of land ownership) did not accurately represent reality. Ironically, many writers were themselves engaging with precisely this issue: men such as Chaucer and his friend John Clanvowe staged debates between conventional, elite language and the language of truth-telling, and meditated long and hard about the relationship between sign and signified, representation and reality, surface and what lies beneath.[36] The irony of the rebels' affinity with the oligarchs can hardly be overestimated: it was, after all, the *other* group in London (the one sponsored by Gaunt!) that sought to open up a new political discourse in London in which the 'small people' had more voting rights and in which more voices could be heard.

Given the similar attitudes of the rebels and the city oligarchs to a whole range of issues—including foreigners, Gaunt, and Crown interference—the accusation made by John More (Northampton's right-hand man) that some of Brembre's associates opened the gates to the city was not an entirely ludicrous idea.[37] Similarly, Usk reported that Northampton's party considered accusing Brembre of supporting Thomas Farndon (or Farringdon).[38] This rebel leader provides a fascinating and bewildering example of the complexities of the politics of the revolt. A disaffected goldsmith from a prominent family, Farringdon had a personal grievance against the prior of St John of Jerusalem, Robert Hales. He led attacks in Essex, just down the road from Bradwell manor; was allegedly the instigator of the murder of Hales and the attack on the priory; and was said to have confronted Richard II, seizing his bridle and demanding

---

[35] Justice, *Writing and Rebellion*; Crane, 'The Writing Lesson of 1381'; Lindenbaum, 'London Texts,' 286–93.

[36] *Book of Cupide* and *Parliament of Fowls*. See chapter 18.

[37] Turner, *Chaucerian Conflict*, chapter 2. John More was a close associate of Northampton's.

[38] Thomas Usk, *The Appeal of Thomas Usk against John Northampton*, appendix 2 in *The Testament of Love*, ed. R. Allen Shoaf (Kalamazoo, MI: TEAMS Middle English Texts, 1998), available online at http://d.lib.rochester.edu/teams/text/shoaf-usk-testament-of-love-appendix-2.

justice. There is little doubt that he was a prominent and violent rebel. He was pardoned in February 1382 at the request of the queen, the aldermen, and the mayor—Northampton.[39]

There are many instances of such strange bedfellows in the Rising of 1381. In February 1381, Chaucer mainprised John Hende, guaranteeing that he would keep the peace with John Ewell and Robert Lenham.[40] This is quite an odd connection for Chaucer to have. John Hende was a London draper and banker who held the usual offices in London that wealthy merchants occupied: he was repeatedly alderman of both Candlewick and Walbrook, he was sheriff in 1381–82, and a decade later he became mayor.[41] So far, so unexceptional: Hende was similar to many of the men with whom Chaucer worked, of the same kind of group as Chaucer's own father. And Chaucer mainprised him in company with Ralph Strode (dedicatee of *Troilus* and discussed in more detail below). The precise details of Hende's activities at this time, however, make it clear that in supporting him, Chaucer was supporting someone who was directly challenging aspects of Crown authority. In the 1370s and 1380s, Hende began to acquire property in Essex and Kent.[42] John Ewell was the king's escheator in Essex: this meant that he represented the king's interests in that county, with responsibility for taking lands into the king's hands when a tenant-in-chief died or forfeited them. Hende was in dispute with Ewell over properties in Essex, and indeed, there was in general a 'radical dissatisfaction with royal justice in Essex' in the years building up to the revolt, and Ewell was

---

[39] *Calendar of the Patent Rolls: Richard II*, Membrane 24, 2:103. Later that year Parliament specifically excluded him from pardon for his behaviour in the Revolt; PROME, Membrane 7, no. 16, 6:284 (October 1382), and in the second version of the November sheriffs' inquisitions that year, he was condemned in detail. Dobson, *The Peasants' Revolt*, 218–20; Turner, *Chaucerian Conflict*, 49–50. A few months later, in March 1383, he was issued with a personal royal pardon. National Archives, KB 27/484 rex 3r.

[40] Crow and Olson, *Chaucer Life-Records*, 281–84. Connections between men are often demonstrated in late-medieval documents by mainprising. This involved procuring the release of a prisoner by guaranteeing that the accused would appear in court at a particular time.

[41] Jenny Stratford, 'Hende, John (d. 1418),' in the *ODNB*, https://doi.org/10.1093/ref:odnb/52249.

[42] Robert Lenham had some kind of claim on the Bradwell manor in Essex. Hende had already been in dispute with Ewell over a property in Essex called the Mascallsbury manor; this was resolved in 1380. The dispute over the manor of Bradwell, however, reached its head in 1381. In 1378, Lenham had been in conflict with Margery Long over this property; after her death the manor was taken into the king's hands, on the advice of Ewell and others, because Margery was found to have been illegitimate. *Calendar of the Patent Rolls: Richard II*, Membrane 25d, 2:136 (11 April 1382).

a representative and enforcer of that justice.[43] On 10 June 1381, Ewell was murdered in Essex, one of the victims of the rising.[44] (Part of Ewell's job had involved enforcing the collection of the poll tax, one of the principal grievances of the rebels.) A couple of weeks after Ewell's death, presumably taking advantage of the upheaval caused by the revolt, John Hende sent a group of men to take over Bradwell manor for himself, and to requisition the revenues.[45] The following year, a royal enquiry, headed by the king's most notorious favourite, Robert de Vere, looked into both the death of Ewell and the seizure of Bradwell.[46] Hende then submitted himself to the king, alongside John Bataill (or Battle), Thomas Bataill, and Nicholas Dagworth.[47] The latter had previously owned the estate and appears to have sold it to Thomas and John Bataill in 1379.[48] The Bataill brothers had also been implicated in Hende's dubious actions with regards to Mascallsbury manor. The details of these cases are somewhat obscure, but it is clear that Hende was acting with these Essex brothers and against the officers of the Crown. Indeed, John Bataill was one of the local men initially appointed in January 1382 to administer part of the Mortimer inheritance (discussed below)—the East Anglian Clare estates.[49] He was then replaced in March by a king's man, Henry English, who had had connections with the Mortimer estate but also frequently worked for the Crown, and who became a client of de Vere himself.[50] Hende's associates are the antiroyalist group—Bataill may have been connected with Gloucester, the future Appellant.[51] And Hende's interests and actions also

[43] Christopher Dyer, *Everyday Life in Medieval England* (London: Bloomsbury, 2003), 215.

[44] He seems to have been executed specifically on the order of one Richard Palmer, who then took the manor of Langdon Hall that Ewell had seized for the Crown. *Calendar of the Patent Rolls: Richard II*, Membrane 8d, 2:507 (6 December 1382).

[45] André Réville, *Le soulevement des travailleurs d'Angleterre en 1381* (Paris: Picard, 1898), xcviii; 218–19.

[46] *Calendar of the Patent Rolls: Richard II*, Membrane 16d, 2:199 (5 October 1382).

[47] PROME, Membrane 7, no. 17, 6:284 (October 1382).

[48] 'Bataill, Thomas' and 'Dagworth, Sir Nicholas,' in J. S. Roskell, L. Clark, and C. Rawcliffe (eds.), *The History of Parliament: The House of Commons, 1386–1421* (Stroud: Alan Sutton, 1992), 2:144–45 and 2:733–36. All *History of Parliament* entries can be found online at http://www.historyofparliamentonline.org.

[49] *Calendar of Patent Rolls: Richard II*, Member 4, 2:65 (16 January 1382).

[50] 'English, Henry,' in Roskell, Clark, and Rawcliffe, *History of Parliament*, 3:27–29; *Calendar of Patent Rolls: Richard II*, Membrane 24, 2:104 (11 March 1382).

[51] 'Bataill, Thomas,' *History of Parliament*, 2:144–45; Anthony Goodman, *The Loyal Conspiracy: The Lords Appellant under Richard II* (London: Routledge & Kegan Paul, 1971), 101.

demonstrate the urban elite's investment in the countryside, and the fact that the royal household, London merchants, and local men might all be struggling for power in the regions.

Hende seems to have been something of a political maverick: he openly condemned Northampton in later years, although he too was a draper, seeing the capitalists as his more natural allies.[52] However, he was not a king's man: in local politics in Essex, he defied the Crown (in a way that Chaucer, as a member of the royal household and an officer of the Crown in the Custom House, certainly would not have done). His anticourt attitude continued after Gaunt left the centre of power (in contrast, say, to Brembre): in 1391 he was mayor during Richard's quarrel with London, and was stripped of his office and imprisoned. It was after this that he became a major royal supplier—initially on credit to appease the king.[53] Chaucer's connection with Hende reminds us that friends, or associates, or people who owe each other favours, do not necessarily have the same politics or interests. Most people are members of multiple communities and have relationships with people of diverse politics and interests. In 1381, Hende, a rich merchant capitalist, found himself in agreement with the poll tax–opposing lower-class rebels: they, like he, found royal 'justice' oppressive, albeit in different ways. In terms of the tenor of London life, it is worth remembering that the fallout from the revolt, including the investigations mentioned here into Ewell's death, Hende's behaviour, and Farringdon's crimes, took place in the same year as Anne's sparkling arrival into London. Chaucer picked a rich historical moment for writing a poem about a divided city, betrayed from within, under siege, yet continuing to construct a shining surface through spectacle, set pieces, and conspicuous display and consumption.

The election of 1383 was a turning point in London. From at least late 1382, Brembre had been attempting to win over Richard himself by making generous loans to the Crown: in September of that year, he lent

---

[52] Thomas, *Calendar, 1381–1412*, Roll A27, Membrane 2, 54 (22 March 1385). As the example of Bamme shows us, however, this does not reveal Hende's allegiances a few years earlier.

[53] Stratford, 'Hende, John'; Caroline Barron, 'The Quarrel of Richard II with London, 1392–1397,' in F.R.H. Du Boulay and Caroline Barron (eds.), *The Reign of Richard II: Essays in Honour of May McKisack* (London: Athlone Press, 1971), 173–201.

Richard £1,333 6s 8d.[54] In 1383, it seems that Richard supported Brembre's bid for the mayoralty.[55] Brembre now employed strong-arm tactics to win the city back for the elite. Amid rumours of armed supporters and mob violence, Gaunt refused to act, presumably realizing that his unpopularity in the city or his nephew's emerging independence, or both, made intervention unwise—and Gaunt was probably particularly cautious about his personal safety in the wake of the revolt. It is only from around this point that Brembre can be seen as a Ricardian, or royalist. For many years he had been the staunch opponent of Gaunt and his brothers, battling against the court when court policy was centred on weakening the power of the London merchants. Now, as Richard stumblingly attempted to shape his own coterie, Brembre entered into a new phase of his political life—a phase that was to be short-lived, and that would end in utter calamity. Chaucer, whose allegiance to Gaunt is not in question, would certainly not follow blindly where Brembre led.[56]

With his public relations triumph in the Rising of 1381, and as a newly married man, Richard now wanted to establish himself and to separate himself from his powerful uncle. Simon Burley, Richard's tutor, one of his key favourites, and future victim of the Merciless Parliament, returned from Germany in late January 1382.[57] In December and January 1381–82, as Anne arrived in pomp and was feted, married, and crowned, events were also taking place that led to one of the first crises of Richard's rule. On 27 December, Edmund Mortimer (widower of Philippa of Clarence, daughter of Chaucer's first employers) had died, leaving a seven-year-old, Roger Mortimer, to inherit his vast estates. On 5 January (the day before Richard II's fifteenth birthday), Philippa Mortimer (Edmund's

---

[54] Saul, *Richard II*, 184. I suggest that it is only in the early 1380s that we see Brembre becoming the 'staunch royalist' that Strohm terms him; Paul Strohm, *Social Chaucer* (Cambridge, MA: Harvard University Press, 1994), 28. Strohm refers to another of Chaucer's associates (indeed friends), William Beauchamp, as a 'member of the young king's party' (33) in 1378–80, but I argue that there was not such a party in these years. There were different influence groups at court, of course, but Richard (aged eleven to thirteen) did not have a clearly defined party. Rather, those gaining favour from the court tended to be gaining favour from Gaunt in the late 1370s.

[55] Bird, *Turbulent London*, 76.

[56] I thus differ from Strohm, who sees Chaucer as 'hand in glove with Brembre.' Strohm, *Poet's Tale*, 179.

[57] T. F. Tout, *Chapters in the Administrative History of Medieval England: The Wardrobe, the Chamber and the Small Seals* (Manchester: Manchester University Press, 1928), 3:382–83.

mother) died, and her dower lands also fell under the control of the Crown. While initially, Mortimer's own officials were appointed to look after these estates, these orders were quickly countermanded, and the huge inheritance was parcelled out to a dozen members of Richard's household.[58] Although it is impossible to piece together all the intricacies of the story, or to know the extent to which Richard was himself directing policy as opposed to being led by men such as Burley, what is clear is that he was *not* following the advice of his magnates and uncles, nor the established practices of wardship and patronage, and that his behaviour gave rise to anxiety about the direction he was taking. As Mark King comments, now and throughout his reign, Richard 'clearly believed that it was his right to use [such] estates as if they were his own private lands during their time in his hands,' and that this kind of thinking eventually precipitated his deposition. In the summer of 1382, the chancellor, Richard le Scrope, fell out with Richard over his behaviour and was dismissed. That autumn, Parliament urged that money from the Mortimer inheritance and from alien priories be used for the expenses of the royal household (not to enrich Richard's cronies). In October 1383, the Lords complained in Parliament that Richard did not listen to them as he should, and in December that year, they forced Richard to give up the Mortimer inheritance to Mortimer himself and a coalition of magnates, headed by Arundel, a future Lord Appellant.[59]

Richard, meanwhile, increasingly turned to his personal friends and away from the magnates of the realm, including his uncles.[60] He started personally to shape royal policy.[61] And this was now the period when the notorious 'favourites' began to emerge. The most infamous of these was Robert de Vere, a long-term friend of the king, knighted alongside him in

[58] Mark King, 'Richard II, the Mortimer Inheritance, and the March of Wales, 1381–1384,' in Hamilton, *Fourteenth-Century England VIII*, 105.

[59] Ibid., 95–118; Tuck, *Richard II*, 171–72; Alastair Dunn, 'Richard II and the Mortimer Inheritance,' in Chris Given-Wilson (ed.), *Fourteenth Century England II* (Woodbridge: Boydell, 2002), 159–70. See also chapter 17.

[60] Goodman comments that '[i]n 1384–5 [Gaunt] had to defend himself against the intrigues of hostile factions at court,' as Richard, 'increasingly assertive after 1381, often appears to have regarded his uncles' influence as a constraint rather than a support.' *John of Gaunt*, 87.

[61] King, 'Richard II,' 97; Chris Given-Wilson, 'Richard II and His Grandfather's Will,' *English Historical Review* 93 (1978): 320–37.

1377, whose rewards became noticeably more lavish, indeed excessive, from 1384.[62] In London, Brembre was now feeling secure, and Northampton was arrested on 7 February. In the Salisbury Parliament held from 29 April to 27 May, both Arundel and Gaunt were in trouble: Arundel had a public confrontation with the king, which Gaunt defused, but he was himself then accused of treason by a Carmelite friar. This odd episode has never been satisfactorily explained, but there were clearly all kinds of murmurings against Gaunt in the court circle. When Northampton asked for Gaunt's presence at his trial in August, he had miscalculated the political climate and only succeeded in infuriating the king, already resentful of Gaunt's perceived power. Early in 1385, there was allegedly a plot by Richard's friends to murder Gaunt. The king's uncles had walked out of the council, enraged by its timid policies in relation to France. Gaunt then confronted Richard at Sheen, accused his nephew of surrounding himself with people who sought Gaunt's life, and withdrew to Hertford. They were reconciled through the agency of Richard's mother, Princess Joan, but the clashes continued: in August they disagreed again on Scottish policy. Meanwhile, Richard continued to promote his nonmagnate cronies: he supported Brembre's reelection to the mayoralty in October and made de Vere marquis of Dublin in December.[63] Gaunt continued openly to spar with Brembre, as can be seen in his correspondence with the city on behalf of Northampton: he terms Brembre's treatment of Northampton, Richard Norbury, and John More 'unreasonable and outrageous.'[64]

These were strange years politically for Chaucer, and he did not have one clear allegiance. His dominant association was with Gaunt, but Chaucer had a royal appointment, many of his friends were also in the king's household, and he worked closely with Brembre.[65] When Chaucer had

[62] '[F]rom 1384' de Vere emerged as the most rewarded courtier. Anthony Tuck, 'Vere, Robert de, ninth earl of Oxford, marquess of Dublin, and duke of Ireland (1362–1392),' in the *ODNB*, https://doi.org/10.1093/ref:odnb/28218.

[63] Hector and Harvey, *Westminster Chronicle*, 69, 93, 103, 113–15, 121, 131, 137, 145.

[64] See the letter from the king of Castile and Leon, duke of Lancaster, to Sir Nicholas Brembre, mayor of London, in Thomas, *Calendar, 1381–1412*, Roll A27, Membrane 26, 109 (7 May 1386).

[65] Strohm's groundbreaking book, *Social Chaucer*, unpicks Chaucer's circle and audience in great detail, and changed the landscape of Chaucer studies. His book provides an anatomy of Chaucer's world that should inform every subsequent analysis of Chaucer. My view is that Chaucer was less clearly associated with the Brembre faction than Strohm believes, and that his colleagues and friends too often had more ambiguous and diverse political ties (see discussions of Strode and Hende in this

been appointed as the court man back in the mid-1370s, Brembre had been in strong opposition to the court; now Brembre had become a thorough king's man—while Chaucer was in an equivocal position with his loyalties to both Gaunt and Richard. Chaucer had a long-term relationship with Gaunt, as indeed did many of his friends in the king's household. Chaucer's children were closely connected with Gaunt, and with Gaunt's children and household: Gaunt had paid lavishly for Elizabeth's transfer to Barking in 1381, and Thomas was to travel with him to Castile in 1386. In England, Gaunt was gradually losing influence as the 1380s progressed, and he was agitating to go to Castile to claim his wife's throne. Richard was to seize on this as a way of getting rid of his uncle, unwittingly sending away the staunchest supporter of the royal prerogative and paving the way for the rebellion of the Lords Appellant.

Chaucer's texts are consistently associated with members of the guilds who supported Northampton, not Brembre (although there is no evidence and little likelihood that Northampton's policies would be appealing to Chaucer).[66] It is very likely that Chaucer's 'Adam scriveyn' poem, in which he makes specific references to Adam copying out *Troilus* and *Boece*, is addressed to Adam Pynkhurst. Although book historians differ in their opinions about Pynkhurst, it is generally agreed that he was a prominent scribe of Ricardian literature, that he worked on some of Chaucer's texts, and that he also worked in Northampton's interest, both for the Mercers and probably for Northampton himself.[67] Lawrence Warner argues that

chapter). Above all, I see Chaucer's connection with Gaunt as his most important tie, particularly before Gaunt absented himself in Castile. Chaucer's political friendships were not consistent or exclusive, and the political climate changed dramatically in short periods of time. Equally, as I have repeatedly argued in this book, other figures, such as Brembre, cannot be consistently marked as royalist, given the changing circumstances of the 1370s and 1380s. In London records we often see men readily changing associations as the political landscape altered.

[66] The three companies at whose halls Northampton and his supporters conspired are the same three companies particularly connected with the early reception of Chaucer's texts: the Tailors, the Goldsmiths, and the Mercers. See 'Usk and the Goldsmiths,' 148–49; and Bird, *Turbulent London*, 135–56.

[67] Linne Mooney argues that Pynkhurst was the scribe of Hengwyrt and Ellesmere; see 'Chaucer's Scribe,' and Linne Mooney and Estelle Stubbs, *Scribes and the City: London Guildhall Clerks and the Dissemination of Middle English Literature, 1375–1425* (York: York Medieval Press, 2013), 67–85. This is disputed by Lawrence Warner, but he does agree that Pynkhurst was the scribe of numerous Ricardian literary texts and that he worked on a *Boece* manuscript. 'Scribes, Misattributed,' 84. For Pynkhurst and the Mercers' Petition, see also Turner, 'Conflict.' For Pynkhurst and Northampton, see Warner, 'Scribes, Misattributed,' 83–84.

Pynkhurst worked on a *Boece* manuscript during Chaucer's lifetime.[68] John Brynchele is another important example. Long known to us as the earliest recorded owner of a *Canterbury Tales* manuscript, Brynchele was clerk to the Tailors' Company (a company associated with Northampton and one of those that petitioned against Brembre).[69] As Martha Carlin has recently shown, Brynchele was embedded in Southwark networks as a hosteler and brothel owner in the last quarter of the fourteenth and first quarter of the fifteenth centuries. He can be linked in several documents to Thomas Spencer, the earliest known owner of a *Troilus* manuscript.[70] Like Brynchele, he was a Southwark brothel owner and scrivener. Interestingly, we find Brynchele—who died possessed of five books, including the *Canterbury Tales* and an English Boethius (almost certainly Chaucer's *Boece*)—in company with John of Gaunt in 1384. An account of a court case, written up on 21 July 1385, mentions that Brynchele went to Calais in January 1384, in the company of the duke of Lancaster.[71] Gaunt was leading the peace negotiations at Leulinghem between Calais and Boulogne that month; they were concluded on 26 January. Given that both men had connections with Chaucer's poetry, it is fascinating to see them together at this date, and it reemphasises Chaucer's connections at this point with the anti-Brembre and pro-Gaunt group in the city.

Troilus and Criseyde is also associated with Ralph Strode, common serjeant of London and Chaucer's associate in mainprising John Hende in 1381. Strohm sees Strode as a Brembreite, 'involved in providing service to the king or supporters of the king.'[72] It is true that Strode lost his apartment during Northampton's mayoralty and was given a pension under Brembre.[73] However, he lost his apartment because the king was repeatedly demanding an apartment over the gates for his emerging favourite—John

[68] Warner, 'Scribes, Misattributed,' 84.

[69] On Brynchele, see Turner, 'Usk and the Goldsmiths,' 140–42. See also F. J. Furnivall (ed.), *The Fifty Earliest English Wills in the Court of Probate, London, A.D. 1387–1439*, EETS 78 (London: Oxford University Press, 1882); and Matthew Davies and Ann Saunders, *The History of the Merchant Tailors' Company* (Leeds: Northern Universities Press, 2004), 43, 275. On the Tailors' Petition, see Robert Ellis, 'Verba Vana: Empty Words in Ricardian London' (PhD thesis, University of London, 2012), 110n55.

[70] See Carlin, 'Thomas Spencer,' 393, 402n31. See also the discussion in chapter 16 in this study.

[71] Thomas, *Calendar, 1381–1412*, Roll A27, Membrane 18, 92–94 (21 July 1385).

[72] Strohm, *Social Chaucer*, 44.

[73] Sharpe, *Calendar of Letter-Books: Letter-Book H*, fol. clx, 208, fol. clxxix, 245 (July 1384).

Beauchamp.[74] This was exactly the time—late 1382 to early 1383—when Richard was trying to assert himself. Beauchamp was one of Richard's prime cronies, and ended up being executed by the Merciless Parliament, like Brembre.[75] So Strode was ousted *by the royal faction*, albeit under Northampton's mayoralty—and according to the *Letter-Book*, he had already given up his job, so losing the tenement might have been a small matter.[76] We might also remember Caroline Barron's detailed argument for Strode as author of the Jubilee Book, Northampton's key governance reform manual, later burnt by Nicholas Exton, a fishmonger who thoroughly opposed Northampton's policies.[77] It is clear, then, that Strode was not unproblematically on one 'side.' He certainly had some patronage from Brembre, both in 1377 and in 1384, but he also lost his rooms at the behest of Richard. I suggest that Strode, like so many scribes and clerks, was not fully politically committed but maintained relative neutrality.[78] In 1384, Brembre worked hard to win people over to his side—most notoriously, Thomas Usk—and his pension grant to Strode may have been part of this policy of developing his friendship base, in this case renewing old relationships. But even though Strode was helped by Brembre in 1384, that does not necessarily mean that he was a committed Brembreite or Ricardian in the preceding years. It was also possible to receive favours from Brembre without being a Ricardian—just as it was possible for Chaucer to receive favours from Gaunt without being a Northampton partisan. Gower, the other dedicatee of *Troilus*, is generally seen as an 'independent' in these years, with Ricardian *and* Lancastrian affiliations.[79]

What did Chaucer do in these stormy years? He wrote *Troilus and Criseyde*. And then he left London. On 25 November 1384, he applied for permission for a temporary deputy at the Custom House, and very

[74] Ibid., fol. clx, 208.

[75] For Beauchamp, see Saul, *Richard II*, 124.

[76] Strode originally had the tenement only while he held his job; in 1377 Brembre had given it to him for life. The *Letter-Book* alleges that he had relinquished his office freely. If this is true, it might have given the city at least a reason not to fight the king's repeated request.

[77] Caroline Barron, 'The Burning of the Jubilee Book,' talk given 17 June 2002 at the Guildhall Historical Association, available at https://guildhallhistoricalassociation.org.uk/papers/papers-2000-to-2009/.

[78] Lindenbaum comments that 'the best-known figures employed in the civic secretariat during these years—Ralph Strode, John Marchaunt, William Cheyne and Thomas Usk—all worked at some time for both of the city's major parties.' 'London Texts,' 287.

[79] Strohm, *Social Chaucer*, 31.

soon after this, and before 17 February 1385, he applied for permission to appoint a permanent deputy. We don't know for certain if he immediately put deputies in place, or if he simply held on to the permission, but it is probable that he did indeed step back from his job. While over the previous several years he had received his own annuities via the wool custom, that stopped happening after April 1385, and he received the annuities from other sources. On two occasions, the sheriffs of London did not name him as controller in documents relating to the customs: this happened first in the autumn term of 1385 and again in June 1386. The most likely explanation for their omission of his name is that he was absent from his post and living in Kent.[80] We know that he was certainly working in Kent for at least part of this time. He was a justice of the peace in Kent from 12 October 1385, and the following year he also acted as MP for Kent. Certainly, the evidence points to Chaucer detaching himself from London in late 1384 or early 1385, and taking little further interest in the Custom House during the last part of his official tenure. This ran until December 1386, when he resigned the post in the wake of the Wonderful Parliament's attack on controllers generally. By early 1385, then, Chaucer had left his office-apartment life.

He may have chosen to leave his London job and life for any number of reasons, and these reasons may not have been political. But if his decisions were political—or were partly influenced by political discomfort—he left because Gaunt was in trouble, *not* because he foresaw that Brembre and Richard's 'party' more generally were going to fall into difficulties. He left at a time when Brembre's hold on power was secure, but when another protégé of Gaunt (Northampton) had fallen into the wilderness, and when Gaunt himself was repeatedly clashing with the king and coming off second best. There is no evidence that Chaucer was either a Brembre supporter or a Northampton supporter—he had obvious sympathies and differences with both. As he was neither a guild member nor a citizen, he could hold himself somewhat aloof from the factional battles around the mayoralty in the early 1380s. Equally, his association with Gaunt always went alongside an association with the king. When Edward III was the king, and in

---

[80] See chapter 15 for further discussion of Chaucer and Kent.

the early years of Richard's reign, these allegiances were completely harmonious—indeed, they were virtually identical. That was no longer the case. Chaucer had to renegotiate his position at this point, and rather than pinning his colours decisively to one mast, he tried hard to keep at least the lukewarm favour of all his patrons.[81]

Many of those around Chaucer were also repositioning themselves, either ostentatiously or carefully in this new political world. Thomas Usk is the best-known example: having worked intensively for Northampton and for the Goldsmiths, he turned state witness and accused Northampton and his associates. Usk eventually gained a royal appointment at the height of Richard's crisis in 1387, and ended up being executed alongside Brembre, as a corrupt Ricardian partisan. Our first known reader of *Troilus*, Usk may well have known the poem while it was in process, in the course of his work as a scribe. Adam Bamme provides an example of more politic and subtle repositioning. An important goldsmith who often appears in Gaunt's accounts (supplying, for instance, gifts for Philippa Chaucer),[82] he ranged himself against the grocers and fishmongers (such as Brembre, Exton, and Walworth) in the 1370s, standing surety for his fellow goldsmith Nicholas Twyford in his violent altercation with Brembre in 1378.[83] Usk repeatedly names Bamme as a Northamptonite in his *Appeal*. By 1383, however, when Brembre was elected, Bamme was dining with Walworth, Philipot, and Brembre himself.[84] He did not, however, associate too enthusiastically with his new associates, and did not suffer from Brembre's downfall. Quite the contrary: he gained some of Brembre's estates and married Philipot's widow, going on to be mayor twice in the 1390s.

What do we call 'betrayal' and what 'adaptation'? What is the difference between treason and making a virtue out of necessity? In *Troilus*, Chaucer shows us sympathetically why Criseyde might change her allegiance in a

[81] As Clementine Oliver comments, 'strange bedfellows were made' at this time, as 'various factions whose interests often conflicted with one another would join together.' *Parliament and Political Pamphleteering in Fourteenth-Century England* (Cambridge: Boydell and Brewer, 2010), 47.

[82] Crow and Olson, *Chaucer Life-Records*, 90–91; Lodge and Somerville, *John of Gaunt's Register, 1379–1383*, fol. 35b, 1:111–12, no. 327 (2 January 1380); fol. 50b–51a, 1:181–83, nos. 556–58 (6 March 1381); fol. 63a, 1:233, no. 715 (6 May 1382).

[83] See Riley, *Memorials of London*, 415–17; and Sharpe, *Calendar of Letter-Books: Letter-Book H*, fol. xcii–xciib.

[84] Bird, *Turbulent London*, 83.

world in which she has to adapt to survive, and where she can do nothing about the downfall of her former friends and might reasonably feel abandoned and betrayed by them. The poem takes political and personal side-switching as its subject, and dwells with the complexities of how to survive in a world where no one else has *your* interests at heart. Criseyde is expected to stay loyal to a city that has rejected and traded her, to an uncle who has prostituted her, and to a lover who failed to speak up for her, all of whom, as she knows, are doomed. Her new associates include a father who abandoned her and a suitor who is entirely self-interested and cynical—but they have the advantage of proximity, and of being on the winning side. *Troilus* is profoundly concerned with examining how a vulnerable individual can survive in political society.

Chaucer's decision to explore this issue through the lens of the exchange of women is entirely appropriate in the political world with which he was deeply familiar. Queen Anne's own arrival was itself not an unequivocally shining surface. Her spectacular entry into London celebrated the handing over of a woman to a man, and to a foreign country, for political and financial reasons. These aspects of the celebrations would have stood out with particular clarity to Chaucer, who had been on several diplomatic trips to try to negotiate a marriage for Richard, then an English child, with various European children. We know that he was involved in discussions with both the French and the Visconti in the 1370s.[85] Richard's marriage had been a major part of Chaucer's life: these journeys abroad were time-consuming, complicated, and presumably exhausting. Given that marriage negotiations for the elite had been part of his job, it is fascinating that in the years immediately following his trip to Lombardy, he wrote *Troilus*, the 'Knight's Tale,' and the *Parliament of Fowls*, all of which are fundamentally *about* the constrained and indeed coerced sexual choices of aristocratic women. And he goes out of his way to alter his sources (Boccaccio's poems, picked up during that very trip to Italy) in such a way as to amplify his heroines' lack of autonomy and victimization. Emily's dismay at the thought of marriage is far more clear-cut than Emilia's. Criseyde's vulnerability and wariness is very different from Criseida's active participa-

---

[85] See chapter 13.

tion in the pre-consummation scheming and her overt sexual availability. In both poems, the patriarchal agents shaping these women's sexual destinies are given more power and prominence than in Boccaccio's versions. Emily's final marriage is determined by Parliament in the 'Knight's Tale,' and Chaucer's single-most obvious change to the *Filostrato* is the dramatic elevation of Pandarus to starring role: he speaks and does far more in Chaucer's poem and, significantly, is no longer Criseyde's cousin but has become her authoritative uncle, a male 'protector' who can direct her life.

The 'Knight's Tale' opens with a glorious procession, a civic entry celebrating the military victory over the Amazons, the rape of Hippolyta, and the imprisonment of Emily. Later we see a dazzling spectacle of men entering an amphitheatre to do battle for the right of one of them to marry someone who does not wish to marry at all. In *Troilus and Criseyde*, the chivalric spectacle of the Trojans riding to encounter the Greeks, equipped with the accessories of chivalry ('hauk on honde' [Book V, 65]) is a vehicle for the enforced sale of Criseyde, a Trojan woman, to a hostile army.[86] Royal entries, descendants of the Roman 'triumph,' often celebrated the forcible imprisonment and subjugation of others, as London had seen, for instance, after Poitiers in 1356, when the Black Prince entered London with the French king as his prisoner. The 'Knight's Tale' makes crystal clear the blurred boundary between prisoner and wife in its opening few lines; *Troilus* does the same when in the first moments of Criseyde being handed over as part of an alleged exchange of prisoners—although, as Hector states, she is *not* a prisoner (Book IV, 179)—she is treated primarily as a sexually available object (another change to Boccaccio). The very reason for London's euphoric celebration in 1382, then, is deeply troubling, and the problem of the exchange of women occupies Chaucer's mind in these years, dominating his texts. The other poem that he may well have written during these years was the tale of St Cecilia—later the 'Second Nun's Tale'—a story about a woman resisting exchange and patriarchal authority.[87]

---

[86] Lynn Staley discusses this episode in conjunction with Gaunt's arrival in Bruges with his retinue, with his own hawk on his hand in 1375. See Staley, *Languages of Power*, 1, 5–6.

[87] In the F-Prologue to the *Legend of Good Women*, Alceste comments that Chaucer has 'maad the lyf also of Seynt Cecile' (426). We therefore know that a stand-alone version of the tale predates the first version of the Prologue. For the dating of the F-Prologue to around 1386, see chapter 14.

The 'Knight's Tale' and *Troilus* share many attributes: both find their principal source in Boccaccio; both are also deeply influenced by Boethius; both have a pagan, classical setting; both centre around the exchange of women between men; and both stage how men, as individuals and in groups, use women as a pretext for violence. Both texts also meditate extensively on the nature of conventional language, and its limitations. While the romance heroes obsessively deploy the conventional tropes of their genre—happily calling 'bauderye' 'compaignye' (Book III, 396–97) for instance—those who briefly speak directly get nowhere. Hector openly terms the so-called exchange of Criseyde a sale when he exhorts the Trojans not to sell women (Book IV, 182). Emily is clear about what she wants: to walk freely and not to enter the sexual economy ('Knight's Tale,' 2304–11). What they say is ignored. But those who are creatures of linguistic convention are trapped too: Troilus cannot escape the excessive and deceptive language of courtly love and cannot get past his obsession with surfaces and performance to see that Criseyde's value lies in her depth, her reality, her complexity, not in her shining, quasi-divine surface. He chooses to infantilise himself at her feet, abject, impotent, needy, and thus avoids responsibility. In the 'Knight's Tale,' the surface values of chivalry and courtly love are devastatingly exposed in the temples, which display the horrors of war and sex—through an aesthetically stunning surface.

Chaucer was fascinated by surfaces: particularly by how a commitment to performance, artifice, and a 'discourse of deception' permits the subjugation of the weak and the ignoring of conflict and violence.[88] For Chaucer, Troy—in its dual incarnations both as the city of *Troilus and Criseyde* and as the city in which he lived—exposed its own inadequacies through its misdirection and its silences. As his poetic career continued, his poetic voice evolved: he was to leave behind the courtly-romance-tragedy mode of *Troilus* as he continued to develop into the poet of the *Canterbury Tales*, building on the experiments of poems such as the *Parliament of Fowls* and the *House of Fame*. And Chaucer ultimately found a poetic way forward through the *political* experimentation that began in the Parliament of 1376 and fundamentally changed politics and literature in England.

[88] Staley, *Languages of Power*, 7.

CHAPTER 12

> \>─┤ ◄►─◦─◄►─┤ ◄

Parliament

Oure is the voys.

—The Parliament of Fowls

Chaucer's poetic voice evolved and changed dramatically during his London years. The petitioning voice of the *Book of the Duchess* was a voice that explicitly presented itself in subjection, a voice dependent on favour, a voice that spoke to its complicit friends. This was a voice that ostentatiously followed the example of poets such as Machaut, who were writing for patrons upon whom they depended. This declaredly hesitant and personal voice gave way to an assertive voice that spoke as if by right, a voice that ventriloquized others, a voice that spoke to a mixed, non-private audience. We see the emergence of this mode most clearly in the *Parliament of Fowls*, and it led directly to the innovations of the *Canterbury Tales*. At the same time, in the Good Parliament of 1376, the Commons changed the nature of *its* voice, substituting an impersonal, assertive voice for the voice of petition that had formerly been its mode.[1] This was not a remarkable coincidence. Rather, literature and the law—specifically, parliamentary law and practice—were fundamentally intertwined during these years as both spheres entered into a period of profound innovation and experimentation. Chaucer's poetic practice and development was, of course, shaped by many different factors, but one of the most decisive influences on him was the radical change in parliamentary practice that unfolded in 1376.

[1] M. V. Clarke, 'The Origins of Impeachment,' in *Fourteenth Century Studies*, ed. L. S. Sutherland and M. McKisack (Oxford: Clarendon Press, 1937), 265.

The Good Parliament altered the political landscape for a generation, and had far-reaching, utterly unexpected consequences. Since the thirteenth century, Parliament had had a key role in English political life, a role far outstripping in importance comparable institutions on the Continent.[2] The Good Parliament (the penultimate parliament of Edward III's reign) inaugurated a new era for Parliament that lasted throughout the reign of Richard II.[3] Parliament became a place of extraordinary legal experimentation. It also emerged as a location of texts, an institution that produced and fed an appetite for news, instigated the production of new kinds of texts, and employed men who both wrote and consumed many kinds of texts.[4] The onslaught of parliament-related texts—newsletters, pamphlets, processes, and broadsides—allowed an emergent public sphere to have unprecedented access to the parliamentary world and contributed to the depiction of parliamentary scenes in many of the great poems of the day.[5] Parliament also became a place for the development and manipulation of the idea of a common, representative voice, a voice that became characteristic of Ricardian poetry.[6]

The English Parliament was unusual in Europe in its inclusion of the House of Commons as a central part of the institution: most importantly, the Commons had the power to grant or to withhold taxation. This contrasted strongly with, for instance, the Third Estate in France, which had only advisory powers.[7] The Commons comprised knights of the shire and urban burgesses who represented their local communities. In contrast to

---

[2] Gwilym Dodd, 'Parliament and Political Legitimacy in the Reign of Edward II,' in Gwilym Dodd and Anthony Musson (eds.), *The Reign of Edward II: New Perspectives* (York: York Medieval Press, 2006), 165–89; David Carpenter, *The Struggle for Mastery: Britain, 1066–1284* (Oxford: Oxford University Press, 2003), 466–94; Michael Prestwich, *Plantagenet England, 1225–1360* (Oxford: Oxford University Press, 2007), 98–99, 131–33, 278–84.

[3] Gwilym Dodd, 'Richard II and the Transformation of Parliament,' in Gwilym Dodd (ed.), *The Reign of Richard II* (Stroud: Tempus, 2000), 71–84; Gwilym Dodd, 'Changing Perspectives: Parliament, Poetry, and the "Civil Service" under Richard II and Henry IV,' *Parliamentary History* 25 (2006): 299–322; and Holmes, *Good Parliament*.

[4] Chris Given-Wilson, *Chronicles: The Writing of History in Medieval England* (London: Hambledon and London, 2004),

[5] Oliver, *Parliament and Political Pamphleteering*.

[6] For the idea of the common voice and public poetry, see Middleton, 'Public Poetry,' 94–114.

[7] John Watts, *The Making of Polities: Europe, 1300–1500* (Cambridge: Cambridge University Press, 2009), 224–38.

the members of the House of Lords, who sat in Parliament either by hereditary privilege (i.e. due to the title they held) or by virtue of the ecclesiastical office they occupied, the members of the Commons were there to put forward the perspective of their community. Although they were men of substance—the Commons were not 'ordinary' people but tended to belong to the landed gentry or the wealthy mercantile class—they were far less privileged than the Lords. The participation of these relatively non-elite men and the concept of a representative assembly were extraordinary. Then, in 1376, the role of the Commons was significantly enhanced. Parliament had not been called for two and a half years: there had not been a comparable gap since 1302–5. In the mid-1370s, as we have seen, a corrupt court coterie had run amok in the dog days of Edward's reign and, to the Londoners' fury, had profited by allowing merchants, in particular Italians, to pay to evade the staple. The advisors around Edward were accruing huge personal wealth through moneylending to the Crown, oppressive monopolistic practices, and dealings with foreign merchants. Gaunt was associated with this group, although they were not all his cronies. Both Edward III and his eldest son were seriously ill—the Black Prince died during this parliament—and Richard of Bordeaux was only nine years old. In the face of this chaos, the Commons closed ranks and asserted themselves in a way unprecedented in English political history.

They were able to do this through the stratagem of choosing a Speaker, an innovation that survives to this day. Parliament itself took place in the palace of Westminster, opening in the Painted Chamber and then moving to the White Chamber, but the Commons held their own deliberations in the chapterhouse of Westminster Abbey. Their mood was angry and belligerent as they gathered their examples of bad government emanating from the king's advisors. They managed to bring together their grievances into coherent and compelling form by choosing one spokesperson—Sir Peter de la Mare—to speak for all of them, and they remained united in their assertion that their chosen Speaker represented their views. Declaring that 'what one of us says, all say and assent to,' they insisted that they should all be allowed to enter Parliament as one block, combatting attempts to divide them. In this way, de la Mare put forward their accusations against Latimer, Lyons, and Perrers, and they then moved to impeach Lyons and Latimer 'a une voyce.'[8]

Impeachment was the key legal innovation of this parliament. This new procedure involved the Commons *as a group*, bringing a legal action against those more powerful than themselves. Emphasising the audacity, novelty, and indeed 'revolutionary' implications of the Commons' actions, Maude Violet Clarke writes that '[t]he Good Parliament broke through the encirclement of statutes and achieved the transition from procedure by petition, with all its implications of grace and favour, to procedure by indictment, which is an assertion of right.'[9] Plucknett, in contrast, argues that impeachment derived not from indictment but from the idea of notoriety or clamour.[10] The legal origins of impeachment are not of great importance here, however: the key piece of information is that the Commons were declaring their unwillingness to depend on the king's pleasure and their belief that by acting as a group they could forcibly bring the king's ministers to justice. Those ministers—and later the new king, when he was a few years older—were alive to the dangerous implications of the Commons' newfound belligerence. Latimer asserted that he would only answer charges brought by particular individuals, challenging the Commons' right to override the common-law rights of subjects. The Parliament Roll tells us that he said 'he willingly would give his answer thereon to anyone who would accuse him individually of any of the aforesaid things,' but that he did not succeed in his challenge, as 'no individual person would publicly accuse the said lord of the same things in parliament, but the commons would maintain the said accusations in common.'[11] Maurice Keen

[8] See the discussion of the univocality of this parliament in Matthew Giancarlo, *Parliament and Literature in Late Medieval England* (Cambridge: Cambridge University Press, 2007), 53–56, 69–73.

[9] Clarke, 'Origins of Impeachment,' 265.

[10] T.F.T. Plucknett, 'The Origin of Impeachment,' *Transactions of the Royal Historical Society*, 4th series 24 (1942): 47–71. See also Wendy Scase, *Literature and Complaint in England, 1272–1553* (Oxford: Oxford University Press, 2007), 62–65. Bellamy argues that the impeachments of 1376 were brought about by appeal, preempting the Merciless Parliament. J. G. Bellamy, 'Appeal and Impeachment in the Good Parliament,' *Bulletin of the Institute of Historical Research* 39 (1966): 35–46. For a recent discussion, see W. M. Ormrod, 'Parliamentary Scrutiny of Royal Ministers and Courtiers,' in Richard W. Kaeuper (ed.), *Law, Governance, and Justice: New Views on Medieval Constitutionalism* (Leiden: Brill, 2013), 178.

[11] PROME, Membrane 3, no. 26, 5:304 (April 1376).

argues that Gaunt saw the procedure as 'an affront to the royal dignity and an unwarranted interference with royal freedom of action.'[12]

Impeachment, however, survived, and has been called 'the crowning achievement of Parliament in the fourteenth century.'[13] Another, more gradual change that also signalled the changing role of the Commons and, in particular, emphasized the idea of a common and representative voice, was the Commons' adopting of private petitions as common. Throughout the fourteenth century, receivers of private petitions passed onto the Commons those petitions that had more general significance, but from the 1370s, private petitioners began directly approaching the Commons to take on their petitions as common.[14] The process arose whereby the Commons could avow or disavow petitions, adopting some petitions as genuinely common in their concern.[15] When Thomas Haxey put forward his famous petition attacking the king's household in 1397, for which he was condemned to death, his petition did not specify a petitioner at all.[16] Another sign of the growing power of the Commons as a group was that rather than themselves *being* the petitioners, as had traditionally been their role, they were now addressed *by* petitioners. In the early fourteenth century, petitions were usually addressed to the king or to the king and his council. By the later years of Edward's reign, they were starting to be addressed to the king and the House of Lords of Parliament, and by the end of the fourteenth century, some were addressed to the king, House of Lords, and the Commons, and some even to the Commons alone. The earliest extant example of a petition that included the Commons in the addressees comes from 1378, when the abbot and convent of Westminster protested against a murder within their sanctuary as an invasion of their

[12] Maurice H. Keen, *England in the Later Middle Ages: A Political History*, 2nd ed. (London: Routledge, 2003), 207.

[13] Clarke, 'Origins of Impeachment,' 188. By contrast, the process of appealing people of treason in Parliament, used in 1388, 1397, and 1399, was abandoned after this date.

[14] A. R. Myers, 'Parliamentary Petitions in the Fifteenth Century: Part I; Petitions from Individuals or Groups,' *English Historical Review* 52 (1937): 398.

[15] Doris Rayner, 'The Forms and Machinery of the "Commune Petition" in the Fourteenth Century,' Part I, *English Historical Review* 56 (1941): 198–233.

[16] For an account of Haxey and his petition, see A. K. McHardy, 'Haxey's Case, 1397: The Petition and Its Presenter Reconsidered,' in James L. Gillespie (ed.), *The Age of Richard II* (Stroud and New York: Sutton / St Martin's Press, 1997), 93–114. See also chapter 19.

liberties, appealing to: 'nostre seigneur le Roy et as seigneurs et communs du parlement.'[17]

In both the legal and the literary arena, this idea of a common voice gained traction during these years and was subject to abuse and manipulation. Even the Speaker of 1376, Sir Peter de la Mare, was the steward of Edmund Mortimer, next in line to the throne (through the female line) after the Black Prince and Richard, and therefore rival of John of Gaunt. In the field of the law, the *sub pena* writ was developed in the 1380s as a tool to be used against the powerful: it did not name a plaintiff and could impose immediate financial penalties for noncompliance, so it had traction against those of high social status.[18] But in practice it was soon viewed with suspicion by the Commons, and seen as a tool of faceless bureaucratic oppression. On the civic side, we might be reminded of Thomas Usk's accusation that Northampton's party did what they liked, under cover of words of common profit.[19]

Chaucer's London years were a period in which the idea of a common voice, representing others, speaking for a community, shot into the political spotlight, and the Good Parliament was the driving force in this development. Parliamentary politics was never the same again. We can hardly overstate the importance of the Good Parliament for someone who was living and working in London, and was a client of Gaunt. The Good Parliament made immediate literary waves: Langland's depiction of the parliament of rats and mice and their inability to bell the cat is a refraction of the events of April 1376, filtered through a contemporary sermon by Thomas Brinton, who used the exact same story when preaching during the parliament itself.[20] Chaucer, predictably, does not write so explicitly. But three of his great poems of the next few years—the 'Knight's Tale,' *Troilus and Criseyde*, and the *Parliament of Fowls*—contain parliament scenes. In *Troilus*, the parliament is clearly separated into a

[17] Myers, 'Parliamentary Petitions,' 399; PROME, 'Appendix: 20 October 1378,' no. 7, 6:106.

[18] See W. M. Ormrod, 'The Origins of the *Sub Pena* Writ,' *Historical Research* 61:144 (1988): 11–20; and Gerald Harriss in *Shaping the Nation: England, 1360–1461* (Oxford: Clarendon Press, 2005), 47–58.

[19] See discussion in Turner, *Chaucerian Conflict*, 26, 93–126.

[20] For a recent discussion of Langland and Brinton's use of the fable, see Elizaveta Strakhov, 'But who will bell the cat?,' *Yearbook of Langland Studies* 30 (2016): 253–76.

group of commons—the uncontrolled, assertive 'peple' (Book IV, 183)—
and the lords, such as Hector and Troilus, with a powerless king presid-
ing. The people have their way and get it all wrong, as mobs so often do in
Chaucer's poetry. In the 'Knight's Tale,' the parliament is perfunctory,
cynically manipulated by Theseus, who has already decided upon his
course of action and seeks only confirmation. As we might expect, the
poem that declares itself to be a parliament poem—the *Parliament of
Fowls*—provides us with the richest depiction of a parliamentary world.
There was a tradition of poems about bird parliaments, but Chaucer does
something very different to his predecessors. While poems such as the *Owl
and the Nightingale* focus on a debate between two individuals, Chaucer
includes many of the elements of the contemporary English Parliament in
his poem. The leisurely debate between aristocrats, structured by endless
repetition and conventional language, is interrupted by the strident voices
of the lower classes, obvious figures for the English Commons. Not only do
the voices of the lower classes intrude and ultimately take over the debate,
emerging successful while the aristocrats achieve only deferral and frustration, but the poem also models the idea of a *representative* voice. After the
lower birds' initial clamouring interruption, Nature tells them to choose
representatives, and they agree. Then the 'foules of ravyne / Han chosen
fyrst, by pleyn eleccioun, / The tercelet' (527–29), and the tercelet then
speaks for his group. When the aristocratic eagles interrupt him, he re-
proves them, reminding them of his role: '*Oure* is the voys that han the
charge in honde' (545; emphasis mine). His voice is plural, it is the voice of
the group. The other birds similarly then choose representatives to speak
for them. In this legalistic poem, densely packed with the technical
language of law and politics, the word 'eleccioun' stands out: this may be
the first occasion when this word is used for the formal nomination of a
political representative—its primary meaning for us today.[21]

These assertive nonaristocratic voices are quite different from the
voices of the *Book of the Duchess* or the later Prologue to the *Legend of
Good Women*. In those dream poems, the poet-narrator is a supplicant,
fully involved in the poem but in a position of weakness, petitioning for

---

[21] See Giancarlo, *Parliament and Literature*, 157–58.

information or pleading for mercy. His voice is cautious and defensive. In the *Parliament of Fowls* and the *House of Fame*, the poet-narrator is less of a participant and more of an observer, not himself taking part in the main action of the poem. In both of these poems, we see insurgent voices: in the *House of Fame*, the voices/texts of the House of Rumour swirl about of their own authority; in the *Parliament of Fowls*, assertive voices are explicitly placed in a political setting. The scene of aristocratic love-talk interrupted by impatient and vulgar lower-class voices obviously anticipates the Miller's interruption of the Knight, as many readers have noted. The Knight/Miller interaction is perhaps less a peasants' uprising than a parliamentary challenge.[22] Indeed, Chaucer found a way to expand which voices could be heard in his poetry through the example of Parliament. If we keep in mind the idea of parliamentary *representation*—both in that the Commons were chosen to represent their communities, and in that the Speaker was elected to represent the Commons—the origins of the Canterbury company itself become clearer. While Chaucer drew on a diverse array of literary sources, Parliament was also a crucial model for him. (And it is striking that the real-life Harry Bailly was an MP for Southwark in the Good Parliament.)[23] I would not argue that the pilgrim group as a whole 'represents' Parliament, but that each figure—somewhat personalized but not fully realized as an individual, representing their estate as well as themselves—is a representative figure in the same way that an MP was (and is) both an individual and a representative of others. In the *Decameron*, the storytellers—all coming from the same social background—represent only themselves. In estates satire, figures are conventionally wholly representative of their estates. Chaucer brings the genre of estates satire into conversation with texts such as the *Decameron* and finds a middle way. That middle way—part individual, part representative—echoes what he did in the *Parliament of Fowls*, which, in turn, draws closely on the unique and changing position of the English Parliament.

The evolution of Chaucer's poetic voice as a voice of representation that took its authority not from itself alone—nor from the weight of authori-

---

[22] Alfred David terms the interruption a 'literary Peasants' Rebellion.' *The Strumpet Muse: Art and Morals in Chaucer's Poetry* (Bloomington: Indiana University Press, 1976), 92.

[23] *Calendar of Close Rolls: Edward III*, Membrane 23, 14:430 (10 July 1376).

tative written sources, but from other human, speaking, contemporary agents—parallels the evolution of the voice of the Speaker as he began to use the device of the protestation (discussed below). Chaucer was already fond of the disclaimer, as were some of his predecessors. In *Troilus and Criseyde*, the narrator ironically emphasizes that he is following his (invented) Latinate source, Lollius.[24] In this, he follows Jean de Meun's slippery assertion that he is merely copying old books and cannot himself be accused of misogyny or indecency; he only repeats.[25] Oral performers in many cultures also claim that they are transmitting old knowledge, that they are not themselves the creators of their texts.[26] In the *Canterbury Tales*, Chaucer does not place the responsibility for his tales on old books or on old folkloric stories; rather, his pilgrim persona makes it clear that he is repeating the words of (fictional) individuals, presented as flawed human beings. These are not figures who are intrinsically authoritative: the point is that they have the right to have their views transmitted, and the Chaucer-figure, as their conduit, has a responsibility, he claims, to convey their views.

This new take on the position of the poet presents him as interested not in old authority or tradition but simply in reproducing and representing, regardless of the intrinsic value or authority of the material. It is not his fault; his role is to represent the views of others. Chaucer developed this persona in the wake of the rapid establishment of the Speaker's protestation. In 1377, when Peter de la Mare returned to the role of Speaker, he 'made protestation' that he was not speaking 'of his own accord but by the will, consent, and express wish of all the commons there present'; he goes on to put his text under correction, requesting that 'he might be corrected by his same companions,' if he departs 'from their intent.'[27] The 'correction' plea is echoed closely in the 'Parson's Prologue,' as Matthew Giancarlo has pointed out. The Parson explicitly states that 'I make protestacioun / That

---

[24] For instance, Book V, 1653; for a more general disavowal, see Book V, 1037–50.

[25] *Romance of the Rose*, 15185–212. For discussion of this passage in relation to Chaucer, see Alastair Minnis, *Magister Amoris: The Roman de la Rose and Vernacular Hermeneutics* (Oxford: Oxford University Press, 2001), 226–29.

[26] Richard Bauman, *Verbal Art as Performance* (Long Grove: Waveland Press, 1977), 22; Leslie K. Arnovick, *Written Reliquaries: The Resonance of Orality in Medieval English Texts* (Amsterdam: John Benjamins, 2006), 180.

[27] PROME, Membrane 2, no. 15, 6:11 (October 1377).

I wol stonde to correccioun' (59–60).[28] The Speaker's protestation quickly became institutionalized. In 1378, Sir James Pickering made a long protestation; protestations are again recorded by the Speakers in 1380 (Sir John Gildeburgh), 1381 (Sir Richard Waldegrave), and 1383 (Pickering again).[29] By 1394, we are told that the Speaker, Sir John Bushy, 'made protestation in the accustomed manner.'[30] These protestations are all slightly different, but they tend to emphasise the need for correction immediately by the Commons should the Speaker get anything wrong, and to request that if the Speaker says anything offensive, it should be 'held at naught and considered unsaid.'[31] In one protestation, the Speaker requests that the Commons not be blamed if the Speaker causes offence—but that the Speaker should not be blamed either and should simply be treated 'as if nothing had been said.'[32] In 1399, the Speaker, John Doreward, explicitly states that what he says should 'not be regarded as something which he did of his own volition or individual will but rather that it was and would be by the common assent and agreement of all his aforesaid companions.'[33] Chaucer's famous protestations that he is merely repeating the views and words of others, and that the audience must 'Blameth nat me,' similarly work to deflect personal responsibility. In the 'Miller's Prologue,' Chaucer requests that we 'demeth nat that I seye / Of yvel entente'; rather, he speaks because he must 'reherce' what others have said (3181, 3172–73). The very idea that the voices of common people should be preserved regardless of their message, simply because they have the right to be heard, is shared by the Speaker and the Chaucerian narrator; both present themselves as a transparent filter for these ordinary people.[34] Where they differ is that Chaucer presents himself as speaking not for one group only but as varying his voice to represent multiple opinions—just as in 1381, the Commons suggested that each estate might debate separately and each group come up with a viewpoint.[35]

[28] Giancarlo, *Parliament*, 176.
[29] PROME, Membrane 7, no. 16, 6:74 (October 1378); Membrane 8, no. 11, 6:149 (January 1380); Membrane 12, no. 9, 6:215 (November 1381); Membrane 2, no. 9, 6:311–12 (February 1383).
[30] PROME, Membrane 8, no. 6, 7:250 (January 1394).
[31] PROME, Membrane 7, no. 16, 6:74 (October 1378).
[32] PROME, Membrane 8, no. 11, 6:149 (January 1380).
[33] PROME, Membrane 16, no. 64, 8:29 (October 1399).
[34] Giancarlo argues that the Host is a Speaker-figure; see *Parliament and Literature*, 169–78.
[35] PROME, Membrane 12, no. 16, 6:217 (November 1381).

The Commons' push to be heard should also be seen in the context of a more general interest in public affairs on the part of the English populace. In the last quarter of the fourteenth century, we see a dramatic increase in the production of 'newsletters,' ephemeral pamphlets circulated for general consumption. Some of these were embedded into chronicles but many have been lost.[36] For the first time, newsletters were produced about parliaments; some texts were produced by clerks of parliaments;[37] some pamphlets may have had their origins in the households of great nobles, who found it worth their while to circulate propaganda.[38] Thomas Favent's exceptionally interesting pamphlet about the Merciless Parliament has survived: it uses vivid detail and imagery to argue its very partisan case.[39] The public fascination with news—and particularly with Parliament—was a novel development: Given-Wilson writes that 'parliaments had, by 1400, entered the public consciousness and historical literature of England to an extent that, twenty-five years earlier, could scarcely have been imagined.'[40] In effect this is the emergence of what would later

---

[36] Given-Wilson writes that Knighton, for instance, 'evidently viewed newsletters as dissoluble texts, to be abridged, rearranged or epitomised in whatever fashion best suited his narrative.' More generally, Given-Wilson comments that in the last quarter of the fourteenth century, 'people now bothered to write newsletters about parliaments,' suggesting that clerks of the Crown may have begun 'to see it as part of their job to produce ... tracts [about Parliament].' See Given-Wilson, *The Writing of History*, 16, 176, 177. See also Douglas Biggs, 'The Appellant and the Clerk: The Assault on Richard II's Friends in Government, 1387–9,' in Dodd, *The Reign of Richard II*, 57–70; and John Taylor, *English Historical Literature in the Fourteenth Century* (Oxford: Clarendon Press, 1987), 203–8.

[37] On the writing activities of clerks and bureaucrats, see Kathryn Kerby-Fulton and Steven Justice, 'Langlandian Reading Circles and the Civil Service in London and Dublin, 1380–1427,' *New Medieval Literatures* 1 (1997): 59. See also Kathryn Kerby-Fulton and Steven Justice, 'Reformist Intellectual Culture in the English and Irish Civil Service: The *Modus tenendi parliamentum* and Its Literary Relations,' *Traditio* 53 (1998): 149–202.

[38] Biggs, 'The Appellant and the Clerk,' 57–140; Oliver, *Parliament and Political Pamphleteering*, 60–61; May McKisack in Thomas Favent, *Historia siue narracio de modo et forma mirabilis parliamenti apud Westmonasterium anno domini millesimo CCCLXXXVJ: Regni vero regis Ricardi Secundi post conquestum anno decimo, per Thomas Fauent clericum indictata*, in *Camden Miscellany 14*, ed. May McKisack (London: Offices of the Society, 1926), vi–vii.

[39] For information about Favent, see Clementine Oliver, 'A Political Pamphleteer in Late Medieval England: Thomas Fovent, Geoffrey Chaucer, Thomas Usk, and the Merciless Parliament of 1388,' *New Medieval Literatures* 6 (2003): 67–98; and *Parliament and Political Pamphleteering*. See Dodd, 'Changing Perspectives,' 314; Turner, 'Imagining Polities,' 399–403; Ruth Evans, 'The Production of Space in Chaucer's London,' in Ardis Butterfield (ed.), *Chaucer and the City* (Cambridge: D. S. Brewer, 2006), 41–56; Frank Grady, '*St Erkenwald* and the Merciless Parliament,' *Studies in the Age of Chaucer* 22 (2000): 179–211.

[40] Given-Wilson, *Writing of History*, 177. Andrew Galloway refers to 'Favent's aggressive eagerness for "news,"' in 'The Literature of 1388 and the Politics of Pity in Gower's *Confessio amantis*,' in Emily

be called the public sphere.[41] Relatively ordinary people's investment in politics and in its discursive expression is further demonstrated in the aftermath of the Good Parliament, when the Londoners pinned a vernacular broadside to the doors of St Paul's, accusing Gaunt of illegitimacy and reversing his arms, coding the supposed story of his changeling status in terms recognizable to any reader of romance.[42] We see here evidence of an insurgent appropriation both of literary modes and of political discourse: textual culture was opening up to new audiences and expanding chaotically in the final decades of the century.

Chaucer was writing at a time when, as Anne Middleton has cogently argued, the 'idea of public poetry' emerged as the decisive mode of Ricardian literature.[43] Middleton's argument is that during the last quarter of the fourteenth century, English poets came to favour a voice that was not courtly, spiritual, or popular. Sitting between the religious and the courtly, the personal and the universal, it was a common voice: a voice that served the common good but was itself embedded in the social world. Public poetry speaks as if to and for the whole community, rather than addressing a coterie or patron. Middleton points to Langland and Gower as the great exponents of public poetry, suggesting that Usk and the Lollard knights also aspired to this public and common voice. She places Chaucer somewhat outside or on the periphery of the trend, suggesting that he cultivates different kinds of personae. More recently, David Lawton has suggested that although Chaucer's voices are multiple and his positioning often indirect, he can nonetheless be grouped with those poets who aspire to speaking in a common voice, a voice that is that of an 'enlightened citizen.'[44] While the voices that he cultivates are more diverse than those of his poetic contemporaries, he is connected to the same group as these poets and, like them, has an interest in 'bourgeois moderation,' as Middleton puts it.[45] He is interested in deflecting violence—both aristocratic and popular—and in

Steiner and Candace Barrington (eds.), *The Letter of the Law: Legal Practice and Literary Production in Medieval England* (Ithaca: Cornell University Press, 2002), 67–104.

[41] David Lawton, 'Public Interiorities,' in Turner, *Handbook of Middle English Studies*, 93–107.

[42] Turner, 'Conflict,' 267.

[43] Middleton, 'Public Poetry,' 94–114.

[44] Lawton, 'Public Interiorities,' 99.

[45] Middleton, 'Public Poetry,' 95.

promoting peace. He spent much of his diplomatic career negotiating peace treaties and marriage alliances. The 'Tale of Melibee,' told in the voice of Chaucer the pilgrim himself, is in many ways a cynical—or at least pragmatic—tale, but it is also a tale about how to avoid violence, and how to resist the urge to take revenge. The *Parliament of Fowls* stages the deflection of the aristocratic urge to fight by the intervention of the lower-class birds and Nature, all of whom are more interested in communion. The idea of Parliament is that it is about talking—'parley'-ing. When it degenerates into 'Kek kek, kokkow' (499), Chaucer satirizes its tendency to become a talking-shop, but there can be no doubt that he thought talking was better than fighting. Every one of the three parliaments that he depicts is essentially about the exchange of a woman as a way of preventing violence. In every case, however, we are starkly shown that there is a victim here. Emily is exchanged entirely against her will. The formel is granted a deferral but has no option of refusal. And Criseyde, we are explicitly told, is being treated as a prisoner of war, and forcibly handed over. So Chaucer did not idealise what Parliament could do: every movement towards peace has casualties and victims. It was not until later in his life, however, that he witnessed the full horror of what Parliament could unleash, in the bloodbath of 1388.

The political situation changed rapidly and unpredictably in the 1380s and beyond. As we have seen, the Good Parliament had seismic effects both on English politics and on English poetry, with its unprecedented promotion of the idea of a common voice. But it was the Wonderful Parliament, a decade later, that provided Chaucer with his firsthand experience of Parliament—almost certainly *after* he had written his explicitly parliamentary texts. The *Parliament of Fowls* only makes sense as a post–Good Parliament but pre–Wonderful Parliament text. It is highly unlikely that Chaucer saw the Good Parliament as straightforwardly 'good.' It challenged John of Gaunt, and it decimated court policies that Chaucer had been heavily involved in promoting. It also attacked foreigners with whom Chaucer worked closely. But its promotion of a common representative voice was of profound importance to Chaucer, and clearly captured his imagination and interest. Although the *Parliament of Fowls* is not a sunnily optimistic text, it does suggest that the Commons can make some progress, while the nobles remain locked in deferral and coercion. The lower-class birds really do assert themselves, and do get somewhere. But Parliament got a whole lot darker in 1386, worsened in 1388, and then reprised the brutality of 1388 in 1397. The tools of the Commons were co-opted, first by the Lords Appellant and then by the king, as they, in turn, appealed their enemies of treason and condemned them in Parliament, killing them without due process of law. The changing nature of the Speakers reflects the darkening mood. In 1386 and 1388, the Commons were in such disarray that there does not seem to have been a Speaker at all. Throughout the 1390s, the Speaker was consistently the same man— John Bushy—a close crony of Richard II who was beheaded in 1399 when Richard was deposed.

The Wonderful Parliament must be understood in the context of Gaunt's very recent departure for Spain.[46] As Richard had begun to assert himself in the first half of the 1380s, three loose political groups around the court and government had emerged. On the one hand, there was the Arundel-Warwick grouping: abrasive magnates who supported war with France. On the other extreme was the nascent Ricardian group, symbolised by men such as Robert de Vere: these were Richard's personal friends, characterised by their interest in courtly pursuits and uninterested in belligerence, famously described by Walsingham in his *Chronicle* as 'knights of Venus not of Bellona.'[47] In the middle were the Lancastrians. Gaunt steered a middle course and often resolved disputes, although, as we saw in chapter 11, Richard increasingly (and foolishly) wanted to free himself from his uncle's influence. Gaunt's departure was massively destabilising to the political balance of government. It unleashed chaos. There was now, as Saul puts it, 'a void at the centre of politics' and the prolonged crisis of 1386 to 1389 can be seen as 'the by-product of the duke's absence.'[48] Many of those who had been in Gaunt's group now had to choose one of the other, more extreme factions. They all had to rethink their position in the newly uncertain situation. Clarke argues that when the Wonderful

[46] He departed on 9 July 1386, returning in November 1389. The Wonderful Parliament opened on 1 October 1386. For discussion of Gaunt's absence, see Saul, *Richard II*, 151.

[47] Walsingham, *Chronica maiora*, 248.

[48] Saul, *Richard II*, 151.

Parliament met, it became clear that with Gaunt gone, 'the middle way could no longer exist,' and that Parliament had the effect of 'driving' the members of his group one way or the other.[49]

It is clear that dissatisfaction within the Lords and Commons had been building up for some time, particularly directed at Richard's management of his household, his treatment of favourites, and the perceived misuse of money. Nonetheless, things need not have turned out the way that they did. The Commons does not seem to have been well organised, nor was it 'packed.'[50] The members of Parliament were anxious and frightened about the growing French threat. France, angered by Gaunt's going to war against Castile (now France's ally) and taking advantage of Gaunt's requisitioning of a large proportion of available English shipping, had built up a sizeable navy and was threatening invasion.[51] England—and especially the southeast and London—was in an uproar. Chaucer gave up his London rooms—which he was no longer living in—at this time, probably in response to the city's anxiety about the strategic importance of defending the gates.[52] The mood was further exacerbated by confusion about where tax money had gone and a suspicion that it was being wasted by the king and his cronies. Richard had been favouring his friends excessively over the previous couple of years, and calls for reform of the household in the 1385 Parliament had not yielded results. In the absence of Gaunt's mediating presence, the belligerent magnates—such as Arundel and Gloucester—were ready to assert themselves. In this context Michael de la Pole, Richard's chancellor, got up and announced ludicrous plans for an English invasion of France, led by Richard. It was a serious misjudgement at a time when the Commons needed reassurance and a promise of sober rule, attention to defence, and sensible expenditure. Hereafter, Parliament was taken up by grievances against the king's household—which

---

[49] M. V. Clarke, 'The Lancastrian Faction and the Wonderful Parliament,' in *Fourteenth Century Studies*, ed. L. S. Sutherland and M. McKisack (Oxford: Clarendon Press, 1934), 48, 52.

[50] Giancarlo, *Parliament and Literature*, 164.

[51] Saul, *Richard II*, 153–55.

[52] Walsingham reports that Londoners were fleeing the city; others were pulling down houses near the walls. *Historia Anglicana*, 2:145–46. If Chaucer, as I argued in chapter 11, was not living in London it makes sense that he gave up his rooms—and that the city wanted him to—so that they could be occupied and used, if necessary, for defence. He had given them up before 5 October. See Crow and Olson, *Chaucer Life-Records*, 146.

would almost certainly have happened anyway, but could perhaps have been moderated had Richard and de la Pole been more conciliatory.[53]

The campaign against the household and the king's rule focused on Michael de la Pole himself, but he was a fall guy. The real target was obviously Richard, and his failure to listen to the nobility or to manage his household. And while the Commons participated in the attack on de la Pole, the campaign was led by the Lords. In this parliament, the Lords and Commons acted together. Richard stormed off to Eltham in Kent, refusing to dismiss de la Pole or to participate any more in Parliament. What seems to have happened next is that Gloucester (his uncle) and Thomas Arundel went to talk to him and threatened deposition if he did not fall into line. This worked, and Richard returned to Parliament and accepted the imposition of a council that would, in effect, govern on his behalf for the next year, and that was charged with the reform of his household.[54]

Chaucer was part of this Commons, the allegedly united group complaining about the king's household. Undoubtedly, this was deeply uncomfortable for Chaucer, who himself held a household appointment. As I argued in chapter 11, he had already left both his rooms and his job (which was being done by a deputy), and his very presence in this parliament as MP for Kent demonstrates that his affiliation was now south of the river. When Parliament ended, he made clear efforts to dissociate himself from the taint of household corruption: he gave up the job, which he was not doing, responding to the Commons' specific attack on customs' officers.[55] In the 1385 Parliament, the Commons had urged that customs' officials should 'remain in their offices rather than exercising them through deputies or attorneys.'[56] In 1386, the critique of customs' officers focused on those who were appointed for their whole lives—this did not, in fact, apply to Chaucer, but given his abandonment of the post, one can understand why he felt it was politic to bow out completely. It may already have been clear to him that the political situation was spinning out of control, as the fledgling Lords Appellant began to spread their wings. In 1387, Richard's

[53] See Saul, *Richard II*, 157.
[54] Knighton, *Knighton's Chronicle*, 360–84.
[55] Parliament closed on 28 November; Adam Yardley took over as controller on 4 December. Crow and Olson, *Chaucer Life-Records*, 268.
[56] PROME, 'Appendix: Westminster, 20 October 1385,' no. 2, 7:28–29.

great riposte to the Lords was his 'questions to the judges,' which redefined and strengthened the royal prerogative. Significantly, one of the issues that he focused on was the use of parliamentary impeachment, which was judged treasonous when done against the king's will.[57] Richard was vigorously moving against the right of others to assert opinions contrary to his, and to get their voices heard.

And his opponents were similarly despotic: in the 1388 Merciless Parliament, the Lords Appellant invented their own laws and refused to be moved, even by the spectacle of the queen on her knees. Parliament descended into total brutality with the summary execution of men including Brembre and Usk. The Lords Appellant were determined to condemn and indeed to kill their opponents, regardless of normal legal procedure. While an appeal could be heard under common or civil law, depending on the court in which the appeal was lodged, the Appellants took aspects from both laws. Thus, they refused to allow Brembre a copy of the accusations, counsel, or time to plead, as would have been his right under civil law, but they also asked for conviction of absent appellees by default, which was not allowed under common law. Ultimately, the Lords in Parliament declared that the case was being judged by Parliament, within a law neither civil nor common—the Appellants allowed themselves 'to invent other procedures.'[58] The Parliament Roll informs us that the Lords requested that matters be 'discussed by the procedures of parliament, and not by civil law, nor by the common law of the land, practised in other lower courts of the realm.'[59] This was an entirely new concept. Elsewhere, the roll makes it clear that the Lords took this step because they could not do what they wanted under civil or common law. The justices and other legal advisors informed them that the appeal 'had not been made or affirmed in accordance with the procedure required by either law.' The Lords discussed this—perhaps with some consternation[60]—and decided that

---

[57] Clarke, *Fourteenth Century Studies*, 266.

[58] See Alan Rogers, 'Parliamentary Appeals of Treason in the Reign of Richard II,' *American Journal of Legal History* 8 (1964): 95–124, for a detailed discussion of the use of the appeal in Parliament at this time; quote is from 110.

[59] PROME, Membrane 5, no. 7, 7:64 (February 1388, Part 1).

[60] However, Biggs argues that the Appellants wanted the lawyers to defer to the Lords. 'The Appellant and the Clerk,' 60.

such high crimes could only be judged by the 'ley et cours du parlement' (law and usage of Parliament).[61] With this declaration, the Lords of Parliament declared themselves above the law.[62] Interestingly, even in this most autocratic and audacious behaviour, the Appellants may have remained somewhat dependent on textual propaganda and parliamentary clerks. Kerby-Fulton and Justice have argued that this declaration of the 'law of parliament' derives from the *Modus tenendi parliamentum*.[63] They suggest that this text was a product of 'reformist civil service culture,' and reflects clerkly modes of thought, further arguing that a copy belonging to one of the Appellants (Mowbray) 'may suggest some kind of concerted and early effort at disseminating the text for political reasons.'[64] The history of this text, then, may also bear witness to the propagandist efforts of the Appellants, and reveal their dependence on parliamentary clerks (both for sourcing and for disseminating such texts), while also underlining their own ability to harness texts for their own uses. In the hands of the Appellants, parliamentary precedence morphed into the rights of great magnates to act above the law. This specific instance exemplifies the more general trend that I have been outlining. Across Richard's reign, parliamentary innovation by the Commons was taken over by the Lords and then by the king: the Commons' punching-*up* impeachment of Richard Lyons and his cronies was taken as a model for the Lords' and then Richard's top-*down* attacks on their enemies in the Merciless and Revenge Parliaments.[65] The Speaker, who in 1376 was a voice against court corruption and was indeed imprisoned for his presumption, became a spokesman of the king in the 1390s. By the time of Richard's deposition, the king was accused of having tampered with the Parliament Roll, in a particularly damning demonstration of his attack on other perspectives and voices.[66]

[61] PROME, Membrane 14, 7:100 (February 1388, Part 3).

[62] Tout writes: 'Nothing in the history of this memorable parliament is more significant than this declaration. It may be put before the judges' enunciation at Nottingham of the theory of the prerogative. It was in substance an answer to the judges for it declared the supremacy of parliament over the lawyers and law courts.' *Chapters*, 3:432.

[63] Kerby-Fulton and Justice, 'Reformist Intellectual Culture,' 169–70.

[64] Ibid., 181, 178, 162, 165, 167.

[65] The Revenge Parliament of 1397 is discussed in chapter 19.

[66] See PROME, '1397 September,' 7:332, and articles of deposition in Chris Given-Wilson (ed.), *Chronicles of the Revolution: 1397–1400* (Manchester: Manchester University Press, 1993), 175, 178, articles 8 and 19.

In the context of the far darker political mood of the late 1380s, the years of Gaunt's absence, it is illuminating to think about the chronology of Chaucer's texts. He was never an optimistic, idealistic writer; nonetheless, the *Book of the Duchess* and the *Parliament of Fowls* are not texts about punishment, and both are, in some ways, hopeful about talking. The *Book of the Duchess* tries out the possibility of a talking cure for grief. In the *Parliament of Fowls*, violence (trial by battle) is explicitly deflected by talking. The *House of Fame* (which I and others have long argued is a later text than *Parliament of Fowls* and was probably written alongside or after *Troilus*) and the Prologue to the *Legend of Good Women* are texts, on the other hand, in which punishment is enforced.[67] Indeed, in the Prologue to the *Legend of Good Women*, self-expression is explicitly met with the threat of violence, and although that too is deflected, oppressive punishment is meted out. These two later poems are themselves quite different in texture and offer different visions of the role of the poet in extreme political circumstances. The *House of Fame* ends with a chaotic portrayal of the possibility of unruly multiple voices, temporarily free from oppressive control, and suggests that there can be a space for insurgent stories. But the right to speak, asserted in the Good Parliament and the *Parliament of Fowls*, comes under threat in the Prologue to the *Legend of Good Women*, written around the same time as the Wonderful Parliament, the questions to the judges, and the Merciless Parliament. The Prologue ends with a bleak depiction of what happens to a servant voice when the sovereign voice will brook no dissent, as I will discuss in chapter 14 ('Garden'). Politically and poetically, Chaucer repeatedly signalled his discomfort with the idea of a hegemonic voice: in the *Canterbury Tales* he found a way to liberate his poetry from a master perspective and to celebrate not *the* common voice but a plethora of common voices.

---

[67] On the date of the *House of Fame*, see Turner, *Chaucerian Conflict*, 12–13n16; Cooper, 'Four Last Things,' 59, 64; Minnis, *The Shorter Poems*, 171.

CHAPTER 13

Empire

[T]he Roman people by Right and not by usurpation took to itself
over all mortals the office of monarchy, which men call the Empire.

—*Dante,* De monarchia

Chaucer travelled to Lombardy—perhaps the most transformative of all
his journeys—in the wake of the Good Parliament of 1376. After the English Commons' extraordinary assertion of the rights of insurgent voices,
Chaucer experienced a regime of absolutism and extreme brutality, a
regime in which only the Visconti voice mattered. And while visiting this
centralizing and terrifying state, Chaucer came into contact with literature that was to change his poetic trajectory completely. He also lived, for
a few weeks, under a regime that simultaneously exalted violence and revered, sponsored, and promulgated culture. What he experienced there can
only have been an assault on the imagination on an enormous scale. The
negotiations of 1378 were part of a complicated European picture, in which
the empire and the split papacy were struggling for dominance. The space
of empire stretched across much of Western Europe. It also dominated the
political imaginations of some of the greatest poets of the fourteenth century, and was increasingly important to England's foreign policy in the
reign of Richard II. When Chaucer visited Lombardy in 1378, he was
swimming in the slipstream of imperial power broking, as the powers of
Europe positioned themselves between the Scylla and Charybdis of Rome
and Avignon. He also visited a state that was itself an imperial fief, and
that was ruled by tyrants with imperial ambitions in their own region.

The idea of empire continued to shape English politics in various ways for the rest of Richard's reign: in 1382, he married the sister of the Holy Roman Emperor; by the later 1380s, he was increasingly styling himself in imperial terms; at the end of his reign, he aspired to become the emperor himself. Chaucer had firsthand experience of secular rulers who attempted to impose a singular, dominant perspective on their subjects; he responded with poems that repeatedly rejected hegemonic ideologies and the idea of the sovereign voice and instead privileged *tidings*—stories, ideas, points of view—in all their messy multiplicity.

Both in his discovery of the ideas of Petrarch and Dante, and in his engagement with Italian politics, Chaucer encountered an ideology of history-as-destiny, a belief that a plan was unfolding in time, in the space of empire. The Holy Roman Empire dominated the political understanding of Petrarch and Dante; it had a particularly acute significance in the century of the Avignon papacy and the Schism, when papal power was moving away from its Italian heartland. From 1378 until 1417, two rival popes ruled from two rival centres, Rome and Avignon. For centuries, Italian city-states had wrestled with imperial-papal conflicts, originally supported by the Ghibelline and Guelf factions, respectively. The Visconti were 'imperial vicars,' originally dependent on imperial patronage for their position, and they increasingly modeled their own claims to authority on the language of imperial power.[1] The negotiations on which Chaucer was engaged in Milan were ultimately disrupted by a more formal Anglo-imperial alliance, cemented by a different marriage, and working against France and the Avignon antipope.[2] This marriage between Richard II and Anne of Bohemia tied England to the empire and inspired Richard's own bid to become the Holy Roman Emperor almost twenty years later.[3] While the lives and writings of Dante and Petrarch were embedded in the politics of empire and papacy, these forces were naturally far more distant from the life of Chaucer. But in the 1370s, when Chaucer made his visits to Genoa, Florence, and Milan, Italian imperial and papal politics were

[1] Jane Black, *Absolutism in Renaissance Milan: Plenitude of Power under the Visconti and the Sforza, 1329–1535* (Oxford: Oxford University Press, 2009), 52.

[2] Saul, *Richard II*, 85; Anthony Tuck, 'Richard II and the House of Luxembourg,' in Anthony Goodman and James Gillespie (eds.), *Richard II: The Art of Kingship* (Oxford: Clarendon Press, 1999), 216.

[3] Saul, *Richard II*, 83–107, 292, 366, 406.

increasingly important in his life and in English political life as a whole, culminating in the alliance formed in direct response to the Great Papal Schism, which took place while Chaucer was in Italy in 1378. And at the same time as England came into closer contact with the empire, Chaucer came into closer contact with the writings of Dante and Petrarch, which strongly supported an exalted secular power.

The Holy Roman Empire had a conceptual heart in Rome and saw itself as the heir of the Roman Empire itself, but of course it was not really 'Roman' in the medieval era: it had its base in Germany and particularly in Bohemia in Chaucer's lifetime; its tentacles reached down into Italy and over to the Low Countries and the borders of France. For Dante, the empire was not geographically bounded at all: 'The glorious power of the Romans cannot be held in check either within the boundaries of Italy or within the three sides of Europe itself . . . it stretches out everywhere by uninfringeable right, as far as the waves of Anphrite, and the inadequate waters of the ocean can scarcely contain it.'[4]

Dante's claims for empire, made in his letters to the emperor, Henry VII, and in his tract *De monarchia*, could hardly be more grandiose: he explicitly links the emperor to a heritage stretching back to Aeneas, and argues that Christ chose to be born at the time of Augustus's census in order to signal the justice of the emperor's earthly authority.[5] Petrarch also corresponded with the emperor of his day, Charles IV (grandson of Emperor Henry VII, and father of Anne), and wrote a number of other texts extolling empire; like Dante, he emphasizes the divine plan of empire and the perpetuity of Roman power, and cites Virgil as an authority. He famously asked, 'What is all of history but the praise of Rome?,' insisting that 'emperors may wander but the empire is "fixed and stable."'[6] Rather than representing a clearly demarcated territory, the empire stood for an understanding of the divinity and order of secular rule emanating from Rome and from Aeneas and checking the ambitions of the papacy; for an

[4] Dante Alighieri, 'Letter to the Emperor Henry VII,' in Clare E. Honess (ed.), *Dante Alighieri: Four Political Letters* (London: Modern Humanities Research Association, 2007), 74.

[5] Ibid., 75.

[6] Francesco Petrarca, 'Invective against a Detractor of Italy,' in *Francesco Petrarch: Invectives*, ed. and trans. David Marsh (Cambridge, MA: Harvard University Press, 2003), 416–17; Giuseppe Mazzotta, *The Worlds of Petrarch* (Durham, NC: Duke University Press, 1993), 25.

idea of history as ordered and driven; for a belief in a transcendent truth and justice behind human history. These were all ideas that Chaucer—along with Boccaccio—comprehensively rejected.

Chaucer travelled to Lombardy at a time when a particularly complicated contest for supreme power in Europe was raging. While pope and emperor had traditionally competed over which one was truly inheriting Roman authority, most famously in the investiture controversy of the eleventh and twelfth centuries, now there was the added problem of the Schism. The ideological conflict between the papacy and secular rulers, especially the emperor, had been acute throughout the fourteenth century, as popes, kings, lords, and emperors alike sought to extend the kind of power that they wielded. At the turn of the thirteenth to the fourteenth century, Boniface VIII had asserted the pope's right to bear the temporal as well as the spiritual sword, claiming a quasi-imperial position emphasized by his assumption of imperial vestments.[7] In response, Dante's *De monarchia* strongly asserted the divine rights of empire, and slightly later in the century (1328), the emperor Louis IV (who was married to Philippa of Hainault's sister Margaret and was thus brother-in-law to Edward III) had himself crowned by a layman and deposed the pope in a spectacular assertion of imperial authority.[8] The bitter conflict between emperor and pope simmered down midcentury when Charles IV took the crown and his former tutor became Pope Clement VI.[9] From 1309 to 1377 the papacy was based at Avignon (which was technically under the rule of Naples), where it reached new heights of corruption and profligacy, but despite its move to a French-Neapolitan heartland, it continued to fight for land and power in northern Italy, coming into conflict both with the Milanese Visconti and with the city-states, especially with Florence. In the early 1370s, Pope Gregory XI was at war against the Visconti, with the English mercenary John Hawkwood's armies providing the manpower. Florence, which opposed the expansion of the Papal States and was supporting rebellion within those states, paid Hawkwood not to fight against them, and allied with Milan as the papacy

[7] Friedrich Heer, *The Holy Roman Empire* (London: Weidenfeld and Nicolson, 1968), 99–100.
[8] Ibid., 110.
[9] Ibid., 114.

declared war. In 1376, the pope excommunicated the Florentine government and placed the whole city under interdict; in 1377 Hawkwood joined the antipapal coalition and married Donnina Visconti, illegitimate daughter of Bernabò Visconti.

These events had knock-on effects in England, itself undergoing an intense period of crisis and change. The heir to the throne, the Black Prince, had died in 1376, during the Good Parliament, and Edward III himself died in 1377. Gaunt was embroiled in his tussle with London (and especially the monopolists), and expatriate Florentines became pawns in the game. As discussed in chapter 10, London and its bishop, William Courtenay, wanted to take advantage of the papal interdict to seize Florentine goods and suspend their privileges, but Gaunt, backed by his protégé John Wycliffe, supported the Florentines and agreed to place them in the Tower for their own protection, later releasing them as the legal chattels of the king.[10] The Florentine Commune would later send thanks to Gaunt and Edward for this treatment of their citizens. Within the English context, this was at least partly about Gaunt asserting his power over London and Courtenay, who were condemning Wycliffe and who had recently dramatically insulted Gaunt himself.

The war with France rumbled on: plans were made for a new expedition, which were then cancelled when Edward died.[11] At the same time, the English were considering a marriage alliance with France instead: Chaucer made several trips in 1376 and 1377 that were related to negotiations for Richard to marry a French princess.[12] In early 1378, English tactics changed. Now Chaucer was sent to Milan, to negotiate with Bernabò Visconti and John Hawkwood, to gain their support in the war against France.[13] The negotiations involved plans for a marriage alliance between

[10] Wallace, *Chaucerian Polity*, 31. Also see chapter 10 in this study.

[11] Goodman, *John of Gaunt*, 63–64.

[12] Chaucer travelled to Paris and Montreuil in February and March 1377 and to parts of France between the end of April and the end of June 1377. Records also suggest another later trip to France, and further overseas trips may be indicated in an issue roll entry of payment for 'divers voyages made to divers parts beyond the seas' in April 1377. It is clear that he was travelling frequently during these months. There are multiple English records of these journeys; Froissart also specifically mentions him—'Jeffrois Cauchiés' and 'Gieffroy Cauchier' in his description of the negotiations for peace and for a marriage between Richard and the French princess Marie. For the records, see Crow and Olson, *Chaucer Life-Records*, 44–53.

[13] Ibid., 53–61.

Bernabò's daughter, Caterina, and Richard II. The countries in Europe were moving into power blocs, which hardened as the Schism developed during the middle of the year. Ultimately, the Roman pope, Urban I, was supported by the empire, England, northern Italy, Denmark, Flanders, Hungary, Ireland, Norway, Portugal, Poland, and Sweden, while the Avignonese Clement VII was backed by France, Naples, Castile, Aragon, Cyprus, Burgundy, Savoy, and Scotland. In this context, Urban sought to strengthen Anglo-imperial ties by promoting a marriage alliance between Charles IV's daughter, Anne of Bohemia, and Richard II; that marriage was thus born out of the big picture of European power relations in the late 1370s. A marriage with Bernabò's daughter would have maintained broadly the same alliances, and have been more lucrative, but far less prestigious. In travelling to Milan, Chaucer was travelling to an imperial fief in the service of Crown anti-French and pro-imperial policy.

At the Lombard court he met rulers of obscure and recent origins who wanted to be treated as if they were emperors, and who were indeed conquering lands across northern Italy during the fourteenth century.[14] At several points in his writings, Chaucer makes reference to this visit. Most explicitly, in the 'Monk's Tale,' Bernabò Visconti is described as 'God of delit and scourge of Lumbardye,' associated with luxurious pleasure and violence (2400). In the Prologue to the *Legend of Good Women*, Alceste urges the God of Love not to behave like 'tirauntz of Lumbardye' (F-Prologue, 374). Such tyrannical courts, she says, are full of liars that gossip and make accusations, insistently drumming on your ears (350–54); envy is the laundress of the court, everywhere amongst the dirty linen, and she never leaves the 'hous of Cesar' (359–60). The Lombards are thus explicitly connected with 'Caesar'—that is, empire. Such tyrants cannot be opposed, refusing to rule with fairness and 'equytee' (398). Lombardye again comes up as the setting of the whole of Fragment IV (the 'Clerk's Tale' and the 'Merchant's Tale'). In the 'Clerk's Tale,' it is associated with a tyrant lord who cares only for 'delit' (68), his 'lust present' (immediate pleasure, 80), and this time the story is explicitly associated with thinkers well known in Lombardy at the time of Chaucer's visit: Petrarch (d. 1374) and

---

[14] Jane Black writes that they were 'embracing the law and language of the pope and the emperor.' *Absolutism*, 2.

Legnano (d. 1383).[15] Both had strong connections with Milan, and while the former was a client of the Visconti and a lover of empire, the latter defended the papacy.[16] After the Schism, when the interests of emperor and Visconti lay in supporting Urban VII, Legnano's work in defence of the Roman pope exactly suited the political agendas of empire and England alike. This work was written and immediately circulated while Chaucer was in Lombardy. It is of great interest that, in translating Petrarch's version of Boccaccio's Griselda story, Chaucer takes pains to set the story in Lombardy (unlike his sources), to flag up Petrarch and Legnano in the 'Prologue,' and to present, through the Clerk, a version of the story that repeatedly criticizes the tyrannical ruler, lauding instead the lowborn victim who is able to rule with great 'equitee' (439).

The Visconti wanted to acquire—even believed that they had acquired—quasi-imperial status. In an attack on the archbishop of Milan, Bernabò Visconti demanded: 'Don't you know that I am pope and emperor as well as signore in all my lands? Not the emperor, not even God, can do anything in my territories unless I wish it.'[17] The absolutist politics, expansionist program, and violent methods of the Visconti were notorious. They were also, however, part of a much broader trend amongst fourteenth-century rulers to establish themselves as holding imperial status.[18] The idea of individual sovereignty—a status that placed a ruler outside legal frameworks—was by no means generally accepted in the late Middle

---

[15] Fraunceys Petrak, the lauriat poete,
Highte this clerk, whos rethorike sweete
Enlumyned al Ytaille of poetrie,
As Lynan dide of philosophie,
Or lawe, or oother art particuler;
But Deeth, that wol nat suffre us dwellen heer,
But as it were a twynklyng of an ye,
Hem bothe hath slayn, and alle shul we dye. ('Clerk's Prologue,' 31–38)

[16] See Wallace, *Chaucerian Polity*, chapter 10, '"Whan She Translated Was": Humanism, Tyranny, and the Petrarchan Academy,' 261–98, for a detailed discussion of Petrarch's politics, poetics, relationship with the Visconti, and treatment of the Griselda story. For Legnano, see John P. McCall, 'Chaucer and John of Legnano,' *Speculum* 40:3 (1965): 484–89.

[17] Francesco Cognasso, 'Istituzioni comunali e signorili di Milano sotto i Visconti,' in *Storia di Milano, Volume VI: Il ducato visconteo e la repubblica ambrosiana (1392–1450)* (Milan: Fondazione Treccani degli Alfieri, 1955), 537.

[18] Anthony Black, *Political Thought in Europe, 1250–1450* (Cambridge: Cambridge University Press, 1992), 113.

Ages.[19] On the contrary, legal historians have written extensively about English antipathy towards the idea of the containment of sovereign power in the person of the king: the reframed coronation oath in the early fourteenth century explicitly emphasized that the king not only had to obey the law, but that the laws were chosen by the people—he was not even the lawmaker.[20] The Good Parliament of 1376 was perceived to be addressing the issue of the kind of power Gaunt wielded, and how the king himself related to the law as Parliament asserted its own rights. Langland's contemporary fictionalization of the Parliament depicts a number of conflicting viewpoints about the relationship between monarch and law, including the idea that 'precepta regis sunt nobis vincula legis' (the king's precepts are law to us).[21]

The idea of 'plenitude of power'—an 'absolutist' form of power that operated outside the law—had been developed in the twelfth century (from earlier origins) to signify the sweeping claims of the papacy. In the subsequent century, emperors too took on the term, and so did other rulers, such as the French king. The imperial chancery started using the term during the rule of Frederick II in the 1230s; by the early 1300s, Henry VII, Dante's political hero, was using it extensively.[22] The essence of plenitude of power and its imperial provenance is described by Baldo degli Ubaldi, a civil law academic from Perugia who worked for the Visconti later in the fourteenth century. He comments that the doctrine is summed up by the ancient saying that 'whatever the prince decrees has the force of law,' adding elsewhere that '[t]he emperor has total plenitude of power in every land in the empire . . . in him all power shines, for the

[19] Frederick Pollock and Frederic William Maitland, *The History of English Law before the Time of Edward I*, 2nd ed. (Cambridge: Cambridge University Press, 1898), 182.

[20] The coronation oath, reframed for Edward II's coronation in 1308, was consistently used in this new form throughout the late-medieval period: 'Sire, grauntez-vous a tenir et garder les leys et les custumes droctureles, *les quiels la communaute de vostre roiaume aura eslu* et les defendrez et afforcerez al honour de Dieu a vostre poer?' (emphasis mine). Cited in H. G. Richardson, 'The English Coronation Oath,' *Speculum* 24 (1949): 64. See also B. Wilkinson, 'The Coronation Oath of Edward II,' in J. G. Edwards, V. H. Galbraith, and E. F. Jacob (eds.), *Historical Essays in Honour of James Tait* (Manchester: Manchester University Press, 1933), 405–16; and Seymour Phillips, *Edward II* (New Haven: Yale University Press, 2010), 140–48. The implications of the key phrase, italicised above, is disputed; I translate it as 'which the people of your realm shall have chosen.'

[21] Line 145 of the 'Prologue,' in Langland, *Piers Plowman: The B Version*, 235.

[22] Black, *Absolutism*, 8–9, 11–12, 36–37.

providence of God has seen that no one and nothing would better protect the well-being of the republic than Caesar.'[23] This kind of ideology directly opposes the Good Parliament's insistence on the right to take action against the will of the king. And the constraint of the king by Parliament and the nobles was precisely Richard's concern in his questions to the judges of 1387, as he tried to establish an exalted royal prerogative.

Increasingly, more minor rulers too started to stake a claim to a grandiose form of power. The Visconti, backed up by legal academics, were at the forefront of this movement.[24] In 1355, their imperial vicariate (the powers granted to them by the emperor) became more detailed than before, and gave them judicial rights more usually claimed by the emperor himself, as well as authority to legislate and to raise imperial taxes. While there were various eddies in the current over the next forty years—times at which they fell out with the emperor—in general they were moving towards a more established status, culminating in Giangaleazzo Visconti's double ducal investitures of 1395 and 1396. As Jane Black writes, the diploma of 1396 'gave the Visconti special status, raising them above the ranks of other rulers who acknowledged imperial authority.'[25] While the first ducal investiture covered only Giangaleazzo's inherited lands, the second one covered the cities and territories that the Visconti had conquered, giving extra legitimacy to their own empire. During these years, the Visconti walked a line between reliance on imperial sanction for their status and declaring that they held power in their own right. Baldo degli Ubaldi and his brother Angelo degli Ubaldi both wrote about this issue: Angelo asserted that the Visconti had their powers as princes, not deriving these powers from the emperor; Baldo argued that although their powers did come from the emperor, they were 'all the same powers as the emperor,' and that Giangaleazzo 'wielded Caesar's sword.'[26] Explicitly, they were aiming at imperial-type power, the power of Caesar.

[23] Baldo degli Ubaldi, *Commentariolum super pace Constantiae*, in *Baldi Perusini in vsus feudorum commentaria doctissima* (Lyons: Pidié, 1552), s.v. 'Libellariae,' no. 3 and *Consiliorum Sive Responsorum* (Venice: H. Polum, 1575), book 3, 359 ('Quemadmodum Imperator'), no.1, cited in Black, *Absolutism*, 19.

[24] Azzone Visconti used the term in 1334. Black, *Absolutism*, 43.

[25] Ibid., 97.

[26] Baldo, *Consilium*, book 3, 359 ('Quemadmodum imperator'), nos. 1–2, cited in Black, *Absolutism*, 62–64.

Chaucer set off for Milan on 28 May 1378. He departed 'de civitate Londonie' and returned to London on 19 September.[27] He was thus away for 115 days—as the accounts specifically note, because he was paid per day. He travelled in company with Sir Edward de Berkeley, a chamber knight. Berkeley, as we might expect given his superior status, was the leader of the mission: he was accompanied by nine mounted men and was paid 20s per day.[28] Chaucer was accompanied by five men and their horses and was paid 13s 4d per day.[29] The wages have clearly been worked out in relation to each other, as Chaucer was receiving exactly two-thirds as much as Berkeley: this, perhaps, is the weighting of knight to esquire. Chaucer was the deputy in this group of sixteen, and Berkeley and Chaucer appear to have been the only two named, chosen members of the embassy. Chaucer thus had a position of considerable importance, and had an entourage in his own right. Over the previous year or so, he had been dispatched on multiple journeys: to Flanders, Paris, Montreuil, and perhaps to other parts of France.[30] The records are not always clear about how many journeys he went on, but there were several, and they dealt with possible treaties and marriage alliances with France. At this moment in his career, he was very much in the diplomatic world as well as in the milieu of the Custom House. His prior trip to Italy in 1373, his familiarity with treaty negotiations, and his knowledge of the Italian language particularly suited him to this trip.[31] He received letters of protection, the equivalent of a passport, and he gave power of attorney to John Gower and Richard Forrester, so they could represent him should a lawsuit be brought against him while he was away.[32] A deputy had been appointed to do his work in the Custom House.[33] Berkeley and Chaucer were tasked with negotiating both with 'Barnabo dominum de Mellan' (Bernabò Visconti, lord of Milan), and with 'Johannem de Haukewode' (John

---

[27] Crow and Olson, *Chaucer Life-Records*, 59.

[28] Ibid., 60–61.

[29] Ibid., 59.

[30] Ibid., 42–53.

[31] It is just possible that Chaucer had visited Lombardy before. He travelled abroad in 1368, and we don't know where he went: he could have attended Lionel's wedding to Violante Visconti.

[32] Crow and Olson, *Chaucer Life-Records*, 53–54.

[33] Ibid., 164–65. The deputy was Richard Barrett.

Hawkwood, English mercenary soldier, in charge of the White Company, and son-in-law of Bernabò).[34]

There were well trodden routes to Italy at this time. This large group crossed the Channel and then proceeded by horseback, roughly following the Rhine, before crossing the Alps into Lombardy. A decent average speed for riders in no particular hurry would be twenty-five miles a day.[35] From London to Milan is around eight hundred miles, so it would take a month or a little more. Chaucer was in his midthirties, travelling at the perfect time of year in terms of climate, so there is no reason to think that the journey would have been particularly arduous—unlike his winter crossings of the Pyrenees in 1366 and the Alps in 1372–73. Nor would it have been particularly exciting; most people would find such a trip somewhat monotonous. We don't know if they told each other stories to pass the time.

Chaucer probably arrived in Milan around the end of June or beginning of July and stayed in Lombardy until mid-August—the height of the summer, and the first time he'd seen Southern Europe in summer light, or experienced the sensual pleasure of this climate. His mission was primarily to Milan, but it is probable that he also visited Pavia, an easy ride from Milan. Pavia was the home of Galeazzo Visconti, closely associated with Petrarch, and site of a great library in the awe-inspiring Visconti fortress. Chaucer arrived in Lombardy at an extraordinary moment. Pope Urban VI had been elected in April, but his cardinals were already regretting his election, and a large group had withdrawn from Rome to Anagni. While Chaucer was still in Lombardy, they pronounced the election void (on 2 August); and the day after Chaucer returned to England, they elected a rival pope, Clement VII. Chaucer was also in Lombardy when Galeazzo Visconti died at Pavia on 4 August. He had ruled jointly with his brother Bernabò, and his death initially allowed Bernabò even freer reign, until Galeazzo's son, Giangaleazzo, executed a coup against his uncle in 1385, a turn of Fortune's wheel memorialized in the 'Monk's Tale.'

Milan was framed by two massive palaces, the residences of the two Visconti brothers. Galeazzo's palace still stands today, a vast fortress that now houses civic museums. Bernabò's has gone, along with most of the

<hr />

[34]Ibid., 58.
[35]Childs, 'Anglo-Italian Contacts,' 66.

magnificent Visconti church, San Giovanni in Conca. Today, part of its wall stands on an island in the middle of a busy road; one can walk down steps into the crypt but can only imagine the previous magnificence of the basilica, later eclipsed by the Duomo and then cut in half to make way for a road. San Giovanni in Conca was a late antique foundation, dating back to the fifth or sixth century. Towards the end of the thirteenth century, radical restoration and rebuilding had added a great rose window and a 24-metre-high bell tower. Lavishly frescoed, it was incorporated into Bernabò's palace in the second half of the fourteenth century when he was dramatically expanding the residence that he had inherited in 1354. In the years following their joint succession to the role of signori of Milan, the two Visconti brothers both built up their rival castles enthusiastically. They also harnessed the power of art and culture to enhance the Visconti image. When Chaucer was in Milan, San Giovanni had recently acquired a huge statue of Bernabò riding his horse and staring ahead, held up by the female figures of Strength and Justice (plate 14). It is a disturbing statue: Wallace has discussed its aggressive promotion of masculine virility and power, particularly demonstrated through the depiction of the horse's genitals swinging behind the small female allegorical figures.[36] Although Strength and Justice are supposed to be supporting Bernabò, they are relatively insignificant in size, and Bernabò's sword suggestively dangles close to the head of Strength—he controls them. Indeed, his dominance of the beleaguered-looking allegorical women is peculiarly appropriate: he promotes not an objective justice but his own idea of justice; he supports strength only if he himself directs and channels it. This statue, shockingly placed on the altar, symbolized the aggressive secular power of the Visconti. Worshipping in that church must have seemed close to idolatry: not for nothing did Bernabò claim to be God in his own realm.

The statue itself also represents the Visconti interest in art and culture: it was carved by Bonino da Campione, the most admired master sculptor of the day.[37] In the 1370s Milan was a place of artistic diversity and innovation,

[36] Wallace, *Chaucerian Polity*, 321.
[37] Serena Romano, 'Milan (and Lombardy): Art and Architecture, 1277–1535,' in Andrea Gamberini (ed.), *A Companion to Late Medieval and Early Modern Milan: The Distinctive Features of an Italian State* (Leiden: Brill, 2014), 221.

described by one critic as 'unrivalled in Europe as an artistic crossroads.'[38] The artistic experiments of Giotto had spread to Lombardy early, demonstrated particularly through the depiction of spatial depth, the representation of architecture, and the portrayal of narrative cogency. Giotto himself had painted frescoes in the older Visconti palace, which was destroyed and rebuilt by Galeazzo. The city was also full of sculpture. The older traditionalist Campionesi style had been replaced by a new fashion as Bonino da Campione and his followers were pioneering a greater naturalism and sense of space and weight in sculptural style. As Chaucer approached the gates, he saw older carvings that celebrated the history of the city and that told stories through art: the sequences on one of the gates, for instance, unfolded the narrative of Ambrose chasing the Arians from Milan. In the churches and palaces of Milan, he saw the newer sculptural style, not least in Bernabò's equestrian statue. New artistic and architectural work was everywhere in Milan and Pavia at the moment of Chaucer's visit. Not only had the great palace fortresses of Milan been rebuilt in the 1360s, but Galeazzo's huge castle at Pavia was built between 1360 and 1365, and it housed an exceptionally rich library. Bonino da Campione was at work in the 1370s, for instance constructing the tomb of Giovanni da Fagnano in 1376. In 1378, a new façade of Santa Maria Maggiore—the cathedral of Milan—was completed (only to be torn down and rebuilt a decade later). This flourishing of the visual arts went hand in hand with the encouragement and patronage of education and poetry. Pavia University had been founded by Emperor Charles IV in 1361. And manuscript production, the cultivation of libraries, and the making of poetry were all central to the Visconti self-image.

We see this emphasis on bookish and literary culture most clearly in the role of Petrarch in the Visconti regime. Petrarch's position gave him space and time in which to write and to devote himself to his studies, but he was deeply compromised as the client of tyrants, a position that was politically and intellectually horrifying to contemporaries such as Boccaccio. Petrarch resided in Milan between 1353 and 1361, and regularly visited Pavia during and after this time, making his last visit to Pavia in May

---

[38] Ibid., 214.

1369, less than a decade before Chaucer's probable visit. He died in 1374.[39] A late fourteenth-century sculpture in Milan represents the figure of a poet laureate: fine-featured, calm, and crowned with laurel, he is an image of confidence and self-possession (plate 12). The very existence of such an image bears witness to the new importance of the figure of the contemporary poet in fourteenth-century Italy. Petrarch was a figure of towering cultural importance: himself a prolific poet, he was also at the forefront of humanist learning, rediscovering classical works that had been lost for centuries, languishing unread in libraries. He encouraged the beginnings of a new interest in Greek: in 1354 he received from the Byzantine ambassador a manuscript containing the *Iliad* in Greek, now MS Ambrosiana I. (By 1397, Manuel Chrysoloras was lecturing on Greek in Florence.[40]) In 1369, Petrarch had his scribe, Giovanni Malpaghini, copy a Latin translation of the *Iliad* and the *Odyssey*. Indeed, he patronized an atelier (workshop) around himself that produced Latin codices.[41] His own library—which later came into the hands of Giangaleazzo Visconti— was extensive, and the Visconti brothers also built up impressive libraries at Milan and Pavia.

We have an inventory of the library at Pavia, made in 1426. Undoubtedly, many of the books there entered the library after Chaucer's 1378 visit. However, critics have noted the extraordinary number of source texts used by Chaucer that are also present in this inventory—many of which were not available in England. The overwhelming likelihood is that Chaucer did indeed get hold of material here. His poetry in the 1380s demonstrates, in particular, extensive knowledge of Boccaccio's poetry at a time when no one else in England seems to have had such knowledge. In Pavia, he could have found Boccaccio's *Filostrato, Amorosa Visione, Decameron, De Genealogia Deorum Gentilium, De Claris Mulieribus, De Casibus Virorum Illustrium,* and *De Montibus.* The 1426 inventory details many other books by various authors that Chaucer certainly read: Virgil, Ovid, St Jerome, Macrobius, St Augustine, Boethius, Dante, Petrarch—although

[39] See discussion in Massimo Zaggia, 'Culture in Lombardy: 1350–1550,' in *A Companion to Late Medieval and Early Modern Milan*, 167.

[40] Boitani, 'Introduction,' in *Chaucer and the Italian Trecento*, 1.

[41] Zaggia, 'Culture in Lombardy,' 168.

he would have had many other opportunities to read the classical and late antique texts.[42] There were a large number of French translations of Latin texts here too, including multiple French translations of Boethius.[43] If he did indeed read books from the Visconti libraries, how did this work? His status as deputy on a mission from the king of England would make it easy for him to gain favour and gifts from the Visconti. When they sent messengers to Richard II at the end of the year, Richard presented the envoys with the generous gift of 200 marks in gold and two silver-gilt cups.[44] This kind of largesse was the norm. Moreover, the Visconti, somewhat surprisingly, were notoriously generous with their books: always happy to lend them out and to allow others to make copies, a practice that was 'altogether exceptional.'[45] In Pavia, there were numerous willing scribes available at the university and at the scriptorium attached to San Pietro in Ciel D'Oro, a famous church very close to the fortress. So Chaucer may well have not only read new texts here but also acquired copies to take back home with him. He got copies of the *Teseida* and the *Filostrato* from somewhere, and this is by far the most likely place. William Coleman has demonstrated the similarities between a particular copy of the *Teseida* described in the inventory (item 881) and the text that Chaucer knew: the parts that are missing from this copy match the parts that Chaucer did not have available.[46] Chaucer very likely gained the cultural knowledge that was to transform his literary practice under the auspices of the most ruthless and feared tyrants of his time.[47]

The library at Pavia was housed in Galeazzo Visconti's fortress, a stone's throw from San Pietro. This church still houses the tombs of two of the greatest writers in history, Boethius and St Augustine. Chaucer, as an extremely cultured English visitor who previously worked for Lionel of Clarence, who was also buried here, probably saw these tombs: they were

---

[42] Robert A. Pratt, 'Chaucer and the Visconti Libraries,' *English Literary History* 6:3 (1939): 195–96.

[43] Wallace, *Chaucerian Polity*, 52.

[44] Crow and Olson, *Chaucer Life-Records*, 61.

[45] Pratt, 'Chaucer and the Visconti Libraries,' 198.

[46] William E. Coleman, 'Chaucer, the *Teseida*, and the Visconti Library at Pavia: A Hypothesis,' *Medium Aevum* 51 (1982): 92–101.

[47] The torture meted out by the Visconti is described in detail in documents; see discussion by Wallace, *Chaucerian Polity*, 324.

enough of an attraction that Giangaleazzo showed them to Henry of Derby when he visited a few years later.[48] The church was made particularly famous in Chaucer's day by contemporary poets. Dante wrote about Boethius in 'Cieldauro' in *Paradiso* (10.128). In Boccaccio's *Decameron* (10.9), the story also centres on San Pietro. Petrarch writes to Boccaccio about the fame of the church, and the tombs of Augustine and Boethius in his *Seniles* (5.1). The tombs of these long-dead writers (who were also revered as saint and martyr, respectively) were given fresh cultural capital in these contemporary writings. At the same time, the tomb of Augustine was itself rebuilt in the 1360s: a magnificent ark was sculpted over the preexisting monument.[49] The fourteenth century thus laid new claim to antiquity and framed the glories of the past through its own new styles and techniques. Although schools and universities focused on classical texts, the cultural world in which Chaucer moved was confident about the value and sophistication of the new. Virgil's works, for instance, were for Dante and Chaucer an inspiration from which they could progress into new areas of literature. The crucial difference between the two authors was that Dante presents himself as surpassing Virgil by virtue of his Christian revelation, while Chaucer depicts himself as a bumbling incompetent—although he also takes pains to undermine an idea of Virgilian infallibility.

There is no doubt that, with the exception of the early *Book of the Duchess*, all of Chaucer's long poems responded to Italian poetry, and that Italian poetry utterly transformed the kind of poet that Chaucer was. That is not to say that he abandoned French or Latin sources. Indeed, Italian literature was itself born out of careful reading of texts in these languages.[50] However, the poetry of Dante and Boccaccio became Chaucer's principal inspiration for the majority of his poetic career. We see this at the level of poetics, as Chaucer plays with Dante's theories of poetry; we see it at the level of genre, as he embraces the vernacular tale collection in the wake of the *Decameron*; we see it at the level of subject matter, ranging

[48] John Capgrave, *Liber de Illustribus Henricis*, ed. Francis Charles Hingeston (London: Longman, 1858), 100; Walsingham, *Historia Anglicana*, 1:306.

[49] Rodney K. Delasanta, 'Chaucer, Pavia, and the Ciel D'Oro,' *Medium Aevum* 54 (1983): 117–21.

[50] See Butterfield, 'Chaucer's French Inheritance,' 26–28.

from the story of Palamon and Arcite, to that of Troilus and Criseyde, to the fabliau stories of the *Decameron*. At a metrical level, the Italian poetic line prompted Chaucer to develop the English decasyllabic line, his most important formal contribution to English poetry. While there were some examples of ten-syllable lines in French poetry, Italian eleven-syllable lines, with their dependence on stress, had more in common with the line that Chaucer invented.[51] And it is profoundly significant that Chaucer did not develop this line until he had encountered, and was imitating, Boccaccio's work. His first poems to use the pentameter are also those poems that draw closely on the *Teseida*; he then continued to use the line in his *Filostrato*-inspired *Troilus and Criseyde*.[52] Seeing the kind of things that the Italian poets were doing inspired a kind of experimental frenzy in Chaucer and liberated him to indulge in his fascination for 'newfangelnesse'—albeit (paradoxically) a 'newfangelnesse' that was ostentatiously imitative in a European context. In poems such as *A Complaint to His Lady* and *Anelida and Arcite*, he tries out different kinds of poetic form within the same poem, experimenting with stanza length, rhyme scheme, and line length.[53] Poetically, Chaucer's consumption of Italian verse was exceptionally productive, generative, and liberating: it energized him and gave him tools and models for innovative literary play. Politically, his encounter with Italian literature and life was more problematic and troubling.

In fourteenth-century Italy, the development of vernacular literature was not a straightforward triumph of the language of the people. In Boccaccio's Naples in the 1330s and Petrarch's Lombardy of the 1360s alike, Tuscan was privileged over local dialects.[54] This 'Tuscanisation' demoted

[51] See Duffell, *A New History of English Metre*, 85–87. See also Wallace, 'Chaucer's Italian Inheritance,' 37–38. The Italian *endecasillabo* is technically dependent on the final stress falling on the tenth syllable, but also had informal patterns of earlier stresses.

[52] The *Parliament of Fowls*, the 'Knight's Tale,' and *Anelida and Arcite* draw heavily on the *Teseida*. It is interesting that the *House of Fame*, which relies much more on Dante, nonetheless does also reveal knowledge of the *Teseida*. See Piero Boitani, 'Style, Iconography, and Narrative: The Lesson of the *Teseida*,' in Boitani, *Chaucer and the Italian Trecento*, 188.

[53] For the experimental nature of these poems, see Wallace, 'Chaucer's Italian Inheritance,' 43–44; and Pearsall, *Life of Geoffrey Chaucer*, 120–21.

[54] On Tuscan and Neapolitan in Naples, see David Wallace, 'Chaucer and Boccaccio's Early Writings,' in Boitani, *Chaucer and the Italian Trecento*, 146–47.

other dialects—Neapolitan, Lombard—that were increasingly viewed as inferior.[55] Under the Visconti, particular kinds of culture were promoted, culture that encouraged homogenization of identity rather than regional diversity. The vernacular poetic voice was thus itself a voice of a particular kind of privilege. The same thing ultimately happened in England, but a little more slowly. We can see the rise of chancery English in Chaucer's day,[56] just as the Visconti chancellery produced documents in Tuscan rather than Lombard,[57] but in late fourteenth-century England there was still a vibrant tradition of 'high' vernacular literature in the alliterative style and northwestern dialect, as well as in the rhymed, southeastern form of Chaucer and Gower's verse.

The master's voice across Europe was also homogenizing. Across the Continent, monarchs were increasingly using the language of imperial power, encouraging the adoption of modes of address that treated them as emperors, and developing more elaborate ceremonial styles that wrapped them in mystique and distanced them from their subjects. This more distant and elevated style of rule perhaps originated at the thirteenth-century court of Frederick II of Sicily[58]—the first emperor to utilize the idea of plenitude of power, as noted above—and by the fourteenth century was spreading across Europe, most notably (in terms of influences on the English monarchy) to Prague and Paris.[59] Richard II's own father, the Black Prince, was also known for the magnificence and ceremony of his court in Aquitaine. Once Richard II reached adulthood, in the second half of his reign, he demanded the use of imperial modes of address—'vostre

---

[55] Zaggia, 'Culture in Lombardy,' 170–72.

[56] See Gwilym Dodd, 'The Spread of English in the Records of the Central Government, 1400–1430,' in Elisabeth Salter and Helen Wicker (eds.), *Vernacularity in England and Wales, c. 1300–1550* (Turnhout: Brepols, 2011), 225–66; Gwilym Dodd, 'Writing Wrongs: The Drafting of Supplications to the Crown in Later Fourteenth-Century England,' *Medium Aevum* 80:2 (2011): 217–46; and Gwilym Dodd, 'The Rise of English, the Decline of French: Supplications to the English Crown, c. 1420–50,' *Speculum* 86:1 (2011): 117–50.

[57] Zaggia, 'Culture in Lombardy,' 170.

[58] This is suggested by Saul, *Richard II*, 347.

[59] Gervase Mathew argued that Prague was the strongest influence on Richard II; Nigel Saul suggests more diffuse influences and gives more emphasis to France. Regardless of the chain of influence, numerous courts in Europe were assuming increasingly elaborate styles of kingship. See Saul, *Richard II*, 343–49; and Mathew, *Court of Richard II*, 17; Vale, *Princely Court*.

hautesse et roiale mageste'—quite different from the traditional ways of addressing English monarchs.[60] The struggle between Richard and the Lords Appellant in 1386–89, and the final years of Richard's 'tyranny' and his deposition, played out a conflict between a king who wanted himself to embody the law and magnates who sought to place legal power either with Parliament or with themselves.[61] Indeed, the articles of deposition alleged that Richard claimed: 'quod leges sue erant in ore suo, et aliquociens in pectore suo, et quod ipse solus posset mutare et condere leges regni sui' (that his laws were in his mouth, or sometimes in his breast: and that he alone could alter and create the laws of his realm).[62]

Richard's models for the kind of kingship to which he aspired were multiple: his own father, the Black Prince, and the Valois kings were potent imaginative presences in his political world. The imperial court, from which his adored wife Anne came, was another key aspirational model for Richard. While the empire and England had historically been friendly, Charles IV's links with France and the Avignon papacy in the mid-fourteenth century had cooled their friendship.[63] The Anglo-imperial alliance formed after the Schism remade the relationship between the two realms for the long term. This alliance, with Richard and Anne's marriage as its cornerstone, also provided wide-reaching trade benefits and enabled increased economic and cultural traffic.[64] Charles IV's cultured court, with its extraordinary architectural and artistic achievements, its promotion of vernacular literature, its connections with the great humanist thinkers of the day, and its foundation of the first Northern European university provided an appealing image of kingship to Richard, and indeed, we see the influence of Prague in some of his own artistic projects.[65]

[60] This comes from the address to the king by the Commons in the Parliament of 1391. PROME, Membrane 4, no. 25, 7:205 (November 1391), cited in Saul, *Richard II*, 340n47.

[61] For the Appellants' invention of the 'law of parliament,' see PROME, Membrane 13, 7:103 (February 1388, Part 3). For discussion of this, see Tout, *Chapters*, 432. See also Kerby-Fulton and Justice, 'Reformist Intellectual Culture,' 169–70.

[62] PROME, Membrane 19, no. 33, 8:18 (October 1399, Part 1). The deposition is discussed in more detail in chapter 19.

[63] Tuck, 'Richard II and the House of Luxemburg,' 205–29.

[64] Michael Van Dussen, *From England to Bohemia: Heresy and Communication in the Later Middle Ages* (Cambridge: Cambridge University Press, 2012), 1–5.

[65] See S. Harrison Thomson, 'Learning at the Court of Charles IV,' *Speculum* 25, no. 1 (1950): 1–20; and Paul Binski, *Westminster Abbey and the Plantagenets: Kingship and the Representation of Power,*

In general, the nature of international high culture of the time means that it can be difficult to separate cultural influences by nation: the French Machaut, after all, had been patronized by Charles IV's father, John of Luxembourg, for whom the poet had written the *Jugement du Roi de Behaigne*. But Prague and the empire were certainly increasingly important to English political and cultural life after the alliance of 1378. Anne and her retinue brought with them an interest in education and in vernacular writings, as well as new fashions both in clothing and in literature: the flowers and pearls that are scattered throughout texts such as the Prologue to the *Legend of Good Women* come in part from Bohemian influence.[66] This text was revised after Anne's death, and the exhortation that it was to be given to 'the quene' at one of her palaces 'at Eltham or at Sheene' (F-Prologue, 496–97) was removed from the poem. Although this reference does not necessarily mean that Anne ever saw the poem, it does give us a more specific link between Chaucer's poetry and Anne than we have between his poetry and Richard; this cultured Bohemian woman may have been more interested in vernacular poetry than her husband was.

The emperor from 1378 was Wenceslas IV, a less competent ruler than his father and someone whose career mirrored Richard's in depressing ways: like Richard he relied on his household officials and favourites, alienating and undermining his magnates, and he too was imprisoned and deposed from some of his titles by those magnates—although he escaped with his life and with some of his powers intact.[67] But Richard, of course, could not foresee that both would have their imperial desires thwarted. In 1397 Richard was set on styling himself in ever-more imperial terms: he both sought the imperial crown (and Walsingham claimed that his movement against the Appellants was motivated by the German envoys' suggestion that he needed to demonstrate that he could control his own subjects before he could be accepted as an emperor),[68] and demonstrated heightened interest in the borderlands of his kingdom—notably Wales and

1200–1400 (New Haven: Yale University Press, 1995), 193.

[66] Alfred Thomas, *A Blessed Shore: England and Bohemia from Chaucer to Shakespeare* (Ithaca: Cornell University Press, 2007), 7–28.

[67] Ibid., 13.

[68] 'Thomas Walsingham on the Tyranny of King Richard,' in Given-Wilson, *Chronicles of the Revolution*, 70–71.

its marches and Ireland.[69] As more than one commentator has suggested, Richard was driven by imperial fantasies.[70]

Chaucer was not. The ideology of the Roman Empire was set out most influentially by Virgil in the *Aeneid*, which depicts a fateful, agonizing conflict between destiny and emotions, progression and digression, masculine duty and feminine errancy, Rome and North Africa. Pius Aeneas's desertion of Dido for the sake of his imperial destiny was the key foundational myth of empire: the Roman Empire was fated, necessary, inevitable, part of a divine plan; it mattered far more than personal affections. Almost immediately, other writers—particularly Ovid—suggested other ways of reading the story of Aeneas and Dido, challenging Virgil's vision, and by the Middle Ages there was a powerful countertradition that emphasized Aeneas's treachery to Troy and to Dido.[71] But for Dante, Virgil was a revered guide and teacher, his master both politically and poetically, as Dante sought both to promote imperial power and to create a great vernacular epic poem. In *Paradiso* 6, the soul of Emperor Justinian describes the history of the empire, symbolized by the imperial eagle, the 'bird of God,' detailing the imperial journey from Troy to Rome, its defeat of the forces that opposed it, its unfortunate swerve to Constantinople, and its rightful role as defender of the Roman Church and of justice. Later on in the *Paradiso*, the blessed souls in the sixth sphere form a biblical verse from the opening of the Book of Wisdom: *diligite justitiam qui judicatis terram* (love justice, you that are the judges of the earth [18.91–93]). The final 'm' then transforms into the imperial eagle, who criticizes unworthy emperors and exalts righteous ones (18–20). In making his own poetry directly imitate God's book of creation, Dante constructs a divinized form of poetry: as one critic writes, 'Dante circumvents the mediacy of ordinary human creativity and instead imitates God directly.'[72] He depicts his political vision as certain in its claims: Henry VII is seated in the

---

[69] Saul, *Richard II*, 270: 'it is possible that he had in mind the "imperial" notion of a crown possessed of many dependencies.'

[70] Thomas, *Blessed Shore*, 13; Federico, *New Troy*, 36; Saul, *Richard II*, 270; Patricia Clare Ingham, *Sovereign Fantasies: Arthurian Romance and the Making of Britain* (Philadelphia: University of Pennsylvania Press, 2001), 119.

[71] James Simpson, 'The Other Book of Troy: Guido delle Colonne's *Historia destructionis Troiae* in Fourteenth- and Fifteenth-Century England,' *Speculum* 73:2 (1998): 397–423.

[72] Taylor, *Chaucer Reads the Divine Comedy*, 24.

highest ranks of the blessed, although he could not achieve success because Italy was not ready for him. Nonetheless he is depicted as a saviour-figure (30). History has a meaning and a trajectory that will win out in the end, and Dante is a poet of truth.

In sharp contrast, in a series of writings that toy with stories of empire and tyranny, Chaucer suggests that when people believe in one truth, sovereign power, and unchallengeable discourse, a lot of other people tend to get damaged, even killed. Ovid was a key influence on Chaucer here—indeed, some critics argue for Ovid as the most consistently important source for Chaucer across his career. Ovid, like Chaucer, was interested not in the masculine march of single-minded empire but in the 'experiential narrative' and the 'female voice [that could] undo the impersonal solidities of epic, and the assurance of accepted, masculine, imperial ideals.'[73] Both authors were fascinated by the proliferation of perspectives and meanings. Chaucer's anti-imperial texts tend to reveal that the idea of a sovereign voice simply cannot be maintained: there will always be other versions of stories, gossip, speculation, alternative perspectives—what Chaucer calls 'tidings.'

The *House of Fame*, Chaucer's most Dantean text by far, tells the story of the foundation of empire in Book I, in a Virgilian-Ovidian hybrid that overtly challenges the idea of literary or historical truth through blending the two mutually irreconcilable versions of Aeneas's story. Dido and Aeneas's story is told through ekphrasis as the narrator sees their histories painted on the walls of the temple. As Marilyn Desmond has commented, the voyeuristic, masculine tone, indicated through the repeated 'Ther sawgh I,' fades away as the Virgilian material morphs into the Ovidian. The narrator now dwells on Dido's perspective and moves away from the sternly male, march-of-empire narrative.[74] The contrast between Virgil and Ovid, Rome and North Africa, Aeneas's perspective and Dido's,

---

[73] Simpson, 'Chaucer as a European Writer,' 62. For Chaucer and Ovid, see also Kathryn McKinley, 'Gower and Chaucer: Readings of Ovid in Late Medieval England,' in James G. Clark, Frank T. Coulson, and Kathryn L. McKinley (eds.), *Ovid in the Middle Ages* (Cambridge: Cambridge University Press, 2011), 197–230; and Jamie C. Fumo, *The Legacy of Apollo: Antiquity, Authority, and Chaucerian Poetics* (Toronto: University of Toronto Press, 2010); for more context, see Rita Copeland (ed.), *The Oxford History of Classical Reception in English Literature, Volume I: 800–1558* (Oxford: Oxford University Press, 2016).

[74] Desmond, *Reading Dido*, 145.

destiny and emotion, is also enacted through style. The Virgilian section is strongly plot-driven. Aeneas acts because of his 'destinee' (145, 188). His progression is clearly signalled in the narrative: the markers 'First,' 'And aftir,' 'And next,' 'And I saugh next' (151, 157, 162, 174), and then the repeated 'Ther sawgh I' (193, 198, 209, 219, 221), all move the story on as Chaucer details the events of the flight from Troy. As he segues into the description of Aeneas's affair with and desertion of Dido, these markers of progress disappear. Instead, the narrative circles—the narrator 'responds emotionally' to the part of the story that is about how empire was nearly derailed by emotion.[75] The description of the beginning of their affair is hedged with multiple evasions and indications of brevity and discomfort: 'shortly of this thyng to pace,' 'shortly for to tellen,' 'What shulde I speke more queynte,' 'Hyt were a long proces to telle' (239–52). After a swerve back to 'Ther sawgh I grave' (253), the narrator returns to the topic of how their love began, detailing it again in lines 256–66. We then move into a long 'digression,' punctuated by 'Allas!,' by proverbs, by Dido's long lament, and eventually by an extensive list of other treacherous men. The betrayal of Dido thus occupies far more narrative time than the story of the fall of Troy and Aeneas's journey to Carthage, reminding us that Aeneas can be viewed in more than one way. The narrator then briefly returns us to the Virgilian story, and we also return to the repeated 'Thoo sawgh I' (433) and, interestingly, to a specific nod to Dante (450). Roman Empire, Virgil, and Dante are strongly associated with a belief in narrative progression, fixity, and truth, while the counterpoint of Dido's story itself challenges that notion of truth. Chaucer, as he would do throughout his poetic career, dwells on the digression, the diversion, revelling in leaving the expected narrative path. The *Canterbury Tales* is not about people getting to Canterbury; it is about them failing to get there and being distracted by what happens on the way.[76] His texts typically fail to end; he refuses to close them. In his comically Ovidian-Virgilian bastardisation of the Aeneas story, Chaucer signals his discomfort with Dantean grandiose ideas about empire and poetic truth. And just after the end of the Aeneas-Dido story, Chaucer's avatar finds himself, fascinatingly, in a barren field that

[75] Ibid., 145.
[76] See chapter 19 in this study.

he compares to the 'desert of Lybye' (488)—home of Dido.[77] Having placed himself in this location that is famous as the location that nearly derailed the empire, that distracted Aeneas from his destiny, that stands for women, other stories, emotion, and digression—but that is, for this narrator, empty of discursive possibility—Chaucer then introduces, hilariously, intriguingly, his own Dantean eagle.[78]

This eagle combines aspects of several figures from the *Divine Comedy*: Virgil as the guide, the eagle of *Purgatorio* 9 that carries Dante, and the imperial eagle of *Paradiso*. Chaucer, however, is not guided through the afterlife, nor is he wisely instructed, nor does he receive divine revelation. The eagle does not prove to be a figure of heavenly justice and rule who can transform the poet's understanding. On the contrary, the eagle is a comic figure who, far from teaching Geffrey about imperial and divine truths, shows him things he already knows, jibes at him for being fat, bores him, and lectures him. The poem presents a comprehensive denunciation of the vagaries of fame and the reputation of the great classical poets. It also depicts, through Fame, a monstrous picture of an arbitrary, absolutist ruler with total control over her subjects. In contrast to the hegemonic voice of Fame, who can make and destroy reputations at will, and in contrast to a Dantean sense of truth and destiny, Chaucer presents us with *tidings*.

'Tidings' is the key word of the *House of Fame*. Indeed, it sums up Chaucer's poetics as a whole. The word occurs twenty-two times in this poem. The poem is about the search for tidings: Geffrey has writer's block, he 'hast no tydynges' (644), 'no tydynge cometh to thee' (648). He seeks 'Somme newe tydynges for to lere' (1886), but the classical stories of Fame's House are 'no suche tydynges' (1894). The House of Rumour, however, is 'fild ful of tydynges' (1957); it is a place 'Where thou maist most tidynges here' (2025). He sees the movement of 'every tydyng fro mouth to mouth' (2076) and that 'lesinges' are 'Entremedled with tydynges' (2123–24). Tidings, then, are unclassified stories, the raw material of literature. They are spoken, they change, they are 'fals and soth' combined

[77] In the Legend of Dido, in the *Legend of Good Women*, Chaucer mentions that she ruled over Libya (959).

[78] See Gillespie, 'Authorship,' 137–54.

(2108).[79] For Chaucer, these varied, unreliable stories are the origins of poetry. This is a very different vision of poetic inspiration from Dante's depiction of divine inspiration and destiny. Chaucer instead gives us an image of chaotic unreliability and randomness.

Although this word is so central to the *House of Fame*, Chaucer does not use it much elsewhere. The only other text in which it occurs more than twice is another text about the Roman Empire: the 'Man of Law's Tale,' which uses the word four times.[80] This is another text that sets Rome against North Africa, and it seems to promote a vision of Christian imperial destiny.[81] Constance, who can be seen as the ship of the church and the ship of empire, is protected by God and returns, inevitably, to Rome, having brought Britain into the Christian and imperial fold. But the tale repeatedly foregrounds the problems of seeking to promote one dominant narrative. As Carolyn Dinshaw has discussed, while the Man of Law declares his unwillingness to tell a story about incest, the Constance story has its roots in a story about a princess's refusal to marry her father, and the ghost of this story lurks underneath the sanitized surface.[82] In the 'Prologue' to the tale, the Man of Law outrageously twists another source—*De Miseria Humanae Conditionis*—inverting its moral.[83] And the tale begins not with the emperor, as do its immediate sources, but with tidings themselves.[84] It is tidings—the gossip and hearsay of merchants— that catalyse the plot as the traders tell the Sultan what they have heard about the beauty of Constance. And the tale turns out to be full of counterstories: both the counterfeit letters of Donegild (746) and the evasions of Constance herself.[85] While the Man of Law presents this as a story of glorious imperial conquest, the material itself shows us Rome and Syria coexisting with happy trading relationships before the business of conver-

---

[79] See also *House of Fame*, 1027, 1888, 1907, 1955, 1983, 2010, 2045, 2066, 2072, 2111, and 2134.

[80] 'Man of Law's Tale,' 129, 181, 726–27.

[81] Destiny and fate are foregrounded in the 'Man of Law's Tale,' 190–96 and 302.

[82] Dinshaw, *Chaucer's Sexual Poetics*, 95, 101–5.

[83] This is discussed in detail in chapter 18.

[84] Wallace, *Chaucerian Polity*, 184–86.

[85] She says she has lost her memory when she arrives in Northumberland (526–27); when she returns to Rome she does not tell her aunt her true identity (972–82); she sends her son to Alla anonymously (1009–15).

sion and cultural colonialism (the imposition of a sovereign voice) leads to mass murder on both sides.

Chaucer tends to use the word 'tiding' in texts that engage with the conflict between a sovereign voice—either imperial or tyrannical—and freer forms of discourse. Sometimes the tidings directly oppose the voice of hegemony; sometimes they refer explicitly to lies peddled by the sovereign ruler, reminding us that his voice is not truthful. As well as occurring frequently in the *House of Fame* and several times in the 'Man of Law's Tale,' 'tiding' occurs twice in the 'Clerk's Tale,' once in the 'Manciple's Tale,' and twice in the *Legend of Good Women*, all texts that are very clearly about tyranny and that associate that tyranny explicitly with the desire to control what people say and to silence protest.[86] The 'Clerk's Tale,' with its Lombard setting, depicts a monstrous ruler who wants his wife to submit wholly to his will, even when he commits the worst possible atrocities. Her refusal to speak against him, even when she believes he is slaughtering their children, stages a horrifying scene of tyranny in action. Chaucer makes it clear to us, however, that tyranny cannot extend into the soul: Griselda only 'semed' (500) to accept Walter's judgements, and her warning to him not to torture another wife (1038), along with her own emotional collapse at the end of the tale (1079–85), demonstrates that her mind remains independent of his. Petrarch's love for the Griselda story and his explicitly allegorical understanding of it as a story about the soul and God, tropes the tyrannical ruler as analogous with the divine, enjoying the kind of special imperial status that he and Dante claimed for the emperors, in sharp contrast to Boccaccio and Chaucer's narrators' distaste for Walter's behaviour.[87]

The 'Manciple's Tale,' with its final exhortation to 'be noon auctour newe / Of tidynges, wheither they been false or trewe' (359–60), emphasizes that a tyrant cares not whether you speak the truth. Earlier in the tale, Phoebus wants to hear only the songs that he has taught his bird; the idea of a multiplication of stories horrifies him, as it would horrify Walter.[88]

---

[86] The word also occurs twice in *Troilus and Criseyde*, both times referring to news carried by Pandarus (Book II, 951, 1113), and three times in the (possibly) Chaucerian translation of the *Romance of the Rose* (Fragment B, 2921, Fragment C, 7478 and 6038).

[87] See Wallace's discussion of the tale in *Chaucerian Polity*, 277–93.

[88] Fradenburg, 'Manciple's Servant Tongue,' 108–10.

Only in Chaucer's version of this much-told story does the god decide that the bird was lying, and that his wife was innocent all along, in a breathtaking rewriting of history. Truth becomes exactly what Phoebus decides it is. His destruction of both his own harp and his crow's voice represents a destruction of the instruments of making, of representation. Similarly, in the Prologue to the *Legend of Good Women*, we see a tyrant (again explicitly associated with Lombardy and with divinity) who is indeed appalled by the multiplication of stories and who accuses Chaucer of writing stories that work against the tyrant's agenda. The god and Alceste's solution is to control the poet's voice and to make his work conform to their wishes.[89] Chaucer goes on to make a strong statement about the impossibility of writing to order and about the tyrant's ultimate inability to control discourse: his legends escape their prescribed moral, their sources will not be suppressed, their puns lead us in multiple directions.[90] Everywhere Chaucer shows us—exuberantly, defiantly—that tidings cannot be made to serve a monolithic, imperial narrative.

Across Chaucer's work, the greatest political and poetic problem is an insistence on a singular idea of truth. The idea of the sovereign, unchallengeable voice is characteristically associated with imperial power. Everywhere he went in Milan and Pavia, Chaucer saw the Visconti emblem adorning tombs, statues, ceilings, walls, and pottery. The emblem (known as the biscione) depicts a dragon-like serpent swallowing a victim whole, feet first (plate 13). The Visconti celebrated their violence and their dominance, and represented themselves as a terrifying mouth, devouring opponents, silencing them through their own insatiable greed and aggression. Endlessly replicated, the image calls attention to the Visconti's delight in their own brutality and their absolute sovereignty. Chaucer experienced the atmosphere of the Visconti court, and did not want to see it imitated at home. As we so often see in Chaucer's writings, his social experience and his reading informed his views in symbiosis—and not only because he likely encountered much of the literature that influenced him while he was travelling on political missions. When he overtly attacks Lombard rule, he is drawing on his own firsthand knowledge of Bernabò Visconti. When

---

[89] See chapter 14.
[90] See Delany, *Naked Text*, 139–50.

he parodies the *Divine Comedy*, he is responding to Dante's grandiose poetics. But poetics and politics are always bound up together. We see this very clearly in a text such as the *Legend of Good Women* or the 'Manciple's Tale,' both of which deal with a ruler's attempt to control the voice of a poet-figure, or in the 'Clerk's Tale,' in which Chaucer reworks Petrarch's literary writings and his political agenda. In the *House of Fame* too, Chaucer's detailed response to Dante is simultaneously a response to Dante's ideas about what poetry could do and a response to Dante's vision of world history and empire. Throughout Chaucer's life, he witnessed European rulers attempting to gain more power and status. This was, of course, an acute problem in England, and led ultimately to the deposition of Richard II. Chaucer's retellings of the story of Aeneas or his meditations on Fame are very far from being abstract comments about Virgilian poetics. These are stories with direct relevance to Chaucer's political world, a world in which a belief in imperial destiny could destroy both speech and lives.

CHAPTER 14

﹥━┤━◆﹥━●━﹤◆﹥━┤━﹤

Garden

O, what pity is it
That he had not so trimm'd and dress'd his land
As we this garden!

—*William Shakespeare*, Richard II

Gardens, in late-medieval poetry and architecture alike, were enclosed, contained, even claustrophobic spaces. They were locations of surveillance and eavesdropping, sites of aristocratic emotion and oppression.[1] Associated with Eden and temptation, with the religious-erotic garden of the Song of Songs, and with the allegory of the *Roman de la Rose*, gardens were female spaces.[2] Metaphorically, they represented the female body itself;[3] socially, they were associated with ludic, female-based or mixed-sex play.[4] They could be spaces of female segregation, but women could also take charge, turning the garden into a 'creative female preserve.'[5] In the poems

[1] Gardens often contained 'gloriettes' (pavilions at the centre) or other observation posts. See John Harvey, *Mediaeval Gardens* (London: Batsford, 1981), 103–6. Poems, including Machaut's *La Fontaine Amoureuse* and Chaucer's *Book of the Duchess*, stage scenes in gardens, in which an aristocrat's personal lament is overheard by the poet.

[2] See, for instance, Laura Howes, *Chaucer's Gardens and the Language of Convention* (Gainesville: University Press of Florida, 1997), esp. 100–101.

[3] For medieval interpretation of the garden of the Song of Songs as Mary's body, see Ann Astell, *The Song of Songs in the Middle Ages* (Ithaca: Cornell University Press, 1995); and Brian E. Daley, 'The Closed Garden and Sealed Fountain: Song of Songs 4.12 in the Late Medieval Iconography of Mary,' in Elizabeth MacDougall (ed.), *Medieval Gardens* (Washington, DC: Dumbarton Oaks, 1986), 263–67.

[4] See discussion of the flower and the leaf below.

[5] Roberta Gilchrist, *Gender and Archaeology: Contesting the Past* (London: Routledge, 1999), x; see also 109–45.

of Machaut and his heirs, the garden is the space of courtly subjectivity and subjection, where the individual is constrained and yet also constituted. The garden is usually the place where poets sleep and dreams begin, and where debates and parliaments take place.[6] It was emphatically not rural: as a cultivated and walled space, it had more affinity with the cage than with the wilderness. Cities, indeed, were full of gardens.[7] Walled gardens, and especially courtyard gardens within quadrangles of buildings, were spaces poised between inside and outside. These gardens were constituted by their connection with buildings. If one looks up from an enclosed quadrangle, the sky is visible but framed by man-made construction; the garden needs its edges to define what it is (plate 15).

Three of Chaucer's dream poems are set mainly in gardens; he translated the *Roman de la Rose*, the key garden poem of the Middle Ages; there are crucial garden scenes in *Troilus and Criseyde*; and several of the *Canterbury Tales* draw on the Song of Songs and Genesis to depict gardens that symbolize sexual temptation—as we see in the 'Franklin's,' 'Shipman's,' and 'Merchant's' Tales. In the English, and possibly Chaucerian, *Romaunt of the Rose*, the lover, having been chased away from the garden by Daunger, is then welcomed in by Bel Acueil, who shows him 'the estres of the swote place' (the interior/inner rooms of the sweet place [3626]).[8] The garden here represents the female body, and indeed the subsequent lines dwell on an erotic description of the swelling rose as the lover spies on her aroused state (3627–48), encouraged by Bel Acueil's loathing of chastity (3667–70).[9] In the opening of Book II of *Troilus and Criseyde*, the garden

---

[6] Poets fall asleep in gardens in, for instance, Machaut's *Fontaine Amoureuse*, *Pearl*, the *Legend of Good Women*, and the *Divine Comedy*. Debates and parliaments take place in gardens in, for instance, *The Owl and the Nightingale*, *The Parliament of Fowls*, and *The Book of Cupide*.

[7] See Teresa McLean, *Medieval English Gardens* (London: Collins, 1981), 24, 42, 46, 64, 66–71; and Caroline M. Barron, 'Centres of Conspicuous Consumption: The Aristocratic Town House in London, 1200–1550,' *London Journal* 20:1 (1995): 12.

[8] Chaucer tells us in the Prologue to the *Legend of Good Women* that he translated the *Roman de la Rose*; Deschamps also comments on the translation. However, there is critical debate about how much of the extant *Romaunt of the Rose* is in fact Chaucer's translation. Most critics agree that Fragments B and C are not by Chaucer, and that Fragment A may represent all or part of his translation. For further discussion, see *The Romaunt of the Rose*, ed. Dahlberg, 3–23. See also Philip Knox, 'The Romance of the Rose in Fourteenth-Century England' (unpublished DPhil thesis, University of Oxford, 2015), 219–46.

[9] Chaucer also uses the word 'estris' in the Legend of Lucrece: when Colatyn takes Tarquin to his house, unwittingly giving Tarquin the means to access Colatyn's own wife's body later in the tale, we

is *socially* a feminine space, a space in which Criseyde and her ladies read, laugh, and talk about love, until a masculine entry disrupts their play.[10] In the 'Knight's Tale,' the garden is a place where women are watched by men. After writing the *House of Fame* and *Troilus*, and just before he embarked on the 'General Prologue,' Chaucer wrote a poem with an intense concentration on the garden: the F-Prologue to the *Legend of Good Women*. This fascinating poem moves from an actual garden to a dream garden, engaging closely with both the marguerite and the flower and leaf traditions.[11] It self-consciously positions itself in relation to Machaut, Boccaccio, and Dante, among others, and comments fairly directly, if ambiguously, on contemporary politics, although it seems to have been written at an extraordinarily fraught political moment: 1386–87. In both its politics and its poetics, it is a startling and confusing poem, and understanding the meanings of the garden is centrally important to interpreting the poem.

Like all of Chaucer's poems, the F-Prologue is a poem that is about poetry (among other things). Indeed, one of the most important uses of the garden image in late fourteenth-century poetry is as a metaphor of poetic making. Throughout his *balade* to Chaucer, almost certainly written in the mid-1380s and brought over to Chaucer by Lewis Clifford by 1386, Deschamps riffs on the idea of Chaucer as a gardener.[12] The poem depicts Chaucer as a prolific and accomplished writer and translator, praising him extravagantly and playfully, in a teasing mode associated with competitive poetic production.[13] Deschamps singles Chaucer out for attention, and in initiating an exchange of poems, he marks his interest in Chaucer's work. At the same time, however, Deschamps's imagining of himself as a nettle in Chaucer's garden is rather like Chaucer's comic

---

are told, 'The husbonde knew the estris wel and fyn' (1715); again the estris symbolizes the female body, and men are spying on the woman within. In this text, the ultimate result of this is a brutal rape.

[10] Pandarus pretends that he and Troilus spent time in the garden, but the scene really took place in a room (Book II, 505–53).

[11] On the marguerite tradition, see James I. Wimsatt, *The Marguerite Poetry of Guillaume de Machaut* (Chapel Hill: University of North Carolina Press, 1970). On the flower and the leaf, see Joyce Coleman, 'The Flower, the Leaf, and Philippa of Lancaster,' in Carolyn P. Collette (ed.), '*The Legend of Good Women*': *Context and Reception* (Cambridge: D. S. Brewer, 2006), 33–58.

[12] The balade is available in Wimsatt, *Chaucer and the Poems of 'Ch,'* 81–82.

[13] For a recent discussion, see Butterfield, *The Familiar Enemy*, 143–51.

depiction of himself as able only to tell the story of Sir Thopas: the great poet constructs himself as incapable, and the joke rests on our knowledge of his actual skill. The idea of Deschamps, in France, dying of thirst unless he gets a drink from the English poet is arch in a late-medieval context in which the richness of the French poetic tradition was unrivalled amongst vernacular poetry. Chaucer is described hyperbolically as a God of Love, in sole charge of English poetry—but also as a maker who is wholly reliant on receiving plants from French nurseries, from poets who write for posterity, rather than simply mediating the works of others (as Chaucer is said to do). The image of the garden structures the whole poem. In the first verse, Chaucer is praised for having sown flowers and the rose tree in England (8); in the second, Deschamps asserts that Chaucer has for a long time ('a ja longtemps' [19]) been constructing ('edifias' [19]) an orchard or garden ('un vergier' [17]). For this, he has requested plants from others—and the refrain of the balade is 'grant translateur, noble Geffroy Chaucer.' In the third stanza, Deschamps refers to the fountain of Helicon as entirely controlled by Chaucer (21), and promises to send his own plants to the English poet (27). The closing envoy asserts that Deschamps would be only a nettle in Chaucer's 'jardin' (32) in comparison with his own plants.

Chaucer himself often uses the trope of planting and reaping in an agricultural context as an image of poetic making: the *Parliament of Fowls* compares the 'newe corn' that comes from 'olde feldes' with the 'newe science' that comes from 'olde bokes' (22–25). Planting, like reading, is a generative activity, and each new text is a direct descendent of the texts that precede it. Similarly, in the F-Prologue, Chaucer bemoans his inability to praise the flower adequately. He complains that other lover-poets have already 'Of makyng ropen, and lad awey the corn' (reaped the fruit of poetic makyng, and taken away the corn). He, then, is stumbling in their wake, picking up what they have left behind: 'glenyng here and there,' delighted if he can find 'an ere [of corn]' that they have neglected (74–76). The idea of poet as gardener or farmer associates poets with the cultivation of nature. It also tends to place poets in a relationship of collaboration or competition with others. In Deschamps's poem, the gardener-poet transplants seedlings across the channel and showcases others' plants in his own garden. And his poem is itself in conversation with another poet, related to the tradition of *puys* and of more vitriolic poetic exchanges.[14] Chaucer's use of the gleaning image is explicitly connected not only to poetic competition but also to competition amongst court factions in the playful rivalry between the flower and the leaf. The lover-poets that 'kan make of sentement' and who sing 'fresshe songes,' are 'with the leef or with the flour' (68–79). The Chaucer-figure himself then dwells on the flower— the daisy—in loving and obsessive detail, before asserting that he, in fact, is retained by neither party, and doesn't favour the 'flour agayn the leef,' any more than he favours 'the corn agayn the sheef' (189–90). Indeed, he doesn't even know 'who serveth leef ne who the flour' (193). This repeated foregrounding of the flower and the leaf locates the poem in a courtly scene of play, in a context of competition, and in a poetic milieu, specifically indeed in the world of Deschamps. Conveniently for Chaucer, Deschamps's poem in praise of the flower was written for the daughter of John of Gaunt, so Chaucer's poetic and sociopolitical interests coincide.

Around 1384 or 1385, when Philippa of Lancaster was being touted as a possible bride for Charles VI of France, Deschamps wrote a balade in praise of her beauty, associating her with the flower. The key stanza is as follows, in English translation:

> And who would wish to have knowledge
> Of the very sweet name that I know from hearsay
> And of the country where she dwells,
> May look in the isle of Albion, hidden away.
> In Lancaster you will find her, I trust,
> Trace the letters P H and E L I P P E
> Assemble them all; these eight letters construe
> You will have the name of the worthy flower
> Who has slender body, beautiful eyes, and sweet face.
> Judging rightly, I hold with the flower.[15]

The poem could have come to Chaucer along with the balade addressed to him, in the bundle conveyed by Lewis Clifford—who was himself

---

[14] Ibid., 234–38.
[15] Coleman prints the original and translation in 'The Flower, the Leaf, and Philippa of Lancaster,' 57–58.

certainly a friend of Chaucer's, a Lancastrian, and very likely godfather to little Lewis Chaucer.[16] Or it might have been sent to Philippa, who then either directly or indirectly transmitted it to Chaucer (who was uncle to her half-brothers and sister).[17] In the summer of 1386, Philippa left for the Iberian peninsula with her father and his retinue—including Thomas Chaucer—and she was married to the king of Portugal in the following year, where she became a literary patron.[18] The Deschamps poem seems to have introduced the flower and the leaf into English court society and literature. Gower also refers to it:

> Some of the lef, some of the flour,
> And some of the grete Perles were;
> The newe guise of Beawme [Bohemia] there.[19]

Both Chaucer in the F-Prologue and Gower here in the *Confessio* cluster together the flower and the leaf, the marguerite (pearl/daisy) tradition, and Queen Anne/Bohemia. The poems are thus carefully located in the contemporary court, albeit in a highly stylized and abstracted version of that court. The game of the flower and the leaf involved choosing sides and debating and defending certain values. Most commonly the flower and the leaf was a gender competition, with the flower associated with women and the leaf with men.[20] It thus was part of a bigger poetic culture that found expression in, for instance, the *demandes d'amour* of Machaut's poems.[21] The *Jugement du Roi de Behaigne* is structured around a question: does

---

[16] In his poem to Chaucer, Deschamps says that he is sending him a bundle of poems 'par Clifford' (29). He also mentions 'amoureux Cliffort,' in a balade addressed to the Seneschal d'Eu. See G. L. Kittredge, 'Chaucer and Some of His Friends,' *Modern Philology* 1:1 (1903): 7; and John Livingston Lowes, 'The Prologue to the *Legend of Good Women* Considered in Its Chronological Relations,' *PMLA* 20:4 (1905): 760–66. See the *ODNB* for information about Clifford's life. I discuss Clifford in more detail in chapter 15.

[17] Coleman, 'The Flower, the Leaf, and Philippa of Lancaster,' 55.

[18] Ibid., 34, 37.

[19] John Gower, *Confessio Amantis*, book 8, 2468–70, in *The Complete Works of John Gower: Vol. 3, The English Works*, ed. G. C. Macaulay (Oxford: Clarendon Press, 1902). See discussion in Thomas, *A Blessed Shore*, 27–28.

[20] See Florence Percival, *Chaucer's Legendary Good Women* (Cambridge: Cambridge University Press, 1998), 315.

[21] On the popularity of the *demande d'amour*, see McDonald, 'Games Medieval Women Play,' in Collette, 'The Legend of Good Women,' 190–92; and Betsy McCormick, 'Remembering the Game: Debating the *Legend*'s Women,' in ibid., 113.

the bereaved woman or betrayed man suffer more? (The 'sequel,' the *Juge-ment du Roi de Navare*, then functions as a trial of the poet, accused of misogyny for having sided with the man in the previous poem; it is thus a close model for the F-Prologue, which features the poet on trial for a simi-lar 'crime.')[22] The flower and the leaf was directly echoed in the holly and the ivy, where the hard, prickly holly represented the male, the malleable ivy the female. Sometimes, the debate was less explicitly gendered: the flower could represent idle, pleasure-seeking sexual love, the leaf chaste, faithful, honourable love.[23] There are analogues with other modes of struc-turing debate: John Clanvowe's *Book of Cupide* pits the cuckoo (male, truth-telling, down to earth) against the nightingale (female figure of courtliness and *fin amor*).[24] Clanvowe quotes the 'Knight's Tale' in this poem and also mentions the queen; he too is personally connected with Chaucer and with Lewis Clifford.[25]

One context for the F-Prologue, then, is a world of courtly, poetic play-fulness, a world that took the garden not only as its setting but as its cen-tral image, with the flower and the leaf. This was not a world imagined and maintained by male poets in a literary realm of their own. Richard's court was noted—indeed notorious—for its inclusion of women.[26] His and Anne's households overlapped a great deal; he was criticized for hav-ing too many women at court; chroniclers complained that his knights were lovers not warriors; and he vastly expanded the Sorority of the

[22] It also should be seen in the context of the debate about the *Roman de la Rose* more generally; in the very early fifteenth century, the texts relating to this debate multiplied hugely, in the so-called *querelle des femmes*. See, for instance, David F. Hult, 'The *Roman de la Rose*, Christine de Pizan, and the *querelle des femmes*,' in Wallace and Dinshaw, *Cambridge Companion to Medieval Women's Writ-ing*, 184–94. James Simpson points out that Chaucer also here writes his biography in Ovidian terms: medieval commentary tradition imagined Ovid as banished by Augustus because of his licentious poetry. 'Chaucer as a European Writer,' 77.

[23] Percival, *Chaucer's Legendary Good Women*, 316.

[24] Scattergood (ed.), *Works of Sir John Clanvowe*; Patterson, 'Court Politics and the Invention of Literature,' 7–41.

[25] He was one of the witnesses of Chaucer's release from further actions by Cecily Champaigne; Crow and Olson, *Chaucer Life-Records*, 343. Clifford and Clanvowe were fellow chamber knights and were both part of the loose group later termed the Lollard knights. See McFarlane, *Lancastrian Kings and Lollard Knights*, 182–85.

[26] See PROME, Membrane 5, no. 14, 7:314 (January 1397); see also Haxey's petition, discussed in chapter 19.

Garter (from two to twenty-two members).[27] In the middle of the 1380s there were two major sex scandals at court. Elizabeth of Lancaster, Philippa's younger sister, had been formally betrothed to John Hastings, heir to the earl of Pembroke and several years her junior. In 1385, she was about twenty-one, and he was thirteen. She embarked on an affair with Sir John Holland (son of Joan of Kent and therefore older half-brother to Richard II) and became pregnant before the summer of 1386. They were hastily married and joined the rest of the Iberian party on their voyage.[28] At the same time, Robert de Vere, now at the height of his influence as Richard's intimate friend, was involved in an affair with one of the queen's ladies, Agnes Lancrona. De Vere was already married to Philippa de Courcy, whose mother was Isabella, daughter of Edward III and thus sister to John of Gaunt and to Thomas of Woodstock, duke of Gloucester—whose antagonism towards Richard and his friends was growing. In 1387, when his position had become precarious indeed after the Wonderful Parliament, de Vere offered a serious insult not only to his wife but also to her uncles when he repudiated her and began lobbying for a divorce; meanwhile, he married Agnes, possibly by force.[29] The years 1385–87—in which the court was presided over by a king and queen who were in their late teens, both turning twenty during this time—were years of extravagance, sexual licence, and fashionable play. Poetic and riddling interludes formed part of the cultural milieu. In fifteenth-century manuscripts, there are two examples of the *Legend of Good Women* being bound with texts that demonstrate medieval erotic play. One of these was *Ragman Roll*, the other the *Chaunce of Dice*. *Ragman Roll* was addressed to an all-female

[27] See Nicola McDonald, 'Chaucer's *Legend of Good Women*, Ladies at Court, and the Female Reader,' *Chaucer Review* 35:1 (2000): 22–42; and James L. Gillespie, 'Ladies of the Fraternity of Saint George and of the Society of the Garter,' *Albion* 17:3 (1985): 259–78.

[28] The *Westminster Chronicle* describes the affair: '[Elizabeth] had been betrothed to the earl of Pembroke a child of tender age, before, having herself come to womanhood, she was introduced into the royal court to study the behaviour and customs of courtly society. Here, Sir John Holland, the present king's uterine brother, fell violently in love with her at first sight and pursued his wooing night and day until at last his constantly renewed campaign of enticement led to such folly that by the time her father the duke left for the coast she was with child. With the duke's approval, Holland made haste to marry her before the baby should be born, and then accompanied his father-in-law to Spain' (192–93).

[29] Ibid., 188–91; Walsingham, *Historia Anglicana*, 2:160–61.

audience, and involved each woman receiving a 'character,' some of which are explicitly sexually licentious: for instance, one woman rewards yeomen and grooms who thrust hard. The *Ragman Roll* is spoken by King Ragman Holly, a phallic figure associated with the gender-play of the holly and the ivy. The *Chaunce of Dice* is addressed to a mixed-sex audience and involves each person receiving a 'fortune,' some of which are obscene. The text is also packed with references to Chaucer: 'Creseyde is here in worde bothes thought and dede,' or 'there Jason falseth oon ye falsen twoo' (quoting the *Legend of Good Women*).[30] While these manuscripts are fifteenth-century compilations, the *Ragman Roll* exists in thirteenth-century versions, and fifteenth-century players and readers were following in earlier traditions. As Nicola McDonald writes, these games and the *Legend* represent 'erotic social exchange that animated fashionable, late medieval circles and their fifteenth-century imitators.' Quoting a filthy riddle, McDonald suggests that Anne of Bohemia did indeed know 'long before we did, the difference between a piglet and a penis.'[31]

The F-Prologue, with its compliment to Anne, its explicit investment in the flower and the leaf, and its staging of a courtly scene, positions itself as a court interlude for a knowing, sophisticated audience. Critics have convincingly argued that this first version of the F-Prologue was written for a coterie audience, for performance, and for an audience dominated by courtly women. The later G-Prologue, written after Anne's death, shifts its emphasis to appeal to a more general audience.[32] In terms of its encoded or aspirational audience, the F-Prologue has closer affinities to the much earlier *Book of the Duchess* than to Chaucer's other texts. While *Troilus* addresses Gower and Strode, and the *Parliament of Fowls* and the *House of Fame* are interested in demotic voices, insurgency, and socially mixed, disruptive scenes, the *Book of the Duchess* and the F-Prologue are both set in courtly gardens that clearly pay homage to Machaut's courtly poems. Both focus attention on an idealized courtly woman;

---

[30] McDonald, 'Games Medieval Women Play'; Percival, *Chaucer's Legendary Good Women*, 316–21.

[31] McDonald, 'Games Medieval Women Play,' 177, 197.

[32] William A. Quinn, 'The *Legend of Good Women*: Performance, Performativity, and Presentation,' in Collette, 'The Legend of Good Women,' 1–32; Percival, *Chaucer's Legendary Good Women*, 8–10, 322–23; McDonald, 'Chaucer's *Legend of Good Women*.'

both pay explicit homage to contemporary women—Blanche and Anne. Chaucer is flirting with court poetry anew—at a time when politically the court was in trouble.

The leisured, static world of courtly self-indulgence and reassuring sameness is appropriately represented by the enclosed garden, the *locus amoenus*, the special place where mundane life does not exist. In the F-Prologue, Chaucer points to the artificiality of such idealization, when he wishes to dwell in the garden in an eternal May, suspending normal human needs for food and sleep (175–77), while reminding us that in fact the seasons do change, death intrudes onto new life (125–37)—that leitmotif of the poetry of Chaucer and his contemporaries. But for the space of the poem, time is suspended in the dazzlingly beautiful garden, where people are able to spend hours contemplating a daisy. The cult of the garden came to England via the Islamic world. Muslims in Spain built extensive and elaborate pleasure gardens, with aqueducts and rare plants often centred on water features.[33] Muslims also took their garden fashions to Sicily, where the Normans learned how to develop these beautiful, stylized spaces. The Persian word *pairidaeza*, meaning 'enclosure,' referred to sculpted parks with pools and trees; the word then evolved into the English 'paradise,' which was used for shaded, porticoed gardens adjoining Byzantine basilicas and then churches and monasteries all over Europe. Other features of English gardens also came from the Islamic world via the Iberian peninsula: the 'gloriette,' for instance, a pavilion at the centre of a garden, was architecturally of Moorish design, and the word derived from Spanish. There were gloriettes at palaces, including Woodstock and Corfe Castle, the latter of which was rebuilt for Richard II in 1377–78.[34] Stylized enclosed gardens with water features, follies, and carefully chosen and designed paths, plants, and recesses became important parts of royal palaces, and symbolically central features of courtly poems.[35] In the late Middle Ages, court gardens often appear in the records, both as scenes of

---

[33] Harvey, *Mediaeval Gardens*, 38. McLean, *Medieval English Gardens*, 16–18.

[34] Harvey, *Mediaeval Gardens*, 103–6.

[35] Creighton writes about the reciprocal relationship between literary and real gardens. See Oliver H. Creighton, *Designs upon the Land: Elite Landscapes of the Middle Ages* (Woodbridge: Boydell, 2009), 1–4.

political encounter—Richard II met the Lords Appellant in the Tower garden vineyard in 1387, Froissart recounts being with Sturry in the garden at Eltham in 1395—and for more mundane reasons (for instance, records demonstrate a second walled garden was made at Eltham in 1388–89 for Richard and Anne to dine in during the summer).[36] They also dominate poetry: the *Roman de la Rose*, *Pearl*, *La Remede de Fortune*, *La Fontaine Amoureuse*, the *Book of the Duchess*, the *Parliament of Fowls*, and the Prologue to the *Legend of Good Women* are all texts in which the garden is central to the poem's meaning.

The garden functions in these poems like a room: in the Chaucerian mid-fifteenth-century *Floure and the Leafe*, the 'herber' (pleasure garden or arbor, 49) has a 'roofe,' and is shaped 'as a pretty parlour,' with a hedge comparable to 'a castel wall' (64–66).[37] Garden rooms are idealized rooms with more opportunities for play: the garden's partial openness and fundamental connection with nature and fertility make it symbolically different from an inside room. There were elaborate gardens in Richard's palaces, including Woodstock, Eltham, Sheen, Kennington, and the Tower. Chaucer also had opportunities to see Iberian and Italian gardens: the Visconti planted one of the first private gardens in Italy. In Olite (in Navarre), Charles the Bad's son later built famous gardens, following in the Iberian tradition of elaborate gardens.[38] The small, paved quadrangles that still survive—surrounded by cloisters, overlooked by galleries, and planted with mulberry or olive trees—give an excellent imaginative parallel for Criseyde's and Deiphoebus's gardens in *Troilus and Criseyde*. These are social spaces of partial privacy rather than places of liberty. The garden tended to be the place furthest away from the public street within a household; it was therefore the 'deepest space' in the complex, and one had to cross multiple thresholds to get there from the public entrance to the house.[39] By providing ways for women to be outside without leaving the

---

[36] See Knighton, *Knighton's Chronicle*, 424–27; Froissart, *Oeuvres*, 15:167; Colvin et al., *History of the King's Works*, 1:934.

[37] 'The Floure and the Leafe,' in Derek Pearsall (ed.), *The Floure and the Leafe, The Assembly of Ladies, The Isle of Ladies* (Kalamazoo, MI: TEAMS Middle English Texts, 1990), 4–27, available online at http://d.lib.rochester.edu/teams/text/pearsall-floure-and-the-leafe.

[38] See Harvey, *Mediaeval Gardens*, 51, 45.

[39] John Schofield, 'Social Perceptions of Space in Medieval and Tudor London Houses,' in Martin Locock (ed.), *Meaningful Architecture: Social Interpretations of Buildings* (Aldershot: Ashgate, 1994), 203.

palace buildings, these gardens work to constrain female movement, but with a light touch.[40] When Criseyde is in the garden, she is with a group, and she can easily be overheard and then interrupted by a male presence. Troilus does not actually go to the garden, but when Pandarus wants to tell a story about Troilus, he makes up a garden setting (Book II, 505–53), deciding that this will sound better to Criseyde than the truth—that he was in his bedroom. Pandarus, like a medieval poet, uses the garden as his setting and, like the poet of the *Fontaine Amoureuse* or the *Book of the Duchess*, imagines himself overhearing Troilus and offering help. The idea of the garden as a place of aristocratic sexual longing and despair, and as a place of eavesdropping and devoted friendship, was so ingrained in the literary imagination that Chaucer shows his own literary character deploying these conventions to fictionalise Troilus's experience. While men can temporarily be alone in the garden, women usually go to gardens in groups: this is the experience of the ladies of the F-Prologue and of Criseyde and her women in *Troilus*.

The literary and stylized elements of the garden, then, were central to the late-medieval imagination. Into this most abstracted, beautiful, fantasy setting, Chaucer inserts some of his most direct political commentary. This makes compelling sense when we consider the garden's representation of control over nature—an obvious metaphor for political as well as poetic control. And the kind of leisure pursuits that took place in the garden were mechanisms for conveying high status: exhibiting your ability to be at play was itself a politicized statement.[41]

The F-Prologue describes the God of Love, surrounded with regalia associated with Richard, as an angry, immoderate figure who needs to learn how not to behave like a Lombard tyrant.[42] He is exhorted to pay attention to the business of kingship, reminded of his responsibilities, told that he is influenced by unreliable cronies, and encouraged to think of his great magnates as themselves half-gods, part of the divine social

---

[40] Emily is imprisoned in the garden while Palamon and Arcite are in the Tower. See chapter 3; also see Kolve, *Chaucer and the Imagery of Narrative*, 93–96; Aers, *Chaucer, Langland and the Creative Imagination*, 175–95; Gilchrist, *Gender and Archaeology*, esp. 111–13 and 120–23.

[41] Creighton comments that leisure activities were 'key mechanisms for the expression of status,' *Designs upon the Land*, 2.

[42] For Ricardian symbolism, see Barr, *Socioliterary Practice*, 80–93.

order. This is hard-hitting stuff, all the more so given that in 1386 the Wonderful Parliament attacked Richard's frivolity, condemned his friends, and forcibly inserted the great men of the kingdom into the political order through the establishment of the governing council. Moreover, over the previous two or three years, Richard had repeatedly figured as an angry man in parliaments and councils. And yet, this potential attack on Richard is placed within a poem that is addressed to Anne and, whether or not it was 'really' intended to reach her, is situated within courtly circles. While the poem articulates political views of which one might expect the fledgling Lords Appellant to approve, the poem is directed towards the queen herself.

We can make sense of this by resisting the pressure of hindsight. In 1387, Richard was only twenty years old. Chaucer was around forty-five. At this point, Richard had not executed anyone or embarked on his 'tyranny.' As he had emerged from the influence of his uncle, he had stumbled in his attempts to assert himself: he had become angry with dominating, warmongering older men and had given out too much favour to older boys that he idolized. But there was no reason for a middle-aged man such as Chaucer, who was becoming established as a poet, was a long-term esquire of the king's household and a client of John of Gaunt, whose children were well placed, and whose wife served in the highest households of the realm, to be frightened of Richard. He was barely out of adolescence. As Lynn Staley has argued, the F-Prologue works 'only if the sovereign is *not* dangerous.'[43] At this point, things seemed entirely redeemable. Chaucer is not calling Richard a tyrant; he is saying 'learn from the example of Bernabò Visconti.' The poem is closely modeled on the *Jugement du Roi de Navare*: its literariness protects it. Richard and Anne had not 'really' taken exception to *Troilus* and the *Roman de la Rose*, as the F-Prologue pretends the God of Love and Alceste have. Rather, there was a literary tradition of poets making previous poems the catalyst for new ones by inventing audience agitation and staging the trial of the poet. So the setting is obviously fictionalized and frivolous—Richard did not really care about *Troilus*, and anyway, it is obvious that *Troilus* is not the

[43] Staley, *Languages of Power*, 21; emphasis mine.

poem that the F-Prologue says it is. So there is an extent to which this is genuine 'advice to princes' material, written by someone who had experience of accessible kings and lords and, crucially, was part of a poetic culture that was licentious and disrespectful. Langland writes about Edward III and Alice Perrers in a way that we cannot imagine Wyatt writing about Henry VIII and Anne Boleyn, for instance[44]. The court was changing but had not yet reached the tipping point. As we saw in chapter 12, in 1376 Parliament chose its first Speaker, symbolizing at least a limited ability for the Commons to speak truth to power. In the 1390s, Richard's crony occupied the role for every parliament. So things changed, and the crucible of that change was precisely the late 1380s. The Wonderful and Merciless Parliaments altered the political world. Richard emerged from the horrors of 1388 with a cautious, determined programme of moderation; having reestablished himself, he turned to different, extreme tactics as the 1390s wore on. This, however, was not foreseeable in 1386.

Most critics agree that the F-Prologue was written between 1386 and 1387.[45] The poem includes a helpful CV-section, in which Chaucer lists the poems he has already written, in addition to the *Roman de la Rose* translation and *Troilus*, which have been the subject of the God of Love's wrath:

He made the book that hight the Hous of Fame,
And eke the Deeth of Blaunche the Duchesse,
And the Parlement of Foules, as I gesse,
And al the love of Palamon and Arcite
Of Thebes, thogh the storye ys knowen lyte;
And many an ympne for your halydayes,
That highten balades, roundels, virelayes;
And, for to speke of other holynesse,
He hath in prose translated Boece,
And maad the lyf also of Seynt Cecile.
He made also, goon ys a gret while,
Origenes upon the Maudeleyne. (417–28)

[44] For Alice Perrers as Lady Mede, see Ormrod, 'Who Was Alice Perrers,' 219 and Trigg, 'Traffic in Medieval Women.'
[45] See, for instance, Pearsall, *Life of Geoffrey Chaucer*, 191; Staley, *Languages of Power*, 16–17.

The F-Prologue thus seems to be poised between the dream poems, the major translations, *Troilus*, and Chaucer's early drafts of what later would become some of the *Tales* on the one hand, and his conceiving of the *Canterbury Tales* as a whole on the other. The references to the flower and the leaf (68–79, 189–90, 193) and *Troilus* suggest the poem could not have been written before 1386. As the poem predates the 'General Prologue,' which was almost certainly written while the staple was at Middleburgh, that is, between 1384 and 1388, a date of 1386 or 1387 seems likely.[46] The arrival at court of Deschamps's poems, and Gower's similar reference to the flower and the leaf at around this time, also suggest a 1386–87 date.[47] The playfulness of the poem and the light, ludic portrayal of the court might also mark it both as a poem connected with the frivolous young court of the mid-1380s and as a pre-Merciless Parliament poem—in other words, a pre-1388 poem. So while we cannot be absolutely certain, there is a great deal of evidence that suggests a date of 1386 or 1387—the years of Richard's crisis.

In my view, the *House of Fame*, the F-Prologue, and the 'General Prologue' to the *Canterbury Tales* were all written fairly closely together.[48] There are parallels and echoes across the three texts. Some of these are specific linguistic similarities. Thus, in the F-Prologue we read: 'No wonder ys thogh Jove hire stellyfye' (525), echoing the *House of Fame* 'Wher Joves wol me stellyfye' (586). The F-Prologue's 'And Zephirus and Flora gentilly / Yaf to the floures, softe and tenderly / Hire swoote breth' (171–73) preempts the famous 'Whan Zephirus eek with his sweete breeth' (5) in the 'General Prologue.' However, the F-Prologue also echoes other Chaucerian texts: its image of the earth forgetting winter (125–26) and indeed the reference to Zepherus also imitates the *Book of the Duchess* (402–15), and the Valentine-inspired birds (145) singing 'Welcome somer' (170)

[46] There is a rather circular argument in Chaucer criticism that asserts that the *Legend of Good Women* was written in 1386, because it clearly predates the *Tales*, which were begun in 1387, because they clearly postdate the *Legend*, which was written in 1386. In other words, there are some shaky datings. However, the reference to the staple's being at Middleburgh ('General Prologue,' 277) does suggest a pre-1388 dating—see chapter 15 in the present study for a more detailed discussion of the dating of the 'General Prologue.'

[47] Coleman, 'The Flower, the Leaf, and Philippa of Lancaster.'

[48] On the date of the *House of Fame*, see Turner, *Chaucerian Conflict*, 12n16; Cooper, 'Four Last Things,' 59; Minnis, *Shorter Poems*, 167–72.

closely mimics the *Parliament of Fowls* (680). It is the broader concerns of the three poems that compellingly link them together as the products of the same period. Indeed, the *House of Fame*, the F-Prologue, and the *Legend of Good Women* serve as crucial preliminaries to the 'General Prologue.' Both dream poems are profoundly concerned with authorial intent and misreading. *Troilus* too is obsessed with this, but for the earlier dream poems, it is less of a concern. In the *House of Fame*, the twisting of the Dido and Aeneas story by both Virgil and Ovid, the dramatization of Lady Fame's ignoring of intent, and the final focus on tidings' independent life in the world, all bespeak an anxiety about and interest in readers' and auditors' interpretations. The poem ultimately rests happily (and resignedly) with the dynamic qualities of texts and their ability to mutate and be reinterpreted. In sharp contrast, the F-Prologue—which is fundamentally about a deliberate and willful misreading—explores, as the 'Manciple's Tale' would later do, what happens when your misreader is also your political master and has no interest in understanding your intentions, nor in the subtleties of texts. These are the two poems (before the *Tales*) that most clearly associate Chaucer the man with his poetic persona: in the *House of Fame* he is named as Geffrey; in the F-Prologue he is described as the author of all of Chaucer's works. Both texts, unlike Chaucer's other poems, are ostentatiously Dantean. Apart from the *Tales*, Chaucer's only two references to Dante by name come in these two poems (F-Prologue, 360; *House of Fame*, 450). While the *House of Fame* mirrors the three-book structure of the *Divine Comedy* and contains a Dantean eagle, the F-Prologue opens with a sly reference to the fact that no poet has actually been to heaven or hell (1–9). Both poems are fascinated by the figure of the tyrant. Fame is an all-seeing, all-hearing monster, totally willful and arbitrary in her actions, governed by whim.[49] The God of Love will not be gainsaid 'in ryght ne wrong' (477); he is implacable, unreasonable, and a terrible reader, who understands nothing beyond plot—hence his instruction to Chaucer to 'Sey shortly' (577). Both poems meditate profoundly on the tension between authority and experience, an issue that was to become of central importance in tales such as 'The Wife of Bath's Tale.'

[49] See Turner, *Chaucerian Conflict*, chapter 1.

The *House of Fame* charts a journey through literary authority to the lived experience of talking, hearing stories, and experiencing city life. The F-Prologue opens with a passage in praise of books, before the narrator bids his books goodbye in order to enjoy Maytime festivities (29–39).

In different ways, each text provided a way for Chaucer to try out ideas and think through methodologies that were to be crucial in the development of the *Canterbury Tales*. The *House of Fame* stages the poet's movement through court and Troy poetry to a new kind of poetry, where he listens to stories and imagines pardoners, shipmen, and pilgrims with their own stories to tell, in an explosion of heterogeneity and diversity. The journey from the House of Fame to the House of Rumour in the poem mirrors both Chaucer's literal journey from noble and royal households to London rooms and his poetic journey from the *dits amoureux* and stories of Troy to the gestation of the *Canterbury Tales*. The F-Prologue preempts the *Tales* in various formal ways. This poem represents an early attempt to use the heroic couplet: the ten-syllable, rhyming couplet that was to become the building block of the *Tales*, and that Chaucer had already deployed in the 'Knight's Tale.' By now, Chaucer had been playing with the ten-syllable line for a number of years, and had perfected rhyme royal. The heroic couplet (or 'riding rhyme,' as the non-end-stopped version of couplets in iambic pentameter that Chaucer used is also known) now became Chaucer's favoured form and was a lasting legacy to English poetry. The *Legend* is also an experiment in gathering together mini-narratives under the umbrella of a framing fiction. In this aspect, it provides a negative example: the identical, repetitive structure of each tale functions as a template of what not to do—as 'The Monk's Tale' was also to enact. Indeed, that tale may also date from around this time (or part of it could have been written earlier): the references to Visconti tyranny in the F-Prologue and to Bernabò's death in 'The Monk's Tale' may both have been written hot on the heels of news of Bernabò Visconti's death, which reached England in 1386.[50]

---

[50] Bernabò died in December 1385. Froissart notes that the news quickly spread abroad and became a topic of debate. Although Froissart is often unreliable, it is inconceivable that such scandalous news would not spread quickly. Froissart, *Oeuvres*, 10:327–28.

Both the *House of Fame* and the *Legend* ostentatiously stall—one on the word 'auctorite,' the other on the word 'conclusioun.' Indeed, the stagey unfinishedness of these poems is part of their fabric and importance— Chaucer could not take either of them forward, and instead took their lessons to the 'General Prologue.' The poems offered two different poetic paths. One was to write poetry that was consciously separate from court influence and from patronage. The new tidings exist in the insurgent space of the wickerwork house, away from the palace and ruler; poetic inspiration comes from a public, civic, porous space. The other path was the path of servility and reassuring repetition. The poet who took this road could say:

> My word, my werk, ys knyt so in youre bond
> That, as an harpe obeieth to the hond
> And maketh it soune after his fyngerynge,
> Ryght so mowe ye oute of myn herte bringe
> Swich vois, right as yow lyst, to laughe or pleyne. (F-Prologue, 89–93)

The poet became the instrument, a thing to be played by the master. We know, of course, that Chaucer did not choose to embrace the servile, courtly voice but instead became a poet of diverse voices and stories. In Wallace's terms, he made a choice between associational form and absolutist poetics, and ended up on the right side of history.[51] It is clear throughout the F-Prologue and the *Legend* that Chaucer was exposing the intellectual limitations and constraints of writing under tyranny; in other words, his choice had already been made.

But this was not a poem criticizing the court to a public audience: this was very clearly a poem designed for performance in an aristocratic, courtly environment, the world of the flower and the leaf—so Chaucer's choice had not been *decisively* made; the enacting of this poem reveals him playing with a courtly milieu. And the choice was not as easy as it might seem: as the F-Prologue shows us, the 'absolutist' route also offered an educated

[51] Wallace, *Chaucerian Polity*. For absolutism and the Prologue to the *Legend of Good Women*, see 337–77. See also Simpson's brief discussion of the appalling violence of Italian republicanism, 'Chaucer as a European Writer,' 83–84.

mixed-sex audience and a highly sophisticated ludic environment that had obvious appeal. This audience did not disappear for Chaucer, but his poems also entered a less exclusive world of brothels and taverns in the 1390s.[52] Anne was a highly educated woman, from a sophisticated court, who had a particular interest in female education and literacy. She sought papal backing for the promotion of the cult of St Anne in England—St Anne was traditionally iconographically represented teaching her daughter to read.[53] And indeed, in the F-Prologue, as in the 'Life of St Cecilia,' written sometime shortly before, we see the emergence of a different kind of woman from the type characteristic of most of Chaucer's early poetry. This shift can be seen as part of a bigger late-medieval cultural shift, as the dominance of courtly love became subsumed within a more expansive idea of love that encompassed common profit, companionate marriage, and early humanist interest in ethics, social practice, and ancient texts.[54] In texts such as the 'Knight's Tale,' *Troilus*, and the *Parliament of Fowls*, women's primary role is as objects of desire and victims of trafficking. These women are presented sympathetically, and the system that treats them in this way is held up for scrutiny, but their function in the text, and in their lives, is as courtly ladies. Women such as Cecilia and Alceste, in contrast, take on public roles: they influence others, speak confidently and reasonably, and are not valued primarily as objects of erotic desire.[55] In this, they preempt women such as Prudence in 'Melibee,' the queen and ladies of the 'Wife of Bath's Tale,' and Griselda, all of whom demonstrate equitable judgement and use their intelligence and reason to deflect violence. Emily, Criseyde, and the formel, by contrast, were expected to use their sexual availability to deflect violence, like the women handed over in peace treaties.[56] Wallace

---

[52] McDonald, 'Chaucer's *Legend of Good Women*'; Carlin, 'Host,' 479.

[53] Saul, *Richard II*, 324.

[54] Carolyn P. Collette, *Rethinking Chaucer's 'Legend of Good Women'* (York: York Medieval Press, 2014), 1–3; ibid., x–xi. Of course, Chaucer is interested in these ideas in his earlier texts too: notably, the *Parliament of Fowls* focuses on common profit and *Troilus and Criseyde* explores Boethian ideas of love as the force that binds the world, rather than an exclusively erotic force. However, in Chaucer's later texts, there is a stronger turn away from *fin amour* and towards a different kind of female power.

[55] For a recent discussion of the hybrid nature of Alceste, see Glenn Burger, ' "Pite renneth soone in gentil herte": Ugly Feelings and Gendered Conduct in Chaucer's *Legend of Good Women*,' *Chaucer Review* 52:1 (2017): 66–84.

[56] Chaucer's growing interest in ethics and gentilesse as a quality not bound by class or gender is discussed further in chapter 18.

goes so far as to term Chaucer's fascination with wifely eloquence, 'the most singular aspect of his oeuvre,'[57] and we see this coming into being in the F-Prologue—written, incidentally, around the time that his own wife died.

But if we think about the F-Prologue and subsequent *Legend*—a courtly text staging a tyrannical assault on creative freedom—as essentially representing the poetic road not taken, its most important characteristic is that it is static. Sophisticated as the humour and play is, with its appeal to a knowing audience, its puns, and its structural irony,[58] this is a text about staying in one place, literally and metaphorically, in stark contrast to the extraordinary journey of the *House of Fame*, and then the *Canterbury Tales*. The *House of Fame*, indeed, is the only dream poem not set in a garden. It moves through the temple of glass, the desert, the House of Fame, and the wickerwork nest-cage of the House of Rumour. The House of Rumour is itself defined by its constant movement. The *Parliament of Fowls* and the *Book of the Duchess* both figure the narrator moving through different locations, but are principally set in a garden: the *House of Fame* is far more varied, the Prologue to the *Legend* far less varied in its use of locations. Equally, the very world of courtly play is an intimate, self-indulgent, inward-looking world. Chaucer satirizes this in the *Parliament of Fowls*: the higher-class birds who speak the language of *fin amor* are castigated by the other birds for their navel-gazing. They are able to spend all day talking about love because they have 'leyser' (484–90).[59] Other people have to go to work. The F-Prologue is staged in a fixed, courtly garden setting, and is the precursor to a tale collection that is structured by repetition: each tale goes back over the same template, nothing moves on. In contrast, the two most innovative aspects of the *Canterbury Tales* (aspects that clearly differentiate it from the *Decameron*) are that

[57] Wallace, *Chaucerian Polity*, 377.

[58] McDonald argues that the sexual banter of the text only works in the context of a knowing female audience, 'Chaucer's *Legend of Good Women*,' 24; Sheila Delany has written about the sexual puns throughout the *Legend* in *The Naked Text*, 139–50. The structural irony lies in the fact that the tales are ludicrously curtailed and homogenized (see, for instance, Dinshaw, *Chaucer's Sexual Poetics*, 67–87), and in the knowing absurdity of deriving universal truths from individual examples, as discussed by McDonald, 'Chaucer's *Legend of Good Women*,' 31.

[59] They speak from morning until sundown; the narrator points out that he himself does not have the 'leyser' (487) to recount their long speeches. On Petrarch and 'otium,' see chapter 16.

Chaucer introduces socially diverse voices and that his frame setting is not an aristocratic garden but a restless journey.

In Chaucer's garden perspective of 1386, we see a man hesitating about what poetic path to take, and a man on the cusp of political change. Chaucer undoubtedly suffered in the years 1386–88 when Richard lost power. But he was not a card-carrying Ricardian. He was not personally embroiled with Richard's corrupt cronies as were de Vere or Brembre, although he was connected with them in his workplace. On the other hand, he was also not connected with Richard's most prominent opponents—the duke of Gloucester, for instance, the earl of Arundel, or the earl of Warwick. His friends were the moderates, educated men who had entered royal service from a background in the affinities of the Black Prince or John of Gaunt—as I'll discuss in detail in chapter 15. In 1386, Chaucer is positioning himself as a voice of moderation, offering critical advice from a position partly within, or on the borders of, the court, as someone who always saw the magnate perspective, as he was himself primarily not a king's man but Gaunt's man. His criticisms, indeed, are exactly the sort of criticisms that Gaunt himself might have offered to his nephew, albeit in far less guarded and allegorical terms. Chaucer is politically bolder here than he is in any other poem, but he burns no bridges; his extravagant praise of Anne and investment in courtly play signals an insider appreciation of court style that encloses a plea to the king to take politics more seriously. While he jokingly imagines himself as an abject, worm-like court servant (F-Prologue, 318), he uses this fool-like position to offer a critique that manages to praise the magnates ('half-goddes,' 387) *and* the sun-like, dazzling king, while pointing out the dangers of an immoderate exercise of power. At this political moment, the battle lines that seem so clear to us in retrospect had not been drawn. Criticising the king did not make one irretrievably 'against' him—even some of his most violent opponents in 1387–88, including the two junior Appellants, Mowbray and Bolingbroke, gained favour from Richard in the 1390s. The garden offered a forum for a ludic style of critique perfectly positioned, in yet another pre-empting of the 'General Prologue,' between earnest and game.

PART III

APPROACHING CANTERBURY

>–⊢◆›–⊙–‹◆⊣–≺

Prologue

After about 1386, Chaucer devoted the majority of his creative energies to the *Canterbury Tales*. In the early part of his adult life, in the 1360s and 1370s, he had travelled abroad frequently; in the early 1380s, he had remained largely based in London, in his counting-house existence. Now he lived mainly in the Kentish hinterlands, a few miles from the city of London. During these years, his patterns of life were different: he crops up witnessing documents in the Greenwich and Woolwich area and in local government roles, such as acting as a commissioner to investigate walls and ditches on the Thames after flooding. He was not always in this corner of Kent, however. In his capacity as clerk of the king's works, as deputy forester for North Petherton, and as a member of the king's household, he needed to travel between various regional centres and, particularly from 1389 to 1391, he was fairly itinerant. Politically, the last years of the fourteenth century were stormy indeed, culminating in Richard's notorious tyranny, the exile of Henry Bolingbroke, Gaunt's death, Richard's deposition by Henry, and Henry's assumption of the throne. Personally, Chaucer was now a widower and the father of a young child—for whom he wrote an educational treatise during these years—and of two older, independent children, one of whom was embarking on a spectacular rise in the service of the house of Lancaster. During the late 1380s and throughout the 1390s, Chaucer was writing with great poetic confidence. His poetry was now written almost exclusively in the ten-syllable line, and his creation of the *Canterbury Tales* gave him abundant opportunities for the juxtaposition and mixing of styles at which he excelled.[1]

When Chaucer was writing the *Canterbury Tales*, his thought-patterns ran in established ways. Most of all, his mind moved *across* ideas and styles, not through them, as he eschewed social and poetic hierarchies. Just as he placed the romance next to the fabliau, so he placed women next to men, the poor next to the noble, the moral next to the fable. More than this, he intertwined these juxtapositions to demonstrate that romance is not so different from fabliau, and each can be found in the other. Equally, a low-class woman can have more gentilesse than a high-class man. And the most important meaning might inhere in form itself, in the very practice of rhetoric, in the experience of performing, debating, and thinking. His refusal to allow his pilgrims to reach Canterbury, to permit one tale to win the competition, or to give us a clear moral or interpretative anchor in the text leaves his text open and radically egalitarian. While Dante tells us to look *through* the veil of verses ('velame de li versi') to find the meaning hidden ('asconde') underneath, Chaucer's Nun's Priest exhorts us to sort the fruit from the chaff in a tale that is fundamentally *about* rhetorical performance and has no obvious centre of gravity.[2] Chaucer demands that readers interact with the text and focus not on a final literal or metaphorical goal but on the journey, the approach, the process of consideration. Chaucer's point is not that everything is of equal importance, but that it is up to each

---

[1] The only poetic Canterbury Tale not written in the decasyllabic line is the 'Tale of Sir Thopas,' a witty parody. For the brilliant jokes embedded in the form of the tale, see J. A. Burrow, '*Sir Thopas*: An Agony in Three Fits,' *Review of English Studies*, n.s., 22:85 (1971): 54–58; and E. A. Jones, 'Loo, Lordes Myne, Heere Is a Fit!': The Structure of Chaucer's *Sir Thopas*.' *Review of English Studies*, n.s., 51:202 (2000): 248–52.

[2] Dante, *The Divine Comedy, Book 1: Inferno*, trans. John D. Sinclair (New York: Oxford University Press, 1961), 9.62–63, 123. McKinley comments that both Boccaccio and Chaucer 'admired yet could not, ultimately, endorse,' the *Divine Comedy*, and goes on to discuss Chaucer's 'strong distaste for allegory.' *Chaucer's House of Fame*, 10, 135. For detailed discussion of the Nun's Priest and of the image of the fruit and chaff in Chaucer's poetry, see chapter 18 in this book.

individual to work out what matters, to engage in critical thought, to discriminate.

In the *Canterbury Tales*, as in other artistic, scientific, and economic endeavours in the late Middle Ages, 'relativity replaces hierarchy as the basis of order and identity.'[3] When the Miller challenges the Knight, his interruption of the proposed order of tale-telling subverts the formal order that the 'General Prologue,' implicitly promised. We realize, in the 'Miller's Prologue,' that the *Tales* is being presented not as an ornately wrought whole but as an entity with its own energy that proceeds according to the demands of its own characters, who will interrupt, speak over each other, tell tales of different lengths, and generally pull the text first into one shape and then into another. Lee Patterson describes this as the replacement of 'the principle of hierarchy' by 'an internally generated and self-sustaining principle of "quiting."'[4] This responsive form is dynamic and unpredictable, resisting externally imposed structure. Of course, the *Tales* does not 'really' have its own energy and is not 'really' directed by the whims of the pilgrims: the appearance of disorder is crafted by Chaucer to reflect a particular social and aesthetic philosophy, a worldview that values multiplicity rather than homogeneity, movement rather than stasis, self-ordering systems rather than hegemonic authority.[5] Chaucer developed a spatial poetics based on relativity: his attitude to the distribution of power across space and the distribution of meaning across texts were both underpinned by a suspicion of traditional hierarchical understandings of what was important and what was peripheral and easy to dismiss. This spatial poetics is a fundamental part of the *Canterbury Tales*.

The first two chapters of this section, 'South of the Thames' and 'Inn,' deal with locations just south of the river in their real and imagined forms. Chaucer moved to the south bank—not, it turns out, to a 'wilderness' but to a location very well connected through the artery of the Thames. The inn that became the imaginative starting point for the *Tales* is a centre in

---

[3] Kaye, *History of Balance*, 7.

[4] Patterson, *Chaucer and the Subject of History*, 245.

[5] Kaye explores the connection between the flourishing of self-regulating economic systems and the expression of a more relativistic view of the world by scientists and artists alike in the thirteenth and fourteenth centuries in *A History of Balance*, especially 267–82.

its own right, not a peripheral civic locale, and its role in the 'General Prologue' becomes a way of thinking about the boundaries between reality and fiction, but also about social mixing and juxtaposition. The next three chapters, 'Peripheries,' 'What Lies Beneath,' and 'Threshold,' focus on the spatial poetics of the *Canterbury Tales*, in conjunction with geographical and conceptual understandings of space in the 1390s. I focus on the conceptual areas of peripheries (forest, region, and far, far away), what lies beneath (politically and hermeneutically), and thresholds (the approach to Canterbury, the liminality of death, and the impending crisis of 1399). Finally, Chaucer's move to the edges of Westminster Abbey signaled a move back to the clear centre of things, to a space where all kinds of power networks converged.

In the final chapter, 'Abbey,' a key text is Chaucer's *Complaint to His Purse*, one of the very few Chaucerian texts that we can date with any accuracy. None of the *Canterbury Tales* can be assigned to a particular year, both because our evidence is limited and because Chaucer treated his texts as works in progress. We can see this in the two versions of the Prologue to the *Legend of Good Women*. Tales were drafted, rewritten, and moved about within the overall structure of the *Tales*, and traces of previous arrangements, cancelled endlinks, and inconsistent speakers sometimes remain. Just as Langland seemed to engage with *Piers Plowman* as a living text throughout his writing life, so Chaucer probably rarely had a sense of tales as definitively 'finished.' For instance, I argue in chapter 17, 'Peripheries,' for a much earlier date for a preliminary version of the 'Wife of Bath's Tale' than has previously been suggested, but Chaucer certainly returned to her section and rewrote it over the next few years. So I am not trying to tie tales to specific moments in Chaucer's life, although we can often make sensible estimates. Rather, I am interested in how Chaucer's habits of mind, conditioned by the world in which he lived, are expressed in his writing. The form that Chaucer developed in the *Canterbury Tales* showcases the mixed style and the centrality of reader response. His concerns increasingly moved towards ethics, as well as poetics, as he focused more and more on issues relating to inner worth, equity, and social estate. In his *Canterbury Tales* years, Chaucer embraced the idea of equivalence—in terms of genre, interpretation, social status, and gender. This ability to equalize without homogenizing is central to Chaucer's ethical stance and to his poetic art. The genius of the *Tales* lies in its valuing of difference qua difference, and its refusal either to collapse those differences or to prioritise saint's life over folktale, man over woman, knight over miller, marquis over peasant girl, moral truth over poetic line, idea over rhetoric. Readers must make decisions for themselves: '*Al* that is writen is writen for oure doctrine' (*Retractions*, 1083; emphasis mine).

CHAPTER 15

>-┼-◆>-•-O-•-<◆-┼-<

South of the Thames

Red sails

Wide

To leeward, swing on the heavy spar.

The barges wash

Drifting logs

Down Greenwich reach

Past the Isle of Dogs.

Weialala leia

Wallala leialala

—*T. S. Eliot,* The Waste Land

As the political crisis hit, Chaucer hunkered down on the southern bank of the Thames. No longer taking the king's shilling, no longer part of the royal household, residing in Kent rather than London, this newly widowed man had very obviously removed himself from the centre of the political storm. Did he do this because he was a target of the Appellants' wrath? No. Were the people in charge Chaucer's enemies? No. Was the change in his life sudden? No. Was it, nonetheless, alarming and disorienting? Yes. Did his position make it wise for him to maintain a low profile for a short time? Yes. And, during these years—as Richard fell, the Appellants floundered, and Richard returned, newly (and temporarily) moderate— Chaucer's mode of life changed permanently. He never again lived in the city. He began to devote the vast majority of his creative energies to the *Canterbury Tales,* a project that occupied him until his death. During the 1390s, he also wrote a few short lyrics and *A Treatise on the Astrolabe*, and he revised the Prologue to the *Legend of Good Women*. But he undertook no major literary projects except for the *Tales*. Compare this with the variety of his output in the 1380s, and the number of projects he left unfinished as he tried to find his way forward, and it is clear that Chaucer had now found a voice and a project that suited him down to the ground. His *working* life was much less settled in the late 1380s and 1390s compared with his years in the Custom House (except for his tenure as clerk of the king's works from 1389 to 1391), but *creatively*, the tale-collection concept allowed him to devote his energies to one coherent undertaking while still indulging his passion for varied modes and voices.

Around 1386–87, then, was an odd moment for Chaucer: he was away from the centre and his life had lost its stability, the monarchy was in real turmoil, and extremism was flourishing on both sides of the political divide. Chaucer's response was to write the 'General Prologue': a poem set on the wrong side of the river, a poem about a journey, a poem that took the temperature of contemporary English society. The 'General Prologue' is not a piece of journalism; its literariness has been well established, most famously by Jill Mann's magisterial work on estates satire.[1] It also oscillates between the out-of-time and the profoundly temporal. We see this very clearly in the opening lines (1–20), when the grand sweep of the seasons, the universe, and nature are juxtaposed with 'in that sesoun on a day, / In Southwerk.' We zoom in on a particular, material location—the Tabard Inn in Southwark—and Chaucer goes on to describe his pilgrim company. This is not a representation of the whole of society but of a particular slice of that society (the middle), described partly in satirical and conventional ways, but packed with specific contemporary details.

---

[1] We do not know exactly when the 'General Prologue' was written. The vast majority of critics place it around 1387, with a terminus ad quem of 1388, when the staple moved from Middleburg (referred to at 277 in the 'General Prologue'). A very cautious *Riverside Chaucer* note (809) makes clear that we cannot be certain that Chaucer's Merchant was not, in fact, a merchant adventurer who was unaffected by the change in staple port, but this seems to me to be reading the figure too much as a real person with a backstory. The 'Prologue' was surely revised, probably many times, but my best guess is that it has its origin around 1387. I note, in passing, in reference to the 'Middleburgh and Orewelle' line, that Chaucer's friends Clanvowe and Neville were in charge of checking the defences of Orwell in 1386. *Calendar of the Patent Rolls: Richard II*, Membrane 29, 3:214 (26 September 1386). For estates satire see Jill Mann, *Chaucer and Medieval Estates Satire* (Cambridge: Cambridge University Press, 1973).

Almost every description abounds in both local detail and international references. The 'Prologue' draws a map for us of Chaucer's world. London dominates: St Paul's and its porch, Cheapside, the guildhall, the Inns of Court, urban taverns. Many other parts of England also feature, including Orwell, Norfolk, Dartmouth, Bath, and, of course, Canterbury, in Kent. The nearer parts of Europe are mentioned over and over again, including Artois, Flanders, Middleburg, Rome, Ypres, and Santiago de Compostela, but references to further corners of the known world also litter the text: Carthage, Jerusalem, Alexandria, Russia. And the most striking aspect of the 'Prologue' is that its characters are not noble or, for the most part, gentle. Chaucer has turned his back on court poetry, on client-patron dream visions and romances, on the noble tellers of the *Decameron*, and is forging a new kind of poetry. As I've argued in previous chapters, it was born out of both the poetic experimentation of the dream visions and contemporary political contexts, notably Parliament. At a political moment in which Richard was claiming that his own voice should be absolute and hegemonic and the Appellants were inventing procedures to promote their own brutal agenda, Chaucer foregrounds the voices of the Commons as the voices of literature. It is hard to see the flourishing of this new mode as unconnected to Chaucer's movement away from the centre. The whole enormous poem is set in the hinterland between the south bank of the Thames and Canterbury, the area in which Chaucer was now living. But perhaps most significant is the idea of movement itself. Chaucer had eschewed stasis for the journey. The idea that life is a process of constant change dominates Chaucer's poetry. Those who cannot or will not change are tragic figures; those who adapt survive. While the courtly garden came to symbolize stasis, as we see in the parodically repetitive *Legend*, the journey of the *Tales*, with its celebration of difference, disagreement, multiple perspectives, and digression, symbolizes, above all, movement—and therefore change.

Why had Chaucer's own life changed? To answer this question, it is important to trace some of the contours of the high politics of the 1380s. The Wonderful Parliament of 1386 had effectively removed Richard from power and appointed a council to govern for him. Richard's furious response was most potently expressed in the questions to the judges of 1387, resulting in a dramatic affirmation of the royal prerogative and an opening up of the possibility of accusing the Appellants of treason. Matters escalated and a pitched battle ensued: de Vere's royalist forces were defeated by the Appellants at the battle of Radcot Bridge in December 1387. The Merciless Parliament opened in February 1388 and resulted in the execution of those of Richard's favourites who had not already fled. The Appellants, though, overreached themselves, and by summer 1389, Richard had won over the junior Appellants (Henry of Derby and Thomas Mowbray) and was able to announce his return to full rule. He requested Gaunt's return, appointed moderates across the political spectrum, and worked hard to reestablish his authority.[2]

During this time Chaucer gave up his London apartment, his job at the Custom House, and his Exchequer allowance. The Appellants were attacking the king's household and his appointees, and many of the king's clients kept their heads down during these years. Chaucer, for a brief period of time, had no job and no Exchequer allowance (although he did still have his allowance from Gaunt). He was pursued for debt. By any standards, these were difficult times for Chaucer, and he had to make tough decisions, what we might think of as 'constrained choices.' However, the precise chronology and context suggests that this was not a *crisis* for Chaucer but a convergence of different circumstances, some personal, some political.[3] Chaucer, as I've already discussed, had physically left his job and his rooms in late 1384 or early 1385, well before Richard's downfall, and was already based in Kent before the Wonderful Parliament. He came into that parliament as MP for Kent, and his customs job had by this point long been performed by a permanent deputy.[4] Parliament singled out the abuses of customs' officers for criticism and demanded that certain officers be removed from their roles.[5] At the same time, there was increased attention

[2] For a fuller discussion of the events of 1386–89, see Saul, *Richard II*, 148–204.

[3] The terms 'constrained choice' and 'crisis' are both borrowed from Strohm, *Poet's Tale*, 183. I differ from Strohm's perspective in the *Poet's Tale* about the seriousness of what happened to Chaucer at this time. But I wholeheartedly agree with his comment in *Social Chaucer* that Chaucer, in both his literary and his political choices, demonstrated 'even-handedness and receptivity to opposed points of view,' 41.

[4] See chapter 11.

[5] 'Also, the commons pray: that all the controllers of the kingdom's ports who hold their office for the term of life by grant of the king, because they perpetrate great oppressions and extortions against the people in their offices, be dismissed and removed.' Chaucer did not actually hold his office for the term of his life, but at the king's pleasure. PROME, Membrane 1, no. 32, 7:51–52 (October 1386).

to the importance of the walls and gates of London during the invasion crisis. On 4 September 1386, the *City of London Letter-Book* records an order to the aldermen to make sure the men in their wards were 'put in array' (i.e. armour) and on 13 September householders were ordered to provision their houses for three months.[6] On 18 September a grant of murage (a tax for repairing the walls and dykes) was made to the mayor, aldermen, and citizens of London for ten years.[7] These defensive measures were taken at exactly the same time as Chaucer gave up his rooms over one of the gates set into the walls: Richard Forster (Chaucer's friend and colleague) was in possession on 5 October.[8] His apartment was given to Forster by Brembre, so this was certainly not part of an attack on Chaucer by the Appellant group. Rather, the city wanted a resident in this crucial defensive position as panic grew about the possibility of a French invasion. And, although the loss of income must have been a sacrifice, these actions were formalizing decisions that had been taken much earlier: Chaucer now officially gave up rooms that he didn't live in, and a job that he didn't do.

The year 1387 opened quietly for Chaucer. He took part in a commission investigating an abduction in Kent.[9] He received his annuities.[10] In July, he seems to have gone to Calais with William Beauchamp, brother of one of the Appellants.[11] Beauchamp was a long-term friend of Chaucer's and supported the Appellant cause in 1387. We don't know what Chaucer was doing in Calais, but he cannot have been there long, as he was present at another hearing for the abduction case on 1 August.[12] At around this time, Philippa died. Chaucer collected his wife's annuity on 18 June, as usual, but that was the last payment made to her. In early November, he collected his own money only, so she must have died between these dates. However much or little time they spent together, Philippa and Geoffrey had been married for more than twenty years and had two or

---

[6] Sharpe, *Calendar of Letter-Books: Letter-Book H*, fol. cci, 285.

[7] *Calendar of the Patent Rolls: Richard II,* Membrane 31, 3:210.

[8] Sharpe, *Calendar of Letter-Books: Letter-Book H*, fol. cciv b, 290. See Crow and Olson, *Chaucer Life-Records*, 60, for Chaucer's connection with Forster in 1378.

[9] Crow and Olson, *Chaucer Life-Records*, 375–83.

[10] Ibid., 312.

[11] Ibid., 61–62.

[12] Ibid., 375.

three surviving children. If Lewis was their child, as he almost certainly was, he was only a few years old. The couple was on good enough terms for Geoffrey to use his advantages at the Custom House to collect Philippa's annuities and (presumably) pass them on to her, as he had been doing regularly for the last few years. Their daughter was at Barking Abbey; their older son absent in Spain with Gaunt—they were both independent. Chaucer's life had lost another one of its moorings, although he was only about forty-five. He was now a single man, for the first time since his early twenties, writing in Kent, somewhat occupied with local government but no longer working regularly.

This, then, was the melancholy situation in Chaucer's life as the political situation spun out of control and the Appellants fought against royal forces led by de Vere at the battle of Radcot Bridge. The country was in a state of civil war: on 20 December, de Vere lost the battle and fled. On 21 December, the five Appellants marched into nearby Oxford to plan their next move. Meanwhile, the disastrous news reached Richard—possibly from de Vere himself before he left the country—and the king removed from Windsor to the Tower.[13] On this same day, Chaucer received an advance of 20s at the Exchequer (a debt that he never paid back)—a typical medieval example of the ordinary business of government continuing smoothly in the face of calamity and chaos.[14] He was thus, at least briefly, back around the capital in this most dramatic time—on the day when news of the battle must have been dominating the conversation of all those around the king's household and offices. Over the next few days, the Appellants arrived at London, entered the Tower, and probably temporarily deposed the king.[15] Chaucer was no longer working or living in London, but he was by no means detached from the centre or the workings of power.

Now, the national drama ramped up yet further. In February the Merciless Parliament opened. De Vere, de la Pole, Tresilian, Neville, and

[13] See Hector and Harvey, *Westminster Chronicle*, 222–24; Chris Given-Wilson, *The Chronicle of Adam Usk* (Oxford: Clarendon Press, 1997), 10–12.

[14] Crow and Olson, *Chaucer Life-Records*, 330. In chapter 1, I discuss the robustness of institutions in the face of the trauma of the Black Death; see also Dyer, *Making a Living*, 273.

[15] See the chronicle of Whalley Abbey, BL, MS Harley 3600, discussed in Clarke, *Fourteenth Century Studies*, 91–95. See also Hector and Harvey, *Westminster Chronicle*, 218–19. This is discussed in more depth in chapter 10.

Brembre were appealed and condemned. Only Brembre was present, but Tresilian was found hiding nearby, and they were executed on 19 February (Tresilian) and 20 February (Brembre). Towards the end of the month, and at the beginning of March, people of lesser importance were impeached: these included Thomas Usk and John Blake (who had drafted the questions to the judges), who were executed on 4 March. On 12 March, a group of Richard's chamber knights, including Burley, was impeached. On Friday, 20 March, Parliament was adjourned for a three-week Easter recess.[16] It recommenced on 13 April; Chaucer, meanwhile, found himself occupied with his own financial affairs. On 16 April, John Churchman (owner of the Custom House) sued him for debt. He initiated the suit in London that day, and nine days later issued a writ in Kent. Churchman issued multiple writs on the same day to many different people, for sums as large as £330. Chaucer's debt was for just £3 6s 8d.[17] This was not a negligible sum of money, but nor was it disastrous for a man whose Exchequer annuities amounted to 40 marks a year, and who had a further £10 annuity from the duke of Lancaster. He was summoned to appear at the Court of the Exchequer on 31 May and again on 1 July, but there is no evidence that he went, or that the debt was ultimately paid or vigorously pursued. It may well have been a government debt, that is, a debt accumulated when Chaucer paid for a work-related expense out of his own pocket (by borrowing money on his own account), as he did with much larger sums when he was clerk of the king's works, and as he had when he went abroad to Lombardy, for instance.[18] In the last weeks of April and the first days of May (with a break for the St George's Day celebrations), Parliament continued to discuss Burley's fate, amongst other business. It had not yet been determined, and Parliament was still in full swing when Chaucer, rather surprisingly, surrendered both his annuities to John Scalby, an esquire of John Waltham, who had been appointed to the governing council by the Appellants. The letters for transferring the annuities (which amounted to 40 marks, or £26 8s) were enrolled on 1 May 1388.

[16] See PROME, '1388 February,' 7:55.
[17] Crow and Olson, *Chaucer Life-Records*, 384–87.
[18] Ibid., 58–59, 441, 469.

He almost certainly exchanged these annuities in return for a sum of money. The question is why? There are many possible explanations, but two are probable. One is that he was acting with great caution. The Merciless Parliament was primarily attacking the recipients of the king's favour and, in particular, members of the household. Later on in the Parliament, the Commons requested that certain annuities be made void, and Chaucer's annuities could have been included within this group. It is possible that the proposal was already circulating and that Chaucer wanted to cut his losses while he could. This would be in keeping with his resigning his customs job when Parliament was moving against customs' officers eighteen months earlier. Some of his friends and colleagues had similarly retrenched and effaced themselves: in October 1386, Philippe de la Vache, for example, had given up his custody of the king's park of Langley.[19] A second possibility relates to Chaucer's new way of life. When he worked at Wool Quay, at the heart of England's economy and taxation system, he was extraordinarily well placed to receive his annuities and indeed received them exceptionally easily and regularly. He did not have to endure delays or inconveniences. But now he lived in Kent and no longer worked at the centre of taxation, so claiming his allowances was likely not going to be as straightforward. Perhaps he simply couldn't be bothered to argue and plead for them twice a year and preferred the bird in the hand in the shape of a large cash sum. He may have had urgent debts to pay or have found that his wife's death and the loss of her annuity (in 1387) had made a significant difference to his life—perhaps he now had to take greater responsibility for Lewis, for instance (which would also fit with his writing a text for him around 1391).[20]

He continues to appear in various documents throughout this period. Towards the end of 1388 and in early 1389, while Henry Atwood (an innkeeper) was pursuing him for debt, and he was ignoring his creditor, Chaucer himself stood surety for an otherwise obscure woman named Matilda Nemeg.[21] Matilda had left her employer, Maria Alconbury,

---

[19] *Calendar of the Patent Rolls: Richard II*, Membrane 15, 3:234 (20 October 1386).

[20] On Lewis, see chapters 9 and 18.

[21] For the Atwood case, see Crow and Olson, *Chaucer Life-Records*, 387–91; for Nemeg, see 289–93.

before the end of the agreed term, and Alconbury was suing her; at the same time, Alconbury also brought a suit against John of Cologne, a clockmaker, for abducting Matilda. We don't know how Chaucer was connected to these people, or what happened in the end. We do know that Chaucer appears here alongside a group of Kentish men.[22] We also know that he is associated with foreigners—John of Cologne and Matilda Nemeg. Given her association with John of Cologne, it is highly likely that 'Nemeg' or 'Nemghen' derives from Nimeguen (now Nijmegen) in Gelderland. One interesting context is that at exactly this time—autumn 1388—a group of Hanse merchants had been arrested in London in reprisal for the arrest of English merchants at La Sounde. These merchants—including two Johns from Cologne—were released when they guaranteed English merchants freedom to trade in Lubyk, Rostok, Wyssemere, and Hamburg.[23] There was manifest tension between London merchants and German merchants at this time: there had been little trade since 1385 and the Appellants had sent an embassy to Prussia a few months earlier. They returned around the end of September to report that they had negotiated a treaty allowing reciprocal trading rights.[24] Given Chaucer's historic associations with pro-foreigner government policies, my best guess is that there was a campaign of harassment against German merchants, and Chaucer was supporting the immigrant traders. As a side note, the fact that John of Cologne was a clockmaker is a reminder of the kinds of objects that were newly being circulated around this time.

Chaucer was out of a job throughout the years of Richard's loss of power, regaining an appointment (as clerk of the works) almost as soon as Richard resumed the reins of government. This does not, however, demonstrate that Chaucer was a fervent Ricardian and an opponent of the Appellants. Chaucer's political position was consistent throughout his life: he was a moderate and a Lancastrian. He had been employed in the king's household and had given up his position when the household was being reduced and critiqued. But he remained on good terms with, for instance, William Beauchamp, brother to one of the Appellants. Indeed, one of the minor

[22] Ibid., 292.
[23] Thomas, *Calendar, 1381–1412*, Roll A29, Membrane 2, 149–50 (20 September 1388).
[24] Hector and Harvey, *Westminster Chronicle*, 330–31, 368–69.

Appellants was Henry, son of Chaucer's principal patron and half-brother to Chaucer's nephews and nieces. Chaucer's own son was closely associated with Henry throughout his life and was, at this time, in the Iberian peninsula with Gaunt. Chaucer was reappointed when Richard was appointing moderates in general, and when Gaunt was returning from Spain.

We can compare Chaucer with others who effaced themselves or lost favour around 1386 but regained it a couple of years later.[25] Throughout his life, Chaucer was connected to a group of men who were later known as the Lollard knights.[26] These well-educated men were connected with the royal household, usually as chamber knights, and were interested in aspects of religious reform. They were around the same age as Chaucer and generally had connections with John of Gaunt, the Black Prince, and Princess Joan (wife of the Black Prince and mother of Richard II). Although they worked in Richard's household, their connection with the royal household predated Richard's accession; they were a generation older than he was and, indeed, their very interest in aspects of Wycliffite thought connected them to Joan, Gaunt, and the intellectual climate of the 1370s (when Richard was a young child). The fluidity of their associations was such that several of them gained appointments under the Appellants, demonstrating the fact that they were not indelibly associated with the kind of Ricardian excesses and favouritism that brought down de Vere and Burley. Although there was an attack on the household in 1386–88, most long-serving courtiers suffered only very minor and temporary setbacks. Some, like Chaucer, came back into prominence in 1389, others a year earlier. This is not because they had changed their politics or because their politics necessarily differed from each other; it is down to chance and circumstances—these were men who could work for Richard *or* for the Appellants.

We have a great deal of information about this group of readers, writers, soldiers, and courtiers who were among Chaucer's earliest readers, and with whom Chaucer travelled abroad and socialized in London and Westminster. Lewis Clifford, for instance, the literary mediator between

---

[25] See also Strohm, *Social Chaucer*, for a discussion of these men's 'restraint' during these years, 36–41.

[26] McFarlane, *Lancastrian Kings and Lollard Knights*, 182–85.

Deschamps and Chaucer, fought for the Black Prince in Najara in 1367 and for Gaunt in France in the 1370s; he worked for Joan right until her death, after which he was one of her executors. He was with her in 1385, went on a peace mission to France in 1386, and then kept a low profile until 1389, after which he frequently attended the king's council.[27] His connections, then, are very similar to Chaucer's (although he was more important, as he was a knight) and, given that they were certainly friends, that Lewis is not a common name, and that children were frequently given the name of their godparent, he may well have been godfather to Chaucer's son, little Lewis. Clifford's own son-in-law was Philippe de la Vache, to whom Chaucer addressed a poem, *Truth*. De la Vache also fought for Gaunt and received gifts from him, was a member of Edward III and Richard II's households, and was one of Joan's executors. He, like Chaucer, removed himself somewhat from public life when the Appellant onslaught on the household began. However, by 1388, he was back in the centre of things: he served as an MP for Buckinghamshire in the Merciless Parliament and was made captain of Calais Castle by the Appellants during this parliament.[28] When Richard returned to power in 1389, Vache remained in favour. We see here an example of someone who was indeed able to negotiate good relations with both sides. Similarly, William Neville, another one of the Lollard knight group, and one of Chaucer's guarantors in the Cecily Champaigne group, did not seem to be affected by the rise of the Appellants. Associated with the court party in the 1370s and thereafter a chamber knight of Richard II, his brother Alexander was one of the targets of the Merciless Parliament and was found guilty of treason (but not executed). We find William being granted several manors in Cornwall on 9 January 1387 in exchange for an allowance (which had

[27] See the *ODNB* for more detail.

[28] His appointment appears in Thomas Carte (ed.), *Catalogue des Rolles Gascons, Normans et Français, conservés dans les Archives de la Tour de Londre* (Paris: Jacques Barois, 1743), Membrane 5, 2:157 (15 May 1388). Strohm follows Rickert in asserting that he disappears from the record between 1386 and 1390 (Strohm, *Social Chaucer*, 39–40; Edith Rickert, 'Thou Vache,' *Modern Philology* 11:2 (1913): 218). However, he did in fact both attend Parliament and receive an appointment. Rickert claims that he could not have been captain of Calais Castle at a later date, because that was Beauchamp's job ('Thou Vache,' 218n4). However, the role of captain of Calais was separate from the role of captain of Calais Castle. See also, for example, *Calendar of Close Rolls: Richard II*, Membrane 30d, 3:627 (22 November 1388): Beauchamp and Vache here co-witness a document dated 20 October 1388 in their respective roles as captain of Calais and captain of Calais Castle.

itself been granted in lieu of a forestership); on 19 April 1388, during the Merciless Parliament, he successfully requested the pardon of John Yoxhale, for stealing a silver dish; on 8 June, a few days after the end of the parliament, he was appointed to a commission of array for Nottinghamshire for the defence of the Scottish Marches.[29] He was also active in 1387 in protecting Nicholas Hereford, Wycliffe's disciple, as was John Montagu (discussed below).[30] William is best known to history as the intimate of Sir John Clanvowe, with whom he was buried near Constantinople. Clanvowe also backed Chaucer in the Cecily Champaigne case and was the author of a poem that quoted from the 'Knight's Tale' and of a radical religious tract in prose. He was with Gaunt repeatedly in the 1370s and worked for Edward III and Richard II. Clanvowe was sent on government business in September 1386 and then kept a low profile in 1387. However, in November 1388, when the Appellants were still in charge but Richard was resurgent, we find him negotiating with the French in a group that included William Beauchamp, John Devereux, and Nicholas Dagworth.[31] Although Chaucer's friends were associated with Richard's household, they were not perceived as his favourites or as antagonistic to the Appellants. They were mature, established men of proven worth. Their earlier connections with Gaunt and the Black Prince and their long careers of military and diplomatic service made them respected and useful civil servants.

Another member of this group leaned more in the Appellant direction but again was able to negotiate between different groups. William Beauchamp, an exact contemporary of Chaucer who also witnessed his release from Cecily Champaigne and whom Chaucer mainprised in 1378, fought with the Black Prince at Najera, worked for Gaunt repeatedly in the 1370s, was a member of the royal household under Edward III and Richard II, and was one of Joan's executors in 1385.[32] As the brother of the earl of

---

[29] *Calendar of the Patent Rolls: Richard II*, Membrane 30, 3:267 (9 January 1387); Membrane 9, 3:449 (19 April 1388); Membrane 2d, 3:475 (8 June 1388). Strohm argues that Neville was inactive between the April supplication for Yoxhale's pardon and 1391. *Social Chaucer*, 39.

[30] McFarlane, *Lancastrian Kings and Lollard Knights*, 198–99.

[31] Carte, *Catalogue des Rolles Gascons, Normans et François*, Membrane 7, 2:159 (26 November 1388).

[32] For his connections with Chaucer, see Crow and Olson, *Chaucer Life-Records*, 343 and 279.

Warwick, he assisted the Appellants in 1387. Although he lost some of his preferment in the early 1390s, he continued to serve on royal commissions and did not fall even when Richard took revenge on the Appellants, including William's brother. Indeed, some men strongly associated with the Appellants in 1386–88 proved their worth and were kept on by Richard. One example is John Waltham, closely associated with the Appellants and appointed as keeper of the privy seal in their council. He lost his job when Richard took over but was reappointed by the king as treasurer two years later, and he became such a close associate of Richard's that he was buried in Edward the Confessor's Chapel at Westminster. Another important figure is John Gilbert, bishop of Hereford (and then of St David's). Like the Lollard knights, Gilbert was closely associated with the Black Prince, acting as his spiritual advisor, and was connected with Gaunt from the late 1370s until his death. He was involved in diplomacy under Edward III and Richard II—at one point alongside Chaucer—and was one of Edward's executors. He was appointed treasurer by the Appellants, serving from 24 October 1386 until 1 May 1389. When Richard resumed power, he initially changed the whole administration but reappointed Gilbert only three and a half months later, on 20 August 1389. He served until 2 May 1391 (when Waltham took over).[33]

The fluid and multiple nature of the connections across the seeming party lines are neatly demonstrated by a social gathering that took place on 25 March 1388.[34] John and Maud Montagu celebrated the birth of their son, Thomas, that day and immediately baptized him (an interesting footnote to this story is that Thomas would, much later, marry Chaucer's granddaughter). We met Maud Montagu earlier in this book, as the daughter of Adam Fraunceys, merchant and mayor of London and patron of St Helen's Bishopsgate. John Montagu, heir to the earldom of Salisbury, was another Lollard knight, and (according to Walsingham) patron of Wycliffe's follower, Nicholas Hereford.[35] Like many of the other men that I have described above, he was a member of the royal household and

---

[33] See his *ODNB* entry.

[34] J. L. Kirby (ed.), *Calendar of Inquisitions Post Mortem: Volume XIX, 7–14 Henry IV (1405–1413)* (London: HMSO, 1992), 234–35, item 655.

[35] Walsingham, *Historia Anglicana*, 2:159, 216; McFarlane, *Lancastrian Kings and Lollard Knights*, 198.

a lover of poetry: the writer Christine de Pisan praised his poetry and sent her son to be educated with John's son, Thomas.[36] John chose Thomas of Woodstock, duke of Gloucester and one of the principal Appellants, luckily now free from his appealing and executing duties for a few weeks during the Easter recess, to act as godfather to the new baby, who took his name. John also chose Sir Richard Sturry, his colleague from the royal household with whom he shared literary and religious interests, to act as another godfather. Gloucester gave the baby 'a golden reliquary with precious stones and a picture of the Trinity,' and Sturry presented him with 'a valuable silver basin.' Sturry, we are informed by a proof of age inquisition from 1409, rode to Shenley for the baptism with Walter Somery 'talking of rumours touching King Richard.'[37] The duke of Gloucester was an extremely cultured man and a great book owner, interested in vernacular religion and courtly poetry.[38] John Montagu, who became a fervent Ricardian in 1397, was, according to later accounts, a close confidant of the duke in this earlier period, while also being associated with the Lollard knight group that gathered around the royal household.[39] Sturry, who was captured and ransomed alongside Chaucer in 1360, participated in diplomatic missions and local commissions with him, was one of the key courtiers in the last years of Edward III's reign alongside Latimer and Lyons, owned a copy of the *Roman de la Rose*, presented Froissart to Richard II in 1395, had long been in the royal household, and had connections with the Black Prince and Joan (he was yet another one of her executors).[40] Sturry was socializing with the Appellants at the exact moment when the fate of members of the household such as Burley hung in the balance. The Appellants were not attacking the men of the household overall, nor the institutions of government. They were pressing for reforms of certain practices and targeting their ire on particular

[36] McFarlane, *Lancastrian Kings and Lollard Knights,* 182.

[37] Kirby, *Calendar of Inquisitions*, 235, item 655.

[38] A. H. Dillon and W. H. St John Hope, 'Inventory of the Goods and Chattels belonging to Thomas, Duke of Gloucester, and Seized in His Castle at Pleshy, Co. Essex, 21 Richard II (1397),' *Archaeological Journal* 54:1 (1897): 280–82; Staley, *Languages of Power*, 165–66.

[39] See PROME, '1399 October,' 7:2–8, 6; and Membrane 3, no. 7, 8:83–84 (October 1399, Part 2); Walsingham, *Chronica maiora*, 1:820–21, 2:12–13.

[40] Froissart, *Oeuvres*, 15:167.

people—but the vast majority of court and government servants emerged from the crisis unscathed.

All of the men that I have been describing here—Chaucer, Clifford, Sturry, Vache, Clanvowe, Beauchamp, Waltham, and Gilbert—could work for Richard *or* for the Appellants. They were not, primarily, partisans; they were competent men, and they were moderates. So, although giving up his allowances must have been tedious for Chaucer, it was not catastrophic. He was temporarily retreating, but he was not penniless or friendless. And the fact that Scalby painstakingly transferred monies owed to him in arrears suggests that he was not in some kind of political wilderness.[41] He was probably confident that he would be able to get another job if he wanted one, either when the drama calmed down or when Gaunt returned.

This poet of change, then, had changed his life and was now looking at London and Westminster from a Kentish perspective, a perspective from south of the river. It is easy to see the river as a barrier and to imagine a dramatic difference between life in the countryside and life in London, to think that Chaucer was decisively separated from his old life. But the Thames was an actual river, not a symbolic one. In contemporary texts such as *Pearl*, the river divides one realm from another; it cannot be crossed. In Gower's *Confessio Amantis*, in contrast, the Thames is a social space, a space for meeting and messing about on boats, but it is also a space that exists out of time, where Richard speaks to Gower in a fantasy world of literary play.[42] The actual Thames—the river that Chaucer looked at every day during his London years from his office on the north bank— was an artery that connected large swathes of the country. It appears in this way in Hoccleve's *Male Regle*, when Hoccleve uses the river as a way of getting from Westminster to London, chatting to the boatmen on the way.[43] In one of his short poems, Chaucer writes to his friend at Windsor, saying that Scogan 'knelest at the stremes hed / Of grace,' while he, Chaucer, is 'In th'ende of which strem' where he is 'dul as ded, / Forgete in

---

[41] In 1389, Scalby paid Chaucer arrears on his annuity due for 1 April to 1 May 1388.

[42] Kendall, *Lordship and Literature*, 262–63.

[43] Thomas Hoccleve, 'La Male Regle de Thomas Hoccleue,' in Roger Ellis (ed.), *'My Compleinte' and Other Poems* (Exeter: University of Exeter Press, 2001), 64–78, lines 193–208.

solytarie wildernesse' (*Lenvoy de Chaucer a Scogan*, 43–46). In all of the manuscripts, the 'stremes hed' is glossed as Windsor and the wilderness as Greenwich.[44] Chaucer is surely seeking some kind of preferment at this point from those at the 'stremes hed.'[45] But a glance at a map, or a cursory knowledge of political and regional life, makes it clear that the 'wilderness' comment is a joke. It is rather like someone in London today moaning about moving to Zone 3, or a New Yorker complaining about relocating from Manhattan to Brooklyn. Greenwich is about four miles from the Tower of London, and one could get a boat all the way. In no context can that be seen as a difficult journey. And indeed, in the part of Kent in which we find Chaucer, he was mixing with many of his old acquaintances from London and from the court.

Chaucer is connected with Kent from the mid-1370s, when we find him being given the wardship of Edmund Staplegate and then William Soles. From the mid-1380s onward he can be placed in Kent in many contexts: as JP, as MP, investigating an abduction case, being sued for debt, participating in a commission to bolster flood defences, as a witness of land transactions. It is likely that he had long owned property in Kent. First, the fact that he was given the wardship of Kentish heirs and later acted as JP and MP in Kent strongly suggests that he was a Kentish property owner.[46] There is also a further piece of circumstantial evidence that supports the Greenwich connection. In 1386 (during the Wonderful Parliament), Chaucer stood surety for Simon Mannyng, a Kentish man based at Cudham (about twelve miles south of Greenwich), and husband of Katherine Mannyng.[47] A later source claims that Katherine was Chaucer's sister.[48] Katherine Mannyng inherited a manor and six acres of land with appurtenances in East Greenwich ('vno mesuagio *et* sex acris te*rr*e cu*m* pertin*en*tiis in Est grenewich') in 1365 and sold it for 20 marks of silver ('viginti marcas argenti').[49] It is made clear that the land was inherited by

---

[44] *Riverside Chaucer*, 1087, note to line 43.

[45] See chapter 18 for further discussion.

[46] Strohm reads the evidence differently, arguing that Chaucer's lack of qualification to be an MP in comparison with his peers suggests that he was given the role as a partisan. See *Poet's Tale*, 141–45.

[47] Crow and Olson, *Chaucer Life-Records*, 285–89.

[48] The comment appears around 1619. London, British Library MS Harley 1548, fol. 29b. Crow and Olson, *Chaucer Life-Records*, 289. It would be a rather eccentric fiction.

[49] National Archives, CP 25/1/106/180.

Katherine, not her husband ('*hereditate predicte Katerine*'). Katherine and Simon sold the land to two men, one of whom, Robert Atwood, was being sued alongside Simon Mannyng twenty years later, on the occasion on which Chaucer mainprised his (likely) brother-in-law. Given Geoffrey's own manifold connections with the Greenwich area, it is possible that he too inherited land in this part of Kent, and that the Chaucer family had various connections with the northern part of the county.[50]

Whether or not this is true—and it cannot be proved, although it would be very strange indeed for Chaucer to be given the kind of roles he held in Kent if he did not own property there—there is no doubt that he was in Kent from the middle of the 1380s. He was especially connected with an area just a few miles from central London, close to the south bank of the Thames. Documents particularly link Chaucer with Greenwich and Woolwich. If you cross the Thames from London to Southwark, and then follow the river east, after about three miles you reach Hatcham, in Deptford, or West Greenwich. This is where Chaucer was robbed in 1390. Another mile or so from Deptford brings you to Greenwich itself—also known as East Greenwich. It is about three miles between Greenwich and Woolwich. Turning away from the river and heading further down into Kent, Eltham Palace, one of Richard's favourite residences, is three or four miles from both Greenwich and Woolwich. Given that Chaucer could have gone between Greenwich and the Tower of London by boat, he was probably about equidistant between the Tower and Eltham, two of the places that he oversaw when he was clerk of the works.[51]

Now that Chaucer lived somewhere along the south bank of the Thames—in the Greenwich-Woolwich area—the river was a vital conduit for him, as he often journeyed over to London, for instance, to the Tower, as well as further afield. In 1390, he was appointed as clerk of the works for St George's Chapel, Windsor, and probably made several trips upriver

[50] Katherine made the agreement to hand over the land in Greenwich on 25 November 1365, although the document was recorded several months later in 1366. She thus possessed the land before John Chaucer died (he was still alive on 16 January 1366). Therefore, unless the land was gifted to her by John, perhaps as a marriage gift, but imprecisely termed an inheritance here, she must have inherited this land from someone else. On the similarities between the marriage portion and inheritance, see Joseph Biancalana, *The Fee Tail and the Common Recovery in Medieval England: 1176–1502* (Cambridge: Cambridge University Press, 2004), 52.

[51] See chapter 10.

to fulfill his duties there, repairing the chapel.[52] The Thames was the most important road in the country; goods travelled along it to or from Reading, Oxford, and Henley at one end, and to or from the ports of Essex and Kent at the other—and also to the world beyond the river's eastern estuary. London was the centre of the Thames-side trade, of course, the place where the boats came in. From Chaucer's new southern perspective, he could take the ferry from locations including Greenwich, Charlton, Upper Woolwich, or Woolwich.[53] Or he could have ridden up to Rotherhithe, or gone on to Southwark where London Bridge was located. The river teemed with activity: there were further ferry embarkation points downriver at Erith, Dartford, Greenhithe, Gravesend, and Higham, before the river emptied into the sea. This part of Kent and London were mutually dependent economically, as one might expect given their close proximity. Goods such as beans, oats, peas, rye, wheat, and faggots of wood were supplied to London from Lewisham Priory, via the Greenwich dock. Deptford (West Greenwich) was a shipbuilding location and the river also provided London with fish.[54] Over and over again, the needs of fishermen clashed with the needs of merchants, as fish weirs obstructed the smooth movement of ships bringing goods to London. Indeed, Magna Carta prohibited the use of fish weirs in the Thames.[55] In 1371, the parliamentary Commons had petitioned that 'each person, of whatever condition he may be, who has a mill, weir, fishery or any other thing whatsoever by which the free passage along the said rivers might be disturbed, shall cause them to be removed within a certain term.'[56] When Chaucer refers to a water mill in the 'Reeve's Tale' (3923), or uses an image of a fish weir as a way of entrapping a victim in courtly love in *Troilus* (III, 35), he is using mundane and political images. The fish weir in particular was something that was seen by many as the tool of profiteering predators, impeding free movement. The fishermen from Woolwich, Greenwich,

---

[52] For this appointment, see Crow and Olson, *Chaucer Life-Records*, 408–10.

[53] G. M. Draper, 'Timber and Iron: Natural Resources for the Late Medieval Shipbuilding Industry in Kent,' in Sheila Sweetinburgh (ed.), *Later Medieval Kent, 1220–1540* (Woodbridge: Boydell Press, 2010), 62.

[54] Ibid., 63, 66.

[55] H. Summerson et al. (trans.), 'The 1215 Magna Carta: Clause 33,' The Magna Carta Project, http://magnacarta.cmp.uea.ac.uk/read/magna_carta_1215/Clause_33.

[56] PROME, Membrane 3, no. 18, 5:239 (February 1371).

and the surrounding area complained to the king in 1394 that they were being prevented from exercising their ancient right to fish from boats and rafts in the Thames, but the ban on their 'trawl-nets' was upheld: the king's interest was consistently focused on maintaining the flow of shipping on the river.[57] So, there were particular kinds of economic activity that were strongly associated with living near the river, and Chaucer, as first a worker on the north bank of the Thames and then a resident of Greenwich on the south bank, was inevitably very familiar with the life of the river and with the river's role as an artery that connected different parts of the body of the country.

Chaucer knew many people who owned property in this area. Indeed, from the middle of the fourteenth century there was a clear increase in mercantile Londoners buying property in precisely the Greenwich-Woolwich-Dartford area, from where it was so easy to go to and from London.[58] Even those who rented out their property or used it for business purposes would have come back and forth to see to their affairs. Adam de Bury, for instance, who gave Chaucer his apartment in 1374 and was one of the court targets of the Good Parliament in 1376, gained the manor of Spittlecombe in Greenwich in 1372, and used it as a residence, executing his will there in 1385.[59] Brembre had a number of Kentish properties, some of which were passed on to Adam Bamme.[60] Henry Vanner, oligarch of London whose path crossed Chaucer's in very many ways, owned and leased property in Lewisham and Greenwich, as well as further down the river in Erith.[61] As well as the mercantile traffic in this area there were also, of course, the established Kentish families, with many of whom Chaucer was connected. In 1385, when Chaucer first became a JP in Kent, his fellow JPs included, for instance, John Cobham, John Devereux, and Arnold Savage. These were all men with Appellant leanings.[62] They also,

[57] PROME, 'Appendix: 27 January 1394,' no. 14, 7:281.

[58] Draper, 'Timber and Iron,' 67.

[59] National Archives, PROB 11/1/11. Crow and Olson, *Chaucer Life-Records*, 506–7n5.

[60] Edward Hasted, *Historical and Topographical Survey of the County of Kent* (Canterbury: W. Bristow, 1797), 2:310, 2:336.

[61] 'Vanner, Henry,' in Roskell, Clark, and Rawcliffe, *History of Parliament*, 4:706.

[62] Cobham in particular was strongly associated with the Appellant cause and was sentenced to death for his involvement when Richard took his revenge in 1397. However, the sentence was commuted to banishment.

like the Lollard knights, had connections with Gaunt, the Black Prince, and Joan.[63] Chaucer had even been in Navarre at the same time as Devereux, back in 1366.[64] Cobham had long had connections with Gower,[65] and we know that Gower and Chaucer had been friends since at least the late 1370s, when Gower looked after Chaucer's interests while Chaucer was in Italy.[66] Cobham is a fascinating figure in his own right. In chapter 10 I discussed his use of an English motto on his castle and his connection with the architect and craftsman Henry Yevele. The fact that he expressed himself through English verse and artistic patronage makes his connections with both Chaucer and Gower particularly interesting in reconstructing the circles that surrounded these poets. Gower himself had Kentish property interests and resided in Southwark, a short ride from the Greenwich area. Southwark, origin point for the Canterbury pilgrims and location of the first known exchange of a Chaucer manuscript in 1394, was clearly an important early home for Chaucer's poetry. Packed with aristocratic and gentry residences,[67] as well as disreputable alehouses and brothels, it was also the location of the real Tabard Inn, run by the real Harry Bailly, taverner and MP. Chaucer may regularly have stayed in one of the inns there or have ridden the few miles over from his Kentish residence. He would have found all kinds of company there—including many people with literary interests.[68]

If he travelled a few miles in a different direction from Greenwich, he could reach Eltham palace, one of Richard's favourite residences, and one of the places of which Chaucer was in charge when he became clerk of the works. Richard spent a lot of time at Eltham: we know that he spent at least sixty-five days there in 1385, during five visits, at least fifty days in 1386, and thirty-one days in 1390.[69] He had bathhouses and a

---

[63] Cobham was another one of Joan's executors; he also repeatedly served with Gaunt. Savage was also in Joan's household: Devereux was a long-term retainer of the Black Prince.

[64] See chapter 4.

[65] For Cobham and Gower's connections, see John H. Fisher, *John Gower: Moral Philosopher and Friend of Chaucer* (London: Methuen, 1964), 51–54, 313–18; and Kendall, *Lordship and Literature*, 39–43.

[66] Crow and Olson, *Chaucer Life-Records*, 54.

[67] Martha Carlin, *Medieval Southwark* (London: Hambledon Press, 1996), 30–35, 44–51.

[68] See chapter 16.

[69] See Saul, 'Appendix: Richard II's Itinerary, 1377–99,' in *Richard II*, 468–74.

dancing chamber constructed there and also allowed many courtiers to have their own personal apartments there.[70] Political meetings and discussions often took place at Eltham; it was also at Eltham that Froissart presented Richard with a book, through the agency of Sturry, in 1395. Chaucer's literary friends were thus spending time at the palace, and even talking about books there, just down the road from Greenwich. One courtier couple with their own apartment at Eltham was Nicholas and Margaret Sarnesfield. Nicholas had been in the retinue of the Black Prince and became Richard's standard-bearer; Margaret probably came over to England with Anne in 1381 as a lady-in-waiting. After Henry IV's accession, he confirmed her life interest in her Eltham apartment and granted her a garden there, so it seems likely that the Sarnesfields treated the palace as at least a part-time home.[71] In 1392 Chaucer witnessed a charter transferring Woolwich manor plus other properties and rents in Kent to Nicholas and Margaret, from John Horn, a major London fishmonger (who later said the release had been extorted from him and his wife).[72] Similarly, in 1395 and 1396 Chaucer repeatedly witnessed documents relating to Thomas Arundel's transfer of the manor of Spittlecombe and other local properties to a group of men, including John Waltham, Philippe de la Vache, and William Courtenay, then archbishop of Canterbury. He then witnessed their transfer to Gregory Ballard in 1396 and acted as Ballard's attorney to take possession of the properties.[73] The cluster of documents all place Chaucer physically in the Combe area. They also reveal a good relationship between Chaucer and Thomas Arundel, the archbishop of York, brother of one of the principal Appellants and a key ally of the Appellants throughout 1386–89. Although Arundel worked harmoniously with Richard for some years after the crisis—serving as his chancellor and as archbishop of Canterbury—he was exiled in 1397 and returned with Henry Bolingbroke in 1399.

---

[70] Colvin et al., *History of the King's Works*, 2:934; Given-Wilson, *Royal Household*, 31.

[71] See Douglas Biggs, 'Patronage, Preference, and Survival: The Life of Lady Margaret Sarnesfield, c. 1381–c.1444,' in Douglas Biggs, Katherine French, and Linda Mitchell (eds.), *The Ties that Bind: Essays in Medieval British History in Honor of Barbara Hanawalt* (Burlington: Ashgate, 2013), 143–58.

[72] Crow and Olson, *Chaucer Life-Records*, 504–6.

[73] Ibid., 506–13.

Chaucer acted as an attorney for Ballard, but this does not imply that he was a lawyer; rather, it suggests that he acted with power of attorney, or in Ballard's stead. Ballard was an esquire and chief butler of the king's household.[74] These Kentish documents demonstrate Chaucer's 1390s identity as a Kentish man, living in the Greenwich-Woolwich area. But they also demonstrate that this identity was not a big change for him: the parties in the Woolwich transaction were a wealthy London merchant and a courtier couple, and those in the Combe transaction included royal officials and a major aristocratic politician and churchman.

Local resentment was often stirred up by the arrival of royal representatives and favourites into Kent.[75] Chaucer does not fall into that category—he had long-term connections with Kent and never received lavish rewards in the county—but he often took the role of outsider, representative of the centre. All members of royal commissions, such as commissions to investigate walls and ditches, took on this role to a certain extent, however local some of the members might be. Their job was to enforce central directives and, where necessary, coerce local men into labour. The area around the banks of the Thames was reclaimed marshland, like much of the eastern part of England. Parts of the Norfolk Broad peatlands, the Humber wetlands, the Lincolnshire marshes, the Pevensey Levels in Sussex, the Romney and Walland marshes, and the marshes around the Thames estuary and tidal river in Essex and East Kent had all been embanked, drained, and converted to farmland during the long medieval period.[76] These areas remained vulnerable to storm damage and flooding and, in the thirteenth and fourteenth centuries, England entered into a stormier period. Some areas reverted to marsh completely.[77] From the middle of the thirteenth century, royal commissions were set up to manage drainage and flood defences, and the commission that Chaucer sat upon in 1390 was one such commission.[78] One way of reading the commissioners' roles is as

---

[74] See, for instance, *Calendar of Close Rolls: Richard II*, Membrane 14d, 6:76 (7 November 1396).

[75] Kendall, *Lordship and Literature*, 42.

[76] James A. Galloway, 'Coastal Flooding and Socioeconomic Change in Eastern England in the Later Middle Ages,' *Environment and History* 19:2 (2013): 176–81.

[77] Galloway, 'Coastal Flooding,' 183–84.

[78] The first was set up in 1257. *Calendar of the Patent Rolls: Henry III*, Membrane 10d, 3:592 (16 April 1257); Galloway, 'Coastal Flooding,' 201.

centralizing enforcers, interfering in local matters and taking poor men away from their own labour to build flood defences. Another is that the royal commissions were enforcing important environmental work for the good of the whole local community: drainage and reinforcing defences were vital for the maintenance of food production and indeed of communities more generally. The commission on which Chaucer sat was set up on 12 March 1390, one week after a great storm. It had the express purpose of reinforcing the walls and ditches on the Thames between Greenwich and Woolwich. Chaucer's fellow commissioners included Henry Vanner and the ubiquitous Richard Sturry. Vanner, as mentioned above, was the leaser of the manors of Lewisham and East Greenwich. He leased them from the priory of Ghent, but the Crown had seized these lands as part of their attack on alien priories more generally, and Richard Sturry was the custodian of the manors on behalf of the Crown.[79] The makeup of the commission reminds us that Chaucer maintained close connections with men such as Sturry into the 1390s. It is notable that we often hear of Sturry in Kent—here in Woolwich with Chaucer in 1390 or four miles down the road at Eltham with Froissart in 1395. The other men on the commission were John Culpepper, a JP from an old Kentish family, and two experienced legal representatives.[80] Records of the work of similar commissions reveal that they summoned local people to report on problems such as breaches in dykes, and then gave detailed orders for repairs, including advising on the planting of willows along the edges of the dykes and the ringing of pigs to protect the banks. They also took bonds to ensure the performance of the repairs.[81] This latter practice put pressure on local gentry to make sure that they did their duty. Chaucer's role was thus one that involved reasonably detailed local knowledge and engagement with the landscape, and an understanding of how the behaviour of humans made an impact upon the seemingly natural features of the environment.

---

[79] A. K. McHardy, 'The Alien Priories and the Expulsion of Aliens from England in 1378,' *Studies in Church History* 12 (1975): 133–41.

[80] Crow and Olson, *Chaucer Life-Records*, 490–93.

[81] Ibid., 493.

The weather was not the only threat along the banks of the Thames. The vignettes that describe an attack on Chaucer in 1390 help us to imagine Chaucer's routine work in Kent (and elsewhere). He was robbed as he rode through Deptford, near his regular stamping ground of Woolwich and Greenwich, probably en route between Westminster and Eltham, taking money to pay workers there. He was violently set upon and left without his transport: his attackers took his horse, other property, and a large sum of the king's money. A few miles south of Greenwich, the area of Shooters' Hill was a notorious spot for brigands.[82] The story reminds us how itinerant Chaucer's job of clerk of the king's works was—he had to travel about to numerous locations, and because those locations were royal palaces, he was in contact with a diverse array of royal officers and courtiers. He may not have needed to travel to some of the further-flung places for which he was responsible—such as Feckenham in Worcester-shire or Hatheberg in the New Forest—but he was certainly frequently travelling around the Thames artery to the Tower, Westminster, Windsor, and Eltham. Although he no longer lived in the capital city, Chaucer's life remained a life at the conceptual centre, representing the Crown. But quite apart from this job, if we look at the people with whom Chaucer was connected in property transactions and through the varied and vibrant cultural and intellectual life taking place both at Eltham Palace and in Southwark taverns and houses, it is clear that northwest Kent was by no stretch of the imagination a backwater. Like the river itself, Chaucer's life was always changing, and always the same.

[82] Draper, 'Timber and Iron,' 63. I discuss the robbery in more detail in chapter 17.

CHAPTER 16

Inn

Assembled was this compaignye
In Southwerk at this gentil hostelrye
That highte the Tabard, faste by the Belle.

—'General Prologue'

Chaucer's decision to begin the *Canterbury Tales* in the Tabard Inn in Southwark was a marked choice. He chose to set his poem in a place of social mixing, where people of different estates could come together. The setting thus facilitated the great change that Chaucer made to the tale-collection genre. In contrast to Boccaccio's *Decameron*, or Gower's *Confessio Amantis*, or his own *Legend of Good Women* or 'Monk's Tale,' this tale collection featured multiple tellers from different social backgrounds, allowing Chaucer to foreground diverse perspectives. This juxtaposition of voices and genres is central to the poetics of the text. The *particular* inn that Chaucer chose as his pilgrims' origin point is also significant: the Tabard was a real location and Harry Bailly, its owner in the *Canterbury Tales*, was also its owner in real life. The Tabard and the Harry Bailly of the *Tales* are, however, by no means identical to the Tabard and the Harry Bailly that Chaucer knew in contemporary Southwark. Chaucer thus confronts, head-on, the tricky boundary between fiction and reality. His inn is neither the actual place that his readers might frequent, nor an allegorical representation of, for instance, earthly vice in contrast to the church, symbolized by Canterbury Cathedral. In moving from more courtly poetry to embrace a more naturalistic aesthetic, Chaucer was not moving from idealism to pragmatism or from fantasy to reality. My earlier discussions of the dream visions and *Troilus* have demonstrated how much these poems are imbued with contemporary politics; conversely the *Canterbury Tales* is a text fascinated by stylized literary form. The real-world setting foregrounds questions of what literature is, of how fiction relates to everyday, lived experience, and of the power of representation and aestheticization. Chaucer's consistent interest in representing experience in multiple ways—through contrasting perspectives, varying genres, and juxtaposed voices—finds its ideal location in the fourteenth-century inn, a place where normal hierarchies were suspended, and various identities could be performed.

The initial lines of the 'General Prologue' form a stunning poetic sequence and are still Chaucer's most-quoted and most influential lines (cited above in chapter 1). The dazzling opening images are images of balance and contrast: spring and winter, water and drought, breath and inertia, health and sickness. In every case, the image of life and hope precedes its opposite. These are lines about desire, about the process of change, about seeking self-understanding. Showcasing the novel ten-syllable line and the fledgling heroic couplet with confidence, Chaucer also draws on traditions well known to his audience. The *reverdie*—or address to the spring—was a common motif in romance and lyric especially; the opening is reminiscent of dream visions including the *Roman de la Rose,* and consciously imitates texts such as Guido de Columnis's *Historia destructionis Troiae.*[1] Chaucer also sets up his tale collection as a competition in the mode of the historical civic Puy. Moving away from Petrarchan and courtly models, Chaucer now draws on estates satire—a genre that critiques and mocks the vices and follies traditionally associated with different social roles and occupations—amongst other generic models.[2] And, as I have argued in earlier chapters, his political awareness of the changes in parliamentary practice and the evolution of the Speaker helped Chaucer to develop

---

[1] See the notes to the *Riverside Chaucer* for an overview of the sources of the 'General Prologue.'

[2] Mann, *Chaucer and Medieval Estates Satire.* Sebastian Sobecki has recently argued that the Southwark poll tax return forms a model for the 'General Prologue' cataloguing of people. 'A Southwark Tale: Gower, the 1381 Poll Tax, and Chaucer's *Canterbury Tales,' Speculum* 92:3 (2017): 630–60.

his own poetic voice and the idea of the mixed voices of the *Canterbury Tales*.

The opening stages a contrast between the eternal and the temporal, the world of cyclical inevitability ('Whan that Aprille') and the world of contingent opportunities ('Bifel') (plate 2).[3] The magisterial rhythms of the first, extraordinary eighteen-line sentence give way to the happenstance of the factual, specific 'Bifel that in that seson, on a day, / In Southwerk at the Tabard as I lay.' This is the reader's introduction to the surprising, real-world setting of the poem. Chaucer had long been experimenting with the division between fiction and fact, as had authors such as Machaut, particularly through the development of narratorial personae.[4] The poet-narrators of the *House of Fame* and the Prologue to the *Legend of Good Women*, the two unfinished experimental poems that, in their different ways, were both crucial precursors to the *Tales*, are comic, fictionalized figures that nonetheless are clearly versions of Chaucer himself. In the dream poems, the world of fiction—the garden court, the bird parliament, the houses of Fame and Rumour—dominates, as it does in *Troilus* too. The contemporary world—intimated through the detailed description of luxury bedding in the *Book of the Duchess* or the evocation of Aldgate in the *House of Fame*, or made explicit through the presentation of the abject poet in the *Legend* or the naming of Geffrey in the *House of Fame*—irrupts into that fictional world, destabilising a clear division between art and life, poet and narrator, fact and fiction. *Troilus and Criseyde* is intensely naturalistic in its depiction of interiority, of everyday incidents, and of material and circumstantial detail, but its setting remains both the legendary world of Troy and the literary world of stylized love.[5] But in the 'General Prologue,' Chaucer does something altogether different. Here, the setting for the text, the world of the *Tales* seems, confusingly, to be the real world itself: a real inn, located in a real place, run by (a fictionalised version of) a real, contemporary personage. This seeming foregrounding of history has caused all kinds of problems for Chaucer critics, some of whom have tried

[3] On time, see Le Goff, 'Merchant's Time and Church's Time'; and Strohm, *Social Chaucer*, 110–43.

[4] The old idea of Chaucerian 'realism' is problematic in its terminology but still useful; see Muscatine, *Chaucer and the French Tradition: A Study in Style and Meaning* (Berkeley: University of California Press, 1957). See also the discussion in chapter 5 in this study.

[5] For more discussion, see chapter 11. See also Wimsatt, 'Realism,' 43–56.

to find 'real' sources for the pilgrims, for instance.[6] The 'General Prologue' is a profoundly literary, self-conscious text, about literary characters,
not real people. But Chaucer chooses to make the boundaries between
reality and fiction deeply unstable, using two key techniques. First, he
develops a style that Cannon has described as an early version of free indirect discourse, as Chaucer blends the first- and third-person perspectives
in the 'General Prologue' descriptions, creating the illusion that the narrator really has spoken to the pilgrims and is repeating their own views of
themselves.[7] Second, he chooses Harry Bailly's Southwark Tabard Inn as
the opening location for the pilgrims' meeting. In making this choice, he
imitates Boccaccio's decision to place his storytellers in Santa Maria No-
vella, a real church well known to his audience. The *Decameron* group
then moves to the countryside garden-estate, which becomes the place of
carnival for their games. The Canterbury pilgrims move into the amorphous zone of pilgrimage, where real life, debts, and day-to-day obligations were suspended, again leaving space for stories and play. The more
concrete the origin point, the greater the contrast between the idea of
ordinary life and play.

The choice to begin the *Tales* in this specific location—the Tabard
Inn—is profoundly important and innovative. But what precisely did
this inn signify to Chaucer and his audience? On the one hand, Chaucer
has chosen a location that is not in the city, not the symbolically central
St Paul's that would have been an obvious imitation of Santa Maria No-
vella. Nor is the location courtly. It is suburban, and this particular suburb was the home of brothels and drinking houses. It is easy to see the
Tabard as signifying a disreputable origin-point for the *Tales*, as a place of
the 'tavern sins'—drinking, dicing, swearing—that were condemned by
contemporaries. Alcohol consumption was clearly one of the defining aspects of the starting point of Chaucer's poem. Indeed, the name of the
Tabard itself has symbolic meaning: we might be more familiar with the

---

[6] J. M. Manly, *Some New Light on Chaucer: Lectures Delivered at the Lowell Institute* (London: Bell,
1926).

[7] Cannon, *Literacy to Literature*, 119–24. Cannon argues that this oscillation between the first and
third person is inspired by school grammar books' layering of teacher's and student's perspectives, linking Chaucer's techniques to those he learnt in school. In a brilliant argument, Cannon suggests that 'a
deft use of pedagogical technique can create a vivid subjectivity' (124).

meaning 'garment,' but it could also refer to a lead tank enclosing a brew-ing vessel, a singularly apt name for an alcohol-providing establishment. The Parson uses tavern signs themselves as metaphors for sin: when ex-plaining that outer pride signifies inner pride, he uses the example that 'the gaye leefsel atte taverne is signe of the wyn that is in the celer' (411). The tavern sign functions as a straightforward illustration of the simple relationship between sign and signified—something about which Chaucer was deeply skeptical—and what a tavern 'means' to the Parson is simply wine. Furthermore, wine here is a metaphor for sin. But the Tabard Inn had many associations other than alcohol, and it was certainly very different in reputation and atmosphere from a low-class alehouse, for in-stance. Martha Carlin, the historian of Southwark, has pointed out the important differences in different kinds of medieval drinking establish-ments that we might now group together as pubs. At the bottom of the scale came the humble alehouse, selling ale by jug or cup; next was the brewhouse, a place that brewed beer and might also sell by retail; the tavern was a somewhat more expensive establishment that was licensed to sell wine; and finally, at the top of the scale, was the inn, sharply differenti-ated from these other establishments principally because it provided lodging.[8] The inn was a hotel, where people could sleep in dormitories or in luxurious private accommodation, where they could get meals and drinks, and fodder and stabling for their horses. It was a respectable gath-ering place. Inns made their profits from food, stabling, and private accommodation—dormitory beds were either free or very cheap.[9] So the relatively poor could stay there as well as the very rich. The word 'inn'— 'hospicium'—was also used for aristocratic townhouses. It was a word, then, that did not have negative connotations. Indeed, in the 'Knight's Tale,' when the royal tourneyers come to Athens and Theseus needs to find them accommodation, we are told that he 'inned hem, everich at his degree' (2192). This could mean that they are lodged in inns or in royal lodgings or in aristocratic houses—the word is neutral.

[8] Carlin, 'Host,' 460.

[9] Martha Carlin, ' "What say you to a piece of beef and mustard?": The Evolution of Public Dining in Medieval and Tudor London,' *Huntingdon Library Quarterly* 71:1 (2008): 205–8.

Rather than being a periphery, then, the inn was a centre, a place of luxurious living and mixed social interaction. Harry Bailly's Tabard Inn was a completely different kind of place from, for instance, the dicing tavern of the 'Pardoner's Prologue' or 'Cook's Tale'; and different again from the alestake that the Summoner resembles and that the Pardoner pauses at before embarking on his tale. Harry Bailly as a historical personage was not a poor beer seller on the make. On the contrary, he was an MP, a tax collector and controller, and a coroner. He was entrusted with large sums of money and was a collector for the notorious poll tax.[10] That is not to say that he did not have connections that were not respectable—he was, for instance, connected with brothel owners. Indeed, one of those brothel owners worked with Harry Bailly, collecting the poll tax, and is known to Chaucer scholars as the first recorded owner of the *Canterbury Tales*—John Brynchele.[11] When we examine the people with whom Bailly was associated, there are other overlaps with Chaucer's circles. William Atte Wode, for instance, was one of the recipients of Arundel's transfer of the Spittlecombe property in 1395, which Chaucer witnessed; he can also be found at Lesnes, a few miles further into Kent, witnessing a document alongside Harry Bailly in 1387.[12] Southwark's identity was bound up with those parts of northwest Kent that it bordered. I do not think that we need to place Chaucer as living in Southwark—when a great deal of evidence points to his living in Kent, as discussed in chapter 15—to believe that he knew Southwark well and probably dined and socialized at the inns there. The parts of Kent in which we find Chaucer were only a few miles from Southwark. It is hard to understand his use of the Tabard and Harry in the 'General Prologue' except as an in-joke, a reference to a place and person that he and part of his primary audience knew reasonably well. It would be very easy for him to ride to Southwark from the Combe area, or to stop there on his way back from the Tower or

---

[10] Carlin, 'Host,' 461–65.

[11] See Sobecki, 'A Southwark Tale,' on Brynchele's connection with Bailly. See Turner, 'Usk and the Goldsmiths,' for discussion of Brynchele's ownership of the *Tales*; and Carlin, 'Thomas Spencer,' for his brothel connections.

[12] Crow and Olson, *Chaucer Life-Records*, 506–9; *Calendar of Close Rolls: Richard II*, Membrane 36d, 3:435 (5 October 1387, recorded 9 October), Membrane 26d, 3:398 (10 September 1387).

Westminster, or to stay overnight occasionally, either at an inn or at the house of a friend such as John Gower or Arnold Savage.

Sebastian Sobecki has argued recently that Southwark had its own urban identity as a vibrant location in its own right, not primarily as an extension of London.[13] It was a quickly growing place in the fourteenth century as aristocrats and ecclesiastics built or bought lavish properties there and inns developed apace. Southwark also became the location for the stews—signifying both the brothels and the fishponds near the Thames—but in the past, critics have perhaps overemphasised these more disreputable aspects. What Southwark, and specifically the Tabard, offered as a location for Chaucer was a place that encouraged juxtaposition and mixing. In all of Chaucer's poems, he plays with mixing registers and generic norms. But in the *Canterbury Tales*, juxtaposition—both social and literary—becomes the life breath of the text. The most striking aspect about his pilgrim company, in contrast to Boccaccio's, is its social variety, and the most striking aspect of the *Tales*—showcased perhaps most clearly in Fragment I and also particularly dramatically in VII—is their diversity and mutual contrast.[14] When Chaucer took the stand-alone story of Palamon and Arcite (a reworking of Boccaccio's *Teseida*, probably written in the first half of the 1380s and listed as an individual text in the F-Prologue to the *Legend of Good Women*, 420), and turned it into the 'Knight's Tale,' a poem defined by its place in a bigger text and, in particular, defined by its relationship to the 'Miller's Tale' and, to a lesser extent, the 'Reeve's' and 'Cook's' Tales, he made a vital move in the history of English poetry. No one who has read Fragment I in its entirety can think of the 'Knight's Tale' as a stand-alone text—its meanings are deeply inflected by its context, and especially by the fact that it is immediately parodied, its generic norms exposed, its teller's worldview questioned

---

[13] Sobecki, 'A Southwark Tale,' 650–52.

[14] The *Canterbury Tales* is divided by editors into ten fragments, each of which consists of tales that are internally linked. The arrangement of the fragments in relationship to each other is a matter of conjecture, as different scribes made different decisions. Therefore, while we can be sure that the 'General Prologue' should be followed by the 'Knight's Tale,' then the 'Miller's Tale,' then the 'Reeve's Tale,' and then the 'Cook's Tale' (Fragment I), we do not know for certain what 'should' come next. Indeed, Chaucer may have changed his mind about the ordering of the tales. The 'Man of Law's Tale' (Fragment II) follows in many manuscripts and in most modern editions, but in the earliest manuscript (Hengwrt), Fragment III follows Fragment I.

and opposed. Chaucer fully understood the power of different literary forms to critique and undermine each other. He knew that multiple forms both expose the inadequacy of each individual form and, together, can present a much fuller and more nuanced perspective.

Mixed social groups, then, facilitate formal variety. As Strohm demonstrated in *Social Chaucer*, in the *Canterbury Tales* social conflict is played out through genre.[15] The opening tales of the Canterbury project tell the same story in different genres—and their generic differences matter enormously. The tales contrast with each other in scale, tone, and worldview: the space of the amphitheatre becomes the window ledge through which Nicholas sticks his bottom; the intervention of the gods in the world becomes Nicholas's pretence of the flood. But they also each contain within themselves aspects of the other: witness the importance of the artisans' construction of Theseus's display of feudal power, or Nicholas and Absolon's deployment of the language of courtly love. Similarly, in the first tale told by Chaucer's own avatar, the 'Tale of Sir Thopas,' mercantile places and ideology are jumbled up with the spaces and ideals of chivalric romance. Thopas was born at Poperyng, in Flanders, wears stockings from Bruges, excels at the low-class sports of archery and wrestling, and spends Genoese money.[16] But he also embarks on a quest, riding through a forest, seeking the land of Faerye, and fighting (or running away from) a giant, all the time motivated by love-longing and chivalric ambitions. We see here, in comic miniature, a reprisal of the juxtapositions of the 'Knight's' and 'Miller's' Tales. Mixing is *the* most characteristic aspect of the style of the *Canterbury Tales*.

The inn provided a location in which social mixing was easy to imagine, where Chaucer could, in a real-life setting very different from the ostentatiously fictional bird parliament and House of Rumour, further develop the idea of the right of all kinds of people to speak on their own authority, an idea that he had explored in his earlier poems and that had captured his imagination. The norms of behaviour at inns also suggest that these were locations of performance, where strangers could choose what kind of personae to project and indeed what kind of genre to employ. The

---

[15] Strohm, *Social Chaucer*, 166–72.
[16] See Wallace, *Premodern Places*, 103.

1396 *Manières de langage* provides a fascinating insight into generic self-consciousness in those who patronized inns.[17] The author euphemistically terms the customer's procuring of a prostitute as an 'aventure galante' (39). He is then given the option of addressing her in two different ways, one using the familiar *tu* and the other the formal *vous*. He could say: 'Isabelle, vien ça, vien' ('Isabel, come here, come'). Or he could say: 'Venez a moy, ma tresdoulce amie, hardiement, car je vous promette que je ne vous fera ja de vilaynie, ains vous ferai, s'il Dieu plest, de bien et de l'oneur' (40) ('Come to me, my very sweet love, quickly, because I promise you that I will not do any villainy to you, but I will, if God pleases, do to you good and honour'). In other words, he can decide whether he is in a fabliau or a romance. Both texts have the same aim and outcome—sex. But in the fabliau everything happens quickly and straightforwardly ('vien ça, vien'); there is no need to pretend that sex is not the aim. This is the world of the 'Miller's Tale,' of Pandarus, of the lower-class birds in the *Parliament of Fowls*. The 'romance' option is quite different. Now the tone is formal, the speaker extravagantly compliments the object of desire ('ma tresdoulce amie'), he invokes God ('s'il Dieu plest'), and uses the language of villainy and honour ('je ne vous fera ja de vilaynie, ains vous ferai . . . de bien et de l'oneur'), swearing that his intentions are indeed honourable, when it is crystal clear that this is not the case, and that the love-object/prostitute knows this as well as he does himself. This is the world of Palamon, Arcite, and Troilus, albeit in a more debased form. But if one function of Fragment I (comprising the 'General Prologue' and the 'Knight's,' 'Miller's,' 'Reeve's,' and 'Cook's' Tales) is to show us that romance utilizes the same plot essentials as fabliau, with the result that we see *both* how much language and form matter, *and* how much language and form deceive, cover up, and twist meanings, then the *Manières de langage* is a fascinating analogue for the Knight-Miller juxtaposition. And as it goes on, we continue to see the client being encouraged to sing songs and make up courtly love poems (40–41). The world of romance, this suggests, could penetrate even the most transactional of sexual encounters. It doesn't matter whether or not people actually behaved in this way, reciting

---

[17] Andres M. Kristol (ed.), *Manières de langage (1396, 1399, 1415)* (London: Anglo-Norman Text Society, 1995); translation mine.

highly conventional romance poems to prostitutes. But it is interesting that it was taken for granted that talk about love, respect, and honour was doublespeak—just as in romance itself words such as 'pity' and 'mercy' are euphemisms for sex. There is something peculiarly appropriate about Chaucer's staging his meditation on genre, class, voice, and register in the contact zone of the inn, a place of performance and elaborate self-fashioning.

Historically, the earliest copies of Chaucer's books that we can trace were also connected with Southwark, with inns, and with prostitution. From at least the last decade of Chaucer's life, continuing into the fifteenth century, we can reconstruct a network of Southwark residents who owned Chaucer's books and were engaged in text work as scribes, associated with cloth workers, and ran brothels. At around the same time that Chaucer was visiting Bernabò Visconti and coming into close contact with Petrarch's cultural milieu, John Brynchele was setting up a drinking house in Southwark. In the last decades of the fourteenth century, and continuing into the 1420s, there are numerous records of Thomas Spencer and Brynchele. These two men were both hostelers and brothel keepers. They both worked as professional scribes. They both lived in Southwark for many years and for a time were next-door neighbours. Both had problems with the law. And while one was our earliest known owner of the *Canterbury Tales*, the other was our first known owner of *Troilus and Criseyde*. Thomas Spencer, who owned a cheap copy of *Troilus* by 1394, signed his name next to Adam Pynkhurst's in the register of the Scriveners' Company, placing him in suggestive connection with a man who worked for Chaucer and whom Chaucer specifically links to the copying of *Boece* and *Troilus*.[18] Spencer, and indeed Brynchele, may well also have come into contact with Chaucer's texts professionally, as scribes.[19] Chaucer's books, both in their fictional contents and their material form, were bound up with taverns and brothels, with eating, drinking, and sex. And they circulated in a mixed community of people with some decidedly disreputable elements.

[18] Mooney, 'Chaucer's Scribe,' 100–101. See also Mooney and Stubbs, *Scribes and the City*, 67–85; and Warner, 'Scribes, Misattributed.'

[19] Carlin, 'Thomas Spencer,' 387–401.

Many critics have suggested that Chaucer's audience changed after 1386–87, when he moved out of London. Strohm suggests that Chaucer needed to invent a new, fictional audience—the pilgrims of the *Canterbury Tales*—in the aftermath of the events of 1386.[20] Pearsall argues that Chaucer's pre-*Canterbury Tales* poems were for a mixed-gender courtly audience and that the *Canterbury Tales* was written for a London audience that was male and 'clubby' in atmosphere.[21] Sobecki concurs that the audience was male and 'clubby,' although he locates it in Southwark.[22] Cooper, in contrast, suggests that in the *Canterbury Tales* Chaucer is rejecting not only courtly poetry but also male, clubby poetry. She argues that the poetry of the all-male Puy focused on the honouring of ladies and was primarily in a French-derived lyric mode. The *Canterbury Tales*, in her view, is breaking with both court and city: its evocation of a mixed-gender, English-speaking group outside the city walls imagines a different kind of reception environment.[23] One of the key issues here is how men write about women. As Pearsall states, Chaucer's earlier poems tend to focus on sexual love, which is much less important in the *Canterbury Tales*. He suggests that this change is explained by the fact that women vanished from Chaucer's audience.[24] His implication, then, is that the poetry of idealized sexual love is poetry that appeals to women. But, as Cooper demonstrates, the all-male poetry of the Puy focuses on this kind of idealizing—and dehumanizing—attitude to women. In that context, 'courtly love'–inspired poetry is indeed the poetry of the all-male club. As Chaucer matured, he increasingly focused on depicting women in a wider range of roles (although he had never been one-dimensional in his treatment of women). In the *Book of the Duchess* and the *Parliament of Fowls*, women primarily function as objects of sexual desire. But we do also see women taking other roles in Chaucer's early writings—St Cecilia, for instance, or the intercessory queens of the 'Knight's Tale.' When Chaucer came to write *Troilus*

[20] Strohm, *Poet's Tale*, 227–30.

[21] Derek Pearsall, 'The *Canterbury Tales* and London Club Culture,' in Butterfield, *Chaucer and the City*, 98–99.

[22] Sobecki, 'A Southwark Tale,' 650.

[23] Helen Cooper, 'London and Southwark Poetic Companies: "Si tost c'amis" and the *Canterbury Tales*,' in Butterfield, *Chaucer and the City*, 113–17.

[24] Pearsall, 'London Club Culture,' 99.

and Criseyde, although Criseyde functions as an object of desire and exchange, Chaucer makes her a fully rounded and realized subject whose perspective is crucial to the poem. In the *Canterbury Tales* Chaucer moves more decisively away from writing about courtly romance heroines and towards writing about different kinds of women and about female perspectives—most famously, of course, in the figure of the Wife of Bath and in her extraordinary tale, which forms an original meditation on what it is to be raped and how rape should be punished.[25] As discussed in other chapters, this change in focus in Chaucer's depiction of women was part of a cultural change as humanist-influenced poets increasingly focused on love as something that encompassed ethics, social practice, and common profit.[26] This is a fruitful context for thinking about tales such as 'Melibee,' the 'Clerk's Tale,' and indeed the 'Wife of Bath.' Chaucer's imagined audience is not female-dominated, as Boccaccio's was (seven of his ten tale-tellers are female), but it does include women (the Wife of Bath, the Prioress, and the Second Nun). It is difficult to see why his actual audience would not also contain women: if his poem was being read at Eltham Palace *or* at the Tabard Inn, there would be women present. Inns were not exclusively male environments: Harry Bailly had a wife, women could stay at the inn, and other aristocratic women lived in Southwark. Chaucer had developed a new kind of poetry and was now writing outside London, in a somewhat different kind of environment. But members of court and city circles were still within his ambit and there is, in my view, no compelling reason for believing that the *Tales* was written for a male coterie.[27]

Given Chaucer's marked decision to set the beginning of the *Tales* within a Southwark inn, and the fact that we know that his texts were owned by Southwark hostelers during and beyond Chaucer's lifetime, the overwhelming probability is that his texts did find one immediate audience within Southwark drinking establishments of various kinds—some of which were very respectable venues, patronized by well-off, educated

[25] There are many versions of this story. Only in Chaucer's is rape the crime under consideration. The rapist's exhortation to the old lady to 'Taak al my good and lat my body go' (1061) suggests a belated realization on his part of the true horror of his crime. For other versions of the story, see Correale and Hamel, *Sources and Analogues*, 2:405–48.

[26] See chapter 14 and also chapter 18.

[27] Wallace, *Chaucerian Polity*, 156–81.

people. The *Tales* were almost certainly read and discussed in environments such as the Tabard and the hostelries owned by Brynchele and Spencer, and were part of a living culture in the 1390s.

The inn or tavern was a place in which conversation and discussion could flourish. For those who did not go to university, the drinking establishment was the successor to the schoolroom as a place of debate, argument, and social mixing. Here, books and ideas circulated, were exchanged, and were brought to life, while the solitary intellectual was 'deed and nayled in his cheste' ('Clerk's Prologue,' 29) or sat 'domb as any stoon' (*House of Fame*, 656). And when reading was done in an inn, it was associated with eating and drinking. Listening to a book while eating dinner was a common medieval practice, a practice that connects books and the body, ingesting knowledge and food together.[28] The book was profoundly connected with the body and its appetites. Indeed, the bodiliness of reading was particularly accentuated in an era in which reading tended to be done out loud.[29] When one speaks a text, the words are rolled on the tongue and from the lips, they are physically felt and experienced; rhetorical techniques cannot be ignored, nor can they merely be noted; they are an inescapable part of the reading experience. The text is not only touched and seen (and smelt), it is spoken and heard; it engages the senses much more fully. When one reads aloud, one performs the text; it becomes a drama. In Chaucer's times, this was often a drama enacted for an audience, as people often read in groups, but even if one were alone, if one read aloud, the text became an embodied performance. Medieval readers engaged with texts in interactive ways: those who were reading or copying Chaucer's poetry frequently added comments or quotations from his sources to the margins. 'Controversial' parts of the *Tales*—notably the 'Wife of Bath's Prologue'—attracted particularly heavy glossing from its scribes (plate 7).

The idea of the book in the inn, prompting competition and exchange, makes the book into a compromised, commercial object. But the

---

[28] Joyce Coleman, *Public Reading and the Reading Public in Late Medieval England and France* (Cambridge: Cambridge University Press, 1996), 82–83; and 'Audience,' in Turner, *Handbook of Middle English Studies*, 155–69.

[29] Coleman, *Public Reading*.

inn-as-book-room also embeds the book in the realm of the social, and the realm of the senses, in tune with the philosophy of social reading that is advocated across Chaucer's texts.[30] In contrast to the Visconti library, which offered a model of cultural production that was decisively rejected by Chaucer (and by Boccaccio), Chaucer chose the Southwark inn as his cultural home. As well as turning away from the poetry of patronage in favour of a more public kind of poetry, Chaucer was also turning his back on the Petrarchan ideal of writing in solitude. Petrarch argued that intellectuals needed *otium* (leisure), ideally in settings of rural beauty, where they could cultivate their minds apart from destructive and distracting *negotium*. He was not arguing for complete isolation; on the contrary, his ideal was to commune with a small group of like-minded, male intellectual friends.[31] When readers have imagined Chaucer in the wilderness, writing coterie poetry, they have come close to imagining Chaucer's living in this Petrarchan mode. But as we have seen, Chaucer repeatedly emphasized in his poetry the need to go to the streets and to listen to all kinds of people. His interest in the street-level perspective, not the privileged view from outside or above, was a constant part of his philosophy of reading and writing. It is important to resist reading any aspect of the *House of Fame* or the 'General Prologue,' with their interests in the voices of pardoners and shipmen, as straightforwardly autobiographical. But given Chaucer's protodemocratic literary choices, the groups amongst which his manuscripts circulated, and his intense suspicion of the ideologies of Petrarch and Dante, it is likely that he did indeed favour a more social and less exclusive model of literary production. In other words, he circulated his poems in inns and other social spaces, not only to a couple of carefully chosen friends. His language choice itself, as

[30] See chapter 7 for a discussion of the problems of reading in isolation in Chaucer's texts.

[31] Petrarch wrote two treatises relevant here: *De vita solitaria* and *De otio religiosa*. See discussions in Julia Conaway Bondanella, 'Petrarch's Rereading of *Otium* in *De Vita Solitaria*,' *Comparative Literature* 60:1 (2008): 14–28; Unn Falkeid, '*De Vita Solitaria* and *De Otio Religioso*: The Perspective of the Guest,' in Albert Ascoli and Unn Falkeid (eds.), *The Cambridge Companion to Petrarch* (Cambridge: Cambridge University Press, 2015), 111–19; Susanna Barsella, 'A Humanistic Approach to Religious Solitude,' in Victoria Kirkham and Armando Maggi (eds.), *Petrarch: A Critical Guide to the Complete Works* (Chicago: University of Chicago Press, 2009), 197–208; and Armando Maggi, ' "You Will be My Solitude": Solitude as Prophecy (*De Vita Solitaria*),' in Kirkham and Maggi, *Petrarch: A Critical Guide*, 179–95.

well as his subject matter, indicates that his desired audience was quite different from Petrarch's—it was more diverse, in terms of both social estate and gender.

Metaphors relating to drinking establishments infuse Chaucer's texts. We frequently come across casual comments such as the Wife of Bath's statement that 'thou shalt drynken of another tonne, / Er that I go, shal savoure wors than ale' ('Wife of Bath's Prologue,' 170–71) or the Host's assertion that he would 'levere than a barel ale' that his wife had heard the 'Tale of Melibee' ('Prologue of the Monk's Tale,' 1893). The Parson and the Pardoner both 'read' the tavern as a straightforward symbol of vice. The Parson attacks those 'that holden hostelries' ('Parson's Tale,' 439); the Pardoner terms the tavern a 'develes temple' ('Pardoner's Tale,' 470), a place of dicing, drunkenness, and swearing. These churchmen figure the tavern as the opposite of the church, as an allegorical location. Their perspectives, however, are unreliable: the Parson peddles an inflexible, rigid, schematic morality while the Pardoner deliberately performs an easy black-and-white interpretation of the world, designed to persuade and frighten the gullible.[32] Perhaps the most interesting metaphor in this image-field comes in the 'Reeve's Prologue,' when the Reeve drearily proclaims that:

> As many a yeer as it is passed henne
> Syn that my tappe of lif bigan to renne.
> For sikerly, whan I was bore, anon
> Deeth drough the tappe of lyf and leet it gon,
> And ever sithe hath so the tappe yronne
> Til that almoost al empty is the tonne.
> The streem of lyf now droppeth on the chymbe. (3889–95)

Death is here imagined as a cellarer who is waiting for the cask to run out. Life is a wait for death, measured out from the moment of birth, and the

---

[32] I discuss the Parson in more detail in chapter 19. For his simplifying stance, see especially Charles Muscatine, 'Chaucer's Religion and the Chaucer Religion,' in Ruth Morse and Barry Windeatt (eds.), *Chaucer Traditions: Studies in Honour of Derek Brewer* (Cambridge: Cambridge University Press, 1990), 258; Donaldson, *Speaking of Chaucer*, 173; Aers, *Chaucer, Langland, and the Creative Imagination*, 109. For a range of perspectives on the 'Parson's Tale,' see David Raybin and Linda Tarte Holley (eds.), *Closure in* The Canterbury Tales: *The Role of The Parson's Tale* (Kalamazoo MI: Medieval Institute Publications, 2000).

Reeve has now reached the bleak moment when only drips are emerging from the barrel. This image is unique to Chaucer and pays interesting testament to the centrality of the imagery of alcohol in the imagination of this vintner's son. It is also comparable to the 'Pardoner's Tale,' in which we also see a personified Death, a drinking scene, and an inevitable march towards death. For the Reeve and for the rioters, there is no escape, no way out, and no consolation. Indeed, in both cases, we see a radical misuse of metaphor. The plot of the 'Pardoner's Tale' hangs on the rioters' relentless literalism. The three rioters fail to understand that Death is not an isolatable figure, or that only Christ can kill death—and that this killing is metaphorical. The Reeve's understanding of metaphor is also ostentatiously limited. As Kolve has shown, imagery of the 'tonne' is usually related to relaxation and joy, and imagery of death is set against Christian hope, or 'the necessary counter-truth.'[33] The Reeve has a distorted understanding of life and death that focuses relentlessly on the negative. The imagery that he uses to describe the ageing process focuses on distasteful images of rotting desire, while in the tale itself, his use of imagery is thin and limited in sharp contrast to the luxuriant sensuality and exuberance of the image-packed 'Miller's Tale.' The difference between these two fabliaux beautifully demonstrates the variety within this genre. The contrast between courtly poetry and poetry set in a recognizable real world, or the contrast between romance and fabliaux, or the contrast between the idealizing language of *fin amor* and the pragmatic language of sexual conquest, is not a clear contrast between profundity and shallowness, nor between philosophical understanding and ruthless cynicism. The Reeve's pared-down tale of brutality is at least as different from the 'Miller's Tale' in terms of style *and* content as the 'Miller's Tale' is from the 'Knight's Tale.' Indeed, one could pair the 'Knight's' and the 'Miller's' Tales together as stories rich in imagery, inviting complex readings, unlike the unremittingly bleak 'Reeve's Tale.' The Miller's simultaneously moving and comic depiction of adulterous pleasure as a 'melodye' (3652) that ultimately chimes with the singing of lauds nearby (3655–56) is markedly different from the horrific description of the frenzied attack of the students on their

---

[33] Kolve, *Chaucer and the Imagery of Narrative*, 217–35.

victims in the 'Reeve's Tale' ('He priketh harde and depe as he were mad' [4231]). The Reeve's unyielding understanding of the 'tappe of lyf' demonstrates the extreme limitations of his almost-nihilistic perspective, and that inflexible perspective is isolated as the joyless point of view of one particular teller, not representative of the genre as a whole.

The drinking establishment or the wine cask meant a range of contradictory things in Chaucer's world. In the experience of the narrator of the *Tales*, the inn is the place where the compaignye is able to form; it is a sociable contact zone that allows conversation to take place. The compaignye that forms here is, however, conflict-ridden, and drinking nearly forces them apart—most notably in the 'Manciple's Prologue.' Alcohol is presented as medicinal—after the 'Physician's Tale,' the Host feels sick to the heart and needs a 'triacle,' or 'a draughte of moyste and corny ale,' or to hear 'a myrie tale' to cure him ('Introduction to the Pardoner's Tale,' 314–16). However, it is also poisonous, as we see in the 'Manciple's Prologue' when the Cook becomes a death-like figure, whose humanity, speech, and ability to function within the group is eroded by wine. The inn presented at the opening of the 'General Prologue' is a place of comfort and safety: 'The chambres and the stables weren wyde / And wel we weren esed atte beste' (28–29). It is a place of life, sociability, and pleasure. But the tavern of the 'Pardoner's Tale' and the wine cask of the 'Reeve's Prologue' are places of death.

This sense of the inn as a mixed space is crucial to Chaucer's presentation of human experience. His text is not an allegory, a straightforward progress from tavern to church, sin to redemption, Tabard to Canterbury, sickness to health. He does not present the inn and the church as allegorical opposites. The Pardoner, who preaches in the *Tales* at an alestake, is repeating the material that he usually preaches in churches, at Mass. Even the Parson reveals an awareness that churches themselves can be corrupt spaces: he compares the woman who commits adultery with someone who steals the chalice from a church. Adulterers, he asserts, 'breken the temple of God spiritually.' He thus draws a comparsion between the body and the church, and between the soul and the 'vessel of grace' (878–79). Real churches were places of business, and sometimes of feasting and drinking. One fourteenth-century archbishop of Canterbury bemoans the fact that after taking the Eucharist, Easter churchgoers would set up a meal in the church, eating 'unconsecrated bread and wine, and there sit down eating and drinking as in a tavern.'[34] In a throwaway reference, the Summoner reminds the Friar that 'wommen of the styves' are prostitutes licenced by the archbishop and therefore out of ecclesiastical jurisdiction ('Friar's Tale,' 1332–33). The bishops of Winchester licenced many Southwark brothels, and the Benedictine nunnery of St Leonard's—Stratford at Bowe—also owned brothels on the south bank of the Thames.[35] Westminster Abbey owned numerous taverns, and the Tabard itself was owned by the abbot of Hyde.[36] And inns, like other institutions, were dependent on various different authorities and constituencies: the Tabard acquired its wine from taverns, paid rent to the abbot of Hyde, and functioned as a stopping point or threshold for people on their way from London to Canterbury or elsewhere. As Chaucer wrote the *Canterbury Tales*, he imagined all kinds of spaces and economies: feudal, mercantile, regional, tyrannical, urban, claustrophobic, courtly, ecclesiastical.

For Chaucer, spaces, like genres, could not easily or productively be hierarchized or separated: in chapter 17, I demonstrate Chaucer's interest in exploring the relationship between spaces, their interdependence, and the way that different kinds of spaces rely on each other. The map that he drew in the *Canterbury Tales* was a map of networks and overlaps; the origin point of the Tabard inaugurates a metaphorical textual space where discourses, genres, estates, economies, and spaces contest, collaborate, conflict, and converse.

---

[34]'oblationes non consecratas et vinum . . . inibique sedentes, edentes, et bibentes quemadmodum in taberna.' The archbishop of Canterbury was Walter Reynolds, writing in 1325. Cited in Clarence H. Miller and Roberta Bux Bosse, 'Chaucer's Pardoner and the Mass,' *Chaucer Review* 6:3 (1972): 176–77. For the Latin, see David Wilkins, *Concilia Magnae Britanniae et Hiberniae* (London, 1737), 2:528.

[35]Carlin, *Medieval Southwark*, 49–50, 213; H. Ansgar Kelly, 'Bishop, Prioress, and Bawd in the Stews of Southwark,' *Speculum* 75:2 (2000): 342–88; and Sobecki, 'Southwark Tale,' 650–51.

[36]For instance, in 1384, John Weston sold a hostelry in King Street to the Abbey; it was later known as the Boar's Head. Gervase Rosser, *Medieval Westminster: 1200–1540* (Oxford: Clarendon Press, 1989), 63. Martha Carlin, Urban Development of Southwark, c. 1200 to 1550 (unpublished DPhil thesis, University of Toronto, 1983), 226–27; and Carlin, 'The Host,' 468.

CHAPTER 17

>·!·‹›·•·⊙·‹›·!·‹

Peripheries

Things fall apart, the centre cannot hold.
— *W. B. Yeats, 'The Second Coming'*

The *Canterbury Tales* as a whole promises a movement from sociable, sub-urban inn through the countryside and pilgrimage site, and back again to the Tabard. But throughout the *Canterbury Tales*—indeed in its very fragmentary fabric—Chaucer destabilizes the idea of centre and periphery. He does this both through his emphasis on multiple, movable centres, and through his interest in networks and in the interdependence of different kinds of places. The *Canterbury Tales* is expansive in its geographical interests: nationally, the text encompasses locations including Northumberland, Dartmouth, Norfolk, and Yorkshire; internationally, it ranges across places such as Morocco, Egypt, Lithuania, and India. Chaucer, and many of his friends and acquaintances, were extremely well travelled, and all men and women of his class depended on the extensive trade routes that traversed Europe, North Africa, the Silk Road, Russia, Central Asia, India, Southeast Asia, and China, for the luxuries that had become essential parts of their lifestyle.[1] Well-travelled, educated English people understood that to many people, England itself was peripheral, on the geographical and cultural borders of Europe.

In 1403, a Spanish embassy travelled into central Asia, to the court of Timur, known to Western posterity as Tamerlane, located at Samarkand

---

[1] Freedman, *Out of the East*, 7–10, 104–29. See also chapter 1 in this study.

(in modern Uzbekistan).[2] The travellers were sent by Henry III of Castile, whose queen was Catherine, daughter of John of Gaunt. One of the ambassadors wrote an account of his journey and of his time at Timur's court. He recounts that Timur welcomed them, saying, 'Here are the ambassadors sent by my son the king of Spain who is the greatest king of the Franks and lives at the end of the world.'[3] Ruy González de Clavijo (the Spanish ambassador) demonstrates here his understanding that what is central and what is peripheral is very much a matter of perspective. Geographically, Timur's view makes a good deal of sense: Spain, like Britain and Ireland, bordered the Atlantic, and it was unclear to Europeans and to inhabitants of Asia if there were lands further west. Those in Central Asia could logically see themselves as central, with Japan and Spain representing the eastern and western edges of the world. As one historian of medieval trade and power puts it, the Indian subcontinent was 'on the way to everywhere.'[4] Traditional Christian *mappae mundi* placed Jerusalem at the centre of the world, again seeing Britain as geographically marginal, although writers such as Mandeville, who wrote about the antipodes, displaced the very concept of a centre. And although Mandeville was an armchair traveller, many of his contemporaries were not. Clavijo's detailed description of his travels and of the habits and customs of Timur's people reminds us that places such as Samarkand were not mythical to educated late-medieval people.[5]

The journey between perceived centre and perceived periphery is the fundamental structure of European medieval narrative. This structure is, of course, common across multiple cultures and periods: the *Odyssey* and *Beowulf* are both variations on this theme. In late-medieval Europe, as medieval romance developed into a master genre, it built on classical and

---

[2] On Timur, see Beatrice Forbes Manz, *The Rise and Rule of Tamerlane* (Cambridge: Cambridge University Press, 1989).

[3] Clements R. Markham (trans.), *Narrative of the Embassy of Ruy González de Clavijo to the Court of Timour at Samarcand, AD 1403–6* (London: Hakluyt Society, 1859), 133.

[4] Abu-Lughod, *Before European Hegemony*, 260–86. On England's marginality, see Kathy Lavezzo, *Angels at the Edge of the World: Geography, Literature, and English Community, 1000–1534* (Ithaca: Cornell University Press, 2006), 2–8.

[5] The Franciscans had houses in Tartary, and the papacy had long been in communication with the khans. Edward I had sent a delegation to Arghan Khan in 1297. See Vincent J. DiMarco, 'The Historical Basis of Chaucer's Squire's Tale,' in Kathryn L. Lynch (ed.), *Chaucer's Cultural Geography* (New York: Routledge, 2002), 56–75.

biblical traditions, incorporating romance's distinctive fascination with mental space and personal growth.[6] The result was a torrent of texts based around this basic movement, a pulse that takes a hero away and back; texts that use marginal space in diverse ways. Peripheral spaces—often forests or wildernesses—became places of adventure, isolation, madness, testing, transition, and regeneration.[7] In text after text we see the knight set forth from the court to undergo adventure, a personal test in the forest, before returning, changed, to the centre.[8] One of the best iterations of this pattern is found in Chrétien de Troyes's *Yvain*. *Sir Orfeo* is one of the most striking Middle English examples. In both of these texts, the marginal forest-wilderness space represents madness and a crisis of identity. The centre-periphery-centre motif is repeated over and over again in central romance texts such as Malory's *Morte Darthur*. Occasionally, the motif is provocatively challenged: in *Sir Launfal*, the hero does not return to the courtly centre but remains in the shadowy otherworld; in *Sir Gawain and the Green Knight*, the poet reveals that the moral centre is located in the social periphery, and foregrounds the problems of returning, transformed, to an unchanged home. As James Simpson argues, in romance the return to the centre is a return predicated on the hero having 'encountered and recognized all that is other to value and order as defined by that ending.' This is not straightforward conservatism, but 'reformist conservatism'; a conservatism that is interested in incorporating alterity and in change.[9] Chaucer frequently deploys this important motif of the movement from centre to periphery and back again. The rapist in the 'Wife of Bath's Tale' goes from court to forest and back to court. Chauntecleer is taken from farmyard to hinterland, and escapes back to the farm. Constance leaves Rome and travels to Syria and Northumberland before returning to Rome.

Chaucer's own life was increasingly decentred after he left the Custom House—or perhaps it would be more accurate to say that it coalesced

[6] Corinne Saunders, *The Forest of Medieval Romance: Avernus, Broceliande, Arden* (Cambridge: D. S. Brewer, 1993).

[7] Corinne Saunders, 'Margins,' in Turner, *Handbook of Middle English Studies*, 331–46.

[8] Eric Auerbach, 'The Knight Sets Forth,' in *Mimesis: The Representation of Reality in Western Literature*, trans. Willard Trask (Princeton: Princeton University Press, 2003), 123–42; Richard Southern, 'From Epic to Romance,' in *The Making of the Middle Ages* (New Haven: Yale University Press, 1953), 219–57.

[9] Simpson, *Reform and Cultural Revolution*, 255–56.

around numerous centres. Although Chaucer's early residence in a constantly moving great household, his extensive travels, and his intense personal and professional involvement with international trade had always made manifest to him the contingency of any idea of a political, cultural, or geographical centre, he himself had, for a decade or so, been living in by far the biggest and most important city in England, adjacent to the principal bureaucratic, legal, and political institutions that governed the country. He had only moved a few miles, but he was now in the hinterlands of that city. This did not mean, however, that he lived a satellite existence. Not only was the English countryside a vibrant and powerful locale, but Chaucer also now moved between various centres. His job as clerk of the king's works placed him in the midst of many royal residences—such as Windsor and Eltham, as well as the London stronghold of the Tower—each of which became the 'centre' when the court was there.

Chaucer, indeed, became a victim of crime precisely when he was transferring funds from the capital to a satellite 'centre' (Eltham). He was robbed of large sums of money in Deptford and in Westminster, seemingly targeted repeatedly by a gang on the same day.[10] The unscrupulous, violent, itinerant gang that robbed him roamed the country, committing robberies in London, its southern borderlands in Kent and Surrey, Hertfordshire, Buckinghamshire, Wiltshire, and Hampshire; one of its members was from Lancaster, one from Ireland.[11] Of course, travelling robbers were not a new problem, but contemporaries certainly associated them with the increased mobility of a post-plague society. In the Commons' petition against vagrants of 1376, they accused labourers and artisans of refusing to abide by the Statute of Labourers, becoming vagrants and then usually becoming robbers, in small gangs. The Commons frame the problem of travelling robber gangs as a problem of itinerant labour: the solution they offer is for people to be physically punished 'until they will

---

[10] Crow and Olson, *Chaucer Life-Records*, 477–89. The several records are confusing: they suggest that Chaucer was robbed at Hatcham, Surrey, also near Le Foul Oak, Kent, also at Westminster. As a glance at a map reveals that Hatcham and Le Foul Oak are very close together, in the parish of Deptford (now in South London), it is probable that there was one robbery in this area, and that the different dates given (3 and 6 September) are a mistake: the robbers were tried for committing one robbery in that area on the 6th, and another robbery at Westminster on the same day.

[11] Ibid., 478–89.

swear to return to their own region and serve their neighbours according to the form of the aforesaid ordinances and statutes.'[12] While the demonization of workers is obviously biased and reactionary, gangs such as that which attacked Chaucer were probably helped by the freer movement of labourers in this period. And they were able to find targets such as Chaucer because of the 'newish' economic conditions that involved more physical moving about of large sums of actual money, both because people were increasingly paid in money, not kind, and because money increasingly came first to the bureaucratic centre through taxation before being moved outwards again.[13]

Chaucer also, however, worked for a regional great household, taking on the role of forester for North Petherton, in Somerset. This role was not a royal or government appointment. He was working for the earl of March, one of the great nobles of the country, whose major estates were on the western borders of England, abutting Wales. The great magnates of the late Middle Ages created their own centres—and indeed we might be reminded that Chaucer's primary loyalty had always been to Gaunt, whose interests were sometimes very much the same as the king's and sometimes quite different. Gaunt himself now returned (in 1389) from his attempt to make Spain his own centre of gravity, and the Spanish gold he had won funded his son's extensive travels in the early 1390s. While on a personal level Chaucer was experiencing an existence outside the obvious 'centre' of England, in its peripheral villages, towns, and forests, many of his friends were travelling to the edges of Christendom and beyond. The truce with France, signed in 1389, freed up English knights for crusading, and made travel across French territory easier. So in these years, Chaucer saw his friends roaming across the eastern edges of Europe, North Africa, and the Middle East. His close friends John Clanvowe and William Neville could be found at Tunis in 1390, and in Galata, next to Constantinople, in 1391. Sir Peter de Bukton, to whom Chaucer addressed a poem (*Lenvoy de Chaucer a Bukton*), accompanied Henry, earl of Derby, to Prussia and Lithuania in 1390, and part of the way to Jerusalem in 1392. Chaucer and his friends were, for

---

[12] PROME, Membrane 15, no. 117, 5:338 (April 1376). Also discussed by David Aers, *Community, Gender and Individual Identity: English Writing, 1360–1430* (London: Routledge, 1988), 28–30, 43, 49.

[13] Spufford, *Money and Its Use*, 378–96; see chapter 10 in this study.

various reasons, increasingly looking outwards in the first half of the 1390s, away from Richard and away from London. Richard himself also looked away from London, as he removed many crucial institutions to York during his quarrel with London in 1392. For many different groups, then, these post-Appellant, post-treaty years were disparate and expansive.

Chaucer was characteristically interested not in the big, important place but in the smaller place next door. Over and over again he writes about suburb rather than city, hinterland rather than town, and the smaller place tends to assert its own powerful identity.[14] Indeed, the seemingly unimportant countryside locations in Chaucer's *Tales* are foregrounded for their economic importance and vibrancy.[15] In the 'Reeve's Tale,' for example, the regional centre and university town, Cambridge, is dependent on the backwater Trumpington (the place where the story begins), because the miller there has the right and the means to mill the Cantabrigians' wheat—which itself must have come from their rural landholdings. And the scholars who represent the centre have come from the far north of England, probably Northumberland on the borders of England. Centres, in other words, are constantly renewed by immigrants from peripheries. The tale demonstrates competition but also dependence between different kinds of place and, as David Wallace has pointed out, the smaller place leaves a permanent mark on the aggressive interloper.[16]

More fundamental still is the way that Chaucer's depiction of space mirrors his poetics. Throughout the *Tales*, Chaucer's radical destabilizing of ideas of centre and periphery reflects his destabilizing of hierarchies of genre. Just as Oxford cannot survive without Osney, or the court without the forest, so the meaning of the 'Knight's Tale' is constructed through the 'Miller's,' 'Reeve's,' and 'Cook's' Tales—and, indeed, through the 'Wife of Bath's Tale,' the 'Tale of Sir Thopas,' and the 'Squire's Tale,' among others. The project of the *Tales* involves a levelling of discourse akin to a levelling out of power across locations that traditionally have very different levels of importance. So when Chaucer locates authority in peripheral

[14] Simpson, 'Chaucer as a European Writer,' 55–56.

[15] This contrasts with, for instance, Boccaccio's depiction of rural locations. See Wallace, *Chaucerian Polity*, 134.

[16] Wallace, *Chaucerian Polity*, 126.

or marginal geographical or topographical spaces, he performs a similar move to his location of equal authority in a Miller's and a Knight's stories, or in a fabliau and a romance. Chaucer's use of the tale-collection genre allows him to demonstrate that one perspective cannot be the whole story: the reader needs to hear multiple perspectives to put together a picture. The central idea of networks and interconnectedness is equally important for Chaucer's sense of space and for his poetics.

The forest, the region, and far, far away are three key kinds of marginal space in Chaucer's work and in his life. The forest meant many different things, both in medieval society and in medieval literature. It often symbolised isolation and separation from society, yet texts also show it as a space inhabited by swineherds, outlaw groups, woodcutters, and other characters. While sometimes the forest does indeed mean a thickly wooded area, forests also often included clearings, groves, and more cultivated areas. Forests can represent the wild, untamed places of the mind, but they are also often recognisable as enclosed, regulated hunting grounds. Jacques Le Goff writes about the forest as 'a place where in a sense the hierarchy of feudal society broke down' and goes on to discuss Yvain's descent into savagery in the forest.[17] The 'Broceliande' of *Yvain* is in many ways an archetypal forest landscape. But in some texts of Chaucer's time in particular, the forest seems to lose its mythic elements. In *Sir Gawain and the Green Knight*, the forest is in fact a place of rigid hierarchy, where the huntsman's role is quite different to the role of the lord.[18] As Saunders notes, the forest of this poem is very different from the 'usually vague *forest avantureuse* of the quest'; instead, it closely resembles 'the actual landscape of Britain.'[19] Hunting was a practice informed by myriad rules and conventions at this time, as tracts such as the *Master of Game* show. In *Gawain*, Bertilak's careful rules about conserving game to allow for a long hunting season reflect the laws of the time.[20] Far from associating the Green Knight with nature, the hunt scenes

[17] Jacques Le Goff, *The Medieval Imagination*, trans. Arthur Goldhammer (Chicago: University of Chicago Press, 1988), 110, 114.

[18] Trevor Dodman, 'Hunting to Teach: Class, Pedagogy, and Maleness in the *Master of Game* and *Sir Gawain and the Green Knight*,' *Exemplaria* 17:2 (2005): 413–44.

[19] Saunders, *Forest of Medieval Romance*, 149.

[20] Saunders comments that Bertilak's rules about conserving game to allow for a long hunting season are in line with the laws of royal hunting forests; ibid., 152.

bind him—in his straightforward seigneurial form of Bertilak—even closer to law, hierarchy, and convention. In the realm of law, the forest was a place of extreme hierarchy and extreme punishments. There was no general right to hunt wild animals in England. After the Norman Conquest, the kings designated huge tracts of land as 'forest,' which meant that in these areas (which included land held by people other than the king), the king had a monopoly on hunting deer and boar, although he could grant to others permission to hunt these animals.[21] In the fourteenth century, the king delegated his rights to local noblemen in various places, who then held their forest privileges directly from the king.[22] Thus, in the 1390s, Chaucer was employed as a forester for North Petherton by the trustees of Roger Mortimer, the earl of March, whose forester rights derived from the king.

As a forester himself—albeit a desk-based one—Chaucer had a thorough understanding of the economics of land management. This job, held by Chaucer in the 1390s, is one of the most obscure and least discussed of his roles. The evidence comes from postmedieval antiquarians: Thomas Palmer, who transcribed the rolls of North Petherton Park in Somerset, and John Collinson, who copied Palmer's work.[23] The rolls list Richard Britte as subforester in 1386; Richard Britte and Geoffrey Chaucer together as subforesters in 1390; and Geoffrey Chaucer again in 1397.[24] This episode in Chaucer's life has received remarkably little attention, perhaps partly because the original documents are now lost. Most importantly, biographers have tended to comment that Chaucer was appointed 'by the family' and that he acted for 'the owner'—but little attention has been paid to who, in fact, had authority over the estate at this time.[25] This appointment, it turns out, came from the heart of the Appellant camp.

[21] The punishments for hunting without permission were extreme, including blinding, castration, and even death, until the Charter of the Forest (1217) legislated against mutilation and execution for forest offences. Robert Bartlett, *England under the Norman and Angevin Kings, 1075–1225* (Oxford: Oxford University Press, 2000), 187, 239, 673–74.

[22] Charles Young, *The Royal Forests of Medieval England* (Leicester: Leicester University Press, 1979), 169.

[23] See John Collinson, *The History and Antiquities of the County of Somerset, Collected from Authentick Records, Volume III* (Bath: R. Cruttwell, 1791), 62. See also W. D. Selby, *The Athenaeum* (20 November, 1886), 672–73.

[24] Crow and Olson, *Chaucer Life-Records*, 494–95, 496.

[25] Donald Roy Howard, *Chaucer and the Medieval World* (London: Weidenfeld & Nicholson, 1987), 459; Pearsall, *Life of Geoffrey Chaucer*, 224.

The Mortimer inheritance was of central importance throughout Richard's reign and beyond, as I've discussed in chapter 11. Edmund Mortimer, husband of Philippa of Clarence (Lionel and Elizabeth's daughter) had died in 1381, leaving his seven-year-old son Roger as his heir. Edmund's mother died shortly afterwards in 1382, adding her dower lands to the child's vast inheritance. Richard, himself only fifteen in 1382, and his advisors largely left out the magnates who expected to control the Mortimer inheritance (Edmund Mortimer had been the ward of the previous earl of Arundel) and instead handed out patronage to a number of household favourites.[26] One of these favourites was Sir Peter Courtenay, who received the farm (i.e. the income) of the forest of North Petherton, together with the income of the forests of Exmoor, Nerechich, and Mendeep.[27] Richard's appointments, however, provoked outrage, and the king backed down in 1383. Now, the Mortimer estate passed to the heir and a new set of trustees: the earls of Arundel, Warwick, and Northumberland, and John, Lord Neville. Arundel also received the rights to arrange Mortimer's marriage, but these were later transferred to Thomas Holland, the king's half-brother, who soon arranged for the young heir to marry Holland's own daughter, Eleanor. Holland himself was married to Arundel's sister, Alice, so Mortimer's wife was Arundel's niece. The four men in charge of the Mortimer lands, then, included two of the three major Appellants (Arundel and Warwick).

In 1386, the guardians of Roger Mortimer brought a suit against Peter Courtenay, claiming that the forest of North Petherton had been granted to them but that Courtenay had trespassed and was still taking the fees and profits. This court case ran for several years and seems to have been settled out of court in some way.[28] It is clear that Courtenay had refused to give up the rights bestowed upon him by Richard in 1382 when those rights were rescinded and the inheritance transferred to the new trustees the following year. But there was some kind of resolution, and in 1393, Roger Mortimer granted the lease of the forestership to Courtenay. The

---

[26] For discussions of the Mortimer inheritance, see Dunn, 'Mortimer Inheritance,' 159–70; and King, 'Richard II, the Mortimer Inheritance, and the March of Wales,' 95–118.

[27] *Calendar of the Patent Rolls: Richard II*, Membrane 1, 2:132 (9 June 1382).

[28] This is discussed in J. M. Manly, 'Three Recent Chaucer Studies,' *Review of English Studies* 10:39 (1934): 259–60. For documents connected with the suit, see National Archives, E 143/18/3.

relationship of Peter Courtenay to both Richard and the Lords Appellant across this period is tangled and confusing. Like so many of the members of the royal household discussed in previous chapters, Peter served with the Black Prince early in his career, fighting at Najera and being knighted by the Black Prince himself. He also, however, served with the earl of Arundel in 1378. Peter was a member of a very important noble family, one of the many children of the earl of Devon and his wife, Margaret Bohun.[29] One of Peter's brothers was William Courtenay, the bishop of London (and later Canterbury) who clashed dramatically with Gaunt and Wycliffe in the later 1370s and early 1380s. Another brother was Philip, a favourite of Richard's in the early years of his reign, who was then (like many others) displaced by de Vere's exceptional dominance from around 1386. In the 1390s, Philip fell out of favour but was rewarded by the Lancastrian regime after 1399. Peter too moved between different groupings. As we have seen, he received favour from Richard in 1382 when he was granted the custody of North Petherton Park, along with the forests of 'Exemore, Nerechich and Mendep.'[30] His refusal to get out of these lands seems to have been part of a more general policy that consistently worked for Peter. In 1387, he received a pardon for entering property without licence, and in the same document was granted that property.[31] Similarly, he ended up receiving the farm of North Petherton that he had refused to give up for so many years. In the mid-1380s Richard used him to help to get preferment for another court favourite. Richard promoted his beloved wife's confessor, Nicholas Hornyk, to be the prior of a lucrative priory in Somerset (the Cluniac priory of Montacute), although it already had a prior, Francis de Baugiaco. The ostensible justification was the ongoing dispute with alien-owned priories, although Francis had good legal reasons for protesting, which he did indeed do. We see Peter Courtenay on numerous commissions relating to this debacle: in December 1385, the commissioners were protecting Francis, in January 1386 letters protecting Francis were revoked, and three weeks later the commissioners were

---

[29] For useful biography, see the 'History of Parliament' entry for Peter's brother, Philip Courtenay: 'Courtenay, Sir Philip,' in Roskell, Clark, and Rawcliffe, *History of Parliament*, 2:670–73.

[30] *Calendar of the Patent Rolls: Richard II*, Membrane 1, 2:132 (9 June 1382).

[31] Ibid., Membrane 11, 3:298 (20 April 1387).

supposed to be putting Hornyk into position (at this point the records state that he had been appointed in June 1385). Somewhat comically, in 1387 Peter and his colleagues were then appointed to arrest those who had expelled Francis (themselves and their proxies). Presumably, at this point he was acting for the commission that was now in charge (since the Wonderful Parliament), rather than for Richard. Hornyk hung on, though: an undated petition from Hornyk requesting Francis's arrest is marked as approved by the king, while Francis's petitions seem to have languished. Indeed, Francis was not restored until after the deposition of Richard II.[32]

This story is entirely in keeping with the politics of the 1380s: Richard was maneuvering, inexpertly, to place his favourites in lucrative positions. Peter Courtenay, as a king's knight to whom Richard had given grants and favour, was the kind of person that Richard used to further his own agenda. But Peter was halfhearted—he was equally able to act for the Appellant-led commission. And indeed, they appointed him chamberlain in 1388. He was probably a kind of compromise candidate whom all parties were reasonably happy to accept. Fascinatingly, though, while the Appellants were willing to appoint him to this important role, two of them—in their roles as trustees for Roger Mortimer—were continuing to prosecute their suit against Peter for his continuing occupation of the North Petherton Park. Allegiances were so flexible that, with one hat on, Arundel could lavish favour on Peter while, wearing his other hat, he took him to court.

Enter Chaucer. Arundel and his associates, acting in Roger Mortimer's name, had first appointed a subforester (Britte) in 1386, when they commenced their lawsuit against Peter Courtenay. They then reappointed Britte and added Chaucer in 1390. At this point, the trustees were trying to get hundreds of pounds back from Peter—the revenues of the estates since 1382.[33] The appointment of Chaucer is interesting—and telling—in a number of ways. First, it demonstrates that he was not perceived as a Ricardian or as anti-Appellant. Indeed, the king had no rele-

---

[32] *Calendar of the Patent Rolls: Richard II*, Membrane 13d, 3:88 (6 December 1385); Membrane 36d, 3:166–67 (21 January 1386); Membrane 21d, 3:174 (28 February 1386); Membrane 9, 3:243 (3 December 1386); Membrane 23d, 3:262 (28 September 1386); Membrane 30d, 3:385–86 (13 July 1387). *Two Cartularies of the Augustinian Priory of Bruton and the Cluniac Priory of Montacute*, Somerset Record Society VIII (London: Harrison & Sons, 1894), lxxiii. National Archives, SC 8/250/12495.

[33] Manly, 'Three Recent Chaucer Studies,' 259. Crow and Olson, *Chaucer Life-Records*, 494–97.

vance in this particular dispute any more. The interests of the handful of really great magnates of this era sometimes were the same but often were specific to their own situation. John of Gaunt, his various brothers, the Mortimer family, the earls of Arundel, the earls of Northumberland: these were men (with enormous retinues) who had their own agendas, and who worked together on some issues and not on others. In this case, Chaucer was given an administrative job that was not a royal or city appointment but was, essentially, for the earl of Arundel. His knowledge of the Mortimer family, of course, went back a long way—to his early employment by Elizabeth de Burgh and Lionel of Clarence, grandparents of the current earl (whose mother was Richard II's first cousin).[34]

Why was Chaucer given this job? It was not a sinecure. The earl of Arundel had no reason to give Chaucer a sinecure. Furthermore, his appointment during this lawsuit makes it clear that there was work to be done, presumably going through accounts, legal documents, and other paperwork. (He was not the kind of forester that his Knight employs as Yeoman, a man engaged in the day-to-day practice of woodcraft.)[35] As such paperwork was likely to be in Somerset, it is probable that Chaucer went there. What we can deduce from this appointment is that Chaucer was competent: there can be no other reason for his being appointed. He was thought of as someone who knew his way around documents and was good at his job. And it reinforces the fact that he was not in political trouble or connected with those Ricardians who had fallen in 1388. The Appellants themselves were perfectly happy to employ him. And this job, like his job as clerk of the king's works, which he held concurrently, involved Chaucer in riding around the country, visiting both metropolitan and regional great houses, palaces, and hunting lodges. His life no longer took place within the compressed, even claustrophobic space of Aldgate and Wool Quay: it was far more fragmented, even itinerant, during the *Canterbury Tales* years. At the same time, he must also have spent a good deal of time in his Kentish home in the Greenwich area, writing his poetry.

[34] There is, however, no reason to think that Chaucer's forestership was connected with his earlier employment by Elizabeth and Lionel, as some critics have argued. Selby, *The Athenaeum*, 672–73.

[35] On different kinds of forester, see Raymond Grant, *The Royal Forests of England* (Stroud: Alan Sutton, 1991), 112–29.

Like *Gawain*, the *Canterbury Tales* injects a note of historicity into its depiction of forest landscapes and the exile-and-return motif. The *Tales* starts from a 'centre,' a social space where the characters are gathered, and moves through peripheral space, the countryside roads of Kent, with the promise of a return back to the dining tables of the Tabard Inn—not quite the Arthurian Round Table, but a comic, unpretentious version of this image of consumption-based togetherness. The return does not happen, however, and neither the *Tales* as a whole nor individual tales conform to the logic of romance. While Chaucer often nods to the literary and mythic conventions of what the forest landscape represents, he also inserts a characteristic scepticism, frequently reminding us of the social and historical realities within this landscape. Fragment III opens with the 'Wife of Bath's Prologue and Tale,' which is followed by the 'Friar's Tale' and the Summoner's angry riposte.[36] The 'Wife of Bath's Tale' and the 'Friar's Tale' both explicitly emphasise 'realistic' aspects of their forest landscapes.

The 'Wife of Bath's Tale' opens with an archetypal romance setting: uniquely amongst Chaucer's works, this tale is set in the time of King Arthur. The landscape is fey and mysterious, filled with 'fayerye' (859). Alison then transports us to the present day—telling us that now there are no otherworldly spirits in the country; rather, women are threatened by friars potentially lurking in wooded spaces, 'In every bussh or under every tree' (879). When we return to Arthur's time, however, it turns out that then too it was not the 'incubus' (880) or demonic spirit who was the threat. Dark forces came not from an otherworld—a forest, hell, far away—but from the court itself, in contrast to romances such as *Sir Gowther* or *Sir Degare* in which the rapist is a faery-demon. The rapist in the 'Wife of Bath's Tale' is a human knight. Not a demon pretending to be a knight, but an actual knight. Right from the start Chaucer tells us that the relationship between centre and periphery is not what we think it is. He also does this in a dramatic change from his sources and analogues.[37] This

---

[36] For a fascinating argument for reading these tales as a patterned trilogy analogous to the Knight-Miller-Reeve structure, see Penn R. Szittya, 'The Green Yeoman as Loathly Lady: The Friar's Parody of the Wife of Bath's Tale,' *Chaucer Review* 90:3 (1975): 386–94.

[37] For discussions of the loathly lady tradition, see S. Elizabeth Passmore and Susan Carter (eds.), *The English 'Loathly Lady' Tales: Boundaries, Traditions, Motifs* (Kalamazoo, MI: Medieval Institute Publications, 2007).

basic story appears in various other forms, most notably in Gower's 'Tale of Florent,' in the *Confessio Amantis* and in the fifteenth-century *Wedding of Gawain and Dame Ragnell*. Only in Chaucer's version is the crime rape. And only in Chaucer's version is the knight unambiguously culpable for what he has done. In Gower's version, the knight has killed somebody, but accidentally and fairly. In *Dame Ragnell*, the knight (Gawain) has done nothing wrong whatsoever but is proxy for the king's land dispute with Ragnell's brother. So Chaucer is ostentatiously foregrounding the idea that the usual hero of romance—the knight who sets forth—is here a criminal, a violent oppressor of women.

Once he has received his punishment, and has embarked on his quest for knowledge, the knight encounters the mysterious, shape-shifting loathly lady in the forest. He rides 'under a forest syde' (990) and sees twenty-four mysterious dancers, who vanish, leaving only the old lady, who gives him the answer he needs. Now the forest functions in a more typical romance way: it is the place of magic and transformation. But we do not forget that the forest is not the origin of dark crimes and marginal experience—those things have come directly from the court. The forest provides recuperation and regeneration, as the loathly lady works in harmony with the courtly ladies who stayed the rapist's execution and gave him the opportunity to change.

The tale that immediately follows echoes and alters various aspects of the 'Wife of Bath's Tale.'[38] The 'Friar's Tale' too features an encounter 'under a forest syde' (1380) with a mysterious shape-shifter, a plighting of troth, and a test of the criminal protagonist. The 'Friar's Tale' seems to set up a classic romance landscape: the forest is inhabited by a demon from hell. The yeoman-demon at first identifies his home as 'fer in the north contree' (1413)—traditional location of hell, but also representing marginal borderlands. Dressed in green, conventionally the colour of the devil in medieval times, he represents those most dangerous and 'other' aspects of the forest. Again, though, there are no straightforward binaries in this tale. The form that the demon takes is the form of a bailiff, representative

---

[38] I discuss the changing order of the tales and the original assigning of the 'Shipman's Tale' to the 'Wife of Bath' in chapter 18.

of the centre.[39] He describes himself to the summoner as a minor official who works for a lord and supplements his wages by extortion. In other words, he is a very recognizable kind of figure with whom it is easy for the summoner to identify, as he is exactly this kind of figure himself. We, the readers, know that when the demon describes his lord as 'hard to me and daungerous' (1427), he is describing the devil himself. The yeoman-demon thus makes clear the parallels between hell and a corrupt earthly household—just as the otherworld of *Sir Orfeo* mirrors Orfeo's court, and the glittering, mysterious world of Hautdesert is profoundly similar to Camelot. This *unheimlich* (uncanny) play between the familiar and the unknown is important in many sophisticated romances. Chaucer, like the *Gawain* poet, then deploys the familiar and legalistic language of trothplight to make the affinities between the supernatural and the ordinary world even clearer.

As the tale goes on, the Friar comprehensively rejects the recuperative, regenerative structures of romance. His summoner is not redeemed; he is actually taken to hell. While in *Sir Orfeo*, Herodis is rescued from a hellish underworld, and in *Sir Launfal*, the hero ends up in a non-hellish otherworld, here there is no gleam of hope for the protagonist. Moreover, the tale makes clear that while the yeoman-demon in fact operates according to a kind of moral code, the summoner does not. He is a *more* dangerous agent in the world than the devil because he preys on the innocent, whereas the yeoman-demon can only have power over those who sinfully give that power to him. As in the 'Wife of Bath's Tale,' the real evil in society is presented as human, not supernatural. Similarly, in the 'Pardoner's Tale,' the rioters seek a mysterious, supernatural figure in a wooded environment, but the place of danger is inside themselves.[40] Each kills the other, but it is their own evil that causes their moral deaths. Chaucer, like the *Gawain* poet, demonstrates that we should fear not what is outside but what is inside. Both poets also emphasise the fact that the centre and the periphery

---

[39] A recent article suggests that the tale is an exploration and critique of centralized bureaucracy and officialdom. See Eric Weiskott, 'Chaucer the Forester: The Friar's Tale, Forest History, and Officialdom,' *Chaucer Review* 47:3 (2013): 323–36.

[40] See Turner, *Chaucerian Conflict*, chapter 5.

are not so different from each other, that the world is not structured by binaries.

Chaucer's depictions of landscapes tend to focus on the landscape's connection with humans, on the environment as shaped through myriad interventions. In the 'Physician's Tale,' he makes a throwaway reference to the forest landscape in the context of arguing that promiscuous women can later become strict guardians of younger girls, in a poacher-turned-gamekeeper analogy. He writes:

> A theef of venysoun, that hath forlaft
> His likerousnesse and al his olde craft
> Kan kepe a forest best of any man. (83–85)

The forest is inextricably bound up with game, with animals bred for human enjoyment and consumption, and with the trespassers and officers who move through the forest landscape. Indeed, Chaucer's primary knowledge of forests was as royal and aristocratic hunting grounds, just as he had extensive experience of outside space in general as managed space: the parks, orchards, and gardens attached to palaces and great households.[41] In the 'Knight's Tale,' while Emily fantasizes about walking 'in the wodes wilde' (2309) and Palamon does indeed escape from his prison to the woods, those woods turn out to be Theseus's hunting ground. Theseus then intervenes in ever more extreme ways on this landscape: he builds an amphitheatre a mile wide in circumference, surrounded by a ditch (1885–88), and later unleashes a graphically described programme of deforestation to build Arcite's funeral pyre (2919–34). The agonies of the trees and their spirits are explicitly emphasized.[42] We see here an aggressive encounter between men and trees, a failure (on Theseus's part) to balance competing interests or to understand the principle of interconnectedness. He enacts violence quite different from the managed violence of much medieval hunting, with its emphasis on game preservation and longevity. While Bertilak or the proverbial forester of the 'Physician's Tale' are engaged

---

[41] See Laura L. Howes, 'Chaucer's Forests, Parks, and Groves,' *Chaucer Review* 49:1 (2014): 125–34.

[42] See Gillian Rudd, *Greenery: Ecocritical Readings of Late Medieval English Literature* (Manchester: Manchester University Press, 2007), especially 58–65.

in extreme violence against animals, they are also concerned with maintaining their habitats and the animal population. In the 'Knight's Tale,' Theseus embarks on single-minded, short-sighted destruction.

In the tale that follows, we see a much more finely grained balance between town, suburb, landowner, and countryside, an economy very different from the politics of domination and conquest that structures Theseus's mentality. The 'Miller's Tale' demonstrates the relationship between town (Oxford), great household (the abbey at Osney), countryside and forest (the farm and its surroundings from where the carpenter gets his timber), and metropolis (where John sends his servants on errands). These different places are clearly presented as part of a network. John moves between his home in Oxford and the abbey at Osney, on the outskirts of Oxford. The abbey was the largest landholder in Oxford at this time, and an important employer.[43] The tale then reminds us that every urban and household centre needs its hinterlands when John goes to the grange where 'he is wont for tymber for to go' (3667). Forests are a resource, but they need to be looked after; they are part of the economy, not something to be destroyed for the sake of political spectacle, as they are in the 'Knight's Tale.' The tale also shows us the overlaps between parish society, with its depiction of the church; trade society, with the blacksmith's shop; and the university, which Nicholas attends. With its rich descriptions of interior rooms, permeable boundaries, and public spaces, the tale weaves a picture of a mutually dependent community in which each thread contributes to the whole tapestry.

Indeed, as we move through Fragment I, Chaucer increasingly focuses on the networks of interests across the economy, on how cities relate to their hinterlands, and on the economies of English regions. If we glance across Chaucer's poetic career, *Troilus* and the *House of Fame* are profoundly London poems, and the *Parliament of Fowls* is a Westminster poem. The *Book of the Duchess* and the Prologue to the *Legend of Good Women* are court or household poems, poems structured around the figure of the lord and his household patronage system. The *Canterbury Tales* is anchored in London and Southwark but looks outwards to regions and

---

[43] Kathryn Kerby-Fulton, 'Oxford,' in David Wallace (ed.), *Europe: A Literary History* (Oxford: Oxford University Press, 2016), 1:208–26, 1:210.

inhabits them comfortably. Chaucer was not a London poet who dismissed the rest of the country. He travelled to many places in England himself. Dartmouth, Southampton, Somerset, Oxford, Woodstock, Leicester, Hertford, Lincoln, and Yorkshire were all places that mattered in Chaucer's cultural geography. Sometimes he travelled as an agent of the Crown, going from the centre to its edges, but at other times he travelled in the company of a great lord, a moving centre. All the magnates and courtiers of Chaucer's time had regional as well as courtly urban identities. They belonged in their regions and tended to go back there. Regional houses were great centres of economic and cultural production and patronage. Indeed, as Emily Steiner has written, in the late fourteenth century, as vernacular literary culture rapidly developed, it was still possible that this culture could 'revolve around a great lord and his dominions rather than around a major city, like London, or a ruler, like Richard II.'[44] She uses the example of John Trevisa, prolific translator and writer, who was based at Berkeley Castle but whose intellectual connections to Oxford provided a link between university and household culture. Lynn Staley has also speculated about the *Gawain* poet's possible connections to the households of John of Gaunt and Thomas of Woodstock: whether these men were or were not his patrons is less important than the emphasis on the multiple centres of culture in England at this time.[45]

Chaucer famously replicates the northern dialect of the students in the 'Reeve's Tale' (4026–45), painstakingly representing their idiosyncratic vocabulary (e.g. 'boes'), pronunciation (especially the 'a' replacing the southern 'o' [e.g. 'gas' for 'goes']), and grammar (e.g. 'is I' for 'am I').[46] This was an era of increasing centralization and the rise of the southeast, and other contemporary authors (notably Ranulph Higden) point to the differences between northerners, southerners, and those in the middle.[47] But this marking

---

[44] Emily Steiner, 'Berkeley Castle,' in Wallace, *Europe: A Literary History*, 1:227–39.

[45] Staley, *Languages of Power*, 188, 211–14.

[46] J.R.R. Tolkien, 'Chaucer as Philologist: *The Reeve's Tale*,' *Transactions of the Philological Society* 33:1 (1934); 1–70; R.W.V. Elliot, *Chaucer's English* (London: Wiley-Blackwell, 1974), 390–93.

[47] Ranulph Higden, *Polychronicon Ranulphi Higden Monachi Cestrensis*, ed. Churchill Babington and J. R. Lumby, Rolls Series 41 (London: Longman, Green, Longman, Roberts, and Green, 1865–86) 2: 158. For discussion, see Robert W. Barrett Jr., 'Chester and Cheshire,' in Wallace, *Europe: A Literary History*, 1:240–55; and Jeffrey Jerome Cohen, *Hybridity, Identity, and Monstrosity in Medieval Britain: Of Difficult Middles* (New York: Palgrave Macmillan, 2006).

of northern otherness is only a small part of Chaucer's interest in the distant regions of England. The idea of a centralized nation, with unimportant and backward margins, where power circled only around London and Westminster, would not have made sense to Chaucer. Not only were the regional courts of magnates vital and diverse economic and cultural centres, but the king himself travelled widely—and this particular king, Richard II, had a penchant for the northwest and enjoyed an especially problematic relationship with the southeast. Of course, the southeast was the most powerful region, with its trade, law courts, and offices of government, but it had nothing like the dominance that it was to achieve over the following century. Chaucer was familiar with the grandeur of Gaunt's many residences, in which his own wife had spent a great deal of her time, and which were located in, for instance, Leicester and Lincolnshire. His forestership connects him with the Mortimer family, whose great landholdings ranged widely and were centred around castles such as Wigmore (in Herefordshire) and Ludlow (in Shropshire)—both in the Western Midlands, near the Welsh borders. Scotland and Wales themselves are only briefly mentioned by Chaucer, but the borders—particularly Northumberland (my own home county)—were central to Chaucer's imagination.[48]

John of Gaunt's Northumbrian holdings and his interventions in border politics had been a bone of contention between himself and the Percy family during the 1380s. The Percy earls of Northumberland were back in control in the later 1380s, and their defence of the borders from their base at Alnwick Castle was well known, especially after the dramatic capture and subsequent ransom of Hotspur, the son of the earl, at Otterburn in 1388. The Neville family was certainly familiar to Chaucer: John, Lord Neville, who had major landholdings in county Durham, in Northumberland, and in Yorkshire, was one of the courtiers impeached by the Good Parliament. He was retained by Gaunt from at least 1366, and was to marry Gaunt's daughter—and Chaucer's niece—Joan Beaufort. We saw him earlier in this chapter as one of the guardians of the Mortimer inheritance.

---

[48] For Chaucer and Wales, see Simon Meecham-Jones, ' "Englyssh Gaufride" and British Chaucer? Chaucerian Allusions to the Condition of Wales in the *House of Fame*,' *Chaucer Review* 44:1 (2009): 1–24. For Chaucer and Scotland, see R. James Goldstein, ' "To Scotlond-Ward His Foomen for to Seke": Chaucer, the Scots, and the "Man of Law's Tale," ' *Chaucer Review* 33:1 (1998): 31–42.

The many impressive castles in Northumberland, including Alnwick, Warkworth, Prudhoe (all owned by the Percys), Dunstanburgh (Gaunt's stronghold), and Bamburgh (under the custody of John Neville) remain as tangible reminders of the deep wealth and power of the families in this region, and of the fact that this region was often the stage on which the biggest internal conflicts and rivalries of the realm were played out. Warkworth, Dunstanburgh, Bamburgh, and Alnwick are all very close to one another—only a few miles apart. Prudhoe abuts Bywell, a barony held by the Nevilles. These families competed over the roles of guardians of the marches, in particular, and these roles changed hands frequently during these years.[49]

Northumberland was a region beset with border troubles between the English and the Scots, but it was not, for Chaucer, an alien marginal place, defined by brutality and otherness. On the contrary, it was a place of great houses and castles, where the richest magnates of the kingdom held court. When Chaucer slips local saints' names into his tales—the Oxford saint, Frideswide, in the 'Miller's Tale' (3449), the Northumbrian saint Cuthbert in the 'Reeve's Tale' (4127)—he demonstrates his understanding of multiple centres. For a Northumbrian, the cult of a local saint provided a spiritual and cultural centre: men and women from this region were not turning their eyes to London or Canterbury saints as the inevitable 'centre' points but to Cuthbert's great shrine and his legacy.[50] These local saints, of course, both hail from an English past that long predates Thomas à Becket. Northumberland had a particular claim to centrality in the English historical imagination. Writing about the 'Man of Law's Tale,'

[49] For instance, around 1380 tension flared up between Gaunt and Percy (who were almost exact contemporaries and were closely associated with each other in the late 1370s). Gaunt was appointed the king's lieutenant in the Marches; Percy subsequently refused to allow Gaunt into Alnwick to protect him during the Rising of 1381. Percy ultimately had to apologise, but John Neville, Gaunt's retainer, was given the wardenship of the eastern march in December 1381. In 1389, Richard made a particularly divisive move when he appointed Mowbray, whom he was trying to win over and who had no local connection, as warden of the eastern march. See Anthony Tuck, 'The Percies and the Community of Northumberland in the Later Fourteenth Century,' in Anthony Goodman and Anthony Tuck (eds.), *War and Border Societies in the Middle Ages* (London: Routledge, 1992), 178–95; Kris Towson, '"Hearts Warped by Passion": The Percy-Gaunt Dispute of 1381,' in W. M. Ormrod (ed.), *Fourteenth Century England III* (Woodbridge: Boydell Press, 2004), 143–54.

[50] In this, England differs from the Italian city-states: Wallace points out that as part of its programme of centralization, Florence suppressed local cults to promote itself as spiritual, as well as political, and economic, centre. Wallace, *Chaucerian Polity*, 136.

Suzanne Conklin Akbari comments that Northumberland went on 'to become not only a Christian country but part of England itself'; Joseph Taylor agrees that Northumberland was 'brought into the English fold.'[51] But in the post-Roman centuries in which the tale is set, there was no 'England,' and Northumberland became the cultural and Christian heart of the island. Converted by Irish and Scottish monks, Northumberland embraced Christianity and developed Christian culture from the extraordinary centres of learning at Lindisfarne, Jarrow, Hexham, and Durham, at a level that far exceeded what was happening in Kent and its surrounds, and at a time when most of the island was pagan. Northumberland, indeed, laid claim to *European* cultural centrality in the long age of the Lindisfarne Gospels, Cuthbert, and Bede. In a famous story recounted by Bede, Gregory is prompted to send missionaries to the land of the Angles because he sees slave boys (who look like 'angels' to him) being sold. The boys come from the land ruled by Alla, known as 'Deira' (the Anglo-Saxon kingdom of Northumbria); Gregory vows to teach them 'alleluia' and to rescue them 'de ira,' from God's anger.[52] It is Alla's Northumberland— the land of the 'Man of Law's Tale'—that prompts the pope to send Augustine to England. In this text, the Angles (who prompt his 'angel' pun) are Northumbrians. The insular section of the 'Man of Law's Tale' is precisely about Northumberland's history as the *centre* of English, Christian identity. It is a place with castles and books, a border country that itself defends the borders and fights the Scots, a realm that ultimately joins with

---

[51] Suzanne Conklin Akbari, 'Orientation and Nation in Chaucer's *Canterbury Tales*,' in Lynch, *Chaucer's Cultural Geography*, 121; Joseph Taylor, 'Chaucer's Uncanny Regionalism: Rereading the North in the Reeve's Tale,' *JEGP* 109:4 (2010): 478.

[52] 'Responsum est quod Angli uocarentur. At ille: "Bene" inquit; "nam et angelicam habent faciem, et tales angelorum in caelis decet esse coheredes. Quod habet nomen ipsa prouincia, de qua isti sunt adlati?" Responsum est quia Deiri uocarentur idem prouinciales. At ille "Bene" inquit "Deiri, de ira eruti et ad misericordiam Christi uocati. Rex prouinciae illius quomodo appellatur?" Responsum est quod Aelle diceretur. At ille adludens ad nomen ait: "Alleluia, laudem Dei Creatoris illis in partibus oportet cantari."' [He was told that they were called Angli. 'Good,' he said, 'they have the face of angels, and such men should be fellow-heirs of the angels in heaven.' 'What is the name,' he asked, 'of the kingdom from which they have been brought?' He was told that the men of the kingdom were called Deiri. 'Deiri,' he replied, 'De ira! Good! Snatched from the wrath of Christ and called to his mercy. And what is the name of the king of the land?' He was told that it was Ælle; and playing on the name, he said, 'Alleluia! The praise of God the Creator must be sung in those parts.'] Bede, *Ecclesiastical History of the English People*, ed. and trans. Bertram Colgrave and R.A.B. Mynors (Oxford: Clarendon Press, 1969), book 1, 132–35.

Rome to allow a happy marriage between England and the Church, symbolized by Alla and Constance, and consolidated in the figure of their son Maurice. Northumberland is not a place that has the capacity to be part of England; it is the heart of English Christian history, and it is people from other regions who later join Northumbrians as English and Christian.

Northumberland is not the only northern location that Chaucer imagines in detail in the *Canterbury Tales*. The 'Summoner's Tale' focuses on Holderness, a place that almost every modern reader of the *Canterbury Tales* will have to look up if they wish to locate it. To the vast majority of modern readers, the tale is set in an obscure, marshy location in a part of England a long way from Chaucer's home. But that is not at all how Chaucer and his contemporaries thought of Holderness. Chaucer names very few of his friends in his poems, but one of them is Sir Peter de Bukton, to whom Chaucer addresses a lyric.[53] Bukton came from Holderness itself, a coastal area in East Yorkshire, bordered on the south by the Humber, which divides it from Lincolnshire.[54] Holderness contains Hull, a prominent port in the Middle Ages, as well as major religious foundations, including Bridlington Priory and the Priory of Swine (where Bukton was buried). In the 'Summoner's Tale,' Chaucer again demonstrates, as he does so brilliantly in the 'Miller's' and 'Reeve's' Tales, his ability to delineate a regional community and its social and economic networks.[55] This community has a manor house, villages, an inn, and a church. The lord and lady, a squire, and a retinue are physically present in the manor. Thomas too—the 'cherl'—has his own retinue of friends that supports him, and his home is vividly realized through small details: there is a cat on the bench and a pig in the sty; the sick man lies on a low couch while his wife works in their garden. At the end of the tale, the community as a whole joins together across class lines to mock the unscrupulous, itinerant friar. The

---

[53] Some critics have suggested that the poem is addressed to a different Bukton, Robert Bukton. However, most agree that Sir Peter Bukton is the addressee. See especially Ernest P. Kuhl, 'Chaucer's "My Maistre Bukton,"' *PMLA* 38: 1 (1923): 115–32. See also Pearsall, *Life of Geoffrey Chaucer*, 184, 333n11.

[54] The *Riverside Chaucer* mistakenly claims that Holderness is a town. See the gloss to line 1710 in *Riverside Chaucer*, 29.

[55] Wallace aptly comments on the 'extraordinary imaginative energies invested in Chaucer's rural landscapes.' *Chaucerian Polity*, 126.

residents of this locality prove more than able to beat the friar at his own games—at wordplay, sophistry, and the language of education. And at the heart of the tale is an exposé of the monstrosity of the representative of an outside institution who seeks to exploit the heart-stopping—albeit everyday—human tragedies of the death of a child and the debilitating illness of his father. Holderness is not sharply delineated as a place different from other areas of England; the point is that small, regional places far from London matter. Chaucer is interested in the power and energies of these rural societies—the North is not a strange other-land to him.

Chaucer wrote his poem to Bukton—and almost certainly sent him some version of the 'Wife of Bath's Prologue' and perhaps also a 'Tale'—early in his *Canterbury Tales* years. His lines 'The Wyf of Bathe I pray yow that ye rede / Of this matere' (29–30) work well if a version of the 'Prologue' (at least) was sent to Bukton at the same time. At this point, the 'Prologue' and 'Tale' might have been very different from their later form: the tale indeed might have been the story that ended up as the 'Shipman's Tale,' as this was almost certainly initially intended for the Wife of Bath.[56] The likelihood is that early in the evolution of the *Canterbury Tales*, the Man of Law told the tale of Melibee, which was followed by an exchange between the Wife of Bath and the Host—the 'Epilogue' or cancelled end-link to the 'Man of Law's Tale'—which led on to the Wife telling the tale now known as the 'Shipman's Tale.' Chaucer may have experimented in many ways with the development of the Wife of Bath and her utterances, and it is impossible to know precisely what Bukton received, or with what version of the Wife of Bath he was familiar. The *Lenvoy de Chaucer a Bukton* has traditionally either not been dated or has been assigned a post-1396 date as it refers to the horrors of being taken prisoner 'in Frise' (23), and there was a raid on Frisia in 1396. Critics have pointed out, however, that the throwaway reference would work without this specific context, and that Frise is a common rhyme word.[57] Chaucer's reference to his own refusal to 'falle eft [again]' (8) into marriage makes it clear that he is a widower

---

[56] See Robert A. Pratt, 'The Development of the Wife of Bath,' in MacEdward Leach (ed.), *Studies in Medieval Literature in Honor of Albert Croll Baugh* (Philadelphia: University of Pennsylvania Press, 1961), 45–79. See also Dinshaw, *Chaucer's Sexual Poetics*, 113–31.

[57] See *Riverside Chaucer*, 1087 and 1088, note to line 23. See also J. L. Lowes, 'The Date of the Envoy to Bukton,' *Modern Language Notes* 27 (1912): 45–48.

(i.e. it is after 1387). He is advising Bukton not to marry, and telling him that if he does, experience will teach him that it is better to be taken prisoner than to marry again. Chaucer advises Bukton to keep his 'fredam' (32) and to read the 'Wyf of Bathe' (29). The poem is clearly written before Bukton married, and when he was contemplating marriage. In July 1410 Bukton's son joined with him in a lawsuit, so he must have been at least twenty-one at that time—and therefore could not have been born later than the summer of 1389.[58] So Bukton must have married no later than 1388. If we imagine this poem as a satirical epithalamium, it dates from very early in the Canterbury period and, given the reference to the Wife of Bath, reveals that Chaucer was circulating tales, or fragments, to his friends at this early date. And the likelihood is that Chaucer was writing prolifically in 1387 and 1388, years when he had no fixed job and the political tectonic plates were shifting. This leaves open the possibility of extensive revision of this material over the subsequent decade. But this dating of Bukton's marriage does place Chaucer's invention of the Wife of Bath at an earlier date than has been previously supposed.

Bukton was not only connected with a particular corner of Yorkshire, but also with Lithuania, Konigsberg, Venice, and the Holy Land. In 1390, Bukton accompanied Henry of Derby to Prussia, in his capacity as steward of Henry's household. Henry had been refused a safe-conduct through France to join the duke of Bourbon's expedition against Tunis—however, others well known to Chaucer, including his wife's nephew, John Beaufort, and his close friends, John Clanvowe and William Neville, did go on this expedition. So while some of Chaucer's circle voyaged to North Africa, others went to the Baltic. Instead of attacking Muslim pirates, Henry and his retinue went to crusade against the Lithuanians. The truce with France thus offered all kinds of violent opportunities for English

---

[58] Bukton's son's participation in the lawsuit is pointed out in the biography of Bukton in the *History of Parliament*: 'by July 1410 the two parties had gone to law at the York assizes ... the eldest of [his sons], Peter, had been involved with him in the litigation at the York assizes, and must therefore have been of age.' The relevant document (referring to Bukton and his son) can be found at the National Archives, JUST 1/1517. It is reproduced at http://aalt.law.uh.edu/AALT4/JUST1/Just1no1517 /aJUST1no1517fronts/IMG_5869.htm. The biography can be found at 'Buckton, Sir Peter,' in Roskell, Clark, and Rawcliffe, *History of Parliament*, 2:404–7. Bukton's 1413 will mentions his wife, Cecilia, and three sons, Peter, Ralph, and William. See James Raine and John William Clay (eds.), *Testamenta Eboracensia, or, Wills Registered at York* (London: J. B. Nichols and Son, 1836–1902), 1:360–61.

and French chivalric men, following on from the Anglo-French jousting tournament at St Inglevert in spring of 1390. Henry and his party set off on 19 July 1390 and returned on 30 April 1391. After a year of conspicuous consumption at home, Henry returned to Prussia in July 1392, only to discover that a truce had just been achieved between the Teutonic knights and Lithuania. So Henry set off for the Holy Land instead, travelling across Europe to Greece, through the Morea and Rhodes to Jerusalem and Jaffa, and then back through Italy and France, returning to England in July 1393. During this second extended journey, Bukton remained in Venice, organizing his funds and directing operations.[59]

When a great noble such as Henry travelled, he did so in a profoundly imperial manner. He captured and 'converted' numerous women and children, and brought back a boy from Lithuania, who he named 'Henry the Lithuanian,' and a boy from the Holy Land named 'Henry the Turk,' in a breathtaking display of appropriation. He travelled with huge retinues and with animals, including a leopard and ostrich, when he went to Jerusalem. His fighting in Lithuania took place in an area known as 'Le Wyldrenesse,' appropriately symbolic for Henry's self-image as a knight of traditional romance, testing and proving himself, and consolidating his identity in the marshy forest landscape.[60] Henry's travels are decidedly not testament to an attitude tolerant of cultural diversity at this time. What they do show us is that Chaucer was well acquainted with people who travelled widely—even more widely than he himself had done. They also demonstrate that, just as magnates travelled around England, making their centre wherever they were, so a man such as Henry was able to recreate his court wherever he went in the world. After the campaigning season, he stayed in Konigsberg from October until February, happily feasting, jousting, hunting, hawking, gambling, and being entertained by minstrels. He had brought vast resources of his own, but international courtly and aristocratic culture meant that from London to Samarkand, rulers shared many interests—particularly hunting, hawking, and riding.

Chaucer was on the edges of a social group for whom long journeys and extended stays in or near non-Christian areas were common. Indeed, the

---

[59] Given-Wilson, *Henry IV*, 61–76.
[60] Ibid., 66, 68–69, 73, and 76n59.

papacy had long maintained relations with the khans of Central Asia, and there had been hopes for an alliance between Western European powers and Central Asia against the Mamluk powers who controlled Jerusalem. Across the *Canterbury Tales*—and Chaucer's other works too—the lands of far, far away appear in myriad forms. He includes a tale about Syrian Muslims, one about Jews, and one about the court of Ghenghis Khan. Those three tales differ hugely in their impact and in the attitude of their tellers. The 'Squire's Tale' depicts the alien court of Ghenghis Khan as sophisticated, luxurious, and courteous, an image of familiar otherness.[61] The 'Prioress's Tale,' with its simultaneous sentimentality and sadism, exposes an extreme anti-Semitism that marks Jews as subhuman and uses hatred to bolster a specific mode of Christian devotion. As Anthony Bale writes, the tale thus reveals 'the compromised cultural authority of this kind of popular religion.'[62] The 'Man of Law's Tale' shows us Muslim merchants and Muslim rulers, decent Muslims and Muslims who are incarnations of pure evil; it offers no way of reconciling Rome/Constantinople and Syria, but it also shows problematic affinities in the violence of the two nations.[63] No one knows what Chaucer thought about Muslims or indeed if he had a view of Muslims as a group. The structure of the *Canterbury Tales* discourages the idea of a hegemonic perspective on anything. The tale-collection genre as Chaucer develops it puts forward a Bakhtinian view of the world, in which the tales appear

> like mirrors that face each other, each reflecting in its own way a piece, a
> tiny corner of the world, forc[ing] us to guess at and grasp for a world be-
> hind their mutually reflecting aspects that is broader, more multi-leveled,

[61] John M. Fyler, 'Domesticating the Exotic in the *Squire's Tale*,' *ELH* 55:1 (1988): 1–26, and DiMarco, 'Historical Basis.'

[62] Anthony Bale, ' "A maner latyn corrupt": Chaucer and the Absent Religions,' in Helen Phillips (ed.), *Chaucer and Religion* (Woodbridge: Boydell & Brewer, 2010), 58. The Prioress and her anti-Semitism have generated a huge amount of scholarship. See Louise O. Fradenburg, 'Criticism, Anti-Semitism, and the Prioress's Tale,' *Exemplaria* 1:1 (1989): 69–115; and Lawton, 'Public Interiorities,' 93–107. For a recent discussion of the 'Tale,' and its contexts, see Geraldine Heng, *The Invention of Race in the European Middle Ages* (Cambridge: Cambridge University Press, 2018), 81–90.

[63] The sultaness and her followers' violence towards the Christian converts is mirrored by the Romans' genocidal revenge; the implicitly incestuous feelings of the Muslim/pagan mothers in the story are mirrored by the semi-suppressed incest of the Constance story. See Dinshaw, *Chaucer's Sexual Poetics*, 88–112. On Rome as Constantinople, see Geraldine Heng, *Empire of Magic: Medieval Romance and the Politics of Cultural Fantasy* (New York: Columbia University Press, 2003), 46–51.

containing more and varied horizons than would be available to a single language or a single mirror.[64]

Bakhtin here uses the language of geography to describe poetics. This is peculiarly apt for Chaucer, whose use of multiple perspectives reflects a conception of the world as a multiple place—not a place with one centre and margins that must be controlled but as a network with centralizing nodes of power that link together. It is the tale-carrying Syrian merchants at the start of the 'Man of Law's Tale' who peddle tidings across the world, or the backstory of the 'Squire's Tale,' through Old French romances back to the *Thousand and One Nights*, that make the most significant statements about cultural connectedness, and the nearness of far, far away in Chaucer's imagination.[65]

Indeed, the deep structures of Chaucer's world reveal how connected the economies and cultures of its disparate parts were. To take one example, the Athens and Thebes of the 'Knight's Tale' may seem to be stock places from the classical and romance traditions with little connection to real fourteenth-century cities. It is easy to assume that they simply represent 'far far away,' 'not here,' fantasy settings distant in time and space. But those cities had been violently connected with Western Europe throughout the Crusades and, indeed, the origins of romance as a genre are intertwined with the history of the Crusades and with the chronicles and accounts of Crusader journeys and battles.[66] Texts such as Chrétien's *Cligès*, Benoît's *Roman de Troie*, or the *Roman de Thèbes* are dependent in all kinds of ways upon Western Crusaders' encounters with the Byzantine Empire in the East as well as with the Muslim states of the Levant.[67] After the Fourth Crusade, Athens and Thebes fell under Western rule so that for much of the thirteenth century, the duchy of Athens (encompassing both cities) was ruled by the Burgundian de la Roche family. For most of the fourteenth century the duchy was under the control of the Catalan

[64] Mikhail M. Bakhtin, *Dialogic Imagination: Four Essays*, ed. Michael Holquist, trans. Caryl Emerson and Michael Holquist (Austin: University of Texas Press, 1981), 414–15.

[65] Dorothy Metlitzki, *The Matter of Araby in Medieval England* (New Haven: Yale University Press, 1977), 140–42.

[66] Heng, *Empire of Magic*, 17–61.

[67] Dominique Battles, *The Medieval Tradition of Thebes: History and Narrative in the Old French 'Roman de Thèbes,' Boccaccio, Chaucer, and Lydgate* (New York: Routledge, 2004), especially 19–60.

Company and the dukedom was held by Aragonese rulers.[68] When Boccaccio wrote the *Teseida*, he was living in Naples, in close contact with Niccolò Acciaioli, a Florentine confidant (and probably lover) of Catherine of Valois, who claimed the title Empress of Constantinople. She gave Acciaioli estates in the Morea (the area of the Peloponnese peninsula) and she herself decamped there with her household in 1338. Catherine was the sister-in-law of Robert, king of Naples. The *Teseida* was written in a context in which the cities of Athens and Thebes and their surrounding areas were centres of conflict, frontiers in struggles for dominance not only between Western Europe and the Byzantine Empire, but between multiple competing forces of Western and Eastern Europe. When Chaucer was writing, it remained a site of territorial competition: in the 1370s, a Navarrese company conquered Thebes, and in 1388 the Acciaioli family took over the duchy. It may have been Niccolò Acciaioli who transmitted Tuscan texts into Greek territory: throughout the fourteenth and fifteenth centuries, Greek versions of Western romances were produced, witnesses to the cultural traffic between Western Europe and its neighbours.[69]

Chaucer, as a highly cultured man, had an excellent understanding of global networks of power and culture. He personally understood how indebted Western culture was to Arabic writings, for example.[70] And Chaucer knew not only that his country and language were 'of lesser cultural significance and authority than their continental competitors,' but also that Europe itself 'was a peripheral player' in global trade networks.[71] He understood that places change their allegiances and their culture, that we live in a world of shifting power blocs and conquest. Indeed, the 'Man

[68] Kevin Brownlee and Marina Scordilis Brownlee, 'Athens, Thebes, and Mystra,' in Wallace, *Europe: A Literary History*, 2:309–22.

[69] Brownlee and Brownlee, 'Athens, Thebes, and Mystra,' 317.

[70] Chaucer relies on the Arabic heritage in *A Treatise on the Astrolabe* in particular. A number of mansucripts of his main source, a Latin translation of the text known as the 'Messahalla,' acknowledge the author by name (e.g. Cambridge, University Library, MS Ii.3.3, Oxford, Bodleian Library, Ashmole MS 1522 and MS 1796), and it seems likely that Chaucer did indeed know that his Latin source had Arabic origins. Elsewhere in Chaucer's writings, he also refers to authorities who wrote in Arabic, including 'Senior' ('Senior Zadith,' another name for Muhammed bin Umail it-Tamimi as-Sadiq, 'Canon's Yeoman's Tale,' 1450), and a number of medical authorities, such as the well-known Avicenna and Averroes ('General Prologue,' 432–33). Eleanor Myerson has also pointed out to me in a personal communication that many early glosses on manuscripts of the *Canterbury Tales* make further references to Islamic authorities.

[71] Simpson, 'Chaucer as a European Writer,' 55; Freedman, *Out of the East*, 105.

of Law's Tale' differs from its sources in referring to England's chequered Briton past: the teller reminds us of early Roman Christianity and the driving out of Christian Celts to the edges of the country.[72] In 1391, Chaucer's friends Clanvowe and Neville died at Galata. Under Byzantine rule, this area had been the Jewish quarter, and had been destroyed in the Fourth Crusade. It then became a Genoese colony—and in the fifteenth century, after the Ottoman conquest of Constantinople, the Dominican church where Clanvowe and Neville were buried became a mosque. At the end of the century, this mosque was known as the Arab Mosque, because it was given to Spanish Moors fleeing the Spanish Reconquista. Galata—also known as Pera—is situated at a particularly important crossroads. But it also reflects the history of Europe more generally: many places have similarly startling histories of takeover and return, bloodshed and accommodation, refugees and imperialism. Earlier in this book we saw Chaucer travelling to Genoa, at the time when the Genoese invaded Cyprus, and to Navarre, home of significant Muslim and Jewish communities. Chaucer's understanding of the rise and fall of empires and individuals underpins the very structure of *Troilus and Criseyde*.[73] In the diversity of the places and genres of the *Canterbury Tales*, he again signals his lack of interest in a triumphalist idea of history, geography, or poetics.[74] Chaucer was never really on the peripheries, nor at the heart of anything: he was a consummate *networker*. And he was fully aware that the centre cannot hold.

[72] Lavezzo, *Angels*, 101.

[73] As Simpson notes, Chaucer is much more interested in the dark side of the Theban and Trojan stories than Boccaccio was. See 'Chaucer as a European Writer,' 73; Patterson, *Chaucer and the Subject of History*, 90–99.

[74] See earlier discussion in chapter 13.

CHAPTER 18

>—I—◆>—◗—O—◖>—I—◀

What Lies Beneath

It semed that alle the rokkes were aweye.

—*'The Franklin's Tale'*

The first few years of the 1390s were the most settled years of Richard's reign, years in which the king appeared to be working harmoniously with his magnates. A lull between the crashing waves of the Wonderful and Merciless Parliaments of the mid- to late 1380s, and the Revenge Parliament, murder of Gloucester, and exile and disinheritance of Henry of Derby in the late 1390s, these years presented a relatively smooth surface. This new political era was inaugurated by Gaunt's return from his Castilian expedition on 19 November 1389. Richard, who had been so keen to get Gaunt out of the way back in the mid-1380s, now knew that Gaunt was not the enemy. Gloucester, Arundel, and Warwick would almost certainly not have challenged the royal prerogative in the way that they had if Gaunt, with his strong respect for the office of kingship, had been there to restrain them.[1] Gaunt, with his Castilian fantasies over and his coffers full of Spanish gold, was turning his attention to Aquitaine and his new dream of long-term Lancastrian rule in Guyenne, a project for which he needed to work closely with the king.[2] When uncle and nephew were reunited after three years apart, Richard took the Lancastrian livery collar from Gaunt's neck and placed it on his own, in a powerful symbolic

---

[1] Goodman, *John of Gaunt*, 14.
[2] Ibid., 144–46.

gesture of unity and mutual allegiance.[3] The stage was set for around five years of dominant Lancastrian influence. In some ways, then, these were years akin to the early mid-1380s, years in which the court and council seemed relatively stable—although now Richard had an older and far more politic head on his shoulders. But they were also similar to those years in that the smooth surface was deceptive and sometimes significantly disturbed. The undercurrents not only did not go away, they intensified, surged up at key moments, and finally unleashed a tsunami in the events of 1397–99. When Richard linked Gaunt's collar of esses around his own neck in 1389, Henry's disinheritance by and subsequent murder of his cousin cannot have been part of any future imagined by the returning elder statesman.

Across these years, Chaucer ultimately regained his financial security from the king but was also specifically rewarded by Henry of Derby, on top of his preexisting annuity from Gaunt. Chaucer's son Thomas laid the foundations of his own considerable wealth and influence during these years, again through Lancastrian patronage. This was also a period of intensive reading and writing for Chaucer; the reworked Prologue to the *Legend of Good Women*, written after Anne's death in 1394, tells us explicitly about some of his literary activities around the late 1380s and early 1390s, including his engagement with texts such as *De Miseria Humanae Conditionis* and Jerome's *Adversus Jovinian*. Most famously, from the late 1380s Chaucer was immersed in the *Canterbury Tales*, a project that moved on from the chivalric world of Troilus and Criseyde's failed love to a world much more expansive in its concerns, a world where the traditional hierarchies of estate and gender were under open attack. Lynn Staley relates the *Tales* to political preoccupations with sacrality and forms of hierarchy and submission during the 1390s, astutely commenting that 'we can catch echoes within [Chaucer's] works of conversations held on much higher levels of power.'[4] We can't date Chaucer's tales precisely, but tales such as the 'Wife of Bath's,' 'Man of Law's,' 'Shipman's,' 'Melibee,'

---

[3] PROME, Membrane 6, no. 11, 7:258 (January 1394): Richard is reported as saying that he 'took the collar from the neck of his same uncle and put it on his own neck and said that he would wear it as a sign of the great love and whole heartedness between them.'

[4] Staley, *Languages of Power*, 147.

'Merchant's,' 'Clerk's,' 'Franklin's,' and 'Pardoner's' probably occupied Chaucer during these years and are certainly connected to the reading he did at this time, and are also connected to one another. The 'Wife of Bath's,' 'Merchant's,' 'Pardoner's,' and 'Franklin's' Tales draw on Jerome; the 'Man of Law's' and 'Pardoner's' draw on *De Miseria*.[5] The Wife of Bath is a figure in the 'Merchant's' and 'Clerk's' Tales, and the Wife of Bath and Pardoner interact in her 'Prologue'; they also are both 'confessional' figures. A cancelled endlink suggests that Chaucer initially imagined a sequence of the 'Man of Law's Prologue,' followed by the 'Tale of Melibee,' followed by the Wife of Bath telling the 'Shipman's Tale.'[6] Indeed, the Wife of Bath, with her revelatory prologue, her brilliantly counterintuitive use of hostile sources, and her focus on ethics, rank, and gender, distills the major concerns of all these tales. She is, in many ways, the beating heart of the *Canterbury Tales*, and although she existed in some form by 1388 (as discussed in chapter 17) the existence of the cancelled endlink demonstrates Chaucer's reworking of his material. Her appearance in so many other tales also suggests Chaucer's continuing preoccupation with her: Carolyn Dinshaw aptly calls her Chaucer's 'favourite character.'[7]

Significantly, as Chaucer got fully down to work on the radical and extraordinary *Canterbury Tales*, his country, in the wake of the Merciless Parliament and Richard's return to rule, was entering into a 'crucial period of English political consciousness.'[8] When Gaunt returned from the Iberian peninsula, Richard, now approaching his twenty-third birthday, had recently (3 May 1389) resumed rule in his own right. He had presented a conciliatory face to the world over the previous year, and indeed had won over the minor Appellants, Derby and Mowbray, who had never been in full agreement with their senior colleagues.[9] A truce had now been signed with France, and Richard was beginning to establish himself as an adult independent ruler for the first time (he had been only nineteen

---

[5] Chaucer also continues to use sources such as the *Roman de la Rose*, which had long been important to him. His crucial recent vernacular influences—in particular Boccaccio's writings—remain, as ever, unacknowledged.

[6] See *Riverside Chaucer*, 862–63.

[7] Dinshaw, *Chaucer's Sexual Poetics*, 116.

[8] Staley, *Languages of Power*, 77. She adds that 'this contestation of sacrality informs the texts ... of the last decade of the fourteenth century, including the *Canterbury Tales*.'

[9] Saul, *Richard II*, 200–204.

at the time of the Wonderful Parliament).[10] He worked hard to gain Gaunt's powerful support. In 1377, Gaunt had been granted palatinate powers in the duchy of Lancaster for life (as noted in chapter 5); now, on 16 February 1390, those powers were entailed on his male heirs. Parliament then moved to grant him the duchy of Aquitaine for life on 3 March.[11] Over the next four years, Gaunt had a 'unique influence' in the realm and, with the prospect of establishing a fief in Aquitaine, the house of Lancaster had 'enormous potential power.'[12] It was also looking increasingly likely that Henry would become Richard's heir, given Edward III's entailing of the Crown on his male heirs (which demoted the earl of March, descended from Edward's granddaughter), and Anne's continued failure to bear a child, now after many years of marriage.[13]

Both Richard and his Lancastrian relatives were particularly concerned with surfaces, with public image during these years. As discussed in chapter 17, Gaunt lavished money on Henry's spectacular chivalric and crusading exploits. It is also likely that he publicized these exploits as part of a textual campaign to promote his son's glossy image.[14] Richard was also increasingly preoccupied with his public identity. From 1390, he started distributing his own livery badge and constructing his own private affinity, retaining large numbers of knights and squires.[15] During these years, he encouraged the use of imperial modes of address towards himself, and around the middle of the decade, he commissioned the extraordinary Westminster portrait of himself: hieratic, commanding, and very much individualized (plate 16).[16] Roger Dymmok's anti-Lollard tract, given to Richard in 1396–67 in response to the radical Wycliffite 'Twelve Conclusions,' presented a robust defence of the surface attributes of majesty, arguing for the importance of the mystifying regalia of kingship.[17] Public

---

[10] Ibid., 205.

[11] Goodman, *John of Gaunt*, 146.

[12] Ibid., 157; Staley, *Languages of Power*, 181. See also Given-Wilson, *Henry IV*, 100.

[13] Michael Bennett, 'Edward III's Entail and the Succession to the Crown, 1376–1471,' *English Historical Review* 113:452 (1998): 582–98.

[14] Staley, *Languages of Power*, 172.

[15] Ibid., 173; Saul, *Richard II*, 259.

[16] Saul, *Richard II*, 238–40; Mathew, *Court of Richard II*. See chapter 13 in this book.

[17] H. S. Cronin (ed.), *Roger Dymock: Liber contra XII errores et hereses Lollardorum* (London: Kegan Paul, Trench, Trübner, 1922). For the idea that the Twelve Conclusions might have been penned by men from within Chaucer's circle, see Steven Justice, 'Lollardy,' 673. See also Anne Hud-

displays of chivalry, such as the 1390 Smithfield tournament for which Chaucer provided the scaffolds in his capacity as clerk of the king's works, were designed to present an aspirational picture of the flower of English nobility.[18] Richard's trip to Ireland (the first time an English monarch had crossed the Irish Sea since 1210) was part of his vision of himself as an imperial ruler; similarly, Gaunt was striving hard to be more than the duke of Lancaster as he pursued his ambitions in Aquitaine.[19] Most importantly, Gaunt and Richard's intimacy ostentatiously demonstrated that the fissures at the centre of English politics had closed up or at least become irrelevant.

When one looks closely at the events of these years, however, it is clear that Richard never accepted what had happened in 1388 or took on board the lessons that he could have learnt about the problems of authoritarian kingship in the English context. He was biding his time, but his resentment was never far below the surface— like the 'sursanure' of the 'Franklin's Tale,' a wound that continues to fester beneath a seemingly healed body (1113). As early as 1390, Richard was testing the water to see if he could invite his exiled cronies (de Vere and Alexander Neville) back to England.[20] Twice in 1391 he planted petitions, whereby the Commons requested that the king should be as free as his predecessors in 'liberty, regality, and royal dignity.'[21] His financial position was rapidly deteriorating, partly because he was working hard to retain and develop his own affinity.[22] Indeed, Richard was now promoting a new group of younger men who would become his supporters in the crisis years of his tyranny. He was trying to control Parliament, and maneuvered to have his own placeman (John Bushy or Bussy) elected as Speaker repeatedly, making a mockery of that role.[23] In 1392, Richard again pushed for the return of de Vere and Neville. There was some kind of confrontation in the council

---

son, *The Premature Reformation: Wycliffite Texts and Lollard History* (Oxford: Clarendon Press, 1988), 112.

[18] Sheila Lindenbaum, 'The Smithfield Tournament of 1390,' *Journal of Medieval and Renaissance Studies* 20 (1990): 1–21.

[19] Saul, *Richard II*, 270.

[20] Hector and Harvey, *Westminster Chronicle*, 440–41.

[21] Saul, *Richard II*, 255n74.

[22] Ibid., 259.

[23] Ibid., 261–62.

at this point, and on 12 February 1392, the king's magnates promised that they were 'loialx subgits' and that they would do nothing violent against the king 'en prive ne en apert.' In return, the king promised that he would not seek to punish anyone for things they had done in the past; nor would he seek to restore anyone who had been judged 'en plein parlement.'[24] The need for these statements strongly suggests that there were significant tensions between Richard and the nobles, and that the former Appellants and their allies were already anxious about possible reprisals. Richard's frustrations bubbled up again, and more violently, in a dramatic quarrel with London later that year, when he showed his penchant for extreme reactions.[25] In the middle of the following year, discontent broke out elsewhere in the realm, in a northern rebellion in Lancashire and Cheshire, largely driven by soldiers dismayed by the proposed treaties with France, and suspecting that Gaunt's Aquitaine ambitions were to blame.[26]

Many of the underlying problems in the realm exploded in 1394. This dramatic year opened with a parliament, at which the seething earl of Arundel, erstwhile Appellant, openly attacked Gaunt and, specifically, Gaunt and Richard's relationship. He said that it was not appropriate for Richard to be 'so often in the close company' of Gaunt, nor to wear his livery collar. He accused Gaunt of dominating the council and Parliament in such a way that others dared not speak, and he condemned the grant of Aquitaine, the funding previously given to the Castilian expedition, and aspects of the French treaty.[27] Parliament went on to reject that treaty. It is also likely that a discussion about the succession took place, a discussion that can only have been deeply unwelcome to Richard.[28] As the year wore on, things worsened: a rebellion broke out in Aquitaine in the spring, and Gaunt's hopes for a Lancastrian duchy in France looked increasingly shaky.[29] And, tragically, three women died suddenly and unexpectedly

[24] John Prophet, 'A Journal of the Clerk of the Council during the Fifteenth and Sixteenth Years of Richard II,' in J. F. Baldwin (ed.), *The King's Council in England during the Middle Ages* (Oxford: Clarendon Press, 1913), 495.

[25] See especially Barron, 'Quarrel of Richard II,' 173–201.

[26] Goodman, *John of Gaunt*, 153–54.

[27] PROME, Membrane 6, no. 11, 7:258 (January 1394).

[28] Given-Wilson, *Henry IV*, 97.

[29] Ibid., 90–91; J.J.N. Palmer, *England, France, and Christendom, 1377–99* (London: Routledge & Kegan Paul, 1972), 152–65.

within three months: Constance of Castile, wife of Gaunt; Mary de Bohun, wife of Henry of Derby; and Anne of Bohemia, wife of the king.[30] The death of Anne was personally traumatic for Richard: he ordered the palace in which she had died to be burnt to the ground, and physically struck the earl of Arundel for arriving late to her funeral.[31] These dramatic outbursts of emotion reveal something of what was going on under his surface. Politically, Anne's death brought the question of the succession even more to the fore: now there was a greater chance of Richard producing heirs with a new wife. By the end of 1394, both Richard and Gaunt, newly widowed, were abroad, in Ireland and Aquitaine, respectively, and their accord would never be properly rebuilt. Indeed, Gaunt remained abroad for most of 1395, while Henry watched over Lancastrian interests at home. Meanwhile, Richard's French marriage was negotiated across the Channel while he campaigned in Ireland during the first half of the year. By early 1396, the house of Lancaster was weakened through the problems in Aquitaine, anxieties about the succession, and the rise of the king's friends.[32] Richard and Gaunt met cordially, but Richard was no longer seeking a special relationship with his uncle and indeed may have been turning his acquisitive eyes to the vast Lancastrian landholdings.[33] No longer able to exert the kind of influence he had wielded just a few years earlier, Gaunt focused his attention on his immediate family circumstances, making the astonishing decision to marry Katherine Swynford, and seeking the legitimation of his Beaufort children. Richard, meanwhile, was preparing to enact his terrible and long-meditated revenge for the events of 1388.[34]

The years between Gaunt's return and the traumas and changes around the middle of the decade, then, had their own character, a seeming lull

---

[30] Constance died on 24 March; Anne on 7 June; Mary also died in June.

[31] G. B. Stow (ed.), *Historia Vitae et Regni Ricardi Secundi* (Philadelphia: University of Pennsylvania Press, 1977), 134; H. T. Riley (ed.), *Johannis de Trokelowe et Henrici de Blaneforde Monachorum S. Albani Necnon Quorundam Anonymorum, Chronica et Annales, Regnantibus Henrico Tertio, Edwardo Primo, Edwardo Secundo, Ricardo Secundo et Henrico Quarto* (London: Longmans, 1866), 168–69.

[32] Given-Wilson, *Henry IV*, 92–93.

[33] Ibid., 95–96.

[34] Given-Wilson writes that in 1397, we see the explosion of 'the clenched resentment of a decade'; *Henry IV*, 100. Goodman comments that Richard's revenge was 'doubtless long premeditated'; *John of Gaunt*, 160.

between two storms, years in which a different future seemed not only possible but likely, but years in which unity was always predicated on a relentless suppression of what was going on beneath the surface. Overall, these were good years for Chaucer. He was clerk of the king's works, earning a very respectable salary, between 1389 and 1391. He also took on the forester job, appointed by the earl of Arundel and the other trustees of the earl of March. He had, we presume, his annuity from Gaunt, but after the end of his government role of clerk of the works in 1391, money was probably thin on the ground. Since 1388 he had been without his regular Crown annuity. He was taken to court for debt by several different people.[35] He was also involved in the court case against the thieves who had robbed him at Foul Oake.[36] However, sometime in 1392, Richard gave him a gift of £10 and, much more significantly, on 28 February 1394, the king granted Chaucer £20 a year for life, effectively reinstating the allowances that Chaucer had given away six years earlier.[37] This was granted in the standard terms of such documents, 'pro bono servicio' (for good service). Did Richard see Chaucer as a useful court servant? Had someone spoken up for Chaucer? We can't know, and the candidates are many: Gaunt himself, the earl of March, Richard Sturry, or even the queen could all be contenders. This annuity gave Chaucer the security that he had lacked for the last few years, and made him comfortable for the forseeable future. Of course, it conveyed certain obligations of loyalty and potential service, now that he was again a paid member of the royal household. In the same week as Richard made this grant to Chaucer, we also see him patronizing rising men such as William le Scrope and John Bushy, as well as Chaucer's old friend and longtime court servant Sturry.[38]

The short poems *Fortune* and *Lenvoy de Scogan* probably date from the early 1390s and relate to Chaucer's attempt to get his annuity reinstated or to seek other forms of royal favour. While the general tone of *Fortune*—with its reliance on Boethius and the *Roman de la Rose*—might suggest that it was partly drafted at an earlier date, the final stanza surely

[35] Crow and Olson, *Chaucer Life-Records*, 391–96.
[36] Ibid., 496.
[37] Ibid., 120; 514–15.
[38] *Calendar of the Patent Rolls: Richard II*, Membrane 36, 5:371 (24 February 1394); Membrane 31, 5:380 (22 February 1394); Membrane 32, 5:378 (24 February 1394).

dates from the early 1390s. Here, Fortune addresses 'Princes' and asks that 'three of you or tweyne' help the supplicant or, if they do not wish to, that they 'preyeth his beste frend of his noblesse / That to som beter estat he may atteyne' (73–79). In March 1390, an ordinance was passed relating to the procedure of the council. It specified that no gift or grant that might reduce the resources of the king could be passed without the agreement of at least two of a group consisting of the royal uncles and the chancellor (the dukes of Lancaster, York, and Gloucester, and William of Wykeham).[39] The reference in *Fortune* to requiring help from 'three of you or tweyne' is almost certainly a reference to this barrier, with the 'beste frend' representing the king. Chaucer is explicit in asking for preferment: 'some beter estat.' In *Lenvoy de Chaucer a Scogan*, Chaucer again asks for favour: he reminds Scogan that he is 'at the stremes hed / Of grace,' while Chaucer is 'dul as ded, / Forgete in solytarie wildernesse' (43–46). I have previously discussed the jokey tone of these lines and the absurdity of the suggestion that Chaucer is really alone in a wasteland.[40] But the comic hyperbole does not alter the fact that Chaucer is indeed asking Scogan to 'Mynne [remember] thy frend' (48), from his superior position at court. It is most likely that this poem too dates from the years when Chaucer had neither his Exchequer annuities nor his position as clerk of the works. The poem suggests that Scogan's offence (13) against love at Michaelmas (18–19), when he gave up his lady, has caused Venus to weep so copiously that she has caused torrential rain (11–14). The reference to 'this diluge of pestilence' (14) only makes sense if there is indeed heavy rain, and the pointed 'this' suggests that the poem was written during the bad weather. There were, of course, many periods of heavy rain in the relevant years, and we can't fix a date to this poem with certainty, but it may be significant that there was flooding in September and October (i.e. around and after Michaelmas) in 1393, a few months before Chaucer received his new annuity.[41]

[39] N. H. Nicolas (ed.), *Proceedings and Ordinances of the Privy Council of England* (London: Eyre and Spottiswode, 1834–37), 1:18a–18b.

[40] See chapter 15.

[41] John Stow, *The Annales of England: Faithfully collected out of the most autenticall authors, records, and other monuments of antiquitie, lately collected, since encreased, and continued, from the first habitation vntill this present yeare 1605. By Iohn Stow citizen of London* (London: Peter Short, Felix Kingston, and George Eld, 1605), 495.

As well as these short poems, Chaucer was also at work on another 'occasional' text during these years: *A Treatise on the Astrolabe*. While the text may have been written over a number of years (as discussed in chapter 9), it was probably begun around 1391, given the specific references to using the astrolabe in March 1391.[42] This fits well with what we know was going on in Chaucer's life: having, for obscure reasons, given up the job of clerk of the works in June 1391, he was at a loose end and may indeed have seized the opportunity to 'spend more time with his family.' His focus on the education of his son and on shared pursuits with Lewis is certainly intriguing. The text suggests that Chaucer gave an astrolabe to Lewis, that Chaucer knows Lewis's abilities at maths, Latin, and science, and that Lewis petitioned his father to help him to understand how to work the astrolabe.[43] All of this reveals that Chaucer was interested in his son and knew something about his abilities; it also shows us Chaucer's willingness to spend time and money on Lewis. Did Lewis live some of the time in Kent with his father? Did Chaucer visit Lewis in Katherine Swynford's household? Was Lewis with his much older brother, since Thomas's return to England?[44] We can only speculate, but Chaucer's role as a father did matter to him during these years. And indeed, the next generation—the children of Chaucer and Philippa, Katherine and Gaunt, Katherine and Swynford, Gaunt and Blanche, and Gaunt and Constance—were starting to inherit the earth. Chaucer's older son had now returned from Spain and was beginning his triumphant route to wealth and influence.

Richard was not the only person extending favour to Chaucer in the middle of the 1390s. Henry of Derby also singled out Chaucer. His accounts for the year preceding 1 February 1396 show that he gave Chaucer fur for a gown, as well as £10.[45] These gifts were presumably given at some point in 1395 and provide the only evidence that we have of Henry's direct contact with Chaucer. Although Henry had personal reasons for patronizing Chaucer, given their familial connection and the close rela-

---

[42] *A Treatise on the Astrolabe*, Part II, 1.7 and 23.16, pp. 669–70.

[43] 'Prologue,' in *Treatise*, 1–10, 27, p. 662.

[44] Our only documentary reference to Lewis places him in Thomas's company and the company of the Beauforts and Swynfords, as discussed in chapter 9. See Crow and Olson, *Chaucer Life-Records*, 544–45. See also National Archives, E 101/43/22, printed in Lewis, 'Carmarthen Castle,' 4–5.

[45] Crow and Olson, *Chaucer Life-Records*, 275.

tionship between all the Lancastrian-Beaufort-Swynford-Chaucer siblings and cousins, he may also have had literary reasons. Henry, whose own grandfather had been an author, had subsequently married into the most cultured family in England (the Bohuns), and he and Mary were both interested in education and books.[46] Chaucer's *Book of the Duchess* had been written about the death of Henry's own mother when Henry was an infant. Henry's particular interest in contemporary English poets is revealed by his patronage of John Gower in 1393. At the end of that year, Henry records that he has given Gower a Lancastrian livery collar—a collar of esses like the one Richard had taken from Gaunt a few years earlier.[47] Gower writes effusively about the meanings of that collar in his poetry.[48] He had also, either in late 1392 or in early 1393, revised his *Confessio Amantis* to include a dedication to Henry. While his first version (1389–90) had included an explicit dedication to Richard—and a reference to Chaucer—the second (1390–91) had deleted both these references. This third version now positioned itself in a broader way, with an address to the country, rather than to the king. It is this version that includes a dedication to Henry, which perhaps had its origins in a presentation copy.[49] It is perfectly possible that Henry was rewarding two vernacular poets at around the same time.

We might also, or alternatively, link Henry's gifts to Chaucer with the situation of Chaucer's son Thomas, a Lancastrian through and through, and first cousin to Henry's Beaufort brothers and sister. Thomas Chaucer had accompanied Gaunt on his Castilian expedition and had been retained for life by Gaunt, for £10 a year, in 1389. In January 1394 his fee as one of Gaunt's esquires was doubled.[50] It can only have been through his Lancastrian connections that he then achieved a brilliant marriage, with Maud Burghersh. We know that they were married before 2 December 1395,

[46] Given-Wilson, *Henry IV*, 77–80, 86–87, 387–90.

[47] Fisher, *John Gower*, 68, 341–42n5. On the Lancastrian livery collar, see also Doris Fletcher, 'The Lancastrian Collar of Esses: Its Origins and Transformations down the Centuries,' in Gillespie, *Age of Richard II*, 191–95.

[48] 'Cronica Tripertita,' in Gower, *The Complete Works*, 315.

[49] Staley, *Languages of Power*, 25–40.

[50] Roskell, 'Thomas Chaucer,' 153. See also K. B. McFarlane, 'Henry V, Bishop Beaufort, and the Red Hat, 1417–1421,' in *England in the Fifteenth Century: Collected Essays* (London: Hambledon Press, 1981), 79–113.

when the Close Rolls record an order to give 'Thomas Chaucer and Maud his wife seisin of the manor of Ewelme'; they had probably been married during 1395, though 1394 is possible.[51] Henry's gift to Chaucer could therefore plausibly have been related to the marriage of Chaucer's son. Thomas Chaucer was now a significant landholder, holding land in Oxfordshire, Hampshire, Essex, Suffolk, Norfolk, Cambridgeshire, and Lincolnshire. Over the next few years, he gained other appointments through Lancastrian patronage, such as the constableship of the castle of Knaresborough and the role of chief forester there.[52] Once Henry became king, Thomas continued to amass property and wealth, and became a stalwart of Parliament, repeatedly serving as Speaker during the early fifteenth century.[53] His daughter, Alice, who never knew her literary grandfather, ended up as duchess of Suffolk, and both Thomas and Alice's wonderful tombs remain at Ewelme, near Oxford (plate 19).

Chaucer gained an heiress for a daughter-in-law at around the same time as he saw the deaths of the three most important women in the realm. He may not have known much of Mary, but Chaucer's own wife had served Constance for many years—and indeed both Mary and Constance were very much in the same circle as Katherine Swynford.[54] Anne certainly meant something to Chaucer, whether his relationship with her was based more on personal contact or on aspirational imaginings. She is one of the very few contemporaries that he mentions in his poems, both in his reference to 'our' new appreciation for 'A' in *Troilus* (Book I, 171),[55] and, more obviously, in his hopeful reference in the F-Prologue to the *Legend of Good Women* to giving the poem to the queen 'at Eltham or at Sheene' (497). It is a specific detail, mentioning two of Richard and Anne's favourite palaces, both near London. After Anne's tragic death, these lines became awkward and anachronistic. Given that Anne's death occurred at Sheen and Richard, in his extreme grief, then ordered its demolition, the line even becomes embarrassingly inappropriate. Sometime after Anne's death, probably in 1394 or 1395, Chaucer revised the Prologue to the *Legend of*

---

[51] *Calendar of Close Rolls: Richard II*, Membrane 15, 5:446.
[52] Roskell, 'Thomas Chaucer,' 153.
[53] Ibid., 156–60.
[54] Given-Wilson, *Henry IV*, 77.
[55] See Lowes, 'Date of Chaucer's *Troilus and Criseyde*,' 285–306.

Good Women, writing what is now known as the G-Prologue. The reference to the queen disappears. The playful, courtly discussion of the flower and the leaf, which spoke so beautifully to the ludic culture of 1386, also vanishes. It became a more general, less 'occasional' kind of poem.[56] It may, however, gesture to the specific idea of a marriage between Richard and Isabella (discussed in 1395) in the insertion of the image of the garland of rose and lily, symbols of England and France (G-Prologue, 160).[57]

The F-Prologue to the *Legend of Good Women* contains a list of Chaucer's 'unproblematic' writings, those that could be used in his defence against accusations of misogyny. Alceste mentions, first, the *House of Fame*, the *Book of the Duchess*, the *Parliament of Fowls*, the story of Palamon and Arcite, and many other short poems made for the God of Love's 'halydayes.' She then adds:

> And, for to speke of other holynesse,
> He hath in prose translated Boece,
> And maad the lyf also of Seynt Cecile. (424–26)

In the G-Prologue, these lines change to:

> And, for to speke of other besynesse,
> He hath in prose translated Boece,
> And Of the Wreched Engendrynge of Mankynde,
> As man may in Pope Innocent yfynde;
> And mad the lyf also of Seynt Cecile. (412–16)

Chaucer here adds a new work to his résumé: a translation of Innocent III's very popular and well-known text *De Miseria Humanae Conditionis*, here called 'Of the Wreched Engendrynge of Mankynde.' Although we do not have Chaucer's translation of this text, its influence is evident in several of the *Canterbury Tales*, some of which include direct translations of parts of *De Miseria*. Another part of the G-Prologue tells us more about what Chaucer had been reading between his two versions of the 'Prologue.'

---

[56] Quinn, 'The *Legend of Good Women*,' 1–32; Percival, *Chaucer's Legendary Good Women*, 8–10, 322–23; McDonald, 'Chaucer's *Legend of Good Women*.' See also chapter 14.

[57] For the negotiations of the marriage, see Saul, *Richard II*, 226–27; for the symbolism of the garland, see Barr, *Socioliterary Practice*, 92.

After line 335 (F)/266 (G), Chaucer adds forty-five lines to the earlier version. These lines emphasise the weight of authority that Chaucer could have called upon to write about good women, suggesting that he has 'sixty bokes olde and newe' on this subject, and that 'al the world of autours' treat the issue of how 'trewe and kynde' women are—far more so than men (273, 308, 303). The lines participate in the poem's concerns with experience versus authority and with ludic love debate. One of the sources mentioned here, Ovid's *Heroides*, had certainly long been known to Chaucer. But the lines are dominated by references to another authority: Jerome. As the *Adversus Jovinian* did not influence Chaucer's earlier work, but is a crucial source for some of the *Canterbury Tales*, its use here seems to signal that this was a text new to Chaucer in the late 1380s and 1390s. And, given that Jerome's monstrous text is driven by both misogyny and misogamy, and compares illicit sexual activity to eating dung, it is startlingly funny that Chaucer here makes the God of Love cite him repeatedly as an example of someone who says good things about women. Admittedly, Jerome does indeed praise virgins and virginity, but he is hardly the best authority to cite in praise of *women*. There are obvious comparisons to make between the God of Love's use of Jerome here and the Wife of Bath's extensive use of Jerome in her own 'Prologue.' We might also compare the God of Love's assertion that 'al the world of autours' (G-Prologue, 308) write about good women with the Wife of Bath's far more accurate comments about clerks' misogyny, the painting of lions, and women's lack of opportunity to tell stories about male perfidy.[58] The Wife of Bath's key point is that stories tend to be told from a dominant male perspective: if the pen was in women's hands, the canon would look different. In these years, Chaucer was particularly preoccupied with issues relating to gender and to social estate as he probed the relationship between surface and depth, both in the sphere of ethics and in the sphere of poetics.

In the G-Prologue, but not the F-Prologue, Chaucer twice uses a well-known image about exterior and interior or surface and depth: the image

---

[58] 'Wife of Bath's Prologue,' 692–96. She refers to a story of a lion looking at a picture of a man triumphing over a lion who points out that the picture was painted by a man; the point is that if a lion had painted the picture, the story would look different.

of the kernel of corn and its husk. This is an image of the relationship between outer form and inner content. It derives from the well-known biblical exhortation to separate the wheat from the chaff (Matthew 3:12). The God of Love asks the Chaucer-figure: 'what eyleth the to wryte / The draf of storyes and forgete the corn?' (311–12), and then urges him to 'Let be the chaf, and writ wel of the corn' (529). Chaucer does not use the image in his earlier poetry, but he uses it several times in the *Canterbury Tales*. The Man of Law explains of his narrative technique that 'Me list nat of the chaf, ne of the stree / Maken so long a tale as of the corn' (701–2), and the Parson similarly asks, 'Why sholde I sowen draf out of my fest, / Whan I may sowen whete, if that me lest?' (35–36). The God of Love, the Man of Law, and the Parson all conventionally emphasise the importance of focusing on the corn or wheat of a tale, and ignoring the chaff. They assume that the two things can be clearly divided and that clear meaning, or stable *sentence*, can be found and separated from the words or metaphorical terms in which it is expressed. But Chaucer's most famous iteration of this image comes at the very end of the startlingly brilliant tour de force of the 'Nun's Priest's Tale' when the priest tells his audience to 'Taketh the fruyt, and lat the chaf be stille' (3443). This comes as the culmination of a tale that has absolutely refused to provide a moral, or to hierarchise the different genres and perspectives on show. In Travis's words, there is an 'overabundance of "fruit" scattered about its narrative field,' as the tale demonstrates, 'the adamantine resistance of all literature to traditional interpretative practices.'[59] Indeed, the tale showcases the importance of not providing a moral, of not closing down meaning through traditional allegory, of arguing for argument's sake, of allowing different opinions and ideas to jostle each other, of focusing on the play of language and rhetoric itself. The Nun's Priest demonstrates that the relationship between outer and inner or surface and depth is complicated, and we need to be wary of the very idea of an integumental text that has an unambiguous meaning, of a form that transparently reveals what lies beneath. Chaucer's focus on the power of rhetoric and language suggests that the medium *is* the message,

---

[59] Travis, *Disseminal Chaucer*, 2, 4.

that there is no distinction between surface and depth—no single, fixed meaning lies hidden beneath the surface.[60]

Chaucer's repeated use of this image in texts of the 1390s neatly points to a number of his concerns during these years, some of which occupied him throughout his career, some of which were newly important to him at this moment. One way in which Chaucer had long been interested in surface and depth was his obsession with the architecture of texts, with how texts are built out of other texts: under the surface of a 'new' work lie the foundations constructed out of myriad other texts. Chaucer was fascinated by questions of authority and influence, the use and misuse of sources, the relationship between his own writings and the writings of those who preceded him. In the *House of Fame*, *Troilus and Criseyde*, and the Prologue to the *Legend of Good Women*, he focuses on the issue of how readers and writers can misinterpret or deliberately twist the meanings of their source texts. In many parts of the *Canterbury Tales*—such as the 'Prologue of the Man of Law's Tale' or the 'Wife of Bath's Prologue'— Chaucer portrays his speakers as outrageously (ab)using their sources.

Tracing his use of the texts new to him in the 1390s that he foregrounds in the G-Prologue to the *Legend of Good Women*—*De Miseria Humanae Conditionis* and *Adversus Jovinian*—reveals something of how he was theorizing the poetics of influence in the *Canterbury Tales*. *De Miseria Humanae Conditionis*, a late twelfth-century tract by Lotario dei Segni, who later became Pope Innocent III, survives in around seven hundred manuscripts (and by 1700 existed in fifty printed editions in many different languages). It is divided into three sections: the miserable entrance upon the human condition, the guilty progress of the human condition, and the damnable exit from the human condition.[61] Approximately half of the text is quotation. It details the sins and failings of man and the sufferings of mankind, with a particular focus on the curial problems that Lotario saw firsthand: thus he focuses far more on the sins of the clergy, and on

---

[60] For a discussion of medieval allegory, and Chaucerian allegory specifically, see Suzanne Conklin Akbari, *Seeing through the Veil: Optical Theory and Medieval Allegory* (Toronto: University of Toronto Press, 2004).

[61] Lotario dei Segni (Pope Innocent III), *De Miseria Condicionis Humane*, ed. Robert E. Lewis (Athens: University of Georgia Press, Chaucer Library, 1978); John C. Moore, *Pope Innocent III, 1160/61–1216: To Root Up and to Plant* (Leiden: Brill, 2003), 275–76.

homosexuality, than on adultery, for example.[62] His attacks on, for instance, ambition, luxury, and greed are fairly standard. Cupidity is the root of all evil; feather beds and canopies are to be condemned; the ambitious man is constantly hypocritical as he 'pretends humility, feigns honesty, displays affability, shows off his kindness, is accommodating, is compliant, honors everyone and bows to everybody' (part 2, xxvi); the magnate 'concludes a miserable life with a miserable end' (part 3, xxix). Lotario's focus on the commonality of man's fate is also in keeping with the mainstream of late-medieval thought, although his imagery is at times particularly memorable: book 3 opens with a chapter 'On the rottenness of corpses,' which details how worms stand, like mourners, by the dead body.[63]

One of the most significant aspects of the *De Miseria*, like the *Adversus Jovinian*, is that it is one-sided. Lotario promised to follow up the *De Miseria* with a tract on the dignity of mankind, but this never materialized. But Chaucer shows us how even a polemical, unbalanced text can be used to argue points contrary to the thrust of the original.[64] The Man of Law turns Lotario's scorning of poor and rich alike into an attack on poverty alone, in keeping with the lawyer's narrow morality, concern with money, and inability to read texts well. The Man of Law spends more than three stanzas expressing his disgust and disdain for the poor ('Prologue of the Man of Law's Tale,' 99–121). He begins: 'O hateful harm, condicion of poverte! / With thurst, with coold, with hunger so confoundid!' The speech ends with the lines:

---

[62] John C. Moore, 'Innocent III's *De Miseria Humanae Conditionis*: A *Speculum Curiae*?,' *Catholic Historical Review* 67:4 (1981): 553–64.

[63] For further discussions of death in the Middle Ages, see Paul Binski, *Medieval Death: Ritual and Representation* (London: British Museum Press, 1996); Ashby Kinch, *Imago mortis: Mediating Images of Death in Late Medieval Culture* (Leiden: Brill, 2013); Nigel Saul, *Death, Art, and Memory in Medieval England: The Cobham Family and Their Monuments, c. 1300–1500* (Oxford: Oxford University Press, 2001); Christopher Daniell, *Death and Burial in Medieval England, 1066–1550* (London: Routledge, 1997); Elina Gertsman, *The Dance of Death in the Middle Ages: Image, Text, Performance* (Turnhout: Brepols, 2010).

[64] Lewis compares Chaucer's more direct use of the text in the 'Man of Law's Prologue and Tale' with the 'Pardoner's Tale,' arguing that by the time Chaucer wrote the 'Pardoner's Tale,' the text had been more assimilated into Chaucer's own thought. *De Miseria*, 8, 31. See also Robert Enzer Lewis, 'Chaucer's Artistic Use of Pope Innocent III's *De Miseria Humane Conditionis* in the Man of Law's Prologue and Tale,' *PMLA* 81:7 (1966): 485–92.

Yet of the wise man take this sentence:
'Alle the dayes of povre men been wikke'
Be war, therfore, er thou come to that prikke!
If thou be povre, thy brother hateth thee,
And alle thy freendes fleen from thee, allas!

The whole speech draws very closely on *De Miseria*. The last four lines quoted above translate: 'All the days of the poor are evil.' 'The brethren of the poor man hate him, and even his friends have departed far from him' (part 1, xiv). Lotario, however, follows his critique of the life of the poor with an attack on the rich: 'The rich man flies away to his pleasure and falls into unlawfulness and they become the instruments of his punishments that had been the pleasures of his sins.' Indeed, later on, he includes a chapter titled, 'How Short and Miserable the Life of Magnates' (part 3, xxix). The Man of Law, however, follows his attack on the poor with a passage *praising* rich merchants: 'O riche marchauntz, ful of wele been yee, / O noble, o prudent folk, as in this cas!' (122–23). He thus takes Lotario's text and utterly changes its meaning, turning it into a passage in praise of sharp business, rather than a pessimistic comment on the evils of any mode of life in this world. If we dig into Lotario's own text, we can see yet another layer of source twisting. The passage from *De Miseria* that Chaucer adapts here itself draws heavily on the Bible. For instance, 'The brethren of the poor man hate him, and even his friends have departed far from him' is a quotation from Proverbs 19:7: 'The brethren of the poor man hate him: moreover also his friends have departed far from him.' This chapter begins with the words: 'Better is the poor man, that walketh in his simplicity, than a rich man that is perverse in his lips, and unwise' (19:1). Subsequent verses warn that friends flock to rich men and flatter them with gifts, but that in the end 'he that keepeth prudence shall find good things' (19:8). In the 'Prologue of the Man of Law's Tale,' Chaucer's pilgrim teller is selectively quoting a source (Lotario) who himself was selectively quoting a source (the Bible). The Man of Law is thus constructing an edifice of authority that crumbles with the slightest touch.

The Pardoner, a far better and cleverer reader than the Man of Law, plays with the same text. He uses *De Miseria* to demonstrate how the meanings of a text are determined by the contexts in which it is read. The Pardoner's exclamation: 'O wombe! O bely! O stynkyng cod, / Fulfilled of dong and of corrupcioun!' (534–35) builds up to a comment about cooks who 'stampe, and streyne, and grynde, / And turnen substaunce into accident' (538–39). He here translates Lotario's comment about cooks: 'One grinds and strains, another mixes and prepares, turns substance into accident' (part 1, xvii). Substance and accident are key terms in Aristotelian philosophy, terms newly important and current in the late twelfth-century environment of scholasticism. Lotario's flippant comment, putting the language of philosophy into a discussion of cooking to criticize gluttony, was not primarily, if at all, Eucharistic. By the late fourteenth century, however, in the wake of Wycliffe's attack on transubstantiation, the comment gains sharper and more controversial meanings.[65] And indeed, these are emphasized by the overall context of the tale: it is structured around a misunderstanding of metaphorical death as literal; wine becomes one of its central symbols; and it is preceded by a Eucharistic parody.[66] The 'substance into accident' detail thus becomes an example of the recontextualising of an authority for a new historical moment.

Chaucer's use of Jerome's text is more extensive and provides a detailed example, not only of how he uses sources but of how the use of sources was *itself* a central theme in the *Canterbury Tales*. Jerome's work—*Adversus Jovinian*—is an attack on Jovinian's claim that virginity is not better than marriage. The text is, as its editors comment, 'heated and personalized,' 'rigid,' 'outrageous,' and 'distasteful'; it became 'a serious personal embarrassment to Jerome,' and Jerome 'frequently and deliberately distorts the context [of his sources] in order to score debating points.'[67] He embeds another text, Theophrastus's 'aureolus liber de nuptis,' within his text, and indeed may have invented this text himself. This text has a 'paranoic tone,' which is 'at the furthest remove from that ideal philosophic rationality which the text purports to advocate.'[68] However, Jerome's text circulated

---

[65] Strohm, *Theory and the Premodern Text*, 168–75.

[66] For the Eucharistic aspects of the tale, see Robert E. Nichols, 'The Pardoner's Ale and Cake,' *PMLA* 82:7 (1967): 498–504.

[67] Ralph Hanna III and Traugott Lawler (eds.), *Jankyn's Book of Wikked Wyves: Volume I, The Primary Texts* (Athens: University of Georgia Press, Chaucer Library, 1997), 18, 19, 23, 17.

[68] Ibid., 8, 16.

very widely in the Middle Ages, mainly in excerpt form, which did something to suppress the illogicality and absurdity of the arguments. It remained, nonetheless, a deeply unpleasant, antifeminist tirade. Its influence is obvious in a number of *Canterbury Tales*, most notably the 'Wife of Bath's Prologue and Tale,' but also in numerous other tales, including the 'Merchant's.' In this tale, Jerome is quoted in the context of a marriage debate between two contrary perspectives—later personified by Placebo and Justinius—both of which are prejudiced and unreliable. The early part of the tale functions as a rhetorical exercise, similar to those that we see in the 'Nun's Priest's Tale' and the 'Melibee,' where authorities are mustered on both sides of a debate and the process of debate is itself the narrative goal. January, indeed, has made his decision and wants only to have it approved. In a wonderfully Chaucerian touch, one of the authorities cited within the Merchant's marriage debate is the Wife of Bath herself, who has also been cited in the preceding tale, the 'Clerk's.' The Wife's life as an authority outside her own tale is without parallel in Chaucer's corpus: he makes her an 'author' in a way that he does for no other character.

In the Wife of Bath's own 'Prologue,' the use of the authoritative Jerome is playful, extensive, and complex. Alison's relationship with antifeminist tracts is a much-debated aspect of Chaucer's writings: she both embodies antifeminist stereotypes and challenges the weight of the antifeminist tradition.[69] One of the most important aspects of her relationship with authorities is the way that she, like Jerome, takes the Bible and uses it in a selective and one-sided way—although she is far less guilty of this than Jerome himself. For instance, Jerome takes Paul's injunction that it is good not to touch a woman but better to marry than to fornicate and turns it into a statement that it is evil to touch a woman. The Wife of Bath takes Paul's statement that 'man shal yelde to his wyf hire dette' (130) but conveniently ignores the next verse that orders wives to yield to their husbands too. She frequently embraces Jerome's words, glorying in being a wooden rather than a golden vessel (98–101), or in the idea of octogamy

[69] For discussion see, for instance, Dinshaw, *Chaucer's Sexual Poetics*; Warren S. Smith, 'The Wife of Bath Debates Jerome,' *Chaucer Review* 32:2 (1997): 129–45; and Mary Carruthers, 'The Wife of Bath and the Painting of Lions,' *PMLA* 94:2 (1979): 209–22.

(33), scathingly suggested by the church father. Towards the end of her 'Prologue' she tells us about her fifth husband's misogynist *Book of Wikked Wyves*, a book similar to many medieval collections, and dominated by Jerome.[70] Readers of the 'Prologue' can see immediately how much the construction of the Wife of Bath and the limits of her knowledge are determined by this imagined book. However, she then steps outside this book—drawing on a fable as her source—to make an explicit comment about the weighty bias and monstrous misreadings of the antifeminist tradition, and indeed of the canon as a whole.[71] Asking 'who peyntede the leon, tel me who?' (692), she emphasizes that the canon has been written by men, and indeed by 'clerkes . . . withinne hire oratories' (694)—men of the church—and that women have not had the chance to write stories. There is, of course, a profound irony in the fact that these lines are written by a man, but there is also something extraordinary about that man's decision to create and foreground this female character. The Wife of Bath here explicitly addresses the problem of the extreme bias of authorities and thus questions the very idea of authoritative sources. Literary tradition is presented as a prisonhouse of misogynist ideas and the reader is surely encouraged to cheer on the Wife's playful appropriation of that tradition for her own ends. This reminder of women's lack of an authoritative tradition also throws into focus the Wife's opening statement about the experience/authority binary (1), a binary that is also foregrounded at the opening of the Prologue to the *Legend of Good Women*, the sister text to the 'Wife of Bath's Prologue' in terms of its explicit treatment of issues of deliberate misreading of sources through the lens of Jerome (in the G-Prologue). In the 'Wife of Bath's Prologue,' Chaucer's lifelong interest in the malleability of 'authorities' reaches its apogee in Alison's attack—literal and metaphorical—on the *Book of Wikked Wyves*. This attack is all the more dazzling for coming from a self-declared embodiment of one of those very 'wikked wyves' who is able to take on the canonical misogynists at their own game and win hands down, exposing their own deliberately bad reading strategies.

---

[70] Hanna and Lawler, *Jankyn's Book*, 2–3.
[71] See Robert M. Correale and Mary Hamel (eds.), ' "Romulus," Fable 44: The Man and the Lion,' in *Sources and Analogues* (Cambridge: D. S. Brewer, 2005), 2:382–83.

Alison's self-declarations, however—as a gossip, a liar, and a manipulator—are not reliable. The surface may not be what it seems to be. While Chaucer's interest in unreliable narrators is evident throughout his career, in the *Canterbury Tales* he developed this interest in a new way through the confessional personae of the Wife of Bath, the Pardoner, and the Canon's Yeoman. All three deliver long prologues about themselves, in which they purport to reveal their secrets. Yet the point of these performances—especially the Pardoner's—is to demonstrate to us that individuals do indeed perform versions of themselves. The Pardoner tells us over and over again that he is a pretender, a fake, someone who convinces people that he is something that he is not. He presents himself as a truthful liar, a hypocrite in the tradition of the *Roman de la Rose*'s Faux Semblant (False Seeming).[72] Similarly, in the *Voir Dit*, Machaut presents what he claims is autobiography, but makes us question its truth value, even telling us that he could have been lying all along and could have sent a false self.[73] Through the disturbing figure of the Pardoner, Chaucer forces his readers to interrogate their own powers of perception and again makes us think about the nature of truth. Just as the *House of Fame* destabilized not only the canon but the very idea of truth, in its images of 'fals and soth compouned' (1029, 2108), so the Pardoner tells us that there is no objective way of determining truth. Indeed, if identity is constructed by performance, the idea of a truthful core is itself destabilized, and it becomes impossible to separate essence from iteration or, some might say, substance from accident. As the Nun's Priest showed us, the fruit and chaff distinction flatters to deceive.

In the 1390s, Chaucer also grappled particularly with the problem of using surface attributes to determine ethical depths. As he worked on the

---

[72] A great deal has been written about the subjectivity of the 'confessional' pilgrims. See in particular Patterson, *Chaucer and the Subject of History*, chapters 7 and 9. See also H. Marshall Leicester, *The Disenchanted Self: Representing the Subject in the Canterbury Tales* (Berkeley: University of California Press, 1990); Mary Flowers Braswell, *The Medieval Sinner: Characterization and Confession in the Literature of the English Middle Ages* (Rutherford, NJ: Fairleigh Dickinson University Press, 1983); and John Ganim, 'Chaucer, Boccaccio, Confession, and Subjectivity,' in Koff and Schildgen, *The 'Decameron' and the 'Canterbury Tales,'* 128–47.

[73] See Laurence de Looze, *Pseudo-autobiography in the Fourteenth Century: Juan Ruiz, Guillaume de Machaut, Jean Froissart, and Geoffrey Chaucer* (Gainesville: University Press of Florida, 1997), chapter 3.

Canterbury Tales, he was increasingly concerned with rank, gender, and inner worth, all wrapped up in the key term 'gentilesse.' This new interest signaled a more urgent interest in ethics than we see earlier in Chaucer's career. In texts such as the *Book of the Duchess*, the *House of Fame*, *Troilus and Criseyde*, and the *Legend of Good Women*, social position or estate—what we might, in very broad terms, call class—was not a major concern, except in terms of the client-patron, poet-master relationship. The *Parliament of Fowls* is a different case: the clash between gentils and churls places social position and rivalry centre-ground, and paves the way for the Knight-Miller confrontation, as discussed earlier in this book.[74] However, this aspect of social positioning is quite different from the emphasis on gentilesse, which becomes so important in the *Canterbury Tales*. Across several tales, Chaucer makes the point that social origins, age, and gender are surface attributes, and are irrelevant to true gentilesse. This new focus on the idea that equitable behaviour, both personal and political, transcends rank, age, and gender, is one of the most significant aspects of Chaucer's intellectual development in the *Canterbury Tales* years. He had certainly long been aware of writings about gentilesse: Boethius writes that when gentilesse relates to 'the dessertes of auncestres,' it is 'veyn' and 'flyttynge'; true gentilesse is 'of thiself' and comes from 'thy deserte.'[75] Many other writers well known to Chaucer, including Dante and Jean de Meun, also wrote about this common idea.[76] In early and mid-career texts such as the 'Second Nun's Tale' and the *Legend of Good Women*, Chaucer wrote about women whose role in society was not determined by their role in the sexual economy, women whose eloquence and ethical stance determined their importance. This interest in women's broader role in society and in their minds and souls preempts Chaucer's engagement with ethical ideas of gentilesse in the *Canterbury Tales*.[77] It is part of a humanist interest in ethics exhibited by many late fourteenth-century European writers.[78] But it was

---

[74] See chapter 12.

[75] Book 3, prosa 6, p. 427.

[76] He cites Dante in the 'gentilesse' passage in the 'Wife of Bath's Tale,' 1125–30.

[77] For Chaucer's interest in stoic ethics, see Alcuin Blamires, *Chaucer, Ethics and Gender* (Oxford: Oxford University Press, 2006), 9–10.

[78] See chapter 14. See also Collette, *Rethinking Chaucer's 'Legend of Good Women,'* 78–94; Wallace, *Chaucerian Polity*, 61.

only when he was writing the *Tales* that Chaucer's radical interest in gentilesse as a quality not connected with rank, age, and gender developed fully.

Gentilesse is important in a number of tales: the Parson makes an explicit statement about it (460–69), the Franklin depicts the clerk demonstrating gentilesse as fully as his social superiors (1607–12),[79] the Squire emphasizes that gentilesse of blood is not sufficient (620). Griselda in the 'Clerk's Tale,' although a poor woman, demonstrates far greater gentilesse and political judgement than any other character: the stanzas in which she dispenses justice through ethical rule form one of the most important passages in the tale (428–41). Chaucer engages with the concept most extensively in the 'Wife of Bath's Tale.' Other versions of the 'loathly lady' story have nothing similar to the lady's long lecture on gentilesse.[80] The basic moral (that decency comes from Christ and is not dependent on social status or background ['Crist wole we clayme of hym oure gentillesse, / Nat of oure eldres for hire old richesse' [1117–18]) is not at all original: this is a standard Christian perspective. It is, however, stated at great length here, and in an unexpected context, in contrast to other iterations of this story. The tale as a whole thus focuses not on the fantasy shape-shifting but on the social aspects of the story: that a young, handsome, rich knight is a rapist who needs to learn from an old, ugly, poor woman—and that society judges people wrongly on their parentage and looks. One of the images that the lady uses emphasizes the discrepancy between exterior and interior: she imagines a fire burning 'in the derkeste hous / Bitwix this and the mount of Kaukasous' (1139–40) and emphasizes that this hidden-away fire, behind closed doors, still burns just as much as if it is seen by the multitudes. An ethical person can be hidden behind any exterior. True 'gentillesse cometh fro God allone' (1162). She focuses on social class, on the fact that 'a lordes sone [can] do shame and vileynye' (1151) and that a 'duc or erl' becomes a 'cherl' when he commits 'synful dedes' (1157–58). Challenging the idea of the division into gentils and cherls, which we see in, for instance, the *Parliament of Fowls* or indeed the Canterbury compaignye,

---

[79] For discussion about the 'Franklin's Tale' and gentilesse, see Mann, *Feminizing Chaucer*, 152–68.

[80] For the analogues, see Correale and Hamel, *Sources and Analogues*, 2:405–48.

she explicitly states that 'Thanne am I gentil, whan that I bigynne / To lyven virtuously and weyve synne' (1175–76).

This straightforward but eloquent defence of the dignity of the individual, regardless of the accident of externals, is then undercut by the choice offered to the rapist knight, a choice that comes straight from Jerome. While other versions of the story offer the man the choice between having his lady fair by night and foul by day, or foul by night and fair by day, in this version the choice is different. He can choose to have his wife ugly and old, but faithful and true, or young and beautiful, but flirtatious and perhaps promiscuous.[81] Theophrastus, via Jerome, writes:

> A beautiful wife will be quickly surrounded by lovers, an ugly one will have difficulty restraining her desires. What many love is hard to keep; to have what no one else wants is irksome. Still, it is less painful to have an ugly wife than to keep a beauty.

Deschamps, in the *Miroir de Mariage*, a text that probably influenced a number of tales, adds:

> If you marry somebody because she's pretty she'll never bring you peace because every man who comes along will want her . . . If you marry an ugly woman no man will envy you . . . A pretty wife is hard to tame, an ugly one too embarrassing.[82]

In offering this choice, the lady of the 'Wife of Bath's Tale' implicitly confirms the stereotype that only lack of opportunity could make a woman honest, and that you can indeed judge a woman by her appearance. However, the tale does not allow the stereotype to stand: the man gives the choice over to the lady, who transforms into somebody both beautiful and virtuous. Once she is treated like a human being, and given autonomy over herself, she demonstrates integrity and, crucially, that people should *not* be judged by appearances (pretty women are not asking for it, as we hope the rapist has now learned). Indeed, this returns us to the beginning of

---

[81] This choice comes from 'a thousand years of antifeminist tradition which made a woman's virtue, her very will, subject to the accident of her physical appearance'; Daniel M. Murtaugh, 'Women and Geoffrey Chaucer,' *ELH* 38:4 (1971): 473–92.

[82] Correale and Hamel, *Sources and Analogues*, 2:354–55, 2:396–99.

the story, where Chaucer, again in a departure from the other versions of the story, made the crime rape, not murder or land acquisition. The crime has become a violent removal of female choice and autonomy over herself. The rapist realized something of what he had done when he cried, 'Taak al my good and lat my body go' (1061). The whole tale is a meditation on the importance of respect and dignity for each human being, and for treating each person as an individual, not judging them according to one's prejudices. The 'Wife of Bath's Tale' is thus a very serious tale indeed, a tale that forcefully puts forward the position that women and men of all ages and estates are moral equivalents.[83] This is also, of course, a compelling message for this tale collection overall, with its levelling of multiple voices and genres.

On a literary level, Chaucer is endlessly fascinated by the mysteries and ambiguities of poetry, by the endless possibilities that lie beneath. For Chaucer, the idea of a 'naked text' (G-Prologue to the *Legend of Good Women*, 86) is an absurd idea—no text is transparent or unproblematic in its meaning. In many of the tales that I have been discussing in this chapter, Chaucer stages a difficulty of interpretation. The 'Clerk's Tale' ends with a pile-up of possible interpretations (1142–1212). The 'Franklin's Tale' ends with a question, a prompt to debate (1621–23). The Host voices his own inadequate readings before the 'Pardoner's Tale' ('Introduction to the Pardoner's Tale,' 287–300)[84] and after the 'Melibee' ('Prologue to the Monk's Tale,' 1889–1923). The Wife of Bath moves seamlessly from a classic 'happy ending' of female obedience causing a happily-ever-after to an exhortation to women to take control, all within the same sentence (1257–64). The Prologue to the *Legend of Good Women*, rewritten in the middle of the 1390s, is based around the idea of multiple interpretations, encouraging readers to read against the meanings imposed by the readers within the text.[85]

Medieval readers were attuned to the idea of reading on many levels, most fundamentally, the literal and the allegorical. Chaucer devastatingly

---

[83] Isabel Davis, 'Class,' in Turner, *Handbook of Middle English Studies*, 285–98.

[84] This is the Host's reading of the 'Physician's Tale.'

[85] Indeed, as Helen Barr writes, the *Legend* 'explores the relationship between the "real" and its representation' precisely through its focus on hermeneutics. *Socioliterary Practice*, 105.

demonstrates the problem of literalism in the 'Pardoner's Tale,' when the rioters fail to understand the fundamental metaphors of Christianity.[86] In tales such as the 'Clerk's Tale' and the 'Tale of Melibee,' Chaucer presents us with allegories that are disturbingly naturalistic.[87] The Host reads both tales as pure narrative, offering models for marriage.[88] This is obviously misguided, but to read the tales only as allegories is to render women and children's lived experience of abuse as unimportant—even productive. The Clerk warns us against interpreting women as allegories in his critique of Petrarch's interpretation of the Griselda story ('Clerk's Tale,' 1142–1212). We need to keep multiple levels in mind at once, not pass through the inferior literal to reach the meaningful destination within.

Chaucer offers us a poetics based on complexity, individual responsibility, and the inseparability of vehicle and tenor, form and content, surface and depth. We need the literal *and* the metaphorical, and we need them *at the same time*. This refusal to partition the things that matter from those that don't, to privilege essentials over inconsequentiality, finds its finest expression in the Nun's Priest's, 'Taketh the moralite' (3440). Here, Chaucer makes it clear that he will not openly guide our interpretation or hierarchize meanings: he encourages his readers to make their own decisions and find their own moral in a deeply troubling world. The very structure of the *Canterbury Tales* privileges digression over progression, the pleasure of the text over a final determined meaning, the means over the end. This fundamentally ethical and egalitarian text is a strange fruit indeed of the 1390s, a troubled decade that built to a bloody tyranny and a dramatic revolution.

---

[86] This is discussed in chapter 16.
[87] I discuss 'Melibee' in detail in *Chaucerian Conflict*, 167–91.
[88] 'Prologue to the Monk's Tale,' 1889–1923; 'Clerk's Tale,' 1212b–12g.

CHAPTER 19

Threshold

But how many daydreams we should have to analyze under the simple heading of Doors!

—*Gaston Bachelard,* Poetics of Space

The last three prologues of the *Canterbury Tales* bring the pilgrims closer and closer to Canterbury, but they never cross the boundaries of the city. Instead, they linger on the threshold—and covering these last few miles takes a wildly disproportionate amount of time in the narrative. Chaucer tantalizes his readers as the pilgrims approach their goal, in ever-slower freeze-frame. However, his focus remains on the journey, not the destination, and the compaignye never goes through the gates. Indeed, the whole of the *Canterbury Tales* exists in a kind of transit lounge: between London and Canterbury but never actually *in* either city. The movement of the pilgrimage is structured by a pull forward and a resistance to that pull. Thresholds—between-spaces—are crucial spaces in many cultures. Often physically marked by charms and spells, they also function symbolically as the conceptual space between one stage of life, or social role, and another.[1] In the 'Miller's Tale,' for instance, when John worries that some kind of dark magic has possessed Nicholas, he blesses the four sides of

[1]Victor Turner is the most famous theorist of liminality; see 'Betwixt and Between: The Liminal Period in *Rites de Passage*,' from *The Forest of Symbols: Aspects of Ndembu Ritual* (Ithaca: Cornell University Press, 1967), 4–20; 'Liminality and Communitas,' in *The Ritual Process: Structure and Anti-Structure* (London: Routledge & Kegan Paul, 1969), 94–113; and 'Passages, Margins, and Poverty: Religious Symbols of Communitas,' from *Dramas, Fields, and Metaphors* (Ithaca: Cornell University

the house and then 'the thresshfold of the dore withoute' (3482). One of the principal functions of sacraments in the Catholic Church—which were under attack from the Lollards in the 1390s in particular—is precisely to take people across a threshold: baptism, confession, marriage, ordination, and extreme unction do this very clearly.[2] When Dymmok rhetorically asks, in his refutation of the 'Twelve Conclusions, 'how does a king differ from all men, or how is a child different after baptism?,' he is appealing to his audience's shared understanding of the transformational power of ceremony and sacrament to take individuals across thresholds, from one state of being to another.[3]

In Chaucer's dream visions, the movement through doorways and into and out of different kinds of spaces reflects the boundaries of different mental states and processes and indeed the transitions between consciousness and the dream.[4] The threshold is a place between two states of being, or two spaces, or two modes of thought. It is a Janus-like space from which one can look forward and backward.[5] One hesitates in the threshold, one waits, one stays still. Chaucer spent much of his life literally on thresholds: living on the walls of the city, the boundary between inside and out; working at the riverside, looking across to Southwark and Kent or inward to the city; moving to the other side of the river and continuing to traverse the liminal waterways.[6] As the son of a merchant who entered the king's household, he also existed on a social threshold. Strohm has written about Chaucer's whole social stratum of knights and esquires as itself transitional, enjoying gentility along with great lords but sharing non-noble status with merchants, citizens, and burgesses, adding that Chaucer was situated 'at a more than ordinarily ambiguous place in

---

Press, 1975), 231–71. See also Arnold van Gennep, *The Rites of Passage*, trans. Monika B. Vizedom and Gabrielle L. Caffee (London: Routledge, 2004).

[2] The remaining sacraments are the Eucharist and Confirmation. They also cross thresholds, but less ostentatiously than the other five sacraments.

[3] Cronin, *Roger Dymock*, 129.

[4] See Turner, 'Chaucer,' in *Oxford Handbooks Online*.

[5] 'Janus sit by the fyr, with double berd' ('Franklin's Tale,' 1252).

[6] The waterfront was a boundary in diverse ways: Hsy comments that, 'Texts associated with London's waterfront frequently expose the porous boundaries between languages and suggest a capacity to inhabit multiple languages at will.' *Trading Tongues*, 51.

this group.'[7] In the late 1390s, he was on the threshold of death, although he did not know this, and the country was poised between two political regimes, on the cusp of the Lancastrian takeover. Across Chaucer's work, his anxiety about conclusions, and his predilection for unfinished, open texts, reflects a poetic affinity for threshold rather than new place, for possibility rather than decision, for hedging one's bets, rather than coming down on one side or the other.

Chaucer uses the image of the threshold to symbolize various different kinds of transition. Those transitions often echo the key 'threshold' scene in medieval art: the Annunciation. When Walter comes to 'translate' ('Clerk's Tale,' 385) Griselda from her poverty to wealth and from virginity to marriage, he finds her on a threshold. Chaucer uses the word twice in one stanza: Griselda is poised, 'as she wolde over hir thresshfold gon' when Walter calls her, and she sets down her water, 'Biside the thresshfold, in an oxes stalle' (288, 291). Chaucer emphasizes the oxen stall motif to draw attention to Griselda's Christological aspects, making the scene a disturbing version of both the Annunciation and the Incarnation.[8] The 'Miller's Tale' features a much more extreme parody, when the window becomes the scene, not for Mary's reception of the Holy Spirit but for Alison and Absolon's anal or genital kiss, and then Nicholas's fart and branding with the 'kultour' (3812). As Helen Barr has proposed, the foundational scene in the *Book of the Duchess*, in which the narrator receives inspiration through the stained glass, is also an 'Annunciation scene retold . . . [as] an originary scene of English vernacular writing that will fuse what has already been written with a new body of work produced by this Chaucerian narrator.'[9] Translation is again linked with an incarnational poetics, and the body and poetry are brought together through the image of the threshold, the space of change. The Annunciation almost always features Mary reading a book in medieval art, as the physical Incarnation of Christ is insistently linked with the ingestion of knowledge: the Word

[7] Strohm, *Social Chaucer*, 11–12.

[8] Wallace, *Chaucerian Polity*, 287; James I. Wimsatt, 'The Blessed Virgin and the Two Coronations of Griselde,' *Mediaevalia* 6 (1980): 188–92; Sarah Stanbury, 'Regimes of the Visual in Premodern England: Gaze, Body, and Chaucer's "Clerk's Tale,"' *New Literary History* 28:2 (1997), 261–89.

[9] Barr, *Transporting Chaucer*, 12.

made flesh.[10] In the 'Miller's Tale,' the thresholds that are crossed are conceptually scandalous, flirting with adultery, sodomy, and homosexuality, and they are also materially realized. The boundary depicted over and over again in exquisite medieval iconography has become a particular kind of window (a low shot-window with a hinge, 3695–96) in a fourteenth-century Oxford street, close to neighbouring houses (3825–27). The tale provides a vivid example of how Chaucer uses literal space symbolically to intensify and transform our understanding of fundamental scenes. And in all of these examples, the master scenes of the Annunciation and the Incarnation remind us that the threshold often represents the loss of virginity and the associated idea of the beginning of new life, whether that new life is a child or, as in the *Book of the Duchess*, a poem.

The other key threshold in the life cycle is the threshold between life and death—and this threshold became more important to Chaucer as he approached the end of the *Canterbury Tales*, and as he aged and neared the end of his own life, although there is no evidence of a *causal* connection between life and works in this regard. The progress towards the tomb of Thomas à Becket, symbol of death, is resisted by the digression of the tale-telling itself, a project that encourages the pilgrims to forget the end point and remain in the threshold space of pilgrimage.[11] Across the *Canterbury Tales* as a whole, there are only a few references to the geographical whereabouts of the pilgrims. At the end of the 'General Prologue,' we are told that they reach the Watering of St Thomas (826), a stream a couple of miles from London, and in the 'Reeve's Prologue,' the Host mentions Deptford and Greenwich, just another couple of miles further on (3906–7). There are further references to Rochester (roughly halfway between Canterbury and London ['The Prologue of the Monk's Tale,' 1926]) and Sittingbourne (about seventeen miles from Canterbury, and forty-five from London ["The Wife of Bath's Prologue," 847]).[12] It is clear, then, that

---

[10] Laura Saetveit Miles, 'The Origins and Development of the Virgin Mary's Book at the Annunciation,' *Speculum* 89:3 (2014): 632–69.

[11] On pilgrimage sites and the ritualizing of death, see Lefebvre, *Production of Space*, 254.

[12] For a discussion of the relevance of the places mentioned by Chaucer to the ordering of the *Tales*, and an analysis of the merits and problems of the 'Bradshaw shift,' which moves Fragment VII to follow Fragment II, see Derek Pearsall, *The Canterbury Tales* (London: Routledge, 1985, reprinted 2005), 19–21.

Chaucer was not very interested in mapping the itinerary, or in cultivating a strong sense of naturalism, in evoking the details of the pilgrimage route. However, when the pilgrims get close to Canterbury, this changes. Just as there were several references to places just outside London, so we linger over the immediate vicinity of Canterbury. Chaucer now tantalizes his readers with the imminence of the destination, the ending, and the crossing of the boundary, but ultimately refuses to take his characters or his readers through the gates of Canterbury.

In the 'Canon's Yeoman's Prologue,' the pilgrims are at Boughton-under-Blee, about five miles from Canterbury and the place from where the towers of Canterbury could first be seen by travellers coming from London. While the end of the journey is drawing inexorably closer, this is the most incident-packed prologue in the entire set of tales, as it features the arrival of two new members of the compaignye, the betrayal of one by another, and the subsequent departure of the Canon. The reader is thus made to linger in this village as the text resists the pull of Canterbury or the sense that the ending is approaching by introducing a wholly unexpected turn of events. The group has moved on just three more miles by the time we reach the 'Manciple's Prologue,' set at Harbledown, known as 'Bobbe-up-and-down,' and again the move forward exists in tension with a plot-rich prologue, this time containing a sadistic confrontation between two rival pilgrims and the silencing of one of them. At no other point in the *Tales* do two neighbouring prologues contain references to the geographical location of the pilgrims so our attention is being carefully focused on this threshold space. In the final prologue, the pilgrims have emerged from the village ('Parson's Prologue,' 12) and, we assume, are within sight of Canterbury. Other aspects of this prologue strongly emphasise its liminality. The sun is sinking and the shadows are lengthening (2–9). The scales of justice are hanging in the sky (11). The Host tells us that his plan is 'almoost' fulfilled (19), and the Parson makes an explicit reference to the liminal qualities of life itself when he tells his audience that he will try to show them the way to the shining destination of 'Jerusalem celestial' (51). But the pilgrims famously remain always on the threshold of their destination. Chaucer's literary heirs imagined them arriving in Canterbury: one depicted their behaviour there in wonderful and imaginative detail; another also described them turning back and beginning their return journey.[13] But Chaucer himself left them in limbo, about to arrive, waiting, desiring, hesitating—but never crossing over.

The 'Second Nun's Prologue and Tale,' 'Canon's Yeoman's Prologue and Tale,' 'Manciple's Prologue and Tale,' and 'Parson's Prologue and Tale' form a coherent sequence. The 'Canon's Yeoman's Prologue' begins with a reference to the 'lyf of Seinte Cecile' (554), and the two tales are closely bound together by their themes.[14] The 'Manciple's Prologue' takes place just a couple of miles further on from the setting of the 'Canon's Yeoman's Prologue'; the 'Parson's Prologue' refers to the Manciple's having just finished his tale in its first line. The Host's subsequent insistence that 'Fulfilled is my sentence and my decree' (17) and the Parson's agreement that he will 'knytte up al this feeste and make an ende' (47) signals that this is the last tale. Of course, the programme initially outlined by the Host (four tales per pilgrim, two on the way to Canterbury and two on the way back to Southwark ['General Prologue,' 791–95]) has by no means been fulfilled, but it is clear that these last four tales were nonetheless conceived of as an ending, even if Chaucer hoped to go back to fill in gaps and do further revisions to the text as a whole. These prologues and tales were certainly conceived of as 'threshold' texts themselves, told when the pilgrims hovered on the outskirts of Canterbury and the reader is on the brink of coming to the end of the *Tales*. We know that the 'Second Nun's Tale' had existed in some form much earlier, as it is mentioned as early as the F-Prologue to the *Legend of Good Women* (426). However, it is probable, if not provable, that much of the rest of the sequence was indeed written

[13] The 'Canterbury Interlude' appears in the Alnwick manuscript of the *Tales* (Alnwick, Alnwick Castle, Collection of the Duke of Northumberland MS 455). The text is rearranged as a two-way journey, with the scene at Canterbury and the 'Tale of Beryn' (the Merchant's second tale) inserted into the middle of the text. Lydgate's *Siege of Thebes* is framed in its 'Prologue' as the first tale on the way back to London. See John M. Bowers (ed.), *The Canterbury Tales: Fifteenth Century Continuations and Additions* (Kalamazoo, MI: TEAMS Middle English Texts, 1992).

[14] For discussion, see Marc M. Pelen, 'Idleness and Alchemy in Fragment VIII (G) of Chaucer's *Canterbury Tales*: Oppositions in Themes and Imagery from the *Roman de la Rose*,' *Forum for Modern Language Studies* 31 (1995): 193–214; Joseph Grennen, 'Saint Cecilia's Chemical Wedding: The Unity of the *Canterbury Tales*, Fragment VIII,' *JEGP* 65 (1966): 466–81; Bruce A. Rosenberg, 'The Contrary Tales of the Second Nun and the Canon's Yeoman,' *Chaucer Review* 2: 4 (1968): 278–91; and Robert M. Longsworth, 'Privileged Knowledge: St Cecilia and the Alchemist in the *Canterbury Tales*,' *Chaucer Review* 27: 1 (1992): 87–96.

towards the end of Chaucer's time working on the *Tales*, and towards the end of his life. The absence of the 'Canon's Yeoman's Prologue and Tale' from the earliest manuscript (Hengwrt) gives particular weight to the idea that this was a late addition and therefore not always circulated with the bulk of the tales.[15] Its belatedness—dealing as it does with someone who arrives late and bursts into the compaignye—may echo its own identity as an afterthought.

Whether or not this 'Prologue' and 'Tale' are an example of Chaucer's late style, they certainly demonstrate what I call 'threshold poetics,' a style that reflects both the liminality of the teller and the pilgrims' position, hovering near their destination.[16] This poetics is comprised of two characteristics working in tension with each other—haste and digression—and they operate both in the 'Prologue' and in the 'Tale.' On the one hand, the stress on haste gives an impression of unstoppable progress, an immoderate desire to press onward. On the other, the description of urgency is itself repetitive and narratively slow; it pulls us back into stasis. We see these techniques at work in the first thirty lines of the 'Prologue,' the passage that describes the arrival of the suburban newcomers (556–86). Their introduction—'us gan atake / A man'—establishes haste as their defining characteristic: we know that they have overtaken the compaignye before we know anything else about them. We are then told that the Canon's horse 'so swatte' that it seemed as if 'he had priked miles three' and that the Yeoman's horse, 'So swatte that unnethe myghte it gon.' The next couplet tells us more about this sweat, that it makes the horse look like a dappled magpie. A few lines later we are again reminded of how fast they have ridden: 'he hadde riden moore than trot or paas; / He hadde ay priked lik as he were wood.' The next five lines return to the subject of sweat in close detail: we are told that the Canon has placed a leaf under his hood to soak up the sweat, and the narrator's exclamation of 'joye' in watching the sweat emphasizes how extreme it was. Indeed, we are now told, in an

[15] Pearsall, *Canterbury Tales*, 113.

[16] For the problematic and controversial idea of late style, see Edward Said, *On Late Style* (London: Bloomsbury, 2006). See also Gordon McMullan, *Shakespeare and the Idea of Late Writing: Authorship and the Proximity of Death* (Cambridge: Cambridge University Press, 2006), and Gordon McMullan and Sam Smiles (eds.), *Late Style and Its Discontents: Essays in Art, Literature, and Music* (Oxford: Oxford University Press, 2016).

image preempting the laboratory of the tale, that he drips 'as a stillatorie.' In case anyone is in doubt, the Canon now announces, 'Faste have I priked.' The excessive emphasis on speed and sweat has slowed up the whole narrative; the audience within and outside the tale has lingered over this spectacle of haste—which has become static.

The tale that follows utilizes the same narrative strategy. The Yeoman peppers his narrative with words such as 'faste,' 'swithe' (quickly), and 'anon,' and repeatedly tells us that he is getting on with his narrative (for instance, 'I go my tale unto,' 'I wol procede' [898, 1019]).[17] The tale is also, however, punctuated by long digressions and interjections; he also spends a great deal of time telling us what he is going to tell us.[18] A typical example of his threshold poetics comes, appropriately enough, in his description of the opening and closing of a door. He says:

The chambre dore, shortly for to seyn,
They opened and shette, and wente hir weye.
And forth with hem they carieden the keye,
And come agayn withouten any delay.
What sholde I tarien al the longe day? (1217–21)

This is a narratorial 'slow-down,' where the time of the narrative exceeds the time described in the story.[19] The Yeoman is describing in laborious detail the opening and closing of the door, but he pretends that he is speaking economically: the phrases 'shortly for to seyen' and 'What sholde I tarien al the longe day?' tell us that he is being quick, when in fact he is wasting narrative time through the very use of these phrases. Indeed, there are several points in the tale at which he describes a departure and return (1110, 1216, 1296), an image that itself reflects the frenetic stasis of the alchemical world where one is always moving and always returning to the same point without making any progress. The alchemists, in other words,

[17] For instance, for 'faste,' see 682, 863, 1192, 1235, 1260; for 'swithe,' 1194, 1309, 1336, 1426; for 'anon,' 1103, 1116, 1127, 1142, 1145, 1198, 1364, 1453.

[18] There are digressions at, for example, 830–51, 862–97, 992–1011, 1065–1100, 1299–1307, 1388–1481; briefer interjections can be found at, for instance, 1172–75 and 1273–75. For examples of his telling us what he is going to tell us, see 1084–87 and 819–21.

[19] Steven Cohan and Linda M. Shires, *Telling Stories: A Theoretical Analysis of Narrative Fiction* (London: Routledge, 1988), 88.

remain always on the threshold. As the Yeoman says, alchemy 'is to seken evere' (874). He remains always on the brink of discovery but will never make progress: the narrative strategies of the tale reflect his position, rooted in the doorway, neither able to go back ('I koude nevere leve it in no wise,' 714) nor forward ('of his science am I never the neer,' 721). The tale's poetics mirror the overall structure of the *Tales*: its progressive movement towards Canterbury is always in tension with the digressive tale-telling competition itself. As a study of the frustrations of attempting transformation, this is also a tale that engages head-on with the problems of unmoored identity that modernity has brought to the late fourteenth-century subject. It is, in the words of Lee Patterson, Chaucer's 'ultimate experiment in the dynamics of self-representation.'[20] It leaves the Yeoman forever on the threshold of identity, unsure who he is, uncertain of his place in the world.

The subsequent 'Prologue' and 'Tale' form a devastating critique of absolutist rule, depicting the unjust suffering of the disbelieved and silenced servant in detail.[21] Again ostentatiously set on the outskirts of Canterbury, the 'Manciple's' sequence approaches the idea of the threshold through the idea of the voice and the mouth, a threshold between self and others, inside the body and outside.[22] The last poetic tale of the collection thus returns to and completes some of the motifs that dominated the opening of the 'General Prologue' itself.[23] The 'General Prologue' introduces perhaps the most powerful image in the entire *Canterbury Tales*: the image of breath. Zephirus, 'with his sweete breeth / Inspired hath in every holt and heeth / The tendre croppes' (5–7). The wind giving life into the world in springtime is explicitly figured as breathing, and breathing is *inspiration*—both literally and metaphorically. To breathe life into something is to give it meaning. And breathing breaks down boundaries: as air

[20] Lee Patterson, 'Perpetual Motion: Alchemy and the Technology of the Self,' *Studies in the Age of Chaucer* 15 (1993): 38. See also Patterson, *Chaucer and the Subject of History* and chapter 10 in this study.

[21] See Fradenburg, 'Manciple's Servant Tongue.'

[22] For a brilliant discussion of orality and the mouth in the 'Manciple's Prologue and Tale,' see Peter Travis, 'The Manciple's Phallic Matrix,' *Studies in the Age of Chaucer* 25 (2003): 317–24.

[23] The tale also returns us to the 'General Prologue' by repeating the idea of the word as cousin to the deed. See P. B. Taylor, 'Chaucer's *Cosyn to the Dede*,' *Speculum* 57, no. 2 (1982): 315–27; and Turner, *Chaucerian Conflict*, 134–36.

comes in and out of the body, breathing symbolizes our connectedness with the world. In the 'Manciple's Prologue,' the idea of the threshold as an open space where aspects of inside and outside mingle yields to an image of contamination. The Manciple's attack on the Cook focuses on his breath: it 'ful soure stynketh' (32) and his open mouth threatens to swallow the rest of the world (35–36). The Manciple orders him to close his mouth, saying that the devil is within it (37–38) and that his 'cursed breeth infecte wole us alle' (39). This anxiety about the open mouth as crossing boundaries and tearing open a door that 'should' remain closed is expressed in the common idea that one should eat with one's mouth closed—as medieval courtesy books, like twenty-first-century parents, advise.[24] As the 'Prologue' goes on, the Cook is comprehensively silenced and humiliated. Silencing also proves to be the theme of the subsequent tale: in a change to his source, Chaucer inserts the loss of the crow's voice (300–306). This is an unnerving story about the end of poetry. Crossing the threshold of the body by opening one's mouth and speaking is dangerous: the mother tells us at the end of the tale that the mouth should be kept closed. Another arresting image represents the teeth and lips as the walls of an enclosure (323), and the mother urges her son to withdraw and keep his tongue to himself (319, 329, 333, 345, 362). Her opinion is certainly not Chaucer's—and this speech about silence is ostentatiously and comically long and repetitive—but the Manciple has exposed the dangers that he perceives of moving to the doorway and speaking across the threshold of the mouth.

This was an issue that occupied Chaucer across his career. I have discussed in earlier chapters his fascination with going to the doorway and listening to his neighbours, rather than writing within a literary ivory tower, his body closed off, his senses deprived.[25] For Chaucer, the open door, the threshold, is a place of possibility that allows the author to collaborate but not to commit. His affinity with the idea of the threshold as a way of not moving forward to closure or conclusions is evident in text

---

[24] For instance, 'The Young Children's Book,' in Edith Rickert and Frederick James Furnivall (eds.), *The Babees' Book: Medieval Manners for the Young* (London: Chatto & Windus, 1923), 24. Indeed, the exhortation, 'Don't eat with your mouth open,' is chosen by Bachelard as an epigraph to his chapter on 'The Dialectics of Outside and Inside.' *Poetics of Space*, 211.

[25] See especially chapters 7, 8, and 9.

after text. Chaucer's long poems are, in general, either unfinished (*House of Fame, Legend of Good Women, Canterbury Tales*) or overfinished (*Parliament of Fowls, Troilus and Criseyde*).[26] The *Parliament of Fowls* ends with a roundel that repeats its cyclical message over and over again, and the dreamer returns to his books.[27] Chaucer thus refuses to move us on and returns us to the threshold of knowledge—reading, hoping, desiring. He always eschews the kind of progress and completion endorsed by a poet such as Dante. This affection for the non-ending, the waiting, the hesitation, is dramatically evident in the *Canterbury Tales*, when it leaves the pilgrims poised to enter Canterbury.

In the 'Parson's Prologue and Tale' and the subsequent *Retractions*, the end of the *Tales* and the approaching end of Chaucer's life coincide. The *Retractions* are prefaced with the words 'Heere taketh the makere of this book his leve'—both from the work and from life (plate 8). He lists his works and asks his readers to pray for him to receive mercy. Chaucer here talks about his own death, asking for grace 'unto my lives ende' (1090), and hopes for salvation to be one of those that, 'at the day of doom that shulle be saved' (1092). At this point, he thinks about the fragments of the *Canterbury Tales* as a text that fits together—'the tales of Caunterbury'—in contrast to the G-Prologue list of his works, where he makes no such reference, although he lists all his other reasonably complete works. It seems clear that he did significant work on the *Tales* after the middle of the decade (when the G-Prologue was written), culminating in the *Retractions*, written when he felt he was pretty much done with the *Canterbury Tales*. While we cannot be absolutely certain that the 'Parson's Tale' itself did not exist at an earlier date, separate from the *Retractions*,

---

[26] For the ending of *Troilus*, famously termed 'a nervous breakdown in poetry,' by Donaldson ('The Ending of Chaucer's *Troilus*,' in Arthur Brown and Peter Foote [eds.], *Early English and Norse Studies* [London: Methuen, 1963], 34), see Rosemarie P. McGerr, 'Meaning and Ending in a "Paynted Proces": Resistance to Closure in *Troilus and Criseyde*,' in R. A. Shoaf and Catherine Cox (eds.), *Chaucer's 'Troilus and Criseyde': 'Subgit to alle Poesye'* (Binghamton, NY: Medieval & Renaissance Texts & Studies, 1992), 179–98. On the (satisfyingly) unsatisfactory nature of Chaucer's endings in general see, for instance, Elizabeth Salter, *Fourteenth-Century English Poetry: Contexts and Readings* (Oxford: Oxford University Press, 1983), 116; Piero Boitani, *Chaucer and the Imaginary World of Fame* (Cambridge: D. S. Brewer, 1984), 208.

[27] A roundel is a French lyric form with a refrain and only two rhymes. It thus has a repetitive and cyclical structure. The precise form of this particular roundel has been reconstructed (by Skeat) as the manuscripts are unclear. See notes in *Riverside Chaucer*, 1002.

the evidence strongly suggests that this tale was indeed his last substantial work. Lee Patterson has traced the passages in the 'Parson's Tale' that echo—or prefigure—passages elsewhere in the tales and, in a compelling argument, has demonstrated the likelihood that the influence runs from the other tales to the 'Parson's Tale.' For instance, he demonstrates how specific passages are coherent and appropriate in their appearance in the 'Pardoner's' and 'Summoner's' Tales and seem much more awkward in the 'Parson's Tale.' The nature of the 'Parson's Prologue' and the *Retractions*, the tale's function as a rejection of poetry and its mirroring of the 'Manciple's Tale,' and the appropriateness of the *Retractions* both to the 'Parson's Tale' and to the *Tales* as a whole make it very probable that this entire sequence was indeed written towards the very end of Chaucer's life.[28] This does not mean that we have to believe that the *Retractions* represents any kind of actual 'repentance' for writing certain poems: it obviously does nothing of the sort. As other critics have pointed out, the 'retraction,' was conventional in European, if not English, poetry, and many aspects of the text run along familiar lines.[29] Chaucer wants to advertise his texts, listed in careful detail here, not to renounce them. But, while the voice of the *Retractions* is not an authentic confessional Chaucer, his leavetaking is nonetheless *connected* to the ageing poet coming to the end of his work on a vast, ambitious, diverse text. There is certainly no reason to think that his request for prayers from his readers is not genuine.

The 'Parson's Tale' is announced to us as the final tale of the collection, the *Retractions* as Chaucer's farewell to the text, literary endeavor, and life. A hundred years ago, some critics began to voice the idea that the 'Parson's Tale' glosses the tales that come before and that the teller reprimands the other pilgrims' sins.[30] A more recent critical viewpoint eschews such imaginative projection but sees the tale as offering meaning relevant to all human experience, voicing an authority that shifts the text away from the

[28] As Patterson writes, 'The evidence is that Parson's Tale was written late in the poet's career and there seems no reason not to accept the obvious biographical implication that it was his last work.' 'The "Parson's Tale" and the Quitting of the *Canterbury Tales*,' *Traditio* 34 (1978): 380.

[29] See Olive Sayce, 'Chaucer's *Retractions*: The Conclusion of the *Canterbury Tales* and Its Place in Literary Tradition,' *Medium Aevum* 40 (1971): 230–46.

[30] See, for example, Frederick Tupper, 'Chaucer and the Seven Deadly Sins,' *PMLA* 29: 1 (1914): 93–123; and Ralph Baldwin, *The Unity of the 'Canterbury Tales'* (Copenhagen: Rosenkilde and Bassen, 1955), 95–105.

play of the tale-telling contest.[31] In these readings, this final tale has a greater authority than the tales that precede it, and it suggests that Chaucer now capitulates to a religious vision of life, crossing a boundary and closing the text.[32] The 'Parson's Tale,' however, is presented to us as the perspective of an individual, like all the other tales, and the teller has a limited vision, like all the other tellers, a vision that codifies the self in relentlessly simplifying ways.[33] Indeed, his assumption of the natural order of social hierarchy—'God ordeyned that som folk sholde be moore heigh in estaat and in degree, and som folk moore lough' (771)[34]—and his emphasis on the inferiority of churls and women contrasts starkly with the ethical and compassionate emphasis on gentilesse as a quality not determined by gender, class, or age in other tales.[35] Across the tale, we are reminded that we are hearing not truth but the Parson's own viewpoint.[36] In contrast to his sources, the Parson repeatedly uses the first and second person, reminding us of his and his audience's presence; he also alters his sources to change their emphasis and to select material that suits a particular worldview.[37] We have not passed through the liminal zone of the

[31] Patterson, 'The "Parson's Tale,"' 347.

[32] Wenzel characterizes this kind of reading as 'teleological.' He claimed (in 2000) that such readings were taking over from 'perspectivist' ones, but I see no evidence for this, quite the contrary. Wenzel argues that if we see the 'Parson's Tale' as concluding the *Tales*, then Chaucer is prioritizing it as taking place on a 'higher plane' than other tales. Siegfried Wenzel, 'The *Parson's Tale* in Current Literary Studies,' in Raybin and Holley, *Closure*, 6, 9–10.

[33] Muscatine terms it 'endless, narrow, small-minded, inveterately enumerative, circumstantially punitive list of sinful acts'; Donaldson describes the tale as 'ill-tempered, bad-mannered, pedantic, and joyless'; Aers refers to the Parson's 'failure of imagination and critical intelligence.' Muscatine, 'Chaucer's Religion and the Chaucer Religion,' 258; Donaldson, *Speaking of Chaucer*, 173; Aers, *Chaucer, Langland, and the Creative Imagination*, 109.

[34] For a discussion of the Parson's extreme social conservatism, see Strohm, *Social Chaucer*, 178–79.

[35] In his excellent and thought-provoking discussion of the Parson, Scanlon discusses the literalization of the metaphor of lord and thrall in the 'Parson's Tale' and the Parson's 'gendered, class-specific understanding of sin.' Scanlon conflates the Parson's perspective with Chaucer's and suggests that Chaucer is here appropriating church authority. I see the Parson and his tale as no more authoritative than any other pilgrim. Scanlon, *Narrative, Authority and Power*, 15–16. For gentilesse, see chapter 18 in the current study.

[36] Critics who argue for the Parson's limited perspective include Helen Cooper, *The Structure of the 'Canterbury Tales'* (London: Duckworth, 1983), 200–207; and Jill Mann, *Geoffrey Chaucer* (New York: Harvester Wheatsheaf, 1991), 121.

[37] On the use of the first and second person, see Judith Ferster, 'Chaucer's Parson and the "Idiosyncracies of Fiction,"' in Raybin and Holley, *Closure*, 130–32. On the Parson's alteration of his sources on the subject of marital sex, see Carol V. Kaske, 'Getting around the *Parson's Tale*: An Alternative to Allegory and Irony,' in Rossell Hope Robbins (ed.), *Chaucer at Albany* (New York: Franklin, 1975), 169.

playful tale-telling contest and ended up in the transcendent world of the spiritual Jerusalem. On the contrary, as Ferster argues, the Parson's perspective is 'one equal voice among many'; he is 'partial—like all the other pilgrims—in both senses of the word.'[38]

Moreover, the 'Parson's Tale' as a penitential manual cannot offer closure or final authority because of the nature of the genre. Larry Scanlon points out that the penitential manual is a 'radically open' text because it is dependent upon the response of the penitent for its purpose to be achieved.[39] The Parson's own focus is on the *way*, the *process* of reaching heaven, not that goal itself.[40] The 'Parson's Tale' and the *Retractions* focus the reader's attention onto the technology of confession, a radical mode of self-fashioning. The essence of confession is the splitting of the self, not only into self past and self present, but into the speaking and spoken self, subject and object. The confessional pilgrims (the Pardoner, Wife of Bath, and Canon's Yeoman) devastatingly demonstrate this split.[41] Penitential manuals such as the 'Parson's Tale' seek to emphasise the self's orientation in God and the Church.[42] But the demonstrably subjective aspects of the tale throw into question the idea that one can find such external objectivity in a human-authored tract. Chaucer's presentation of the Parson's viewpoint as partial suggests that human interpretations of doctrine are not infallible.[43]

Just as the last tales of the *Canterbury Tales* linger on the threshold (of Canterbury, of an ending, of meaning), so Chaucer was personally experiencing years of in-betweenness as Richard's reign drew to its bitter close.

---

[38] Ferster, 'Chaucer's Parson,' 117, 116.

[39] Scanlon, *Narrative, Authority, and Power*, 14.

[40] Drawing on Augustinian theories of time (*expectatio futurorum* and *intentio ad superiora*), Gross argues that the Parson's way of penitence is oriented towards the eternal but that the way has to be accomplished in linear time, suggesting that his way leads to speech, diversity, and temporality, not silence, unity, and eternity. In the same volume, Raybin emphasizes the Parson's interest in the 'movement through life,' and on diversity, rather than one, singular way. Charlotte Gross, '"The goode weye": Ending and Not-Ending in *The Parson's Tale*,' in Raybin and Holley, *Closure*, 181–85 and 193; David Raybin, '"Manye been the weyes": The Flower, Its Roots, and the Ending of the *Canterbury Tales*,' in Raybin and Holley, *Closure*, 17.

[41] See chapter 18 for a discussion of the confessional pilgrims. For an overview of the technology of confession, see Christopher Cannon, *Middle English Literature: A Cultural History* (Cambridge: Polity, 2008), 27–35.

[42] See Gregory Roper, 'Dropping the Personae and Reforming the Self: *The Parson's Tale* and the End of *The Canterbury Tales*,' in Raybin and Holley, *Closure*, 151–75.

[43] This is, of course, quite different from calling the sacraments themselves into question. For discussions about Chaucer, orthodoxy, and dissent, see the essays in Phillips, *Chaucer and Religion*.

The years from 1397 to 1399 were the dog days of Richard's rule, years of uncertainty, fear, and transition. England was playing a waiting game, and no one knew when or how it would end. With hindsight, these years— the years of Richard's 'tyranny'—were a threshold between the Plantagenet and the Lancastrian regimes. They were also transitional years for Chaucer, the threshold between his life and death, although he was presumably unaware of this. There is no evidence that he was ill, and he was certainly still writing until very shortly before he died in 1400. Although Henry's usurpation of the throne was by no means inevitable, anyone could see that these were crisis years, years in which Richard was crossing a boundary and redefining English kingship and the English aristocracy. He came out the other side, not into a new era of absolutist kingship but into disgrace, dethronement, and death. Chaucer was not at the forefront of the traumas of these years, but he was certainly involved in various ways in the shocking and extraordinary events of 1397–99.

The political temperature was rising from the very beginning of 1397. In the parliament held in January, a petition attacked the cost of the royal household and the number of bishops and ladies in it. Richard reacted with fury, claiming that this was an offence against 'his regality and his royal majesty, and the liberty of himself and his honourable progenitors.'[44] He demanded that the petitioner be named and brought forward: Thomas Haxey, a king's clerk, was then condemned to death as a traitor, in an extraordinary interpretation of treason, but Thomas Arundel, his longtime patron, intervened to save his life.[45] This incident was a taste of things to come in its demonstration of Richard's increasingly imperial understanding of his own kingship. In the same parliament, Richard indicated that he was still bound to Gaunt and his family, when he agreed to the parliamentary legitimation of the Beaufort children.[46] And indeed, the two junior Appellants—Mowbray and Derby—were safe that summer and autumn, while Richard crushed the three senior Appellant lords. He arrested them on 10 July; at the same time he began, in Walsingham's words,

[44] PROME, Membrane 5, no. 15, 7:314 (January 1397).

[45] For discussion of Haxey, see McHardy, 'Haxey's Case,' 93–114. See also Dodd, 'Richard II and the Transformation of Parliament,' 71–84.

[46] See Given-Wilson, *Henry IV*, 101.

'to tyrannize' his people, extorting forced loans and controlling Parliament.[47] On 17 September, the Revenge Parliament began, opening with the bishop of Exeter's sermon on the appropriately sinister theme, 'There shall be one king for all.'[48] By this point Gloucester—Richard's uncle—was already dead, murdered in Calais. A few days later, the earl of Arundel had been executed, his brother (Thomas, the archbishop of Canterbury) exiled, and Warwick also banished. Richard arraigned John Cobham and Sir Thomas Mortimer and embarked on dramatic redistribution of land.[49] He liberally dispensed titles and honours to his supporters—who became known as the 'duketti'—the little, pretend dukes. At this point, Mowbray and Derby were still, at least seemingly, in favour, and became the dukes of Norfolk and Hereford, respectively.[50] Richard, in full biblical throttle, wrote to Manuel Paleologus, emperor of Byzantium, smugly noting that he had ground down offenders to the root.[51] As discussed earlier in this book, Richard may himself have been partly motivated at this point by his imperial ambitions.[52]

In December that same year, Richard granted Chaucer a tun of wine a year for life. The records that survive relating to this grant are Chaucer's petition for the letters patent relating to the grant, the privy seal warrant for those letters patent, their enrolment, and an order for the waiving of the fee for the letters. All date from October 1398.[53] The documents state that the grant had been made in December 1397 ('en le moys de Decembre de lan de vostre regne vingt et primer') and state that the wine was due on 1 December each year, at the port of London. Chaucer had formerly enjoyed a similar grant and, as a member of the household, this was the kind of favour that he might expect. It is probable that Chaucer was in attendance on the royal household at around this time; indeed, perhaps Richard made the grant in person to Chaucer. As it was not written down in December 1397, it may have been an oral promise from the king, or one

---

[47] For the events of the summer and autumn of 1397, see Saul, *Richard II*, 366–84. Given-Wilson, *Chronicles of the Revolution*, 71.

[48] PROME, '1397 September,' 7:333.

[49] Saul, *Richard II*, 381, 383.

[50] Given-Wilson, *Henry IV*, 107 and 107n34.

[51] A. R. Myers (ed.), *English Historical Documents* (London: Eyre & Spottiswoode, 1969), 174–75.

[52] See chapter 13.

[53] Crow and Olson, *Chaucer Life-Records*, 116–18.

of his more senior attendants, to Chaucer as a member of the household, although it is also possible that the promise was made to an advocate or intermediary. What we know of Richard's movements places him in Oxfordshire for much of November and December that year (and nowhere else until Christmas): he was in Woodstock on 1 November, Abingdon on 11–12, Woodstock on 15–21 (where Henry visited him), Banbury on 23–26, Woodstock again on 15 December, Banbury on 22 December, and then Coventry (in Warwickshire, the neighbouring county) for Christmas.[54] Indeed, as Richard embarked on his political excesses, he increasingly eschewed London and over the next two years spent much of his time in the West Midlands and the Northwest.[55] But it is particularly interesting that Chaucer may have been attending the court in Oxfordshire in the winter of 1397, given the fact that his son Thomas was now an Oxfordshire gentlemen of considerable property and influence with a substantial manor at Ewelme, just a few miles from Oxford. Perhaps Chaucer spent some time—or a great deal of time—with his newly wealthy son.

Whether or not Chaucer was in Oxfordshire in late 1397, we do know that he was travelling during these months. On 4 May 1398, Chaucer received a royal protection against lawsuits for two years, to free him to travel around England ('in diversis partibus infra regnum nostrum Anglie') on the king's urgent business ('ardua et urgencia negocia nostra tam').[56] We do not know either the nature of the business or the reason for the unusual clause protecting him from lawsuits. Another document relating to lawsuits provides further evidence of the change in Chaucer's mode of living since his return to the king's household. At some point in the regnal year 1397–98, a debt that he owed to the Exchequer (which he never paid) was transferred from Kent to London, which suggests he was no longer residing in Kent.[57] Perhaps he was spending more time actually with the royal household. As for what he was doing for the king during 1398, we can only speculate, but he was working for the royal household in some way. At the same time, he also returned to his previous job as

[54] Saul, 'Appendix: Richard II's Itinerary,' in *Richard II*, 473. For Henry's visit on 19 November, see Given-Wilson, *Henry IV*, 108n41.

[55] Saul, *Richard II*, 392.

[56] Crow and Olson, *Chaucer Life-Records*, 62–64.

[57] Ibid., 334.

forester for North Petherton. While Peter Courtenay had returned to his position there after Roger Mortimer attained his majority, the earl of March died in the summer of 1398, leaving his wife, Eleanor, in control of North Petherton.[58] Eleanor was the daughter of Thomas Holland (half-brother of Richard II) and Alice, sister of the recently murdered earl of Arundel. She was therefore Richard's niece and sister of the recently elevated duke of Surrey. The likelihood is that Chaucer was appointed to sort out some of the paperwork and cast his eye over the accounts during this transitional period following the sudden, unexpected death of the young earl of March. It is clear that he was still viewed as a competent administrator.

The political climate darkened considerably for Gaunt and his son in 1398. The month in which Chaucer had received his new grant of wine was also the month in which the future began to look increasingly murky for the house of Lancaster. Complicit, even active, in the demise of the senior Appellants a few months earlier, Henry and Gaunt were now themselves in fear of their lives.[59] Henry and Thomas de Mowbray (now the duke of Norfolk), the two Appellants who were still alive and at large, became embroiled in a mess of accusation and counteraccusation. There may have been a Ricardian plot to bring them down, or one of them may have been scheming against the other. Derby, who went to his father after Mowbray approached him with his story of plots, got to the king in January with his version of events and remained precariously in favour during the first half of the year.[60] Indeed, in May 1398, when Chaucer received his safe-conduct, Henry was confirmed in various land grants, while Mowbray was in the Tower.[61] In the summer of that year, both Richard and Henry were restless. Henry moved around his estates, accompanied by his core retinue, including his steward, Bukton, Chaucer's friend.[62] Richard

[58] Manly argues that the Collinson-Palmer date of 1397 for Chaucer's second forestership is incorrect and makes a convincing case for 1398–99 being the correct date. See Manly, 'Three Recent Chaucer Studies,' 261.

[59] For their complicity, see Given-Wilson, *Henry IV*, 103. For plots against Gaunt's life in late 1397 and early 1398, see ibid., 107, 110.

[60] For accounts of these months, see Given-Wilson, *Henry IV*, 108–14; Saul, *Richard II*, 394–400.

[61] *Calendar of Close Rolls: Richard II*, Membrane 10, 6:263 (26 April 1398); Membrane 7, 6:266 (20 May 1398).

[62] Given-Wilson, *Henry IV*, 113.

also spent most of his time far from the southeast, in his western heart-lands.[63] The date for the trial by battle between Mowbray and Derby was set for 16 September, and although Henry had plenty of reasons to be worried, there was no reason to think that things were going to go as badly as they did. Famously, Richard stopped the battle as it began and sentenced Mowbray to permanent exile, Henry to ten years' exile, with the right to inherit property. Both were to depart England by 20 October.[64] Now things moved quickly. Around December, Gaunt fell seriously ill. On 3 February 1399, the greatest nobleman in England, and the other half of the longest close relationship of Chaucer's life, died. He was almost Chaucer's exact contemporary, and whether or not their relationship was very personal, they were bound together by tie upon tie—professional, poetic, and familial. And there is a particular kind of melancholy attached to the death of a contemporary: Gaunt was fifty-eight when he died, Chaucer was probably about fifty-six at this time, and they had known each other since at least 1357, when both were teenagers (around seventeen and fifteen).

If Chaucer needed further impetus to focus his mind on the way of all flesh and the realities of death, he got it in spades. Now, the threshold between life and death was displayed in spectacular fashion. Gaunt had specified that his body should remain unburied for forty days, an extraordinarily impractical request.[65] The rotting corpse stayed above the ground, graphically demonstrating the democracy of death, while Richard deliberated over whether to deal what he hoped would be a conclusive blow—not only to the house of Lancaster but to the established interests of the English nobility. He had recently and repeatedly shown his willingness to strike at the heart of inheritance and to reopen questions of land distribution.[66] His treatment of Henry, however, was audacious in the extreme and signaled a determination to centralize and to accrete more and more authority to himself. Before Gaunt had been buried, Richard decreed that Henry was now banished for the term of his life, and that he could not inherit his father's estates, which Richard was taking into his own

[63] Saul, *Richard II*, 392.
[64] Given-Wilson, *Henry IV*, 114–15.
[65] Goodman, *John of Gaunt*, 367.
[66] Given-Wilson, *Henry IV*, 102, 111.

hands.[67] England now stood on the brink of a confrontation between these two cousins. It was clear that only one could survive, and that the survivor would be king.

England remained on the threshold of a new regime for another six months. By June 1399 Henry and Thomas Arundel had forged an alliance, and Henry now signed a treaty with the duke of Orleans. By the end of June, he was at the English coast, while Richard was occupied in Ireland. A tense six weeks followed as Henry mustered forces across England and a reluctant army was mustered against him. Henry's victory was relatively easy, and by 15 August Richard had been captured; on 16 August he resigned his throne to his cousin. At the end of September, this was formalized: on 29 September of that month, Richard removed his signet ring and publicly renounced his throne. Henry was now acclaimed as king, and on 13 October he was crowned.[68] England had crossed the boundary and a new dynasty had taken over the monarchy. What did this mean for Chaucer? He must have felt unmoored: Gaunt, his constant protector, was dead, and his allowance from Gaunt had gone; he had also lost his allowances from Richard. Henry, of course, had favoured Chaucer in the past and was closely connected with Chaucer's older son, so there is no reason to think that things were particularly worrying for Chaucer. He knew many of Henry's associates—such as Bukton and perhaps Thomas Arundel—fairly well. But, while Henry had decisively crossed his Rubicon and transformed himself from man into king through the solemn anointing and elaborate ceremonies of the coronation, everyone else was still waiting to see what the new order would mean for them. Chaucer himself, a couple of months after Henry's coronation, was living on the edge of a Benedictine community, in the precincts of the symbolic centre of the monarchy itself: Westminster Abbey.

[67] As Saul writes, 'Richard had taken a step which struck at the heart of the aristocracy's most vital interests.' *Richard II*, 404.

[68] Given-Wilson, *Henry IV*, 122–54.

CHAPTER 20

> ━◆◆◆━○━◆◆◆━

Abbey

[A]ll that's written is written to inspire us.

— *Patience Agbabi,* Telling Tales

Parliamentary politics, religion, economics, government, bureaucracy, craftsmanship, architecture, the visual arts, musical composition and performance, book production, and the monarchy all found a vibrant centre at medieval Westminster.[1] In the late fourteenth century, visiting Westminster involved an assault on the senses.[2] The extraordinary buildings were lavishly decorated with paintings, sculptures, tiles, and bronzework; the great offices of state were based here; and Parliament met here. In the second half of the fourteenth century, bureaucratic institutions were established in Westminster Hall, and Westminster also became Parliament's most usual meeting place, with the Commons meeting in the abbey chapterhouse and then in the refectory.[3] In the later years of the century, Richard's extensive patronage of the abbey ensured its artistic development: the choir was formed, his portrait was painted and hung here (see plate 16), and he continued the tradition of elaborate funerary monuments.[4] At Westminster Hall, Hugh Herland was constructing the

[1] See W. R. Lethaby, *Westminster Abbey and the King's Craftsmen: A Study of Mediaeval Building* (London: Duckworth, 1906).

[2] Edward Carpenter describes the 'blaze of bright colours' of the abbey in *A House of Kings: The Official History of Westminster Abbey* (London: John Baker, 1966), 64.

[3] See Rosser, *Medieval Westminster*, 37–39.

[4] Nigel Saul, 'Richard II and Westminster Abbey,' in John Blair and Brian Golding (eds.), *The Cloister and the World: Essays in Medieval History in Honour of Barbara Harvey* (Oxford: Oxford University Press, 1996), 197–219.

breathtaking hammer-beam roof. At the same time, the abbey encouraged commerce by renting out its land for shops, taverns, and tenements. Itinerant sellers, immigrant workers, and beggars flocked here, adding to the dizzying sense of chaos, opportunity, and exploitation.[5] Both a place of governmental bureaucracy and a place of spectacular beauty, Westminster was the centre of the business of the nation *and* of the business of imagining the nation. This was where Chaucer chose to be based for the last ten months of his life.

Chaucer's house was in the gardens of Westminster Abbey, near the Lady Chapel. The town of Westminster was dominated by the abbey and the palace, which abutted each other near the river (as they still do). The palace at this time comprised both a residence for the royal family and the massive Westminster Hall, where the business of government was carried out. The hall was the home of the Courts of Common Pleas, King's Bench, and Chancery. The Exchequer was located in a building next to the hall, and the whole area was thronged with lawyers and clerks. A poem written around 1400, *London Lickpenny*, vividly describes the experience of a countryside dweller arriving in the crowds of Westminster.[6] The poem is structured around the refrain 'For lacke of money, I may not spede,' and it evokes the narrator's experience of being an outsider in the incomprehensible world of Westminster. Straight away, as he pushes 'thrughe-out the thronge' (9), he finds his hood stolen. He tries to get his case heard at all three courts, but none will help him. One of the 'grete rowt' (17) of clerks calls out so fast and loud that the narrator 'wist not wele what he ment' (21); the petitioner insistently tells us that 'In all Westminstar Hall I could find nevar a one / That for me would do, thowghe I shuld dye' (49–50). The chaotic cut-and-thrust of the area is further emphasized by the description of stallholders and itinerant sellers swirling around the business of the courts. Immediately at the doors are crowds of immigrant Flemings, trying to sell him 'felt hatts' and 'spectacles' (54); at the gate are the victuallers with food and drink on offer (59–63).

[5] Rosser, *Medieval Westminster*, 68–73.
[6] The poem is edited in Dean, *Medieval English Political Writings*, 222–25. It is also available online at http://d.lib.rochester.edu/teams/text/dean-medieval-english-political-writings-london-lickpenny.

The world of commerce was also an integral part of the abbey area. The palace had literally intruded on the abbey in 1365, when Edward III had the Jewel Tower constructed by Yevele on land requisitioned from the abbey. There was no clear separation between religion and government; indeed, the great church was part of political life, most notably through its role in Parliament. In 1386, when Chaucer sat in Parliament, he sat in the abbey refectory, along with the rest of the Commons, for deliberations.[7] In the same month he also gave evidence regarding the Scrope-Grosvenor enquiry in the same location, when the Court of Chivalry took its statements in the abbey refectory. The abbey itself was a very large and complex institution. A venerable Benedictine foundation, it had generally housed forty-eight monks, although this number expanded to around sixty in the late fourteenth century.[8] They were assisted by a great number of servants, some of whom lived on site. Other people paid to have corrodies, whereby they received food and fuel, and some of these people lived in the abbey precincts. Women served the abbey, doing jobs such as laundry, gardening, and repairing vestments.[9] The abbey was divided into numerous departments and areas, and was run by many officers with their own responsibilities.[10] It owned a great deal of land and rented out many properties in the town of Westminster itself. Increasingly, land within the abbey, especially in the almonry and sanctuary, was rented out as tenements and shops, as the abbey maximized the commercial potential of this land, particularly the land that fronted the street and the rest of the town.[11] The growing number of lay residents in the precincts was further supplemented by those seeking sanctuary and, at almsgiving times, by crowds of needy beggars.[12] The abbey's pragmatic interaction with the

[7] Rosser notes that in the 1380s, the Commons' meeting place moved from chapter house to refectory; *Medieval Westminster*, 39.

[8] Barbara Harvey, 'The Monks of Westminster and the Old Lady Chapel,' in Tim Tatton-Brown and Richard Mortimer (eds.), *Westminster Abbey: The Lady Chapel of Henry VII* (Woodbridge: Boydell Press, 2003), 16.

[9] Barbara Harvey gives examples of servants who lived on site, of laypeople with corrodies living within Westminster, and of women working for the abbey, in *Living and Dying in England, 1100–1540: The Monastic Experience* (Oxford: Clarendon Press, 1993), 166–67, 248–49.

[10] See Barbara Harvey, *The Obedientiaries of Westminster Abbey and Their Financial Records, c. 1275 to 1540*, Westminster Abbey Records Series 3 (Woodbridge: Boydell Press, 2002).

[11] Rosser, *Medieval Westminster*, 67–73.

[12] Ibid., 156; Harvey, *Living and Dying*, 74.

town over which its buildings loomed is well demonstrated by the existence of a brothel set up specifically to cater to the monks.[13]

The symbolic centre of the monarchy since the time of Edward the Confessor, Westminster enjoyed a particularly golden age in the 1380s and 1390s. In the late 1370s, the abbey had had to stand up for its privileges after a shocking murder in the church itself, for which Gaunt was blamed. The debate about the right of sanctuary became part of the struggle between royal and church power in which Gaunt was mobilizing Wycliffe.[14] But as Richard II grew up, he focused on Westminster as the stage for his theatrical conception of kingship, ceremonially visiting the abbey on many important occasions and focusing on Edward the Confessor as his inspiration.[15] He lavished gifts on the monastery, engaged in extensive artistic patronage, and enabled the expansion of the community: in 1397–98 nine new novices joined, which was an unprecedented number.[16] Although Richard had initially opposed the election of William Colchester as abbot in 1386 when he was pushing the claims of another candidate,[17] the two men became close allies, with Colchester even accompanying Richard to Ireland in 1399. Presumably, they saw mutual benefit in the glorification of Westminster as the symbolic home of sanctified English monarchy.

This image was increasingly promoted through artistic endeavour. The abbey buildings were, of course, already decorated with exquisite tiles, paintings, and sculptures. But now, artistic projects intensified. From 1384, Westminster had broken new ground for English monasteries when it began to employ professional musicians, based at the Lady Chapel. Walter Whitby was their first cantor, or choirmaster, joining the boy singers supplied by the abbey's almonry grammar school.[18] In 1393, singing men were employed, and their numbers were doubled in 1397.[19] John Tyes was

[13] Rosser, *Medieval Westminster*, 144.

[14] For a discussion of the case, see Thomas Prendergast, *Poetical Dust: Poets' Corner and the Making of Britain* (Philadelphia: University of Pennsylvania Press, 2015), 28–33. See also Gervase Rosser, 'Sanctuary and Social Negotiation in Medieval England,' in Blair and Golding, *The Cloister and the World*, 58–80.

[15] Saul, 'Richard II and Westminster Abbey.'

[16] Harvey, 'Monks of Westminster,' 16.

[17] See E. H. Pearce, *The Monks of Westminster: Being a Register of the Brethren of the Convent from the Time of the Confessor to the Dissolution* (Cambridge: Cambridge University Press, 1916), 104, 130.

[18] Bowers, 'The Musicians and Liturgy,' in Tatton-Brown and Mortimer, *Westminster Abbey*, 37–38.

[19] Harvey, 'Monks of Westminster,' 16; Bowers, 'Musicians and Liturgy,' 40.

employed as a polyphonic singer and organ player; his compositions include a three-part setting of the Gloria and a four-part setting of the Sanctus.[20] From 1388, Henry Yevele was supervising the 'new work' on the Gothic nave, and from 1394 he was also supervising the reconstruction of Westminster Hall, a stone's throw away. In the abbey, Yevele also constructed Anne and Richard's joint tomb after Anne's death in 1394.[21] Towards the end of the century, Richard commissioned his extraordinarily powerful, hieratic portrait.[22] Glaziers, bronze workers, and sculptors all found ample work at the Westminster complex.[23] Copyists, binders, and book repairers worked at the abbey; specialist scribes were brought in for particular projects, such as the Litlington Missal, made in 1384–85.[24] The historian of Westminster, Gervase Rosser, speculates that there may have been a generally 'bookish atmosphere' in the town.[25] At the abbey itself, Chaucer found many monks who wrote their own texts and who owned both sacred and secular texts. Westminster had a long tradition of chronicle writing and compiling and sent several monks to Gloucester College in Oxford. John Scarle, clerk of Parliament for many years was a long-term pensioner of the abbey. Thomas Merks, composer of a dictaminal treatise, was a Westminster monk; Richard Cirencester, who wrote the *Speculum Historiale*, was at Westminster from 1354 to 1400. William of Sudbury, a monk between 1373 and 1415, wrote a treatise on the coronation regalia, composed a letter for Richard II to Urban VI, and wrote an index of the works of Aquinas, a treatise on the authenticity of the relic of the precious blood of Christ, and probably a treatise on sanctuary. Richard Exeter, a Westminster monk between about 1358 and 1397, owned books including a *Polychronicon*, a *Historia de Troia*, several maps, and a book about Marco Polo. When he died, a 'liber de jocondio amoris' (book on the pleasure of love) was being copied for him and an astronomical work was being bound.[26]

---

[20] Bowers, 'Musicians and Liturgy,' 41–42.
[21] Lethaby, *King's Craftsmen*, 204–5, 215–19.
[22] Saul, 'Richard II and Westminster Abbey,' 210.
[23] Lethaby, *King's Craftsmen*, 254, 289, 304.
[24] Carpenter, *House of Kings*, 72; Rosser, *Medieval Westminster*, 209.
[25] Rosser, *Medieval Westminster*, 210.
[26] See *Westminster Chronicle*, xxxi–xlvii; translation mine.

This community, then, was at the forefront of many kinds of artistic activity, was commercially highly astute and engaged, was involved in high politics, and had members who were interested in all kinds of literature and writing. Taking a longer view, Benedictine communities across Europe had increasingly focused on affect, emotion, and Marian devotion since the so-called twelfth-century renaissance, in which the ideas and writings of Anselm and Bernard had changed the intellectual climate of monasticism.[27] One of the effects of this changed climate was an increased focus on individual, private prayer and devotion. By the late fourteenth century, orthodox religious communities and followers of Wycliffe alike were interested in ways of expressing personal devotion. In Westminster, where Simon Langham owned books of meditative prayers by Anselm and Bernard, individual members of the community offered wall paintings; celebrants were given long, private prayers to recite; anchorites were supported and maintained; and connections were formed with the individualistic, eremetical Carthusians.[28] Thus, while the community had no truck with Wycliffe's branch of reform, which aimed to lessen the wealth and influence of church institutions, they had much in common with the so-called Lollard knights around Richard's court, with whom Chaucer may well have shared sympathies. Chaucer lived and wrote before the era of Lollard burnings, at a time when many men and women were interested in aspects of Wycliffite thought without wanting to leave the established church. In the cancelled endlink to the 'Man of Law's Tale,' removed in the process of revision but still surviving in some manuscripts, the Host refers to the Parson as a potential 'Lollere' after he criticises swearing (1173). Another speaker—initially the Wife of Bath, later replaced by the Shipman, Squire, or Summoner, depending on the scribe—supports the Host's jibe saying: 'He wolde sowen som difficulte, / Or springen cokkel in our clene corn' (1182–83).[29] This image of the weed (often referred to as a 'lollius') amongst the corn is taken from Matthew 13:24–30, and was

[27] See the classic account in Southern, *The Making of the Middle Ages*, 219–57. See also R. N. Swanson, *The Twelfth Century Renaissance* (Manchester: Manchester University Press, 1999); and the essays in Robert Louis Benson, Giles Constable, and Carol Dana Lanham (eds.), *Renaissance and Renewal in the Twelfth Century* (Toronto: University of Toronto Press, 1999).

[28] Carpenter, *House of Kings*, 73–74.

[29] See *Riverside Chaucer*, 863, note to 1179.

beloved of critics of Lollardy.[30] It is used here as an attack on Bible interpretation, reinforcing the idea that the Parson will 'gospel glosen' (1180) and thus make the Bible more difficult. As a comment on Lollardy, the whole passage exposes the ignorance of those criticizing the Parson: the Lollards were against glossing and supported literal reading.[31] Similarly, the speaker triumphantly promises to speak in English, not Latin—something with which Lollards would be entirely in sympathy. The point, surely, is the same as that made by Chaucer's friend, Sir John Clanvowe, in his prose religious tract, *The Two Ways*: that ascetically pious people are insulted as Lollards ('lollers') in the current religious climate.[32] Having some sympathy with such people and with their views certainly did not preclude friendship and sympathy with monks as well.

Chaucer took a lease on 24 December 1399 for a tenement in the garden of the Lady Chapel.[33] This garden was subsequently subsumed into the larger Lady Chapel built a century later. When Chaucer took the lease, the house either adjoined or was right next to the chapel. It had previously been inhabited by an employee of the Exchequer with an annuity from Richard, and it was subsequently inhabited by a king's clerk and physician, and then by a wealthy skinner who supplied furs, cloaks, and hoods.[34] By 1411, Chaucer's son, now a substantial man, had taken it over, presumably finding it particularly convenient for Parliament.[35] So this property was generally inhabited by men not dissimilar to Chaucer in situation. It placed him at the centre of things, giving him easy access to the institutions of government and to all kinds of cultural production and books. Its location also made it easy for him to live: he may have been able to buy basics such as bread and ale from the monastery kitchens, and there were victuallers and taverns aplenty very close by. The sanctuary privileges may

---

[30] See, for instance, Thomas Wright (ed.), *Political Songs and Poems Relating to English History* (London: Longman, 1859–61), 1:232.

[31] See John Wycliffe, *Selected English Works of John Wyclif*, ed. Thomas Arnold (Oxford: Clarendon Press, 1869), 1:376.

[32] Scattergood, *Works of Sir John Clanvowe*, 70.

[33] Crow and Olson, *Chaucer Life-Records*, 535–36.

[34] Pearsall discusses these other inhabitants, and also suggests that Chaucer took on the lease specifically in the hope of being buried in Westminster Abbey. Derek Pearsall, 'Chaucer's Tomb: The Politics of Reburial,' *Medium Aevum* 64:1 (1995), 52–53.

[35] Crow and Olson, *Chaucer Life-Records*, 538–40.

have been an incentive for Chaucer too: the inclusion of the unusual and special clause protecting him from lawsuits for two years in his 1398 safe-conduct bespeaks some kind of particular anxiety about debt.[36] Perhaps he felt pursued by unjust claims and wanted an extra guarantee of impunity. But he did not need a special reason for moving here; it was an eminently attractive and convenient location for him. Its convenience indeed suggests that he was probably more rather than less politically engaged than in recent years. And living in a religious community would not have seemed strange. It imposed no particular restrictions and actually offered easy access to commercial locations.

Chaucer, like most medieval people, was used to living his life cheek by jowl with religious institutions. As discussed earlier in this book, his daughter was a nun, first at St Helen's Bishopsgate and then at Barking Abbey. When Chaucer lived on Aldgate, he lived next door to the Holy Trinity Priory at Aldgate, and very close to Aldgate Abbey and Eastminster Abbey. His scribe, Adam Pynkhurst, worked out of the Mercers' base at St Thomas Acon, home of the Hospitallers of St Thomas, a religious order following the Augustinian rule.[37] Chaucer's long-term friend and colleague, John Gower, was living in a house in the priory of St Mary Overy in Southwark—perhaps his lifestyle there provided a desirable model for Chaucer. And, although not a monastic institution but a cathedral church, Chaucer's connections with Lincoln also remind us of his intimacy with religious institutions throughout his life. Philippa regularly received her allowances in Lincolnshire,[38] where Gaunt (one of whose titles was earl of Lincoln) owned extensive property; Henry IV was born at Bolingbroke Castle in Lincolnshire; Katherine Swynford also lived in the county, at Kettlethorpe and then near the cathedral itself. Philippa was inducted into the prestigious fraternity at the cathedral alongside numerous others, including Henry, and Gaunt and Katherine were married there.[39] Thomas Chaucer's wife's family also had strong Lincoln connections: the Burghersh family had a chantry and funeral monuments in the cathedral, and Thomas

[36] Prendergast emphasizes the importance of sanctuary for Chaucer; for his argument, see *Poetical Dust*, 39.

[37] See Mooney, 'Chaucer's Scribe,' 109, 111; and Turner, 'Usk and the Goldsmiths,' 146.

[38] Crow and Olson, *Chaucer Life-Records*, 87–88.

[39] Ibid., 91–93.

held lands in Lincolnshire.[40] It is, of course, possible that Chaucer did not spend time in Lincolnshire himself. Aspects of the 'Prioress's Tale,' however, do suggest that his reference to Hugh of Lincoln at the end of that tale is not merely throwaway. The references to the punishment of the Jews by drawing and hanging, and the specific detail of the marble tomb, link this particular version of the 'boy singer' story to narratives of Hugh of Lincoln.[41] Hugh was rather obscure in Chaucer's day in comparison to other 'boy martyrs,'[42] so it is likely that Chaucer's connections with Lincoln, via his wife and Gaunt, prompted him to centre the Prioress's brutal sentimentalism on Lincoln. Philippa's participation in the ceremony of 19 February 1386 reminds us of how engagement with major religious institutions was a fundamental part of the fabric of Chaucer's life.

Throughout the *Canterbury Tales*, it is clear that monastic institutions were embedded in everyday European life in a number of ways. In the 'Miller's Tale,' John the carpenter works for Osney Abbey, and the abbot sends him to outlying farms for timber (3665–68). Similarly, in the 'Shipman's Tale,' Daun John the monk rides about the countryside on the instructions of his abbot, surveying the 'graunges' (farms) that provided so much income for religious institutions (66). It is this freedom of movement and economic involvement that enables Daun John to visit his friend's house and ultimately to engage in flirtation and a sexual encounter with his friend's wife.[43] Abbeys' and convents' role as providers of education is glimpsed in the 'Reeve's Tale,' as the priest's illegitimate daughter is brought up in a nunnery, where she receives 'nortelrie' (3967). In the 'Prioress's

[40] For the Burghersh monuments in Lincoln Cathedral, see Anne M. Morganstern, 'The Bishop, the Young Lion, and the Two-Headed Dragon: The Burghersh Memorial in Lincoln Cathedral,' in *Memory and Oblivion: Proceedings of the XXIXth International Congress of the History of Art Held in Amsterdam, 1–7 September 1996*, ed. Wessel Reinink and Jeroen Stumpel (Dordrecht: Springer, 1999), 515–35. For Thomas Chaucer's Lincolnshire lands, see his entry in Roskell, Clark, and Rawcliffe, *History of Parliament*, 2:524–32.

[41] See Roger Dahood, 'The Punishment of the Jews, Hugh of Lincoln, and the Question of Satire in Chaucer's "Prioress's Tale,"' *Viator* 36 (2005): 465–92, and 'English Historical Narratives of Jewish Child Murder, Chaucer's "Prioress's Tale," and the Date of Chaucer's Unknown Source,' *Studies in the Age of Chaucer* 31 (2009): 125–40.

[42] Sumner Ferris, 'Chaucer at Lincoln (1387): The "Prioress's Tale" as a Political Poem,' *Chaucer Review* 15:4 (1981): 300.

[43] See Elliot Kendall, 'The Great Household in the City: The *Shipman's Tale*,' in Butterfield, *Chaucer and the City*, 148–54.

Tale,' the dead child is taken to the nearby abbey (624), which becomes a centre for exclusive grieving and commemoration. Casual references, such as the brief mention of the 'abbey orlogge' (clock) in the 'Nun's Priest's Tale' (2854), bear witness to how familiar the physical layouts of such institutions were to Chaucer and his contemporaries.[44]

It is well known that Chaucer heavily satirizes members of religious or-ders in the *Canterbury Tales*, drawing on established models of estates satire. Figures such as the Monk, Prioress, and Friar lack both intellectual seriousness and empathetic understanding. They flagrantly fail to keep their religious vows and are sinfully worldly in their interests and occupa-tions. This literary stereotyping tells us nothing, however, of Chaucer's relationships with members of such orders in his own life. Men such as William Colchester were serious intellectuals and politicians, and Col-chester was also known for his generosity to the poor[45]—and a pragma-tist such as Chaucer would not expect men of the church to separate themselves wholly from the world. Chaucer's burial in the abbey strongly suggests he had a warm relationship with the Benedictine community. Westminster Abbey was a monastic institution, not a parish church. Chau-cer was a parishioner of St Margaret's, Westminster, and would logically have been buried there. He was not buried in Westminster as a poet—Poets' Corner was inaugurated much later, and his tomb was moved there in 1556 (plate 17).[46] Nor was he buried in Westminster as a royal servant: he was not nearly important enough, and was not buried in the part of the church where Richard had had favourites such as John Waltham in-terred.[47] Rather, he was buried near St Benedict's Chapel, a gesture that suggests he was accepted as a friend by the monks, and enjoyed close and warm ties with them.[48] He had lived there for less than a year; the tradi-tional date for his death is 25 October 1400. This may not be accurate,

---

[44] See Travis, *Disseminal Chaucer*, chapter 6 (267–301) on telling the time in the 'Nun's Priest's Tale.'

[45] See Barbara F. Harvey, 'Colchester, William (d. 1420),' in the *ODNB*, https://doi.org/10.1093/ref:odnb/54431.

[46] See Pearsall, 'Chaucer's Tomb: The Politics of Reburial,' 51–73; and Thomas A. Prendergast, *Chaucer's Dead Body: From Corpse to Corpus* (New York: Routledge, 2004). I discuss this further in the epilogue.

[47] For John Waltham's career, see chapter 15.

[48] Barron, 'Chaucer the Poet and Chaucer the Pilgrim,' 38–39.

but it is about right; he disappears from the record after the summer of 1400, and did not receive payments on the Michaelmas portion of his annuities.[49]

Chaucer had moved to Westminster at a time when the monks were experiencing a tense and difficult few months. In December, when Chaucer signed his lease, the plots that led to the Epiphany Rising were fomenting, and their crucible seems to have been the abbey itself. This failed rebellion was a pro-Ricardian movement that aimed to dethrone Henry in the first months of his reign. According to one—not very reliable— source, the chief plotters actually met on 17 December 'in the rooms of the abbot of Westminster [William Colchester],' to make their plans and to swear allegiance to each other and to the plot.[50] Although this may not be true, several Westminster monks were implicated in the rebellion, led by the earls of Kent, Huntingdon, and Salisbury, and Thomas Despenser. Clerics accused of complicity included Thomas Merks, the monk of Westminster who had been promoted to the episcopate of Carlisle by Richard, and Roger Walden, another Westminster monk made archbishop of Canterbury by Richard after the exile of Thomas Arundel. William Colchester was imprisoned in the Tower in January, after the failure of the rebellion.[51] The Westminster community must have been in a state of extreme anxiety: Richard had lavished patronage on them and now not only was he deposed, but their abbot was locked up, accused of treason. For Colchester, however, the dust settled. He was swiftly released and continued as abbot until his death in 1420. But Henry's accession marked a change at Westminster more generally. He never gave the abbey the kind of favour and patronage that his predecessor had, and Westminster had to reduce its expenditure, in some cases dramatically. From the date of Henry's succession, the salary provision for the singers in the Lady Chapel, for instance, was reduced by more than 50 per cent, from £47 to £22 13s 4d.[52]

While Westminster Abbey was suffering straitened and stressful times, its new tenant was sitting pretty. Chaucer and his family's primary alle-

---

[49] Crow and Olson, *Chaucer Life-Records*, 547–49.

[50] Given-Wilson, 'The Epiphany Rising and the Death of the King according to the *Traison et Mort*,' 230.

[51] On the Epiphany Rising, see Given-Wilson, *Henry IV*, 160–65.

[52] Bowers, 'Musicians and Liturgy,' 43; Harvey, 'Monks of Westminster,' 17.

giance had always been to the house of Lancaster, and the Lancastrians were now in control. Chaucer's son received several valuable grants in the early weeks of the new reign: he was appointed as constable for life of Wallingford Castle, and steward of the honours of Wallingford and St Valery, and of four and a half of the hundreds of Chiltern, for instance. The importance of his role at Wallingford is demonstrated by the fact that the young queen and her household were residing there and were, effectively, in his custody.[53] Chaucer himself, having lost the paperwork confirming his Exchequer grants, nonetheless successfully petitioned for their confirmation on 18 October, and received a promise of a gift of £10 from Henry on 9 November. He received his tun of wine at some point during Henry's first regnal year, and Henry also increased his allowance, making Chaucer an extra grant of 40 marks a year for life.[54] Although the patent rolls record that this grant was made on 13 October, Sumner Ferris has shown that this date is incorrect. Many documents were backdated to significant dates, such as the first day of a reign, as in this case, but the fact of their backdating can generally be spotted by their nonchronological appearance in the records. This was standard Chancery practice. In this case, the entry appears in a cluster of February documents and, almost certainly, February 1400 is the actual date of its issue. At around the same time, on 21 February, Chaucer received the £10 that he had been promised in November.[55]

This payment in fact provides a vital clue as to what Chaucer was doing at this moment. He was paid this money by the hands of Nicholas Usk, treasurer of Calais. Why might Chaucer have been in Calais in early February 1400? Throughout his life, Chaucer had been going on diplomatic missions for the Crown and had, in particular, been a member of embassies negotiating marriage alliances and peace treaties. At this precise moment, Henry had dispatched envoys to France to try to confirm the 1396 truce in the war, and to negotiate marriage alliances between Henry's family and the family of the king of France. At first, Charles—who was

[53]'Thomas Chaucer of Ewelme,' in Roskell, *Parliament and Politics*, 154.
[54]For the documents, see Crow and Olson, *Chaucer Life-Records*, 119, 525–34.
[55]Sumner Ferris, 'The Date of Chaucer's Final Annuity and of the "Complaint to His Empty Purse,"' *Modern Philology* 65:1 (1967): 45–52.

the father-in-law of Richard II—refused to see Henry's ambassadors in Paris. However, at the end of January, he confirmed the truce and sent his ambassadors to negotiate with the English at Leulinghem, near Calais, the site of many earlier peace negotiations.[56] On 19 February, Henry issued orders specifically mandating his representatives to negotiate marriages between the two royal families.[57] It was also around this time that Richard died, or was killed, under the supervision of Thomas Swynford, Chaucer's nephew by marriage and first cousin of Thomas Chaucer.[58] Isabella, Richard's child-widow, was herself now a pawn in the marriage negotiations: Henry was keen to keep her person and dowry for the Crown, perhaps via a marriage with his son; Charles wanted her, and her dowry's, return. Chaucer was back in his element. He, of course, had been prominent in the negotiations for Richard's first wife, some twenty years earlier. And indeed, Henry was calling upon other old hands with long-term knowledge of marriage and peace negotiations with France to advocate for him. One of the leaders of the current negotiations was Thomas Percy, earl of Worcester. Thomas was the younger brother of the earl of Northumberland and the first cousin of Henry's mother, Blanche. He had a long career as a soldier and diplomat, having fought in the retinue of the Black Prince and John of Gaunt. He had accompanied Gaunt on his Spanish expedition, and was an executor of Gaunt's will. He had also been in favour with Richard and towards the end of the reign had served as steward of Richard's household and had travelled with him to Ireland. In 1378, he had been one of those who particularly supported Wycliffe's attack on Westminster's sanctuary rights.[59] In 1377, Thomas Percy and Geoffrey Chaucer were sent to Flanders 'in secretis negociis domini regis versus partes Flandrie.'[60] They also both spent time in Montreuil, negotiating for

[56] Rymer, *Foedera*, 8:108, 8:125–26, 8:132; Jonathan Sumption, *The Hundred Years War III: Divided Houses* (London: Faber & Faber, 2009), 774–883; Stephen Pistono, 'The Diplomatic Mission of Jean de Hangest Lord of Hugueville (October 1400),' *Canadian Journal of History* 13:2 (1978): 193–207.

[57] Rymer, *Foedera*, 8:128–29.

[58] National Archives, E 403/564. This document records that one of Thomas Swynford's servants took news of Richard to Henry on 17 February. See Given-Wilson, *Chronicle of Adam Usk*, 90–91.

[59] For a sketch of his life, see A. L. Brown, 'Percy, Thomas, earl of Worcester (c. 1343–1403),' in the *ODNB*, https://doi.org/10.1093/ref:odnb/21955.

[60] Crow and Olson, *Chaucer Life-Records*, 44–45. The advances for Percy and Chaucer appear next to each other in the record. The wording quoted above is from Percy's entry, it is identical in Chaucer's

peace between France and England, during the first part of that year.[61] Thomas Percy also appears at other points in Chaucer's life, for instance, as one of the feoffees at Spittlecombe in 1395.[62] He was Chaucer's exact contemporary. It makes complete sense for Chaucer to have been part of Percy's negotiating team in early 1400, and his presence at Calais demonstrates that he was employed by Henry early on in his reign. It is even possible that Chaucer went to Calais on 19 February, with the new orders that Henry issued that day, as he would just about have had time to get there before the 21st, when he received his payment from Nicholas Usk. Percy and Chaucer's employment on this mission demonstrates, yet again, medieval rulers' fondness for continuity. Chaucer had not gained a higher position than he had held twenty years earlier, but he had maintained that position, at the heart of English diplomacy.

At some point during these months, he wrote his *Complaint to His Purse*. The last verse specifically addresses Henry as king, so it must have been written after the end of September 1399. Almost certainly Chaucer's last poem, although he may have been revising and adding bits to the *Canterbury Tales*, it merits quoting in full:

> To yow, my purse, and to noon other wight
> Complayne I, for ye be my lady dere.
> I am so sory, now that ye been lyght;
> For certes but yf ye make me hevy chere,
> Me were as leef be layd upon my bere,
> For which unto your mercy thus I crye,
> Beth hevy ageyn, or elles mot I dye.
>
> Now voucheth sauf this day or hyt be nyght
> That I of yow the blisful soun may here,
> Or see your colour lyk the sonne bryght
> That of yelownesse hadde never pere.
> Ye be my lyf, ye be myn hertes stere.

---

except for the addition of 'easdem' (the same): 'versus easdem partes Flandres,' which makes clear they were going to the same places.

[61] Ibid., 45–53.

[62] Ibid., 506.

Quene of comfort and of good companye,
Beth hevy ageyn or elles moot I dye.

Now purse that ben to me my lyves lyght
And saveour as doun in this world here
Out of this toune helpe me thurgh your myght,
Syn that ye wole nat ben my tresorere;
For I am shave as nye as any frere.
But yet I pray unto your curtesye,
Beth hevy agen, or elles moot I dye.

Lenvoy de Chaucer

O conquerour of Brutes Albyon,
Which that by lyne and free eleccion
Been verray kyng, this song to yow I sende,
And ye, that mowen alle oure harmes amende,
Have mynde upon my supplicacion.

This is a petitioning poem. Chaucer is asking for money, but he is also wittily playing with the language of courtly love and sexual innuendo by punning on terms such as 'purse' (wallet or scrotum), 'hevy' (heavy or pregnant), and 'lyght' (weighing little or promiscuous). The poem closes with an explicit address to Henry, termed king by right of conquest, lineage, and election. It was most likely written either at the beginning of the reign, when Chaucer requested the confirmation of his existing grants, or early in 1400, as Chaucer sought to remind Henry that he had not received payment. But as the king consistently remained behind on payments to Chaucer, the poem could be dated at any point in the last year of Chaucer's life. The king's slowness in paying Chaucer is entirely in keeping with usual practice; more significant is his choosing to increase Chaucer's annuity, a symbolic gesture of patronage (although it might, of course, be preferable to have a smaller allowance that actually got paid).[63]

---

[63] For a different view of Chaucer's relationship with the new regime, see Terry Jones et al., *Who Murdered Chaucer? A Medieval Mystery* (London: Methuen, 2003).

There is nothing in this poem to suggest an end-of-life seriousness, a turning away from poetic playfulness. On the contrary, Chaucer maintains the sexual puns throughout the poem, and continually plays with metaphor and different levels of discourse. The object of his desire is bright and sun-like, its sound is blissful. These are conventional descriptions for a courtly lady, such as Emily, but here the description also refers to a gleaming, jangling coin, such as Alison.[64] The puns on genitals and pregnancy also give the poem a fabliau mood. Death is referenced throughout in the refrain, as we might expect from a late poem, but it is mentioned only flippantly: he will die without money/sexual success, and 'die' itself may have a sexual connotation.[65] Chaucer also comically declares that he would rather be laid upon his funeral bier than continue without the favour of his lady/money. His reference to himself as metaphorically tonsured might gain an extra edge from his current residence within a monkish community. The poem is also decidedly Chaucerian in its intertextuality. Froissart too had written a 'Dit dou florin,' in which he bemoans the loss of a heavy purse, and Lady Mede, one of the most memorable characters in *Piers Plowman*, is both a woman and coinage. Chaucer's address to Henry also closely mirrors Gower's tripartite reference to the king in the *Chronica Tripertita*: 'Regnum conquestat ... / Regno succedit heres ... / Insuper eligitur a plebe' (He conquered the realm ... / He succeeded as heir to the kingdom ... / In addition, he was chosen by the people [3.333–35]).[66] This specific address also marks the explicit politics and purpose of the poem: Chaucer is using poetry to make a real-life request. As the poem unfolds, Chaucer shifts from addressing the purse/lady, to addressing the king. In the literature of *fin amor*, the lady often represents the feudal lord, to whom the knight is subjected. Here we see the lady both as the saviour,

---

[64] See chapter 10 for a discussion of Chaucer's use of coin imagery.

[65] 'Die' as a euphemism for 'climax' becomes common in early-modern texts; however, there may have been an earlier association between death and sexual pleasure. See, for instance, my discussion of Troilus's 'O quike deth, O swete harm so queynte' (Book I, 411), in Turner, *Chaucerian Conflict*, 85–90.

[66] For a discussion of the two texts and of the language and texts surrounding the Lancastrian takeover, see Paul Strohm, 'Saving the Appearances: Chaucer's "Purse" and the Fabrication of the Lancastrian Claim,' in *Hochon's Arrow: The Social Imagination of Fourteenth-Century Texts* (Princeton: Princeton University Press, 1992), 75–94.

morphing into the king in the final stanza, and as the mediator, the circulating coin, the woman who persuades her husband to kindness and moderation. We might be reminded of Chaucer's double identity throughout his life as feudal subject and mercantile actor, member of the king's household and salaried civil servant, client of Gaunt and part of the urban, money economy. Now, indeed, Chaucer lived at the intersection of church time and merchant's time, between abbey and shops, monarchy and parliament, palace and legal bureaucracy.[67]

We can draw interesting comparisons between one of Chaucer's early poems, the *ABC to the Virgin*, a translation of part of Deguileveile's *Pèlegrinage*, and his last poem. Indeed, although Speght's claim that the *ABC* was written for Blanche of Lancaster is unlikely to be correct, given its verse form (the use of the ten-syllable line suggests it was written a little later), it may nonetheless be a 'Lancastrian' poem.[68] Speght may well have seen the poem in a Lancastrian manuscript so, like the *Complaint*, it may be a poem addressed to someone connected with Gaunt. When the *Complaint* refers to the purse/lady as the narrator's 'Quene of comfort,' punning on the meaning of 'quene' as 'whore,' Chaucer is quoting his own *ABC to the Virgin*, in which he repeatedly refers to Mary herself as the 'queen of comfort' (77, 121). It is instructive to put these two poems side by side: the first focusing on the image of the Virgin Mary, the second written when Chaucer lived in the shadow of the Lady Chapel of Westminster Abbey. They frame Chaucer's adult life, a life dominated by his relationship with Henry's father, a poetic career driven by an interest in subjection, mediation, and identity, as both poems illustrate.

The early poem is a poem about learning to read, becoming an individual away from the maternal body (a haven, temple, castle, tent; 14, 145, 154, 41), a poem about the experience of fragmentation ('whider may I flee?' [124]).[69] The late poem is a poem about avoiding death ('or elles mot I dye'), a fallen, commercial poem in which wholeness and purity have

---

[67] Le Goff, 'Merchant's Time and Church's Time.'

[68] Speght's 1602 edition says that the *ABC* was made as a prayer for Blanche; if this is true then the poem would be very early (before 1368). It is more probably a production of the 1370s. See *Riverside Chaucer*, 1076.

[69] For a discussion of these spaces as offering 'womb-like and sacral shelter,' see Georgia Ronan Crampton, 'Chaucer's Singular Prayer,' *Medium Aevum* 59 (1990): 197.

no place. While the *ABC* opens with an image of plenitude in which all the world can flee for 'socour' to the 'al merciable queene' (1–2), by the last line, the onus is firmly on each individual, who can gain the kingdom of heaven, the 'palais' (183), only if they themselves are 'to merci *able*' (184; emphasis mine), that is, capable/deserving of gaining/seeking mercy.[70] The word 'merciable' has itself fragmented, and the poem reads as a meditation on the end of infant innocence. Learning to read (the *ABC*) becomes a metaphor for taking responsibility for interpreting one's own life. Like the Marian *ABC*, the *Complaint* is a poem about intercession—but not religious intercession. Unlike the *ABC*, the *Complaint* does not journey from plenitude to separation—it takes as its premise the fallenness of the world and the unreliability of language, flagged through its sexual puns. And while the *ABC* moves to a position that emphasizes the individual's active role in salvation (merci *able*), the *Complaint* ends on 'my supplicacion,' just as the *Retractions* emphasizes grace and the speaker's 'unkonnynge' (1082).[71] Chaucer stresses how much he needs his purse/ lady/Henry to listen and respond to his plea. His broader depiction of the world as a world of circulating money illustrates his understanding of the essentially social and connected nature of selfhood.

Furthermore, his financial plea is also a poetic statement. Chaucer has chosen, after all, to couch this request in the form of a poem. Or, to put it another way, he has chosen to write a poem that demands a response, an effect, a consequence that has to come from someone else outside the poem. For Chaucer, his texts lacked meaning until they were acted upon by others: the creation of meaning was a collaborative activity—and the petition poem literalizes this idea. Henry's hoped-for response to the poem—probably the confirmation or payment of Chaucer's grants— thus functions as a metaphor for interpretation. In setting up his poem as a petition, with an envoy and a request, Chaucer demonstrates to us yet again his interest in what poems do after they leave the author's control.[72]

---

[70] For further discussion, see Helen Phillips, 'Chaucer and Deguileville: The *ABC* in Context,' *Medium Aevum* 62 (1993): 1–19.

[71] Gower uses the same word—supplicacion—to describe his written request to Venus in the *Confessio Amantis*. See book 8, 2301, in *Complete Works: Vol. 3*.

[72] On the literature of petition, see J. A. Burrow, 'The Poet as Petitioner,' in *Essays on Medieval Literature* (Oxford: Oxford University Press, 1984), 162–77. See also Scase, *Literature and Complaint*.

If Chaucer's earlier poem tells us to take responsibility and interpret our own lives (be *able*), his latest reminds us that it is the job of readers, not writers, to interpret poems. He imagines poetry as a conversation that reaches across doorways and blurs boundaries between social estates and genders, genres and styles, interiors and exteriors, readers and writers. It is entirely appropriate that the last line of Chaucer's last poem is an injunction to the reader to think, actively, about what Chaucer has written: *'Have mynde.'* By throwing responsibility onto his reader, Chaucer emphasizes his own dependency on others, eschewing the role of teacher, patriarch, or authoritative Author.

In this context, I turn again to the end of the *Canterbury Tales*, and the juxtaposition between the end of the 'Parson's Tale' and the end of the *Retractions*. Strikingly, in the *Retractions*, Chaucer places himself in a subjected position in relation both to God and to his readers, thus imagining his earthly and divine audiences in parallel positions. While the Parson focuses on sin and penance, Chaucer's *Retractions* shifts the emphasis onto humility and grace.[73] There is an extraordinary and stark contrast between the two endings. While the last sentence of the 'Parson's Tale' tells us how we can actively 'purchace' heaven and concludes with an emphasis on 'death and mortificacion of synne' (1080), in the last (and longer) sentence of the *Retractions* (before the Latin prayer), Chaucer mentions grace three times, reminds us that Christ has already actively 'boghte us with the precious blood of his herte,' and concludes with the hope that he 'shulle be saved' (1088–92).[74] While there is no doctrinal difference between the two texts, and the *Retractions* also mentions penitence, confession, and satisfaction, the emphasis is very different, encapsulated in the contrast between purchasing and being bought. The 'Parson's Tale' encourages an active striving on the part of the individual. Chaucer, in the *Retractions*, also encourages the *reader* to be active, but, crucially, he places *himself* in a more passive, liminal position, both in terms of waiting for grace that God must actively 'sende' and 'graunte' (1090) and in terms of the author's relationship to the reader. He refuses to specify which of the *Canterbury Tales* might lead one to sin, for instance, demanding that the

[73] Cooper discusses this in *Structure*, 202, 205–7.
[74] For a discussion of the economic metaphor, see Ferster, 'Chaucer's Parson,' 149.

reader participate in the work of interpretation.[75] And he tells us of his own 'unkonnynge' (1082), placing this lacuna at the heart of his whole authorial project. He doesn't know, he's not sure, readers must decide for themselves. The role of God and the role of the reader overlap in surprising ways as Chaucer imagines the author under the control of both of these audiences. Throughout his work, not least in this paragraph of leavetaking, Chaucer resists closure by leaving the work of art on the threshold, not finished, not inherently meaningful, dependent on the reader or listener to decide what they want to do with the text. Unlike Dante, Chaucer actually *refuses* to have his vision. According to his poetics, that is simply not the role of the artist. Instead, he waits and looks both ways.

[75] Grudin similarly argues that Chaucer here 'evades structural closure in favor of a continuing process that involves listener as well as speaker, reader as well as writer.' Michaela Paasche Grudin, *Chaucer and the Politics of Discourse* (Columbia: University of South Carolina Press, 1996), 180.

Tomb

Writing . . . is the principle of death.

—*Jacques Derrida,* Of Grammatology

Chaucer became a monumental poet, enclosed in a monumental tomb, with monumental volumes of his *Complete Works* functioning as the bedrock of the English national canon (see plate 17). In his own poetry, he often writes about tombs: from Arcite's lament at his approaching burial 'Allone, withouten any compaignye' in his grave ('Knight's Tale,' 2779) to the boy singer silenced and 'enclosen' in 'a tombe of marbul stones cleere' ('Prioress's Tale,' 681–82) to Petrarch, 'deed and nayled in his cheste' ('Clerk's Prologue,' 29). To be dead and buried seals off the corpse: for an author, being entombed can both cut off their voice and elevate them to a more authoritative stance—traditionally, the only good author was a dead author.[1] Throughout his poetry, Chaucer refuses to allow the dead author to have precedence; the Clerk's comic insistence on Petrarch's death frees him to criticize Petrarch's poetic choices (53–55), for instance, and the *House of Fame* reveals the arbitrariness of what survives the test of time. In this poem, Chaucer comments directly on canon formation. The image of the names carved in ice, which melt if they happen to be in the sun, and

---

[1] Alastair Minnis, *Medieval Theory of Authorship: Scholastic Literary Attitudes in the Later Middle Ages*, 2nd ed. (Philadelphia: University of Pennsylvania Press, 1988), 12.

survive if they happen to be on the other side, is a striking reminder of how unfair posterity can be (1136–47).[2]

Chaucer was buried in a relatively insignificant way after his death in 1400, around the entrance to St Benet's Chapel in Westminster Abbey. In the fifteenth century, however, Chaucer became the Father of English Literature. Lancastrian poets lauded him (plate 18), and when print arrived in England in 1476, Caxton published his writings and eulogised him. At the same time, his tomb was adorned with a pillar and an epitaph. In the middle of the sixteenth century (1556), Chaucer's place of burial was moved, he was reburied in a new tomb, and a new epitaph and portrait decorated this monument.[3] This followed the elevation of his writings as new major editions of his 'Works' were printed (notably, Thynne's 1532 edition), marking Chaucer as an Author with a capital A.[4] At the same time, the Chaucer biography industry was also inaugurated with John Leland's Latin biographical sketch (ca. 1540) and then Thomas Speght's English biography of 1598.[5]

In subsequent centuries, the new tomb became a locus of anxiety. First, there were rumours that someone else (Dryden) was buried in his tomb. Then, people speculated that the tomb itself had originally been someone else's and had been recycled. Catholics and Protestants competed to claim him as a fellow traveller.[6] These anxieties all bear witness to concerns about authenticity. Was Chaucer's tomb what it was supposed to be? But the real question should be, does it represent what it is supposed to represent? Two impressive tombs at Ewelme remind us that tombs tell stories. The tomb of Chaucer's son, Thomas, does not acknowledge his father at all. Instead, it is decorated with the coats of arms of Thomas's more important relatives, by blood and by marriage.[7] It thus bears witness to an aspirational social identity. Next to his tomb is the spectacular monument to his daughter, Alice, duchess of Suffolk (plate 19). While the tomb

[2] See Isabel Davis and Catherine Nall (eds.), *Chaucer and Fame: Reputation and Reception* (Cambridge: D. S. Brewer, 2015) for essays about the afterlife of the *House of Fame* itself.

[3] See Pearsall, 'Chaucer's Tomb: The Politics of Reburial,' 51–73.

[4] Cooper, 'Poetic Fame,' 368.

[5] See Turner, 'Chaucer,' in *A Companion to Literary Biography*, 375–80, especially 376.

[6] Prendergast, *Chaucer's Dead Body*, especially 54–75.

[7] E. A. Greening Lamborn, 'The Arms on the Chaucer Tomb at Ewelme,' *Oxoniensia* 5 (1940): 78–93; for Geoffrey Chaucer's coat of arms, see 80.

represents Alice in peaceful, noble form, in beautiful alabaster, it is a 'transi' or cadaver tomb: underneath the idealized image is a carved depiction of a rotting corpse, as a reminder of the way of all flesh and of the reality beneath every tomb monument.[8] In death, Chaucer came to represent Englishness, patriarchy, authority. As founder member of Poets' Corner, he is by definition the cornerstone of English poetry, impressive, important, but decidedly of the past.[9] In life, Chaucer did not represent the canon; he certainly wasn't a figure of Englishness; nor was he monumental or grandiose. When I think of Chaucer, I think about the boy in his fashionable skintight leggings and paltok; the man riding across the snowy mountains to multicultural Navarre; the experimental poet who thought he'd try adding extra syllables to his poetic line; the father (of actual children, not a national literature) who wrote a scientific tract for his son and visited his daughter in her nunnery; the seventeen-year-old prisoner of war in France; the man in his room of books at Aldgate, moving towards the doorway where he could hear his neighbours' chatter; the traveller in Italy, devouring manuscripts in a Pavian library. He was many things.

Biographies tend to end with death, and perhaps a postscript about the next generations. For a writer—whose texts are very much living—ending with death and monuments is singularly inappropriate. Chaucer, indeed, has been much resurrected in ever more inventive ways in recent years. No longer entombed and monumental, he is an inspiration for diverse writers around the globe. Rather than thinking about Chaucer in his tomb, I'd like to think about him as the starting point for *Refugee Tales*, a collection published in 2016 that brings together contemporary politics, current writers, and Chaucer's *Canterbury Tales*.[10] I've written about many of Chaucer's places in this book—one of those places is the here and the now.

---

[8] For a discussion of transi tombs, see Binski, *Medieval Death*, 139–52.

[9] For Chaucer's afterlife, see Trigg, *Congenial Souls*.

[10] David Herd and Anna Pincus (eds.), *Refugee Tales as Told to Ali Smith, Patience Agbabi, Abdulrazak Gurnah, Inua Ellams, and Many Others* (Great Britain: Comma Press, 2016).

BIBLIOGRAPHY

Manuscript and Documentary Sources

Alnwick, Alnwick Castle, Collection of the Duke of Northumberland MS 455
Guildhall Record Office, Husting Roll 77, item 66
London, British Library MS Harley 1548
London, British Library MS Harley 3600
London British Library MS Harley 4016
Kew, The National Archives
    Court of Common Pleas, General Eyres and Court of King's Bench: Feet of Fines Files,
    Richard I–Henry VII, Kent: Feet of Fines for 40 Edw III: 1551–75
        CP 25/1/106/180
    Court of King's Bench: Plea and Crown Sides: Coram Rege Rolls
        KB 27/484
    Duchy of Lancaster: Various Accounts
        DL 28/3/1
    Exchequer: King's Remembrancer; Accounts Various
        E 101/43/22
        E 101/93/12
    Exchequer: King's Remembrancer and Lord Treasurer's Remembrancer: Sheriffs'
    Accounts, Petitions, etc.
        E 199/25/72
    Exchequer: King's Remembrancer: Extents and Inquisitions
        E 143/18/3
    Exchequer: King's Remembrancer; Particulars of Customs' Accounts
        E 122/71/4
        E 122/71/9
    Exchequer: Treasury of Receipt: Diplomatic Documents
        E 30/264
        E 30/273
    Exchequer of Receipt: Issue Rolls and Registers
        E 403/564
    Justices in Eyre, of Assize, of Oyer and Terminer, and of the Peace, etc: Rolls and Files
        JUST 1/1517
    Prerogative Court of Canterbury and Related Probate Jurisdictions: Will Registers
        PROB 11/1/11
    Special Collections: Ancient Petitions
        SC 8/250/12495

Primary Sources

Agbabi, Patience. *Telling Tales.* Edinburgh: Canongate, 2014.

Alan of Lille. *Anticlaudianus, or, The Good and Perfect Man.* Translated by J. J. Sheridan. Toronto: Toronto University Press, 1973.

Albert of Saxony. *Quaestiones et decisiones physicales insignium virorum.* Paris: Iodoci Badii & Conradi Resch, 1518.

Alighieri, Dante. 'Letter to the Emperor Henry VII.' In *Dante Alighieri: Four Political Letters*, edited by Claire E. Honess, 69–81. London: Modern Humanities Research Association, 2007.

———. *The 'De monarchia' of Dante Alighieri.* Edited and translated by Aurelia Henry. Boston: Houghton Mifflin, 1904.

———. *The Divine Comedy, Book 1: Inferno.* Translated by John D. Sinclair. New York: Oxford University Press, 1961.

———. *The Divine Comedy, Book 2: Purgatorio.* Translated by John D. Sinclair. New York: Oxford University Press, 1961.

———. *The Divine Comedy, Book 3: Paradiso.* Translated by John D. Sinclair. New York: Oxford University Press, 1961.

Altmann, Barbara K., and R. Barton Palmer, eds. and trans. *An Anthology of Medieval Love Debate Poetry.* Gainesville: University Press of Florida, 2010.

Armitage-Smith, Sydney, ed. *John of Gaunt's Register, 1372–1376.* Camden Third Series. Vols. 20–21. London: Offices of the Society, 1911.

Aristotle. *Physics.* In *The Complete Works of Aristotle*, edited by Jonathan Barnes. 2 vols. Princeton: Princeton University Press, 1984.

Augustine. *The Confessions.* Translated by R. S. Pinecoffin. London: Penguin Books, 1961.

Austin, Thomas, ed. *Two Fifteenth Century Cookery Books.* Early English Text Society 91. London: Oxford University Press, 1888; reprinted in 1964.

Baldo degli Ubaldi. *Commentariolum super pace Constantiae.* In *Baldi Perusini in vsus feudorum commentaria doctissima.* Lyons: Pidié, 1552.

———. *Consiliorum Sive Responsorum.* Venice: H. Polum, 1575.

Bartholomaeus Anglicus. *On the Properties of Things: John Trevisa's Translation of Bartholomaeus Anglicus, 'De Proprietatibus Rerum.'* Edited by M. C. Seymour. Oxford: Clarendon Press, 1975.

Bede. *Ecclesiastical History of the English People.* Edited and translated by Bertram Colgrave and R.A.B. Mynors. Oxford: Clarendon Press, 1969.

Berry, H. F., ed. *Statutes and Ordinances, and Acts of the Parliament of Ireland: King John to Henry V.* Dublin: HMSO, 1907.

Boccaccio, Giovanni. *Amorosa Visione: Bilingual Edition.* Translated by Robert Hollander, Timothy Hampton, and Margherita Frankel. Introduction by Vittore Branca. Hanover: University Press of New England, 1986.

———. *The Decameron.* Translated by Guido Waldman. Oxford: Oxford University Press, 1993.

Boethius. *Boethius: De Consolatione Philosophiae.* Bibliotheca Polyglotta Graeca et Latina, University of Oslo. https://www2.hf.uio.no/polyglotta/index.php?page=volume&vid=216.

Bond, Edward. 'New Facts in the Life of Geoffrey Chaucer.' In *Life-Records of Chaucer: Volume III*, edited by Edward A. Bond and Walford D. Selby, 97–113. London: N. Trübner, 1886.

Bond, Edward, and Walford D. Selby, ed. *Life-Records of Chaucer: Volume III*. London: N. Trübner, 1886.

Bowers, John M., ed. *The Canterbury Tales: Fifteenth Century Continuations and Additions*. Kalamazoo, MI: TEAMS Middle English Texts, 1992.

Brutails, Jean-Auguste, ed. *Documents des Archives de la Chambre des Comptes de Navarre*. Paris: É. Bouillon, 1890.

Calendar of Close Rolls Preserved in the Public Record Office: Edward II. 4 vols. London: HMSO, 1891–1998.

Calendar of Close Rolls Preserved in the Public Record Office: Edward III. 14 vols. London: HMSO, 1896–1913.

Calendar of Close Rolls Preserved in the Public Record Office: Richard II. 6 vols. London: HMSO, 1914–27.

Calendar of Fine Rolls Preserved in the Public Record Office. 19 vols. London: HMSO, 1911–39.

Calendar of the Patent Rolls Preserved in the Public Record Office: Henry IV. 4 vols. London: HMSO, 1903–9.

Calendar of the Patent Rolls Preserved in the Public Record Office: Edward II. 5 vols. London: HMSO, 1894.

Calendar of the Patent Rolls Preserved in the Public Records Office: Edward III. 16 vols. London: Eyre and Spottiswoode, 1891–1916.

Calendar of the Patent Rolls Preserved in the Public Record Office: Richard II. 6 vols. London: HMSO, 1895–1909.

Carte, Thomas, ed. *Catalogue des Rolles Gascons, Normans et François, conservés dans les Archives de la Tour de Londres*. 2 vols. Paris: Jacques Barois, 1743.

Castro, José Ramón, ed. *Catálogo del Archivo General de Navarra: Seccion de Comptos; Documentos: Vol. VI, Años 1366–1367*. Pamplona: Editorial Aramburu, 1954.

Chaucer, Geoffrey. *The Book of Troilus and Criseyde*. Edited by Robert Kilburn Root. Princeton: Princeton University Press, 1959.

———. *The Riverside Chaucer*. Edited by Larry Dean Benson. 3rd edition. Oxford: Oxford University Press, 2008.

———. *The Romaunt of the Rose*. Edited by Charles Dahlberg. Norman: University of Oklahoma Press, 1999.

Christine de Pisan. *The Vision of Christine de Pizan*. Translated by Glenda McLeod and Charity Cannon Willard. Cambridge: D. S. Brewer, 2005.

Coleman, William. 'The Knight's Tale.' In *Sources and Analogues of the Canterbury Tales*, edited by Robert M. Correale and Mary Hamel, 2:86–247. Cambridge: D. S. Brewer, 2005.

Collinson, John. *The History and Antiquities of the County of Somerset, Collected from Authentick Records, Volume III*. Bath: R. Cruttwell, 1791.

Colvin, H. M., R. Allen Brown, and A. J. Taylor, eds. *The History of the King's Works: Part I: The Middle Ages*. 2 vols. London: HMSO, 1963.

Cooper, Helen. 'The Frame.' In *Sources and Analogues of the 'Canterbury Tales,'* edited by Robert M. Correale and Mary Hamel, 1:1–22. Cambridge: D. S. Brewer, 2002.

Correale, Robert M., and Mary Hamel, eds. *Sources and Analogues of 'The Canterbury Tales.'* 2 vols. Chaucer Studies 28. Cambridge: D. S. Brewer, 2002 and 2005.

Cronin, H. S., ed. *Roger Dymock: Liber contra XII errores et hereses Lollardorum*. London: Kegan Paul, Trench, Trübner, 1922.

Crow, Martin, and Clair Olson, eds. *Chaucer Life-Records*. Oxford: Clarendon Press, 1966.

Dean, James M., ed. *Medieval English Political Writings*. Kalamazoo, MI: TEAMS Middle English Texts, 1996.

De Certeau, Michel. *The Practice of Everyday Life*. Translated by Steven Rendall. Berkeley: University of California Press, 1988.

Derrida, Jacques. *Of Grammatology*. Translated by Gayatri Chakravorty Spivak. Baltimore: Johns Hopkins University Press, 1976.

Deschamps, Eustache. *Eustache Deschamps: Selected Poems*. Edited by Ian S. Laurie and Deborah M. Sinnreich-Levi. Translated by David Curzon and Jeffrey Fiskin. New York: Routledge, 2003.

Devillers, Léopold, ed. *Cartulaire des Comtes de Hainaut, de l'avènement de Guillaume II à la mort de Jacqueline de Bavière*. Vol. 1 of 6. Brussels: F. Hayez, 1881.

Devon, Frederick, ed. *Issues of the Exchequer: Being a Collection of Payments Made out of His Majesty's Revenue, from King Henry III to King Henry IV Inclusive*. London: John Murray, 1837.

Dillon, A. H., and W. H. St. John Hope. 'Inventory of the Goods and Chattels Belonging to Thomas, Duke of Gloucester, and Seized in His Castle at Pleshy, Co. Essex, 21 Richard II (1397).' *Archaeological Journal* 54, no. 1 (1897): 275–308.

Dobson, R. B. *The Peasants' Revolt of 1381*. London: Macmillan, 1970.

Duff, J. Wight, and Arnold M. Duff, trans. *Minor Latin Poets*. Vol. 2. Loeb Classical Library 434. Cambridge, MA: Harvard University Press, 2014.

Dugdale, William. 'Charthe longynge to the Office of the Celeresse of the Monasterye of Barkynge.' In *Monasticon Anglicanum*. Vol. 1. London: Longman, 1817–30.

———. *Monasticon Anglicanum*. 6 vols. London: Longman, 1817–30.

Dunbar, William. 'In Honour of the City of London.' In *The Oxford Book of English Verse: 1250–1900*, edited by Arthur Quiller-Couch, 26–27. Oxford: Clarendon Press, 1919.

Eliot, T. S. *The Waste Land*. New York: Horace Liveright, 1922.

Favent, Thomas. *Historia siue narracio de modo et forma mirabilis parliamenti apud Westmonasterium anno domini millesimo CCCLXXXVJ: Regni vero regis Ricardi Secundi post conquestum anno decimo, per Thomas Fauent clericum indictata*. In *Camden Miscellany 14*, edited by May McKisack. London: Offices of the Society, 1926.

Forni, Kathleen, ed. *The Chaucerian Apocrypha: A Selection*. Kalamazoo, MI: TEAMS Middle English Texts, 2005.

Froissart, Jean. *Chronicles*. Translated by Geoffrey Brereton. London: Penguin, 1968.

———. *Le Joli Buisson de Jonece*. Edited by Anthime Fourrier. Genève: Droz, 1975.

———. *Oeuvres de Froissart: Chroniques*. Edited by Joseph Kervyn de Lettenhove. 25 vols. Brussels: V. Devaux, 1867.

———. *La Prison Amoureuse*. Edited by Laurence De Looze. Garland Library of Medieval Literature 96A. New York: Garland, 1994.

Furnivall, F. J., ed. *The Fifty Earliest English Wills in the Court of Probate, London, A.D. 1387–1439*. Early English Text Society 78. London: Oxford University Press, 1882.

Furnivall, F. J., and Edith Rickert, eds. *The Babees' Book: Medieval Manners for the Young*. London: Chatto & Windus, 1923.

Galbraith, V. H., ed. *The Anonimalle Chronicle: 1333 to 1381*. Manchester: Manchester University Press, 1970.

Given-Wilson, Chris, ed. *The Chronicle of Adam Usk*. Oxford Medieval Texts. Oxford: Clarendon Press, 1997.

———, ed. *Chronicles of the Revolution: 1397–1400*. Manchester: Manchester University Press, 1993.

———, ed. 'The Epiphany Rising and the Death of the King according to the *Traison et Mort*.' In *Chronicles of the Revolution: 1397–1400*, 230–34. Manchester: Manchester University Press, 1993.

———, ed. *Parliament Rolls of Medieval England, 1275–1504*. 16 vols. Woodbridge: Boydell & Brewer, 2005.

Gower, John. *The Complete Works of John Gower: Vol. 3, The English Works*. Edited by G. C. Macaulay. Oxford: Clarendon Press, 1902.

———. *The Complete Works of John Gower: Vol. 4, The Latin Works*. Edited by G. C. Macaulay. Oxford: Clarendon Press, 1902.

———. *The Major Latin Works of John Gower: The Voice of One Crying, and the Tripartite Chronicle*. Translated by Eric W. Stockton. Seattle: University of Washington Press, 1962.

Gray, Thomas. *Scalacronica: The Reigns of Edward I, Edward II, and Edward III, as Recorded by Sir Thomas Gray and Now Translated by Sir Herbert Maxwell*. Glasgow: Glasgow University Press, 1907.

Hanna, Ralph, and Traugott Lawler, eds. *Jankyn's Book of Wikked Wyves: Volume 1, The Primary Texts*. Athens: University of Georgia Press, Chaucer Library, 1997.

———. '"Romulus," Fable 44: The Man and the Lion.' In *Sources and Analogues*, edited by Robert M. Correale and Mary Hamel, 2:382–83. Cambridge: D. S. Brewer, 2005.

Hart, W. H., ed. *Historia et cartularium monasterii Sancti Petri Gloucestriæ*. 3 vols. Rerum Britannicarum medii aevi scriptores, no. 33. London: Longman, Green, Longman, Roberts, and Green, 1863.

Harvey, Barbara, ed. *The Obedientiaries of Westminster Abbey and Their Financial Records, c. 1275 to 1540*. Westminster Abbey Record Series 3. Woodbridge: Boydell Press, 2002.

Haydon, Frank Scott. *Eulogium historiarum sive temporis*. 3 vols. Rolls Series 9. London: Longman, Brown, Green, Longmans and Roberts, 1858.

Hector, L. C., and Barbara F. Harvey, eds. and trans. *The Westminster Chronicle, 1381–1394*. Oxford: Clarendon Press, 1982.

Henry of Lancaster. *Le livre de seyntz medicines: The unpublished devotional treatise of Henry of Lancaster*. Edited by E. J. Arnould. Anglo-Norman Texts 2. Oxford: Anglo-Norman Text Society, Blackwell, 1940.

———. *The Book of Holy Medicines (Le Livre de Seyntz Medicines)*. Edited by Catherine Batt. Tempe, Arizona: Arizona Centre for Medieval and Renaissance Studies, 2014.

Herd, David, and Anna Pincus, eds. *Refugee Tales as Told to Ali Smith, Patience Agbabi, Abdulrazak Gurnah, Inua Ellams, and Many Others*. Great Britain: Comma Press, 2016.

Higden, Ranulph. *Polychronicon Ranulphi Higden Monachi Cestrensis*. Edited by Churchill Babington and J. R. Lumby. 9 vols. Rolls Series 41. London: Longman, Green, Longman, Roberts, and Green, 1865–86.

Hoccleve, Thomas. 'La Male Regle de Thomas Hoccleue.' In *'My Compleinte' and Other Poems*. Edited by Roger Ellis, 64–78. Exeter: University of Exeter Press, 2001.

Hodgett, G.A.J., ed. *The Cartulary of Holy Trinity Aldgate*. Leicester: London Record Society, 1971.

Jefferson, Lisa, ed. *Wardens' Accounts and Court Minute Books of the Goldsmiths' Mistery of London, 1334–1446*. Woodbridge: Boydell, 2003.

John of Reading. *Chronica Johannis de Reading et Anonymi Cantuariensis, 1346–1367*. Edited by James Tait. Publications of the University of Manchester 88. Manchester: University Press, 1914.

Kirby, J. L., ed. *Calendar of Inquisitions Post Mortem: Volume XIX, 7–14 Henry IV (1405–1413)*. London: HMSO, 1992.

Knighton, Henry. *Knighton's Chronicle*. Edited by G. H. Martin. Oxford: Clarendon Press, 1995.

Kristol, Andres Max, ed. *Manières de langage (1396, 1399, 1415)*. Anglo-Norman Texts 53. London: Anglo-Norman Text Society, 1995.

Kurath, Hans, Sherman M. Kuhn, and Robert E. Lewis, eds. *Middle English Dictionary*. Ann Arbor: University of Michigan Press, 1952–2001. https://quod.lib.umich.edu/m/med/.

Lakoff, George, and Mark Johnson. *Metaphors We Live By*. Chicago: University of Chicago Press, 1980.

Langland, William. *Piers Plowman: The B Version; Will's Visions of Piers Plowman, Do-Well, Do-Better and Do-Best*. Edited by George Kane and E. Talbot Donaldson. London: Athlone Press, 1975.

Lewis, E. A., ed. 'Carmarthen Castle: A Collection of Historical Documents Relating to Carmarthen Castle from the Earliest Times to the Close of the Reign of Henry VIII.' *West Wales Historical Records* 4 (1914): 4–5.

Lodge, Eleanor Constance, and Robert Somerville, eds. *John of Gaunt's Register, 1379–1383*. Camden Third Series. Vols. 56–57. London: Offices of the Society, 1937.

López de Ayala, Pedro. *Cronicas de los Reyes de Castilla: Don Pedro, Don Enrique II, Don Juan I, Don Enrique III*. 2 vols. Madrid: Antonio de Sancha, 1779.

Lorris, Guillaume de, and Jean de Meun. *Le Roman de la Rose*. Translated by Armand Strubel. Paris: Librarie General Française, 1992.

———. *The Romance of the Rose*. Translated by Charles Dahlberg. 3rd edition. Princeton: Princeton University Press, 1995.

Lotario dei Segni (Pope Innocent III). *De Miseria Condicionis Humane*. Edited by Robert E. Lewis. Athens: University of Georgia Press, Chaucer Library, 1978.

Machaut, Guillaume de. *The Judgement of the King of Navarre*. Edited and translated by R. Barton Palmer. Garland Library of Medieval Literature 45, Series A. New York: Garland, 1988.

Macdonald, Helen. *H is for Hawk*. London: Vintage, 2014.

Macrobius. *Commentary on the Dream of Scipio*. Translated by William Harris Stahl. New York: Columbia University Press, 1952.

Maidstone, Richard. *Concordia (The Reconciliation of Richard II with London)*. Edited by David R. Carlson. Translated by A. G. Rigg. Kalamazoo, MI: TEAMS Middle English Texts, 2003.

Markham, Clements R., trans. *Narrative of the Embassy of Ruy González de Clavijo to the Court of Timour at Samarcand, AD 1403–6*. London: Hakluyt Society, 1859.

Menner, Robert J., ed. *Purity: A Middle English Poem*. New Haven: Yale University Press, 1920.

Myers, A. R., ed. *English Historical Documents*. London: Eyre and Spottiswoode, 1969.

Nicolas, N. H., ed. *Proceedings and Ordinances of the Privy Council of England*. 7 vols. London: Eyre and Spottiswoode, 1834–37.

O'Connor, Stephen, ed. *Calendar of the Cartularies of John Pyel and Adam Fraunceys: Mayors and Merchants of London, 14th Century*. Camden Fifth Series 2. Cambridge: Cambridge University Press, 1995.

Oresme, Nicole. *Le Livre du Ciel et du Monde*. Edited by Albert Douglas Menut and Alexander Denomy. Madison: University of Wisconsin Press, 1968.

Pearce, E. H. *The Monks of Westminster: Being a Register of the Brethren of the Convent from the Time of the Confessor to the Dissolution*. Notes and Documents Relating to Westminster Abbey 5. Cambridge: Cambridge University Press, 1916.

Pearsall, Derek, ed. 'The Floure and the Leafe.' In *The Floure and the Leafe, The Assembly of Ladies, The Isle of Ladies*. Kalamazoo, MI: TEAMS Middle English Texts, 1990.

Petrarch, Francesco. 'Invective against a Detractor of Italy.' In *Francesco Petrarch: Invectives*, edited and translated by David Marsh, 365–475. Cambridge, MA: Harvard University Press, 2003.

———. *Prose*. Edited by Guido Martellotti. Letteratura italiana. Storia e testi 7. Milan: Ricciardi, 1955.

Prophet, John. 'A Journal of the Clerk of the Council during the Fifteenth and Sixteenth Years of Richard II.' In *The King's Council in England during the Middle Ages*, edited by J. F. Baldwin, 489–505. Oxford: Clarendon Press, 1913.

Raine, James, and John William Clay, eds. *Testamenta Eboracensia, or, Wills Registered at York*. Vol. 1. London: J. B. Nichols and Son, 1836–1902.

Register of Edward the Black Prince, Preserved in the Public Record Office: Part IV, 1351–1365. London: HMSO, 1933.

Riley, H. T., ed. *Johannis de Trokelowe et Henrici de Blaneforde Monachorum S. Albani Necnon Quorundam Anonymorum, Chronica et Annales, Regnantibus Henrico Tertio, Edwardo Primo, Edwardo Secundo, Ricardo Secundo et Henrico Quarto*. London: Longmans, 1866.

———, ed. *Memorials of London and London Life in the XIIIth, XIVth, and XVth Centuries*. London: Longmans, Green, 1868.

Root, Robert Kilburn, ed. *The Book of Troilus and Criseyde*. Princeton: Princeton University Press, 1959.

Rye, Walter. 'Chaucer's Grandfather, Robert Le Chaucer.' In *Life-Records of Chaucer: Volume III*, edited by Edward A. Bond and Walford D. Selby, 125–31. London: N. Trübner, 1875.

Rymer, Thomas. *Foedera*. 20 vols. London, 1704–35.

Scattergood, V. J., ed. *Works of Sir John Clanvowe*. Cambridge: D. S. Brewer, 1975.

Sharpe, Reginald R., ed. *Calendar of Letter-Books of the City of London: Letter-Book F, 1337–1352*. London: John Edward Francis, 1904.

———, ed. *Calendar of Letter-Books of the City of London: Letter-Book H*. London: John Edward Francis, 1907.

———, ed. *Calendar of Wills Proved and Enrolled in the Court of Husting, London, A.D. 1258–A.D. 1688*. 2 vols. London: John C. Francis, 1890.

Skelton, John. *The Complete English Works of John Skelton*. Edited by John Scattergood. Revised edition. Liverpool: Liverpool University Press, 2015.

Stahl, William Harris, Richard Johnson, and E. L. Burge, eds. *Martianus Capella and the Seven Liberal Arts*. 2 vols. New York: Columbia University Press, 1971.

Stow, G. B., ed. *Historia Vitae et Regni Ricardi Secundi*. Philadelphia: University of Pennsylvania Press, 1977.

Stow, John. *The Annales of England: Faithfully collected out of the most autenticall authors, records, and other monuments of antiquitie, lately collected, since encreased, and continued, from the first habitation vntill this present yeare 1605. By Iohn Stow citizen of London*. London: Peter Short, Felix Kingston, and George Eld, 1605.

———. 'Vintrie Warde.' In *A Survey of London Reprinted from the Text of 1603*, edited by C. L. Kingsford, 238–50. Oxford: Clarendon Press, 1908. http://www.british-history.ac.uk/no-series/survey-of-london-stow/1603/pp238-250.

Summerson, H., et al., trans. 'The 1215 Magna Carta: Clause 33.' The Magna Carta Project. http://magnacarta.cmp.uea.ac.uk/read/magna_carta_1215/Clause_33.

Thomas, A. H., ed. *Calendar of Plea and Memoranda Rolls Preserved among the Archives of the Corporation of the City of London at the Guild-Hall*. 6 vols. Cambridge: University Press, 1926.

———. *Calendar of Plea and Memoranda Rolls, 1323–1364, Rolls A1a–A9*. Cambridge: University Press, 1926.

———. *Calendar of Plea and Memoranda Rolls, 1381–1412*, Roll A29. Cambridge: University Press, 1926.

Trigg, Stephanie, ed. *Wynnere and Wastoure*. Early English Text Society 297. London: Oxford University Press, 1990.

Two Cartularies of the Augustinian Priory of Bruton and the Cluniac Priory of Montacute. London: Harrison & Sons, 1894.

Usk, Thomas. *The Appeal of Thomas Usk against John Northampton*. Appendix 2 in *The Testament of Love*, ed. R. Allen Shoaf. Kalamazoo, MI: TEAMS Middle English Texts, 1998.

Walsingham, Thomas. *The Chronica Maiora of Thomas Walsingham, 1376–1422*. Translated by David Preest. Woodbridge: Boydell Press, 2003.

———. *Historia Anglicana*. 2 vols. London: Longman, 1863–64.

Wilkins, David. *Concilia Magnae Britanniae et Hiberniae*. 4 vols. London, 1737.

Wimsatt, James I., ed. *Chaucer and the Poems of 'Ch.'* Revised edition. Kalamazoo, MI: TEAMS Middle English Texts, 2009.

Wright, Thomas, ed. *Political Songs and Poems Relating to English History*. 2 vols. London: Longman, 1859–61.

Wycliffe, John. *Selected English Works of John Wyclif*. Edited by Thomas Arnold. Vol. 1. Oxford: Clarendon Press, 1869.

Yeats, W. B. *Collected Poems*. London: Macmillan, 2016.

Secondary Sources

Abulafia, David. 'Genoa and the Security of the Seas: The Mission of Babilano Lomellino in 1350.' *Papers of the British School at Rome* 45 (1977): 272–79.

Abu-Lughod, Janet L. *Before European Hegemony: The World System, A.D. 1250–1350*. New York: Oxford University Press, 1991.

Aers, David. *Chaucer, Langland, and the Creative Imagination*. London: Routledge and Kegan Paul, 1980.

———. 'Class, Gender, Medieval Criticism and *Piers Plowman*.' In *Class and Gender in Early English Literature: Intersections*, edited by Britton Harwood and Gillian Overing, 59–75. Bloomington: Indiana University Press, 1994.

———. *Community, Gender and Individual Identity: English Writing, 1360–1430*. London: Routledge, 1988.

Akbari, Suzanne Conklin. 'Orientation and Nation in Chaucer's *Canterbury Tales*.' In *Chaucer's Cultural Geography*, edited by Kathryn L. Lynch, 102–34. New York: Routledge, 2002.

——. *Seeing Through the Veil: Optical Theory and Medieval Allegory.* Toronto: University of Toronto Press, 2004.

Akehurst, F.R.P., and Stephanie Cain Van D'Elden, eds. *The Stranger in Medieval Society.* Minneapolis: University of Minnesota Press, 1997.

Allen, Martin. *Mints and Money in Medieval England.* Cambridge: Cambridge University Press, 2012.

Ambühl, Rémy. *Prisoners of War in the Hundred Years War: Ransom Culture in the Late Middle Ages.* Cambridge: Cambridge University Press, 2013.

Anderson, Benedict. *Imagined Communities: Reflections on the Origin and Spread of Nationalism.* London: Verso, 1996.

Archer, Rowena E. 'Mowbray, John (I).' In *Oxford Dictionary of National Biography.* Online edition. Oxford: Oxford University Press, 2008. https://doi.org/10.1093/ref:odnb/19450.

——. 'Mowbray, John (II).' In *Oxford Dictionary of National Biography.* Online edition. Oxford: Oxford University Press, 2008. https://doi.org/10.1093/ref:odnb/19451.

——. 'Mowbray, John (III).' In *Oxford Dictionary of National Biography.* Online edition. Oxford: Oxford University Press, 2008. https://doi.org/10.1093/ref:odnb/19452.

Armitage-Smith, Sydney. *John of Gaunt: King of Castile and Leon, Duke of Aquitaine and Lancaster, Earl of Derby, Lincoln and Leicester, Seneschal of England.* London: Constable, 1964.

Arnovick, Leslie K. *Written Reliquaries: The Resonance of Orality in Medieval English Texts.* Amsterdam: John Benjamins, 2006.

Astell, Ann. *The Song of Songs in the Middle Ages.* Ithaca: Cornell University Press, 1995.

Auerbach, Erich. *Mimesis: The Representation of Reality in Western Literature.* Translated by Willard Trask. Princeton: Princeton University Press, 2003.

Axworthy, Roger L. 'Lyons, Richard.' In *Oxford Dictionary of National Biography.* Online edition. Oxford: Oxford University Press, 2008. https://doi.org/10.1093/ref:odnb/52191.

Bachelard, Gaston. *The Poetics of Space.* Translated by Maria Jolas. Boston: Beacon Press, 1994.

Bahr, Arthur W. 'The Rhetorical Construction of Narrator and Narrative in Chaucer's the *Book of the Duchess.' Chaucer Review* 35, no. 1 (2000): 43–59.

Baker, Robert L. 'The Establishment of the English Wool Staple in 1313.' *Speculum* 31, no. 3 (1956): 444–53.

Bakhtin, Mikhail M. *The Dialogic Imagination: Four Essays.* Edited by Michael Holquist. Translated by Caryl Emerson and Michael Holquist. Austin: University of Texas Press, 1981.

Baldwin, F. E. *Sumptuary Legislation and Personal Regulation in England.* Baltimore: Johns Hopkins University Press, 1926.

Baldwin, Ralph. *The Unity of the 'Canterbury Tales.'* Copenhagen: Rosenkilde and Bassen, 1955.

Bale, Anthony. '"A maner latyn corrupt": Chaucer and the Absent Religions.' In *Chaucer and Religion*, edited by Helen Phillips, 52–64. Woodbridge: Boydell & Brewer, 2010.

Barber, Richard. *The Black Prince.* Stroud: Sutton, 2003.

Barr, Helen. *Socioliterary Practice in Late Medieval England.* Oxford: Oxford University Press, 2001.

——. *Transporting Chaucer.* Manchester: Manchester University Press, 2015.

Barrett, Robert W., Jr. 'Chester and Cheshire.' In *Europe: A Literary History.* Vol. 1, edited by David Wallace, 240–55. Oxford: Oxford University Press, 2016.

Barron, Caroline M. 'The Burning of the Jubilee Book.' Guildhall Historical Association, 17 June 2002. https://guildhallhistoricalassociation.org.uk/papers/papers-2000-to-2009/.

———. 'Centres of Conspicuous Consumption: The Aristocratic Town House in London, 1200–1550.' *London Journal* 20, no. 1 (1995): 1–16.

———. 'Chaucer the Poet and Chaucer the Pilgrim.' In *Historians on Chaucer: The 'General Prologue' to the 'Canterbury Tales,'* edited by S. H. Rigby and A. J. Minnis, 24–41. Oxford: Oxford University Press, 2014.

———. 'The "Golden Age" of Women in Medieval London.' In *Medieval Women in Southern England*, edited by A. K. Bate and Malcolm Barber, 35–58. Reading Medieval Studies 15. Reading: Graduate Centre for Medieval Studies, University of Reading, 1989.

———. *London in the Later Middle Ages: Government and People, 1200–1500*. Oxford: Oxford University Press, 2004.

———. 'The Quarrel of Richard II with London, 1392–1397.' In *The Reign of Richard II: Essays in Honour of May McKisack*, edited by Caroline M. Barron and F.R.H. Du Boulay, 173–201. London: Athlone Press, 1971.

Barron, Caroline M., and Anne F. Sutton, eds. *Medieval London Widows, 1300–1500*. London: Hambledon Press, 1994.

Barsella, Susanna. 'A Humanistic Approach to Religious Solitude.' In *Petrarch: A Critical Guide to the Complete Works*, edited by Victoria Kirkham and Armando Maggi, 197–208. Chicago: University of Chicago Press, 2009.

Bartlett, Robert. *England under the Norman and Angevin Kings, 1075–1225*. Oxford: Oxford University Press, 2000.

Baswell, Christopher. 'Aeneas in 1381.' *New Medieval Literatures* 5 (2002): 7–58.

Battles, Dominique. *The Medieval Tradition of Thebes: History and Narrative in the Old French 'Roman de Thèbes,' Boccaccio, Chaucer, and Lydgate*. New York: Routledge, 2004.

Baudrillard, Jean. *Symbolic Exchange and Death*. Translated by Iain Hamilton Grant. London: Sage, 1993.

Baugh, Albert Croll. 'Kirk's Life Records of Thomas Chaucer.' *PMLA* 47, no. 2 (1932): 461–515.

Bauman, Richard. *Verbal Art as Performance*. Long Grove: Waveland Press, 1977.

Baxandall, Michael. *Giotto and the Orators: Humanist Observers of Painting in Italy and the Discovery of Pictorial Composition, 1350–1450*. Oxford: Clarendon Press, 1971.

———. *Painting and Experience in Fifteenth-Century Italy*. Oxford: Clarendon Press, 1972.

Bellamy, J. G. 'Appeal and Impeachment in the Good Parliament.' *Bulletin of the Institute of Historical Research* 39 (1966): 35–46.

Bennett, Michael. 'Edward III's Entail and the Succession to the Crown, 1376–1471.' *English Historical Review* 113, no. 452 (1998): 580–609.

Bennett, Philip E. 'The Mirage of Fiction: Narration, Narrator, and Narratee in Froissart's Lyrico-Narrative *Dits*.' *Modern Language Review* 86, no. 2 (1991): 285–97.

Benson, Robert L., Giles Constable, and Carol Dana Lanham, eds. *Renaissance and Renewal in the Twelfth Century*. Toronto: University of Toronto Press, 1999.

Berry, Craig A. 'Flying Sources: Classical Authority in Chaucer's *Squire's Tale*.' *English Literary History* 68, no. 2 (2001): 287–313.

Bestul, Thomas H. 'Did Chaucer Live at 177 Upper Thames Street? The *Chaucer Life-Records* and the Site of Chaucer's London Home.' *Chaucer Review* 43, no. 1 (2008): 1–15.

Bevington, David. 'The Obtuse Narrator in Chaucer's *House of Fame*.' *Speculum* 36, no. 2 (1961): 288–98.

Biancalana, Joseph. *The Fee Tail and the Common Recovery in Medieval England: 1176–1502.* Cambridge: Cambridge University Press, 2004.

Biddick, Kathleen. 'Becoming Collection: The Spatial Afterlife of Medieval Universal Histories.' In *Medieval Practices of Space*, edited by Barbara A. Hanawalt and Michal Kobialka, 223–41. Minneapolis: University of Minnesota Press, 2000.

Biggs, Douglas. 'The Appellant and the Clerk: The Assault on Richard II's Friends in Government, 1387–9.' In *The Reign of Richard II*, edited by Gwilym Dodd, 57–70. Stroud: Tempus, 2000.

———. 'Patronage, Preference, and Survival: The Life of Lady Margaret Sarnesfield, c. 1381–c.1444.' In *The Ties that Bind: Essays in Medieval British History in Honor of Barbara Hanawalt*, edited by Linda Mitchell, Katherine French, and Douglas Biggs, 143–58. Burlington: Ashgate, 2013.

Binski, Paul. *Medieval Death: Ritual and Representation.* London: British Museum Press, 1996.

———. *Westminster Abbey and the Plantagenets: Kingship and the Representation of Power, 1200–1400.* New Haven: Yale University Press, 1995.

Birch, Julian, and Peter Ryder. 'Hatfield Manor House, South Yorkshire.' *Yorkshire Archaeological Journal* 60 (1988): 65–104.

Bird, Ruth. *The Turbulent London of Richard II.* London: Longmans, Green, 1949.

Black, Antony. *Political Thought in Europe, 1250–1450.* Cambridge: Cambridge University Press, 1992.

Black, Jane. *Absolutism in Renaissance Milan: Plenitude of Power under the Visconti and the Sforza, 1329–1535.* Oxford: Oxford University Press, 2009.

Blamires, Alcuin. *Chaucer, Ethics and Gender.* Oxford: Oxford University Press, 2006.

Boitani, Piero. *Chaucer and the Imaginary World of Fame.* Cambridge: D. S. Brewer, 1984.

———. 'Style, Iconography, and Narrative: The Lesson of the *Teseida*.' In *Chaucer and the Italian Trecento*, edited by Piero Boitani, 185–99. Cambridge: Cambridge University Press, 1983.

Bondanella, Julia Conaway. 'Petrarch's Rereading of Otium in *De Vita Solitaria*.' *Comparative Literature* 60, no. 1 (2008): 14–28.

Bowers, Roger. 'The Musicians and Liturgy of the Lady Chapels of the Monastery Church, c. 1235–1540.' In *Westminster Abbey: The Lady Chapel of Henry VII*, edited by Tim Tatton-Brown and Richard Mortimer, 33–57. Woodbridge: Boydell Press, 2003.

Braddy, Haldeen. 'Messire Oton de Graunson, Chaucer's Savoyard Friend.' *Studies in Philology* 35, no. 4 (1938): 515–31.

Branca, Vittore. *Boccaccio: The Man and His Works.* Translated by Richard Monges. New York: Harvester Press, 1976.

Brantley, Jessica. *Reading in the Wilderness: Private Devotion and Public Performance in Late Medieval England.* Chicago: University of Chicago Press, 2008.

Braswell, Mary Flowers. *The Medieval Sinner: Characterization and Confession in the Literature of the English Middle Ages.* Rutherford, NJ: Fairleigh Dickinson University Press, 1983.

Briggs, Charles F. 'The Clerk.' In *Historians on Chaucer: The 'General Prologue' to the 'Canterbury Tales,'* edited by S. H. Rigby, 187–205. Oxford: Oxford University Press, 2014.

Brodie, Saul. 'Making a Play for Criseyde: The Staging of Pandarus's House in Chaucer's *Troilus and Criseyde*.' *Speculum* 73, no. 1 (1998): 115–40.

Brotton, Jerry. *A History of the World in Twelve Maps.* London: Allen Lane, 2012.

Brown, A. L. 'Percy, Thomas, Earl of Worcester (c. 1343–1403).' In *Oxford Dictionary of National Biography*. Online edition. Oxford: Oxford University Press, 2008. https://doi.org/10.1093/ref:odnb/21955.

Brown, Peter. *Chaucer and the Making of Optical Space*. Oxford: Peter Lang, 2007.

———. 'The Containment of Symkyn: The Function of Space in the "Reeve's Tale."' *Chaucer Review* 14, no. 3 (1980): 225–36.

Brownlee, Kevin. *Poetic Identity in Guillaume de Machaut*. Madison: University of Wisconsin Press, 1984.

Brownlee, Robert W., and Marie Scordilis Brownlee. 'Athens, Thebes, and Mystra.' In *Europe: A Literary History*. Vol. 2, edited by David Wallace, 309–22. Oxford: Oxford University Press, 2016.

Brusegan, Rosanna. 'Le Jeu de Robin et Marion et l'ambiguïté du symbolism champêtre.' In *The Theatre in the Middle Ages*, edited by H. Braet, J. Nowé, and G. Tournoy, 119–29. Leuven: Leuven University Press, 1985.

Burger, Glenn. ' "Pite renneth soone in gentil herte": Ugly Feelings and Gendered Conduct in Chaucer's *Legend of Good Women*.' *Chaucer Review* 52, no. 1 (2017): 66–84.

Burrow, J. A. *Essays on Medieval Literature*. Oxford: Oxford University Press, 1984.

———. '*Sir Thopas*: An Agony in Three Fits.' *Review of English Studies*, n.s., 22:85 (1971): 54–58.

Butterfield, Ardis. 'Chaucer's French Inheritance.' In *The Cambridge Companion to Chaucer*, ed. Piero Boitani and Jill Mann, 20–35. Revised edition. Cambridge: Cambridge University Press, 2004.

———. *The Familiar Enemy: Chaucer, Language, and Nation in the Hundred Years War*. Oxford: Oxford University Press, 2009.

Bynum, Caroline Walker. *Christian Materiality: An Essay in Religion in Late Medieval Europe*. New York: Zone Books, 2011.

Camille, Michael. 'Before the Gaze: The Internal Senses and Late Medieval Practices of Seeing.' In *Visuality Before and Beyond the Renaissance: Seeing as Others Saw*, edited by Robert Nelson, 197–223. Chicago: University of Chicago Press, 2000.

Cannon, Christopher. 'Chaucer and Rape: Uncertainty's Certainties.' *Studies in the Age of Chaucer* 22 (2000): 67–92.

———. 'Chaucer's Style.' In *The Cambridge Companion to Chaucer*, edited by Piero Boitani and Jill Mann, 233–50. Revised edition. Cambridge: Cambridge University Press, 2004.

———. 'Enclosure.' In *The Cambridge Companion to Medieval Women's Writing*, edited by Carolyn Dinshaw and David Wallace, 109–23. Cambridge: Cambridge University Press, 2003.

———. *From Literacy to Literature: England, 1300–1400*. Oxford: Oxford University Press, 2016.

———. *The Making of Chaucer's English: A Study of Words*. Cambridge: Cambridge University Press, 1998.

———. *Middle English Literature: A Cultural History*. Cambridge: Polity, 2008.

———. '*Raptus* in the Chaumpaigne Release and a Newly Discovered Document Concerning the Life of Geoffrey Chaucer.' *Speculum* 68, no. 1 (1993): 74–94.

———. ' "Wyth her owen handys": What Women's Literacy Can Teach Us about Langland and Chaucer.' *Essays in Criticism* 66, no. 3 (2016): 277–300.

Capgrave, John. *Liber de Illustribus Henricis*. Edited by Francis Charles Hingeston. London: Longman, 1858.

Carlin, Martha. 'The Host.' In *Historians on Chaucer: The 'General Prologue' to the 'Canterbury Tales,'* edited by S. H. Rigby, 460–81. Oxford: Oxford University Press, 2014.

———. *Medieval Southwark*. London: Hambledon Press, 1996.

———. 'Thomas Spencer, Southwark Scrivener (d. 1428): Owner of a Copy of Chaucer's *Troilus* in 1394?' *Chaucer Review* 49, no. 4 (2015): 387–401.

———. *Urban Development of Southwark, c. 1200 to 1550*. Unpublished PhD thesis, University of Toronto, 1983.

———. ' "What say you to a piece of beef and mustard?": The Evolution of Public Dining in Medieval and Tudor London.' *Huntington Library Quarterly* 71, no. 1 (2008): 199–217.

Carpenter, David. *The Struggle for Mastery: Britain, 1066–1284*. Oxford: Oxford University Press, 2003.

Carpenter, Edward. *A House of Kings: The Official History of Westminster Abbey*. London: John Baker, 1966.

Carruthers, Mary. *The Book of Memory: A Study of Memory in Medieval Culture*. 2nd edition. Cambridge: Cambridge University Press, 2008.

———. 'The Poet as Master Builder: Composition and Locational Memory in the Middle Ages.' *New Literary History* 24, no. 4 (1993): 881–904.

———. 'The Wife of Bath and the Painting of Lions.' *PMLA* 94, no. 2 (1979): 209–22.

Cervone, Cristina Maria. 'John de Cobham and Cooling Castle's Charter Poem.' *Speculum* 83, no. 4 (2008): 884–916.

Chambers, E. K. *The Medieval Stage*. 2 vols. Mineola, NY: Dover Publications, 1996.

Childs, Wendy. 'Anglo-Italian Contacts in the Fourteenth Century.' In *Chaucer and the Italian Trecento*, edited by Piero Boitani, 67–87. Cambridge: Cambridge University Press, 1983.

Christianson, C. Paul. 'The Rise of the Book-Trade.' In *The Cambridge History of the Book in Britain, Volume 3: 1400–1557*, edited by Lotte Hellinga and J. B. Trapp, 128–47. Cambridge: Cambridge University Press, 1999.

Clanchy, Michael. *From Memory to Written Record: England, 1066–1307*. 3rd edition. Oxford: Wiley-Blackwell, 2013.

Clarke, M. V. 'The Lancastrian Faction and the Wonderful Parliament.' In *Fourteenth Century Studies*, edited by L. S. Sutherland and M. McKisack. Oxford: Clarendon Press, 1934.

Cognasso, Francesco. 'Istituzioni comunali e signorili di Milano sotto i Visconti.' In *Storia di Milano, Volume VI: Il ducato visconteo e la repubblica ambrosiana (1392–1450)*, 449–544. Milano: Fondazione Treccani degli Alfieri, 1955.

Cohan, Steven, and Linda M. Shires. *Telling Stories: A Theoretical Analysis of Narrative Fiction*. London: Routledge, 1988.

Cohen, Jeffrey Jerome. *Hybridity, Identity, and Monstrosity in Medieval Britain: Of Difficult Middles*. New York: Palgrave Macmillan, 2006.

Cole, Andrew. 'Chaucer's English Lesson.' *Speculum* 77, no. 4 (2002): 1128–67.

Coleman, Joyce. 'Audience.' In *A Handbook of Middle English Studies*, edited by Marion Turner, 155–69. Oxford: Wiley-Blackwell, 2013.

———. 'The Flower, the Leaf, and Philippa of Lancaster.' In *'The Legend of Good Women': Context and Reception*, edited by Carolyn P. Collette, 33–58. Cambridge: D. S. Brewer, 2006.

———. *Public Reading and the Reading Public in Late Medieval England and France*. Cambridge: Cambridge University Press, 1996.

Coleman, Olive. 'The Collectors of Customs in London under Richard II.' In *Studies in London History Presented to Philip Edmund Jones*, edited by A.E.J. Hollaender and William Kellaway, 181–94. London: Hodder and Stoughton, 1969.

Coleman, William. 'Chaucer, the *Teseida*, and the Visconti Library at Pavia: A Hypothesis.' *Medium Aevum* 51 (1982): 92–101.

Collette, Carolyn P. *Rethinking Chaucer's 'Legend of Good Women.'* York: York Medieval Press, 2014.

Cooper, Helen. 'Four Last Things in Dante and Chaucer: Ugolino in the House of Rumour.' *New Medieval Literatures* 3 (2000): 39–66.

———. 'London and Southwark Poetic Companies: "Si tost c'amis" and the *Canterbury Tales*.' In *Chaucer and the City*, edited by Ardis Butterfield, 109–26. Cambridge: D. S. Brewer, 2006.

———. 'Poetic Fame.' In *Cultural Reformations: Medieval and Renaissance in Literary History*, edited by Brian Cummings and James Simpson, 361–78. Oxford: Oxford University Press, 2010.

———. *The Structure of the Canterbury Tales*. London: Duckworth, 1983.

Cooper, Lisa. *Artisans and Narrative Craft in Late Medieval England*. Cambridge: Cambridge University Press, 2011.

———. 'Figures for "Gretter Knowing": Forms in the *Treatise on the Astrolabe*.' In *Chaucer and the Subversion of Form*, edited by Thomas A. Prendergast and Jessica Rosenfeld, 99–124. Cambridge: Cambridge University Press, 2018.

Copeland, Rita, ed. *The Oxford History of Classical Reception in English Literature, Volume 1: 800–1558*. Oxford: Oxford University Press, 2016.

Cox, Catherine S. *Gender and Language in Chaucer*. Gainesville: University Press of Florida, 1997.

Crampton, Georgia Ronan. 'Chaucer's Singular Prayer.' *Medium Aevum* 59 (1990): 191–213.

Crane, Susan. *Animal Encounters: Contacts and Concepts in Medieval Britain*. Philadelphia: University of Pennsylvania Press, 2013.

———. 'The Writing Lesson of 1381.' In *Chaucer's England*, edited by Barbara A. Hanawalt, 201–21. Minneapolis: University of Minnesota Press, 1992.

Crawford, Anne. *A History of the Vintners' Company*. London: Constable, 1977.

Creighton, Oliver H. *Designs upon the Land: Elite Landscapes of the Middle Ages*. Woodbridge: Boydell Press, 2009.

Dahood, Roger. 'English Historical Narratives of Jewish Child Murder, Chaucer's "Prioress's Tale," and the Date of Chaucer's Unknown Source.' *Studies in the Age of Chaucer* 31 (2009): 125–40.

———. 'The Punishment of the Jews, Hugh of Lincoln, and the Question of Satire in Chaucer's "Prioress's Tale."' *Viator* 36 (2005): 465–92.

Daley, Brian E. 'The Closed Garden and Sealed Fountain: Song of Songs 4.12 in the Late Medieval Iconography of Mary.' In *Medieval Gardens*, edited by Elisabeth MacDougall, 254–78. Washington, DC: Dumbarton Oaks, 1986.

Daniell, Christopher. *Death and Burial in Medieval England, 1066–1550*. London: Routledge, 1997.

Da Rold, Orietta. 'Materials.' In *The Production of Books in England, 1350–1500*, edited by Alexandra Gillespie and Daniel Wakelin, 12–33. Cambridge: Cambridge University Press, 2011.

David, Alfred. *The Strumpet Muse: Art and Morals in Chaucer's Poetry*. Bloomington: Indiana University Press, 1976.

Davies, Matthew, and Ann Saunders. *The History of the Merchant Tailors' Company*. Leeds: Northern Universities Press, 2004.

Davis, Isabel. 'Class.' In *A Handbook of Middle English Studies*, edited by Marion Turner, 285–98. Oxford: Wiley-Blackwell, 2013.

Davis, Isabel, and Catherine Nall, eds. *Chaucer and Fame: Reputation and Reception*. Cambridge: D. S. Brewer, 2015.

Davis, Rebecca. 'Fugitive Poetics in Chaucer's *House of Fame*.' *Studies in the Age of Chaucer* 37 (2015): 101–32.

Dean, Trevor, trans. *The Towns of Italy in the Later Middle Ages*. Manchester: Manchester University Press, 2000.

Delany, Sheila. *Medieval Literary Politics: Shapes of Ideology*. Cultural Politics. Manchester: Manchester University Press, 1990.

———. *The Naked Text: Chaucer's 'Legend of Good Women.'* Berkeley: University of California Press, 1994.

Delasanta, Rodney K. 'Chaucer, Pavia, and the Ciel D'Oro.' *Medium Aevum* 54 (1985): 117–21.

Deletant, Dennis. 'Genoese, Tatars and Rumanians at the Mouth of the Danube in the Fourteenth Century.' *Slavonic and East European Review* 62, no. 4 (1984): 511–30.

De Looze, Laurence. *Pseudo-Autobiography in the Fourteenth Century: Juan Ruiz, Guillaume de Machaut, Jean Froissart, and Geoffrey Chaucer*. Gainesville: University Press of Florida, 1997.

Denny-Brown, Andrea. *Fashioning Change: The Trope of Clothing in High and Late-Medieval England*. Columbus: Ohio State University Press, 2012.

Desmond, Marilynn. *Reading Dido: Gender, Textuality, and the Medieval 'Aeneid.'* Minneapolis: University of Minnesota Press, 1994.

Devaux, Jean. 'From the Court of Hainault to the Court of England: The Example of Jean Froissart.' In *War, Government and Power in Late Medieval France*, edited by C. T. Allmand, 1–20. Liverpool: Liverpool University Press, 2000.

DiMarco, Vincent J. 'The Historical Basis of Chaucer's Squire's Tale.' In *Chaucer's Cultural Geography*, edited by Kathryn L. Lynch, 56–75. New York: Routledge, 2002.

Dinshaw, Carolyn. *Chaucer's Sexual Poetics*. Madison: University of Wisconsin Press, 1989.

Dodd, Gwilym. 'Changing Perspectives: Parliament, Poetry, and the "Civil Service" under Richard II and Henry IV.' *Parliamentary History* 25 (2006): 299–322.

———. 'Parliament and Political Legitimacy in the Reign of Edward II.' In *The Reign of Edward II: New Perspectives*, edited by Gwilym Dodd and Anthony Musson, 165–89. York: York Medieval Press, 2006.

———. 'Richard II and the Transformation of Parliament.' In *The Reign of Richard II*, edited by Gwilym Dodd, 71–84. Stroud: Tempus, 2000.

———. 'The Rise of English, the Decline of French: Supplications to the English Crown, c. 1420–50.' *Speculum* 86, no. 1 (2011): 117–50.

———. 'The Spread of English in the Records of the Central Government, 1400–1430.' In *Vernacularity in England and Wales, c. 1300–1550*, edited by E. Salter and Helen Wicker, 225–66. Turnhout: Brepols, 2011.

———. 'Writing Wrongs: The Drafting of Supplications to the Crown in Later Fourteenth-Century England.' *Medium Aevum* 80, no. 2 (2011): 217–46.

Dodman, Trevor. 'Hunting to Teach: Class, Pedagogy, and Maleness in the *Master of Game* and *Sir Gawain and the Green Knight*.' *Exemplaria* 17, no. 2 (2005): 413–44.

Donaldson, E. Talbot. 'The Ending of Chaucer's *Troilus*.' In *Early English and Norse Studies*, edited by Arthur Brown and Peter Foote, 26–45. London: Methuen, 1963.

———. *Speaking of Chaucer*. New York: Norton, 1970.

Donavin, Georgiana. *Scribit Mater: Mary and the Language Arts in the Literature of Medieval England*. Washington, DC: Catholic University of America Press, 2012.

Draper, G. M. 'Timber and Iron: Natural Resources for the Late Medieval Shipbuilding Industry in Kent.' In *Later Medieval Kent, 1220–1540*, edited by Sheila Sweetinburgh, 55–109. Woodbridge: Boydell Press, 2010.

Duffell, Martin J. *A New History of English Metre*. London: Legenda, 2008.

Duhem, Pierre. *Études sur Léonard de Vinci, ceux qu'il a lus et ceux qui l'ont lu*. 2 vols. Paris: A. Hermann, 1906.

Dunn, Alastair. 'Richard II and the Mortimer Inheritance.' In *Fourteenth-Century England II*, edited by Chris Given-Wilson, 159–70. Woodbridge: Boydell, 2002.

Dyer, Christopher. *Everyday Life in Medieval England*. London: Bloomsbury, 2003.

———. *Making a Living in the Middle Ages: The People of Britain, 850–1520*. New Haven: Yale University Press, 2002.

———. *Standards of Living in the Later Middle Ages: Social Change in England, c. 1200–1520*. Revised edition. Cambridge: Cambridge University Press, 1998.

Eisner, Sigmund, and Marijane Osborn. 'Chaucer as Teacher: Chaucer's *Treatise on the Astrolabe*.' In *Medieval Literature for Children*, edited by Daniel T. Kline, 155–87. New York: Routledge, 2003.

Edwards, A.S.G. 'The Unity and Authenticity of *Anelida and Arcite*: The Evidence of the Manuscripts.' *Studies in Bibliography* 41 (1988): 177–188.

Edwards, Robert R., ed. *Art and Context in Late-Medieval English Narrative: Essays in Honor of Robert Worth Frank, Jr.* Cambridge: D. S. Brewer, 1994.

———, ed. 'Italy.' In *Chaucer: Contemporary Approaches*, edited by Susanna Fein and David Raybin, 3–24. University Park: Pennsylvania State University Press, 2010.

Elliott, R.W.V. *Chaucer's English*. London: Wiley-Blackwell, 1974.

Ellis, Robert. *Verba Vana: Empty Words in Ricardian London*. Unpublished PhD thesis, University of London, 2012.

Ellmann, Maud. 'Blanche.' In *Criticism and Critical Theory*, edited by Jeremy Hawthorn, 99–110. London: Edward Arnold, 1984.

Engel, Pál. *The Realm of St. Stephen: A History of Medieval Hungary, 895–1526*. Edited by Andrew Ayton. Translated by Tamás Pálosfalvi. London: I. B. Tauris, 2001.

Epstein, Robert. ' "With many a floryn he the hewes boghte": Ekphrasis and Symbolic Violence in the *Knight's Tale*.' *Philological Quarterly* 85 (2006): 49–68.

Epstein, Steven. *Genoa and the Genoese, 958–1528*. Chapel Hill: University of North Carolina Press, 1996.

Estow, Clara. *Pedro the Cruel of Castile: 1350–1369*. Medieval Mediterranean. Vol. 6. Leiden: Brill, 1995.

Evans, Ruth. 'The Production of Space in Chaucer's London.' In *Chaucer and the City*, edited by Ardis Butterfield, 41–56. Cambridge: D. S. Brewer, 2006.

Falkeid, Unn. '*De Vita Solitaria* and *De Otio Religioso*: The Perspective of the Guest.' In *The Cambridge Companion to Petrarch*, edited by Albert Ascoli and Unn Falkeid, 111–19. Cambridge: Cambridge University Press, 2015.

Federico, Sylvia. *New Troy: Fantasies of Empire in the Late Middle Ages*. Minneapolis: University of Minnesota Press, 2003.

Fein, Susanna, and David B. Raybin. *Chaucer: Contemporary Approaches*. University Park: Pennsylvania State University Press, 2010.

Fermosel, José Luis A. 'Jorge Luis Borges: "No Estoy Seguro de Que Yo Exista En Realidad."' *El País* (Buenos Aires, 26 September 1981).

Ferris, Sumner. 'Chaucer at Lincoln (1387): The "Prioress's Tale" as a Political Poem.' *Chaucer Review* 15, no. 4 (1981): 295–321.

———. 'The Date of Chaucer's Final Annuity and of the "Complaint to His Empty Purse."' *Modern Philology* 65, no. 1 (1967): 45–52.

Ferster, Judith. 'Chaucer's Parson and the "Idiosyncracies of Fiction."' In *Closure in 'The Canterbury Tales': The Role of 'The Parson's Tale*, edited by Linda Tarte Holley and David Raybin, 115–50. Kalamazoo, MI: Medieval Institute Publications, 2000.

Fisher, John H. *The Emergence of Standard English*. Lexington: University Press of Kentucky, 1996.

———. *John Gower: Moral Philosopher and Friend of Chaucer*. London: Methuen, 1964.

Fleming, Peter. 'Clifford, Sir Lewis (c. 1330–1404).' In *Oxford Dictionary of National Biography*. Online edition. Oxford: Oxford University Press, 2008. https://doi.org/10.1093/ref:odnb/50259.

Fletcher, Doris. 'The Lancastrian Collar of Esses: Its Origins and Transformations down the Centuries.' In *The Age of Richard II*, edited by James L. Gillespie, 191–204. Stroud and New York: Sutton / St Martin's Press, 1997.

Foster, Michael. 'On Dating the Duchess: The Personal and Social Context of *Book of the Duchess*.' *Review of English Studies*, n.s., 59:239 (2008): 185–96.

Fowler, David C. *The Life and Times of John Trevisa, Medieval Scholar*. Seattle: University of Washington Press, 1995.

Fowler, Kenneth. *The King's Lieutenant: Henry of Grosmont, First Duke of Lancaster, 1310–1361*. London: Elek, 1969.

———. *Medieval Mercenaries*. Oxford: Blackwell, 2001.

Fradenburg, L. O. Aranye. 'Criticism, Anti-Semitism, and the Prioress's Tale.' *Exemplaria* 1, no. 1 (1989): 69–115.

———. 'The Manciple's Servant Tongue: Politics and Poetry in *The Canterbury Tales*.' *English Literary History* 52, no. 1 (1985): 85–118.

———. *Sacrifice Your Love: Psychoanalysis, Historicism, Chaucer*. Minneapolis: University of Minnesota Press, 2002.

Freedman, Paul. *Out of the East: Spices and the Medieval Imagination*. New Haven: Yale University Press, 2008.

Freeman, Jessica. 'The Mistery of Coiners and the King's Moneyers of the Tower of London, c. 1340–c. 1530.' *British Numismatic Journal* 70 (2000): 67–82.

French, Katherine. *The People of the Parish: Community Life in a Late Medieval English Diocese*. Philadelphia: University of Pennsylvania Press, 2001.

Fryde, E. B. *William de la Pole: Merchant and King's Banker*. London: Hambledon Press, 1988.

Fumo, Jamie. *The Legacy of Apollo: Antiquity, Authority, and Chaucerian Poetics*. Toronto: University of Toronto Press, 2010.

———. *Making Chaucer's 'Book of the Duchess': Textuality and Reception*. Cardiff: University of Wales Press, 2015.

Fyler, John M. 'Domesticating the Exotic in the *Squire's Tale*.' *ELH* 55, no. 1 (1988): 1–26.

Galloway, Andrew. 'Chaucer's *Former Age* and the Fourteenth-Century Anthropology of Craft: The Social Logic of a Premodernist Lyric.' *English Literary History* 63, no. 3 (1996): 535–54.

———. 'The Literature of 1388 and the Politics of Pity in Gower's *Confessio amantis*.' In *The Letter of the Law: Legal Practice and Literary Production in Medieval England*, edited by Emily Steiner and Candace Barrington, 67–104. Ithaca: Cornell University Press, 2002.

Galloway, James A. 'Coastal Flooding and Socioeconomic Change in Eastern England in the Later Middle Ages.' *Environment and History* 19, no. 2 (2013): 173–207.

Ganim, John. 'Chaucer, Boccaccio, Confession, and Subjectivity.' In *The 'Decameron' and the 'Canterbury Tales': New Essays on an Old Question*, edited by Leonard Michael Koff and Brenda Deen Schildgen, 128–47. Madison, NJ: Fairleigh Dickinson University Press, 2000.

Geddes, Jane. 'Iron.' In *English Medieval Industries: Craftsmen, Techniques, Products*, edited by John Blair and Nigel Ramsay, 167–88. London: Hambledon Press, 1991.

Gennep, Arnold van. *The Rites of Passage*. Translated by Monika Vizedom and Gabrielle L. Caffee. London: Routledge, 2004.

Gertsman, Elina. *The Dance of Death in the Middle Ages: Image, Text, Performance*. Turnhout: Brepols, 2010.

Giancarlo, Matthew. *Parliament and Literature in Late Medieval England*. Cambridge: Cambridge University Press, 2007.

Gilchrist, Roberta. *Gender and Archaeology: Contesting the Past*. London: Routledge, 1999.

———. *Gender and Material Culture: The Archaeology of Religious Women*. New York: Routledge, 1994.

———. 'Medieval Bodies in the Material World: Gender, Stigma and the Body.' In *Framing Medieval Bodies*, edited by Sarah Kay and Miri Rubin, 43–61. Manchester: Manchester University Press, 1994.

Gillespie, Alexandra. 'Books.' In *Middle English*, edited by Paul Strohm, 86–103. Oxford: Oxford University Press, 2007.

Gillespie, James L. 'Ladies of the Fraternity of Saint George and of the Society of the Garter.' *Albion: A Quarterly Journal Concerned with British Studies* 17, no. 3 (1985): 259–78.

Gillespie, Vincent. 'Authorship.' In *A Handbook of Middle English Studies*, edited by Marion Turner, 135–54. Oxford: Wiley-Blackwell, 2013.

Given-Wilson, Chris. *Chronicles: The Writing of History in Medieval England*. London: Hambledon and London, 2004.

———. *Henry IV*. New Haven: Yale University Press, 2016.

———. 'Richard II and His Grandfather's Will.' *English Historical Review* 93 (1978): 320–37.

———. *The Royal Household and the King's Affinity*. New Haven: Yale University Press, 1986.

Goldberg, P.J.P. 'The Fashioning of Bourgeois Domesticity in Later Medieval England: A Material Culture Perspective.' In *Medieval Domesticity: Home, Housing, and Household in Medieval England*, edited by Maryanne Kowaleski and P.J.P. Goldberg, 124–44. Cambridge: Cambridge University Press, 2008.

Goldberg, P.J.P., and Maryanne Kowaleski, eds. *Medieval Domesticity: Home, Housing, and Household in Medieval England*. Cambridge: Cambridge University Press, 2008.

Goldie, Matthew Boyd. *Scribes of Space: Place in Middle English Literature and Late Medieval Science.* Ithaca: Cornell University Press, 2019.

Goldstein, R. James. ' "To Scotland-Ward His Foomen for to Seke": Chaucer, the Scots, and the "Man of Law's Tale." ' *Chaucer Review* 33, no. 1 (1998): 31–42.

Goodman, Anthony. *John of Gaunt: The Exercise of Princely Power in Fourteenth-Century Europe.* Harlow: Longman, 1992.

———. *The Loyal Conspiracy: The Lords Appellant under Richard II.* London: Routledge & Kegan Paul, 1971.

Grady, Frank. '*St Erkenwald* and the Merciless Parliament.' *Studies in the Age of Chaucer* 22 (2000): 179–211.

Grant, Raymond. *The Royal Forests of England.* Stroud: Alan Sutton, 1991.

Green, David. *The Black Prince.* Stroud: Tempus, 2001.

Green, Richard Firth. 'A Poem of 1380.' *Speculum* 66, no. 2 (1991): 330–41.

———. *Poets and Princepleasers: Literature and the English Court in the Late Middle Ages.* Toronto: University of Toronto Press, 1980.

Greenblatt, Stephen. *Renaissance Self-Fashioning: From More to Shakespeare.* Chicago: University of Chicago Press, 2005.

Grennen, Joseph. 'Saint Cecilia's Chemical Wedding: The Unity of the *Canterbury Tales,* Fragment VIII.' *Journal of English and Germanic Philology* 65 (1966): 466–81.

Gross, Charlotte. ' "The goode weye": Ending and Not-Ending in *The Parson's Tale.*' In *Closure in* The Canterbury Tales: *The Role of The Parson's Tale,* edited by Linda Tarte Holley and David Raybin, 177–97. Kalamazoo, MI: Medieval Institute Publications, 2000.

Grudin, Michaela Paasche. *Chaucer and the Politics of Discourse.* Columbia: University of South Carolina Press, 1996.

Hagiioannu, Michael. 'Giotto's Bardi Chapel Frescoes and Chaucer's *House of Fame*: Influence, Evidence, and Interpretations.' *Chaucer Review* 36, no. 1 (2001): 28–47.

Hanawalt, Barbara. 'Childrearing among the Lower Classes of Late Medieval England.' *Journal of Interdisciplinary History* 8, no. 1 (1977): 1–22.

———. *Crime and Conflict in English Communities, 1300–1348.* Cambridge, MA: Harvard University Press, 1979.

———. *Growing Up in Medieval London: The Experience of Childhood in History.* New York: Oxford University Press, 1993.

———. 'Medievalists and the Study of Childhood.' *Speculum* 77, no. 2 (2002): 440-60.

———. *The Wealth of Wives: Women, Law, and Economy in Late Medieval London.* Oxford: Oxford University Press, 2007,

———. *Women and Work in Pre-Industrial Europe.* Bloomington: Indiana University Press, 1986.

Hanawalt, Barbara, and Kathryn L. Reyerson, eds. *City and Spectacle in Medieval Europe.* Minneapolis: University of Minnesota Press, 1994.

Hansen, Elaine Tuttle. *Chaucer and the Fictions of Gender.* Berkeley: University of California Press, 1992.

Harben, Henry A. *A Dictionary of London.* London: Herbert Jenkins Limited, 1918.

Harriss, Gerald. *Shaping the Nation: England, 1360–1461.* Oxford: Clarendon Press, 2005.

Harte, N. B. 'State Control of Dress and Social Change in Pre-Industrial England.' In *Trade, Government and Economy in Pre-Industrial England: Essays Presented to F. J. Fisher,* edited by D. C. Coleman and A. H. John, 132–65. London: Weidenfeld & Nicolson, 1976.

Harvey, Barbara. 'Colchester, William (d. 1420).' In *Oxford Dictionary of National Biography*. Online edition. Oxford: Oxford University Press, 2008. https://doi.org/10.1093/ref:odnb/54431.

———. *Living and Dying in England, 1100–1540: The Monastic Experience*. Oxford: Clarendon Press, 1993.

———. 'The Monks of Westminster and the Old Lady Chapel.' In *Westminster Abbey: The Lady Chapel of Henry VII*, edited by Tim Tatton-Brown and Richard Mortimer, 5–31. Woodbridge: Boydell Press, 2003.

Harvey, John. *Henry Yevele, c. 1320–1400: The Life of an English Architect*. 2nd edition. London: Batsford, 1946.

———. *Mediaeval Gardens*. London: Batsford, 1981.

Harvey, L. P. *Islamic Spain, 1200–1500*. Chicago: University of Chicago Press, 1990.

Hassall, W. O. 'Plays at Clerkenwell.' *Modern Language Review* 33 (1938): 564–67.

Hasted, Edward. *Historical and Topographical Survey of the County of Kent*. Vol. 2. Canterbury: W. Bristow, 1797.

Havely, Nick. 'The Italian Background.' In *Chaucer: An Oxford Guide*, edited by Steve Ellis, 313–31. Oxford: Oxford University Press, 2005.

Heawood, Edward. 'Sources of Early English Paper-Supply.' *The Library* 10, no. 3 (1929): 282–307.

Heer, Friedrich. *The Holy Roman Empire*. London: Weidenfeld and Nicolson, 1968.

Heller, Sarah-Grace. *Fashion in Medieval France*. Cambridge: D. S. Brewer, 2007.

Helmholtz, Richard H. 'Infanticide in England in the Later Middle Ages.' *History of Childhood Quarterly* 1 (1974–75): 282–90.

Heng, Geraldine. *Empire of Magic: Medieval Romance and the Politics of Cultural Fantasy*. New York: Columbia University Press, 2003.

———. *The Invention of Race in the European Middle Ages*. Cambridge: Cambridge University Press, 2018.

Hiatt, Alfred. 'Genre without System.' In *Middle English*, edited by Paul Strohm, 277–94. Oxford: Oxford University Press, 2007.

Holley, Linda Tarte. *Reason and Imagination in Chaucer, the 'Perle'-Poet, and the 'Cloud'-Author: Seeing from the Centre*. New York: Palgrave Macmillan, 2011.

Holley, Linda Tarte, and David Raybin, eds. *Closure in* The Canterbury Tales: *The Role of* The Parson's Tale. Kalamazoo, MI: Medieval Institute Publications, 2000.

Holmes, George. *The Good Parliament*. Oxford: Clarendon Press, 1975.

Horobin, Simon. 'Adam Pinkhurst, Geoffrey Chaucer, and the Hengwrt Manuscript of the *Canterbury Tales*.' *Chaucer Review* 44, no. 4 (2010): 351–67.

Horrox, Rosemary, ed. and trans. *The Black Death*. Manchester: Manchester University Press, 1994.

Howard, Donald Roy. *Chaucer and the Medieval World*. London: Weidenfeld & Nicolson, 1987.

Howes, Laura L. 'Chaucer's Forests, Parks, and Groves.' *Chaucer Review* 49, no. 1 (2014): 125–33.

———. *Chaucer's Gardens and the Language of Convention*. Gainesville: University Press of Florida, 1997.

Hsy, Jonathan. 'City.' In *A Handbook of Middle English Studies*, edited by Marion Turner, 315–29. Oxford: Wiley-Blackwell, 2013.

——. *Trading Tongues: Merchants, Multilingualism, and Medieval Literature*. Columbus: Ohio State University Press, 2013.

Hudson, Anne. *The Premature Reformation: Wycliffite Texts and Lollard History*. Oxford: Clarendon Press, 1988.

Hudson, Anne, and Anthony Kenny. 'Wyclif [Wycliffe], John.' In *Oxford Dictionary of National Biography*. Online edition. Oxford: Oxford University Press, 2008. https://doi.org/10.1093/ref:odnb/30122.

Hult, David F. '*The Roman de la Rose*, Christine de Pizan and the *querelle des femmes*.' In *The Cambridge Companion to Medieval Women's Writing*, edited by Carolyn Dinshaw and David Wallace, 184–94. Cambridge: Cambridge University Press, 2006.

Hunt, Edwin S., and James M. Murray. *A History of Business in Medieval Europe, 1200–1550*. Cambridge: Cambridge University Press, 1999.

Ilardi, Vincent. *Renaissance Vision from Spectacles to Telescopes*. Philadelphia: American Philosophical Society, 2007.

Impey, Edward, and Geoffrey Parnell. *The Tower of London: The Official Illustrated History*. Revised edition. New York: Merrell, 2006.

Ingham, Patricia Clare. *The Medieval New: Ambivalence in an Age of Innovation*. Middle Ages Series. Philadelphia: University of Pennsylvania Press, 2015.

——. *Sovereign Fantasies: Arthurian Romance and the Making of Britain*. Philadelphia: University of Pennsylvania Press, 2001.

James, Margery Kirkbride. *Studies in the Medieval Wine Trade*. Edited by Elspeth M. Veale. Oxford: Clarendon Press, 1971.

Jewell, Helen M. *Women in Medieval England*. Manchester: Manchester University Press, 1991.

Johnson, Andrew James. 'Ekphrasis in the *Knight's Tale*.' In *Rethinking the New Medievalism*, edited by R. Howard Bloch, Alison Calhoun, Jacqueline Cerquiglini-Toulet, Joachim Küpper, and Jeanette Patterson, 181–97. Baltimore: Johns Hopkins University Press, 2014.

Johnson, Eleanor. 'Chaucer and the Consolation of Prosimetrum.' *Chaucer Review* 43, no. 4 (2009): 455–72.

——. *Practicing Literary Theory in the Middle Ages: Ethics and the Mixed Form in Chaucer, Gower, Usk, and Hoccleve*. Chicago and London: University of Chicago Press, 2013.

Johnson, Matthew. *Behind the Castle Gate: From Medieval to Renaissance*. London: Routledge, 2002.

Jones, E. A. '"Loo, Lordes Myne, Heere Is a Fit!": The Structure of Chaucer's *Sir Thopas*.' *Review of English Studies*, n.s., 51:202 (2000): 248–52.

Jones, Terry, Robert Yeager, Alan Fletcher, Juliette Dor, and Terry Dolan. *Who Murdered Chaucer? A Medieval Mystery*. London: Methuen, 2003.

Justice, Steven. 'Lollardy.' In *The Cambridge History of Medieval English Literature*, edited by David Wallace, 662–89. Cambridge: Cambridge University Press, 1999.

——. *Writing and Rebellion: England in 1381*. Berkeley: University of California Press, 1994.

Kaske, Carol V. 'Getting around the *Parson's Tale*: An Alternative to Allegory and Irony.' In *Chaucer at Albany*, edited by Rossell Hope Robbins, 147–77. New York: Franklin, 1975.

Kaye, Joel. *A History of Balance, 1250–1375: The Emergence of a New Model of Equilibrium and Its Impact on Thought*. Cambridge: Cambridge University Press, 2014.

Kay, Sarah. *The Place of Thought: The Complexity of One in Late Medieval French Didactic Poetry*. Philadelphia: University of Pennsylvania Press, 2007.

Kay, Sarah, Terence Cave, and Malcolm Bowie. *A Short History of French Literature*. Oxford: Oxford University Press, 2003.

Keen, Maurice H. *England in the Later Middle Ages: A Political History*. 2nd edition. London: Routledge, 2003.

Kelly, H. A. 'Bishop, Prioress, and Bawd in the Stews of Southwark.' *Speculum* 75, no. 2 (2000): 342–88.

———. *Inquisitions and Other Trial Procedures in the Medieval West*. Aldershot: Ashgate, 2001.

Kendall, Elliot. 'The Great Household in the City: The *Shipman's Tale*.' In *Chaucer and the City*, edited by Ardis Butterfield, 145–61. Cambridge: D. S. Brewer, 2006.

———. *Lordship and Literature: John Gower and the Politics of the Great Household*. Oxford: Oxford University Press, 2008.

Kerby-Fulton, Kathryn. 'Oxford.' In *Europe: A Literary History*. Vol. 1, edited by David Wallace, 208–26. Oxford: Oxford University Press, 2016.

Kerby-Fulton, Kathryn, and Steven Justice. 'Langlandian Reading Circles and the Civil Service in London and Dublin, 1380–1427.' *New Medieval Literatures* 1 (1997): 59–83.

———. 'Reformist Intellectual Culture in the English and Irish Civil Service: The *Modus tenendi parliamentum* and Its Literary Relations.' *Traditio* 53 (1998): 149–202.

Kibler, William W., and James I. Wimsatt, eds. 'The Development of the Pastourelle in the Fourteenth Century: An Edition of Fifteen Poems with an Analysis.' *Mediaeval Studies* 45 (1983): 22–78.

Kinch, Ashby. *Imago Mortis: Mediating Images of Death in Late Medieval Culture*. Leiden: Brill, 2013.

———. ' "Mind Like Wickerwork": The Neuroplastic Aesthetics of Chaucer's House of Tidings.' *postmedieval* 3 (2012): 302–14.

King, Mark. 'Richard II, the Mortimer Inheritance, and the March of Wales, 1381–1384.' In *Fourteenth-Century England VIII*, edited by J. S. Hamilton, 95–118. Woodbridge: Boydell, 2014.

Kingsford, C. L. 'The Feast of the Five Kings.' *Archaeologica* 67 (1916): 119–26.

Kipling, Gordon. *Enter the King: Theatre, Liturgy, and Ritual in the Medieval Civic Triumph*. Oxford: Oxford University Press, 1998.

Kittredge, G. L. 'Chaucer and Some of His Friends.' *Modern Philology* 1, no. 1 (1903): 1–18.

———. 'The Date of Chaucer's Troilus and Other Chaucer Matters.' London: K. Paul, Trench, Trübner, 1905.

Knapp, Ethan. *The Bureaucratic Muse: Thomas Hoccleve and the Literature of Late Medieval England*. University Park: Pennsylvania State University Press, 2001.

Knapp, Peggy. 'Aesthetic Attention and the Chaucerian Text.' *Chaucer Review* 39, no. 3 (2005): 241–58.

Knox, Philip. *The Romance of the Rose in Fourteenth-Century England*. Unpublished DPhil thesis, University of Oxford, 2015.

Knox, Philip, Jonathan Morton, and Daniel Reeve, eds. *Medieval Thought Experiments: Poetry, Hypothesis, and Experience in the European Middle Ages*. Turnhout: Brepols, 2018.

Koff, Leonard Michael, and Brenda Deen Schildgen. *The 'Decameron' and the 'Canterbury Tales': New Essays on an Old Question*. Madison, NJ: Fairleigh Dickinson University Press, 2000.

Kolve, V. A. *Chaucer and the Imagery of Narrative: The First Five Canterbury Tales*. Stanford, CA: Stanford University Press, 1984.

Krasner, James. *Home Bodies: Tactile Experience in Domestic Space.* Columbus: Ohio State University Press, 2010.

Kuhl, Ernest P. 'Chaucer's "My Maistre Bukton."' *PMLA* 38, no. 1 (1923): 115-32.

Kwakkel, Erik. 'Commercial Organization and Economic Innovation.' In *The Production of Books in England, 1350–1500,* edited by Alexandra Gillespie and Daniel Wakelin, 173–90. Cambridge: Cambridge University Press, 2011.

Labarge, Margaret Wade. *Gascony: England's First Colony, 1204–1453.* London: Hamish Hamilton, 1980.

Laird, Edgar. 'Chaucer and Friends: The Audience for the "Treatise on the Astrolabe."' *Chaucer Review* 41, no. 4 (2007): 439–44.

Lamborn, E. A. Greening. 'The Arms on the Chaucer Tomb at Ewelme.' *Oxoniensia* 5 (1940): 78–93.

Lancashire, Anne. *London Civic Theatre: City Drama and Pageantry from Roman Times to 1558.* Cambridge: Cambridge University Press, 2002.

Latour, Bruno. *We Have Never Been Modern.* Translated by Catherine Porter. Cambridge, MA: Harvard University Press, 1993.

Lavezzo, Kathy. *The Accommodated Jew: English Antisemitism from Bede to Milton.* Ithaca: Cornell University Press, 2016.

———. *Angels at the Edge of the World: Geography, Literature, and English Community, 1000–1534.* Ithaca: Cornell University Press, 2006.

Lawton, David. *Chaucer's Narrators.* Woodbridge: D. S. Brewer, 1985.

———. 'Public Interiorities.' In *A Handbook of Middle English Studies,* edited by Marion Turner, 93–107. Oxford: Wiley-Blackwell, 2013.

———. *Voice in Later Medieval English Literature: Public Interiorities.* Oxford: Oxford University Press, 2017.

Lee, Paul. *Nunneries, Learning, and Spirituality in Late Medieval English Society: The Dominican Priory of Dartford.* York: York Medieval Press, 2001.

Lees, Clare. 'Gender and Exchange in *Piers Plowman.*' In *Class and Gender in Early English Literature: Intersections,* edited by Britton Harwood and Gillian Overing, 112–30. Bloomington: Indiana University Press, 1994.

Lefebvre, Henri. *The Production of Space.* Translated by Donald Nicholson-Smith. Oxford: Blackwell, 1991.

Le Goff, Jacques. *The Medieval Imagination.* Translated by Arthur Goldhammer. Chicago: University of Chicago Press, 1988.

———. 'Merchant's Time and Church's Time in the Middle Ages.' In *Time, Work, and Culture in the Middle Ages,* trans. Arthur Goldhammer, 29–42. Chicago: University of Chicago Press, 1982.

———. 'Reims: City of Coronation.' In *Realms of Memory: The Construction of the French Past III: Symbols,* edited by Pierre Nora. English edition edited by Lawrence D. Kritzman, translated by Arthur Goldhammer, 193–251. New York: Columbia University Press, 1998.

———. *Time, Work, and Culture in the Middle Ages.* Translated by Arthur Goldhammer. Chicago: University of Chicago Press, 1982.

Leicester, H. Marshall. *The Disenchanted Self: Representing the Subject in the Canterbury Tales.* Berkeley: University of California Press, 1990.

Le Patourel, John. 'The Treaty of Brétigny, 1360.' *Transactions of the Royal Historical Society* 10 (1960): 19–39.

Lerer, Seth. *Boethius and Dialogue: Literary Method in 'The Consolation of Philosophy.'* Princeton: Princeton University Press, 1985; reprinted in 2014.

———. 'Chaucer's Sons.' *University of Toronto Quarterly* 73 (Summer 2004): 906–15.

———. *Children's Literature: A Reader's History from Aesop to Harry Potter.* Chicago: University of Chicago Press, 2008.

Leroy, Béatrice. *The Jews of Navarre.* Jerusalem: Magnes Press, Hebrew University, 1985.

Lethaby, W. R. *Westminster Abbey and the King's Craftsmen: A Study of Mediaeval Building.* London: Duckworth, 1906.

Lewis, Robert Enzer. 'Chaucer's Artistic Use of Pope Innocent III's *De Miseria Humane Conditionis* in the Man of Law's Prologue and Tale.' *PMLA* 81, no. 7 (1966): 485–92.

Liddy, Christian Drummond. *War, Politics and Finance in Late Medieval English Towns: Bristol, York and the Crown, 1350–1400.* Woodbridge: Boydell Press, 2005.

Lilley, Keith D. *City and Cosmos: The Medieval World in Urban Form.* London: Reaktion, 2009.

Lillich, Meredith Parsons. *The Gothic Stained Glass of Reims Cathedral.* University Park: Pennsylvania State University Press, 2011.

Lindenbaum, Sheila. 'Ceremony and Oligarchy: The London Midsummer Watch.' In *City and Spectacle in Medieval Europe*, edited by Barbara A. Hanawalt and Kathryn Reyerson, 171–88. Minneapolis: University of Minnesota Press, 1994.

———. 'London Texts and Literate Practice.' In *The Cambridge History of Medieval English Literature*, edited by David Wallace, 284–310. Cambridge: Cambridge University Press, 1999.

———. 'The Smithfield Tournament of 1390.' *Journal of Medieval and Renaissance Studies* 20 (1990): 1–21.

Linehan, Peter. 'Castile, Navarre, and Portugal.' In *The New Cambridge Medieval History: Volume VI, c. 1300–c. 1415*, edited by Michael Jones, 619–50. Cambridge: Cambridge University Press, 2000.

Lloyd, T. H. *The English Wool-Trade in the Middle Ages.* Cambridge: Cambridge University Press, 1977.

Lochrie, Karma. *Covert Operations: The Medieval Uses of Secrecy.* Philadelphia: University of Pennsylvania Press, 1999.

Lockhart, Jessica. *Everyday Wonders and Enigmatic Structures: Riddles from Symphosius to Chaucer.* Unpublished PhD thesis, University of Toronto, 2017.

Longsworth, Robert M. 'Privileged Knowledge: St Cecilia and the Alchemist in the *Canterbury Tales.*' *Chaucer Review* 27, no. 1 (1992): 87–96.

Lopez, Robert S., and Irving W. Raymond, eds. *Medieval Trade in the Mediterranean World: Illustrative Documents.* New York: W. W. Norton, 1967.

Lowes, John Livingston. "The Date of Chaucer's *Troilus and Criseyde.*" *Publications of the Modern Language Association of America* 23 (1908): 285.

———. 'The Date of the Envoy to Bukton.' *Modern Language Notes* 27 (1912): 45–48.

———. 'The Prologue to the *Legend of Good Women* Considered in Its Chronological Relations.' *Publications of the Modern Language Association of America* 20, no. 4 (1905): 749–864.

Luce, Richard, ed. and trans. 'Injunctions Made and Issued to the Abbess and Convent of the Monastery of Romsey after His Visitation by William of Wykeham, 1387.' *Hampshire Field Club and Archaeological Society Proceedings* 17, part 1 (1949): 31–44.

Lynch, Kathryn L. 'The Meaning and Importance of Walls in Chaucer's Poetry.' In *Art and Context in Late-Medieval English Narrative*, edited by Robert Edwards, 107–25. Cambridge: D. S. Brewer, 1994.

Maggi, Armando. '"You Will Be My Solitude": Solitude as Prophecy (*De Vita Solitaria*).' In *Petrarch: A Critical Guide to the Complete Works*, edited by Victoria Kirkham and Armando Maggi, 179–95. Chicago: University of Chicago Press, 2009.

Manly, J. M. *Some New Light on Chaucer: Lectures Delivered at the Lowell Institute*. London: Bell, 1926.

———. 'Three Recent Chaucer Studies.' *Review of English Studies* 10, no. 39 (1934): 257–73.

Mann, Jill. *Chaucer and Medieval Estates Satire*. Cambridge: Cambridge University Press, 1973.

———. *Feminizing Chaucer*. New edition. Woodbridge: D. S. Brewer, 2002.

———. *Geoffrey Chaucer*. New York: Harvester Wheatsheaf, 1991.

Manz, Beatrice Forbes. *The Rise and Rule of Tamerlane*. Cambridge: Cambridge University Press, 1989.

Martines, Lauro. *Power and Imagination: City-States in Renaissance Italy*. Baltimore: Johns Hopkins University Press, 1988.

Matheson, Lister M. 'Chaucer's Ancestry: Historical and Philological Re-Assessments.' *Chaucer Review* 25, no. 3 (1991): 171–89.

Mathew, Gervase. *The Court of Richard II*. New York: W. W. Norton, 1968.

Mazzotta, Giuseppe. *The Worlds of Petrarch*. Durham, NC: Duke University Press, 1993.

McCall, John P. 'Chaucer and John of Legnano.' *Speculum* 40, no. 3 (1965): 484–89.

McCormick, Betsy. 'Remembering the Game: Debating the *Legend*'s Women.' In *'The Legend of Good Women': Context and Reception*, edited by Carolyn P. Collette, 105–31. Cambridge: D. S. Brewer, 2006.

McDonald, Nicola. 'Chaucer's *Legend of Good Women*, Ladies at Court and the Female Reader.' *Chaucer Review* 35, no. 1 (2000): 22–42.

———. 'Games Medieval Women Play.' In *'The Legend of Good Women': Context and Reception*, edited by Carolyn P. Collette, 176–97. Cambridge: D. S. Brewer, 2006.

McFarlane, K. B. 'Henry V, Bishop Beaufort, and the Red Hat, 1417–1421.' In *England in the Fifteenth Century: Collected Essays*, 79–113. London: Hambledon Press, 1981.

McFarlane, Kenneth Bruce. *Lancastrian Kings and Lollard Knights*. Oxford: Clarendon Press, 1972.

McGerr, Rosemarie. *Chaucer's Open Books: Resistance to Closure in Medieval Discourse*. Gainesville: University Press of Florida, 1998.

———. 'Meaning and Ending in a "Paynted Proces": Resistance to Closure in *Troilus and Criseyde*.' In *Chaucer's 'Troilus and Criseyde': 'Subgit to Alle Poesye,'* edited by Catherine S. Cox and R. A. Shoaf, 179–98. Binghamton, NY: Medieval & Renaissance Texts & Studies, 1992.

McGrady, Deborah. 'Guillaume de Machaut.' In *The Cambridge Companion to Medieval French Literature*, edited by Simon Gaunt and Sarah Kay, 109–22. Cambridge: Cambridge University Press, 2009.

McHardy, A. K. 'The Alien Priories and the Expulsion of Aliens from England in 1378.' *Studies in Church History* 12 (1975): 133–41.

———. *The Church in London, 1375–1392*. London: London Record Society, 1977.

——. 'Haxey's Case, 1397: The Petition and Its Presenter Reconsidered.' In *The Age of Richard II*, edited by James L. Gillespie, 93–114. Stroud and New York: Sutton / St Martin's Press, 1997.

McKinley, Kathryn, *Chaucer's 'House of Fame' and Its Boccaccian Intertexts: Image, Vision, and the Vernacular*. Toronto: Pontifical Institute of Medieval Studies, 2016.

——. 'Gower and Chaucer: Readings of Ovid in Late Medieval England.' In *Ovid in the Middle Ages*, edited by James G. Clark, Frank T. Coulson, and Kathryn L. McKinley, 197–230. Cambridge: Cambridge University Press, 2011.

McLean, Teresa. *Medieval English Gardens*. London: Collins, 1981.

McMullan, Gordon. *Shakespeare and the Idea of Late Writing: Authorship and the Proximity of Death*. Cambridge: Cambridge University Press, 2007.

McMullan, Gordon, and Sam Smiles, eds. *Late Style and Its Discontents: Essays in Art, Literature, and Music*. Oxford: Oxford University Press, 2016.

Meecham-Jones, Simon. ' "Englyssh Gaufride" and British Chaucer? Chaucerian Allusions to the Condition of Wales in the *House of Fame*.' *Chaucer Review* 44, no. 1 (2009): 1–24.

Mercer, Malcolm. 'King's Armourers and the Growth of the Armourers' Craft in Early Fourteenth-Century London.' In *Fourteenth-Century England VIII*, edited by J. S. Hamilton, 1–20. Woodbridge: Boydell, 2014.

Mertes, Kate. *The English Noble Household, 1250–1600: Good Governance and Politic Rule*. Oxford: Basil Blackwell, 1988.

Metlitzki, Dorothy. *The Matter of Araby in Medieval England*. New Haven: Yale University Press, 1977.

Middleton, Anne. 'The Idea of Public Poetry in the Reign of Richard II.' *Speculum* 53, no. 1 (1978): 94–114.

Milbourn, Thomas, ed. *The Vintners' Company, Their Muniments, Plate, and Eminent Members*. London: Vintners' Company, 1888.

Miles, Laura Saetveit. 'The Origins and Development of the Virgin Mary's Book at the Annunciation.' *Speculum* 89, no. 3 (2014): 632–69.

Miller, Anne-Helene. 'Guillaume de Machaut and the Forms of Pre-Humanism in Fourteenth-Century France.' In *A Companion to Guillaume de Machaut*, edited by Deborah L. McGrady and Jennifer Bain, 33–48. Leiden: Brill, 2012.

Miller, Clarence H., and Roberta Bux Bosse. 'Chaucer's Pardoner and the Mass.' *Chaucer Review* 6, no. 3 (1972): 171–84.

Minnis, Alastair J. *Magister Amoris: The Roman de la Rose and Vernacular Hermeneutics*. Oxford: Oxford University Press, 2001.

——. *Medieval Theory of Authorship: Scholastic Literary Attitudes in the Later Middle Ages*. 2nd edition. Philadelphia: University of Pennsylvania Press, 1988.

——. *The Shorter Poems*. Oxford: Oxford University Press, 1995.

Mitchell, J. Allan. *Becoming Human: The Matter of the Medieval Child*. Minneapolis: University of Minnesota Press, 2014.

Mooney, Linne R. 'Chaucer and Interest in Astronomy at the Court of Richard II.' In *Chaucer in Perspective: Middle English Essays in Honour of Norman Blake*, edited by Geoffrey Lester, 139–60. Sheffield: Sheffield Academic Press, 1999.

——. 'Chaucer's Scribe.' *Speculum* 81, no. 1 (2006): 97–138.

——. 'Locating Scribal Activity in Late Medieval London.' In *Design and Distribution of Late Medieval Manuscripts in England*, edited by Margaret Connolly and Linne R. Mooney, 183–204. York: University of York Press, 2008.

Mooney, Linne, and Estelle Stubbs. *Scribes and the City: London Guildhall Clerks and the Dissemination of Middle English Literature, 1375–1425*. York: York Medieval Press, 2013.

Moore, John C. 'Innocent III's *De Miseria Humanae Conditionis*: A *Speculum Curiae?*' *Catholic Historical Review* 67, no. 4 (1981): 553–64.

———. *Pope Innocent III (1160/61–1216): To Root Up and to Plant*. Leiden: Brill, 2003.

Morgan, Hollie L. S. *Beds and Chambers in Late Medieval England: Readings, Representations and Realities*. York: York Medieval Press, 2017.

Morganstern, Anne M. 'The Bishop, the Young Lion, and the Two-Headed Dragon: The Burghersh Memorial in Lincoln Cathedral.' In *Memory and Oblivion: Proceedings of the XXIXth International Congress of the History of Art Held in Amsterdam, 1–7 September 1996*, edited by Wessel Reinink and Jeroen Stumpel, 515–35. Dordrecht: Springer, 1999.

Morrison, Susan S. 'The Use of Biography in Medieval Literary Criticism: The Case of Geoffrey Chaucer and Cecily Chaumpaigne.' *Chaucer Review* 34, no. 1 (1999): 69–86.

Munro, John H. 'Bullionism and the Bill of Exchange in England.' In *The Dawn of Modern Banking*, 169–239. New Haven: Yale University Press, 1979.

Murray, Alexander. 'Purgatory and the Spatial Imagination.' In *Dante and the Church: Literary and Historical Essays*, edited by Paolo Acquaviva and Jennifer Petrie, 61–92. Dublin: Four Courts Press, 2007.

Murtaugh, Daniel. 'Women and Geoffrey Chaucer.' *English Literary History* 38, no. 4 (1971): 473–92.

Murton, Megan. 'Secular Consolation in Chaucer's *Complaint of Mars*.' *Studies in the Age of Chaucer* 38 (2016): 75–107.

Muscatine, Charles. *Chaucer and the French Tradition: A Study in Style and Meaning*. Berkeley: University of California Press, 1957.

———. 'Chaucer's Religion and the Chaucer Religion.' In *Chaucer Traditions: Studies in Honour of Derek Brewer*, edited by Ruth Morse and Barry Windeatt, 249–62. Cambridge: Cambridge University Press, 1990.

———. 'Locus of Action in Medieval Narrative.' *Romance Philology* 17, no. 1 (1963): 115–22.

Myers, A. R. 'Parliamentary Petitions in the Fifteenth Century: Part I; Petitions from Individuals or Groups.' *English Historical Review* 52 (1937): 385–404.

———. 'The Wealth of Richard Lyons.' In *Essays in Medieval History Presented to Bertie Wilkinson*, edited by T. A. Sandquist and M. R. Powicke, 301–29. Toronto: University of Toronto Press, 1969.

National Archives. http://blog.nationalarchives.gov.uk/blog/civil-servants-tale-geoffrey-chaucer-archives-part-two/.

Nelson, Robert S. 'A Byzantine Painter in Trecento Genoa: The *Last Judgment* at S. Lorenzo.' *Art Bulletin* 67 (1985): 548–66.

Newhauser, Richard. 'Inter scientiam et populum.' In *Nach Der Veruteilung von 1277/After the Condemnation of 1277*, edited by Jan A. Aertsen, Kent Emery, and Andreas Speer. Berlin: Walter de Gruyter, 2001.

Newman, Paul B. *Growing Up in the Middle Ages*. Jefferson, NC: McFarland, 2007.

Newton, Stella Mary. *Fashion in the Age of the Black Prince*. Woodbridge: Boydell Press, 2002.

Nichol, Charles. *The Lodger: Shakespeare on Silver Street*. London: Penguin Books, 2007.

Nichols, Robert E. 'The Pardoner's Ale and Cake.' *PMLA* 82, no. 7 (1967): 498–504.

Nightingale, Pamela. 'Capitalists, Crafts and Constitutional Change in Fourteenth-Century London.' *Past and Present* 124, no. 1 (1989): 3–35.

———. *A Medieval Mercantile Community: The Grocers' Company and the Politics and Trade of London, 1000–1485*. New Haven: Yale University Press, 1995.

Nolan, Barbara. *The Gothic Visionary Perspective*. Princeton: Princeton University Press, 1977.

Nolan, Maura. 'Beauty.' In *Middle English*, edited by Paul Strohm, 207–21. Oxford: Oxford University Press, 2007.

O'Connor, Stephen. 'Finance, Diplomacy, and Politics: Royal Service by Two London Merchants in the Reign of Edward III.' *Historical Research* 67 (1994): 18–39.

———. 'Fraunceys, Adam.' In *Oxford Dictionary of National Biography*. Online edition. Oxford: Oxford University Press, 2008. https://doi.org/10.1093/ref:odnb/52176.

Oggins, Robin S. *The Kings and Their Hawks: Falconry in Medieval England*. New Haven: Yale University Press, 2004.

Oliva, Marilyn. *The Convent and the Community in Late Medieval England: Female Monasteries in the Diocese of Norwich, 1350–1540*. Cambridge: Boydell Press, 1998.

Oliver, Clementine. *Parliament and Political Pamphleteering in Fourteenth-Century England*. Cambridge: Boydell & Brewer, 2010.

———. 'A Political Pamphleteer in Late Medieval England: Thomas Fovent, Geoffrey Chaucer, Thomas Usk, and the Merciless Parliament of 1388.' *New Medieval Literatures* 6 (2003): 67–98.

Origo, Iris. 'The Domestic Enemy: The Eastern Slaves in Tuscany in the Fourteenth and Fifteenth Centuries.' *Speculum* 30, no. 3 (1955): 321.

———. *The Merchant of Prato: Francesco Di Marco Datini, 1335–1410*. Boston: Nonpareil Books, 1986.

Orme, Nicholas. *Medieval Children*. New Haven: Yale University Press, 2001.

———. *Medieval Schools: From Roman Britain to Renaissance England*. New Haven: Yale University Press, 2006.

Ormrod, W. M. *Edward III*. New Haven: Yale University Press, 2013.

———. 'In Bed with Joan of Kent: The King's Mother and the Peasants' Revolt.' In *Medieval Women: Texts and Contexts in Late Medieval Britain; Essays for Felicity Riddy*, edited by Jocelyn Wogan-Browne, Rosalynn Voaden, Arlyn Diamond, Ann Hutchison, Carol M. Meale, and Lesley Johnson, 277–92. Turnhout: Brepols, 2000.

———. 'The Origins of the *Sub Pena* Writ.' *Historical Research* 61, no. 144 (1988): 11–20.

———. 'Parliamentary Scrutiny of Royal Ministers and Courtiers.' In *Law, Governance, and Justice: New Views on Medieval Constitutionalism*, edited by Richard W. Kaeuper, 161–88. Leiden: Brill, 2013.

———. 'The Trials of Alice Perrers.' *Speculum* 83, no. 2 (2008): 366–96.

———. 'Who Was Alice Perrers?' *Chaucer Review* 40, no. 3 (2006): 219–29.

Palmer, J.J.N. *England, France and Christendom, 1377–99*. London: Routledge & Kegan Paul, 1972.

Parkes, M. B., and A. I. Doyle. 'The Production of Copies of the *Canterbury Tales* and the *Confessio Amantis* in the Early Fifteenth Century.' In *Medieval Scribes, Manuscripts and Libraries: Essays Presented to N. R. Ker*, edited by M. B. Parkes and Andrew G. Watson, 163–210. London: Scolar Press, 1978.

Partington, J. R. *A History of Greek Fire and Gunpowder*. Baltimore: Johns Hopkins University Press, 1999.

Passmore, S. Elizabeth, and Susan Carter, eds. *The English 'Loathly Lady' Tales: Boundaries, Traditions, Motifs*. Kalamazoo, MI: Medieval Institute Publications, 2007.

Patterson, Lee. *Chaucer and the Subject of History*. Madison: University of Wisconsin Press, 1991.

———. 'Court Politics and the Invention of Literature: The Case of Sir John Clanvowe.' In *Culture and History, 1350–1600: Essays on English Communities, Identities and Writing*, edited by David Aers, 7–41. Detroit: Prentice-Hall, 1992.

———. *Negotiating the Past: The Historical Understanding of Medieval Literature*. Madison: University of Wisconsin Press, 1987.

———. 'The "Parson's Tale" and the Quitting of the Canterbury Tales.' *Traditio* 34 (1978): 331–80.

———. 'Perpetual Motion: Alchemy and the Technology of the Self.' *Studies in the Age of Chaucer* 15 (1993): 25–57.

———. *Temporal Circumstances: Form and History in the Canterbury Tales*. New York: Palgrave Macmillan, 2006.

Pearsall, Derek. *The Canterbury Tales*. London: Routledge, 1985; reprinted in 2005.

———. 'The *Canterbury Tales* and London Club Culture.' In *Chaucer and the City*, edited by Ardis Butterfield, 95–108. Cambridge: D. S. Brewer, 2006.

———. 'Chaucer's Tomb: The Politics of Reburial.' *Medium Aevum* 64 (1995): 51–73.

———. *The Life of Geoffrey Chaucer: A Critical Biography*. Oxford: Blackwell, 1992.

Pelen, Marc M. 'Idleness and Alchemy in Fragment VIII (G) of Chaucer's *Canterbury Tales*: Oppositions in Themes and Imagery from the *Roman de la Rose*.' *Forum for Modern Language Studies* 31 (1995): 193–214.

Percival, Florence. *Chaucer's Legendary Good Women*. Cambridge: Cambridge University Press, 1998.

Phillips, Helen. 'Chaucer and Deguileville: The *ABC* in Context.' *Medium Aevum* 62 (1993): 1–19.

Phillips, Seymour. *Edward II*. New Haven: Yale University Press, 2010.

Pistono, Stephen. 'The Diplomatic Mission of Jean de Hangest, Lord of Hugueville (October 1400).' *Canadian Journal of History* 13, no. 2 (1978): 193–207.

Platt, Colin. *Medieval Southampton: The Port and Trading Community, A.D. 1000–1600*. London: Routledge & Kegan Paul, 1973.

———. *The Parish Churches of Medieval England*. London: Chancellor, 1995.

Plucknett, T.F.T. 'The Origin of Impeachment.' *Transactions of the Royal Historical Society*, 4th Series, 24 (1942): 47–71.

Pollock, Frederick, and Frederic William Maitland. *The History of English Law before the Time of Edward I*. 2nd edition. Cambridge: Cambridge University Press, 1898.

Pounds, Norman. *Medieval Castle in England and Wales: A Political and Social History*. Cambridge: Cambridge University Press, 1990.

Power, Eileen. *Medieval English Nunneries, c. 1275 to 1535*. Cambridge: Cambridge University Press, 1922.

Pratt, Robert A. 'Chaucer and the Visconti Libraries.' *English Literary History* 6, no. 3 (1939): 191–99.

———. 'The Development of the Wife of Bath.' In *Studies in Medieval Literature in Honor of Albert Croll Baugh*, edited by MacEdward Leach, 45–79. Philadelphia: University of Pennsylvania Press, 1961.

Prendergast, Thomas. *Chaucer's Dead Body: From Corpse to Corpus*. New York: Routledge, 2004.

———. *Poetical Dust: Poets' Corner and the Making of Britain*. Philadelphia: University of Pennsylvania Press, 2015.

Prestwich, Michael. 'Italian Merchants in Late Thirteenth and Early Fourteenth Century England.' In *The Dawn of Modern Banking*, 77–104. New Haven: Yale University Press, 1979.

———. *Plantagenet England, 1225–1360*. Oxford: Oxford University Press, 2007.

Prevenner, Walter. 'The Low Countries, 1290–1415.' In *The New Cambridge Medieval History: Volume VI, c. 1300–c. 1415*, edited by Michael Jones, 570–94. Cambridge: Cambridge University Press, 2000.

Quinn, William A. 'The *Legend of Good Women*: Performance, Performativity, and Presentation.' In *'The Legend of Good Women': Context and Reception*, edited by Carolyn P. Collette, 1–32. Cambridge: D. S. Brewer, 2006.

Raybin, David. ' "Manye been the weyes": The Flower, Its Roots, and the Ending of the *Canterbury Tales*.' In *Closure in* The Canterbury Tales*: The Role of* The Parson's Tale, edited by Linda Tarte Holley and David Raybin, 11–43. Kalamazoo, MI: Medieval Institute Publications, 2000.

Rayner, Doris. 'The Forms and Machinery of the "Commune Petition," in the Fourteenth Century.' Part I. *English Historical Review* 56 (1941): 198–233.

Reddan, Minnie, and Alfred W. Clapham. *Survey of London, Vol. IX: The Parish of St Helen Bishopsgate*. London: Batsford, London County Council, 1924.

Redstone, V. B., and L. J. Redstone. 'The Heyrons of London.' *Speculum* 12, no. 2 (1937): 182–95.

Reed, Thomas L. *Middle English Debate Poetry and the Aesthetics of Irresolution*. Columbia: University of Missouri Press, 1990.

Rees Jones, Sarah. 'Women's Influence on the Design of Urban Homes.' In *Gendering the Master Narrative: Women and Power in the Middle Ages*, edited by Mary C. Erler and Maryanne Kowaleski, 190–211. Ithaca: Cornell University Press, 2003.

Reisner, Thomas A., and Mary E. Reisner. 'Lewis Clifford and the Kingdom of Navarre.' *Modern Philology* 75, no. 4 (1978): 385–90.

Réville, André. *Le soulevement des travailleurs d'Angleterre en 1381*. Paris: Picard, 1898.

Richardson, H. G. 'The English Coronation Oath.' In *Historical Essays in Honour of James Tait*, edited by J. D. Edwards, V. H. Galbraith, and E. F. Jacobs, 405–16. Manchester: Manchester University Press, 1933.

Richardson, Roland Thomas. 'The Medieval Inventories of the Tower Armouries, 1320–1410.' Unpublished PhD thesis, University of York, 2012.

Rickert, Edith. 'Chaucer at School.' *Modern Philology* 29, no. 3 (1932): 257–74.

———. 'Thou Vache.' *Modern Philology* 11, no. 2 (1913): 209–25.

Riddy, Felicity. ' "Burgeis" Domesticity in Late-Medieval England.' In *Medieval Domesticity: Home, Housing, and Household in Medieval England*, edited by Maryanne Kowaleski and P.J.P. Goldberg, 14–36. Cambridge: Cambridge University Press, 2008.

Robertson, Anne Walters. *Guillaume de Machaut and Reims: Context and Meaning in His Musical Works*. Cambridge: Cambridge University Press, 2002.

Robertson, Kellie. 'Authorial Work.' In *Middle English*, edited by Paul Strohm, 441–58. Oxford: Oxford University Press, 2007.

———. *The Labourer's Two Bodies: Labour and the 'Work' of the Text in Medieval Britain, 1350–1500*. New York: Palgrave Macmillan, 2006.

———. 'Medieval Things: Materiality, Historicism, and the Premodern Object.' *Literature Compass* 5, no. 6 (2008): 1060–80.

———. *Nature Speaks: Medieval Literature and Aristotelian Philosophy*. Philadelphia: University of Pennsylvania Press, 2017.

Rogers, Alan. 'Parliamentary Appeals of Treason in the Reign of Richard II.' *American Journal of Legal History* 8, no. 2 (1964): 95–124.

Romano, Serena. 'Milan (and Lombardy): Art and Architecture, 1277–1535.' In *A Companion to Late Medieval and Early Modern Milan: The Distinctive Features of an Italian State*, edited by Andrea Gamberini, 214–47. Leiden: Brill, 2014.

Roper, Gregory. 'Dropping the Personae and Reforming the Self: *The Parson's Tale* and the End of *The Canterbury Tales*.' In *Closure in* The Canterbury Tales*: The Role of The Parson's Tale,* edited by Linda Tarte Holley and David Raybin, 151–75. Kalamazoo, MI: Medieval Institute Publications, 2000.

Rosenberg, Bruce A. 'The Contrary Tales of the Second Nun and the Canon's Yeoman.' *Chaucer Review* 2, no. 4 (1968): 278–91.

Roskell, J. S. *Parliament and Politics in Late Medieval England, Volume III*. London: Hambledon Press, 1983.

Roskell, J. S., L. Clark, and C. Rawcliffe, eds. *The History of Parliament: The House of Commons, 1386–1421*. 4 vols. Stroud: Alan Sutton, 1992.

Rosser, Gervase. *Medieval Westminster: 1200–1540*. Oxford: Clarendon Press, 1989.

———. 'Sanctuary and Social Negotiation in Medieval England.' In *The Cloister and the World: Essays in Medieval History in Honour of Barbara Harvey*, edited by John Blair and Brian Golding, 58–80. Oxford: Oxford University Press, 1996.

Rubin, Miri. *Mother of God: A History of the Virgin Mary*. London: Allen Lane, 2009.

Rudd, Gillian. *Greenery: Ecocritical Readings of Late Medieval English Literature*. Manchester: Manchester University Press, 2007.

Ruddock, Alwyn A. *Italian Merchants and Shipping in Southampton, 1270–1600*. Southampton: University College, 1951.

Russell, J. Stephen. *The English Dream Vision: Anatomy of a Form*. Columbus: Ohio State University Press, 1988.

Russell, P. E. *The English Intervention in Spain and Portugal in the Time of Edward III and Richard II*. Oxford: Clarendon Press, 1955.

Said, Edward. *On Late Style*. London: Bloomsbury, 2006.

Salter, E. 'Chaucer and Internationalism.' *Studies in the Age of Chaucer* 2 (1980): 71–79.

———. *Fourteenth-Century English Poetry: Contexts and Readings*. Oxford: Oxford University Press, 1983.

Saul, Nigel. *Death, Art, and Memory in Medieval England: The Cobham Family and Their Monuments, c. 1300–1500*. Oxford: Oxford University Press, 2001.

———. *Richard II*. New Haven: Yale University Press, 1997.

———. 'Richard II and Westminster Abbey.' In *The Cloister and the World: Essays in Medieval History in Honour of Barbara Harvey*, edited by John Blair and Brian Golding, 197–219. Oxford: Oxford University Press, 1996.

Saunders, Corinne. *The Forest of Medieval Romance: Avernus, Broceliande, Arden*. Cambridge: D. S. Brewer, 1993.

———. 'Margins.' In *A Handbook of Middle English Studies*, edited by Marion Turner, 331–46. Oxford: Wiley-Blackwell, 2013.

Sayce, Olive. 'Chaucer's *Retractions*: The Conclusion of the *Canterbury Tales* and Its Place in Literary Tradition.' *Medium Aevum* 40 (1971): 230–46.

Scanlon, Larry. *Narrative, Authority, and Power: The Medieval Exemplum and the Chaucerian Tradition.* Cambridge: Cambridge University Press, 2007.

Scase, Wendy. *Literature and Complaint in England, 1272–1553.* Oxford: Oxford University Press, 2007.

Scattergood, John. 'The Love Lyric before Chaucer.' In *A Companion to the Middle English Lyric*, edited by Thomas G. Duncan, 39–67. Cambridge: D. S. Brewer, 2005.

Schofield, John. *Medieval London Houses.* New Haven: Yale University Press, 2003.

———. 'Medieval Parish Churches in the City of London: The Archaeological Evidence.' In *The Parish in English Life, 1400–1600*, edited by Katherine L. French, Gary G. Gibbs, and Beat A. Kümin, 35–55. Manchester: Manchester University Press, 1997.

———. 'Social Perceptions of Space in Medieval and Tudor London Houses.' In *Meaningful Architecture: Social Interpretations of Buildings*, edited by Martin Locock, 188–206. Aldershot: Ashgate, 1994.

Selby, W. D. *The Athenaeum* (20 November 1886): 672–73.

Simpson, James. 'Chaucer as a European Writer.' In *The Yale Companion to Chaucer*, edited by Seth Lerer, 55–86. New Haven: Yale University Press, 2006.

———. 'The Other Book of Troy: Guido Delle Colonne's *Historia destructionis Troiae* in Fourteenth- and Fifteenth-Century England.' *Speculum* 73, no. 2 (1998): 397–423.

———. *The Oxford English Literary History: Volume 2, 1350–1547; Reform and Cultural Revolution.* Oxford: Oxford University Press, 2004.

Skemer, Don C. *Binding Words: Textual Amulets in the Middle Ages.* University Park: Pennsylvania State University Press, 2006.

Smail, Daniel Lord. 'The Linguistic Cartography of Property and Power in Late Medieval Marseilles.' In *Medieval Practices of Space*, edited by Barbara A. Hanawalt and Michal Kobialka, 37–63. Minneapolis: University of Minnesota Press, 2000.

Smith, D. Vance. *Arts of Possession: The Middle English Household Imaginary.* Minneapolis: University of Minnesota Press, 2003.

———. 'Chaucer as an English Writer.' In *The Yale Companion to Chaucer*, edited by Seth Lerer, 87–121. New Haven: Yale University Press, 2006.

———. 'Institutions.' In *Middle English*, edited by Paul Strohm, 160–76. Oxford: Oxford University Press, 2007.

———. '*Piers Plowman* and the National Noetic of Edward III.' In *Imagining a Medieval English Nation*, edited by Kathy Lavezzo, 234–57. Minneapolis: University of Minnesota Press, 2004.

Smith, R. M. '"Mynstralcie and Noyse" in the *House of Fame*.' *Modern Language Notes* 65, no. 8 (1950): 521–30.

Smith, Warren S. 'The Wife of Bath Debates Jerome.' *Chaucer Review* 32, no. 2 (1997): 129–45.

Smyser, H. M. 'The Domestic Background of *Troilus and Criseyde*.' *Speculum* 31, no. 2 (1956): 297–315.

Sobecki, Sebastian. 'A Southwark Tale: Gower, the 1381 Poll Tax, and Chaucer's *Canterbury Tales*.' *Speculum* 92, no. 3 (2017): 630–60.

Southern, Richard. *The Making of the Middle Ages.* New Haven: Yale University Press, 1953.

Spearing, A. C. *Textual Subjectivity: The Encoding of Subjectivity in Medieval Narratives and Lyrics.* Oxford: Oxford University Press, 2005.

Spruyt, Hendrik. *The Sovereign State and Its Competitors: An Analysis of Systems Change*. Princeton: Princeton University Press, 1994.

Spufford, Peter. *Money and Its Use in Medieval Europe*. Cambridge: Cambridge University Press, 1988.

Staley, Lynn. 'Enclosed Spaces.' In *Cultural Reformations: Medieval and Renaissance in Literary History*, edited by Brian Cummings and James Simpson, 113–32. Oxford: Oxford University Press, 2010.

———. *Languages of Power in the Age of Richard II*. University Park: Pennsylvania State University Press, 2005.

Stallybrass, Peter. 'Patriarchal Territories: The Body Enclosed.' In *Rewriting the Renaissance: The Discourses of Sexual Difference in Early Modern Europe*, edited by Margaret W. Ferguson, Maureen Quilligan, and Nancy Vickers, 123–42. Chicago: University of Chicago Press, 1986.

Stanbury, Sarah. 'The Place of the Bedchamber in Chaucer's *Book of the Duchess*.' *Studies in the Age of Chaucer* 37 (2015): 133–61.

———. ' "Quy la?": The Counting House in the *Shipman's Tale*, and Architectural Interiors.' In *Chaucer: Visual Approaches*, edited by Susanna Fein and David Raybin, 37–56. University Park: Pennsylvania University Press, 2016.

———. 'Regimes of the Visual in Premodern England: Gaze, Body, and Chaucer's "Clerk's Tale." ' *New Literary History* 28, no. 2 (1997): 261–89.

Starkey, David. 'The Age of the Household.' In *The Later Middle Ages*, edited by Stephen Medcalf, 225–90. London: Methuen, 1981.

Steel, Anthony. 'The Collectors of the Customs in the Reign of Richard II.' In *British Government and Administration: Studies Presented to S. B. Chrimes*, edited by H. Hearder and H. R. Loyn, 27–39. Cardiff: University of Wales Press, 1974.

Steiner, Emily. 'Berkeley Castle.' In *Europe: A Literary History*. Vol. 1, edited by David Wallace, 227–39. Oxford: Oxford University Press, 2016.

Strakhov, Elizaveta. 'But who will bell the cat?' *Yearbook of Langland Studies* 30 (2016): 253–76.

Stratford, Jenny. 'Hende, John (d. 1418).' In *Oxford Dictionary of National Biography*. Online edition. Oxford: Oxford University Press, 2008. https://doi.org/10.1093/ref:odnb/52249.

Strohm, Paul. *Hochon's Arrow: The Social Imagination of Fourteenth-Century Texts*. Princeton: Princeton University Press, 1992.

———. *The Poet's Tale: Chaucer and the Year that Made 'The Canterbury Tales.'* London: Profile Books, 2016.

———. *Social Chaucer*. Cambridge, MA: Harvard University Press, 1994.

———. 'The Space of Desire in Chaucer's and Shakespeare's Troy.' In *Love, History and Emotion in Chaucer and Shakespeare: 'Troilus and Criseyde' and 'Troilus and Cressida,'* edited by Andrew James Johnston, Russell West-Pavlov, and Elisabeth Kempf, 46–60. Oxford: Oxford University Press, 2016.

———. *Theory and the Premodern Text*. Minneapolis: University of Minnesota Press, 2000.

Sumption, Jonathan. *The Hundred Years War II: Trial by Fire*. London: Faber & Faber, 1999.

———. *The Hundred Years War III: Divided Houses*. London: Faber & Faber, 2009.

Swanson, R. N. *The Twelfth Century Renaissance*. Manchester: Manchester University Press, 1999.

Swift, Helen. 'The Poetic I.' In *A Companion to Guillaume de Machaut*, edited by Deborah L. McGrady and Jennifer Bain, 15–32. Leiden: Brill, 2012.

Szittya, Penn R. 'The Green Yeoman as Loathly Lady: The Friar's Parody of the Wife of Bath's Tale.' *PMLA* 90, no. 3 (1975): 386–94.

Tatton-Brown, Tim. 'Excavations at the Custom House Site, City of London, 1973.' *Transactions of the London and Middlesex Archaeological Society* 25 (1974): 117–219.

Taylor, John. *English Historical Literature in the Fourteenth Century*. Oxford: Clarendon Press, 1987.

Taylor, Joseph. 'Chaucer's Uncanny Regionalism: Rereading the North in the Reeve's Tale.' *Journal of English and Germanic Philology* 109, no. 4 (2010): 468–89.

Taylor, Karla. *Chaucer Reads the Divine Comedy*. Stanford, CA: Stanford University Press, 1989.

Taylor, P. B. 'Chaucer's *Cosyn to the Dede*.' *Speculum* 57, no. 2 (1982): 315–27.

Thomas, Alfred. *A Blessed Shore: England and Bohemia from Chaucer to Shakespeare*. Ithaca: Cornell University Press, 2007.

Thomson, S. Harrison. 'Learning at the Court of Charles IV.' *Speculum* 25, no. 1 (1950): 1–20.

Toivanen, Juhana. 'The Fate of the Flying Man: Medieval Reception of Avicenna's Thought Experiment.' In *Oxford Studies in Medieval Philosophy*. Vol. 3, edited by Robert Pasnau, 64–97. Oxford: Oxford University Press, 2015.

Tolkien, J.R.R. 'Chaucer as Philologist: *The Reeve's Tale*.' *Transactions of the Philological Society* 33, no. 1 (1934): 1–70.

Tout, T. F. *Chapters in the Administrative History of Medieval England: The Wardrobe, the Chamber and the Small Seals*. Vol. 3. Manchester: Manchester University Press, 1928.

———. 'Firearms in England in the Fourteenth Century.' In *The Collected Papers of Thomas Frederick Tout*, 2:233–75. Manchester: Manchester University Press, 1932.

———. *The Place of the Reign of Edward II in English History*. Manchester: Manchester University Press, 1914.

Towson, Kris. ' "Hearts Warped by Passion": The Percy-Gaunt Dispute of 1381.' In *Fourteenth Century England III*, edited by W. M. Ormrod, 143–54. Woodbridge: Boydell Press, 2004.

Trachtenberg, Marvin. *Dominion of the Eye: Urbanism, Art, and Power in Early Modern Florence*. Cambridge: Cambridge University Press, 1997.

Travis, Peter. *Disseminal Chaucer: Rereading the Nun's Priest's Tale*. Notre Dame: University of Notre Dame Press, 2010.

———. 'The Manciple's Phallic Matrix.' *Studies in the Age of Chaucer* 25 (2003): 317–24.

Trexler, Richard C. *The Spiritual Power: Republican Florence under Interdict*. Leiden: Brill, 1974.

Trigg, Stephanie. *Congenial Souls: Reading Chaucer from Medieval to Modern*. Minneapolis: University of Minnesota Press, 2001.

———. *Shame and Honour: A Vulgar History of the Order of the Garter*. Philadelphia: University of Pennsylvania Press, 2012.

———. 'The Traffic in Medieval Women: Alice Perrers, Feminist Criticism and *Piers Plowman*.' *Yearbook of Langland Studies* 12 (1998): 5–29.

Tuan, Yi-Fu. *Topophilia: A Study of Environmental Perception, Attitudes, and Values*. Englewood Cliffs, NJ: Prentice-Hall, 1974.

Tuck, Anthony. 'The Percies and the Community of Northumberland in the Later Fourteenth Century.' In *War and Border Societies in the Middle Ages*, edited by Anthony Goodman and Anthony Tuck, 178–95. London: Routledge, 1992.

———. *Richard II and the English Nobility*. London: Edward Arnold, 1973.

———. 'Richard II and the House of Luxemburg.' In *Richard II: The Art of Kingship*, edited by Anthony Goodman and James Gillespie, 205–29. Oxford: Clarendon Press, 1999.

———. 'Vere, Robert De, Ninth Earl of Oxford, Marquess of Dublin, and Duke of Ireland (1362–1392).' In *Oxford Dictionary of National Biography*. Online edition. Oxford: Oxford University Press, 2008. https://doi.org/10.1093/ref:odnb/28218.

Tupper, Frederick. 'Chaucer and the Seven Deadly Sins.' *PMLA* 29, no. 1 (1914): 93–123.

Turner, Marion. 'Chaucer.' In *A Companion to Literary Biography*, ed. Richard Bradford, 375–90. Oxford: Wiley-Blackwell, 2018.

———. 'Chaucer.' In *Oxford Handbooks Online*, edited by James Simpson. http://www.oxford handbooks.com/view/10.1093/oxfordhb/9780199935338.001.0001/oxfordhb-97801999 35338-e-58.

———. *Chaucerian Conflict: Languages of Antagonism in Late Fourteenth-Century London*. Oxford: Oxford University Press, 2007.

———. 'Conflict.' In *Middle English*, edited by Paul Strohm, 258–73. Oxford: Oxford University Press, 2007.

———. 'Imagining Polities: Social Possibilities and Conflict.' In *Medieval Literature: Criticism and Debates*, edited by Holly A. Crocker and D. Vance Smith, 398–406. Abingdon: Routledge, 2014.

———. 'The Senses.' In *A New Companion to Chaucer*, edited by Peter Brown. Oxford: Wiley-Blackwell, forthcoming.

———. 'Usk and the Goldsmiths.' *New Medieval Literatures* 9 (2007): 139–77.

Turner, Victor. 'Betwixt and Between: The Liminal Period in *Rites de Passage*.' In *The Forest of Symbols: Aspects of Ndembu Ritual*, 4–20. Ithaca: Cornell University Press, 1967.

———. 'Liminality and Communitas.' In *The Ritual Process: Structure and Anti-Structure*, 94–113. London: Routledge & Kegan Paul, 1969.

———. 'Passages, Margins, and Poverty: Religious Symbols of Communitas.' In *Dramas, Fields, and Metaphors*, 231–71. Ithaca: Cornell University Press, 1975.

Underhill, Frances. *For Her Good Estate: The Life of Elizabeth de Burgh*. Basingstoke: Palgrave Macmillan, 2000.

Unwin, George, ed. *Finance and Trade under Edward III*. Manchester: Manchester University Press, 1918.

Vale, Juliet. 'Philippa [Philippa of Hainault] (1310x15?–1369).' In *Oxford Dictionary of National Biography*. Online edition. Oxford: Oxford University Press, 2008. https://doi.org/10.1093/ref:odnb/22110.

Vale, Malcolm. *The Princely Court: Medieval Courts and Culture in North-West Europe, 1270–1380*. Oxford: Oxford University Press, 2001.

Vance, Eugene. *Mervelous Signals: Poetics and Sign Theory in the Middle Ages*. Lincoln: University of Nebraska Press, 1986.

Van Dussen, Michael. *From England to Bohemia: Heresy and Communication in the Later Middle Ages*. Cambridge: Cambridge University Press, 2012.

Viereck Gibbs Kamath, Stephanie A. 'The *Roman de la Rose* and Middle English Poetry.' *Literature Compass* 6, no. 6 (2009): 1109–26.

Wakelin, Daniel. *Scribal Correction and Literary Craft: English Manuscripts, 1375–1510*. Cambridge: Cambridge University Press, 2014.

Walker-Meikle, Kathleen. *Medieval Pets*. Woodbridge: Boydell Press, 2012.

Walker, Simon. *The Lancastrian Affinity, 1361–1399*. Oxford: Oxford University Press, 1990.

Wallace, David. 'Chaucer and Boccaccio's Early Writings.' In *Chaucer and the Italian Trecento*, edited by Piero Boitani, 141–62. Cambridge: Cambridge University Press, 1983.

———. *Chaucer and the Early Writings of Boccaccio*. Woodbridge: D. S. Brewer, 1985.

———. 'Chaucer and the European Rose.' *Studies in the Age of Chaucer* 1 (1984): 61–67.

———. *Chaucerian Polity: Absolutist Lineages and Associational Forms in England and Italy*. Stanford, CA: Stanford University Press, 1997.

———. 'Chaucer's Italian Inheritance.' In *The Cambridge Companion to Chaucer*, edited by Piero Boitani and Jill Mann, 36–57. Revised edition. Cambridge: Cambridge University Press, 2004.

———. *Premodern Places: Calais to Surinam, Chaucer to Aphra Behn*. Malden, MA: Blackwell, 2004.

Warner, Lawrence. 'Scribes, Misattributed: Hoccleve and Pinkhurst.' *Studies in the Age of Chaucer* 37 (2015): 55–100.

Warren, Nancy Bradley. *Spiritual Economies: Female Monasticism in Later Medieval England*. Philadelphia: University of Pennsylvania Press, 2001.

Watts, John. *The Making of Polities: Europe, 1300–1500*. Cambridge: Cambridge University Press, 2009.

Weever, John. *Antient Funeral Monuments of Great Britain, Ireland, and the Islands Adjacent*. London: William Tooke, 1767.

Weiskott, Eric. '*Adam Scriveyn* and Chaucer's Metrical Practice.' *Medium Aevum* 86:1 (2017): 147–51.

———. 'Chaucer the Forester: The "Friar's Tale," Forest History, and Officialdom.' *Chaucer Review* 47, no. 3 (2013): 323–36.

Wenzel, Siegfried. 'The *Parson's Tale* in Current Literary Studies.' In *Closure in* The Canterbury Tales: *The Role of The Parson's Tale,* edited by Linda Tarte Holley and David Raybin, 1–10. Kalamazoo, MI: Medieval Institute Publications, 2000.

Wetherbee, Winthrop. 'The Consolation and Medieval Literature.' In *The Cambridge Companion to Boethius*, edited by John Marenbon, 279–302. Cambridge: Cambridge University Press, 2009.

Wheelis, Mark. 'Biological Warfare at the 1346 Siege of Caffa.' *Emerging Infectious Diseases* 8, no. 9 (2002): 971–75.

Wilkins, Nigel. 'En Regardant Vers Le Pais de France: The Ballade and the Rondeau, a Cross-Channel History.' In *England in the Fourteenth Century: Proceedings of the 1985 Harlaxton Symposium*, edited by W. M. Ormrod, 298–323. Woodbridge: Boydell Press, 1986.

Wilkinson, B. 'The Coronation Oath of Edward II.' In *Historical Essays in Honour of James Tait*, edited by J. G. Edwards, V. H. Galbraith, and E. F. Jacob, 405–16. Manchester: Manchester University Press, 1933.

Wilson, Christopher. 'The Royal Lodgings of Edward III at Windsor: Form, Function, Representation.' In *Windsor: Medieval Archaeology, Art, and Architecture of the Thames Valley*, edited by Laurence Keen and Eileen Scarff, 15–94. Leeds: British Archaeological Association, 2002.

Wimsatt, James I. *Allegory and Mirror: Tradition and Structure in Middle English Literature*. New York: Pegasus, 1970.

———. 'The Blessed Virgin and the Two Coronations of Griselde.' *Mediaevalia* 6 (1980): 187–207.

———. *Chaucer and His French Contemporaries: Natural Music in the Fourteenth Century*. Toronto: University of Toronto Press, 1991.

———. *Chaucer and the French Love Poets: The Literary Background of the 'Book of the Duchess.'* Chapel Hill: University of North Carolina Press, 1968.

———. *The Marguerite Poetry of Guillaume de Machaut.* Chapel Hill: University of North Carolina Press, 1970.

———. 'Realism in *Troilus and Criseyde* and the *Roman de la Rose.*' In *Essays on Troilus and Criseyde*, edited by Mary Salu, 43–56. Cambridge: D. S. Brewer, 1979.

Windeatt, Barry. *Oxford Guides to Chaucer: Troilus and Criseyde.* Oxford: Clarendon, 2002.

Winston-Allen, Anne. *Stories of the Rose: The Making of the Rosary in the Middle Ages.* University Park: Pennsylvania State University Press, 1997.

Wogan-Browne, Jocelyn, et al., eds. *Medieval Women: Texts and Contexts in Late Medieval Britain; Essays for Felicity Riddy.* Turnhout: Brepols, 2000.

Woods, William F. *Chaucerian Spaces: Spatial Poetics in Chaucer's Opening Tales.* Albany: State University of New York Press, 2008.

Woolgar, C. M. *The Great Household in Late Medieval England.* New Haven: Yale University Press, 1999.

Young, Charles. *The Royal Forests of Medieval England.* Leicester: Leicester University Press, 1979.

Zaggia, Massimo. 'Culture in Lombardy: 1350–1550.' In *A Companion to Late Medieval and Early Modern Milan: The Distinctive Features of an Italian State*, edited by Andrea Gamberini, 166–89. Leiden: Brill, 2014.

INDEX

Acciaioli, Niccolò, 437

Adelard of Bath, 213–14, 236

adultery, 53, 196, 200, 202, 408, 469. *See also* sex/sexuality

Aeneas, 159, 267, 316, 334, 335–36, 337, 341

Aesop, *Fables*, 40–41

Affrikano Petro (African Peter), 189

Agbabi, Patience, *Telling Tales*, 486

Akbari, Suzanne Conklin, 430

Alain de Lille, 223, 238; *Anticlaudianus*, 220–21, 225; arithmetic in, 220; arts in, 220; astral flight in, 238; *De Planctu Naturae*, 198

Albert, Duke of Bavaria, 103

Albert of Saxony, 218–19

Alberton, Thomas de, 108, 114

alchemy, 249, 473–74

Alconbury, Maria, 375–76

Aldgate, 242, 246, 271, 394. *See also* Chaucer, Geoffrey, residences

Aldgate Abbey, 493

Aldgate Ward, 181–82

alehouses, 19, 387, 396. *See also* brewhouses; drinking establishments; inns; pubs; taverns

alestake, 397, 408

Alexander the Great, 223

Alexandria, 157, 370

Alfonso XI of Castile, 105

Alhudaly, Amet, 112

aliens. *See* foreigners/aliens

Alla, 430

allegory, 392, 408, 453, 464, 465; and Boethius, 198, 216; in 'Clerk's Tale,' 465; and Griselda story, 339; in 'Knight's Tale,' 86, 88; naturalistic, 465; and *Roman de la Rose*, 74, 342; in 'Tale of Melibee,' 465; and taverns, 406; and women, 465

Alnwick Castle, 428, 429, 429n49

Amanieu, Arnaud, lord of Albret, 114

Amazons, 293

Ambrose, 326

Ancrene Wisse, 63n65

Anderson, Benedict, *Imagined Communities*, 95

Anglo-Castilian treaty, 106

Anglo-Irish, 97

animals, 41, 55, 86, 191–92, 201, 215, 239

Anjou, 92

Anne, St, cult of, 360

Anne Boleyn, 355

Anne of Bohemia, 212, 316, 347, 446, 450; ceremonial entry of into London, 274–76, 283, 284, 292; and children, 442; death of, 440, 445, 450; education and background of, 360; and Eltham garden, 352; and empire, 319; and erotic social exchange, 350; and imperial court, 332; and *Legend of Good Women* (F-Prologue), 333, 350, 351, 354, 362, 450; and *Legend of Good Women* (G-Prologue), 333, 450; and Merciless Parliament, 311; negotiations for, 498; and Richard II, 274–75, 284, 315, 319, 332, 333, 348, 450, 498; and *Roman de la Rose*, 354; and Margaret Sarnesfield, 388; tomb of, 490; and *Troilus and Criseyde*, 354, 450; wedding of, 276

Annunciation, 468–69

Anonimalle Chronicle, 243, 244

Anselm of Canterbury, 491

anti-Semitism, 435

Appleton, William, 242, 243

Aquitaine, 117; change in, 119; G. Chaucer in, 109, 119; and Edward (Black Prince), 97; and Edward III, 92; and England, 109–10; and John of Gaunt, 439, 442, 443, 444, 445; and Navarre, 105, 109; and Pedro I, 106; rebellion in, 444

Arabic writings, 437

Aragon, 113, 437; and Castile, 106; and Enrique de Trastámara, 106; and mercenaries, 106; and Navarre, 105; and Pedro I, 106. *See also* Spain

Archer, Agnes, 53

architecture, 258, 342; allegory of, 63n65; and Charles IV, 332; Giotto's depiction of, 161, 163, 326; of Hatfield Manor House,